ITALY

Chief Editor   Cynthia Clayton Ochterbeck

THE GREEN GUIDE ITALY

Editor   Jonathan P. Gilbert
Principal Writer   Anna Melville-James
Production Coordinator   Natasha G. George
Cartography   Alain Baldet, Michèle Cana, Peter Wrenn
Photo Editor   Lydia Strong
Proofreader   Gaven R. Watkins
Layout & Design   Heinrich Grieb and John Higginbottom
Cover Design   Laurent Muller and Ute Weber

Contact Us: The Green Guide
                                    Michelin Maps and Guides
                                    One Parkway South
                                    Greenville, SC 29615
                                    USA
                                    www.michelintravel.com
                                    michelin.guides@us.michelin.com

                                    Michelin Maps and Guides
                                    Hannay House
                                    39 Clarendon Road
                                    Watford, Herts WD17 1JA
                                    UK
                                    ☎ (01923) 205 240
                                    www.ViaMichelin.com
                                    travelpubsales@uk.michelin.com

Special Sales: For information regarding bulk sales,
                                    customized editions and premium sales,
                                    please contact our Customer Service
                                    Departments:
                                    USA   1-800-432-6277
                                    UK   (01923) 205 240
                                    Canada 1-800-361-8236

Note to the Reader

One Team ...
A Commitment to Quality

There's just one reason our team is dedicated to producing quality travel publications—you, our reader.

Throughout our guides we offer **practical information**, **touring tips** and **suggestions** for finding the best places for a break.

Michelin driving tours help you hit the highlights and quickly absorb the best of the region. Our descriptive **walking tours** make you your own guide, armed with directions, maps and expert information.

We scout out the attractions, classify them with **star ratings**, and describe in detail what you will find when you visit them.

Michelin maps featured throughout the guide offer vibrant, detailed and easy-to-follow outlines of everything from close-up museum plans to international maps.

Places to stay and eat are always a big part of travel, so we research **hotels and restaurants** that we think convey the essence of the destination, and arrange them by geographic area and price. We walk you through the best shopping districts and point you towards the host of entertainment and recreation possibilities on offer.

We **test, retest, check and recheck** to make sure that our guidebooks are truly just that: a personalized guide to help you make the most of your visit. And if you still want a speaking guide, we list local tour guides who will lead you on all the boat, bus, guided, historical, culinary, and other tours you shouldn't miss.

In short, we remove the guesswork involved with travel. After all, we want you to enjoy traveling with Michelin as much as we do.

The Michelin Green Guide Team

PLANNING YOUR TRIP

INTRODUCTION TO ITALY

SYMBOLS

🛈	**Tourist Information**
🕐	**Hours of Operation**
🕐	**Periods of Closure**
🖐	**A Bit of Advice**
👁	**Details to Consider**
💳	**Entry Fees**
🧒	**Especially for Children**
👣	**Tours**
♿	**Wheelchair Accessible**

CONTENTS

DISCOVERING ITALY

HOW TO USE THIS GUIDE

Orientation

To help you grasp the "lay of the land" quickly and easily, so you'll feel confident and comfortable finding your way around the region, we offer the following tools in this guide:

- Detailed table of contents for an overview of what you'll find in the guide, and how the guide is organized.
- Maps of Italy with the Principal Sights highlighted for easy reference.
- Detailed maps for major cities and villages, including driving tour maps and larger-scale maps for walking tours.
- Map of Italian Regional Driving Tours, each one numbered and color coded.
- Principal Sights organized alphabetically for quick reference.

Practicalities

At the front of the guide, you'll see a section called "Planning Your Trip" that contains information about planning your trip, the best time to go, different ways of getting to the region and getting around, and basic facts and tips for making the most of your visit. You'll find driving and themed tours, and suggestions for outdoor fun. There's also a calendar of popular annual events. Information on shopping, sightseeing, kids' activities and sports and recreational opportunities is included as well.

LODGINGS

We've made a selection of hotels and arranged them within the cities by price category to fit all budgets (*see the Legend on the cover flap for an explanation of the price categories*). For the most part, we've selected accommodations based on their unique regional quality, their Italian feel, as it were. So, unless the individual hotel embodies local ambience, it's rare that we include chain properties, which typically have their own imprint. If you want a more comprehensive selection of accommodations, see the red-cover **Michelin Guide Italy.**

RESTAURANTS

We thought you'd like to know the popular eating spots in Italy's cities and regions. So we selected restaurants that capture the experience of the Italian love of a good meal — those that have a unique regional flavor and local atmosphere. We're not rating the quality of the food per se. As we did with the hotels, we selected restaurants for many towns and villages, categorized by price to appeal to all wallets (*see the Legend on the cover flap for an explanation of the price categories*). If you want a more comprehensive selection of dining recommendations, see the red-cover **Michelin Guide Italy**.

Attractions

Principal Sights are arranged alphabetically. Within each Principal Sight, attractions for each town, village, or geographical area are divided into local Sights or Walking Tours, nearby Excursions to sights outside the town, or detailed Driving Tours—suggested itineraries for seeing several attractions around a major town. Contact information, admission charges and hours of operation are given for the majority of attractions. Unless otherwise noted, admission prices shown are for a single adult only. Discounts for children, seniors, students, teachers, etc. may be available; be sure to ask. If no admission charge is shown, entrance to the attraction is free.
If you're pressed for time, we recommend you visit the three- and two-star sights first: the stars are your guide.

STAR RATINGS

Michelin has used stars as a rating tool for more than 100 years:

★★★ Highly recommended
★★ Recommended
★ Interesting

SYMBOLS IN THE TEXT

Besides the stars, other symbols in the text indicate sights that are closed to the public ⊶; on-site eating facilities ✕; also see ⓒ; breakfast included in the nightly rate ☕; on-site parking P; spa facilities Spa; camping facilities ⛺; swimming pool 🏊; and beaches ⛱.
See the box appearing on the Contents page and the Legend on the cover flap for other symbols used in the text.
See the Maps explanation below for symbols appearing on the maps.
Throughout the guide you will find peach-coloured text boxes or sidebars containing anecdotal or background information. Green-coloured boxes contain information to help you save time or money.

Maps

All maps in this guide are oriented north, unless otherwise indicated by a directional arrow. The term "Local Map" refers to a map within the chapter or Tourism Region. See the map Legend at the back of the guide for an explanation of other map symbols. A complete list of the maps found in the guide appears at the back of this book.
Addresses, phone numbers, opening hours and prices published in this guide are accurate at press time. We welcome corrections and suggestions that may assist us in preparing the next edition. Please send your comments to:

Michelin Maps and Guides
Hannay House
39 Clarendon Road
Watford, Herts WD17 1JA
UK
travelpubsales@uk.michelin.com
www.michelin.co.uk

Michelin Maps and Guides
Editorial Department
P.O. Box 19001
Greenville, SC 29602-9001
USA
michelin.guides@us.michelin.com
www.michelintravel.com

Principal Sights

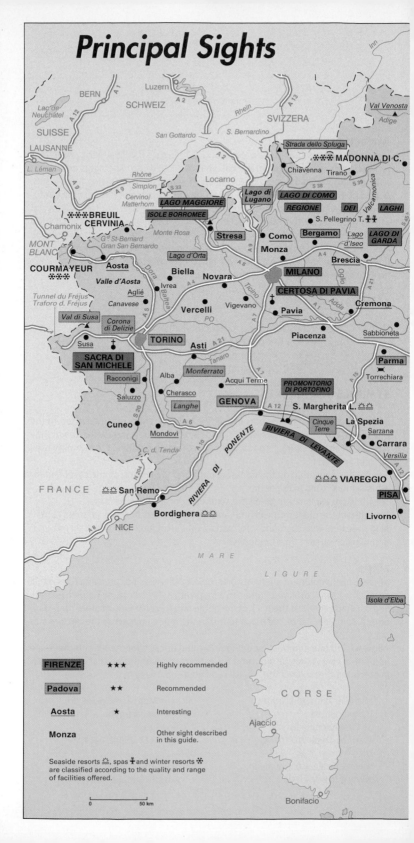

FIRENZE	★★★	Highly recommended
Padova	★★	Recommended
Aosta	★	Interesting
Monza		Other sight described in this guide.

Seaside resorts ⚏, spas ⚎ and winter resorts ✵ are classified according to the quality and range of facilities offered.

0   50 km

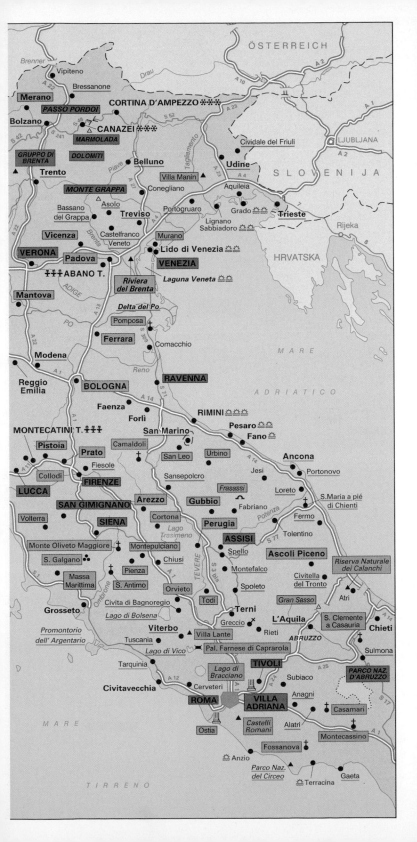

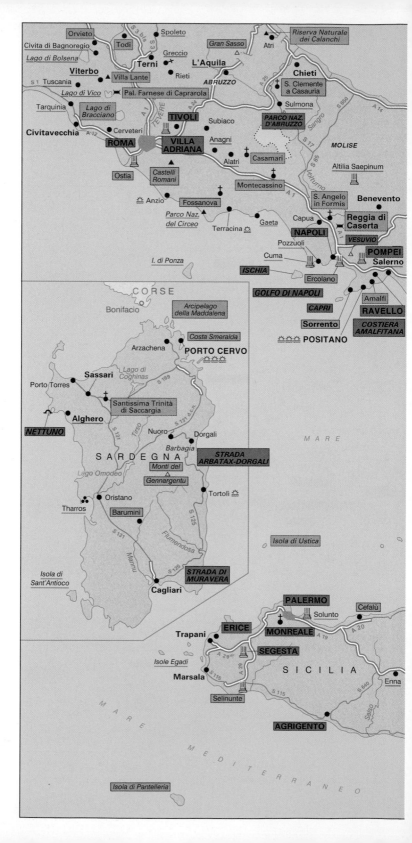

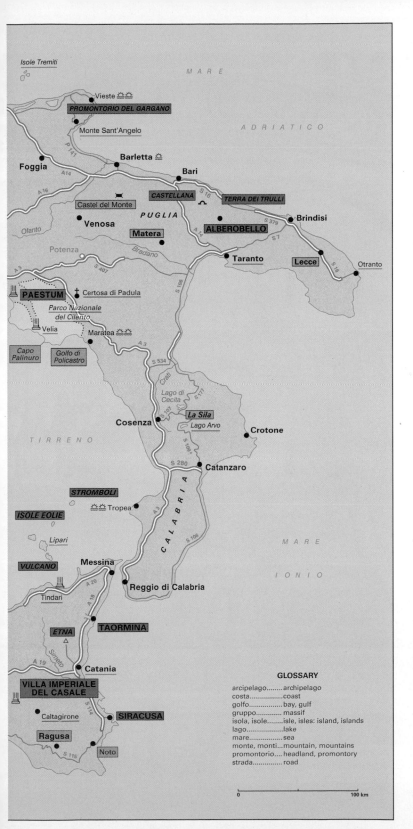

MARE

Isole Tremiti

Vieste ⚎⚎
PROMONTORIO DEL GARGANO

ADRIATICO

Monte Sant'Angelo

P 141

Foggia

Barletta ⚎

A14

Bari

A 16

CASTELLANA

TERRA DEI TRULLI

Castel del Monte

PUGLIA

S 16

ALBEROBELLO

S 379

Brindisi

Ofanto

Venosa

Matera

A 14

S 7

Lecce

S 18

Otranto

Potenza

Bradano

Taranto

S 407

S 106

PAESTUM

† Certosa di Padula

Parco Nazionale del Cilento

A 3

Velia

Maratea ⚎⚎

Capo Palinuro

Golfo di Policastro

A 3

S 534

Crati

Lago di Cecita

S 177

La Sila

Lago Arvo

TIRRENO

S 107

Cosenza

S 109

Crotone

S 280

Catanzaro

STROMBOLI

⚎⚎ Tropea

A 3

C
A
L
A
B
R
I
A

S 106

MARE

ISOLE EOLIE

Lipari

IONIO

VULCANO

Messina

A 20

A 18

Tindari

Reggio di Calabria

ETNA △

TAORMINA

Simeto

A 19

Catania

VILLA IMPERIALE
DEL CASALE

S 114

SIRACUSA

Caltagirone

Ragusa

Noto

S 115

GLOSSARY

arcipelago........archipelago
costa................coast
golfo................bay, gulf
gruppo.............massif
isola, isole........isle, isles: island, islands
lago..................lake
mare................sea
monte, monti...mountain, mountains
promontorio.... headland, promontory
strada..............road

0   100 km

Majolica decoration, the Cloisters,
Chiesa di Santa Chiara, Naples
Lara Pessina/ MICHELIN

MICHELIN DRIVING TOURS

The map of **Driving Tours** (☟*see following pages*) shows recommended itineraries. *The Green Guides* to Rome, Tuscany and Venice provide even more detail on these destinations.

THE GULF OF GENOA AND THE ITALIAN RIVIERA

This itinerary follows the Ligurian coast. Stop and stroll the seaside paths between the Cinque Terre, five coastal villages. Then survey the French-infused chic of the Côte d'Azur before moving inland, passing through the Colle di Tenda *(not recommended for those prone to travel sickness!)*.

VALLE D'AOSTA TO THE WINE-GROWING MONFERRATO AREA

A route for mountain lovers, this loop reaches the French Alps and in−cludes a cultural stop in Turin, with its splendid museums and Baroque architecture, the nearby Sacra di S. Michele, the Olympic Val di Susa, and a stop in the wine-growing Monferrato region.

FROM THE PO VALLEY TO THE GREAT LAKES OF LOMBARDY

This tour begins in the heart of Lombardy, the frenetic city of Milan. Look past the glamorous shops to discover an equally rich cultural heritage. The route continues to the Bassa Padana, a land of mist and fog with a melancholy charm, poetically described in the stories of Giovannino Guareschi. Finally, Verona is an ideal starting point for the lake district.

FROM THE DOLOMITES TO VENICE AND TRIESTE

Start in Venice (☟*see The Green Guide Venice*) before exploring this area's blend of Italian and Central European culture. In Trieste savor the literary atmosphere in the Caffè San Marco. The route continues through the harsh

and atmospheric Dolomites between Cortina and Bolzano, with the sounds of the German- and Latin-accented local dialect, before descending to Trent, dominated by the Buonconsiglio castle with its ancient fresco cycle of the Months. The itinerary concludes in the Palladian town of Vicenza.

THE PLAINS' RICH CITIES TO THE ADRIATIC LAGOONS

This itinerary straddles the Veneto, Lombardy and Romagna. A Byzantine atmosphere infuses this area, which embraces the Po Delta, Bologna, the mosaics of Ravenna, the noble city of Ferrara, the Palladian villas of the Brenta and the Venetian lagoon.

ART, SPIRITUALITY AND NATURE IN TUSCANY AND UMBRIA

This program takes in the art cities of Tuscany (☟*see the Green Guide Tuscany for more detailed information*), starting from Florence and progressing through the area around Lucca with its fine villas, Pisa, the Balze of Volterra and San Gimignano. The heart of Tuscany is embodied by Siena, a city at once gentle and aggressive (home of the *palio* horserace). Here the route explores some of the region's saints: St Bernardino with his sermons that shook the walls (☟*see Fashion in the Introduction*), St Catherine and, in Umbria, Saints Francis and Clare.

UMBRIA TO THE ADRIATIC

A journey of contrasting landscapes, from gentle Umbrian countryside and its treasures of art and spirituality (Gubbio, Perugia, Assisi and Spoleto), to the Abruzzi Mountains, the last refuge of bears, wolves and other indigenous wildlife. The route continues to the Adriatic Sea, with a stopover in the piazza of Ascoli Piceno. From Rimini move inland to San

Marino and the palace of the Duke of Montefeltro in Urbino. Italy's capital requires several days even for an introduction (*consult The Green Guide Rome)*. Once dubbed the *caput mundi*, head of the world, the Eternal City is rich in history and passion. Explore on foot and by public transport - traffic is intense. Afterwards, explore the region's lakes, castles, gardens and the Etruscan remains of Tarquinia. Finally, proceed to the Parco Nazionale d'Abruzzo and the abbeys of Casamari, Monte Cassino and San Clemente a Casauria. Nearby, the beach town of Sperlonga, reminiscent of a Greek white-washed village, sits above the Villa of Tiberius.

THE TREASURES OF THE NEAPOLITAN COAST

This colorful itinerary combines the intense blue of the sea, magenta bougainvillea and pastel houses overlooking the winding Amalfi coast (its splendid views are a frequent backdrop for thrillers such as the James Bond film *For Your Eyes Only*). Visit Naples and the surrounding bay, Capri, Mount Vesuvius and its illustrious victims Herculaneum and Pompeii, and then onto Paestum before reaching Calabria and the Gulf of Policastro. The island of Ischia is a restful detour; Capri's cheaper neighbor contains ancient ruins and volcanic hot springs.

PUGLIA

This route combines the sea with unusual architecture. Gargano – the "chicken spur" of Italy's boot – is a favorite holiday spot for natives, thanks to the sparkling Adriatic. Pilgrims flock to San Giovanni Rotondo, once home to the new saint Padre Pio. Drive south to the Terra dei Trulli, with its beehive-shaped stone huts, then explore the Baroque town of Lecce and down to the Ionian sea and the Sassi di Matera.

SICILY AND CALABRIA

Retrace some of Odysseus's epic journey. At the Strait of Messina, gaze out at the Sirens' rocks, Scylla (a tentacled mythological monster) and Charybdis (a whirlpool). Inland lies Mount Aspromonte, where mushrooms and ski chalets bloom in the mist. Greek ruins line the Ionian shore, but the colonists' descendants still dwell in the Graecanico, five bilingual mountain villages. Ancient monasteries line the road down to Sicily.

SARDINIA

In the north, trace the Costa Smeralda, where pink bluffs contrast with the green sea. Mysterious stone structures dot the west coast; Nuraghe Su Naraxi is the most famous. Museums in Sassari and Cagliari, the island's main town to the south, explore this ancient culture.

A view of the Tuscan countryside in Val d'Orcia

B. Morandi/ MICHELIN

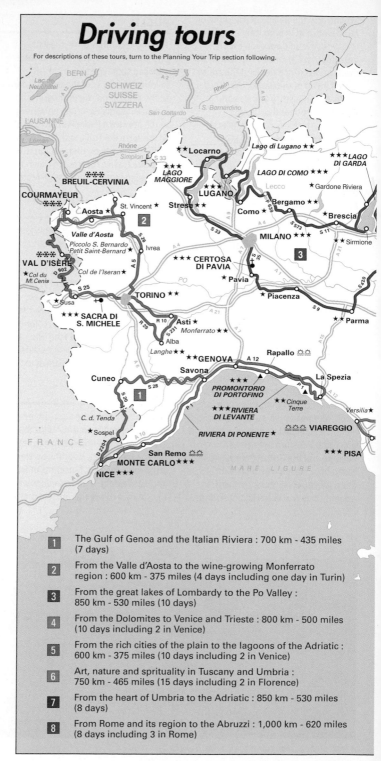

Driving tours

For descriptions of these tours, turn to the Planning Your Trip section following.

1 The Gulf of Genoa and the Italian Riviera : 700 km - 435 miles (7 days)

2 From the Valle d'Aosta to the wine-growing Monferrato region : 600 km - 375 miles (4 days including one day in Turin)

3 From the great lakes of Lombardy to the Po Valley : 850 km - 530 miles (10 days)

4 From the Dolomites to Venice and Trieste : 800 km - 500 miles (10 days including 2 in Venice)

5 From the rich cities of the plain to the lagoons of the Adriatic : 600 km - 375 miles (10 days including 2 in Venice)

6 Art, nature and sprituality in Tuscany and Umbria : 750 km - 465 miles (15 days including 2 in Florence)

7 From the heart of Umbria to the Adriatic : 850 km - 530 miles (8 days)

8 From Rome and its region to the Abruzzi : 1,000 km - 620 miles (8 days including 3 in Rome)

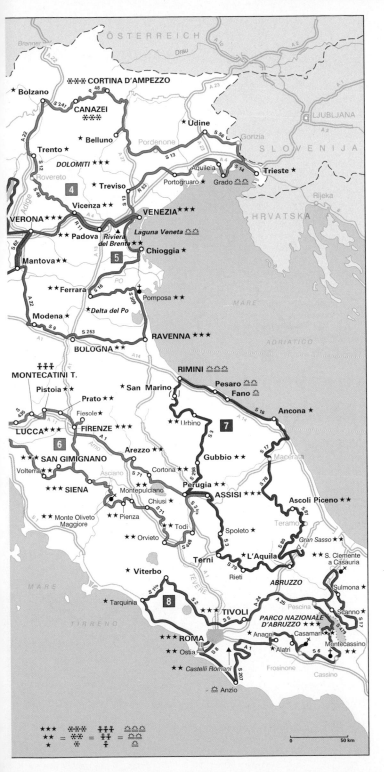

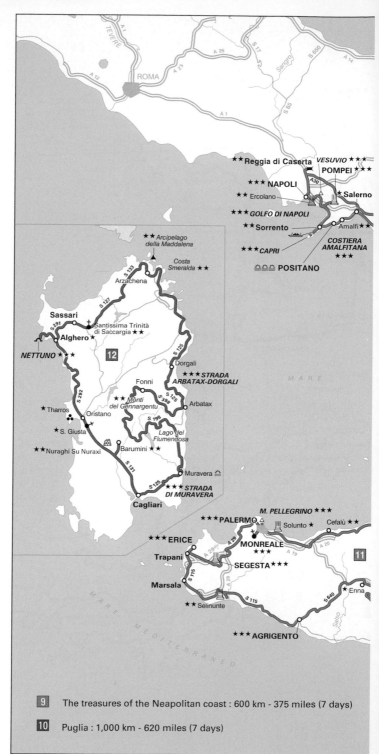

★★ **Reggia di Caserta**   *VESUVIO* ★★★
                            POMPEI ★★★
★★★ NAPOLI   ★ **Salerno**
★★ Ercolano
★★★ *GOLFO DI NAPOLI*
★★ **Sorrento**   Amalfi ★★
                           COSTIERA
★★★ *CAPRI*   *AMALFITANA*
                              ★★★
🏠🏠🏠 **POSITANO**

★★ *Arcipelago della Maddalena*

Costa Smeralda ★★
Arzachena

Sassari
† *Santissima Trinità di Saccargia* ★★
Alghero ★
NETTUNO ★★★   **12**

Dorgali
★★★ *STRADA ARBATAX-DORGALI*
Fonni
★★ *Mónti del Gennargentu*   **Arbatax**
★ **Tharros**   **Oristano**
★ **S. Giusta**   *Lago del Flumendosa*
★★ **Nuraghi Su Nuraxi**   **Barumini** ★★

                            Muravera
                     ★★★ *STRADA DI MURAVERA*
                  Cagliari

                        M. PELLEGRINO ★★★
           ★★★ PALERMO △ Solunto ★   Cefalù ★★
★★★ ERICE   **MONREALE**
Trapani   ★★★
                        SEGESTA ★★★   **11**
Marsala
                                            ★ Enna
           ★★ **Selinunte**
                        ★★★ AGRIGENTO

MARE MEDITERRANEO

9 The treasures of the Neapolitan coast : 600 km - 375 miles (7 days)

10 Puglia : 1,000 km - 620 miles (7 days)

11   Sicily and Calabria : 1,800 km - 1,120 miles (10 days including 7 in Sicily)

12   Sardinia : 1,100 km - 685 miles (7 days)

WHEN AND WHERE TO GO

When to Go

April, May, September and October, are best for city breaks, with cooler temperatures and thinner crowds. However, many Italian cities use the seasons to theatrical advantage and are worth visiting off peak – Venice's winter mists (and floods) lend it an air of mystery, while a crisp winter morning in a deserted Florentine piazza is exceptionally pleasant. June and September are best for beach holidays, providing sultry heat without uncomfortable humidity, high prices and peak crowds. However, in the Alps and Apennines short, cool summers between May to September are optimum times for walking and outdoor activity holidays. The Italian ski season is typically from December to late March, with year-round skiing on the higher reaches of Mont Blanc.

Themed Tours

HISTORIC ROUTES

Italy has a wide network of roads laid down by some illustrious historical inhabitants. Listed here are a few, beginning with a pilgrim route.

Via Francigena

Watch for the Via Francigena logo: a pilgrim who looks like a Roman statue, a little squat, with a cane in his hand and a bundle on his shoulder.
The Via Francigena ran from Canterbury to Rome, and was used by medieval pilgrims who managed to cover about 20km/12.5mi a day on foot.
The stopovers were: Canterbury, Calais, Bruay, Arras, Reims, Chalons sur Marne, Bar sur Aube, Besançon, Pontarlier, Lausanne, Gran San Bernardo, Aosta, Ivrea, Santhià, Vercelli, Pavia, Piacenza, Fiorenzuola, Fidenza, Parma, Fornovo, Pontremoli, Aulla, Luni, Lucca, S. Genesio, S. Gimignano, Siena, S. Quirico, Bolsena, Viterbo, Sutri and Rome. An alternative route into Italy passed through the Val di Susa. For more information see www.viafrancigena.com.

Via Aurelia

Of ancient Roman origin, the Via Aurelia (S 1) has linked Rome to Genoa since 109 BC.

Via Appia

Construction of this road began in 312 BC. At its longest, it linked Rome to Brindisi. Nowadays it is limited to Rome and its surrounding area.

Via Cassia

Laid down in the 2C BC, this road runs through Etruria, linking Rome to Arezzo and then extending to Florence and Modena and, in another direction, to Luni. The current S 2, which still bears the same name, links Rome and Florence.

Via Emilia

This road links Rimini to Piacenza and gave its name to the region. It was built in 187 BC. During the period of the Roman Empire it extended to Aosta and Aquileia. Today the Via Emilia follows the same route.

Via Flaminia

Built in 220 BC, the Via Flaminia linked Rome to Rimini. Nowadays it is one of the principal arteries of the capital.

KNOW BEFORE YOU GO

Useful Websites

The Internet is a useful source of information, enabling visitors to contact tourist offices, consult brochures and make bookings on line.

www.italiantouristboard.co.uk
Website of the Italian State Tourist Board. Accommodation, events, museums and Italian holiday experiences. Tour operator search

www.italiantourism.com
Website of the Italian State Tourist Board in North America. Travel tips and holiday planning, plus region-by-region information

www.initaly.com
Travel tips, accommodation, transport, day tours, photo library museum reservations and useful web sites.

www.discoveritalia.com
Tourist information on Italian cities and destinations, with 'virtual visits', specialist itineraries and road map

www.museionline.it
Information on museums and historic sites, website links and news on exhibitions and special events (in Italian only)

www.italianculture.net
Information on all facets of Italian culture, including art, design, music, opera, language, cinema and cuisine

www.beniculturali.it
Website of the Ministry of Culture (in Italian only). Museum details, cultural event programmes, news on restorations and publications

International Visitors

EMBASSIES AND CONSULATES

ITALIAN EMBASSIES
UK – 14 Three Kings' Yard, London W1K 4EH, ☎ (020) 7312 2200; Fax (020) 7312 2230; ambasciata. londra@esteri.it; www.amblondra.esteri.it.

Tourist Organisations

Italian State Tourist Office – ENIT (Ente Nazionale Italiano per il Turismo)For information, brochures, maps and assistance in planning a trip to Italy, apply to the ENIT in your country or consult the ENIT website, www.enit.it. The main tourist offices in Italy are given at the beginning of each chapter in the Selected Sights section, preceded by the symbol ▯.

UK	1 Princes Street, London W1B 2AY	☎ (020) 7408 1254	italy@italiantouristboard. co.uk
USA	630 Fifth Avenue, Suite 1565, New York, NY 10111	☎ 212-245-5618	enitny@italiantourism. com
	12400 Wilshire Boulevard, Suite 550, Los Angeles, CA 90025	☎ 310-820-1898	enitla@italiantourism.com
	500 North Michigan Avenue, Suite 2240, Chicago, IL 60611	☎ 312-644-0996	enitch@italiantourism. com
Canada	175 Bloor Street East, Suite 907 – South Tower, Toronto M4W 3R8	☎ 416-925-4882	enit.canada@on.aibn.com

USA – 3000 Whitehaven Street, NW Washington, DC 20008, ☎(202) 612 4400; Fax (202) 518 2151; www.ambwashingtondc.esteri.it.
Canada – 275 Slater Street, 21st Floor, Ottawa, Ontario, K1P 5H9, ☎(613) 232 2401; Fax (613) 233 1484; ambasciata.ottawa@esteri.it; www.ambottawa.esteri.it.

ITALIAN CONSULATES
UK – 38 Eaton Place, London SW1X 8AN; ☎(020) 7235 9371; Fax (020) 7823 1609; www. conslondra.esteri.it. Rodwell Tower, 111 Piccadilly Street, Manchester M1 2HY, ☎(0161) 236 9024; Fax (0161) 236 5574; www.consmanchester.esteri.it. 32 Melville Street, Edinburgh EH3 7HA, ☎(0131) 220 3695/226 3631; Fax (0131) 226 6260; www.consedimburgo.esteri.it. 7-9 Greyfriars, Bedford MK40 1H, ☎(0)1234 356 647; Fax (0)1234 269 699; www.consbedford.esteri.it
USA – 690 Park Avenue, New York, NY 10021, ☎(212) 737 9100; Fax (212) 249 4945; info.newyork@ esteri.it; www.consnewyork.esteri.it.
Canada – 3489 Drummond Street, Montreal, Quebec, H3G 1X6, ☎(514) 849 8351; Fax (514) 499 9471; consolato.montreal@esteri.it; www.consmontreal.esteri.it. 136 Beverly Street, Toronto, Ontario, M5T 1Y5, ☎(416) 977 1566; (416) 977 1119; archivio.toronto@esteri.it; www.constoronto.esteri.it. 110-510 West Hastings Street, Vancouver, BC, V6B 1L8, ☎(604) 684 7288; (604) 685 4263; consolato.vancouver@esteri.it; www.consedmonton.esteri.it.

FOREIGN EMBASSIES AND CONSULATES IN ITALY
Australia – Via Antonio Bosio, 5, 00161 Rome, ☎06 85 27 21; www.italy.embassy.gov.au
Canada – Via G.B. de Rossi 27, 00161 Rome, ☎06 85 44 42 911; www.dfait-maeci.gc.ca

Ireland – Piazza di Campitelli 3, 00186 Rome, ☎06 69 79 121; www.ambasciata-irlanda.it
UK – Via XX Settembre 80a, 00187 Rome, ☎06 42 20 00 01; www.fco.gov.uk
USA – Via Vittorio Veneto 119a, 00187 Rome, ☎06 46 741; www.usembassy.it

DOCUMENTS

Passport – Visitors entering Italy must be in possession of a valid national passport. Citizens of European Union countries need only a National Identity Card. Report loss or theft to the embassy or consulate and the local police.
Visa – Entry visas are required by Australian, New Zealand, Canadian and US citizens (if their intended stay exceeds three months). Apply to the Italian Consulate (visa issued same day; delay if submitted by mail). US citizens should obtain the booklet A Safe Trip Abroad ($2.75), which provides useful information on visa requirements, customs regulations and medical care for international travellers. Published by the Government Printing Office, it can be ordered by phone (☎(202) 512-0000) or consulted on-line at www.access.gpo.gov.
Driving Licence – Nationals of EU countries require a valid national driving licence. Nationals of non-EU countries require an International Driving Permit. This is available in the US from the American Automobile Association for US$10 (an application form can be found at www.aaa.com) and in Canada from the Canadian Automobile Association for $15 (see www.caa.ca for details). If you are bringing your own car into the country, you will need the vehicle registration papers.
Car insurance – If you are bringing your own car to Italy, an International Insurance Certificate (Green Card), although no longer a legal require-ment, is the most effective proof of insurance cover and is internationally

recognised by the police and other authorities. This is available from your insurer.

CUSTOMS REGULATIONS

As of 30 June 1999, those travelling between countries within the European Union can no longer purchase "duty-free" goods. For further information on customs regulations, travellers should contact Her Majesty's Revenue & Customs (HMRC) ☎0845 010 9000; Enquiries. estn@hmrc.gsi.gov.uk; www.hmrc.gov.uk.
The US Customs Service offers a free publication entitled Know Before You Go, which can be downloaded at www.customs.gov.

HEALTH

British citizens should apply to the Department of Health for a European Health Insurance Card (EHIC), which entitles the holder to urgent treatment for accident or unexpected illness in EU countries. It does not provide cover for repatriation in the event of an emergency. The EHIC is free, and can be obtained by calling ☎0800 555 7777 or at www.dh.gov.uk. Nationals of non-EU countries should check that their insurance policy covers them specifically for overseas travel, including doctor's visits, medication and hospitalisation in Italy (most take out supplementary insurance).
American Express offers its cardholders a service called Global Assist to help in financial, legal, medical or personal emergencies. For further information, consult their website: www.americanexpress.com.
All prescription drugs should be clearly labelled, and it is recommended that you carry a prescription copy.

Duty-Free Allowances	
Spirits (whisky, gin, vodka etc)	10 litres
Fortified wines (vermouth, port etc)	20 litres
Wine (not more than 60 sparkling)	90 litres
Beer	110 litres
Cigarettes	3200
Cigarillos	400
Cigars	200
Smoking tobacco	3 kg

Chemists' shops (*farmacia* – green cross sign) post a list of colleagues open at night or on Sundays. First Aid service (pronto soccorso) is available at airports, railway stations and in hospitals.

Accessibility

Many of the sights described in this guide are accessible to people with special needs. Sights marked with the symbols ♿ or (♿) offer full or partial access for wheelchairs. However, it is advisable to check beforehand by telephone.
For further information contact CO.IN (Consorzio Cooperative Integrate), Via di Torricola 87, 00178 Rome, ☎800 27 10 27, Fax 06 71 29 01 25, www.consociale.it. ⏰Offices are open Mon-Fri, 9am-5pm and 9am-1pm Sat and on the eve of public holidays. Visit the website at www.coinsociale.it.
The website www.italiapertutti.it also provides information on hotels, restaurants, museums and monuments that are accessible to disabled travellers.

GETTING THERE

By Plane

Many international carriers operate services to Rome and the country's major provincial airports (Milan, Turin, Verona, Venice, Genoa, Bologna, Florence, Pisa, Naples, Catania and Palermo). Numerous no-frills airlines now offer low-cost flights from many regional airports in the UK, Ireland and other European cities. These usually connect to more remote urban airports or those in regional capitals like Pescara or Verona.

Alitalia
2A Cains Lane, Bedfont, Middesex TW14 9RL, ☏0870 544 8259; www.alitalia.co.uk
4-5 Dawson Street, Dublin 2; ☏(01) 677 5171; www.alitalia.ie
350 Fifth Avenue, Suite 3600, New York, NY 10118, ☏800 223 5730; alitaliasupport@alicos.net; www.alitaliausa.com
Viale Marchetti 111, 00148 Rome, ☏06 22 22.

British Airways
Waterside, P.O. Box 365, Harmondsworth, Middlesex UB7 0GB, ☏0870 850 9850; www.ba.com
USA – ☏(1-800) AIRWAYS.
Via Bissolati 11, 00187 Rome, ☏524 92 800 (in Italy only).

British Midland
Flights from London Heathrow to Naples and Venice, ☏0870 607 0555; www.flybmi.com.

Easyjet
Flights to Caligari, Catania, Milan, Naples, Olbia, Palermo, Rome, Turin, Pisa and Venice from London Stansted and regional airports in the UK, ☏0871 244 2366; www.easyjet.com.

Ryanair
Flights to Alghero (Sardinia), Ancona, Bari, Brindisi, Bologna, Genoa, Milan, Palermo, Pescara, Pisa, Rome, Trieste, Turin, Venice and Verona from London Stansted; and to Milan and Rome from London Luton.
☏0871 246 0000; www.ryanair.com.
For information on discounts on flights to Italy, see "Concessions".

By Ship

Details of passenger ferry and car ferry services from the UK and Republic of Ireland to the Channel ports, linking up with the European rail and motorway network can be obtained from travel agents and from the main operators:
P & O Ferries – Channel House, Channel View Road, Dover CT17 9TJ, ☏08705 980 333; www.poferries.com.
Stena Line – Stena House, Station Approach, Holyhead, Anglesey LL65 1DQ, ☏08705 70 70 70; www.stenaline.com.
For details of crossing via the **Channel Tunnel** (35-minute high-speed undersea rail link between Folkestone and Calais), ☏08705 35 35 35; www.eurotunnel.com.
Norfolkline – Export Freight Plaza, Eastern Dock, CT16 1JA Dover, Kent, ☏0870 870 1020; www.norfolkline-ferries.co.uk.

By Train

From London and the Channel ports there are rail services to many Italian towns including many high-speed passenger trains and motorail services. Tourists residing outside Italy can buy rail passes that offer unlimited travel, during a specific period. Parties may purchase discounted group-travel tickets on the Italian Railways network.
Italian State Railway – www.trenitalia.com; ☏89 20 21
Rail Europe – www.raileurope.com, ☏08708 371 371

Eurostar – www.eurostar.com;
☏08705 186 186
Tickets are also available from the main British and American Rail Travel Centres and travel agencies.
Rail is a particularly good way of getting to Milan, Venice and Florence, as the stations are within easy reach of the cities' centres.

By Coach/Bus

Regular coach services operate from London to Rome and to other large provincial Italian towns and cities. Services from Victoria Coach Station in London to Italy are operated by **Eurolines**, ☏08705 143 219; www.eurolines.co.uk.
Alternatively, contact **National Express**, ☏08705 80 80 80; www.nationalexpress.com.

By Car

See "Documents" for details of credential requirements in Italy.
Roads from France into Italy, with the exception of the Menton/Ventimiglia (Riviera) coast road, are dependent on Alpine passes and tunnels. The main roads go through the Montgenèvre pass near Briançon, the Fréjus tunnel and Mont-Cenis pass near Saint-Jean-de-Maurienne, the Petit-Saint-Bernard pass near Bourg-Saint-Maurice and the Mont-Blanc tunnel near Chamonix. Via Switzerland, three main routes are possible – through the tunnel or pass at Grand-Saint-Bernard, through the Simplon pass, and through the St Gottard pass which goes via Ticino and Lugano to the great lakes of Lombardy. Be sure to budget for the Swiss road tax (*vignette*), which is levied on all motor vehicles and trailers with a maximum weight of 3.5 tons, instead of charging tolls on the motorways.
The *vignette* costs 40 Swiss francs and can be bought at border crossings, post offices, petrol stations, garages and cantonal motor registries, or in advance from the Switzerland Travel Centre, 30 Bedford Street, London WC2E 9ED; ☏0207 7420 4900; www.stc.co.uk.
The Brenner pass south of Innsbruck greets drivers from Germany and Austria.
Remember that most of these tunnels or passes levy tolls (*see "By Car" in Getting Around, below*).

Use Michelin maps 719, 721 and 735 or the Michelin Atlas Europe to help plan your route.

GETTING AROUND

By Plane

Frequent domestic flights cover the whole country. There are transfer buses to town terminals and railway stations.
For further information, contact:
Air Dolomiti: ☏045 28 86 140 (+39 0452 886 140 from abroad); www.airdolomiti.it.
Airone: ☏199 20 70 80; www.flyairone.it.
Alitalia: ☏06 22 22; www.alitalia.it.
Meridiana: ☏89 29 28 (+39 0789 52 682 from abroad); www.meridiana.it

By Ship

SICILY AND SARDINIA

These two islands are linked to the mainland by ferries and hydrofoils and are very popular, especially during the summer months. Visitors are therefore advised to book early, especially if travelling with a car or if a cabin is required. Deck tickets are available until a few hours before departure at the terminal. Again, it's wise to book ahead, even for these less luxurious spots.

The main ferry services to Sicily are operated from Genoa by Grandi Navi Veloci (20hr); from Livorno by Grandi Navi Veloci (3 times/week, 17hr); from Naples by Tirrenia (10hr) and SNAV (11hr; a fast service operates from April to October, 5hr 30min); and from Cagliari by Tirrenia (once a week, 13hr 30min). For information and reservations, contact:

Genoa: Grandi Navi Veloci, Via Fieschi 17, 16121 Genova, ☎010 55 091, www1.gnv.it, infopax@grimaldi.it.

Naples: SNAV, Stazione Marittima, 80142 Napoli, ☎081 42 85 555, mergelli@tin.it, www.snav.it; Tirrenia, Molo Angioino, 80133 Napoli; ☎892 123 (from Italian land lines) or ☎081 01 71 998 (from mobile phones or abroad); www.gruppotirrenia.it.

CAPRI

Ferry and hydrofoil services operate from Reggio di Calabria and Villa San Giovanni to Messina. Ferries run from Reggio Calabria (45min, Stazione Ferrovie Stato, ☎0965 75 60 99), Villa S. Giovanni (20min, Caronte Shipping, Via Marina 30, ☎0965 75 82 41) and Ferrovie dello Stato (Piazza Stazione, ☎0965 75 60 99). For hydrofoil services (15min) contact SNAV, Stazione Marittima, Reggio Calabria, ☎0965 29 568, www.snav.it.

CROSSINGS TO SARDINIA FROM THE FOLLOWING CITIES

Civitavecchia: Cosica-Sardinia Ferries, Calata Laurenti, ☎0766 50 07 14, Fax 0766 50 07 18 (7hr to Golfo Aranci), Tirrenia Navigazione, Stazione

Marittima (to Cagliari, Olbia, Arbatax) ☎081 01 71 998 or 892 123 (in Italy), www.tirrenia.it.

Fiumicino: Tirrenia Navigazione, Agenzia DA.NI.MARI Shipping, Via Bignami 43 (to Arbatax and Golfo Aranci). ☎081 01 71 998, or 892 123 (in Italy), www.tirrenia.it.

Genoa: Tirrenia Navigazione, Nuovo Terminal Traghetti, Via Milano 51 (20hr to Cagliari, 15hr to Olbia, 19hr to Arbatax, 10hr to Porto Torres) ☎081 01 71 998 or 892 123 (in Italy), www. tirrenia.it.; Grimaldi, Grandi Navi Veloci, Via Fieschi 17, ☎010 58 93 31, Fax 010 50 92 25.

La Spezia: Tirrenia Navigazione, Agenzia Lardon, Viale S. Bartolomeo 109 (5hr 30min to Golfo Aranci), ☎081 01 71 998 or 892 123 (in Italy), www.tirrenia.it.

Livorno: Corsica-Sardinia Ferries, Calata Carrara, ☎0586 89 89 79, Fax 0586 89 61 03 (9hr to Golfo Aranci).

Palermo: Tirrenia Navigazione, Calata Marinai d'Italia, ☎081 01 71 998 or 892 123 (in Italy), www.tirrenia.it.

Trapani: Tirrenia Navigazione, Agenzia Salvo, Molo Sanità (11hr to Cagliari), ☎081 01 71 998 or 892 123 (in Italy), www.tirrenia.it.

By Train

The railway network (www.trenitalia. it) also enables visitors to travel the length and breadth of Italy. Ticket machines usually have English-language displays and accept credit cards, eliminating long waits and confusing conversations. Whenever possible, reserve a seat or you may wind up huddled in the aisle. Also, be aware that Italy has ten different services, from the posh Eurostar (ES) to the slow, local Regionale (R). Mix-ups could result in costly fines and upgrades. Abbreviations indicate a train's type on the display boards and schedules (printed on large yellow and white posters).

Special train tickets can be bought once in the country. The *biglietto chilometrico* (kilometre ticket) is valid

Capri

for a distance of 3 000km/1 875mi (for a maximum of 20 journeys) and allows travellers to save approximately 15% off the full price of a ticket. It is valid for two months from the date of the first journey and can be bought up to a month prior to travelling.

A *carnet* allows the purchase of a minimum of four tickets with a 10% discount (if the distance is between 71km/44mi and 350km/218mi) or 20% (for longer journeys). Other special railcards include the *Carta Verde* (for those under 26) and the *Carta d'Argento* (for those over 60) which give 10 and 15% discounts on all journeys. The *Pendolino* or high-speed train runs between Milan-Rome (4hr), Turin-Rome (5hr), Genoa-Rome (4hr), Rome-Venice (4hr) and Rome-Bari (4hr 30min). Bicycles can be taken on trains with a guard van (usually all local services) for a supplement of about 3.50 € or an additional second-class ticket. Dismantled bikes ride free if loaded into Trenitalia sacks, but are not covered by lost luggage policies.

For discounts on train fares ⓒsee the "Discounts" section.

By Car

Italian roads are excellent, and there is a wide network of motorways (*autostrade*) (ⓒ*see map on following pages)*. The Italian motorway website can be found at www.autostrade.it.

HIGHWAY CODE

The minimum driving age is 18. Traffic flows on the right. Drivers and front-seat passengers must wear seat belts, also mandatory in the back where they are fitted. Children under 12 must travel in the back seats, unless the front seat is fitted with a child restraint system. Full or dipped headlights should be switched on in poor visibility and at night; use sidelights only when a stationary vehicle is not clearly visible. In the event of a breakdown, a red warning triangle must be displayed in the road; these can be hired from the ACI (Automobile Club Italia) offices at the frontier (deposit refunded).

Drivers should watch out for unfamiliar road signs and take great care on the road (there's much truth in the joke that Italian drivers prefer using their horn to their brakes!). At crossroads, cars coming from the right have priority. Flashing lights indicate a driver is not slowing down.

Severe penalties are applicable for drunk-driving offences.

Speed limits: in built-up areas, 50kph/31mph; on country roads, 90kph/55mph; on motorways, 90kph/55mph for vehicles up to 1,000cc and 130kph/80mph for vehicles over 1,100cc.

PARKING

Car parks with attendants are common. The crime rate is high, so the extra expense is often worthwhile, especially in the south (Naples is most notorious). Obviously, check rates before parking to avoid unpleasant surprises.

Many large towns limit traffic in their historic town centers (only authorised vehicles may enter), indicated by large rectangular signs saying "*Zona a traffico limitato riservata ai veicoli autorizzati.*" Parking outside town is advisable anyway, as Italy's old, narrow streets usually have no pavements or sidewalks.

ROAD SIGNS

Motorways (autostrade – subject to tolls) and dual carriageways (*super-strade*) are indicated by green signs; ordinary roads by blue signs; tourist sights by yellow signs.

ROAD TOLLS

Tolls are payable on most motorways (www.autostrade.it). The amount is calculated according to the distance between the car axles and engine capacity.

At an unmanned booth, press the button for a ticket, which must be presented at the exit.

Motorway fees can be paid in cash (look for lanes with signs representing toll collectors), with the Via Card and by

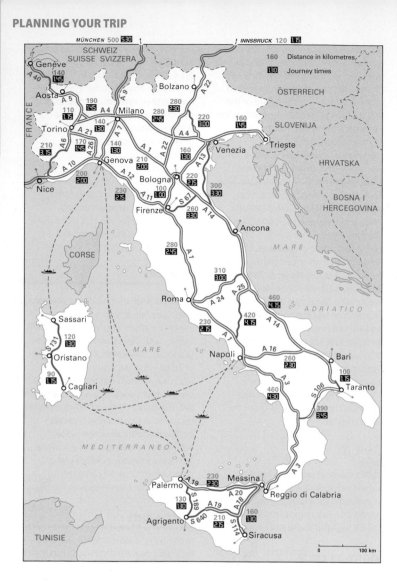

credit card (look for lanes with the Via Card sign and blue stripes on the road surface). The Telepass (www.telepass.it) is a toll pre-pay system that allows cars to pass through the roadtolls quickly. Unless you have a Telepass don't stray into the signed lane by mistake – it is usually on the far left.

PETROL

Gasolio =diesel.
Super =super leaded (98 octane).
Senza piombo =premium unleaded gas (95 octane).

Super Plus or *Euro Plus* =super unleaded gas (98 octane).
Gas stations are usually open from 7am to 7pm. Many close at lunchtime (between 12.30pm and 3pm), on Sundays and public holidays, and many refuse payment by credit card. Attendants do not expect tips and often refuse to issue receipts. Self-service stations have squat machines that don't give change and have a reputation for malfunctioning. Sometimes a start button or lever activates the flow, however; look around.

MAPS AND PLANS

Michelin map 735 at a scale of 1:1 000 000 covers the whole country. At 1:400 000, Michelin map 561 covers the northwest, 562 the northeast, 563 the centre, 564 the south, 565 Sicily and 566 Sardinia; at 1:200 000, 553 covers Bolzano and Aosta to Milan; at 1:100 000, 115 covers the westernmost stretch of the Italian Riviera. The Michelin Atlas Italy (1:300 000) contains a complete index of towns, 80 plans of the largest cities and covers all of Italy; it is also available in mini format. Folded maps 38 (1:10 000) and 46 (1:15 000) cover Rome and Milan. The Touring Club Italiano (TCI), Corso d'Italia 10, 20139 Milan, ☎02 85 26 72, publishes a regional map series at 1:200 000. www.touringclub.it. Michelin Travel Publications has created a website to help motorists prepare for their journey. The service enables travellers to select their preferred route (fastest, shortest etc) and to calculate distances. Consult www.ViaMichelin.com.

MOTORING ORGANISATIONS

Road Rescue Services – In case of breakdown, contact ACI (Automobile Club Italia), ☎116 (24hr). This breakdown service (tax levied) is operated by the ACI for foreign motorists. The ACI also offers a telephone information service in English (and other languages) for road and weather conditions as well as for tourist events: ☎803 116, www.aci.it.

CAR RENTAL

There are car rental agencies at airports, railway stations and in all large towns and resorts throughout Italy. The main agencies are Avis, Hertz, Eurodollar, Europcar and Maggiore Budget. Fly-drive schemes or train-and-car packages are available.
European cars usually have manual transmissions, but automatic cars are available on demand.
Many companies won't rent to drivers under 21 or 23 – or insist upon large cash deposits.
An International Driving Permit could be required for non-EU nationals; both the **American Automobile Association** ($15; www.aaa.com/vacation/idpf.html) and **Royal Auto Club** (£5.50; www.rac.co.uk/travelservices/int_driving_permit/) issue these.

WHERE TO STAY AND EAT

Budget

The euro is rapidly eroding Italy's reputation for good value. Bills steadily rise and tourists are the first to pay the price. However, savvy travelers can still find bargains. Avoid tourist centers and explore off-season. Hotels, in particular, hike up rates in the summer, especially mid-July to the end of August, when Italians go on holiday en masse.
The accommodations and restaurants in the **Address Books** in the guide have been ordered by price categories to suit all budgets.

Lodgings marked by the symbol ⊖ include campsites, youth hostels, and modest but decent hotels and pensioni with double rooms for under under 80€. Restaurants indicated by the symbol ⊖ will charge less than 15 € for a three-course meal (excluding drinks) without sacrificing quality: this is Italy, after all, where poor quality food is scandalous. Those on a larger budget will find more charming and comfortable hotels and better quality restaurants marked by the symbol ⊖⊖. Rooms in this category will cost from 80 € to 130 € for a double and expect to pay between 25 € and 45 € for a meal. For those in search of a truly memorable stay, the category high-lighted by the symbol ⊜⊜⊜ includes luxurious hotels, B&Bs and guest farmhouses with great atmosphere, as well as a wide range of facilities. Restaurants in this bracket will satisfy the most demanding taste buds with prices to match. *For all price categories, see the Legend at the back of the guide.*

Basic meals are cheap and easy to find in Italy: for a meal in a pizzeria, expect to pay about 15€ per person, including drinks; a quick snack, especially at lunchtime, will cost around 6€ for a sandwich and 11€ for a simple dish and beverage.

Address Books

Hotel and restaurant listings fall within the description of each region; they can be found in this guide in green boxes titled Address Books. To enhance your stay, these selections have been chosen for their location, comfort, value for the money and in many cases, their charm. Italian cuisine is as varied as it is exquisite. We have highlighted an array of eateries for their atmosphere, location and/or regional delicacies.

Where to Stay

See the Places to Stay map on the following pages.

CHOOSING WHERE TO STAY

The map of Places to Stay *(on the following pages)* highlights destinations suitable for various interests. Cultural tourists should seek names framed in green. Visitors on brief trips – touring cities of artistic interest – may wish to overnight in places underlined in green. Nature parks are shaded in green, while symbols indicate spas, as well as seaside and winter sports resorts.

For coin ranges see the Legend on the cover flap.

Book accommodations well in advance for popular regions and cities, especially from April to October. Typically, prices are far lower – and many hotels offer discounts or special weekend deals – from November to March (though not the art cities such as Florence, Venice and Rome). Always check prices before booking, as rates can vary depending on the time of year and availability of rooms.

HOTELS AND PENSIONI

Generally, the word *pensione* describes a small family-run hotel. Sometimes situated within residential buildings, these offer basic rooms, often with shared bathrooms.

A hotel may also be labelled an *albergo* or *locanda*.

RURAL ACCOMMODATION

Rural guesthouses were originally conceived as an opportunity to combine accommodation and home-made, home-cooked delicacies (among them olive oil, wine, honey, vegetables and meat). Recently some regions have enjoyed an *agriturismo* boom. Some guesthouses are as elegant as the best hotels, with prices to match. Catering could range from a DIY kitchenette to breakfast or a complete menu celebrating the farm's produce.

The guesthouses included in the guide usually accept bookings for one night only, but in high season the majority prefer weekly stays or offer half or full board, as well as requiring a minimum stay. Prices for the latter are only given when this formula is compulsory. Many rural guesthouses only have double rooms and prices reflect two people sharing. Solo travelers should ask for, but not expect, a discount. In any case, due to agritourism's ever-increasing popularity, book well in advance.

Consult the following guides for further details: **Vacanze e Natura** *(published by Associazione Terranostra,* ☏06 46 82 370, www.terranostra.it), **Agriturismo e Vacanze Verdi** *(published by Associazione Agriturist, www.agriturist.it)*, **Guida all'Agriturismo**, *(published by Demetra)* and **Vacanze Verdi** (*published by Edagricole, which offers a selection of over 400 addresses*). Information is also available from **Turismo Verde**, *Via Mariano Fortuny 20, 00196 Roma,* ☎*06 32 40 111, www.turismoverde.it.*

BED AND BREAKFAST

Sometimes indistinguishable from a hotel, a bed and breakfast may be the hosts' home – an apartment, house or villa with rooms to rent (usually between one and three). Guests are usually required to stay for a minimum period and credit cards are rarely accepted. Normally, a bed and breakfast offers a cosier atmosphere than a hotel. In Italy the experience is often delightful and reasonably priced. Enquire about curfews before booking, however. Contact **Bed & Breakfast Italia,** *Palazzo Sforza Cesarini, Corso Vittorio Emanuele II 282, 00186 Rome,* ☎*06 68 78 618, www.bbitalia.it,* or **Bed & Breakfast Bon Voyage,** *Via Procaccini 7, 20154 Milan,* ☎*02 33 11 814. Also visit the websites at: www. bedandbreakfast.it, www.primitaly.it/ bb/, www.bedebreakfast.it, www. dolcecasa.it.*

SHORT-TERM RENTAL OR SWAP

For privacy and authenticity, a short-term rental is ideal. Generally cheaper than hotels, apartments also have basic cooking implements and facilities. Start your search with companies like **Real Rome** *(www.realrome.com)*, **Life in Italy** *(www.lifeinitaly.com/rent)* and **ExpatExchange** *(www.expatexchange. com)*.

Homeowners can also swap spaces. Find a reputable service, like **Home Exchange** *(Post Office Box 787, Hermosa Beach, CA, 90254, USA,* ☎*310 798 3864, www.homeexchange.com)* or **HomeLink International** *(Italian office: Viale Frassinetti 84, 31046 Oderzo (Treviso);* ☎*422 815 575. www.homelink.org).* Check references before trading places.

HOSTELS AND BUDGET ACCOMMODATION

Hostel accommodation is only available to members of the **Youth Hostel Association**. Join at any YHA branch for worldwide access. There is no age limit for membership, which must be renewed annually. Apart from official youth hostels there are many establishments, mainly frequented by young people, with dormitories or rooms with several beds all of which have very reasonable prices. Visit the websites: *www.italiayhf.org* and *www.hostels-aig.org. For more youth hostelling information contact www.hiusa.org or www.yha. org.uk* Italian hostels sometimes inhabit spectacular spaces: villas, fortresses, palaces and old monasteries. Most are run by the **Associazione Italiana Alberghi per la Gioventù** (AIG), *situated at Via Cavour 44, 00184 Rome,* ☎*06 48 71 152, www.ostellionline.org. Case per ferie* (holiday homes), more common in the big cities, offer decent, cheap accommodations; the only disadvantage being a curfew (typically 10.30pm). For more information, contact the tourist offices and **CITS, Centro Italiano Turismo Sociale, Associazione dell'ospitalità religiosa**, ☎*06 48 73 145.*

CAMPSITES

Campsites offer a reasonably priced way of staying close to the city while still enjoying green surroundings and the open air. Few wilderness options exist in Italy; Outdoor athletes can shelter in the *rifugi* (refuges), some 700 mountain huts, campsites and shelters run by the **Club Alpino Italiano** (☎*02 614 1378; www.cai.it*). Otherwise, expect manicured grounds crowded with tents, caravans (RVs) and bungalows, alongside arcades, shops, discos, pools and restaurants. Happy hordes descend on these pleasure parks in summertime; reserve well in advance.
Prices shown in the guide are daily rates for two people, one tent and one car.

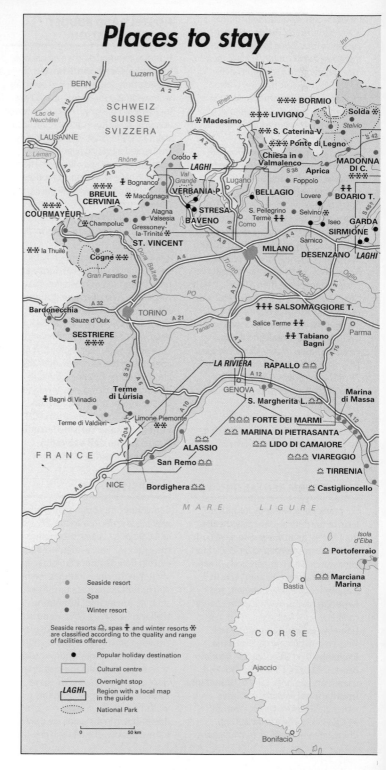

Places to stay

BERN
Luzern
Lac de Neuchâtel
LAUSANNE
L. Léman
SCHWEIZ
SUISSE
SVIZZERA
✴ Madesimo
Rhein
Rhône
Crodo ✚
LAGHI
Val Grande
Lugano
Bognanco ✚
✴✴✴ BREUIL CERVINIA
✴ Macúgnaga
VERBANIA-P.
✴✴✴ COURMAYEUR
Champoluc
Alagna Valsesia
Gressoney-la-Trinité ✴
✴✴ la Thuile
ST. VINCENT
Cogne ✴✴
Gran Paradiso
Dora Baltea
A 5
✴✴✴ BORMIO
✴✴✴ LIVIGNO
Solda
Stelvio
✴✴ S. Caterina-V.
✴✴✴ Ponte di Legno
Chiesa in Valmalenco
S 38
Aprica
Foppolo
MADONNA DI C. ✴✴✴
BELLAGIO
Lovere
S. Pellegrino Terme ✚✚
Selvino
Como
BAVENO
STRESA
Sarnico
MILANO
Iseo
✚✚ BOARIO T.
GARDA
SIRMIONE
DESENZANO
LAGHI
Adda
Oglio

Inn
A 13
A 2
S 42
A 457

Bardonecchia
Sauze d'Oulx
A 32
TORINO
A 21
SESTRIERE ✴✴✴
PO
Tanaro
A 7
✚✚✚ SALSOMAGGIORE T.
Salice Terme ✚✚
Parma
A 15
✚✚ Tabiano Bagni

✚ Bagni di Vinadio
Terme di Lúrisia
Terme di Valdieri
Limone Piemonte ✴✴
N 20
ALASSIO
San Remo
Bordighera ⚱⚱
FRANCE
NICE
A 8
LA RIVIERA
A 12
GENOVA
A 10
RAPALLO ⚱⚱
S. Margherita L. ⚱⚱
Marina di Massa
FORTE DEI MARMI ⚱⚱⚱
MARINA DI PIETRASANTA ⚱⚱
LIDO DI CAMAIORE ⚱⚱
VIAREGGIO ⚱⚱⚱
⚱ TIRRENIA
⚱ Castiglioncello

MARE   LIGURE

Isola d'Elba
⚱ Portoferraio
⚱⚱ Marciana Marina
Bastia
CORSE
Ajaccio
Bonifacio

● Seaside resort
● Spa
● Winter resort

Seaside resorts ⚱, spas ✚ and winter resorts ✴
are classified according to the quality and range
of facilities offered.

● Popular holiday destination
▢ Cultural centre
── Overnight stop
LAGHI Region with a local map in the guide
⬭ National Park

0 ⊢────────⊣ 50 km

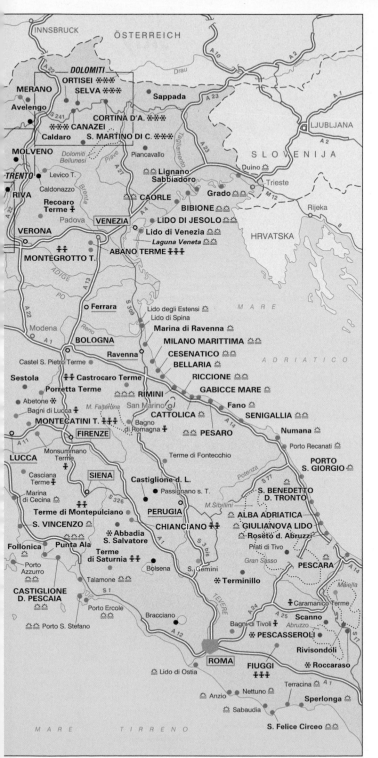

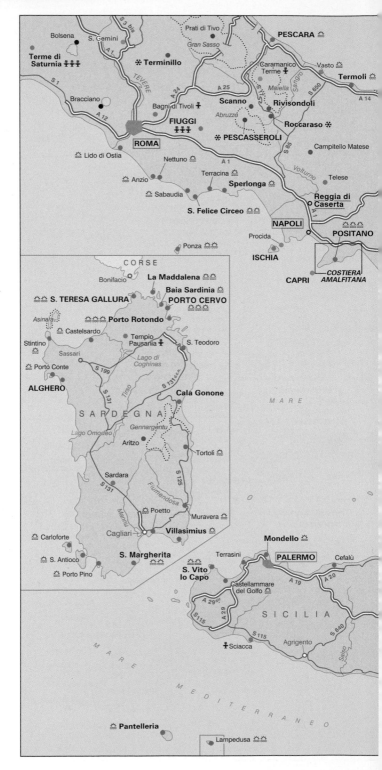

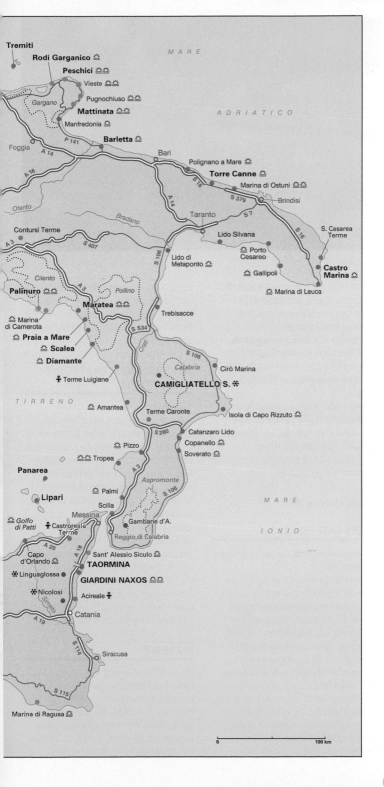

B. Morandi/MICHELIN

Tuscan tomatoes

An International Camping Carnet for caravans is useful, but not compulsory; it can be obtained from the motoring organisations or the **Camping and Caravanning Club,** Greenfields House, Westwood Way, Coventry CV4 8JH, ☎02476 694 995; www.campingandcaravanningclub. co.uk
For more information contact the **Federazione Italiana del Campeggio e del Caravanning,** *Via Vittorio Emanuele 11, 50041 Calenzano (FI), ☎055 88 23 91, Fax ☎055 88 25 918; www.federcampeggio.it.*

Where to Eat

PRICES AND HOURS

For all price ranges, ☾see the Legend on the cover flap.
Restaurant opening times vary from region to region (in the centre and south of Italy they tend to open and close later). Generally lunch is from 12.30pm to 2.30pm and dinner from 7.30pm to 11pm. Service is usually included, but tip in proportion to customer satisfaction (a few euros at most, unless the establishment is elite). Restaurants where service is not included, a rarity, are marked; an appropriate percentage for a tip is suggested after the meal's price. By law, the bread and the cover charge should be included in the price, but in some *trattorie* and especially in *pizzerie* they are calculated separately.
☾*For more information on Italian food, see Introduction.*

RESTAURANTS, TRATTORIE AND OSTERIE

The distinction is eroding, but traditionally a *ristorante* offers fine cuisine and service, while a *trattoria* or *osteria* is more likely to be a family-run establishment serving home-made fare in a more relaxed, informal setting. In typical *trattorie*, the waiter or owner explains the dishes on offer (ask about pricing to avoid a shock when the bill arrives; seafood, in particular, is sold by weight and expenses mount quickly). Be wary of tourist menus, which offer little choice. *Trattorie* used to exclusively serve house wine by the carafe, but now many have proper wine lists, which highlight local vintages.

PIZZERIE

It's hard to go wrong with a pizza in Italy, even from the tiniest back-street counter. Tasty, quick and affordable, this meal is a staple for tourists and locals alike. We selected exceptional *pizzerie*, but welcome reports of "authentic" establishments from readers.

WINE BARS

Wine bars *(enoteche)* are becoming increasingly popular in Italy. Like *osterie* they often have a kitchen and serve daily specials and light starters, as well as a varied choice of wines served by the glass or bottle.

For a more exhaustive list of hotels consult the red *Michelin Guide Italia* which details Italy's hotels and restaurants. Establishments that offer particularly good value are marked with the 🍴 symbol (good food and service at a reasonable price) or coin symbols (a simple meal for under 20 €).

The succulent lemons of the Amalfi coast

WHAT TO SEE AND DO

Leisure Activities

Italy's varied landscape has something for everyone. The Alps provide footpaths and mountains suitable for all levels of athletic expertise. The lake district, the mountain streams and rivers are ideal for fishing. Trentino-Alto Adige, the Riviera del Brenta, Tuscany and Umbria are among the more suitable regions for cycling. The Maremma offers a perfect landscape for horse riding.

The entire coast of Italy is an Eden for those who enjoy swimming, windsurfing and the beach: the Adriatic coast with its shallow waters and long beaches is ideal for families with children, while the waters of the Gargano, the Gulf of Policastro, Sicily and Sardinia are renowned for their crystalline purity and splendid colours, notably the emerald greens of the Costa Smeralda. The Amalfi coast and the Faraglioni of Capri are perhaps the best known Italian coastlines; Versilia, with the Apuan Alps as a backdrop, is an essential venue for habitués of the beach, and the Ligurian Riviera offers striking views and beaches that nestle between the hills that lead down to the sea.

For information on sporting and leisure activities see the addresses of information offices for each region or sight in the introduction to each chapter in the guide.

NATURE PARKS

National nature parks are the ideal destination for holidaymakers who prefer nature to regular tourist pursuits. Further information is available online at www.cts.it (in Italian only) and www.parks.it.

The principal Italian nature parks are:

Parco Nazionale del Gran Paradiso – See *VALLE D'AOSTA*.

Parco Nazionale della Val Grande Near Lago Maggiore, this is one of the largest wilderness areas in Italy.

To reach the park, follow the A 26 to Gravellona Toce. For information, contact Villa San Remiglio 19, 28922 Verbania (VB), ☎0323 55 79 60, www.parcovalgrande.it.

Parco Nazionale dello Stelvio –
This includes the Ortles-Cevedale
and Valfurva massifs and the Martello,
Ultimo, Solda and Trafoi valleys. The
park can be reached via Lombardy
on the SS 38 to Bormio, or via Trentino
by taking first the motorway, then
the SS 43 to Rabbi. Contact the tourist
offices of Solda ☎0473 61 30 15
or Malè ☎0473 90 12 80, or Associazione Turistica Val Martello,
☎0473 74 45 98, www.stelviopark.it.

**Parco Nazionale delle Dolomiti
Bellunesi** – This park runs along the
right bank of the Piave river, between
Feltre and Belluno, and covers three
main mountain ranges: the Vette
Feltrine, the Monti del Sole and the
Schiara massif. The park can be
reached by taking the SS 50 from
Grappa, or the SS 348 from Treviso as
far as Feltre. The park authority office
is in Feltre, Piazzale Zancanaro 1,
☎0439 33 28, www.dolomitipark.it.

Parco Nazionale dei Monti Sibillini
A large limestone massif stretches
from the Marches to Umbria. Reach
the park from Macerata on the S 78 to
Sarnano and Amandola and from
Spoleto the Forca di Cerro pass on the
S 209, S 320 and S 396 to Norcia. For
information on the park, contact the
Marches regional tourist office:
Servizio Turismo della Regione
Marche, Via Gentile da Fabriano 9,
60125 Ancona, ☎071 80 61,
www.sibillini.net.

Parco Nazionale del Gran Sasso –
🛈See ABRUZZO.

Parco Nazionale d'Abruzzo –
🛈See ABRUZZO.

Parco Nazionale della Maiella –
This can be reached via the A 5
motorway, exits Sulmona, Bussi, Torre
de' Passeri and Scafa. For information,
contact the park authorities (Ente
Parco) at Piazza Alberto Duval Casa
Nanni, 67030 Campo di Giove (AQ),
☎0864 40 851, Fax 0864 40 85 350,
www.parcomajella.it.

Parco Nazionale del Circeo –
🛈See GAETA.

**Parco Nazionale del Cilento
e Vallo di Diano** –
🛈See Parco Nazionale del CILENTO.

Parco Nazionale del Gargano –
This park runs along the promontory
of the same name and also includes
the Tremiti islands. There are visitor
centres at San Marco in Lamis, Piazza
Carlo Marx 1, ☎0882 83 32 82 and at
Monte Sant'Angelo, loc. Foresta
Umbra, ☎0884 56 09 44. Information
is also available from the Azienda di
Promozione Turistica di Foggia, Via
E. Perrone 17, ☎0881 72 31 41,
www.parcogargano.it.

Parco Nazionale del Pollino – This
park covers the area around Monte
Pollino (2 248m/7 380ft), which is part
of the Calabrian Apennine chain. The
park also contains several museums:
the Museo del Lupo di Alessandria del
Carretto, the Museo Naturalistico del
Pollino di Rotonda, the Museo Albanese
di Civita and the Museo della Cultura
Arberesh di San Paolo Albanese. For
further information, contact the Ente
Parco Nazionale del Pollino, Via delle
Frecce Tricolori 6, 85048 Rotonda
(PZ), ☎0973 66 93 11,
www.parco-pollino.it.

Parco Nazionale della Calabria and
Parco Nazionale dell'Aspromonte –
🛈See CALABRIA.

**Parco Nazionale del Golfo di
Orosei, Gennargentu e Asinara** –
The best base for trips into the
park is Nuoro. For information,
contact the Ente Provinciale per il
Turismo, Piazza Italia 19, Nuoro,
☎0784 30 083,
www.parcogennargentu.it.

THEME PARKS

The following is a list of the main
theme parks in Italy. Log onto
www.parksmania.it for further details,
including discount offers on tickets.

Edenlandia – Viale Kennedy 76,
80125 Naples, ☎081 23 94 090,
www.edenlandia.it. Over 25 attractions
include a zoo, theater and renowned
steel roller coaster.

Fantasy World Minitalia – Via
Vittorio Veneto 52, 24042 Capriate
(MI), ☎02 90 90 169, www.fantasy-
world.it A 4 motorway, exit at
Capriate. The Wild West theme

stretches from a Mississippi paddle-boat to an old-time train and a covered-wagon ferris wheel.

Fiabilandia – 47900 Loc. Rivazzurra di Rimini, ☎0541 37 20 64, www.fiabilandia.it A 4 motorway, exit at Rimini Sud. Ride concepts include Peter Pan's beach, Merlin's castle, and a gold mine.

Gardaland – 37014 Castelnuovo del Garda, loc. Ronchi, ☎045 64 49 777, www.gardaland.it Take the A 4 motorway and exit at Peschiera del Garda or take A 22 and exit at Affi, then take the road to Peschiera. Italy's largest theme park boasts about its Robot World and Sequoia Adventure roller coaster.

Italia in Miniatura –Via Popilia 239, 47900 Viserba (RN), ☎0541 73 67 36, www.italiainminiatura.com Take A 14 motorway, exit at Rimini Nord. A canoe splash-ride and monorail enliven the "Little Italy" idea.

Le Navi – Piazzale delle Nazioni 1/a, 47841 Cattolica (RN), ☎0541 83 71, www.lenavi.com Take the A 14 motorway, exit at Cattolica. This maritime theme park is housed in old holiday camps from the 1930s.

Mirabilandia – Statale Adriatica 16, km 162, 48100 Savio di Ravenna, ☎0544 56 11 11, www.mirabilandia.it Take the A 14 motorway and exit at Ravenna (from the north) or Cesena Nord, then take the E 45, exiting at Mirabilandia; from Rome, take the A 1 as far as Orte, then the E 45. Rides include a dinosaur tour, car splash, ferris wheel and a London bus (more exciting than it sounds).

Oltremare – Viale Pistoia (near the motorway toll booths), 47838 Riccione, ☎0541 42 71, www.oltremare.org This impressive and enjoyable theme park provides information on the Adriatic and its conservation.

OUTDOOR FUN

🏃 Mountaineering and Hiking
Contact the Club Alpino Italiano (CAI), Via Petrella 19, 20124 Milan, ☎02 20 57 231, www.cai.it.

Hunting
Contact Federazione Italiana della Caccia, Via Salaria 298/a, 00199 Rome, ☎06 84 40 941, www.fidc.it.

Canoeing
Contact Federazione Italiana Canottaggio, Viale Tiziano 74, 00196 Rome, ☎06 36 85 86 50, www.canottaggio.org and Federazione Italiana Canoa e Kayak, Viale Tiziano 70, 00196 Rome, ☎06 36 85 84 18, www.federcanoa.it.

🚴 Cycling
Contact Federazione Ciclistica Italiana, Stadio Olimpico, Curva Nord, Via dei Gladiatori, 00194 Foro Italico, Rome, ☎06 36 85 78 13, www.federciclismo.it.

🐎 Riding and Pony Trekkin
Contact Federazione Italiana di Turismo Equestre, Piazza Antonio Mancini 4, 00196 Rome, ☎06 32 65 02 30, www.fiteec-ante.it.

Golf
Contact Federazione Italiana Golf, Viale Tiziano 74, 00196 Rome, ☎06 32 31 825, www.federgolf.it.

⛵ Sailing and windsurfing
Contact Federazione Italiana Vela, Piazza Borgo Pila 40, Corte Lambruschini, Torre A, 16129 Genoa ☎010 54 45 41, www.federvela.it.

🎣 Fishing
Contact Federazione Italiana Pesca Sportiva e Attività Subacquee, Viale Tiziano 70, 00196 Rome, ☎06 36 85 82 38, www.fipsas.it.

🎿 Skiing
Contact Federazione Italiana Sport Invernali, Via Piranesi, 44b, 20137 Milan, ☎02 75 731, www.fisi.org.

Water skiing
Contact Federazione Italiana Sci nautico, Via Piranesi, 44/b, 20137 Milan, ☎02 75 29 181, www.scinautico.com.

Speleology
Contact Società Speleologica Italiana, Via Zamboni, 67, 40127 Bologna, ☎051 25 00 49, www.ssi.speleo.it.

Spas

The map of Places to Stay on pp 32-35 gives an overview of the location of Italian spas. For further information consult the Italian Tourist Board website (☝see "Useful Web Sites").

Abano
Shaded by pines, this spa town near Padova numbers among Italian's favorites. Terme Montegrotto, Largo Marconi 8, ☎049 866 66 09, free phone in Italy 800 255 161, www.abanomontegrotto.it.

Ferentino
The chic, professional Terme di Pompeo targets acne, rheumatism and respiratory conditions just southeast of Rome. Via Casilina km 76, ☎0775 244 114; www.termepompeo.it.

Fiuggi
The Terme di Fiuggi inhabits a large, ornate complex – including a buggy train, bocce court, minigolf, play-grounds, theater and a dance floor – near the Abruzzi National Park. Piazza Frascara, ☎0775-5451, www.termefiuggi.it.

Montecatini
South of Bologna stands this town which boasts 9 spas. The most grand is Tettuccio, known as the "temple of European spas". Viale Verdi 41, ☎0572 7781, free phone in Italy 800 132 538, www.termemontecatini.it.

Sant' Angelo, Ischia
Baths cascade down a cliff to the hot sand beach at the Aphrodite Apollon, Via Fondolillo, ☎081 999 219, www.aphrodite.it.

Viterbo
The grandiose Terme dei Papi – "baths of the popes" – has a magnificent pool, grotto and hotel. Strada Bagni 12, ☎0761 350 555, www.termedei-papi.it. The Pianeta Benessere is more a "beauty farm with a mix of tradition and modern technology." Strada Tuscanese 26/28, ☎0761 3581, www.grandhoteltermesalus.com.

Activities for Children

In this guide, sights of particular interest to children are indicated with a KIDS symbol [Kids]. Some attractions may offer discount fees for children.

Calendar of Events

JANUARY

30 and 31 January
St Orso Fair: Craft fair with sale of articles from the Valle d'Aosta. Aosta

FEBRUARY

First two weeks of February
Almonds in bloom festival. Agrigento
Carnival
Parties and events in the *calli* and *campi* of Venice. Venice
Folk festival, including the famous battle of the oranges. Ivrea
Procession of allegorical floats Viareggio
"Venerdì gnocolar" procession. Verona

APRIL

1 April
Investiture of the regents of the Republic San Marino
Holy Week (Maundy Thursday and Good Friday)
Holy Week rites: procession of Our Lady of Sorrows and the Mysteries. Taranto

Easter Day
Scoppio del Carro: At noon, in
Piazza del Duomo, fireworks
display from a decorated float –
the fireworks are set off by a dove
sliding along a wire from the high
altar of the cathedral to the float.
Parade in Renaissance costume.
Florence
**Feast of the "Madonna che
scappa in piazza"**
Sulmona

MAY

First Sunday of May
    **Feast of the Miracle of St
    Januarius** in the cathedral.
    Naples
    Feast of Sant'Efisio
    Cagliari
First Thursday after 1 May
    Calendimaggio.   Assisi
First week of May
    Feast of St Nicholas: 7 May:
    procession in period costume
    through the city; 8 May: Mass and
    procession along the shore; the
    statue is taken out to sea and
    worshipped.
    Bari
15 May
    Ceri ("candle") race.
    Gubbio
May
    Vogalonga
    Venice
Last Sunday in May
    Cavalcata Sarda
    Sassari
    **Palio della Balestra in Piazza
    Grande**
    Gubbio
Late May-early June
    **Festival of Sicilian costumes
    and carts.**
    Taormina

JUNE

Early June
    **Cavalcata Oswald von Wolken-
    stein:** tournament and medieval
    fair inspired by the south Tyrolese
    poet. Castelrotto, Siusi and Fiè
    allo Scilia

June-November, even years
    Biennale art festival.
    Venice
16-17 June
    Feast of St Ranieri
    Pisa
**24 June and two other days
of the month**
    Calcio Storico fiorentino: ball
    game in costume in Piazza S.
    Croce, accompanied by a
    procession in 16C costumes.
    **Fireworks in Piazzale
    Michelangelo.**   Florence
    Penultimate Sunday in June
    Giostra del Saracino – Saracen's
    Tournament.   Arezzo

JULY

    Spoleto Festival: international
    theatre, music and dance festival.
    Spoleto
    Umbria Jazz Festival.   Perugia
Late June-late August
    **Opera season in the Roman
    amphitheatre.**   Verona
2 July
    Palio delle Contrade – historic
    horse race.
    Siena
Second Saturday in July
    Festa della Quintana: procession
    of representatives of the various
    districts in 15C costumes; jousting.
    Ascoli Piceno
Third Saturday in July
    Feast of the Redeemer: fireworks
    display on Saturday night;
    religious services and regatta on
    Sunday.
    Venice

AUGUST

First Sunday in August
    Festa della Quintana; jousting.
    Ascoli Piceno
14 August
    Feast of the candles.
    Sassari
16 August
    Palio delle Contrade.
    Siena

29 August and previous Sunday
Feast of the Redeemer.
Nuoro

Last week in August
Ferrara Buskers Festival: street
music festival.
Ferrara

Late August-early September
International Film Festival at
the Lido.   Venice

SEPTEMBER

Palio della Balestra: crossbow
competition in medieval costume.
Sansepolcro
**Festival delle Sagre and "Douja
d'or" wine festival**   Asti
Luminara di S. Croce.   Lucca

First Sunday in September
Giostra del Saracino – Saracen's
Joust.
**Historical Regatta on the Grand
Canal**. Arezzo
Venice

7 September
Feast of the Rificolona (coloured
paper lanterns). Musical and
folklore events in the various
districts.   Florence

7 and 8 September
**Feast of the Nativity of the
Virgin.**   Loreto

**Second weekend in September in
even years**
Partita a scacchi – chess
tournament with human chess
pieces.Marostica

Second Sunday in September
Giostra della Quintana –
jousting competition in medieval
costume.   Foligno

19 September
**Feast of the Miracle of St
Januarius, in the cathedral.**
Naples

Third Sunday in September
Corsa del Palio   Asti

OCTOBER

1 October
**Investiture of the Republic's
regents**.
San Marino

October
Barcolana: sailing regatta.
Trieste

NOVEMBER

Mid-November
Truffle festival   Asti

21 November
Madonna della Salute Feast
Venice

Late November-December
Christmas markets.
Bolzano, Bressanone, Merano

DECEMBER

Night of the 9 to 10 December
**Feast of the Translation of the
Santa Casa.**   Loreto

Shopping

Most shops in Italy open from
8.30/9am to 12.30/1pm and 3.30/4pm
to 7.30/8pm, although in the centre of
large towns and cities, shops usually
remain open at lunchtime. Credit
cards are accepted in most stores, with
the exception of small food shops.

In northern Italy, shops often take a
shorter midday break and close earlier.
Late-night shopping is frequent in
seaside resorts. Many tourist resorts
have a regular open-air market.
Italy is noted for its luxe retail goods -
shop for handmade leather items in
Florence and high fashion in Milan, in
the so-called Golden Triangle around
Via Montenapoleone, or on Via
Condotti in Rome. If you're on a
budget, Italy's best kept shopping
secrets are its designer factory outlet
stores clustered around the big cities -
you will need a car to reach most of
them (*www.factoryoutletsitaly.com*).
For a lower key shopping experience,
every region produces beautiful crafts
of which it is justly proud.

Alabaster and stone – Alabaster is
mostly crafted in Volterra in
Tuscany. Liguria crafts slate
objects.

Paper and papier mâché – These can be found in Fabriano in the Marches, in Florence, Amalfi, Syracuse in Sicily, Lecce in Puglia, Verona and Bassano del Grappa in the Veneto region.

Ceramics – Mainly these appear in Romagna (Faenza), Umbria (Deruta, Gubbio, Orvieto, Città di Castello) and Sicily (Caltagirone).

Coral – Coral is popular in Naples, Torre del Greco and Alghero on the island of Sardinia.

Filigree – Liguria (Genoa) and Sardinia produce fine metalwork.

Wood – Trentino-Alto Adige (particularly in Val Gardena) and Valle d'Aosta are the most notable regions for carvings.

Lace – Lovers of lace should head for the Paese di Bengodi in Burano, the colourful Venetian island, and also for Tuscany and Umbria.

Porcelain – Campania, Capodimonte, and Bassano del Grappa in the Veneto produce this.

Glass – Watch the almost magical creation of glass objects on the island of Murano in the Venetian lagoon, known the world over. Glassblowers also work in Liguria, at Altare, near Savona.

One should not of course forget the vast array of food products: pasta, Parmesan, Parma and San Daniele ham. *See the Introduction.*

Sightseeing

Information on admission times and museum- and monument-charges is given in the "Selected Sights" section of the guide. All are liable to alteration. Due to fluctuations in the cost of living and often in opening times, as well as possible closures for restoration work, the information given here should merely serve as a guideline. Visitors should phone ahead to confirm details. The admission prices indicated are for single adults benefiting from no special concession; reductions for children, students, the over 60s and parties should be requested on site and be endorsed with proof of ID.

The culinary delights of Norcia

Special conditions often exist for groups, with advance notice. For nationals of European Union member countries, many institutions provide free admission to visitors under 18 and over 65 with proof of identification, and a 50% reduction for visitors under 25 years of age. Many museums require visitors to leave bags and backpacks in a luggage deposit area at the museum entrance. Taking photos with a flash is usually forbidden. During **National Heritage Week** (*Settimana dei Beni Culturali*), which takes place at a different time each year, access to a large number of sights is free of charge. Contact the tourist offices for details. When visits to museums, churches or other sights are accompanied by a guide, a donation is customary.

CHURCHES

Churches and chapels are usually closed from noon to 4pm. Notices ask visitors to dress appropriately to a place of worship (no sleeveless and low-cut tops, miniskirts, shorts aor bare feet). Tourists should avoid intruding on services. Visit churches early for the best natural light; also some close in the afternoons due to lack of staff. Artworks often have coin-operated lighting.

Books

Italy has long been a favourite subject with writers, both of fiction and non-fiction, and there are many excellent books that will give you a flavour of the country and its culture. Some of the following books may be out of print and therefore only available from libraries.

HISTORY AND ART

A Concise Encyclopaedia of the Italian Renaissance. JR Hale. (Thames and Hudson).
A comprehensive look at the history and culture of the Renaissance period, covered in over 750 alphabetical entries.
A History of Italian Renaissance Art. F Hartt. (Thames and Hudson). The development of Italian Renaissance art is charted from it's beginnings and influences through to its maturity at the height of the revolution that was the Renaissance.
Italy: The Unfinished Revolution. Matt Frei. (Mandarin). BBC correspondent Matt Frei takes an indepth look at the complex and tumultuous world of contemporary Italian politics, including the rise of neo-fascists to power and the election of media tycoon Silvio Berusconi, to prime minister.
Leonardo da Vinci. Martin Kemp, Jane Roberts and Philip Steadman. (Yale University Press). This classic survey of the life and work of Leonardo da Vinci is illuminated by 128 superb illustrations.
Michelangelo. Howard Hibbard. (Penguin). Comprehensive and well written look at the work and passion of the Renaissance master.
Rise and Fall of the House of Medici. Christopher Hibbert (Penguin). An enthralling journey following the influence of Florence's most famous mercantile patrons, the Medici family, on the city's economic, political and cultural fabric from the early 1430s to the end of the dynasty in 1737.
Roman Italy. TW Potter. (British Museum Publications Ltd) A fascinating combination of history and modern archaeology, looking at the implications of recent findings and their controversies, illustrated with sumptuous photos.
Siena: A City and its History. Judith Hook. (Hamish Hamilton). A classic exposition of the city of Siena through its rich culture, art and politics.
The Art of the Renaissance. Linda and Peter Murray. (Thames and Hudson). Superlative and comprehensive catalogue of the art of the Renaissance, covering everything from the arts of Florence, printing and early illustrated books, the Late Gothic period, Leonardo da Vinci, the Milanese Renaissance, Early Classicism and the beginning of High Renaissance.

TRAVEL

An Italian Affair. Laura Fraser. (Vintage). A touching and semi-autobiographical story of a woman who escapes to Italy at the end of her marriage, only to begin a passionate and consuming affair with a professor she meets there.
DH Lawrence and Italy. (Penguin). These three evocative essays are based loosely on journals written by DH Lawrence as he traveled through mainland Italy and Sardinia with his then wife Frieda.
Italian Neighbours. Tim Parks. (Grove Press) A candid, warm portrait of Italy and Italians through the eyes of an expat married to an Italian woman and living in Italy.
Living Abroad in Italy. John Moretti. (Avalon Travel). A useful guide to all aspects of living and working in Italy.
Love And War in the Apennines. Eric Newby. (Lonely Planet).

Travel writer, Eric Newby reflects back on his experiences in Italy during WWII, from tales of courage in a time of battle, to his emergent love for a local Italian girl.

Old Calabria. Norman Douglas. (Marlboro Travel).
This witty, sophisticated travelogue was first published in 1915, and is an account of the rugged – and at the time, largely unexplored – countryside of southern Italy in the early part of the 20th century.

The Path to Rome. Hilaire Belloc. (Penguin).
Belloc walked from France to Rome, across the Apennines and Alps, and chronicled his journey to create a vivid glimpse of Western Europe after WW1.

Stones of Florence and Venice. Mary McCarthy. (Penguin).
Two great Italian cities come under the sharply observational eye of Mary McCarthy, who charts their influence and evolution through their history and art.

Under the Tuscan Sun. Frances Mayes. (Bantam Books).
Story of the personal and practical odyssey undertaken by Frances Mayes when she buys and restores an abandoned Tuscan villa.

FOOD AND WINE

Life beyond Lambrusco (Understanding Italian Fine Wine). N Belfrage. (Sidgwick and Jackson).
A thorough grounding in Italian viticulture, covering wines from all the country's main wine areas.

The Food of Italy. Claudia Roden. (Steerforth Italia).
Food writer Claudia Roden spent a year in Italy researching Italian food, and this book covers everything from regional recipes to pastas, seafood and authentic Italian desserts.

The Fratelli Camisa Cookery Book. Elizabeth Camisa. (Penguin).
A collection of recipes from friends and family of Elizabeth Camisa, that reflect the produce and traditions of North West Italy. Also included are useful tips on what to look for when buying traditional ingredients to make sure you get the best.

FICTION

A Room with a View. EM Forster. (Penguin)
An elegant tale of social comedy, romantic longing and travel among the middle classes of the 19C that was made into an Academy Award winning Merchant Ivory film in 1985.

Christ Stopped at Eboli. Carlo Levi. (Farrar, Straus and Giroux).
Carlo Levi was exiled to a remote corner of Italy for his opposition to Mussolini, and enters a timeless, eternally patient life long since forgotton by modern life.

Garden of the Finzi-Continis. Giorgio Bassani. (Penguin).
Set in the last summers of the 1930s in Italy, this poignant story, which was turned into an Academy Award-winning film in 1970, follows the movements of an aristocratic Jewish family in the run up to WWII.

Jack Frusciante Has Left the Band. Enrico Brizzi . (Grove Press).
A coming of age story about the powerful effect of first love on a young boy from Bologna.

Sicilian Carousel. Lawrence Durrell. (Faber).
Takes the reader on a bus tour around Sicily, looking at the historical legacies of the island's many occupants, from the Greeks to the Arabs, Normans and Spanish.

The Leopard. Giuseppe Tomasi di Lampedusa. (Flamingo).
This beautifully recounted story, which EM Forster called "One of the great lonely books", is the story of a proud Sicilian prince dealing with the waning power of the aristocracy and and the changes he observes in the society of 19C Italy.

The Name of the Rose. Umberto Eco (Vintage).

Eco's dark murder investigation in a 14C Italian monastery is also an exposition on the history of religious conflict, monastic orders and the idea of heresy in Italy.

Films

⚹ *See CINEMA in the Introduction.*

The Last Days of Pompeii (1935).

An epic tale of ancient Roman family politics interrupted by the fatal eruption of Vesuvius.

Ladri di biciclette (1948).

A poor father in post-war Rome finds work only to have his bicycle stolen on the first day.

Francesco, Giullare di Dio (1950).

Vignettes depicting the life of St Francis.

September Affair (1950).

When a plane crashes a pianist and an industrialist are mistakenly presumed dead. Free of their former lives they begin a love affair in a villa in Florence.

Quo Vadis (1951).

Love story between a Roman general and a Christian during the reign of Emperor Nero.

The Little World of Don Camillo (1951).

The mayor and the priest of a small village in the Po Valley struggle to reconcile their differences of opinion and live in harmony with each other.

Roman Holiday (1953).

An errant princess (Audrey Hepburn) trys to explore Rome incognito, aided by a scheming journalist (Cary Grant).

Summertime (1955).

An American middle-aged secretary's life is turned upside down when she meets a handsome antiques-shop owner in Venice's Piazza San Marco.

Le Notti Cabiria (1957).

A wistful story of Roman prostitute, Cabiria, who falls in love with an accountant that pursues her after seeing her being hypnotized on stage.

La Dolce Vita (1960).

A portrait of decadence in the Eternal City, following a week in the life of a louche Roman journalist, obsessed with a visiting movie star.

Spartacus (1960).

A classic swords and sandals epic charting a slave rebellion against the Roman Empire, led by the gladiator, Spartacus.

Il Gattopardo (1963).

A story of waning aristocratic power in 19C Sicily as told through the eyes of a proud Italian prince.

Il Conformista (1969).

A young man, working for Mussolini, is given a gun on honeymoon and an assignment to look up an old professor of his, who fled Italy when the Facists came to power.

Novecento (1976).

The rise of Fascism as seen through the eyes of a landowner's son and a peasant.

Un giornata particolare (1977).

Sophia Loren ignites a profound friendship with her gay neighbour that is to have a profound impact on both their lives.

A Room with a View (1985).

E M Forster's tale of elegant travel, young love and self-discovery among the English middle classes, set in 19C Florence.

Cinema Paradiso (1989).

A famous film director revisits his childhood Sicilian home, and in doing so comes face to face with his own past.

Il Postino (1994).

The story of an unlikely friendship between a famous exiled Chilean poet and his local postman.

La vita è bella (1997).

A Jewish bookkeeper protects his son in a WWII concentration camp by pretending it's all a game.

The Talented Mr Ripley (1999).

A conman murders a rich American playboy and assumes his identity and life with devestating consequences.

Pane e Tulipani (2000).
> A housewife from Pescara is left behind by a tour bus at a highway cafe, and decides not to wait for her husband to come and get her, but to hitchhike to Venice instead for an adventure.

L'Ultimo Bacio (2002)
> A coming of age, angst-ridden film about a man who finds out his girlfriend is pregnant, yet is reluctant to move into adulthood.

Buongiorno, notte (2003).
> This docu-drama chronicles the real-life 1970s kidnapping of the Italian Prime Minister.

Dopo mezzanotte (2004).
> Love blooms between a museum nightwatchman and a woman on the run from the police.

USEFUL WORDS & PHRASES

ON THE ROAD AND IN TOWN

a destra	to the right
a sinistra	to the left
aperto	open
autostrada	motorway
banchina	pavement
binario	(railway) platform
corso	boulevard
discesa	descent
dogana	customs
fermata	(bus-) stop
fiume	river
ingresso	entrance
lavori in corso	men at work
neve	snow
passaggio a livello	level crossing
passo	pass
pericolo	danger
piazza, largo	square, place
piazzale	esplanade
stazione	station
stretto	narrow
uscita	exit, way out
viale	avenue
vietato	prohibited

PLACES AND THINGS TO SEE

abbazia, convento	abbey, monastery
affreschi	frescoes
arazzi	tapestries
arca	monumental tomb
biblioteca	library
cappella	chapel
casa	house
cascata	waterfall
castello	castle
cena	The Last Supper
chiesa	church
chiostro	cloisters
chiuso	closed
città	town
cortile	courtyard
dintorni	environs
duomo	cathedral
facciata	façade
funivia	cablecar
giardini	gardens
gole	gorges
lagootto	altar frontal
passeggiata	walk, promenade
piano	floor, storey
pinacoteca	picture gallery
pulpito	pulpit
quadro	picture
rivolgersi a	to apply to
rocca	feudal castle
rovine, ruderi	ruins
sagrestia	sacristy
scala	stairway
scavi	excavations
seggiovia	chairlift
spiaggia	beach
tesoro	treasure
torre, torazzo	tower
vista	view

COMMON WORDS

si, no	yes, no
Signore	Sir
Signora	Madam
Signorina	Miss
oggi	today
ieri yesterday	
domani mattina	tomorrow morning
mattina	morning
sera	evening

pomeriggio	afternoon
per favore	please
grazie tante	thank you very much
mi scusi	excuse me
basta	enough
buon giorno	good morning
arrivederci	goodbye
quanto?	how much?
dove? quando?	where? when?
dov'è?	where is?
molto, poco	much, little
più, meno	more, less
tutto, tutti	all
grande	large
piccolo	small
caro	dear
la strada per ...?	the road to ...?
si può visitare?	may one visit?
che ora è?	what time is it?
non capisco	I don't understand
desidero	I would like

NUMBERS

zero	0
uno	1
due	2
tre	3
quattro	4
cinque	5
sei	6
sette	7
otto	8
nove	9
dieci	10
undici	11
dodici	12
tredici	13
quattordici	14
quindici	15
sedici	16
diciassette	17
diciotto	18
diciannove	19
venti	20
trenta	30
quaranta	40
cinquanta	50
sessanta	60
settanta	70
ottanta	80
novanta	90
cento	100
mille	1000
cinquemila	5000
diecimila	10,000

GASTRONOMIC TERMS

Caffè corretto: *espresso* laced with brandy or *grappa*

Caffè decaffeinato (caffè "Hag"): decaffeinated coffee

Caffè latte: mainly hot milk, with a splash of coffee

Caffè lungo: coffee which is not quite as strong as *espresso*

Caffè macchiato: *espresso* with a splash of milk

Cannelloni: large pasta tubes filled with a meat or other sauce

Cappellini: very thin spaghetti

Cappuccino (or *cappuccio*): coffee topped with frothy milk and a dusting of cocoa

Cassata: ice cream containing chopped nuts and mixed dried fruit (similar to tutti-frutti)

Crema: vanilla (ice cream)

Farfalle: pasta bow-ties

Fettuccine: slightly narrower, Roman version of tagliatelle

Fior di latte: very creamy variety of ice cream

Fusilli: small pasta spirals

Gnocchi: tiny potato dumplings

Lasagne: sheets of pasta arranged in layers with tomato and meat sauce (or other) and cheese sauce, topped with Parmesan and baked

Maccheroni: small pasta tubes

Panino: type of sandwich (bread roll)

Panna: cream; similar to *fior di latte*

Prosciutto: cured ham

Ravioli: little pasta cushions, enclosing meat or spinach

Schiacciata: type of sandwich (on a pizza-type base)

Spaghetti: the great classic

Stracciatella: chocolate chip (ice cream)

Tagliatelle: long narrow pasta ribbons

Tiramis: coffee-flavoured frozen gateau (*semifreddo*)

Tortellini: small crescent-shaped pasta rolls filled with a meat or cheese stuffing, often served in a clear meat broth

Tramezzino: type of sandwich (on slices of bread)

Zabaglione: dessert made from egg yolks and Marsala wine

Zuppa inglese: trifle

BASIC INFORMATION

Discounts

Visitors trying to keep costs down will find information on budget accommodation (pensioni, youth hostels, campsites, convents and monasteries) in the Where to Stay section.

TRAINS

Italy honors the Eurail and Inter-rail passes (though a *supplemento*, an additional fee, may be charged for some services). Ferrovie dello Stato – the train system – also offers its own discounts, well worth investigating.
Argento: 15% discount for those 60 and over
Amico: 50% discount on local trains, also applies to companion
Club Eurostar: 20% discount on first-class travel
Flexi: unlimited travel within 8, 15, 21 or 30 days
Kilometric: valid for two months over 3,000km, up to five travelers
Prima: 20% discount on first-class travel
Rail Plus: 25% discount on international second-class travel
Verde: 10% domestic discount, 25% international for those 26 and under.

AIRLINES

Low budget, no-frills airlines have forced fares down in Europe. It's now possible to fly London to Pisa for five euros, plus taxes, on a special deal. Travelers should research the airport's location, transport options and their expense before booking, however. Senior citizens aged 60 or over are eligible for discounts on some airlines, as are children and young adults aged between 12 and 26 on the day of travel.

FAMILY AND GROUP DISCOUNTS

Trains – Children under 12 accompanied by two adults travel free. Tickets are always free for children under 4.

Airlines – Families qualify for discounted tickets on certain airlines under the following conditions: the family must travel together and comprise at least four people, with a maximum of two adults and a minimum of two children (between the ages of two and eleven). One of the adults must be a parent of the children, while the second does not need to be related to the family.

Electricity

The voltage is 220ac, 50 cycles per second; the sockets are for two-pin plugs. Pack an adaptor to use for hairdryers, shavers, computers etc.

Emergencies

The following emergency numbers are all free of charge:
113: General emergency services *(soccorso pubblico di emergenza)*; to be called only in cases of real danger.
112: Police *(carabinieri)*.
115: Fire Brigade *(vigili del fuoco)*.
118: Emergency Health Services *(emergenza sanitaria)*.
1515: Forest Fire Service. Environmental emergencies.
803 116: Automobile Club d'Italia Emergency Breakdown Service.

Public Holidays

Offices and shops are closed in Italy on the following days:

Jan 1	New Year's Day
Jan 6	Epiphany
Mar/Apr	Easter
Apri 25	Liberation Day
May 1	Labour Day
June 2	Anniversary of the Republic
Aug 15	Assumption of the Virgin
Nov 1	All Saints' Day

Dec 8   Day of the Immaculate
             Conception
Dec 25 - Christmas Day
Dec 26 - Boxing Day (Santo Stefano)

Holidays are also observed in cities on local feast days honouring patron saints, including: Apr 25 (St Mark) - Venice, June 24 (St John the Baptist) - Florence, Turin, Genoa, June 29 (Saints Peter and Paul) - Rome, Oct 4 (St Petronio) - Bologna and Dec 7 (St Ambrose) - Milan.

Mail/Post

OPENING HOURS

Post offices are open 8.15am-1.30pm on weekdays, 8.15am-12.30pm on Saturdays. Some branches in city centres and shopping centres are also open on Saturday afternoons. For information, contact ☎800 160 000 or log onto www.poste.it. Stamps are also sold at tobacconists *(tabacchi)* which display a black *valori bollati* sign.

STAMPS

Stamps for letters or postcards cost €0.39 to anywhere within the European Union, and 0.41 € to other countries. Express service stamps *(posta prioritaria)* cost 0.60 € to countries within the European Union.

Money

The unit of currency is the euro which is issued in notes (5 €, 10 €, 20 €, 50 €, 100 €, 200 € and 500 €) and in coins (1 cent, 2 cents, 5 cents, 10 cents, 20 cents, 50 cents, 1 € and 2 €). Correct change is something of a commodity in Italy. Many bars, for example, are unable to break a 20 € or 50 € note. Keep a stock of small bills.

BANKS

Banks are usually open Monday to Friday, 8.30am-1.30pm and 2.30pm-4pm. Some branches are open in city centres and shopping centres on Saturday mornings; almost all are closed on Sundays and public holidays. Most hotels will change travellers' cheques. Money can be changed in post offices (except travellers' cheques), money-changing bureaux and at railway stations and airports. Commission is always charged.

CREDIT CARDS

Payment by credit card is widespread in shops, hotels and restaurants and also some petrol stations. The *Michelin Guide Italia* and *Michelin Guide Europe* indicate which credit cards are accepted at hotels and restaurants. Money may also be withdrawn from a bank, but may incur interest and charges. Some companies now add a 1-3% conversion fee to credit purchases; avoid using these cards abroad. Finally, inform the company of your itinerary, so a "suspicious activity" block doesn't freeze the account.

Newspapers

The main Italian newspapers (available throughout Italy) are *Il Messaggero* and *Il Giorno*. The two national newspapers are *Il Corriere della Sera* and *La Repubblica*. The *Osservatore Romano* is the official newspaper of the Vatican City. Foreign newspapers are available in the cities and large towns. The International Herald Tribune no longer has an Italian section, but Wanted in Rome magazine keeps expatriates connected in the capital.

Pharmacies

Crosses (typically in green neon) mark pharmacies (chemists). When closed, each will advertise the name of the duty pharmacy and a list of doctors on call.

Telecommunications

The telephone service is organized by TELECOM ITALIA (formerly SIP, www.telecomitalia.it).

CELL/MOBILE PHONES

Telecom Italia Mobile (TIM) has a "world in touch" service that enables visitors' phones. It also sells pay-as-you-go handsets.

Rome in Context, a tour company, rents cell phones for 7 € a day (long-term discounts available). Incoming calls are free; Italian calls cost 0.15 € per minute, calls to the US 0.40 €. The price includes phone delivery and collection to a Roman hotel (☎06 482 0911, www.contextrome.com). High Level Communications offers a similar service (☎06 419 0600, www.hlc.it).

INTERNET

Many hotels provide a public PC or permit modem hook-ups.

Try the following for free access via a laptop: Caltanet (www.caltanet.it), Libero (www.libero.it), Tiscali (www.tisca-linet.it) and Telecom Italia (www.tin.it). Easy Internet is a reliable connection cafe; its main outlets are open 24 hours (www.easyeverything.com).

PHONECARDS

Phonecards *(schede telefoniche)* are sold in denominations of 1 €, 2.50 €, 5 € and 8 € and are supplied by CIT offices and post offices as well as tobacconists (sign bearing a white T on a black background). Often, users must tear off a pre-cut corner to activate the card.

PUBLIC PHONES

Telephone boxes may be operated by telephone cards (sold in post offices and tobacconists) and by telephone credit cards. To make a call: lift the receiver, insert payment, await dialling signal, punch in the required number and wait for a response.

TELEPHONING

When making a call within Italy, the area code (e.g. 06 for Rome, 055 for Florence) is always used, both from outside and within the city you are calling.

For international calls dial 00 plus the following country codes:
- ☎ 61 for Australia
- ☎ 1 for Canada
- ☎ 64 for New Zealand
- ☎ 44 for the UK
- ☎ 1 for the USA

If calling from outside the country, the international code for Italy is 39. Dial the full area code, even when making an international call; for example, when calling Rome from the UK, dial 00 39 06, followed by the correspondent's number.

USEFUL NUMBERS

(🕐 See also "Emergencies" above)
The following numbers are subject to a charge:
- ☎ 12: Directory Enquiries.
- ☎ 176: International Directory Enquiries. Provides phone numbers outside of Italy in English and Italian.
- ☎ 170: Operator Assisted International Calls.

Time

Italy lies in the Central European Time Zone and is one hour ahead of Greenwich Mean Time (GMT +1).

CONVERSION TABLES

Weights and Measures

EU	US	UK	
1 kilogram (kg)	**2.2 pounds (lb)**	**2.2 pounds**	*To convert*
6.35 kilograms	14 pounds	1 stone (st)	*kilograms*
0.45 kilograms	16 ounces (oz)	16 ounces	*to pounds,*
1 metric ton (tn)	**1.1 tons**	**1.1 tons**	*multiply by 2.2*
1 litre (l)	**2.11 pints (pt)**	**1.76 pints**	*To convert litres*
3.79 litres	1 gallon (gal)	0.83 gallon	*to gallons, multiply*
4.55 litres	1.20 gallon	1 gallon	*by 0.26 (US)*
			or 0.22 (UK)
1 hectare (ha)	**2.47 acres**	**2.47 acres**	*To convert*
1 sq. kilometre	**0.38 sq. miles**	**0.38 sq. miles**	*hectares to*
(km²)	**(sq.mi.)**		*acres, multiply*
			by 2.4
1 centimetre (cm)	**0.39 inches (in)**	**0.39 inches**	*To convert metres*
1 metre (m)	**3.28 feet (ft) or 39.37 inches**		*to feet, multiply*
	or 1.09 yards (yd)		*by 3.28; for*
			kilometres to miles,
1 kilometre (km)	**0.62 miles (mi)**	**0.62 miles**	*multiply by 0.6*

Clothing

Women	EU	US	UK
	35	4	2½
	36	5	3½
	37	6	4½
Shoes	38	7	5½
	39	8	6½
	40	9	7½
	41	10	8½
	36	6	8
	38	8	10
Dresses	40	10	12
& suits	42	12	14
	44	14	16
	46	16	18
	36	06	30
	38	08	32
Blouses &	40	10	34
sweaters	42	12	36
	44	14	38
	46	16	40

Men	EU	US	UK
	40	7½	7
	41	8½	8
	42	9½	9
Shoes	43	10½	10
	44	11½	11
	45	12½	12
	46	13½	13
	46	36	36
	48	38	38
Suits	50	40	40
	52	42	42
	54	44	44
	56	46	48
	37	14½	14½
	38	15	15
Shirts	39	15½	15½
	40	15¾	15¾
	41	16	16
	42	16½	16½

Sizes often vary depending on the designer. These equivalents are given for guidance only.

Speed

KPH	10	30	50	70	80	90	100	110	120	130
MPH	6	19	31	43	50	56	62	68	75	81

Temperature

Celsius (°C)	0°	5°	10°	15°	20°	25°	30°	40°	60°	80°	100°
Fahrenheit (°F)	32°	41°	50°	59°	68°	77°	86°	104°	140°	176°	212°

To convert Celsius into Fahrenheit, multiply °C by 9, divide by 5, and add 32.
To convert Fahrenheit into Celsius, subtract 32 from °F, multiply by 5, and divide by 9.
NB: Conversion factors on this page are approximate.

UNESCO World Heritage List

"Our cultural and natural heritage are irreplaceable sources of life and inspiration," insists the United Nations Educational, Scientific and Cultural Organization (UNESCO). This nonprofit group has helped preserve over 800 sites of "outstanding universal value" on the World Heritage List since 1972. A site must be nominated by its home country, with annual evaluations.

Cultural heritage may be monuments (buildings, sculptures, archaeological structures); groups of buildings (religious communities, ancient cities); or sites (settlements, exceptional landscapes). Well-known entries include: Australia's Great Barrier Reef (1981), India's Taj Mahal and Peru's Macchu Pichu (1983), the Vatican City and the USA's Statue of Liberty (1984), Canada's Rocky Mountain Parks (1984), Jordan's Petra (1985), The Great Wall of China and Greece's Acropolis (1987), Russia's Kremlin and Red Square (1990), England's Stonehenge (1986), Indonesia's Komodo National Park and France's Banks of the Seine (1991), Cambodia's Angkor Wat (1992) and Japan's Hiroshima Peace Memorial (1996).

Italy's latest UNESCO sites are Tivoli's Villa Adriana (1999), Assisi's Basilica of San Francesco and other Franciscan Sites (2000), the City of Verona (2000), the Aeolian Islands (2000), Tivoli's Villa d'Este (2001), Southeastern Sicily's late Baroque Towns of the Val di Noto (2002), the Sacri Monti of Piedmont and Lombardy (2003), Etruscan Necropolises of Cerveteri and Tarquinia (2004), Val d'Orcia (2004), and Syracuse and the Rocky Necropolis of Pantalica (2005).

UNESCO World Heritage Sites included in this guide are:	
Valcamonica cave paintings	Historic centre of Rome, the Vatican City and San Paolo fuori le Mura
Santa Maria delle Grazie church and refectory, Milan	Historic centre of Florence
Venice and the Venetian lagoon	Piazza del Duomo, Pisa
Historic centre of San Gimignano	Rock dwellings, Matera
Vicenza and the Palladian villas	Historic centre of Siena
Historic centre of Naples	Crespi d'Adda
The Renaissance city of Ferrara	Castel del Monte
Trulli dwellings, Puglia	Palaeo-Christian monuments, Ravenna
Historic centre of Pienza	Residence of the House of Savoy, Turin
La Reggia palace and gardens, Vanvitelli aquaduct and San Leucio buildings, Caserta	Botanical gardens, Padua
Portovenere, the Cinque Terre and Palmaria, Tino and Tinetto islands	Pompeii, Herculaneum and Torre Annunziata
The Cathedral, Torre Civica and Piazza Grande, Modena	The Amalfi Coast
Agrigento archaeological site	Villa Romana del Casale
Su Nuraxi, Barumini	Historic centre of Urbino
The Cilento region and Vallo di Diano, the archaeological sites of Paestum and Velia, and Padula Carthusian monastery	Aquileia Basilica and archaeological site

Sunflower Fields, Tuscany
B.Morandi/MICHELIN

THE REGIONS OF ITALY

The boot of Italy, which stretches some 1 300km/808mi from north to south, juts out into the Mediterranean between Greece and Spain. The country's rugged relief rises from great swathes of plain that cover about a quarter of its total area of 301 262km²/116 317sq mi. Its coastline (almost 7 500km/4 660mi long) is washed by four inner seas: the Ligurian, Tyrrhenian, Ionian and Adriatic.

Geographical Notes

The **Alps**, which were created as the earth's crust folded in the Tertiary Era, form a gigantic barrier with northern Europe and are a formidable source of hydroelectric power. Several passes and tunnels cross the Alps, which peak at Mont Blanc (4 810m/15 780ft), to link Italy with France and northern Europe. On the southern side of the Alps between the fertile Po valley and the foothills there are several lakes of glacial origin.

The **Apennines**, a range of limestone hills formed by a more recent Tertiary geological movement, extend from Genoa down into Sicily, dividing the country into two zones. The peaks of this limestone chain are generally lower than those of the Alps. The Corno Grande at 2 914m/9 566ft is the highest mountain of the chain's tallest massif, the Gran Sasso. The section between Naples and Sicily is subject to tectonic plate movements resulting in earthquakes, volcanoes and marked changes in sea level. Such activity has altered the relief of this southern part of the peninsula.

Exploring the Regions

The 1948 constitution established 20 regions, although it was not enacted until 1970. Five of these (Sicily, Sardinia, Trentino-Alto Adige, Friuli-Venezia Giulia and Valle d'Aosta) have a special statute and enjoy greater administrative autonomy. The regions are subdivided into 95 provinces, which are themselves composed of districts, each headed by a *Sindaco*.

AOSTA VALLEY (VALLE D'AOSTA)

This great deep furrow between the highest mountains in Europe is watered by the Dora Baltea River, whose tributar-

Italy has some of the highest mountains in Europe

Lara Pessina / MICHELIN

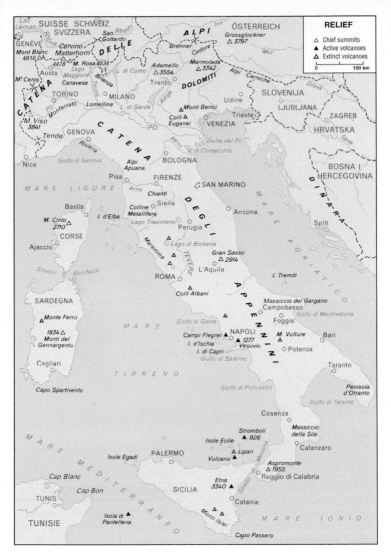

RELIEF

△ Chief summits
▲ Active volcanoes
△ Extinct volcanoes

0   100 km

ies run along picturesque lateral valleys: the Valtournenche, Val di Gressoney, Val d'Ayas, Val Grisenche. The **Parco Nazionale del Gran Paradiso** is found in the southwest of the region.

Aosta, well situated in the centre of the valley, is the capital of this region and has enjoyed a degree of administrative autonomy since 1947. In addition to the pastoral activities of the mountain people, the valley's economy depends primarily on tourism which has developed as a result of the Great St Bernard and

Mont Blanc tunnels and the hydroelectric and iron and steel industries.

From Pont-St-Martin to Courmayeur the towns and villages have retained French names; many of the local inhabitants still speak French and other varied dialects.

PIEDMONT (PIEMONTE)

Piedmont, at the foot of the mountain range, consists mainly of the extensive Po Delta. Surrounded on three sides by

the Alps and the Apennines this fertile area is made up of grassland alternating with fields planted with cereals and rice (three-fifths of the Italian rice production is concentrated in the districts of Vercelli and Novara). The many rivers which cross the region (the Ticino, Sesia, Dora Baltea and Riparia, Tanaro, Bormida and Scrivia) are mainly found in the valley of the river **Po**, which has its source at Pian del Re on Monviso (approximately 100km/62mi southwest of Turin), and which flows for 652km/407mi before joining the Adriatic. Numerous hydroelectric power stations supply electricity to local industry: textile factories in Biella and the metal, engineering and chemical works in Turin.

LOMBARDY (LOMBARDIA)

Lombardy's emphasis on commercial activity is mainly due to its favourable geographical location in the green Po Delta between the Ticino and the Mincio, which together with the Adda feed Lakes Maggiore, Como and Garda. To the north the great lake valleys give access to the Alpine passes. Lombardy, with the mulberry bushes of the **Brianza** district, takes first place in the production of silk. The permanent grazing and grasslands are used by modern dairy farming and processing industries. In the **Lomellina** district, large areas are given over to rice growing.

The many towns, scattered throughout the countryside, were important banking and trading centres in medieval and Renaissance times and spread the

B. Morandi/ MICHELIN

The landscape around Pienza in Tuscany

name of the Lombards all over Europe. Today Como is the centre of the silk industry, Brescia has steel, chemical and engineering industries, Bergamo textile and engineering works, Mantua petrochemicals and plastics, Cremona is the agricultural focus and Pavia the seat of an important university.

It is **Milan**, the economic capital of Italy, that has the highest density of population and businesses. This town with its modern architecture and numerous commercial enterprises and cultural institutions has an outer ring of industrial suburbs which are the home base of textile, oil, chemical, steel and food industries.

VENETIA (VENETO)

This area comprises mainly the vast alluvial Po Delta and its tributaries which are overlooked in the north by the Venetian Pre-Alps, and further north again in the **Cadore** district by the western massifs of the Dolomites. It is an agricultural region growing wheat, maize, mulberry bushes, olives, fruit trees and vines. The industrial sector includes oil refineries, smelting works and chemical plants which are concentrated in the vicinity of Venice at Mestre-Marghera, as well as a large production of hydroelectric energy in the valleys of the Pre-Alps. The latter supplies the textile industry.

The landscape is punctuated by two small volcanic groups, the **Berici Mountains** south of Vicenza and the **Euganean Hills** near Padua. The slopes of these blackish heights support vines and peach orchards, and there are several hot springs.

In the **Po Delta** and that of the Adige lie impoverished and desolate areas, subject to flooding. Following reclamation certain areas are farmed on an industrial scale for wheat and sugar beet. The coastline takes the form of lagoons (*lagune*) separated from the sea by spits of sand pierced by gaps (*porti*). It is one of these lagoons that both provides and threatens the survival of Venice.

TRENTINO-ALTO ADIGE

This is one of five Italian regions to enjoy special autonomy. The people are partly of Germanic culture and German-speaking. The area includes the Adige and Isarco valleys and the surrounding mountains. The Adige Valley, at the southern exit from the Brenner Pass, has always been easily accessible and much used by traffic. Though deep, it opens out towards the sunny south and is very fertile. Cereals are grown on the flatter areas of the valley bottom, with vines and fruit trees on the lower slopes and pastures above. Avelengo in the vicinity of Merano is well known for its breed of horses.

The highly-eroded limestone massif of the **Dolomites** extends across the Veneto and Trentino-Alto Adige.

FRIULI-VENEZIA GIULIA

This region is an extension of the Veneto to the east; it forms the Italian boundary with Austria and Slovenia. The area enjoys a large degree of autonomy in administrative and cultural affairs. In the north is the schistose massif of the **Carnic Alps** with its forests of conifers and alpine pastures. Friuli-Venezia Giulia is an important silkworm breeding and spinning area. Traditional farming activites have been superseded by heavy industry which has grown up around Udine and Pordenone. **Trieste**, the region's capital, was once Austria's busy port.

EMILIA-ROMAGNA

The plain skirting the Apennines derives its name from the Via Emilia, a straight Roman road that crosses it from Piacenza to Rimini. South and east of Bologna the district is known as **Romagna**. Its soil, which is intensively cultivated, is among the best in Italy for wheat and beet. The rhythm of the landscape of extensive fields is punctuated at intervals by rows of mulberries and vines clinging to tall poles, and of maples or elms. Other vines grow on the Apennine slopes.

The towns are strung out along the Via Emilia: **Bologna**, famous for its ancient university, is today a centre of communications and industry (steel, engineering and food) and a market for wheat and pigs.

East of Ferrara, where the Po river runs, the region is devoted to rice growing. To the south is an area of great lagoons, **Valli di Comacchio**, where fishermen catch eels.

LIGURIA

Liguria, furrowed by deep, narrow valleys at right angles to the coast, had a maritime civilisation before the Roman era. The steep slopes of the inner valleys are dotted with poor hilltop villages, watching over groves of chestnut or olive trees and cultivated terraces. The rocky, indented coastline has few fish to offer but has enjoyed heavy coastal traffic since the time of the Ligurians, facilitated by many small deep-water ports. The Roman Empire gave its present appearance to the country, with olive groves and vineyards, now complemented by vegetables, fruit (melons and peaches) and flowers grown on an industrial scale.

The **Riviera di Ponente** (Western Riviera) west of Genoa is sunnier and more sheltered than the **Riviera di Levante**

Basilica of Madonna di San Luca, Bologna

© Bologna Turismo photographic archive/Luciano Leonotti

(Eastern Riviera), but the latter has a more luxuriant vegetation. The chief towns are Imperia, Savona and **Genoa** (shipyards, steel production, oil terminal and thermal power station) and La Spezia (naval base, commercial port, thermal power station and arms manufacture).

TUSCANY (TOSCANA)

The harmony of the beautiful Tuscan landscape of low-lying hills with graceful curves affording wide views and planted with olive groves, vineyards and cypress trees bathed in the soft, golden light, reflects the great artistic sense of the Tuscan people.

The region has a variety of soils. The Tuscan Archipelago, with the mountainous **Island of Elba** and its rich iron-bearing deposits, faces a shore which is sometimes rocky (south of Livorno), sometimes flat and sandy as in the Viareggio area, known as **Versilia**. North of the Arno, the **Apuan Alps** are quarried for marble (Carrara).

In the heart of Tuscany lies the fertile and beautiful **Arno Basin**, an ideal setting for **Florence**. Vines and silvery olives alternate with fields of wheat, tobacco and maize. Peppers, pumpkins and the famous Lucca beans grow among the mulberries. The old farms, with their distinctive grand architectural style, often stand alone on hilltops.

Southern Tuscany is a land of hills, soft and vine-clad in the **Chianti** district south of Florence, quiet and pastoral near Siena, dry and desolate round Monte Oliveto Maggiore, and massive and mysterious in the area of the **Colli Metalliferi** (metal-bearing hills) south of Volterra. Bordering Lazio, **Maremma**, with its melancholy beauty, was once a marshy district haunted by bandits, cowboys and shepherds. Much of the area has now been reclaimed.

UMBRIA

The land of St Francis is a country of hills, valleys and river basins, where the poplars raise their rustling heads to limpid skies. This is the green Umbria of the Clitumnus Valley (**Valle del Clitunno**), whose pastures were famous in ancient times. Umbria has two lakes, **Trasimeno** and Piediluco, and many rivers, including the Tiber. Medieval cities which succeeded Etruscan settlements overlook ravines and valleys: grim Gubbio, haughty **Perugia**, the capital of Umbria, Assisi, Spoleto and Spello. Others stand in the centre of a plain, such as Foligno and Terni, the metallurgical centre.

MARCHES (MARCHE)

So called because they were formerly frontier provinces of the Frankish Empire and papal domains, the Marches form a much subdivided area between San Marino and Ascoli Piceno, where the parallel spurs of the Apennines run down into the Adriatic, forming a series of deep, narrow valleys. There is, however, a flat and rectangular coastal belt dotted with beaches and canalports.

Apart from the capital, **Ancona**, a busy port, most of the old towns are built on commanding sites; Urbino (centre of the arts), Loreto (pilgrimage centre) and Macerata (manufacture of musical instruments).

LAZIO

Latium, the cradle of Roman civilisation, lies between the Tyrrhenian Sea and the Apennines, from Tuscan Maremma to Gaeta. The province borders a sandy coast whose ancient harbors, such as Ostia at the Tiber's mouth, have silted. Civitavecchia today is the only modern port. In the centre of Lazio, **Rome**, the capital and seat of the Catholic Church, is mainly a residential city and epicenter of both public and religious organisations.

To the east and north, volcanic hills, with lonely lakes in their craters, overlook the **Roman Campagna**. Writers and painters have often described its great, desolate expanses, dotted with ancient ruins. Today this area, formerly a hotbed of malaria, has regained a degree of activity: the drainage of the Pontine

Marches, near Latina, was a spectacular achievement.

To the south is the distinctive **Ciociaria**. This area takes its name from the shoes (ciocie), which are part of the traditional costume. They have thick soles and thongs wound round the calf of the leg. The main centres are Frosinone and Casino.

ABRUZZI (ABRUZZO)

This is the part of the Apennines which most suggests a country of high mountains, grand and wild, with its **Gran Sasso** and **Maiella Massifs**. The **Parco Nazionale d'Abruzzo**, the doyen of the Italian national parks, was established in the Upper Sangro Valley in 1921. In basins sheltered from the wind are vineyards, and almond and olive groves, while industry is concentrated in the Chieti-Pescara zone and other areas such as Vasto (glass making), Sulmona (car factories), L'Aquila (steel works) and Avezzano (textile and food industries). The tourist industry is also important for the coastal regions and the winter resorts of the Gran Sasso massif.

MOLISE

Molise, with its capital, **Campobasso**, extends south of the Abruzzi, with which it has several common features: a mountainous relief, dark valleys and wild forests which are still haunted by wolves. The region is bordered to the west by the Maiella. The main industry can be found in the Termoli area, although agriculture still forms the basis of the local economy. The main crops are wheat, oats, maize, potatoes and vines.

CAMPANIA

Campania forms a fertile crescent around the Bay of Naples, where hemp, tobacco and cereals alternate with olive groves and vineyards. The charm and mystery of the **Bay of Naples**, which once stirred the imagination of the ancients, is domi-nated by the characteristic silhouette of **Vesuvius**. Although the coast has lost much of its charm owing to building developments, the **Sorrento Peninsula** and the **Island of Capri** are two notable beauty spots.

PUGLIA, BASILICATA AND CALABRIA

These three regions cover the foot of the Italian "boot". Puglia, on the east side, facing the Adriatic, has many assets. Cereals are grown in the plain between Foggia and Manfredonia and in the plains of Bari, Taranto, Lecce and Brindisi. Vines flourish almost everywhere, often alongside olive trees (the Apulian production of olive oil is very important to the world market) and almonds on the coast. The elevation of the **Gargano Promontory**, otherwise known as the "boot's spur," is distinctive.

Bari, the capital of Puglia, is a busy port, which still enjoys numerous trading links with the Middle East. Along with Taranto and Brindisi it is one of the three main industrial centres in the region. Basilicata or **Lucania**, and Calabria, comprise very different types of country; the rocky corniche from the Gulf of Policastro to Reggio; the grim, grand mountains of the **Sila Massif** with its extensive mountain pastures and wide horizons; and at the southern extremity of the peninsula between two inner seas, lies the **Aspromonte Massif** clad with pine, beech and chestnut forests.

Between Basilicata and Calabria is the **Parco Nazionale del Pollino** (inaugurated in 1990) which is covered in pine forests. Formed by the Pollino Massif it boasts an interesting array of fauna and flora. There are also several natural history museums in the area. ⚭ *See also CALABRIA.*

SARDINIA AND SICILY

⚭ *See SARDEGNA and SICILIA near the end of the guide.*

HISTORY

Since 2000 BC, Italy has been a cross-roads of cultures, the intermingling of Etruscan, Greek and Latin civilisations.

Greeks

After the **Phoenicians** had settled at Carthage and set up trading posts, the Greeks founded a large number of colonies on the coasts of Sicily and southern Italy (8C BC), known as **Magna Graecia**. It included Ionian, Achaean and Dorian colonies, named after the Greek peoples who had colonised them. The social unit was the "city". The 6C and 5C BC marked the zenith of Greek civilisation in Italy, corresponding to the period of Pericles in Athens. Greek seaborne trade was so successful that Syracuse soon rivalled Athens. Syracuse and Taranto were the two main centres of this refined civilisation. Philosophers, scientists and writers settled in Sicily. Aeschylus lived at Gela. Theocritus defined the rules of bucolic poetry and Archimedes was murdered by a Roman soldier in Syracuse.

But rivalry between these many and varied cities led to warfare, which, with Carthaginian raids, led to decline, culminating in the Roman conquest at the end of the 3C BC.

CITIES

Territory in the Greek settlements was roughly divided into three different areas from the 8C BC onwards, when the first colonists arrived in Italy: places of worship, public spaces and residential areas. Generally the city was laid out in an octagonal grid – designed by **Hippodamus of Miletus**, a Greek philosopher and town planner who lived in Asia Minor in the 5C BC – organised around

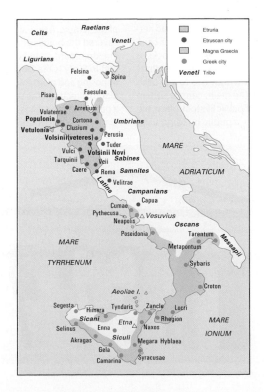

Greek mythology

The shores of Sicily and southern Italy held a sort of fascination for the ancient Greeks, who regarded them as the limits of the inhabited earth. Many mthological scenes unfold there: the Phlegrean Fields, near Naples, hid the entrance to the Kingdom of Hades; Zeus routed the Titans, with the help of Hercules, on Etna, where the Cyclops lived and Hephaestus, the god of fire, had his forges; Kore, the daughter of Demeter, was kidnapped by Hades, who had emerged from the River Tartara near Enna. In the *Odyssey*, Homer (9C BC) relates the adventures of Ulysses (Odysseus) after the siege of Troy, sailing between Scylla and Charybdis in the Straits of Messina and resisting the temptations of the Sirens in the Gulf of Sorrento. Pindar (5C BC) describes these mysterious shores, to which Virgil (1C BC) also refers in the *Aeneid*.

two main axes, the **cardo**(*stenopos* in Greek), which ran from north to south, and the **decumanus** (*plateia* in Greek), running from east to west. The road network was completed with minor *cardi* and *decumani*, which formed blocks. A number of public areas and buildings were situated within the town, such as the *agorà*, the main, central square where much of public life took place, the *ekklesiastérion*, a public building used for the meeting of the public assembly (*ekklesìa*), and the *bouleutérion*, which housed meetings of the citizens' council (the *boulé*). The temples, sometimes built outside the city limits, were often surrounded by other sacred buildings. The monumental structures included porticoes, gymnasia, theatres and votive monuments. The city itself was usually protected by fortifications, outside of which lay the agricultural land, subdivided into family plots, and the area used for burials.

TEMPLES

The focus of the building was the *naos*, also known as the *cella*, which housed the statue of the god; the temple faced east so that the statue was illuminated by the rising sun, considered to be the source of all life. In front of the *naos* was the *pronaos*, a kind of antechamber, while the back of the temple, the *opistodomos*, acted as a treasury room. The temple was surrounded by columns **(peristyle)** and supported by a base; the columns which supported the entablature rested on the last steps **(stylobate)** of the temple. A two-sided sloping roof covered the building.

The dominant style in Magna Graecia and in Sicily is the Doric style, with its imposing and plain columns, which are placed directly on the stylobate without a base. The capital has no sculpted carvings, but consists simply of a round

The Doric harmony and elegance of Neptune's Temple at Paestum

R. Mattes/MICHELIN

buffer (echinus) placed on a square block (abacus). The Doric entablature comprises a smooth architrave. Its upper section presents a frieze with alternating metopes (panels of sculpted low reliefs) and triglyphs (panels depicting two deep vertical grooves in the centre and two smaller grooves on each side). Many consider Doric temples to be the prototype of ideal beauty due to their simple structure and perfect harmony of proportions. The human eye distorts large buildings' lines, so architects made optical corrections to the conventional structure. The entablatures, whose upper sections seemed to lean forward slightly, were raised in the centre, thus acquiring an imperceptible arched shape. To create an impression of perfect equilibrium, the columns situated to the sides of the temple façade were bent slightly towards the inside of the building, in order to avoid the effect of leaning outwards. Finally, in very large buildings (such as the Temple of Concord in Agrigento and the Basilica in Paestum) where the columns seemed to contract towards the top of the temple, this optical illusion was addressed by increasing the shaft's diameter at about two-thirds of its height.

The temples were often decorated with groups of sculptures and low reliefs and were usually painted in red, blue and white in order to provide the sculptures and columns with maximum relief.

Compared with the architecture of mainland Greece, the temples of Magna Graecia and Sicily are more monumental, pay more attention to spatial effect and show a particular taste for abundant decoration.

SCULPTURE

The scarcity of marble and the particular Italian taste for pictorial and chiaroscuro effects resulted in the predominant use of limestone and sandstone as raw materials. Clay was widely used in the pediments and acroteria of the temples, as well as for votive statues. The colonies employed the Ionic style from the end of the 6C BC. This introduced a greater individualisation of features, an increasingly dramatic sense of pathos and the use of softer shapes. The main artistic centres were Taranto, Naples, Paestum, Agrigento and Syracuse.

PAINTING AND CERAMICS

Painting was considered by the Greeks to be the most noble and eloquent form of art; unfortunately the perishable nature of the pigments used means that little remains of this art. The only surviving examples are inside tombs or on the façades of *hypogea* (underground chambers).

Vases with black figures painted against a red or yellow background date from the Archaic and beginning of the Classical periods. The detail on the figures was obtained by simply engraving the black varnish with a steel tip. Mythological subjects or scenes depicting daily life were the most common designs. Red figure vases appeared in southern Italy towards the end of the 5C BC. The black varnish, previously only for figures, now infused the background, with the figures 'reserved' in the natural brick red clay and painted with touches of black and white. This reversal, which gave artists a greater freedom of expression, constituted a revolutionary discovery and allowed artists to produce more subtle designs. The themes used remained much the same. From the 3C BC the art of the native Italian peoples and of Magna Grecia became more decorative in style.

Etruscans

While the Greeks were disseminating their civilisation throughout the south of the peninsula and Sicily, the Etruscans flourished in central Italy, from the 8C BC onwards. This powerful empire'sgrowth was checked only by that of Rome (3C BC). They are a little-known people whose alphabet, along with certain tombstone inscriptions, has now been partially deciphered. Some authorities think they were natives; others, following the example of Herodotus, insist they came from Lydia in Asia Minor. The Etruscans at first occupied the area between the Arno and the Tiber (see map) but later spread into Campania and the Po Plain. They reached their zenith in the 6C BC. Etruria then comprised a federation of 12 city-states known as *lucumonies,* which comprised the cities of Tarquinia, Vulci, Vetulonia, Cerveteri, Arezzo, Chiusi, Roselle, Volterra, Cortona, Perugia, Veii and Volsinii (present-day Bolsena). Grown rich from ironwork, copper and silver mines, and trade in the western Mediterranean, these excellent artisans and technicians enjoyed a highly refined civilisation.

ART

The Etruscan towns, built on elevated sites with walls of huge stones, show an advanced sense of town planning, often based on Greek models. Near the towns are vast burial grounds. These necropolises – cities of the dead – mimicked the streets, blocks, houses and furnishings of everyday life, often carved into the soft tufa.

Etruscan art is strongly influenced by the Orient and especially by Greece from the 6C BC onwards. It has a marked individuality sustained by realism and expressive movement. Vivid frescoes adorn the tombs at Tarquinia; the scenes range from saucy to the sublime. These mysterious artists were also accomplished sculptors, archi-tects, engineers and gold- and iron-workers.

FIGURATIVE ARTS

Sculpture makes up the main body of Etruscan art. The great period is the 6C BC, when large groups of statuary adorned the pediments of temples: the famous Apollo of Veii (in the Villa Giulia museum in Rome), of obvious Greek influence, belongs to this period. Some portrait busts are more original in their striking realism, intensity of expression and stylised features: their large prominent eyes and enigmatic smiles are typical of the Etruscan style. The same applies to the famous groups of semi-recumbent figures on the sarcophagi, many of which are portraits. They also excelled in bronze sculpture, as demonstrated by the Arezzo Chimera (in Florence's Archaeological Museum) and elongated votive figurines.

The only surviving **paintings** are in burial chambers (Cerveteri, Veii and especially Tarquinia). These frescoes were supposed to remind the dead of the pleasures of life: banquets, games, plays, music, dancing, hunting etc. These colourful and delicate wall paintings show amazing powers of observation and form a good record of Etruscan habits and customs.

POTTERY AND GOLDWORK

The Etruscans were artisans of genius. In pottery they used the little known **bucchero** technique, producing black earthenware with figures in relief. Initially decorated with motifs in *pointillé,* the vases developed more elaborate shapes with a more complicated ornamentation, although in general these were not of the same quality as the earlier work. In the 7C BC they modelled beautiful burial urns, *canopae,* in animal or human shape. Both men and women wore heavy – often solid gold – ornaments that often showcased exceptional skill in the filigree and granulation techniques.

Romans

ARCHITECTURE

Roman towns

Roman towns often had military roots. Walled in periods of trouble, they were generally divided into four quarters by two main streets, the *decumanus* and the *cardo*, intersecting at right angles and ending in gateways. Other parallel streets created a grid.

The **streets** were edged with footpaths, sometimes 50cm/18in high, and lined with porticoes to shelter pedestrians. Large flagstones, which fitted together perfectly, paved the roads. Stepping-stones crossed the right-of-way, but grooves allowed horses and cartwheels to pass.

A Roman house

Excavations at Herculaneum, Pompeii and especially Ostia have uncovered two main types of houses. An *insula* was a dwelling of several storeys divided into apartments, often with shops open to the street. A domus was a luxurious, single-family mansion with an atrium, which had evolved from the earlier Greek model.

The latter had a modest external appearance owing to bare walls and few windows. But the interior – adorned with mosaics, statues, paintings and marbles and sometimes including private baths and a fish pond – revealed the riches of its owner. A vestibule overlooked by the porter's lodge led to the *atrium*.

The *atrium*, originally the domus's heart, later referred to the internal courtyard around the *impluvium*, a basin which caught rainwater. The bedrooms (*cubiculae*) opened off the atrium, which was the only part of the house where strangers were usually admitted. At the far end was the *tablinum*, or the living and dining room. The atrium and adjoining rooms constituted the oldest form of the Roman house, later inhabited by less wealthy citizens.

The *peristyle* was a central court surrounded by a portico. Reserved for the family, it generally featured a garden with fountains, statues and mosaic-lined basins. The living quarters opened on to it. The *cubiculae* were simple sleeping chambers with a stone platform built against the wall or a movable bed. There were mattresses, cushions and blankets but no sheets. The dining room or *triclinium*, takes its name from the three couches for the guests. Adopting a Greek custom, Romans ate reclined on cushions and leaning on one elbow. Slaves attended the central table.

Lastly, there was the great hall or *oecus*, which was sometimes embellished with a colonnade. The outbuildings included the kitchen with a sink and drain, and built-in stove and oven; baths, which were like the public baths on a smaller scale, and the slaves' quarters, barns, cellars, stables etc. The latrines were usually in a kitchen corner to simplify drainage systems.

The Forum

Roman life revolved around the forum, each town's center of politics, leisure and commerce. Originally a market, the large square usually stood at a major intersection and was often surrounded by a portico during the Imperial period.

Government offices also flanked a forum. These included the *curia* or headquarters of local government; the voting hall for elections; the public tribune where candidates harangued crowds; the "basilica of finance" or exchange (*argentaria*); the municipal treasury; the public granaries; the "basilica of justice" or law courts; the prison; temples and many commemorative monuments.

As they became less content with the Forum, ancient Roman emperors built auxilliary centers nearby. Trajan, Nerva and Augustus all constructed opulent additions, now collectively known as the *Fori Imperiali*.

The tombs

Roman cemeteries lined major roads at some distance from town. The tombs were marked by an altar, simple stele (a slab or pillar), or even a mausoleum for the most important families. Less affluent Romans rested in a *columbarium*, a vault with niches for funerary urns, named for its resemblance to a dovecote. The most famous cemetery is on the Via Appia Antica, south of Rome. Directly after death, the body was exhibited on a funeral couch surrounded with candlesticks and wreaths. Then the family buried or cremated the remains. The deceased was provided with objects thought useful in the after life: clothes, arms and tools for men, toys for children, and jewellery and toilet articles for women.

Architecture

The Romans borrowed elements from Greek architecture, but created their own art. Innovations included softer, more flexible curved shapes, such as the arch, dome and vault. Walls and pilasters replaced columns, the foundation of the Greek trilithic system. **Concrete**, thrown into moulds, allowed huge covered spaces like the Pantheon, the world's largest unreinfored solid concrete dome at 43.4m/142 ft in diameter. Also noteworthy were the Romans many public civil engineering projects: bridges, aqueducts, roads, tunnels, sewers, baths, theatres, amphitheatres, stadia, circuses, basilicas, nymphaea, gymnasia, colonnades, triumphal arches, and both public and private monuments (often rivals in terms of size and splendour).

Temples

Temples honored gods or emperors, raised to divine status from the time of Augustus. The Roman version, again inspired by the Greek, consists of a closed chamber, the *cella*, containing the image of the god, and an open vestibule. The building is surrounded, partly or completely, by a colonnade and is built on a podium. Romans also imported circular temple-plans. The most stunning example remains the Pantheon, dedicated to all the gods. This engineering marvel has an eye (*oculus*) in its grand concrete dome. Originally built in 27 BC, it has been a place of worship for over 2,000 years and this Catholic church now contains the tombs of the artist Raphael and Italian royalty.

Triumphal arches

In Rome these commemorated the victories by generals or emperors. The low reliefs on the arches recorded their feats of arms. In the provinces, such as Aosta, Benevento and Ancona, there are municipal arches commemorating important events or erected in honour of some member of the Imperial family.

Again, Rome has a concentration of superb structures, including the Forum's 203 AD Arch of Septimius Severus, the worn 81 AD Arch of Titus, which commemorates the capture of Jerusalem (and thus is shunned by many Jews) and the pollution-scarred, 315 AD Arch of Constantine, which the dictator Benito Mussolini further damaged in a megalomaniac desire for a triumphal procession.

Aqueducts

Nowhere is the Roman arch better employed than these waterways, many of which stand today (though an argument could perhaps be made for the Colosseum). These stone streambeds stride across the countryside and plunge underground. Rome alone built

11 between 312 BC and 206 AD, which funnelled more than a million cubic meters a day into the city (35m cubic feet). Three ancient aqueducts still supply the capital's fountains and streetside faucets.

The baths

The Roman baths doubled as fitness centers, casinos, social clubs, libraries, lecture halls and meeting-places. The free amentities explain the amount of time people spent there. Decoration in these great buildings was lavish: mosaic ornaments, coloured marble facings, columns and statues.

The bather followed a medically prescribed circuit. From the gymnasium (*palestra*), he entered a lukewarm room (*tepidarium*) to prepare for the hot baths (*caldarium*). He then returned to a lukewarm room before plunging in the cold baths (*frigidarium*) to tone the skin. Underground furnaces (*hypocausts*) heated the water and air, which also circulated inside the walls and floors.

The amphitheatre

This typical Roman structure, several storeys high, encircles an elliptical arena with seats. A huge adjustable awning, the *velarium*, sheltered the spectators from the sun and rain. Inside, a wall protected the front rows from the wild animals in the ring. A complex of circular galleries, staircases and corridors enabled all the spectators to reach their seats quickly without crowding through the *vomitaria* (passageways).

Always popular, the performances included fighting of three kinds: between animals, between gladiators and animals, and between gladiators. In principle, a human duel always ended in the death of one opponent. The public could ask for a gladiator's life to be spared and the President of the Games would indicate a reprieve by turning up his thumb. The victorious gladiator received a sum of money if he was a professional; a slave or a prisoner would be freed.

In some amphitheatres the stage could be flooded for naval spectacles (*naumachia*), where actors battled in flat-bottomed boats.

Naturally, the Colosseum is the star of this genre. Three tiers high, it covers about 2.5ha/6 acres of drained marshland in Rome's heart. Over 50 000 people could squash onto the marble and tufa benches with standing room at the top. Known as the Flavian Amphitheatre until the eighth century, the Colosseum is the model for modern sports stadiums.

The circus

Usually connected to the Imperial palace, the circus hosted horse and chariot races. Its shape was long and narrow, with a short curved side and a straight side, where the races started. Spectators sat on the terraces, while the competitors whipped around the track. In the later Roman Empire, many different types of games took place here. The circus resembled the smaller **stadium**, which was copied from the Greek model. The Circus Maximus, near Rome's Forum, is among the most famous examples. However, the landmark Piazza Navona also began as a chariot track: the 86 AD circus known as *domitianus* or *agonalis* (from the ancient Greek for "games," which was corrupted into the modern name). Baroque churches, fountains and palaces have since encrusted the ruins, but the shape remains evident.

The theatre

Theatres had rows of seats, usually ending in colonnades, a central area or **orchestra** for performance or elevating distinguished spectators, and a raised **stage**. Action unfolded before a wall – the building's finest part, which imitated a palace façade: decoration included several tiers of columns, niches containing statues, mosaics and marble facings. The perfect acoustics were getnerally due to a combination of sophisticated devices. The scenery was either fixed or mobile and there was an ingenious array of machinery either in the wings or below stage. Special effects were also impressive, including smoke, lightning, thunder, and the sudden appearance of gods – the famous *deus ex machina* – or heroes.

Comedies and tragedies were the theater's chief function; however, the space also hosted competitions, lottery draws and the distribution of bread or money.

Until the end of the 2C BC, all actors wore wigs of different shapes and colours, according to their character's nature. After that date, they adopted distinctive pasteboard masks, often represented in theater sculptures. Tragic actors, to make themselves more impressive, wore buskins or sandals with thick cork soles.

Time Line

The Romans ignited the Italian peninsula, inhabited by Greek colonists, the gentle Etruscans and various Indo-European tribes. They rewrote the rules, from the she-wolf rescuing abandoned babies to Caesar storming across the Rubicon. The Romans spread peace and prosperity from Upper Mesopotamia to the British Isles. Eventually barbarian invasions and plague weakened the empire, which split in two and converted to Christianity. Lombards, Franks and Normans ruled the ruins, and later popes and emperors. City states squabbled through the Dark Ages; then blossomed in the Renaissance. Italians finally cast off foreign rulers – the French and Spanish – under the dashing leadership of Giuseppe Garibaldi in 1871. Following the horrors of Fascism and 1970s political terrorism, Italy stabilized and joined the European Union. The tumultuous journey from "head of the world" to member-state left behind a rich cultural and historical legacy, treasured by travellers.

FROM THE ORIGINS TO THE EMPIRE (753-27 BC)

BC

753	Foundation of Rome by Romulus, according to legend. (However, archaeologists unearthed Latin and Sabine villages on the Tiber Island from the early 8C.)
750	Rape of the Sabine women.
7C-6C	Royal dynasty of the Tarquins, Etruscan rulers. Power is divi-

509 ded between the king, the senate and the people.

509 Tarquins expelled after the rape of Lucretia. Establishment of the Republic: the king's powers are conferred on two consuls.

451-449 The Law of the XII Tables institutes equality between patricians and plebeians.

390 The Gauls sack Rome.

281-272 War against Pyrrhus, King of Epirus; southern part of the peninsula submits to Rome.

264-241 **First Punic War**: Carthage abandons Sicily to the Romans.

218-201 Second Punic War. **Hannibal** crosses the Alps and defeats the Romans at Lake Trasimeno. Hannibal routs the Romans at Cannae and halts at Capua.
In 210 **Scipio** carries war into Spain, and in 204 he lands in Africa. Hannibal is recalled to Carthage. Scipio defeats him at Zama in 202.

146 Macedonia and Greece become Roman provinces. Capture of Carthage.

133 Occupation of Spain, end of Mediterranean campaigns.

133-121 Failure of the policy of the Gracchi, who promoted popular agrarian laws.

122 Senate assassinates democrtic reformer Gaius Gracchus.

118 The Romans in Gaul.

112-105 War against Jugurtha, King of Numidia (now Algeria).

102-101 Marius, the vanquisher of Jugurtha, stops the invasions of Cimbri and Teutoni.

88-79 Sulla, Marius' rival, triumphs over Mithridates (King of Pontus) and establishes his dictatorship in Rome.

70 **Pompey** and **Crassus** become masters of Rome.

63 Catiline's plot against the Senate exposed by Cicero.

60 The first Triumvirate: Pompey, Crassus, **Julius Caesar**. Rivalry of the three rulers.

59 Julius Caesar as Consul.

58-51 The Gallic War (52: Surrender of Vercingetorix at Alesia).

49 Caesar crosses the Rubicon, driving Pompey from Rome.

49-45 Caesar defeats Pompey and his partisans in Spain, Greece and Egypt. He writes his history of the Gallic War and meets Cleopatra.

Early 44 Caesar appointed Dictator for life.

15 March 44 Caesar is assassinated by Brutus, his adopted son.

43 The second Triumvirate: **Octavian** (great-nephew and heir of Caesar), **Mark Antony**, Lepidus.

41-30 Struggle between Octavian and Antony. At Actium, lovers Anthony and Cleopatra suffer defeat and suicide.

THE EARLY EMPIRE (27 BC – AD 284)

27 Octavian takes the title "**Augustus Caesar**" and plenary powers.

AD

14 Death of Augustus.

14-37 Reign of Tiberius.

41 **Caligula assassinated.**

64 **Nero rules. Rome burns.**

67 **Saints Peter and Paul martyred.**

68 **Julio-Claudian Dynasty** (Augustus, Tiberius, Caligula, Claudius, Nero) ends.

69-96 **Flavian Dynasty**: Vespasian, Titus, Domitian.

96-192 Century of the Antonines, marked by the successful reigns of Nerva, Trajan, Hadrian, Antoninus and Marcus Aurelius, who consolidated the Empire.

193-275 **Severus Dynasty**: Septimius Severus, Caracalla, Heliogabalus, Alexander Severus, Decius, Valerian, Aurelian.

235-68 Military anarchy; a troubled period. The legions make and break emperors.

270-75 Aurelius re-establishes the unity of the Empire.

THE LATER EMPIRE AND DECLINE (AD 284-476)

284-305 Reign of **Diocletian** ("the age of martyrs"). Empire split into East and West.

306-37 Reign of **Constantine**. By the **Edict of Milan** (313), Constantine decrees religious freedom. Constantinople, the eastern capital, thrives. Rome declines.

379-95 Reign of Theodosius the Great, the Christian Emperor, who establishes Christianity as the state religion in 382. At his death the Empire is divided between his sons, Arcadius (Eastern) and Honorius (Western).

5C The Roman Empire is repeatedly attacked by the barbarians: in 410, Alaric, King of the Visigoths, captures Rome. Capture and sack of Rome in 455 by the Vandals under Genseric.

475 Byzantium is the seat of the Empire. Goths rule Rome.

476 Deposition by **Odoacer** of Emperor Romulus Augustus ends the Western Empire.

FROM ROMAN EMPIRE TO THE GERMANIC HOLY ROMAN EMPIRE

493 Odoacer is driven out by the Ostrogoths under Theodoric.

535-53 Reconquest of Italy by the Eastern Roman Emperor **Justinian** (527-65).

568 **Lombards**, a Germanic tribe, invade led by King Alboin.

590-604 Papacy of Gregory the Great, who evangelised the Germans and Anglo-Saxons.

752 Threatened by the Lombards, the Pope appeals to Pepin the Short, King of the Franks.

756 Donation of Querzy-sur-Oise. Pepin the Short returns the Byzantine territories conquered by the Lombards to Pope Stephen II, leading to the birth of the Patrimonium Petri (Papal States) and temporal power of the Pope.

774 Pepin's son, **Charlemagne** (Charles the Great), becomes King of the Lombards.

800 Charlemagne is proclaimed Emperor of the **Holy Roman Empire** by Pope Leo III.

9C The break-up of the Carolingian Empire causes complete anarchy and the formation of many rival States in Italy. This is an unsettled period for the Papacy, which is often weak and dissolute. Widespread corruption among the ecclesiastical hierarchy.

951 Intervention in Italy of Otto I, King of Saxony, who becomes King of the Lombards.

962 **Otto I**, now crowned Emperor, founds the Germanic Holy Roman Empire.

THE CHURCH VERSUS THE EMPIRE

9C Establishment of **Normans** in Sicily and the south.

1076 The Gregorian Reform of Pope Gregory VII tries to re-establish the Church's influence. Dispute between the Pope and Emperor Henry IV leads to the Investiture Controversy.

1077 Humbling of the Emperor before the Pope at Canossa.

1097 First Crusade begins.

1155 **Frederick Barbarossa** crowned Emperor. The struggle between the Empire and the Papacy resumes, with the **Ghibellines** supporting the Emperor and the **Guelphs** supporting the Pope.

1167 Creation of the **Lombard League**, an association of Guelph leaning cities.

1176 Frederick Barbarossa and Pope Alexander III reconcile.

1216 Triumph of the Papacy on the death of Pope Innocent III.

1227-50 A new phase in the struggle for Empire (Frederick II) and the Papacy (Gregory IX).

Colosseum

B. Morandi/MICHELIN

FRENCH INFLUENCE AND THE DECLINE OF IMPERIAL POWER

13C	Peak of economic prosperity of the Communes.
1265	Charles of Anjou, brother of St Louis, crowned King of Sicily.
1282	Sicilian Vespers: massacre of French settlers in Sicily.
1300	First Jubilee declared by Pope **Boniface VIII**.
1302	The **Anjou Dynasty** establishes itself in Naples.
1303	Attack of Anagni, instigated by King Philip of France, on Pope **Boniface VIII**. (*see ANAGNI*).
1309-77	The popes established at Avignon, France. The Avignon popes included Clement V to Gregory XI who took the Papacy back to Rome at the instigation of St Catherine of Siena. This period is referred to as the **Avignon Captivity**.
1328	Failure of the intervention in Italy by the Emperor Ludwig of Bavaria.
1378-1418	The **Great Schism of the West** (anti-popes in Pisa and Avignon) is brought to an end by the Council of Constance (1414-18).
1402	Last German intervention in Italy (the Lombard militia defeats the Emperor).
1442	Alfonso V, King of **Aragon,** becomes King of the Two Sicilies.
1453	Constantinople, capital of the Christian Eastern territories, falls to the Turks.

1492	Death of **Lorenzo de' Medici**. **Christopher Columbus** discovers America.
1494	French King Charles VIII intervenes for Ludovico Il Moro.

ECONOMIC AND CULTURAL GOLDEN AGE (15C, EARLY 16C)

Trade transformed the north and centre of the peninsula, while the south kept its feudal structures. The economic importance of Italy derived from the large-scale production of consumer goods (cloth, leather, glass, ceramics, arms etc), as well as commerce.

Merchants and bankers who settled in countries throughout Europe spread their civilization, which bloomed brightest at the Italian courts. Wealthy patrons vied to support artists and commission splendid palaces. Foremost among them ranked the Medici of Florence, the Sforza of Milan, the Montefeltro of Urbino, the Este of Ferrara, the Gonzaga of Mantua and the Popes in Rome (Julius II, Leo X).

Decline set in as trade shifted towards the Atlantic, crippling the maritime republics that prospered during the Middle Ages. **Genoa** soon faced ruin, **Pisa** was taken over by its age-old rival Florence, and **Amalfi** and **Venice** were in serious trouble as the Turks advanced westwards. Additionally, political fragmentation made Italy an inevitable target for the powerful nation-states that emerged within Europe.

FROM THE 16C TO THE NAPOLEONIC ERA

16C	France and Spain struggle for the supremacy of Europe.
1515-26	François I, victor at Marignano, vanquished at Pavia, is forced to give up the Italian heritage.
1527	Capture and **sack of Rome** by the troops of the Constable of Bourbon, in the service of Charles V.
1545-63	The Church attempts to re-establish its authority and credibility, damaged by the Protestant Reformation, with the Council of Trent.
1559	Treaty of Cateau-Cambrèsis: Spanish domination over Naples, Milan, Sicily and Sardinia until early 18C.
17C	Savoy becomes northern Italy's most powerful State.
1713	Victor-Amadeus II of Savoy acquires Sicily and the title of King. The Duke of Savoy swaps Sicily for Sardinia (1720).
1796	**Napoleon's campaign** in Italy. Creation of Cispadan Republic.
1797	Battle of Rivoli. Treaty of Campo-Formio. Cisalpine and Ligurian Republics created.
1798	Proclamation of the Roman Republic. The French occupy Rome. Pope goes into exile.
1799	Parthenopaean (Naples) Republic declared.

The "Roman question"

The Papacy became involved in the Risorgimento during the 19C, when it became clear that the Unification of Italy could not take place unless the Pope was willing to relinquish the temporal power that he exercised over part of the country. When the troops of Victor Emmanuel II entered Rome in 1870, Pope Pius IX retired to the Vatican, declaring himself a prisoner of the Italian State. The "Roman Question" was only finally resolved in 1929, under the papacy of Pius XI, with the **Lateran Treaty** drawn up between the Holy See and the Fascist government of **Benito Mussolini**. These pacts recognised the sovereignty of the Pope within the Vatican City, as well as over certain buildings and organisations in Rome, and granted the Church specific authority regarding education and marriage in Italy. The Lateran Pacts were then included in the new Constitution of the Italian Republic in 1947. They have continued to govern relations between the Italian State and the Church since the end of the Second World War, and were modernised in a new Concordat in 1984.

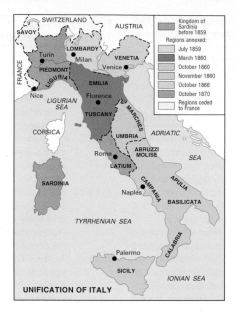

UNIFICATION OF ITALY

1801	The Cisalpine Republic becomes the Italian Republic.
1805	Napoleon transforms the Italian Republic into a Kingdom, assumes the crown of the Lombard kings.
1808	Rome occupied by French troops. Murat becomes King of Naples.
1809	The Papal States are attached to the French Empire.
1812	Pius VII is taken to France as a prisoner.
1814	Collapse of the Napoleonic regime. Pius VII returns to Rome.

TOWARDS ITALIAN UNITY (1815-70)

Niccolò Machiavelli dreamed of a united Italy in the 16C, but no action unfolded for centuries. After the 1815 Congress of Vienna, many revolts by the "Carbonari" – patriots opposed to the Austrian occupation – were crushed. In 1831 **Giuseppe Mazzini** founded the Young Italy movement. This period, known as the **Risorgimento**, inspired the **First War of Independence** against Austria, led by Charles Albert of Savoy, King of Sardinia. Initial Italian successes were followed by a violent Austrian counter-attack, the abdication of Char-les

Albert in 1849 and the accession of Victor **Emmanuel II** to the throne.

Europe finally took notice, thanks to the skilful campaigning of his minister **Camillo Cavour**, an ardent advocate of Italian liberty, and the participation of Piedmont in the Crimean War as France's ally. The Plombières agreement signed by Cavour and Napoleon III in 1858 led to the outbreak of the **Second War of Independence** in the following year, with combined Franco-Piedmontese victories in Magenta and Solferino.

Following popular uprisings in central and northern Italy, the Kingdom of Sardinia annexed Lombardy, Emilia-Romagna and Tuscany. In 1860, after **Garibaldi** liberated Sicily and southern Italy from the domination of the Bourbons, the emerging State added southern Italy, the Marches and Umbria. On 17 March 1861, the Kingdom of Italy was proclaimed with Turin as the capital and Victor Emmanuel as king. In 1866 the capital moved to Florence.

In the same year, the **Third War of Independence** – with the Prussians as Italy's allies against Austria – led to the annexation of the Veneto. Four years later, on 20 September 1870, General Cadorna's troops entered Rome through Porta Pia. Rome finally joined Italy and became the capital in 1871.

FROM 1870 TO THE PRESENT DAY

1882 Italy, Germany and Austria sign the **Triple Alliance.**

1882-85 Italians gain a footing in Eritrea and the Somali Coast.

1900 Umberto I asassinated. Accession of Victor Emmanuel III.

1904-06 Rapprochement of Italy with Britain and France.

1911-12 War breaks out between Italy and the Turks. Occupation of Libya and the Dodecanese.

1915 Outbreak of the **First World War**. Italy enters WWI on 24 May 1915. It joins France, Great Britain and Russia (the Triple Entente) against Austria-Hungary, then Germany (28 August 1916).

1918 The Battle of Vittorio Veneto marks the end of the First World War for Italy (4 November).

1919 Treaty of St Germain-en-Laye: Istria and the Trentino are attached to Italy.

1920-21 Social disturbances fomented by the Fascist Party led by **Benito Mussolini**.

1922-26 Mussolini's squads terrorize opponents, then march on Rome. He becomes Prime Minister, then Il Duce.

1929 **Lateran Treaty** concluded between the Italian Government and the Papacy. This defined the relationship between Church and State and brought to an end the age-old "Roman Question".

1936 Italy occupies Ethiopia. Rome-Berlin Axis formed.

1939 **Second World War** erupts.

1940 Italy enters the Second World War, allied with Germany against Britain and France.

1943 – 10 July: The Allies land in Sicily. 25 July: Overthrow and arrest of Mussolini. 8 September: Armistice. German occupation in much of the country. 12 September: Mussolini is freed by the Germans and

"You are Peter and on this rock I will build my church" (Matthew 16: 18)

The title of "Pope," derived from the Greek *pápas* meaning father, was originally used for patriarchs and bishops from the Orient. From the 5C on, it became widely used in the west, where with the increasing importance of the Roman See, it was eventually reserved for the Bishop of Rome alone. The Bishop of Rome maintained that his See in the traditional capital of the Empire had been founded by the Apostles, Peter and Paul, and therefore claimed first place in the ecclesiastical hierarchy. The Pope was initially chosen by both the people and the clergy, until the Conclave of the Cardinals was established in 1059. Strict regulations regarding this method of election were set out by Gregory X in the 13C. Nowadays the cardinals meet in conclave in the Sistine Chapel and a vote is held twice a day; after each inconclusive vote the papers are burned so as to produce dark smoke. A majority of two thirds plus one is required for an election to be valid; then a plume of white smoke appears above the Vatican. The senior cardinal appears at the window in the façade of St Peter's from which papal blessings are given and announces the election in the Latin formula: Annuntio vobis gaudium magnum: habemus papam (I announce to you with great joy: we have a Pope).

Over the centuries the Pope gradually assumed greater political power so that the history of the Papacy is inevitably linked with that of the relationship between the Church and the main political powers of the time. After the Unification of Italy, the Lateran Pacts of 1929 defined the present configuration of the Vatican City, which constitutes a separate State within the Italian State, of which the Pope is the sovereign ruler. The Holy Father is the undisputed leader of the Roman Catholic church and exercises absolute infallibility over all ecclesiastical dogma, as set out in the first Vatican Council in 1870. Through the figure of the Pope, the spiritual influence of the Roman Catholic church can be felt throughout the world.

sets up the **Italian Socialist Republic** in the north.

1944-45 The Allies slowly reconquer Italy. The country is liberated (25 April 1945) and the war ends. Mussolini is arrested while trying to flee into Switzerland, tried and shot.

1946 Victor Emmanuel III abdicates. Accession of Umberto II. Proclamation of **The Re-public** after a referendum.

1947 **Treaty of Paris**: Italy loses its colonies as well as Albania, Istria, Dalmatia and the Dodecanese. Frontier redefined to the benefit of France.

1948 – 1 January: New Constitution comes into effect.

1954 Trieste is attached to Italy.

1957 Treaty of Rome institutes the European Economic Community (now the EU): Italy is one of six founding members.

1960 Rome hosts Olympic Games.

1962 The Second Vatican Council reforms church policy.

1963-8 Strikes and protests over the socio-economic system: *autunno caldo* (hot autumn). Prime Minister Aldo Moro tries to bring together the socialists and conservatives.

1970-80 Riots due to political unrest. The "Years of Lead."

1970 Regional system instituted.

1978 Left-wing terrorist groups (the **Red Brigades**) kidnap and assassinate Aldo Moro.

1980 Bologna station bombing.

1981 Attack on Pope John Paul II in St Peter's Square by Turkish terrorist Mehmet Alì Agca.

1982 Prefect of Palermo, Alberto Dalla Chiesa killed.

1991 Italian Communist Party (PCI) splits into two new parties, the Democratic Party of the Left (PDS) and the Communist Refoundation (RC). First wave of Albanian refugees arrives in Puglia.

1992 Operation to fight economic and political corruption in Italy commences, and leads to the collapse of the ruling classes of the Republic. Two judges, Giovanni Falcone and Paolo Borsellino, are assassinated in Sicily.

1994 The centre-right led by Silvio Berlusconi wins the first political elections under the new majority electoral system. Second Republic begins.

1996 Teatro La Fenice destroyed by fire in Venice. Electoral victory of the Ulivo alliance. The left governs for the first time in the Republic's history.

1997 Earthquakes in Umbria damage the Basilica of St Francis of Assisi.

27 March 1998 Italy signs up to the single European currency.

13 May 1999 Carlo Azeglio Ciampi, Governor of the Bank of Italy, becomes the 10th President of the Italian Republic.

13 May 2001 Electoral victory for the central-right alliance and Berlusconi.

1 January 2002 Italy adopts the euro.

2002 Prices rise and the economy dips. Fiat plans to lay off 20% of its workforce.

2003 Berlusconi on trial for corruption charges relating to business dealings in the 1980s. Protests against the government and Iraq involvement intensify.

2004 Berlusconi's trial resumes. He is cleared of corruption.

2005 Pope Jean Paul II dies and German cardinal Joseph Ratzinger becomes Pope Benedict XVI. EU constitution ratified. Voters throw out Berlusconi's coalition. He resigns, forms a new government and resumes rule.

2006 Giorgio Napolitano, a former Communist Party member, becomes Italy's 11th postwar president. Romano Prodi becomes Prime Minister.

2007 Romano Prodi resigns after a defeat on a foreign policy vote, but continues with a re-formed coalition government.

ART AND CULTURE

ABC of Architecture

Ancient Art

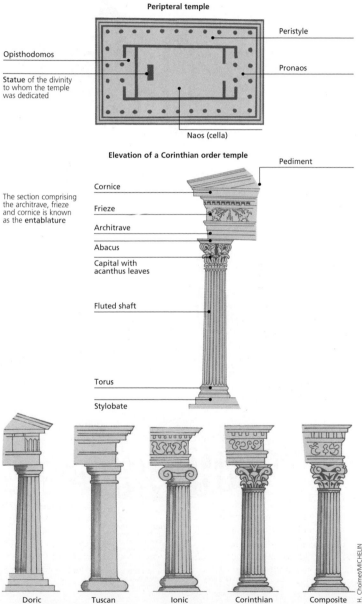

Peripteral temple

Peristyle

Opisthodomos

Pronaos

Statue of the divinity to whom the temple was dedicated

Naos (cella)

Elevation of a Corinthian order temple

Pediment

Cornice

The section comprising the architrave, frieze and cornice is known as the **entablature**

Frieze

Architrave

Abacus

Capital with acanthus leaves

Fluted shaft

Torus

Stylobate

Doric   Tuscan   Ionic   Corinthian   Composite

H. Choimer/MICHELIN

Baths of the Villa Romana del Casale (3-4C A.D.)

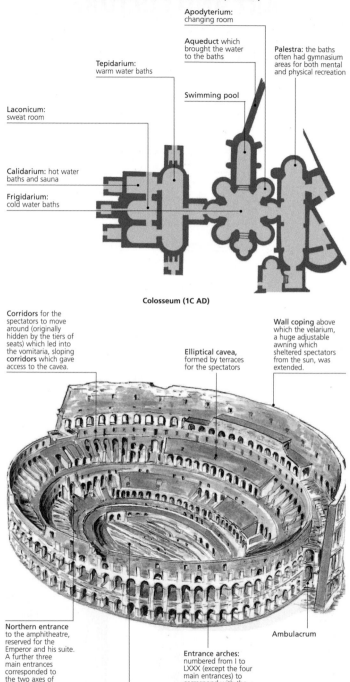

Apodyterium: changing room

Aqueduct which brought the water to the baths

Palestra: the baths often had gymnasium areas for both mental and physical recreation

Tepidarium: warm water baths

Swimming pool

Laconicum: sweat room

Calidarium: hot water baths and sauna

Frigidarium: cold water baths

Colosseum (1C AD)

Corridors for the spectators to move around (originally hidden by the tiers of seats) which led into the vomitaria, sloping **corridors** which gave access to the cavea.

Elliptical cavea, formed by terraces for the spectators

Wall coping above which the velarium, a huge adjustable awning which sheltered spectators from the sun, was extended.

Northern entrance to the amphitheatre, reserved for the Emperor and his suite. A further three main entrances corresponded to the two axes of the ellipsis.

Ambulacrum

Arena: originally covered by a wooden floor.

Entrance arches: numbered from I to LXXX (except the four main entrances) to correspond with the entrance number on the spectator's ticket; seating was arranged according to social status.

R. Corbel

Religious architecture

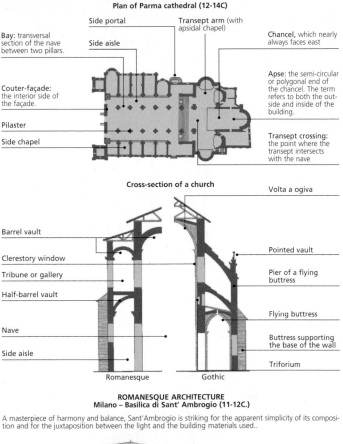

Plan of Parma cathedral (12-14C)

Bay: transversal section of the nave between two pillars.

Side portal

Side aisle

Transept arm (with apsidal chapel)

Chancel, which nearly always faces east

Couter-façade: the interior side of the façade.

Apse: the semi-circular or polygonal end of the chancel. The term refers to both the outside and inside of the building.

Pilaster

Side chapel

Transept crossing: the point where the transept intersects with the nave

Cross-section of a church

Volta a ogiva

Barrel vault

Clerestory window

Tribune or gallery

Half-barrel vault

Nave

Side aisle

Pointed vault

Pier of a flying buttress

Flying buttress

Buttress supporting the base of the wall

Triforium

Romanesque   Gothic

ROMANESQUE ARCHITECTURE
Milano – Basilica di Sant' Ambrogio (11-12C.)

A masterpiece of harmony and balance, Sant'Ambrogio is striking for the apparent simplicity of its composition and for the juxtaposition between the light and the building materials used..

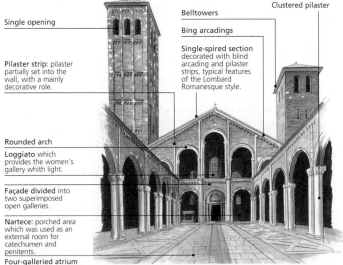

Single opening

Belltowers

Bing arcadings

Clustered pilaster

Pilaster strip: pilaster partially set into the wall, with a mainly decorative role.

Single-spired section decorated with blind arcading and pilaster strips, typical features of the Lombard Romanesque style.

Rounded arch

Loggiato which provides the women's gallery whith light.

Façade divided into two superimposed open galleries.

Nartece: porched area which was used as an external room for catechumen and penitents.

Four-galleried atrium

H. Chormet/MICHELIN

GOTHIC
Milano – Cathedral apse (14-15C)

Milano cathedral is a unique and extraordinary example of the late-Gothic style in Italy. It was started in 1386 and was not finished until the façade was completed in the 19C. The building, commissioned by Gian Galeazzo Visconti, clearly demonstrates a transalpine cultural influence far removed from contemporary Tuscan architecture.

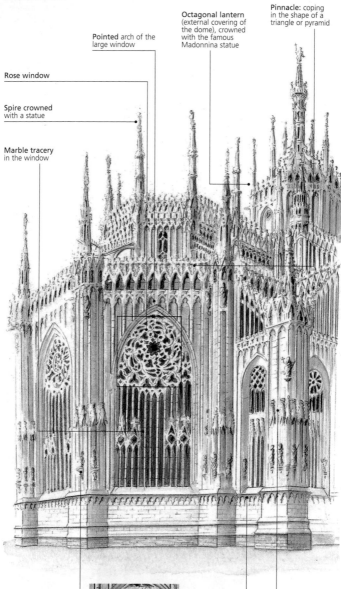

Octagonal lantern (external covering of the dome), crowned with the famous Madonnina statue

Pinnacle: coping in the shape of a triangle or pyramid

Pointed arch of the large window

Rose window

Spire crowned with a statue

Marble tracery in the window

Console bearing a statue

Decorative canopies

Trefoil-arched cornice

Rose window: circular shaped tracery, decorated with different stylised floral motifs

H. Choimet

THE RENAISSANCE
Rimini – Tempio Malatestiano (Leon Battista Alberti, 15C)

Built in honour of Sigismondo Malatesta, this church is a celebration of classical cultures and civilisations, from which many of its structural and decorative features are taken, re-interpreted and adapted to the religious role of the building.

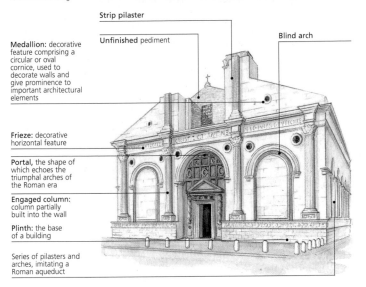

Strip pilaster

Unfinished pediment

Blind arch

Medallion: decorative feature comprising a circular or oval cornice, used to decorate walls and give prominence to important architectural elements

Frieze: decorative horizontal feature

Portal, the shape of which echoes the triumphal arches of the Roman era

Engaged column: column partially built into the wall

Plinth: the base of a building

Series of pilasters and arches, imitating a Roman aqueduct

Firenze – The interior of the Cappella dei Pazzi (Filippo Brunelleschi, 1430-1445)

The harmony of the proportions and the elegant play on colours between the grey of the *pietra serena* stone (which emphasises the architectural features) and the white of the plaster create an atmosphere of dignified and austere simplicity.

Ribbing of the dome: a structural element, which constitutes the framework of the building. It may be hidden or visible.

Ceramic medallion

Oculus: circular opening

Pendentive: connecting piece positioned at a corner of a square space to support an octagonal or circular dome.

Square apsidal chapel

Pilaster strip in *pietra serena* stone

Corinthian capital: decorated with acanthus leaves

Frieze

H. Cholmet

Civil architecture

Castel del Monte (13C)

Built by Frederick II, probably as a leisure residence, the castle is dominated by the number eight: the ground plan is octagonal, there are eight octagonal towers and eight rooms on each floor.

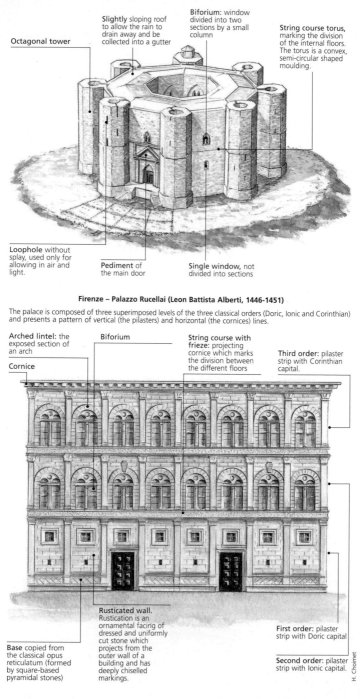

Slightly sloping roof to allow the rain to drain away and be collected into a gutter

Biforium: window divided into two sections by a small column

String course torus, marking the division of the internal floors. The torus is a convex, semi-circular shaped moulding.

Octagonal tower

Loophole without splay, used only for allowing in air and light.

Pediment of the main door

Single window, not divided into sections

Firenze – Palazzo Rucellai (Leon Battista Alberti, 1446-1451)

The palace is composed of three superimposed levels of the three classical orders (Doric, Ionic and Corinthian) and presents a pattern of vertical (the pilasters) and horizontal (the cornices) lines.

Arched lintel: the exposed section of an arch

Cornice

Biforium

String course with frieze: projecting cornice which marks the division between the different floors

Third order: pilaster strip with Corinthian capital.

Rusticated wall. Rustication is an ornamental facing of dressed and uniformly cut stone which projects from the outer wall of a building and has deeply chiselled markings.

Base copied from the classical opus reticulatum (formed by square-based pyramidal stones)

First order: pilaster strip with Doric capital

Second order: pilaster strip with Ionic capital.

H. Choimet

BAROQUE
Lecce – Basilica di Santa Croce (15-17C)

The Baroque style of Lecce is influenced both by Roman and Spanish architecture. The exuberant, highly-worked decoration evokes the Spanish Plateresque style (15-16C), in which façades were decorated with the precise detail of a goldsmith (platero in Spanish).

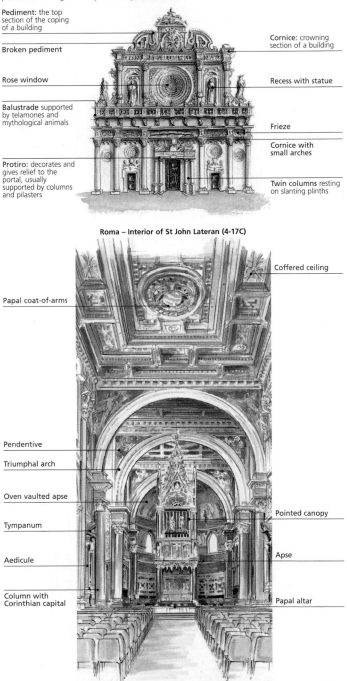

Pediment: the top section of the coping of a building

Broken pediment

Rose window

Balustrade supported by telamones and mythological animals

Protiro: decorates and gives relief to the portal, usually supported by columns and pilasters

Cornice: crowning section of a building

Recess with statue

Frieze

Cornice with small arches

Twin columns resting on slanting plinths

Roma – Interior of St John Lateran (4-17C)

Coffered ceiling

Papal coat-of-arms

Pendentive

Triumphal arch

Oven vaulted apse

Tympanum

Aedicule

Column with Corinthian capital

Pointed canopy

Apse

Papal altar

H. Choimet

Torino – Palazzo Carignano (Guarino Guarini, 1679-1681)

The façade is striking for the juxtaposition of its straight and curved lines, while the use of brick is a reminder of the Emilian origins of the architect.

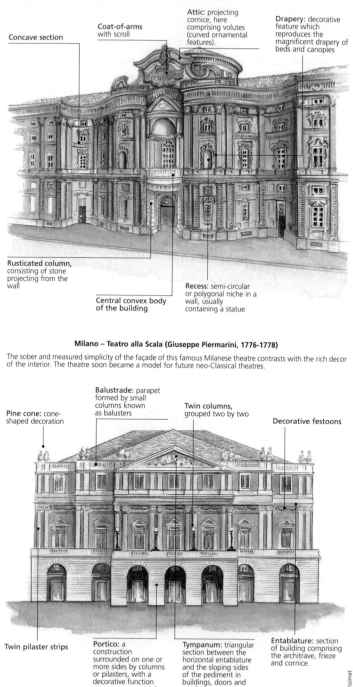

Concave section

Coat-of-arms with scroll

Attic: projecting cornice, here comprising volutes (curved ornamental features).

Drapery: decorative feature which reproduces the magnificent drapery of beds and canopies

Rusticated column, consisting of stone projecting from the wall

Central convex body of the building

Recess: semi-circular or polygonal niche in a wall, usually containing a statue

Milano – Teatro alla Scala (Giuseppe Piermarini, 1776-1778)

The sober and measured simplicity of the façade of this famous Milanese theatre contrasts with the rich decor of the interior. The theatre soon became a model for future neo-Classical theatres.

Pine cone: cone-shaped decoration

Balustrade: parapet formed by small columns known as balusters

Twin columns, grouped two by two

Decorative festoons

Twin pilaster strips

Portico: a construction surrounded on one or more sides by columns or pilasters, with a decorative function or as a monumental entrance.

Tympanum: triangular section between the horizontal entablature and the sloping sides of the pediment in buildings, doors and windows.

Entablature: section of building comprising the architrave, frieze and cornice.

H. Choimet

Architectural Terms

Some of the terms given below are further explained by the illustrations on the previous pages.

Altarpiece (or **ancona**): a large painting or sculpture adorning an altar.

Ambulatory: extension of the aisles around the chancel for processional purposes.

Apse: semicircular or polygonal end of a church behind the altar; the outer section is known as the chevet.

Architrave: the lowermost horizontal division of a Classical entablature sitting directly on the column capital and supporting the frieze.

Archivolt: arch moulding over an arcade or upper section of a doorway.

Atlantes (or **telamones**): male figures used as supporting columns.

Atrium (or **four-sided portico**): a court enclosed by colonnades in front of the entrance to a early Christian or Romanesque church.

Bastion: in military architecture, a polygonal defensive structure projecting from the ramparts.

Buttress: external support of a wall, which counterbalances the thrust of the vaults and arches.

Caisson (or **lacunar**): decorative square panel sunk into a flat roof or vaulted stonework.

Cappella: chapel.

Cathedra: high-backed throne in Gothic style.

Ciborium: a canopy (baldaquin) over an altar.

Corinthian: *see Order*.

Cortile: interior courtyard of a palace.

Counter-façade: internal wall of church façade.

Cross (church plan): churches are usually built either in the plan of a Greek cross, with four arms of equal length, or a **Latin cross**, with one arm longer than the other three.

Crypt: Underground chamber or vault usually beneath a church, often used as a mortuary, burial place or for displaying holy relics. Sometimes it was a small chapel or church in its own right.

Diptych: *see Polyptych*.

Duomo: cathedral.

Entablature: in certain buildings, the section at the top of a colonnade consisting of three parts: the architrave (flat section resting on the capitals of a colonnade), the frieze (decorated with carvings) and the cornice (projecting top section).

Exedra: section in the back of Roman basilicas containing seats; by extension, curved niche or semicircular recess outside.

Fresco: mural painting applied over a fresh undercoat of plaster.

Ghimberga: a triangular Gothic pediment adorning a portal.

Grotesque: a decorative style popular during the Renaissance in which parts of human, animal and plant forms are distorted and mixed. The term comes from the old Italian word grotte, the name given in the Renaissance period to the Roman ruins of the Domus Aurea.

High relief: sculpture or carved work projecting more than one half of its true proportions from the background (half-way between low relief and in-the-round figures).

Ionic: see *Order*.

Jamb or **pier**: pillar flanking a doorway or window and supporting the arch above.

Lantern: turret with windows on top of a dome.

Lesene (or **Lombard strips**): decorative band of pilasters joined at the top by an arched frieze.

Low relief: bas-relief, carved figures slightly projecting from their background.

Merlon: part of a crowning parapet between two crenellations.

Modillion: small console supporting a cornice.

Moulding: an ornamental shaped band which projects from the wall.

Narthex: interior vestibule of a church.

Nave: the area between the entrance and chancel of a church, with or without aisles.

Oculus: round window.

Ogee arch: a pointed arch of double curvature: Cyma Recta where the lower curve is convex and the upper curve concave; Cyma Reversa where the reverse is true.

Order: system in Classical architecture ensuring a unity of style characterised by its columns (base, shaft, capital) and entablature. The orders used in Tuscany are: Doric (capitals with mouldings – the Tuscan Doric order is a simplified version of this), Ionic (capitals with volutes), Corinthian (capitals with acanthus leaves) and the Composite, derived from the Corinthian but more complex.

Pala: Italian term for altarpiece or reredos.

Palazzo: a town house usually belonging to the head of a noble family; the word derives from the Palatine Hill in Rome where the Caesars had their residences and came to mean the official residence of a person in authority.

Pediment: ornament in Classical architecture (usually triangular or semi-circular) above a door or window.

Pendentive: connecting piece positioned at a corner of a square space to support an octagonal or circular dome.

Piano nobile: the principal floor of a palazzo raised one storey above ground level.

Pieve: Romanesque parish church.

Peristyle: the range of columns surrounding a Classical building or courtyard.

Pilaster strip: structural column partially set into a wall.

Pluteus: decorated balustrade made from various materials, separating the chancel from the rest of the church.

Polyptych: a painted or carved work consisting of more than three folding leaves or panels (diptych: 2 panels; triptych: 3 panels).

Portico: an open gallery facing the nave in early Christian churches; it later became a decorative feature of the external part of the church.

Predella: base of an altarpiece, divided into small panels.

Pronaos: the space in front of the cella or naos in Greek temples; later the columned portico in front of the entrance to a church or palace.

Pulpit: an elevated dais from which sermons were preached in the nave of a church.

Pyx: cylindrical box made of ivory or glazed copper for jewels or the Eucharistic host.

Retable: large and ornate altarpiece divided into several painted or carved panels, especially common in Spain after the 14C.

Rose-window: A circular window usually inserted into the front elevation of a church, often filled with stained glass, and decorated with tracery arranged symmetrically about its centre.

Splay: a surface of a wall that forms an oblique angle to the main surface of a doorway or window opening.

Tambour: a circular or polygonal structure supporting a dome.

Tempera: a painting technique in which pigments are ground down and bound usually by means of an egg-based preparation. The technique was replaced by oil.

Tondo: a circular picture, fashionable in Italy in the mid-15C.

Triforium: an open gallery above the arcade of the nave, comprised mainly of three-light windows.

Triptych: see *Polyptych*.

Trompe l'oeil: two-dimensional painted decoration giving the three-dimensional illusion of relief and perspective.

Tympanum: the section above a door (or window) between the lintel and archivolt.

Vault: arched structure forming a roof or ceiling; **barrel vault**: produced by a continuous rounded arch; **cross vault**: formed by the intersection of two barrel vaults; **oven vault**: semicircular in shape, usually over apsidal chapels, the termination of a barrel-vaulted nave.

Volute: architectural ornament in the form of a spiral scroll.

Visual Arts

A tour of Italy's art and architectural treasures can be disorientating, given the country's huge contributions to culture over the centuries. From saints and symbols to glistening mosaics, Italy boasts an impressive array of imagery. Historical context is vital to properly appreciate Italian art in all its diversity and richness. The rightful heir of the Greek, Etruscan and Roman civilisations, Italian art has adopted essential principles and characteristics from each period.

Italy has always been open to foreign influences. This melting pot was fueled in part by its extensive geographical area, stretching from the Alps in the north to Sicily. After the fall of the Western Roman Empire, Byzantium held sway and greatly influenced the northern Adriatic shores for several centuries. Invaders – including the Ostrogoths, Lombards, Franks, Arabs and Normans – all left their imprint on conquered territory in southern Italy. The extraordinarily malleable Italian character absorbed these varied and exotic influences. One after another, the cities of Florence, Siena, Verona, Ferrara, Milan, Rome, Venice, Naples, Genoa – and many other centres of minor or major importance – became cradles of artistic movements.

By the 12C, Italian artists were already beginning to show certain common characteristics: in particular, a shared taste for **harmony and solidity of form**, and an innate sense of space inherited from the Classical world. This restrained style tried to depict the rational and intelligible order of things. The Italians rejected the naturalistic art popular with northern schools, and tempered the abstraction and decoration of Oriental artists. Slowly a representational technique evolved that reflected the artist's emotions. Idealisation – greatly prized in antiquity – continued to play a role as well.

In spite of this scholarly and well-mastered image, Italian art had a strong social component. Parallel to the artist's intellectual attempt to impose order on reality, art gradually developed a feeling

Associazione Turistica di Naturno

8C fresco depicting S. Procolo

for naturalism, influenced by Classical models. A good example of this was the medieval square, or 'piazza'. Following in the tradition of the Roman Forum, it contained the main public buildings, such as the church, baptistery, town hall or princely seat. Law courts, a hospital or a fountain were sometimes added.

Often designed to look like stage scenery, with extensive embellishment and ornamentation, the piazza was the social theatre for business, local markets, meetings, political decision-making and other important events. A typical Italian **piazza** is usually the result of centuries of construction. As a record of aesthetic influences and social moods, it can be used to interpret history. Scholars examine how certain elements were reused, ornamental motifs copied and styles mingled or superimposed. Aspiring architects, sculptors and painters could best exercise and promote their talents in this public arena.

Italy's excellent town planners, however, retained a **harmonious relationship with nature**. From Roman times onward, they embellished the countryside with sumptuous **villas and splendid terraced gardens**, skilfully designed to create shade and please the eye. Fountains, springs and follies invitedv the passer-by to rest, meditate or simply enjoy nature's beauty. Thus the Italian architects and landscape gardeners, often indifferent to the solemn grandeur of French classicism, have created many places that capture an architectural rapport with nature.

These range from Hadrian's Villa near Rome, to the flower-bedecked terraces of the Borromean Islands, including the Oriental charm of the Villa Rufolo in Ravello. This harmony also echoes through the elegant buildings of the Florentine countryside, the fantastic Mannerist creations of Rome, Tivoli or Bomarzo, the urban and regional projects designed by Juvarra in Piedmont, and Palladio's work on the delightful mansions of the Brenta Riviera.

BYZANTINE INFLUENCE

Barbarian invasions triggered the decline of the late Roman Imperial tradition and encouraged the popular and narrative early Christian art, which later formed the basis of the Romanesque style.

Honorius and his sister Galla Placidia chose Ravenna as the capital of the Empire. After the death of Theodoric and the Gothic invasions, the town came under direct Byzantine rule in the reign of Justinian (AD 527-65). The Byzantine Emperors ruled the region of Ravenna and Venezia Giulia only until the 8C, but they held sway in Sicily and part of southern Italy until the 11C. Byzantine art inherited a legacy of naturalism and sense of space from the Greek and Latin artistic traditions, and a rich decorative style from its Oriental roots.

Byzantine architects inherited the vault and dome from the late-Roman period. They developed the style's potential, often with extraordinary results, culminating in the basilica of San Vitale in Ravenna. Simpler structures were also built, combining plain, sober exteriors with dazzling interior decoration in mosaic and marble. The bas-reliefs on sarcophagi, chancel parcloses, ambos and pulpits, assume an essentially decorative character.

Painting

Animals and figures became stylized and symbolic. Byzantine paintings often have a "**cartoon**" quality to the modern eye. Flat, stiff figures – with large eyes – appear to float. Rich hues were frequently paired with gold-leaf backgrounds. Scenes are simple, so illiterate viewers could easily learn religious lessons.

Mosaics

Byzantine artists excelled at this sumptuous form. Precious materials made mosaic the perfect technique for portraying Bible characters or courtly figures. The tiles (*tesserae*) were fragments of hard stone or glass that were glazed and irregularly cut to catch the light. They covered oven vaults, walls and cupolas, where their gold highlights could sparkle in the mysterious semi-darkness. Enigmatic, grandiose figures stood out against midnight blue backgrounds and landscapes filled with trees, plants and animals. The mosaics of Ravenna (5C-6C) are perhaps the most famous examples

Mosaic in the apse of Santa Maria in Trastevere

B. Kaufmann/MICHELIN

of the period. However, the Byzantine style continued to prevail during the 11C-12C at St Mark's in Venice, in Sicily (Cefalù, Palermo, Monreale) and in various forms up to the 13C in Rome.

ROMANESQUE AND GOTHIC (11C-14C)

The Italian predilection for harmony and monumental ensembles meant that architecture did not reach the sublime heights of the great Gothic achievements of northern Europe.

Romanesque Period

Round Roman arches – based on thick, heavy basilica walls – grounded an 11C architectural renaissance. New cathedrals and Benedictine monasteries drew on Carolingian and Ottonian traditions, as well as regional influences. Alternating columns and pilasters provided buildings with rhythm, space and depth. These continued into the roof structure, where archivolts and ribs support the square vaults. In Romanesque style, the structural function of architectural features is always visible. The most flourishing school was initially in northern Italy. Here, master masons included the **Maestri Comacini**, who created exceptional stone buildings in the mountains and brick edifices in the valleys. The **Maestri Campionesi** hailed from the Lugano region and the Lombard lakes. The regions of central Italy were influenced by other cultural models and produced quite different styles. Florence's highly original medieval style is characterised by delicate colors and a subtle intellectual character. Rome, however, drew on the early Christian tradition of the magnificent Constantinian basilicas. In Tuscany – especially in Pisa, Lucca and Pistoia – the Romanesque style shows strong Lombard and classical Florentine influences, embellished by decorative details. Typical features include tiers of arcades with a multitude of small columns on the façades, tall blind arcades on the side walls and east end, decorative lozenges and different coloured marble encrustations. The **Maestri Cosmati**, a Roman guild of mosaic and marble workers, held

sway in 12-13C Latium. They specialised in assembling fragments of multicoloured marble (pavings, episcopal thrones, ambos or pulpits and candelabra) and the encrustation of columns and friezes in the cloisters with enamel mosaics. Finally, southern Italy and Sicily show a mixture of Lombard, Saracen, Byzantine and Norman influences, the result of which was the monumental and noble **Sicilian-Norman style** (👁 see SICILIA). This style also displays Oriental influence in its highly decorative façades, and Classical influence in the perfectly poised rhythm of its colonnades.

Sculpture was closely linked with architecture. Low reliefs presented both Biblical and secular stories, often intended to educate.

Painting bloomed alongside mosaics in the large cathedrals, where the vast walls and vaults were covered with colour. The bare, austere walls seen in many churches today are almost always the result of the ravages of time or restoration work. Originally, bright and imaginative frescoes illustrated stories from the Bible, mixing new experimental artistic forms with old Byzantine influences. Finally, this period saw the rise of illustrated manuscripts, another learning aid.

Gothic Period

"Then arose new architects who after the manner of their barbarous nations erected buildings in that style which we call Gothic (dei Gotthi)," complained Florentine historiographer Giorgio Vasari (1511–1574). The style has since earned respect and even adoration, but the perogative label – evoking barbarian hordes – stuck.

These ambitious builders wanted to push stone steeples closer to God. Romanesque barrel and groin vaults were better suited to squat, solid and dark structures. From the 11C, experiments began with pointed arches, stone ribs and flying buttresses, which propped up constructions with bridge-like arches. Interiors opened out and larger windows poured "divine" light inside.

The **pointed arch** allowed more height above the transept. Tall, spectacular pilasters – formed by bands of columns – supported the weight. Storey upon storey drew the gaze to the vault's highest point, symbolizing Christians' yearning for heaven.

No longer bearing the entire load, the walls could be pierced with glass panels. While the solid structure of the building and the omnipresent Classical heritage remained vital, light became an important element. Lavish **stained-glass** scenes were common, as well as rose windows, which most famously adorn Notre-Dame in Paris.

The buildings reached unimagined heights, supported externally by a mass of buttresses and **flying buttresses**. These were hidden from sight inside the church, accentuating the impression of space and vertical movement.

The Cistercians introduced Gothic architecture into Italy, but its widespread adoption was due to the many new religious orders, especially the Franciscans and Dominicans. These groups often used the traditional model of the early Christian basilica, so practical and economical, and adapted it to current trends. The era's civil architecture showed more originality. Numerous prosperous towns displayed their civic pride with municipal palaces and loggias. The Venetian Gothic style relieved bare façades with windows and loggias, and persisted until the late 15C.

The **Pisano** family from Pisa combined ancient traditions, seen through the classicism championed by Frederick II (**Nicola**, 1215?- c 80), and their vigorously expressive realism, explicitly Gothic in tone (**Giovanni**, 1248-after 1314). These masters and the architect and sculptor **Arnolfo di Cambio** (c 1245-1302) introduced new iconography and ambitious projects for pulpits and funerary monuments. All exhibited the new humanism.

The painted Crucifixes in relief that appeared in the 12C were the first specimens of Italian painting. The rigidity inherited from Byzantine art gradually melted away. In the 13C a Roman, **Pietro Cavallini**, (1273-1321) executed frescoes and mosaics with a greater breadth of style, reminiscent of Antique art. His Florentine contemporary, **Cimabue** (1240-1302), adorned the Upper Basilica of Assisi with frescoes displaying a new sense of pathos. This inspired **Giotto** (1266-1337), who added naturalism to the mix. Movement, depth and atmosphere were indicated or suggested. Emotion flickered across his frescoes in Assisi, Padua and Florence. Giotto's masterful works influenced all successive painting, including that of Masaccio and Michelangelo.

At the same time in Siena, **Duccio di Buoninsegna** (c 1255-1318) still showed a strong Byzantine influence. He founded the **Siena school**, which exployed a graceful linear technique and much decorative colour. Exponents of this delicate school included **Simone Martini** (c 1284-1344) and the brothers **Pietro**

The Cathedral (11C-12C) and the Leaning Tower(12C-14C), uilt in Pisan Romanesque Style

(c 1280-1348?) and **Ambrogio Loren-zetti** (1285-1348?).

The masters of the Florentine Trecento period (14C) developed a mystical and realistic style far removed from the lively work of Giotto. They stressed harmonies of line and colour, and a great refinement in the decorative elements. At the same time the **International Gothic** style, developed in the courts of Europe, was practiced by artists from central and northern Italy and perfected in the frescoes painted by Simone Martini and Matteo Giovannetti (?-1367) in Avignon. Other exponents of this refined, stately and occasionally decadent artistic movement, which lasted until the 15C, include **Stefano da Zevio** (c 1379-after 1438) from Verona, **Pisanello** (c 1380-1455) a portraitist, animal painter and distinguished medallist and **Gentile da Fabriano** (c 1370-1427).

QUATTROCENTO (15C)

Artists, scholars and poets flourished during this era, characterised by a passion for Antiquity, well-organised city-states governed by a noble or princely patron, and a new vision of man's place at the centre of the universe. The Medici city of Florence was the epicenter of this cultural movement, much later designated the **Renaissance (Rebirth)**.

Architecture

A new art concept was introduced by Florentine sculptor and architect **Filippo Brunelleschi** (1377-1446), an enthusiastic admirer of Antiquity. His strong personality transformed the practical approach of the medieval master builder into the creative role of the architect who designed on the drawing board. Brunelleschi was both an artist and an intellectual. His invention of geometrical perspective allowed him to plan harmonious and rationally designed buildings. His intuitive reproduction of three-dimensional objects on two-dimensional canvas provided the foundation for all future painting.

His intellectual abilities and the abstract character of his architectural creations were imitated and made commonplace by his followers, but were never fully understood. **Leon Battista Alberti** (1406-1472) also used his knowledge of ancient art to create a new expressive style. His vision was based on an emotional relationship between objects and space, which most likely inspired the architect Donato Bramante.

Sculpture

The magnificent doors of Florence's Baptistery, designed by **Lorenzo Ghiberti** (1378-1455), show the influence of Gothic tradition and ancient art. However, the most powerful sculptor of the period was undoubtedly **Donatello** (1386-1466), who eschewed

The Imposing Gothic Ruins of San Galgano Abbey, built 13C

G.Bludzin/MICHELIN

intellectual speculation. His focus was on interpreting Classical forms with a free and innovative spirit, breathing dynamism into his work and bringing it to the height of expressive power. After Padua, where he created works that set a standard for all of northern Italy, Donatello returned to Florence. Here, in the changing climate of the second half of the century, he explored the idea that humanity is acquired through suffering, presaging the crisis of the century's end. His contemporary, **Luca della Robbia** (1400-1482), specialised in coloured and glazed terracotta works, while **Agostino di Duccio** (c 1418-1481), **Desiderio da Settignano** (c1430-1464) and **Mino da Fiesole** (1429-1484) continued in the Donatello tradition, at the same time moving away from the extremes of his intense dramatical style.

Painting

The third major figure of the 15C was the painter **Masaccio** (1401-1428). He applied Brunelleschi's laws of perspective and added light. For the first time in centuries, figures cast a shadow, creating perspective and the notion of space. His substantial characters thus acquired a certain realism and a solidity that lent them a moral dignity. **Paolo Uccello** (c 1397-1475) took another tact: perspective based on two vanishing points. Uccello also demonstrated that more than one method exists for reproducing reality, with the philosophical implications all this entails.

At the same time, the Dominican friar **Fra Angelico** (1387-1455), who remained very attached to Gothic tradition, was attracted to the new theories of the Renaissance, while **Benozzo Gozzoli** (1420-1497) adapted his style to the portrayal of brilliant secular festivities. **Andrea del Castagno** (1419-1457) emphasised modelling and monumental qualities (see FIRENZE).

Sandro Botticelli (1444-1510) produced a miraculous purity of line, giving a graceful and almost unreal fragility to his figures and a deep sense of mystery to his allegorical scenes. At the turn of the century, amid the crisis in humanist values, he created dazzling figures of sharp lines and muted colours.

Domenico Ghirlandaio (1449-1494) revealed a gift for narrative painting in monumental frescoes that depicted the ruling class of Florence in an atmosphere of stately serenity.

The work of **Piero della Francesca** (1415-1492) from Sansepolcro is a supreme example of Tuscan Renaissance art. Here, he displays faultless harmony and draughtsmanship with his use of form, colour and light (see AREZZO).

The Annunciation by Filippino Lippi - Capella Carafa

At the Gonzaga court in Mantua, **Andrea Mantegna** (1431-1506) painted scenes full of grandeur and vigour, using ancient models to create Renaissance paintings of strong and inscrutable heroes. In the esoteric, astrological and alchemical atmosphere of the court of Ferrara, **Cosmè (Cosimo) Tura** (1430-1495) created original and challenging compositions in which men and objects are hurled together in a mix of colours that resemble sharp metals and semiprecious stones.

The second major center of art at this time was Venice, where **Giovanni Bellini** (1432-1516) created a sense of optical and empirical space in his paintings. He did this by using colour and tones, in contrast to the geometric, intellectual and anti-naturalist painting of Florence.

Bellini was much influenced by the work of **Antonello da Messina** (1430-1479) in the 1470s, who had in turn drawn on the work of the Flemish masters and his knowledge of Piero della Francesca.

CINQUECENTO (16C)

The 16C saw the development of the previous century's sensibility, infused even more with Antiquity, mythology and the discovery of humanity. The artistic centre of the Renaissance moved from Florence to Rome, where the popes rivalled one another in embellishing palaces and churches. Artists became more independent, acquiring social prestige. The canons of Renaissance art were already being exported and put into practice elsewhere in Europe. However, this golden age of poets and humanists was disrupted by political and religious upheavals in Europe, many linked to Lutheranism.

Architecture

The century began with the return of **Donato Bramante** (1444-1514) from Milan to Rome, where he laid the foundations for the new basilica of St Peter's, later completed by Michelangelo. Despite appearances, Bramante's architectural style was not completely Classical in tone; he made use of trompe l'oeil effects (such as the false chancel created in Milan's San Satiro church) that feigned depth. As a result, architecture became more than a rational representation of what exists. This development would find perfect expression in the later Baroque style.

Michelangelo, partly inspired by Bramante's ideas, attempted to give moulded form to large architectural structures – treating them as sculptures. **Giacomo da Vignola** (1507-1573) also worked in Rome, while **Andrea Palladio** (1508-1580) designed a number of buildings in Vicenza (&see VICENZA). In his important works on architecture, he advocated the Classicism of ancient art and was himself responsible for many churches, palaces and luxury villas in Venetia.

Sculpture

Michelangelo (1475-1564) did most of his life's work in either Florence or Rome. He was the most outstanding character of the century, owing to his creative, idealistic and even troubled genius, which found expression in masterpieces of unsurpassed vitality. His art explored questions like divine revelation, the human longing for something beyond its dissatisfying earthly existence, the soul trying to release itself from the prison of the body, and the struggle between faith and the intellect. He drew inspiration from ancient art and the work of Donatello, which he reinterpreted with impressive moral tension. Michelangelo towered above his contemporaries, including the elegant and refined **Benvenuto Cellini** (1500-1571), a skilled goldsmith and sculptor known for his Perseus (now in Florence) and the powerful sculptor **Giovanni Bologna** (or Giambologna) (1529-1608), who followed the dictates of a stately and courtly art.

Painting

The 16C was an important period for painting. Numerous outstanding artists produced works in the new humanist vein. Rome and later Venice replaced Florence as artistic centers. The century began with exceptional, but complementary, masters. **Leonardo da Vinci** (1452-1519) was the archetype of the new enquiring mind. He is famous for his sfumato (literally translated as 'mist'), an impalpable, luminous veil effect that created an impression of distance between persons and objects or surroundings. His insatiable desire for knowledge, interest in mechanics, and attempt to form observations into a coherent system make him a precursor of modern scientists. His reflections on the soul – interpreted in paintings such as *The Last Supper* in Milan – had a lasting effect on future painters.

Raphael (1483-1520) was not only a prodigious portraitist and painter of gently drawn madonnas, but also a highly inventive decorator with an exceptional mastery of composition, given free rein in the Stanze of the Vatican. His style is classical in the fullest sense. He communicated the most intellectual and sophisticated ideas in logical, fascinating and deceptively simple paintings.

Michelangelo (1475-1564), the last of the three great men, was primarily a sculptor, yet famously frecoed the ceiling of the Sistine Chapel. Here, his skill with relief and power were triumphant. The master's paintings portray a magnificent and heroic humanity, which appears devastated by the message of God. The bright optimism of contemporary Humanist Classicism was thus shattered and future artists were forced to choose between the divine Raphael or the terrifying Michelangelo.

Pietà by Michelangelo

B. Kaufmann/MICHELIN

The 16C Venetian school produced many great colourists. **Giorgione** (1478-1510) explored the relationship between man and nature by creating a wonderful sense of landscape and atmosphere. **Titian** (c 1490-1576), a disciple of Bellini, was influenced as a youth by Giorgione and imbued with his skill for both mythological and religious compositions. He was also a fine portraitist and was commissioned by numerous Italian princes and European sovereigns. His later work, characterised by bold compositions and densely-coloured brushwork, is the impressive and personal document of one of the greatest artists of the century. **Tintoretto** (1518-1594) added a tormented violence to his predecessors' luminosity, and ably exploited this in dramatic religious compositions. **Paolo Veronese** (1528-1588) was foremost a decorator in love with luxury and sumptuous schemes. He delighted in crowd scenes with grandiose architectural backgrounds. In contrast, **Jacopo Bassano** (1518-1592) handled rustic and nocturnal scenes, heightened with a new sense of reality and a freedom of touch and composition.

THE UNSETTLED YEARS

The end of the 15C was a time of crisis: the invasion of Italy by foreign armies, with the resulting loss of liberty for many states, the increase in religious tensions, leading to the Lutheran Protestant movement, the sack of Rome and the Counter-Reformation all had a dramatic effect on artists. In northern Italy, **Lorenzo Lotto** (1480-1556) interpreted the spiritual anxieties of the provincial aristocracy and bourgeoisie with sharp psychological insight. In Brescia, following Foppa, artists explored reality and morality. **Romanino** (1484-1559) exploded with expressive violence. **Giovanni Girolamo Savoldo** (c 1480-1548) demonstrated a deep, lyrical intensity, while the paintings of **Alessandro Moretto** (1498-1554) were humble in their touching spirit of faith. But the most obvious examples of the anti-Classical crisis were in Florence, where **Jacopo Pontormo** (1494-1556) was the typical incarnation of a genial, yet tormented and neurotic artist, a visionary given to bouts of insanity. Influenced by the works of Raphael and Michelangelo, his paintings disturbed the harmony of the Renaissance with their troubled tension, sharp colours and unreal sense of space.

MANNERISM

The art of the Counter-Reformation – which often tweaked the canon in an exaggerated or 'mannered' way – marked the transition between Renaissance and Baroque. It attempted to voice the preoccupations of the previous generation. This refined genre pursued ideals of supreme and artificial beauty by copying the stylistic solutions of Raphael and Michelangelo. Mannerist art involved complex compositions of muscular and elongated figures. The period is generally considered to be one of technical accomplishment, but also of formulaic, theatrical and over-stylized work. A typical exponent of this style was **Giorgio Vasari** (1511-1574), author of the *Lives of the Artists*, who had a strong influence on historical and critical judgement up to the present day. While Mannerism was widely adopted throughout Europe, it was countered in Italy by the Roman Catholic Church, which, following the Council of Trent, proposed that religious art be subjected to greater doctrinal clarity.

NATURALISM, CLASSICISM AND BAROQUE: THE 17C

Painting

Reacting against Mannerism, a group of Bolognese artists founded the **Accademia degli Incamminati** (Academy of the Eclectic), under the leadership of the **Carracci** family (**Annibale**, the most original, **Lodovico** and **Agostino**). They proposed a less artificial style that was truer to nature and paved the way for future artistic trends.

Classicism evolved first in Bologna and Rome, and later throughout Italy, following the premises laid down by the Carracci. One of the basic concepts is that certain forms – used in ancient art and by Raphael – constitute models of perfection and should be paradigms for any creation of high spiritual content. The vault of Palazzo Farnese in Rome, painted by Annibale Carracci, presages the Baroque style with its overwhelming dynamics and trompe-l'œil.

Fanciful and frilly, the Baroque style introduced a sense of movement, broken perspectives, scrolls and false reliefs. Painting paired with architecture to create disturbing visions of impressive verisimilitude. A good example is the ceiling of the Gesù church in Rome, where **Baciccia** (1639-1709) created a credible illusion of the sky in the physical architectural space of the ceiling.

The swashbuckling **Michelangelo da Caravaggio** (1573-1610) overthrew several centuries of Italian idealism. His intense and often cruel realism, inspired by the artistic traditions of Lombardy and Brescia, drew inspiration from everyday life in Rome. Contrasting light and shadow gave a dramatic visual impact to his work and often highlighted the moral reasons behind human actions and sentiments. He was widely imitated in Italy, France and the Netherlands – and was without doubt the most influential artist in 17C Europe.

Architecture and sculpture

Unlike Mannerist architecture – static and intellectual – Baroque sought spatial dynamism. Spectators were amazed and confused by scenic devices, the continual intermingling of exterior and interior, curved and broken lines, and the role of light as a vehicle of divine intervention. The true Baroque style, which is structural and found mainly in Rome, is often the creation of artists who worked as architects, painters, sculptors and scenographers. The transformation of St Peter's basilica by **Gian Lorenzo Bernini** (1598-1680) offers typical examples: the famous colonnade solves the problem of the inharmonious extension of the church and makes the monumental but static façade the background to a dynamic piazza. The square then turns towards Rome and opens its arms to welcome the faithful.

Inside the cathedral, the flooding light and the immense bulk of the baldaquin compensate for the loss of centrality.

Ornate Façade of Basilica dei Santi Pietro e Paolo, 17C-18C, Acireale, Sicily

B. Kaufmann/MICHELIN

The extension of the nave is transformed into an extraordinary tunnel of perspective of increasing tension. An interesting variation of Baroque architecture can also be seen in Puglia (especially Lecce) and in Sicily, where buildings of ornate and imaginative decoration clearly show the influence of the Spanish Plateresque style.

SETTECENTO (18C)

The deep cultural changes of the new century, with its emphasis on rational and enlightened thinking, were reflected in art. Now, the Baroque style, exhausted of its most intimate religious content, became even more secular and decorative in tone. Art was departing from symbolic significance and becoming more autonomous. It was more inclined to entertain rather than to educate – a trend that began in France, where the style was known as *rocaille*.

Italy had by now relinquished its leading role, although the peninsula still produced some important artistic figures, especially in Piedmont. The era's most extraordinary project was the urban revival of Turin, which raised the city to the status of a European capital. Here, **Filippo Juvarra** (1678-1736) moved beyond the drama of his predecessor

Guarino Guarini (1624-1683). Instead, he designed a town plan (long tree-lined avenues surrounding the buildings) of grandiose theatricality: the perfect backdrop for the fine costumes of the Court of Savoy. Art took another important step away from a mere representation of physical objects with the Venetian painter **Giovanni Battista (Giambattista) Tiepolo** (1696-1770), who created trompe l'oeil perspectives for pure visual pleasure and no real regard for verisimilitude or the content of the stories represented: art was now being valued for its artistic qualities alone.

OTTOCENTO (19C)

In the late 18C and early 19C, the vogue for all things Classical spread throughout Italy and Europe, following the excavations of Herculaneum and Pompeii. The style's sober, simple and harmonious lines – modelled on the Antiquity – contrast starkly with the exuberant, irregular Baroque fashion. The Italian neo-Classical style is exemplified by the sculptor **Antonio Canova** (1757-1822), whose works follow perfectly the "noble simplicity and quiet grandeur" of Greek art as described by Winckelmann (and only really observed through Roman copies). In his most famous sculpture, *The Three Graces* (in the Victoria & Albert

Museum, London), the extreme formal perfection is transformed into an ambiguous sensuality that resonates with nostalgia for a perfect world lost forever. It is a subtle allusion to the impalpable screen between life and death that characterises all of his work, as well as the period's poetry.

Neo-Classicism also infiltrated architecture, alongside the eclectic style. This free-for-all lasted throughout the century, often with erratic results. An exception is **Alessandro Antonelli** (1798-1888), who enlivened the idiom with new engineering principles, binding the academic tradition to the boldest experiments in Europe.

In painting, the often academic tone of **Francesco Hayez** (1791-1882) demonstrates the Romantic style, which existed alongside the neo-Classical tradition. This friend of Canova created paintings of medieval history, highly sentimental in tone, which referred to the contemporary events of the Risorgimento. The **Macchiaioli** group, founded in 1855, started a revolt against academicism that lasted about 20 years. Also known as the "spotters", they were in some ways the precursors of the Impressionists; they often worked outdoors, using colour and simple lines, and drawing inspiration from nature. The main figures included **Giovanni Fattori** (1825-1908), **Silvestro Lega** (1826-1895) and **Telemaco Signorini** (1835-1901). Some artists worked with the Impressionists in Paris, and their influence had an indirect, but powerful, effect on Italian art.

At the end of the 19C, in parallel with the growth of a flowing and sketch-like style of painting, **Giovanni Segantini** (1858-18899), **Pellizza da Volpedo** (1868-1907) and **Gaetano Previati** (1852-1920) developed the Divisionist school. This art reflected the theories of the French Post-Impressionists; on the one hand developing a deeper analysis of reality, with strong connotations of a social character, while at the same time lending itself to allegorical and symbolist themes. This was in line with artistic developments in the rest of Europe, and their solutions were of fundamental importance for the avant-garde trends of the 20C.

NOVECENTO (20C)

The 20C began in an explosive manner with the sensational and anti-aesthetic style of the **Futurists**, Under the leadership of the poet **Filippo Tommaso Marinetti** (1876-1944), the movement's theorist, they celebrated speed, crowds and machinery. This was an explicit and anarchic reaction to bourgeois traditionalist values, which were attacked with vehemence and a sometimes superficial vitality. The movement soon adopted a nationalist tone, which in some cases developed into a sympathy for the Fascists. The Futurists tried to render the dynamism of the modern world, often with fragmented forms similar to Cubism's. However, they differed in their marked sense of rebellion, which was influenced both by contemporary philosophers such as Bergson, and by the violent and impassioned disharmony of the Expressionist movement.

The members of this avant-garde movement were **Umberto Boccioni** (1882-1916), **Giacomo Balla** (1871-1958), **Gino Severini** (1883-1966), **Carlo Carrà** (1881-1966) and the architect **Antonio Sant'Elia** (1888-1916). **Giorgio de Chirico** (1888-1978), together with Carrà, created metaphysical painting, a disturbing form where objects are placed in unlikely but credible positions in an ambiguous and enigmatic atmosphere. Giorgio Morandi was inspired by some of the same ideas. His still-lifes of everyday objects invite meditation on history and the meaning of the painting.

After the First World War, the return to peace revived artistic activity both in Italy and abroad. This included the founding of the Novecento group, which developed naturalistic premises through Magical Realism, interpreted through a re-reading of metaphysics and of Italian medieval and classical art. The results were often highly poetic and stylised. Most of the painters, sculptors and architects in Italy either belonged to, or were influenced by this group, especially when the political regime declared itself in favour of this stylistic trend in the 1920s, opposing any relationship with contemporary European art. A

Unique Forms of Continuity in Space by Umberto Boccioni (created 1913, cast 1931)

few isolated voices, often criticised by the authorities, were raised in explicit or tacit opposition to these trends and in favour of a less provincial approach. Some of the most important forces were involved in the **Corrente** group from Milan, the **Scuola romana**, and the **Sei di Torino**.

These groups shared a common interest in Expressionism, which often gave their art a highly dramatic realism, a social tension and a deeply humane content. A good example is the painter **Renato Guttoso** (1912-1987), with his personal interpretation of post-Cubist art, combined with explicitly anti-fascist material. Even in the general post-war crisis, he nearly always managed to avoid the risks of socialist realism, thanks to his openness to different cultural influences. One of the most important contemporary sculptors was **Giacomo Manzù** (1908-1991), who succeeded in breathing new life into Christian art. A clear and luminous sensitivity gave his works, especially the low reliefs, an almost Donatellian vitality. As such, Manzù succeeded in making a sorrowful and humane statement against violence.

The Post-War Period

The tragedy of war always makes an indelible impression. Artists query the significance of creation in a world where all moral values have been brutally set aside. The phrase "the death of art" also surfaced in the new consumer society of the 1950s and 1960s. The classical artistic language was no longer understood as a system of signs able to give form to the aesthetic experience of reality. New expression was therefore anti-aesthetic and mirrored trends which previously had no influence.

Canvases were sometimes tossed aside or much abused. Alberto Burri (1915-1995), who came to painting later in life, avoided the traditional academic circles. By pasting old torn bags onto his canvas, Burri's intention was not to represent ideas or objects, but to exhibit a fragment of reality. This matter only acquired significance because it had been transformed by the artist and therefore became part of his personal experience. **Lucio Fontana** (1899-1968) also stretched the physical limits inherent in the traditional method of creating art. He cut canvases, seeking new solutions to the old problem of space, which can be created, but not represented. In doing so, he emphasised the importance of the "gesture" and of the action that puts the here and now in contact with the other world of the canvas and destroys the classical pretence of space.

Other artists belonged to the movement known as **arte povera**, which opposed the "rich" world. Their break with the classical method of creating and understanding art was complete. The apex was the artist's radical refusal to develop a role; something he believes to be a hoax, dominated by the system against which he is struggling.

Literature

BIRTH OF ITALIAN LITERATURE

The Italian language acquired a literary form in the 13C. At Assisi **St Francis** (1182-1226) wrote his moving Canticle of the Creatures in the vernacular instead of the traditional Latin, so that the people could read the word of God. The 13C also gave rise to the **Sicilian School** which, at the court of Frederick II, developed a language of love inspired by traditional ballads from Provence. The most famous of the 13C poetical trends was, however, that of the dolce stil nuovo ("sweet new style"): followers included Guinezzelli and Cavalcanti. The term was appropriated by **Dante Alighieri**(1265-1321), author of *Vita Nuova* (New Life), *Convivio* (The Banquet) and *De vulgari eloquentia* (Concerning Vernacular Eloquence), to indicate the lyrical quality of this poetry which would celebrate a spiritual and edifying love for an angel-like woman in verse. It was with this new tool that he wrote one of the most powerful masterpieces of Italian literature: the *Divine Comedy* is the account of a lively, enquiring and impassioned visitor to Inferno, Purgatory and Paradise (Inferno, Purgatorio, Paradiso). It is also an epic account of the Christianised Western world and the height of spiritual knowledge of the period. During the 14C **Petrarch** (1304-74), the precursor of humanism and the greatest Italian lyrical poet (☾see PADOVA), and his friend **Giovanni Boccaccio** (1313-75), the astonishing storyteller who seems almost modern at times (☾see SAN GIMIGNANO: Certaldo), continued in the tradition of Dante. Each enriched the Italian language in his own way.

HUMANISM AND RENAISSANCE

Florentine humanism reinterpreted the ancient heritage and invented a scholarly poetry in which the tension of the words and images reflected the aspiration of the soul to attain an ideal. **Politian**, **Lorenzo de' Medici** (1449-92) and especially **Michelangelo** were exponents of the neo-Platonic notion of ideal poetry. However the Florentine Renaissance also favoured the development of other quite different lines of thought: scientific with Leonardo da Vinci, theorist with Leon Battista Alberti, philosophical with Marsile Fincin and encyclopaedic with the fascinating personality of Pico della Mirandola. Later Giorgio Vasari (☾see FIRENZE) became the first-ever art historian.

In the 16C writers and poets perfected the Italian language to a height of refinement and elegance rarely attained, and all this in the service of princes whom they counselled or entertained. The most famous was **Niccolò Machiavelli** (1469-1527) , the statesman and political theorist whose name now symbolises cunning and duplicity. In his work entitled The Prince he defined with clarity and intelligence the processes which control society, and the moral and political consequences of these relationships.

At the court in Ferrara, **Matteo Maria Boiardo** (1441-94) fused the epic poetry of the Carolingian cycles with the courtly poetry of the Breton cycles in the poem celebrating chivalry, *Orlando Innamorato (Roland in Love)*. **Ludovico Ariosto** (1475-1533) and **Torquato Tasso** (1544-95) provided an element of intellectual brilliance. The former wrote *Orlando Furioso (Roland the Mad)*, an epic poem in episodes which enjoyed an extraordinary vogue, and Tasso, his successor at court in this genre, published his *Jerusalem Delivered (Gerusalemme Liberata)*.

At Urbino, **Baldassare Castiglione** (1478-1529) was the author of one of the great works of the period *The Courtier (Il cortegiano)* which was read throughout Europe. In Venice, **Aretino** (1492-1556) sketched the unsentimental portrait of his contemporaries *(Letters)* while in Padua, **Ruzzante** (1502-42) favoured realism in the local dialect.

COUNTER-REFORMATION AND BAROQUE PERIOD

After the discovery of America in 1492, an event which affected the Mediterranean economy adversely, and the spread of Lutheran Protestantism, the 17C to the early 18C marked a period of decadence for Italian literature. The exception was **Galileo** (1564-1642), a scientist, who, taking Archimedes as his point of reference rather than Aristotle, made a distinction between scientific methods and those applicable to theology and philosophy. He was implacably opposed by the Church in an attempt to reassert its influence under the onslaught of the Reformation. The fear of the Inquisition hampered original thought and favoured the development of Baroque poetical concepts in a quest for fantasy.

THE AGE OF ENLIGHTENMENT AND ROMANTICISM

The early 18C was marked by Arcadia, a literary academy which preached "good taste" inspired by the purity of Classical bucolic poetry, in opposition to the "bad taste" of the Baroque period.

The philosopher **Giambattista Vico** (1668-1744) elaborated the theory of the ebb and flow of history based on three stages (sense, imagination and reason). The dramatist **Pietro Metastasio** (1698-1783) was also a leading figure of the period whose biting yet well-thought out vision advanced scientific and philosophical thought.

In Venice, the 18C was dominated by the dramatist **Carlo Goldoni** (1707-93), known as the Italian Molière, who peopled his plays in an amusing, alert and subtle manner with the stock characters and situations of the *Commedia dell'Arte* (see BERGAMO), an art form which was then highly popular in Venice.

From the end of the 18C writers began to express a new national spirit (consciousness which developed until the upheaval of the Risorgimento). **Giuseppe Parini** (1729-99), a didactic writer, and **Vittorio Alfieri** (1749-1803) who became known for his tragedies on the themes of liberty and opposition to tyranny,

were the precursors of the violent and tormented **Ugo Foscolo** (1778-1827) whose patriotic pride is given full vent in *Of the Sepulchres.*

It was **Giacomo Leopardi** (1798-1837) who in some of the finest poems of his verse collection *Canzoni* expresses with a certain lucidity and lyrical purity the growing gulf between the old faith and a fear of the unknown future. He was the main exponent of Italian romanticism and of the theory of historical pessimism based on the contrast between a happy natural state and reason (or civilisation) which brings unhappiness. This was followed by cosmic pessimism which posits the condemnation of Nature and unhappiness as an intrinsic human condition. The Milanese author, **Alessandro Manzoni** (1785-1873), wrote one of the most important novels of 19C Italian literature, *The Betrothed (I promessi sposi)*, a grandiose epic of ordinary folk based on the notion of providence in human existence.

REALISM AND DECADENCE

The Sicilian **Giovanni Verga** (1840-1922) assured the transition between the 19C and 20C with his novels. He was one of the most important members of the Italian Realist *(Verismo)* school of novelists which took its inspiration from the French naturalist movement. In his extravagant fiction series entitled

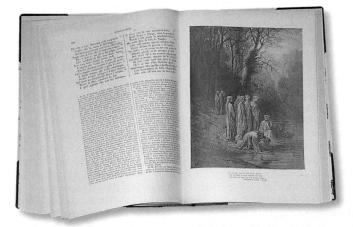

Dante explaining the Divine Comedy to the city of Florence

S. Senini/MICHELIN

Vinti he presents his pessimistic vision of the world and his compassion for the disinherited.

In the field of lyrical poetry in the second half of the 19C **Giosuè Carducci** (1835-1907), a Nobel prize winner in 1906, drew inspiration from Classical poetry. He was a melancholy figure who criticised the sentimentality of the romantic movement. **Gabriele d'Annunzio** (1863-1938) adopted a refined and precious style to express his sensual love of language. The complex and anxious voice of the poet **Giovanni Pascoli** (1855-1912) filled the early years of the century. His nostalgic poetry recalls the age of innocence and a sense of wonder.

AUTHORS MODERN AND CONTEMPORARY

In the early 20C, magazines devoted to political, cultural, moral and literary themes were published. Giuseppe Prezzolini (1882-1982) and Giovanni Papini (1881-1956) were among the contributors.

Futurism, which influenced other forms of artistic expression, was the most important of the contemporary literary movements. In his *Manifesto* (1909) **Filippo Tommaso Marinetti** (1876-1944), the leader and theoretician of the movement, exalted the attractions of speed, machines, war and "feverish insomnia", ideas which were echoed by the disjointed syntax, punctuation and words employed in this literary style.

In line with the European sensibility expressed by Musil, Proust and Joyce, Italian letters favoured the theme of discovery which was influenced by studies on repression and the unconscious in the early years of psychoanalysis. In *Zeno's Conscience*, **Italo Svevo** (1861-1928) examines the alienation of the main protagonist as past and present unfold in a long internal monologue. The Sicilian dramatist **Luigi Pirandello** (1867-1936) also analyses man's tragic solitude and the way in which the identity of the individual is eclipsed by the perceptions of the different persons with whom he associates. The only escape is madness.

© Hulton-Deutsch Collection/CORBIS

Luigi Pirandello

Traces of realism and the influence of D'Annunzio can be detected in the work of **Grazia Deledda** (1871-1936), who shrouds her portrayals of Sardinian society in mythology. Her tales are dominated by passionate emotions and a deep religious sense of life and death.

The **Hermetic Movement**, which developed after the First World War, celebrated the essential nature of words, liberated from the burden of a grandiloquent and commemorative tradition. The poetry of **Giuseppe Ungaretti** (1888-1970) is evocative and intense, while another leading figure of this movement, **Salvatore Quasimodo** (1901-68), produced successful translations of Greek and Latin Classical literature and of Shakespeare.

The poetry of **Eugenio Montale** (1896-1981) relates with sharp and incisive eloquence the anguish which afflicts human nature. **Umberto Saba** (1883-1957), whose native Trieste was strongly marked by Central European culture, uses both noble language and everyday vocabulary in his intensely lyrical and autobiographical work.

After the Second World War, **neo-Realism** – which was ideally suited to the cinema with its popular appeal – gave a graphic account of the life and misery of the working class, of peasants and street children.

The recurring themes in the works of **Cesare Pavese** (1908-50) are the loneliness and difficulty of existence, described with anguish in his diary which was published posthumously with the title *This Business of Living*.

During recent decades the Italian novel has shown a strong vitality with such diverse personalities as Pratolini *(A Tale of Poor Lovers)*, Guido Piovene *(Pietà contro pietà)*, Ignazio Silone *(Fontarama)*, Mario Soldati *(A cena col commendatore)*, Carlo Levi *(Christ stopped at Eboli)* and Elsa Morante *(Arthur's Island)*.

In the 20C, a handful of Italian authors have achieved international fame: **Alberto Moravia** (1907-90) is regarded as a significant narrator of modern Italy identifying thte importance of such issues as sex and money. His book, *The Time of Indifference*, recounts the decline and forbearance of a bourgeois Roman family. Another well-known neo-Realist author was **Italo Calvino** (1923-85) who experimented with the mechanisms of language and who wrote short stories tinged with subtle irony.

Leonardo Sciascia (1921-89) concentrated on revealing some of the ills of Italian society, such as the Mafia. He wrote essays, detective stories, historical memoirs and romantic surveys. **Carlo Emilio Gadda**, known as the "engineer", experimented with language and portrayed the hypocrisy, follies and obscure ills of contemporary society. Pier **Paolo Pasolini** (1922-75) provoked and contested the received ideas of his time, contrasting Marxist ideology with Christian spirituality and peasant values.

Dino Buzzati (1906-72), an original figure, was a poet, writer, illustrator and journalist. His penchant for fantasy and surrealism is tinged with scepticism and is reminiscent of Kafka and Poe.

The 1980s saw the huge success of *The Name of the Rose* (1980), a Gothic thriller written by the semiologist and essayist **Umberto Eco** (b 1932). The century came to a triumphant close with the awarding of the 1997 Nobel Prize for literature to the playwright and actor **Dario Fo** (b 1926), a kind of latter-day court jester who in his plays attacks the powerful and defends the oppressed.

Italian Nobel Prize Winners

Literature – Dario Fo (1997); Eugenio Montale (1975); Salvatore Quasimodo (1959); Luigi Pirandello (1934); Grazia Deledda (1929); Giosuè Carducci (1906).

Physics – Riccardo Giacconi (discovery of cosmic X-ray sources, 2002) Carlo Rubbia (discovery of the subatomic W and Z particles, 1984); Emilio Segrè (discovery of the antiproton, 1959); Enrico Fermi (nuclear reactions produced by the actions of slow neutrons and the resulting fission of uranium, 1938); Guglielmo Marconi (wireless telegraphy, 1909). **Chemistry** – Giulio Natta (polymer structures and technology, 1963).

Medicine and Physiology – Rita Levi-Montalcini (growth mechanisms of nerve cells, 1986); Renato Dulbecco (discovery of the interaction between tumoral viruses and the genetic material of cells, 1975); Salvador Edward Luria (mechanisms of genetic repetition and structure of viruses and bacteria, 1969); Camillo Goigi (structure of the nervous system, 1906).

Economics – Franco Modigliani (analysis of saving cycles and the financial markets, 1985).

Peace - Ernesto Teodoro Moneta (1907).

Music

Italy has played a significant role in the evolution of music with the invention of the musical scale and the development of the violin. It is the birthplace of Vivaldi, who inspired Bach and who was surprisingly neglected until the beginning of the 20C, and of Verdi who created operatic works to celebrate the Risorgimento in the 19C.

EARLY MUSICAL COMPOSITION AND RELIGIOUS MUSIC

As early as the end of the 10C, a Benedictine monk, **Guido** of Arezzo (997-c 1050), invented the scale, naming the notes with the initial syllables of the first six lines of John the Baptist's hymn *"Ut queant laxis / Resonare fibris / Mira gestorum / Famuli tuorum / Solve polluti / Labii reatum Sancte Johannes"*. The "Si" formed by the initials of *Sancte Johannes* was added to these and the Ut was changed to Do in the 17C.

In the 16C, the golden age of vocal polyphony which was then very popular was marked by **Giovanni Pierluigi da Palestrina** (c 1525-94), a prolific composer of essentially religious music (105 masses). During that period, **Andrea Gabrieli** (c 1510-86) and his nephew **Giovanni** (c 1557-1612) who were the organists at St Mark's in Venice were masters of sacred and secular polyphonic music. The latter composed the first violin sonatas.

EFFIGIES ANTONII VIVALDI

© Bettmann/CORBIS

Portrait of Antonio Vivaldi by James Caldwall

FROM THE BAROQUE PERIOD TO THE 18C

It was only in the 17C and 18C that a proper musical school (for operatic as well as instrumental works) was born in Italy, characterised by charm and freshness of inspiration and melodic talent. The old and new musical forms evolved with the expressive and stylistic innovations of **Girolamo Frescobaldi** (1583-1643) for the organ and harpsichord, Corelli (1653-1713) for the violin and **Domenico Scarlatti** (1685-1757) for the harpsichord. The talented Venetian, **Antonio Vivaldi** (1675-1741), composed a wealth of lively music greatly admired by Bach, particularly his concertos divided into three parts, *allegro/adagio/allegro* and with descriptive interludes as in the *Four Seasons*. **Baldassare Galuppi** (1706-85), a native of Burano near Venice composed the music for the librettos of Goldoni as well as sonatas for harpsichord with a lively tempo. Although Venice was in its final period of glory, her musical reputation grew with the **Marcello** brothers, **Benedetto** (1686-1739) and **Alessandro** (1684-1750). The latter composed a famous concerto for oboe, stringed instruments and organ with a splendid adagio. The instrumental compositions of **Tomaso Albinoni** (1671-1750) are reminiscent of Vivaldi's masterpieces.

In the 18C important Italian composers worked outside Italy. In the field of chamber music, **Luigi Boccherini** (1743-1805), a native of Lucca working in Spain, was famous for his melodies and minuets. He also wrote a powerful symphony, *The House of the Devil*.

Antonio Salieri (1750-1825) from the Veneto was an active composer and a famous teacher who taught Beethoven, Schubert and Liszt. Towards the end of his life, he became mentally disturbed and blamed himself for Mozart's death. This is the theme of the film *Amadeus* by Milos Forman (1984). The Piedmontese **Giovanni Battista Viotti** (1755-1824), Salieri's contemporary, enriched the violin repertory with 29 fine violin concertos. He lived in Paris and London; he died when his wine business failed.

Although not a musician, **Lorenzo Da Ponte** deserves a mention for his poetic contribution to great musical works. His love of adventure took him not only to New York where he died, but also to Vienna, Europe's musical capital at that time. He collaborated with Mozart and wrote librettos for *The Marriage of Figaro, Don Giovanni* and *Così fan tutte* which won him great fame. This great period ended with the Romantic movement which is wonderfully celebrated by the great violinist **Niccolò Paganini** (1782-1840) although by that time the

The Piano

The piano was invented by Bartolomeo Cristofori (1655-1732), who modified the harpischord by replacing the plectra, which "plucked" the strings, with hammers which struck them. The first Italian to introduce this new instrument to the rest of Europe was Muzio Clementi (1752-1832), a rival of Mozart. He wrote a hundred studies for the piano, including Gradus ad Parnassum, and Six Sonatas, which were influenced by the work of both Mozart and Beethoven. The piano's wide range of tones and notes made it the ideal instrument for the Romantics, who composed a number of melancholic and passionate pieces for it. In more recent times some of Bach's compositions were adapted for the piano by Ferruccio Busoni (1866-1924).

piano had become more popular than the violin. His adventurous life, genius of interpretation and legendary virtuosity as well as his slim, tall build turned him into a demonic figure. His most famous works include 24 **Capricci** and six concertos; the finale of the second concerto is the well-known *Campanella*.

OPERA

Modern opera originated with **Claudio Monteverdi** (1567-1643) from Cremona whose masterpiece was *Orfeo*. Monteverdi heralded this musical idiom combining words and music, which was immediately very successful and became a popular pursuit influencing the whole cultural scene in Italy.

At the end of the 17C, Neapolitan opera with **Alessandro Scarlatti** established the distinction between arias which highlight virtuoso singing and recitatives which are essential for the

development of the action. In the 18C, **Giovan Battista Pergolese, Domenico Cimarosa** and **Giovanni Paisiello** were the leading composers of comic opera *(opera buffa)*.

In the 19C there were few great composers of instrumental music apart from Paganini, as lyrical art was made to reflect the intense passions of the Risorgimento. **Gioacchino Rossini** (1782-1868) marked the transition from the classical to the romantic period *(Othello, William Tell* and the comic operas *The Italian Girl in Algiers, The Thieving Magpie* and *The Barber of Seville)*. **Vincenzo Bellini** (1801-35) composed undistinguished orchestral music but admirable melodies and arias *(La Somnambula, Norma)*. His rival **Gaetano Donizetti** (1797-1848) wrote several melodramas *(Lucia di Lammermoor)* where the action takes second place to the singing, as well as some charming comic operas: *L'Elisir d'Amore, Don Pas-*

The Violin

The violin was created as a new and improved model of the viola da braccio. Nowadays its fame is so closely linked to that of the old stringed instrument workshops (second half of the 16C – beginning of the 18C), almost all of which were based in Cremona, that the manufacturer's name (Gasparo da Salò, Amati, Guarneri, Stradivari, etc) is almost synonymous with that of the instrument and is often mentioned on concert programmes. The most important composers for the violin include Arcangelo Corelli (1653-1713), who wrote a number of sonatas for the violin and basso continuo (the bass part over which the solo instrument plays the melody), including the well-known La Follia; Giuseppe Torelli (1658-1709), the composer of many concerti grossi (compositions for an orchestra and a group of soloists); Giuseppe Tartini (1692-1770), who wrote the anguished sonatas The Devil's Trill (the devil appears to have been the inspiration for many musical pieces, especially those composed for the violin) and Dido Abandoned; Pietro Locatelli (1695-1764), who perfected violin techniques in his Capricci and Sonate; Giovanni Battista Viotti, and the incomparable Niccolò Paganini.

© Andrea Tamoni - Teatro alla Scala

La Scala

quale. **Amilcare Ponchielli** (1834-86) is remembered mainly for his successful opera *La Gioconda*.

The greatest composer of the genre during the fight for independence from Austria was **Giuseppe Verdi** (1813-1901) with his dramatic, romantic works: *Nabucco, Rigoletto, Il Trovatore, La Traviata, Aida* etc; he also wrote an admirable *Requiem*. The Realist movement *(Verismo)* then became popular, with Mascagni *(Cavalleria Rusticana)*, Leoncavallo *(I Pagliaci)*, and especially **Giacomo Puccini** (1858-1924) whose *Tosca, Madame Butterfly*, and *La Bohème* crowned the era.

MODERN MUSIC

In reaction, the next generation concentrated on orchestral music; it included **Ottorino Respighi** (1879-1937) who composed symphonic poems *(The Fountains of Rome, The Pines of Rome, Roman festivals)*. 20C composers include Petrassi who explored all musical forms and **Dallapiccola** (1904-75), the leader of the dodecaphonic movement (the 12 notes of the scale are used) in Italy. The passionate **Luigi Nono** (1924-90) used serial music to express his political and liberating message; he wrote instrumental, orchestral and vocal works.

VENUES AND ARTISTS

The only relatively recent unification of the country accounts for the numerous and famous opera houses and concert halls: the prestigious La Scala in Milan, for which Visconti created marvellous sets, the Rome Opera House, the San Carlo theatre in Naples, the Poncielli in Cremona, the Politeama in Palermo, the Fenice in Venice (destroyed by fire in January 1996), the Carlo Fenice in Genoa, and the Regio and the modern Lingotto in Turin. In spring Florence hosts a renowned music festival, and in summer splendid performances are held in the amphitheatre at Verona and in Caracalla's Baths in Rome.

Among the great orchestras and chamber music groups, the Orchestra of the Accademia di Santa Cecilia in Rome, the Filarmonica of La Scala in Milan, the Solisti Veniti and the Orchestra of Padua and the Veneto are noteworthy.

Among the great Italian conductors, Arturo Toscanini was renowned for the verve and originality of his interpretations. Other famous names include Victor De Sabata and nowadays, Claudio Abbado, Carlo Maria Giulini, Riccardo Muti, who perform all over the world. Artists of international reputation include the violinists Accardo and Ughi, the pianists Campanella, Ciccolini,

Giuseppe Sinopoli

When he died in Berlin during a performance of Aida that he was conducting on 20 April 2001, this great Italian conductor was only 54 years old. Sinopoli was a man of many talents. Not only was he an accomplished musician and scholar of Wagner he was passionate about psychiatry and archaeology and achieved professional qualifications in both these fields.

Lucchesini and Maria Tipo, the cellists Brunello and Filippini and the ballet dancers Carla Fracci, Luciana Savignano and Alessandra Ferri.

The famous singers Cecilia Bartoli, Renato Bruson, Fiorenza Cossotto, Cecilia Gasdia, Katia Ricciarelli, Renata Scotto, Lucia Valentini Terrani as well as Ruggiero Raimondi and Luciano Pavarotti are worthy successors to La Malibran, Renata Tebaldi, Maria Callas, Caruso and Beniamino Gigli.

Cinema

THE EARLY YEARS AND NEO-REALISM

The Italian cinema industry was born in Turin at the beginning of the 20C and grew rapidly (50 production companies in 1914) with great successes on the international scene. Film-makers specialised first in historical epics, then in the 1910s they turned to adventure films and in the 1930s to propaganda and escapist films subsidised by the State, which distracted spectators temporarily from the reality of the Fascist State.

In 1935 the Cinecittà studios and the experimental cinematographic centre which numbered Rossellini and De Santis among its pupils were founded in Rome. During the years of Fascist rule the cinema had become divorced from real life, and to bridge the gap film directors advocated a return to realism and close observation of daily life. The first major theme of **neo-Realism** was the war

and its aftermath. **Roberto Rossellini** denounced Nazi and Fascist oppression in Rome Open City and Germany Year Zero. **Vittorio de Sica's** *Sciuscia* (1946) and *Bicycle Thieves* (1948) depicted the unemployment and misery of the post-war years. In *Bitter Rice* (1949) and *Bloody Easter* (1950) **De Santis** portrays the working class divided between the prevailing ideology and revolutionary ambitions.

Neo-Realism ended in the early 1950s as it no longer satisfied the public who wanted to forget this bleak period, but its influence was still felt by future generations of film-makers.

1960S TO THE PRESENT DAY

In the 1960s Italian cinema flourished and a large number of films (over 200 a year), generally of very high quality, was made with the support of a strong industrial infrastructure. Three great directors dominated this period. **Federico Fellini** (1920-93) shot the hugely successful *La Strada (The Street)* in 1954 and *La Dolce Vita* in 1960. His fantasy world is reflected in the original camerawork. **Michelangelo Antonioni** (1912-2007) made his debut in 1959 with *L'Avventura,* and his work (*The Red Desert,* 1960 and *Blow Up*, 1967) underlines the ultimate isolation of the individual. **Luchino Visconti** (1906-76) made *Rocco and his brothers* in 1960 and *The Leopard* in 1963. His films, which are characterised by opulence and beauty, examine closely the themes of impermanence, degradation and death.

During the same period a new generation of film-makers made a political and social statement: **Pier Paolo Pasolini, Ermanno Olmi,** Rosi, Bertolucci and the Taviani brothers.

Italian cinema won great international success with several masterpieces until the mid-1970s: *Death in Venice* (1970) and *Ludwig* (1972) by Visconti; *Casanova* (1976) by Fellini, *The Passenger* (1974) by Antonioni; *L'Affare Mattei* (1971) by **Francesco Rosi** and *The Last Tango in Paris* by **Bernardo Bertolucci**. Since the late 1970s the industry has been in a state of crisis, as it faces competition from television and the collapse of the market. However, some films made by famous directors have won acclaim: *The Night of San Lorenzo* (1982) by the **Taviani brothers**, *The Ball* (1983) by **Ettore Scola**, *The Last Emperor* (1987) by Bertolucci, *Cinema Paradiso* (1989) by **Giuseppe Tornatore**.

An introduction to Italian cinema would be incomplete without the *"Italian comedies"*, which include masterpieces such as *Guardie e ladri* (1951), *I soliti ignoti* (1958), *La grande guerra* (1959), *L'Armata Brancaleone* (1966) and *Amici miei* (1975) by **Mario Monicelli** and *Divorzio all'Italiana* (1962) by **Pietro Germi**.

The younger generation of film-makers embraced realism and their protagonists are engaged in the social struggle. The most interesting films include *Bianca* (1984), *La messa è finita* (1985) and *Caro Diario* (1993) by **Nanni Moretti**, *Il portaborse* (1990) and *La Scuola* (1995) by **Daniele Luchetti**; *Regalo di Natale* (1986) by **Pupi Avati**; *Mery per sempre* (1989), *Ragazzi fuori* (1989) and *Il muro di gomma* (1991) by **Marco Risi** and *Notte italiana* (1987) and *Vesna va veloce* (1996) by **Carlo Mazzacurati**. In 2000, **Silvio Soldini** made a name for himself with a charming film, *Pane e tulipani*, in which the rather eccentric protagonists go about their daily life in Venice (and not a tourist in sight).

A number of talented actor-writers have succeeded in exporting Italian comedies abroad. Examples include *Ricomincio da tre* (1981), *Non ci resta che piangere* (1984), *Le vie del Signore sono finite* and *The Postman* (1994) by **Massimo Troisi**; *Un sacco bello* (1980), *Compagni di scuola* (1988) and *Maledetto il giorno che ti ho incontrato* (1992) by **Carlo Verdone**; *Il ciclone* (1996) by **Leonardo Pieraccioni**, and *Il piccolo diavolo* (1988), *Johnny Stecchino* (1991) and *Il mostro* (1994) by **Roberto Benigni**, who also produced the 1999 Oscar-winning masterpiece *Life is beautiful* (1997).

The success of Italian cinema is above all due to its famous stars, such as Vittorio Gasmann, Gina Lollobrigida, Sophia Loren, Anna Magnani, Giulietta Masina, Marcello Mastroianni, Alberto Sordi, Ugo Tognazzi, Totò and many others.

Federico Fellini and Marcello Mastroianni hold up a poster for their film "La DolceVita", ca. 1960

AWARDS AND OSCARS

Oscar Academy Awards

Life is beautiful by Roberto Benigni – 3 Oscars, including Best Foreign Film 1998

Mediterraneo by Gabriele Salvatores – Best Foreign Film 1992

Cinema Paradiso by Giuseppe Tornatore – Best Foreign Film 1990

The Last Emperor by Bernardo Bertolucci – 9 Oscars, including Best Film and Best Director 1988

Amarcord by Federico Fellini – Best Foreign Film 1975

Il Giardino dei Finzi-Contini by Vittorio De Sica – Best Foreign Film 1972

Indagine di un cittadino al di sopra di ogni sospetto by Elio Petri – Best Foreign Film 1971

Ieri, oggi, domani by Vittorio De Sica – Best Foreign Film 1965

8½ by Federico Fellini – Best Foreign Film 1964

Le notti di Cabiria by Federico Fellini – Best Foreign Film 1958

La Strada by Federico Fellini – Best Foreign Film 1957

Cannes Film Festival

La stanza del figlio by Nanni Moretti, 2001

L'albero degli zoccoli (The Tree of Wooden Clogs) by Ermanno Olmi, 1978

Padre padrone by Paolo and Vittorio Taviani, 1977

Il Caso Mattei by Francesco Rosi and *La classe operaia va in Paradiso* by Elio Petri, 1972
Signore e signori by Pietro Germi, 1966
Il Gattopardo (The Leopard) by Luchino Visconti, 1963
La dolce vita by Federico Fellini, 1960
Due soldi di speranza by Renato Castellani, 1952
Miracolo a Milano by Vittorio De Sica, 1951

Venice Film Festival

Così ridevano by Gianni Amelio, 1998
La leggenda del santo bevitore by Ermanno Olmi, 1988
La Battaglia di Algeri by Gillo Pontecorvo, 1966
Vaghe stelle dell'orsa by Luchino Visconti, 1965
Deserto rosso by Michelangelo Antonioni, 1964
Le mani sulla città by Francesco Rosi, 1963
Il generale Della Rovere by Roberto Rossellini and *La grande guerra* by Mario Monicelli, 1959
Giulietta e Romeo by Renato Castellani, 1954

Berlin Film Festival

La casa del sorriso, Marco Ferreri, 1991
The Canterbury Tales by Pier Paolo Pasolini, 1972
Il Giardino dei Finzi-Contini by Vittorio De Sica, 1971
Il diavolo by Luigi Polidoro, 1963
La notte by Michelangelo Antonioni, 1961

Fashion

The term "costume" dates back to the 16C. Its meaning, "way of dressing", had traditional and lasting connotations. "Fashion" is a 17C term which refers to novelty in dress codes and implied something short-lived.

COSTUME OR FASHION?

"Fashion" is now synonymous with Italy, but its connotations – of status, grandstanding and conspicuous consumption – have their roots in Late Medieval Europe and the early Renaissance.

A trend toward greater extravagance started in the 11C and gathered momentum in the 14C, sweeping away the austerity of past centuries and the idea of "costume", with its traditional and lasting connotations, as a way of dressing.

In Italy this move toward increased consumption flourished due to the importance of fine fabric production and importation to the Northern Italian economy.

Merchants and manufacturers who made huge fortunes in the Florentine and Venetian city republics sought to buy the status they coveted, funding art and architecture and dressing ostentatiously to make statements of wealth and social standing.

By the 16th century, this competition in dress had gained another aspect to it – that of the idea of "fashion".

Ever mindful of their desire to establish a new social hierarchy, rich Italians began to fit fabrics together in complex and highly stylized ways. This gave clothing a recognizable "cut" that could be embraced or discarded, according to whim. Clothing now had a novel, transitory value and an built-in obsolescence, where it could go "out of fashion" long before it wore out.

Thus the imperative to continuously update one's wardrobe was born, and with it new social status based on the ability to finance it. This new order was powerful enough to challenge even the inherited entitlement of nobility, who fought back valiantly with various sumptuary laws until the mid-16th century, but to no real avail – fashion as a force and an expression had arrived in Europe, and was there to stay.

FADS AND TRENDS

Flamboyance and confidence characterized the Italian approach to fashion from the 13C onward. Two new developments that were of great influence were **buttons** and **glasses** (Cardinale Ugo di Provenza is depicted wearing spectacles in a 1352 fresco in Treviso's Capitolo di San Nicolò, a first in the history of art). Hair also became longer and more carefully styled, while cosmetics gained in popularity. For nobles and the rich, personal expression became more important than conformity. This partly accounted for extremes of style, such as heels as high as 60cm/2ft! In Venice, it was said that, "such was the height of the heels they wore, the Venetian ladies passing through Piazza San Marco looked like dwarfs dressed up as giants". From the early Renaissance on, hats became a key part of the Italian man's wardrobe. The beret originated in Renaissance Italy as a piece of cloth on a embroidered band, with a string inside to adjust the fit to any head. Women also began to wear earrings again, something that had previously been denounced as unbecoming, as it was a Moorish influence. In the 18C black veils, masks, fans and three-cornered hats were the height of fashion in Venice. By the 19C jackets and coats were worn long and straight with a high waistline, and clothing was under the spell of romanticism. Huge puffed sleeves were in vogue for women, as were corsets designed to make the waist as small as possible (creating the *vitino di vespa* or wasp waist). Next followed the popular crinoline, worn over ornately decorated undergarments.

COLOUR, AN ESSENTIAL ELEMENT

The trend for **color** was particularly evident during the Renaissance, but tastes changed from century to century. Until the 13C, fashion favoured the dark blue of the Byzantine mosaics at San Vitale (Ravenna), giving way to a vogue for two-tone clothes. Pink was all the rage in the Quattrocento; in the 16C the fashion for gold, silver and black gave clothes a more solemn air (as exemplified in portraits by Titian). Pale colors were popular in the late 16c and 17C. So too was 'slashing' on sleeves, doublets and hose to expose bright linings. This circumvented laws that commoners only wear clothes of one color.

The 18C progressed to a preference for white and pastel shades, while the last word in 19C fashion was black and white – a monochromatic look that continued to be popular into the early 20C.

TODAY, AS IN THE PAST

Italy continues to influence global fashion, most notably from the haute couture fashion capital of Milan. Its twice-yearly Fashion Weeks, showing the new collections, rank beside those of Paris and New York for industry importance.

Away from the catwalks, looking good in Italy is a democratic art. Italians take immense pride in their appearance. Many seem to have inherently good taste: opting for classic, well-made clothes, rather than experimental, disposable fashion. Italy is not the place to find new street trends, rather to cut "*la bella figura*" and embrace a consistent elegance through all walks of life. The style imperative applies as much to those who can afford to shop in Via Monte Napoleone (Milan) or Via dei Condotti (Rome) as the locals who go to the market. And there is no off-duty; for Italians, dressing casually is no excuse for shabby, slovenly attire.

The big names

Italy is home to some of fashion's biggest names, and the "Italian look" is a phrase that now means many things. Styles may be diverse, but the emphasis remains on good cuts and fine fabrics. The contemporary trend of many labels to promote both a look and a 'lifestyle' means designer products and lines extend from clothes, to perfumes, jewelry and furnishings. The most iconic fashion houses include:

Giorgio Armani, whose signature style is understated elegance, and who believes that clothes are made to be worn, not just seen. For quintessential Italian chic, an Armani suit lasts many seasons, and his diffusion line, Emporio Armani, is good for quality separates and accessories (www.giorgioarmani.com).

The Benetton label is recognized all over the world, in part thanks to its often controversial publicity campaigns shot by Oliviero Toscani. The label excels at competitively priced knitwear and basics like T-shirts and accessories (www.benetton.com).

Laura Biagiotti is known for clean lines and elegant separates. She has made a particular name in cashmere (www.laurabiagiotti.it).

King of 1960s haute couture, directional designer **Pierre Cardin** was born in Italy to French parents. He introduced geometric designs and experimented with the unisex style (www.pierrecardin.com).

The **Enrico Coveri** brand is about bold patterns and a typically Italian luxe look. Fabrics are sensual; attitude is glitzy (www.coveri.com).

The designs of **Dolce and Gabbana** celebrate the female form. Renowned for their show-stopping eveningwear, the duo fashions daywear that is equally confident, with an emphasis on corseting, figure-sculpting pencil skirts and décolletage. The diffusion line, D&G, is good for well-cut jeans (www.dolcgabbana.it).

Luxury brand **Fendi** is best known for its leatherwork; for style kudos, look for bags, wallets and shoes with the classic Fendi logo (www.fendi.com).

Gianfranco Ferré focuses on "quality, comfort, individuality and simplicity." Trademark pieces include crisply-cut white shirts, stylish eyewear and women's trouser suits (www.gianfrancoferre.com).

Gucci has reigned for some as the must-have label for the fashion faithful. Its look is sexy, streetwise and expensive. A Gucci bag is a key investment: still considered shorthand for style in A-list circles (www.gucci.com).

The family-owned label **Missoni** is best known for sumptuous knitwear in colorful stripes. Its distinctive swimwear is popular with chic sunbathers on Mediterranean beaches. (www.missoni.com)

The **Moschino** style has remained true to the ethos of the late designer. The Cheap and Chic line is always full of surprising designs, with bright colors and quirky detailing (www.moschino.it).

Miuccia Prada designs grown-up, stylish clothes fashioned from fine materials, which frequently dictate the next fashion trends. Her understated bags and shoes are global best sellers (www.prada.com).

Trussardi favors simple lines and a focus on high quality tailoring and finishing (www.trussardi.com).

The designer **Valentino** recognized that women should cultivate their own style to enhance their self-confidence. His label's designs lean toward elegant and classical, many incorporating the famous "V" logo (www.valentino.com).

After her brother Gianni's death in 1997, Donatella **Versace** has taken the family business to new heights. The Versace label is adored by rock and film stars, with a signature style that is glamorous and glitzy, with colorful prints, sequins, attitude and plenty of suntanned skin on show (www.versace.com).

THE COUNTRY TODAY

Land of saints, poets, heroes and navigators, Italy's traditions are rooted in an ancient faith. Scars attest to a long struggle for freedom, but the people remain appreciative of life's finer things: art, architecture, cuisine, wine, fashion, design, opera and sultry siestas. Italophile, Stendhal noted the Italian predeliction for the "art of being happy", something that continues to infuse the modern Italian psyche, despite tumultuous politics and economic uncertainty.

Economy and Government

Italian politics has long had a reputation for its passionate and precarious nature. Elections in April 2006 produced a victory for a centre-left coalition under the leadership of Romano Prodi, former EU commission president and Italian Prime Minister in 1998. Having won the closest election in postwar Italian history, Prodi stayed in power just nine months before resigning following a surprise parliamentary defeat over his coalition government's role in Nato and its alliance with the US. His resignation threw the Italian parliament into crisis, with many fearing a return to "revolving door" politics, but following talks with President Giorgio Napolitano, Prodi agreed to remain in office and face a vote of confidence in parliament – winning by two votes and ending seven days of political uncertainty.

On the international stage, Prodi's predecessor, Silvio Berlusconi, participated in the US-led military coalition in Iraq, amid much public controversy, a decision that Prodi reversed when he withdrew Italian forces in 2006. At home, Prodi's domestic focus has been one of economic liberalization and public debt reduction, in direct response to the country's sluggish economic growth. Italy's economy has been facing increasing difficulties, with rising inflation and the impact of fierce international competition on the medium-sized family-owned companies that make up the bulk of its manufacturing industries. Protests against public spending cuts and pension reforms have also been vehement. However, green shoots may finally be appearing with an acceleration in GDP growth after a period of stagnancy, estimated at two per cent in 2006, the highest since 2000.

FILM, FASHION AND A FABULOUS LIFE

Italy has long enchanted and inspired the world's imagination. As travel writing's grande dame Jan Morris once observed: "For a thousand years and more, it has been one of the most interesting corners of the earth – not always admirable, but never boring."

Indeed, even the peninsula's missteps such as Caligula's cruelties, Christian persecution and the Medici poisonings) are the stuff of legend. But Italy is most famous for its sumptuous lifestyle, and rightly so.

One film personifies the country's modern character best: Federico Fellini's *La Dolce Vita*. This 1960 feature captured the glitterati's nightlife in its heyday. As Anita Ekberg frolicked in the Fontana di Trevi, an icon of excess was born. The title – translating as "the sweet life" – passed into everyday English, as did *"paparazzo."*

Of course, most Italians do not live silver-screen-style, but most try to infuse a little glamour, a little Good Life, into ordinary existence. Extra virgin olive oil, fresh-baked breads and fine wines are staples. Shoppers select farm-fresh produce among the overflowing stalls in outdoor markets. Pastry shops wrap cakes in lavish paper and ribbons. The sight, the smell, the texture and presentation of food is vital.

The same care translates to fashion. Cashmere, silk and leather hold sway here. Brand names are coveted (and copied frequently by knock-off artists). Through make-up and grooming, the average Italian strives for high style daily. Such *bella figura* – good showing – is only gracious, they believe.

Ascoli Piceno: Piazza del Popolo

G. Bludzin/ MICHELIN

Who wants to look at an unkempt person?

People promenade in the evenings, seeing and being seen. Long, languid lunch breaks are common – or even siestas. And the whole country heads to the seashore or mountains for six weeks each summer. Italians, as the cliché stresses, work to live, rather than living to work.

The formula is not without problems. Exuberant drivers make Italy's road infamous for illegal maneuvers and frequent accidents. Passion collides with the Catholic Church's ban on birth control. Governments rise and fall with bewildering regularity. Protests frequently freeze a nation already burdened by Byzantine bureaucracy.

Yet western civilization still eagerly takes cues from this small country. Perhaps, as Morris notes, "the world recognizes in Italy an essential idea of beauty: beauty of landscape, beauty of learning, beauty of art, beauty of human romance and affectition.

ITALY, THE BEL PAESE

Bel Paese is an affectionate term for Italy, drawn from a book by the Abbot Antonio Stoppani (1824-91) and borrowed by the Galbani dairy in 1906.

Cheese jokes aside, everybody agrees on how beautiful (*bel*) and surprisingly varied the country (*paese*) is. Jutting into the sea, the coastline offers sandy coves and pinewoods, and inlets lapped by emerald water. Inland misty, haunting plains rise to form a wild and rugged terrain where even the snow struggles to settle. Frenetic cities contrast sharply with sleepy hilltop villages, where little has changed since the Middle Ages.

Against this backdrop are mapped the different lives, characters and dialects of this land's inhabitants. For example, Sicilians tease the Milanese about their obsessive punctuality and efficiency. A Neapolitan might marvel over the rhythm, tone and humor in the lyrical chatter of the Venetians. And the Romans pity anyone unable to live in the Eternal City, the *caput mundi* – head of the world.

PIZZA AND MANDOLINS

Compliments can easily blur into caricatures – and Italy suffers its share of misconceptions. "Pizza, spaghetti and mandolins" is the tourist's knee-jerk perception, jokes Paolo Villaggio in the *Fantozzi* film series.

Many Italian traditions – from wheezy accordions to checkered tablecloths and Catholic schoolgirls – are the butt of jokes abroad. A classic example is Dean Martin's song *That's Amore*, which distorts Italian phrases into clumsy immigrant English.

The macho Latin lover stereotype is best interpreted in *Un Americano a Roma* by **Alberto Sordi**. He apes the xenophile Italian who denounces his origins, but cannot tear himself away from his plate of spaghetti.

Yet many long-despised traits have found new vogue: the country's garlic-laden, healthy cuisine, the sensual fashion, family values, opportunistic economics and sense of melodrama. Pop culture once again celebrates the *Bel Paese* from Patricia Highsmith's 1992 *The Talented Mr. Ripley* to Frances Mayes' 1997 *Under the Tuscan Sun* and Laura Fraser's 2002 *An Italian Affair*.

They join a long tradition of writers who venerate la dolce vita, including the literary legend Goethe and his *Italian Journey*, as well as the more lighthearted Mark Twain with his book *The Innocents Abroad*.

Never an easy study, Italy often eludes definition. But that's the charm that leads artists and tourists back to her beauty again and again.

Food and Drink

Italian kitchens have produced some of the world's best-known dishes. Yet the cuisine has no national flavour. Rather, it is a lavish buffet of regional recipes, precisely defined and fiercely defended by each province. The overall theme is Mediterranean to the south, while the north reflects hearty Alpine menus. Naples boasts of its pizza and Umbria of its truffles, while the capital is disparaged for simple "peasant" fare. The cooking styles are so distinct that gourmand travelers plot whole trips around elusive delicacies.

REGIONAL SPECIALITIES: FROM NORTH TO SOUTH

Piedmont

Cooking here is done with butter. A popular dish is **fonduta**, a melted cheese dip of milk, eggs and white truffles (*tartufi bianchi*). Typical of the region are *cardi* (chards), prepared *alla bagna cauda*, ie with a hot sauce containing oil, anchovies, garlic and truffles. Other dishes include **agnolotti** (a kind of ravioli), braised beef in red Barolo wine, boiled meat, **fritto misto alla Piemontese** and **bonet** dessert (a type of chocolate pudding). Monferrato and the Langhe hills are also famous for their excellent cheeses, such as **robiola, castelmagno** and **bra**, and delicious wines: **Barolo** (used for braising), Barbaresco, **Barbera**, Grignolino, red Freisa wines, white Gavi and dessert wines such as **Asti**, still or sparkling (*spumante*) and Moscato.

Lombardy

Milan, where cooking is done with butter, gives its name to several dishes; *minestrone alla milanese*, a soup of green vegetables, rice and bacon; *risotto alla milanese*, rice cooked with saffron; **costoletta** *alla milanese*, a fillet of veal fried in egg and breadcrumbs with cheese; **osso buco**, a knuckle of veal with the marrow-bone. **Polenta**, maize semolina, is a staple food in traditional country cooking. Also worth trying are the **tortelli di zucca** (pumpkin fritters) from Mantua. The most popular cheeses are the creamy **Gorgonzola**, the hard **Grana Padana** and **Taleggio**. **Panettone** is a large fruit cake containing raisins and candied lemon peel and **torrone** (nougat) is a speciality of Cremona. Wines produced include Franciacorta (red, white and sparkling) and the red wines of the Valtellina and Pavia districts. The Valtellina is also renowned for its **pizzoccheri** (a type of large tagliatelle made from buckwheat) and its **bitto** cheese.

Bottles of Chianti

B. Juge/MICHELIN

Veneto

As in the Po Delta, the people of the Veneto eat **polenta**, **bigoli** (a type of spaghetti), **risi e bisi** (rice and peas), **risotto** with chicory and **fegato alla veneziana** (calf's liver fried with onions). The excellent fish dishes include shellfish, eels, dried cod (*baccalà*) and **sardelle in saor** (sardines in brine). Black spaghetti made with squid ink is a popular Venetian dish. The most örenowned cheese of the region is **asiago**. **Pandoro**, a star-shaped cake delicately flavoured with orange-flower, is a speciality of Verona. The best wines come from the district of Verona: **Valpolicella** and **Bardolino**, rosé or red, perfumed and slightly sparkling, and **Soave**, which is white and strong.

Trentino-Alto Adige and Friuli-Venezia Giulia

In the Alto Adige, **canederli** is a type of gnocchi (dumplings) made with bread and flour served separately or in a broth. Other specialities include **gröstl** (potato and meat pie) and smoked pork served with sauerkraut. There are delicious pastries, in particular the **Strüdel** cake. Friuli is famous for **cialzons** (a type of ravioli), **jota** (meat soup), pork-butchers' specialities (ham – **prosciutto di San Daniele**), fish dishes (**scampi**, **grancevole** – spider crabs), **frico** (fried cheese) and montasio cheese. Trentino-Alto Adige is an important wine-producing region: white wines include Chardonnay,

Pinot Bianco, Müller-Thurgau and Riesling, while Pinot and Cabernet are two of the best-known red wines. Friuli produces white Sauvignon, Pinot and Tocai and red Cabernet and Merlot wines.

Liguria

Genoa's chief speciality is **pesto**, a sauce made with olive oil, basil, pine-kernels, garlic and ewes' cheese. It is served with **trenette** (long, thin noodles) and lasagne (flat pasta leaves). Other dishes include **cima** (stuffed meat parcels) and the excellent **pansotti** (a type of ravioli) served with a walnut sauce. The delicious seafood includes buridda (fish soup), **cappon magro** (fish and vegetable salad) and **zuppa di datteri**, a shellfish soup from **La Spezia**, with which the Ligurians drink Vermentino or Pigato, strong white wines. Sciacchetrà is an excellent dessert wine from the region.

Emilia-Romagna

The region has a gastronomic reputation; its pork-butchers' meat is the most famous in Italy: Bologna **salami** and **mortadella**, Modena **zamponi** (pigs' trotters), Parma **prosciutto** (ham). *Pasta* is varied and tasty when served *alla bolognese* – that is, with a meat and tomato sauce. **Parmesan cheese** (*parmigiano*), hard and pale yellow, is strong yet delicate. Emilia produces **Lambrusco**, a fruity, red, sparkling wine, and white Albano.

Tuscany

This is where Italian cooking was born, at the court of the Medici. The most typical first courses of the region are minestrones and soups, including the famous **ribollita**, and **pappardelle**, a type of lasagna. Florence also offers its *alla fiorentina* specialities: dried cod (**baccalà**) with oil, garlic and pepper, **bistecca**, grilled steak fillets with oil, salt and pepper, **fagioli all'uccelletto** (beans with quails), or fagioli "al fiasco" with oil, onions and herbs cooked in a round bottle (*fiasco*) on a coal fire. Livorno produces **triglie** (red mullet) and **cacciucco** (fish soup) and Siena offers **panforte**, a cake containing almonds, honey and candied melon, orange and

lemon. Tuscan cheeses include **pecorino** and **caciotta**. **Chianti** (both red and white) is the most popular wine but there are other notable red (**Brunello di Montalcino, Nobile di Montepulciano**) and white (**Vernaccia di San Gimignano, Vin Santo**) wines.

Umbria and Marches

Norcia is the capital of Umbrian cuisine with the black truffles (**tartufo nero**) and pork dishes. The regional dish is the **porchetta**, a whole suckling pig roasted on the spit. Specialities from the Marches include *vincigrassi* (pasta cooked in the oven with a meat and cream sauce), **stringozzi** (a type of hollow spaghetti), stuffed olives, **brodetto** (a fish soup), and **stocco all'anconetana** (dried cod). The region is renowned for both white wine (**Orvieto** and Verdicchio) and red (Rosso Conero and Rosso Piceno).

Lazio

Rome produces many specialities, though sometimes accused of "crude cooking": **fettuccine** or flat strips of pasta, **spaghetti all'amatriciana** (with a spicy sauce) or **alla carbonara** (with a creamy sauce), **gnocchi** *alla Romana*, **saltimbocca** (a fillet of veal rolled in ham and flavoured with sage, fried in butter and served with a Marsala sauce), and **abbacchio al forno** (roast lamb) or lamb *alla cacciatora* (with an anchovy sauce). Vegetables include *carciofi alla Giudia*, artichokes cooked in oil with garlic and parsley, which take their name from their origins in the Jewish quarter of Rome. **Pecorino** (ewes' milk cheese), **caciotta**, **ricotta** and the famous white wines of Montefiascone and the **Castelli** (Frascati) will satisfy any gourmet.

Abruzzi and Molise

Among the pasta note **maccheroni alla chitarra**, made by hand and cut into strips. **Latticini** (fresh mountain cheeses) are popular.

Campania

Naples is the home of **spaghetti**, which is often prepared with shellfish (*alle vongole*). *Trattorie* and *pizzerie* serve *costata alla pizzaiola*, a fillet steak with tomatoes, garlic and wild marjoram, **mozza-**

rella in *carrozza* (cheese savoury) and especially **pizza** and **calzone** (a folded pizza), topped with cheese (*mozzarella*), tomato and anchovy and flavoured with capers and wild marjoram. The local **mozzarella di bufala** (buffalo mozzarella cheese) is especially delicious. Other specialities include cakes and pastries, often made with ricotta cheese and candied fruit. Wines from volcanic soil have a delicate, slightly sulphurous taste: red and white Capri, white Ischia, **Lacryma Christi,** Fiano di Avellino and Greco di Tufo and red Gragnano and Taurasi.

Puglia, Basilicata and Calabria

Orecchiette con cime di rapa (pasta with turnip tops), rice with mussels (*cozze*), stuffed cuttlefish (*seppia*), the delicious oysters (*ostriche*) of Taranto and **capretto ripieno al forno** (roast kid stuffed with herbs) are among the typical dishes of the Apulia region. Wines include the white Locorotondo and San Severo and the rosé Castel del Monte. The specialities of Basilicata include **pasta alla potentina** and a range of lamb and mutton dishes, as well as a good selection of cheeses (*caciocavallo, scamorza* and ricotta), while Calabria is famous for its stuffed macaroni, pork and roast kid cooked on a spit. Red Cirò is the most popular local wine.

Sicily

Specialities include **pasta con le sarde** (with sardines) and **alla Norma** (with aubergines, tomatoes and ricotta cheese), swordfish dishes and, in the Trapani region, **cuscusu** (couscous), a dish inherited from the Arabs and served with a type of fish soup. The island is rich in fruit (lemons, oranges, mandarins, olives, almonds), pastries and ices. The real Sicilian **cassata** is a partly-frozen cream cake containing chocolate cream and candied fruits. Other traditional sweets and pastries include **cannoli** (filled with ricotta and candied

fruit), almond cakes and marzipan. The best-known wine is **Marsala**, which is dark and strong, but **Malvasia** and the white wines of Etna and Lipari are also delicious.

Sardinia

The island of Sardinia is famous for **malloreddus** (pasta shells with sausage and tomato), delicious lobster soup and pork cooked on a spit. Meals are accompanied by **carasau**, the local sheet-thin bread (known as *carta da musica* in the rest of Italy). The many cheeses include goats' cheese, Sardinian **fiore** and Sardinian **pecorino**. **Sebadas** are round doughnuts which are fried and covered with honey. The best-known local wines are the red **Cannonau** and the white Vermentino.

VEGETARIAN OPTIONS

Vegetarians (*vegetariani*) still draw confused looks. Be very clear: *Non mangio la carne* (I don't eat meat). *Antipasti misti* (mixed starters) often include marinated or fried mushrooms (*funghi*), sweet peppers (*peperone*), zucchini/courgette (*zucchine*), eggplant/aubergine (*melanzane*). *Insalata mista* (mixed salad) is another good bet: this dish may feature *rughetta* (arugula/rocket), chicory-like *radicchio* and sometimes corn.
Meat-free standbys include *insalata caprese* (slabs of tomato, bufala mozzarella and basil) and *fagioli all'uccelletto* (white beans) and *bruchetta* (pronounced "bru-SKET-ah"; tomato-topped toast).
Pastas showcase *pomodoro fresco* (fresh tomatoes) or pesto (a sauce of pine nuts, pecorino cheese and basil). Also look for *spaghetti cacio e pepe* (sheep cheese and pepper), *penne al arrabbiata* (fiery garlic-tomato sauce with pasta quills), *ravioli ricotta e spinaci* (ricotta and spinach ravioli, often served with butter and sage) and *orecchiette* (ear-shaped pasta, usually with broccoli).

Ponte di Rialto, Venice
© Philip Coblentz/Brand X Pictures

ABRUZZO

MICHELIN MAP 563 N-R 21-26

The splendours of the Abruzzi region lie in the grandeur and diversity of the wild and rugged terrain it occupies: stark karst formations give way to lush woodland, and barren plateaux to fertile pastures. Enclosed by three national parks – the long-established Parco Nazionale d'Abruzzo, the Parco Nazionale del Gran Sasso and Parco Nazionale della Maiella – the region also offers plenty of variety for both summer holidays and winter sports. Other attractions include a number of well-known seaside resorts including Alba Adriatica, Giulianova Lido, Roseto degli Abruzzi, Silvi Marina and Vasto.

- **Information:** Via N. Fabrizi 171, 65122 Pescara, ☎085 42 90 01. Freephone (in Italy): 800 502 520; www.regione.abruzzo.it/turismo.
- ▶ **Orient Yourself:** The Abruzzi is easily accessible from Rome, taking A 24, and the Adriatic coast, taking A 25. The main access routes are Bisegna, Barrea and Forca d'Acero.
- **Parking:** Parco Nazionale d'Abruzzo has parking areas at valley entrances.
- **Don't Miss:** The Parco Nazionale d'Abruzzo and Grand Sasso, the Warrior of Capestrano at Chieti.
- **Organizing Your Time:** Allow at least four days for the region.
- **Also See:** ASCOLI PICENO (MARCHE), MOLISE

A Bit of History

Various Italic populations dominated the region until the 3C BC when Rome took over the territory. After the fall of the Roman Empire the region became a Lombard, then a Frankish territory. In the 12C it became part of the Kingdom of Naples, until the Unification of Italy. In the Middle Ages the diffusion of Benedictine rule from the neighbouring abbey at Monte Cassino (see *ABBAZIA DI MONTECASSINO*) led to the construction of cathedrals, abbeys and churches whose beautifully ornate *ciboria* and pulpits constitute the definitive glory of Abruzzi art. In the 15C-16C the finest examples of Renaissance art were to be found in the work of the painter and architect **Cola dell'Amatrice**, the painter **Andrea de Litio**, the sculptor **Silvestro dell'Aquila** and the goldsmith **Nicola da Guardiagrele**.

Notable figures of the Abruzzi region include Publius Ovidius Naso (43 BC-AD 17), poets Ovid and Gabriele D'Annunzio (1863-1938), philosopher and statesman Benedetto Croce (1866-1952) and novelist Ignazio Silone (1900-78).

Parco Nazionale d'Abruzzo★★★

Visitors are advised to call the park for opening times. By car the main access routes are Bisegna in the north, Barrea to the east and Forca d'Acero in the west. The park is best seen on foot, and there are car parking areas at the bottom of the valley. For information on park activities contact Centro Operativo Accoglienza Turisti (CAOT) or local offices at Villetta Barrea, Civitella Alfedena, Villavallelonga and Alvito. The main office is temporarily situated in Pescasseroli, Viale S. Lucia, ☎0863 91 131; www.parcoabruzzo.it.

A nature reserve was founded in 1923 in the heart of the massif to protect the region's fauna, flora and outstanding landscapes. The park extends over 40 000ha/100 000 acres, not including the 4 500ha/11 119 acres of the Mainarde territory (in the Molise region), and is surrounded by an external protected area of 60 000ha/150 000 acres. Two-thirds of the park is made up of forests (mainly beech, maple, oak and black pine) and it offers the last refuge for animals that

Address Book

For coin ranges see the Legend on the cover flap.

WHERE TO STAY

Hotel Il Vecchio Pescatore – *Via Benedetto Virgilio – 67030 Villetta Barrea – 15.5km/10mi east of Pescasseroli on S 83 – ☎0864 89 274 – Fax 0864 89 255 – www.ilvecchiopescatore.net – 12 rm – Restaurant 15/23 €.*
A simple but comfortable hotel situated in the heart of the Parco Nazionale d'Abruzzo. Warm welcome. Rooms are small but light and airy. Pale-coloured modern furnishings. A stone's throw from the restaurant of the same name which is run by the same people.

Albergo Archi del Sole – *Largo Porta di Berardo 9 – 67033 Pescocostanzo – ☎0864 64 00 07 – Fax 0864 64 00 07 – www.archidelsole.it – Closed Mon (winter), 15-30 June– 10 rm.* A charming hotel in this village frozen in time. All the rooms are named after a flower, with colour-coordinated decor and furnishings. Parquet floors and beamed ceilings add to the atmosphere.

Hotel Villino Mon Repos – *Via le Colli dell'Oro – 67032 Pescasseroli – ☎0863 91 28 58 – Fax 0863 91 28 30 – 13 rm – .* A fine early-20C villa which used to be the summer residence of Benedetto Croce. Set in splendid parkland with some magnificent old trees. Comfortable rooms, tastefully furnished, with

much attention to detail. A touch of class.

WHERE TO EAT

Al Focolare di Bacco - *Via Solagna 18 – 64026 Roseto degli Abruzzi – 31km/19mi northeast of Pescara on S 16 – ☎085 89 41 004 – Closed Tue, Wed, at lunchtime (except public holidays).*
A popular spot, tucked away in the peace and tranquillity of the Abruzzi hills. Well-known for its cooking *alla brace* (flame grilled). A curious mix of rustic and elegant – with panoramic sea views and earthy aromas wafting from the kitchen. Attractive rooms. A unique base for a seaside vacation.

Peppe di Sora – *Via Benedetto Croce 1 – 67032 Pescasseroli – ☎0863 910 023 – – Closed Mon (winter).* Riverside setting.
A classic trattoria serving hearty local fare. Warmed by a roaring fire during the winter months. Also has rooms to let, simple but clean.

Don Ambrosio – *Contrada Piomba 49 – 64029 Silvi Marina – 14km/8.5mi northeast of Pescara on S 16 – ☎085 93 51 060 – www.donambrosio.it – Closed Tue, 20 days in Nov.* A short trip into the hinterland brings you to this old farmhouse. Inside, the walls of exposed stonework bear witness to its agricultural heritage. Regional dishes and specialities, generous servings. Al fresco dining in summer.

once lived all over the Apennine range: brown bears, Apennine wolves, Abruzzi chamois, wild cats, otters, martens and royal eagles. **Pescasseroli** is the principal town in the Sangro valley and the park headquarters.

Tours

1 Gran Sasso★★

From L'Aquila to Castelli
160km/99mi – allow 1/2 day, excluding tour of L'Aquila and surrounding area.

This is the highest massif in the Abruzzi and its main peak is **Corno Grande** (alt 2 912m/9 560ft). On the northern side, spines with many gullies slope away gently, while on the southern face Gran Sasso drops to the great glacial plateaux edged by deep valleys.

L'Aquila★ *See L'AQUILA*

Campo Imperatore★★
Access by cable car, 8.30am-sunset. Sat and public holidays €10 return ticket (roundtrip). ☎0862 60 61

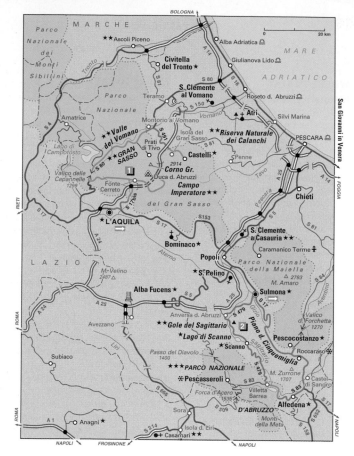

43 (winter) or 0862 40 00 07. 🚗 Access also by car from Fonte Cerreto taking S 17 (⚠ closed Dec-Apr).

The road passes through mountainous landscape grazed by sheep and wild horses. It was from here that Mussolini escaped in 1943, in a daring raid by German airmen whose plane landed and took off near the Duce's hotel.

▶ Return to Fonte Cerreto, follow directions for the Valico delle Capannelle road (⚠ closed Dec-Apr); then take the S 80 for Montorio al Vomano.

The road then skirts the lower slopes of the Gran Sasso, as it follows the long green valley, **Valle del Vomano★★**, before entering the magnificent gorges with their striking stratified rock walls.

▶ On leaving Montorio, take the S 491 to the right, the road to Isola del Gran Sasso. At Isola del Gran Sasso follow directions for Castelli.

Castelli★

This town at the foot of Monte Camicia, has been famous since the 13C for its ceramics of which the 17C **ceiling★** in the **Church of San Donato** is a fine example. Just outside the town, the ex-Franciscan convent (17C) houses the **Museo delle Ceramiche**, which relates the history of Castelli ceramic production from the 15C to the 19C through the display of works of its leading exponents.(♿) ⏱Open May-Aug daily, 10am-1pm and 3-7.30pm, rest of the year 10am-1pm; Sat, Sun and festivals 10am-1pm and 3-6pm. Closed Mon (winter). ⚠3 €. ☎0861 97 93 98.

2 Great Plateaux

Round trip leaving from Sulmona.
140km/87mi – allow at least 1 day excluding tour of Sulmona.

Sulmona★ *⚫ See SULMONA*

Piano delle Cinquemiglia

Beyond, the road sometimes runs along a corniche that affords good views of the Sulmona valley, and eventually reaches the **Piano delle Cinquemiglia**, largest of the Great Plateaux situated between Sulmona and Castel di Sangro. With an average altitude of more than 1 200m/ 3 900ft, the plateau, 5 Roman miles long (8km/5mi), was once the obligatory route for stage-coaches journeying to Naples and was much feared for its harsh winter climate and highway robbers.

▶ *Near the village of Rivisondoli, take S 84 to the left.*

Pescocostanzo★

This attractive village is a flourishing craft centre specialising in wrought-iron work, gold, woodwork and lace.
The **Collegiate Church of Santa Maria del Coll**, although built to a Renaissance plan, has Romanesque features and Baroque additions (organ loft and grille of the north aisle). *⚫Open 7am-midday and 5-6pm. ⊗Donations welcome. ⬛For information, contact Padre Giovanni ☎347 06 34 669 (mobile).*

Alfedena★

The houses of this small town are grouped about the ruined castle. Paths lead to the ancient city of Alfedena with its cyclopean walls and burial grounds.

Scanno★

From its high mountain site, Scanno overlooks the lovely Lake Scanno (**Lago di Scannoa★**). The steep, narrow streets of this resort are lined with old houses and churches. Continuing towards Anversa degli Abruzzi, the road hollowed out of the rock, skirts deep gorges (**Gole del Sagittario★★**) and affords 10km/6mi of spectacular nature.

Visit

Alba Fucens
50km/30mi south of L'Aquila.
These are the **excavations** of a Roman colony founded in 303 BC. Amid the foundations (of Italic origin) are the remains of a basilica, the forum, baths, the covered market complete with paved streets, wells, latrines and an **amphitheatre**. Above the ruins rises the **church of San Pietro★**, erected in the 12C on the remains of a temple of Apollo of the 3C BC. The **interior** houses two notable examples of **Cosmati** work, unusual in Romanesque Abruzzi buildings: the **ambo★★** and the stunning **iconostasis★★** of the 13C. ⬛ *To visit the excavations and the church, contact the Cooperative Alba Fucens prior to your visit: ☎0863 44 96 42 or 338 87 89 548 (mobile); www.albafucens.info.*

Atri
40km/24mi northwest of Chieti.
The ancient settlement of *Hatria-Picena*, founded by an Italic people and later becoming a Roman colony, has a beautiful hillside setting and overlooks the Adriatic sea. The historic centre of the city has splendid medieval, Renaissance and Baroque buildings as well as scenic vistas.

Cathedral★
⚫Open Jun-Sep 10am-noon and 4-8pm, the rest of the year 10am-noon and 3-5pm. ⚫Closed Wed (winter).⊗3 €. ☎085 87 98 140.
Built in the 13C-14C on the foundations of a Roman edifice, the cathedral is a good example of the transitional Romanesque-Gothic style, with a series of sculpted **doorways★** that became a model on which later work in the Abruzzi region was based. The **interior** has tall Gothic arches and, in the apse, **frescoes★★** by the Abruzzi artist, **Andrea de Litio** (1450-73). These depict scenes from the life of Joachim and Mary and fuse Gothic formal opulence with the solid geometry and realism of the Tuscans.
The adjoining cloisters lead to the Roman cistern and the **Chapter Museum** with its collection of Abruzzi ceramics.

In Piazza Duomo traces of the ancient Roman city are still visible.

Bominaco

30km/18mi southeast of L'Aquila. Churches: For information on opening times, call ☎ 0862 93 764 or 0862 93 765; www.webabruzzo.it/bominaco Donations welcome.

Two Romanesque churches stand about 500m/1 640ft above the hamlet of Bominaco, and are all that remain of a Benedictine monastery which was destroyed in the 15C. The church of **San Pellegrino**★ is a 13C oratory decorated with contemporary **frescoes**★ portraying the Life of Christ and St Pellegrino. Two elegant 10C plutei demarcate the chancel whose central wall is decorated with the delightful **Calendario Bominacense**, depicting courtly scenes which are influenced by the French tradition. The **Church of Santa Maria Assunta**★ (11C and 12C), with its beautifully ornamented apses, is one of the most significant examples of Romanesque architecture in Abruzzi. The interior, with its Benedictine imprint, has a graceful Romanesque colonnade that makes skilful use of light and volume. Note the striking 12C **ambo**★.

Chieti

Chieti is built on the summit of a hill planted with olive trees and enclosed by imposing mountains. Due to its panoramic position it is known as "Abruzzi's balcony." **Corso Marrucino**, bordered by elegant arcades, is the town's principal street.

Museo Archeologico Nazionale d'Abruzzo★★

(♿) Open 9am-8pm (last admission 7pm). 8 €. ☎0871 33 16 68.
The archaeological museum is housed in the neo-Classical town hall (**Villa Comunale**) set in lovely **gardens**★, and possesses the most important collection of artefacts excavated in the Abruzzi region. The ground floor has displays from Roman Abruzzi. Statues and portraits (note the **Seated Hercules** discovered at Alba Fucens) relate local history and customs. An interesting coin display, the collection formed by the

Sulmonese **Giovanni Pansa** (ex-votos, domestic objects and bronze figures such as the **Venafro Hercules**) and the stunning bone **bier**★ (1C BC-1C AD) complete the section. The first floor is dedicated to funerary cults of pre-Roman Abruzzi (10C-6C BC). The famous **Warrior of Capestrano**★★ (6C BC) has come to symbolise the Abruzzi region and is the most significant artefact of Picenum civilisation. Both disturbing and magical, it was used to protect royal tombs as can be seen in the inscription on the right pilaster: "Me, beautiful image, made by Aninis for King Nevio Pompuledonio."

Civitella del Tronto★

See ASCOLI PICENO

Riserva Naturale dei Calanchi★★

2km/1.2mi northwest of Atri on SS 353. Calanchi, known locally as *scrimoini* (streaks) are the result of the natural phenomenon that occurred in the Tertiary Era when a plateau was eroded by water. Comparable to scenes from Dante's *Inferno* this lunar landscape is characterised by precipices descending for hundreds of metres, sparse vegetation and white sediment.

Abbazia di San Clemente a Casauria★★

30km/18mi southwest of Chieti on SS 5. Open mid-Apr to Sep, 8am-8pm; rest of the year, 8am-5.30pm. ☎085 88 85 828.
This imposing abbey was founded in 871 for Emperor Ludovic II. After devastating Saracen attacks it was restored in the 12C by Cistercian monks who rebuilt the church in a style that was a crossover between Romanesque and Gothic. The principal doorway is embellished by an exceptional sculptural decoration and a bronze door, dated 1191, whose borders depict the castles belonging to the abbey. Note the monumental **paschal candelabrum**★ and the splendid **pulpit**★★★ (12C); these are two of the finest examples of the Romanesque style in Abruzzi. The high altar consists of an early Christian tomb dating from the 5C and is surmounted by a Romanesque **ciborium**★★★. The 9C crypt is one of the few remains of the original abbey.

Chiesa di San Clemente al Vomano

15km/9mi northwest of Atri. ☞ *Currently closed for restoration.* ☎085 89 81 28.
This church was founded in the 9C although it has undergone reconstruction since then. In the simple interior the **ciborium**★ (12C) stands out.

Abbazia di San Giovanni in Venere

35km/21mi southeast of Pescara on S 16. ⏰*Open May to mid-Oct, Mon-Fri 8am-8pm, Sat 8am-noon and 2-8pm, Sun and public holidays 9.15-11am and 2-4pm; mid-Oct to Apr, Mon-Fri 8am-6.30pm, Sat 8-11am and 2-5pm, Sun and public holidays 9.15-11am and 2-4pm.* ☎0872 60 132.
This abbey, founded in the 8C on the site of a temple dedicated to Venus and remodelled in the 13C, is situated in a panoramic **setting**★ on the Adriatic Sea. On the façade note the 13C **Portale della Luna**★ (Moon Doorway), with low reliefs depicting sacred and profane subjects.

ANAGNI★

POPULATION 19 000
MICHELIN MAP 563 Q 21 – LAZIO.

Anagni is a small medieval town and the birthplace of several popes, including the infamous **Boniface VIII** (1235-1303). In 1303, after years of conflict, the French king, Philip the Fair, who had been excommunicated by the pope, sent a delegation to Anagni to assess its administration and to evaluate accusations of heresy and corruption. Boniface VIII was ignobly humiliated and this is what gave birth to the legend of the insult to the pope which became known as the "Slap (or Outrage) of Anagni."

- **Information:** Piazza Innocenzo III Papa, ☎0775 72 78 52.
- **Orient Yourself:** Situated on a rocky spur that overlooks the Sacco Valley. Anagni is not far from the A1, 30km/19mi from Frosinone.
- **Don't Miss:** The cathedral, Abbazia di Casamari and Monastero di San Benedetto.
- **Organizing Your Time:** Allow two days to explore the town and surrounding area.
- **Also See:** *GAETA, ROME, TiVOLI.*

Worth a Visit

Cathedral★★

⏰*Open 9am-1pm and 4-7pm (winter 6pm). Crypt and the Museo del Tesoro (* ☞ *guided tours only), Museo Lapidario:* ☜*3€ (for each museum); 8€ inclusive ticket.* ☎0775 72 83 74.
The town's most important building stands on the site of the former acropolis. This Romanesque cathedral was built in the 11C and 12C and remodelled in the 13C with Gothic additions. Walk round the outside to admire the three Romanesque apses with Lombard mouldings and arcades, the 14C statue of Boniface VIII over the loggia on the north side and the Romanesque *campanile*. Inside, the 13C **paving**★ was the work of the Cosmati. The high altar is surmounted by a Romanesque ciborium or canopy. The **paschal candelabrum** is adorned with multicoloured encrustations; it rests on two sphinxes and is crowned by an infant holding a cup. The work, like the nearby **episcopal throne,** is by Pietro Vassaleto. The **crypt**★★★ also has magnificent 13C **frescoes** depicting the Old Testament and the lives of the saints and men of science such as Galen and Hippocrates.

Medieval Quarter★

This quarter consists almost entirely of 13C buildings and is particularly evocative. The façade of **Boniface VIII's Palace** has two pierced galleries one above the other. One has wide round-headed arches while the other consists of attractive twinned windows with small columns. In Piazza Cavour is the 12C-13C **Palazzo Comunale** with a great **vault**★ at ground level.

Excursions

Abbazia di Casamari★★
35km/22mi southeast of Anagni on S 6 and S 214. 561. ⏱*Open 9am-noon and 3-6pm.* 💰*Donations welcome.* ☎*0775 28 273; www.casamari.it.*

The abbey occupies a lonely site, originally a Benedictine foundation. It was consecrated in 1217 by Pope Honorius III, and later taken over by the Cistercians who rebuilt the abbey in accordance with the order's rules of austerity and self-sufficiency.

This is a lovely example of early Italian Gothic architecture. Above the entrance porch of the abbey church is a gallery of twinned openings, which served as the abbots' lodging during the Renaissance. The simplicity of the façade is typically Burgundian with a round-headed doorway, the rose window, and rising above all the typically Cistercian transept tower. The interior is spacious, austere and solemn. Built to a Latin cruciform plan, it has a nave and two aisles separated by massive cruciform piers with engaged columns supporting the lofty pointed vaulting. On the south side of the church are the cloisters with their twin columns, a well and a flower garden. On the east side, in its traditional position, is the remarkable chapter house with delicate ribbed, pointed vaulting.

Alatri
25km/15.5mi northwest of Casamari on S 214 and S 155.

This important city, which was built in the 6C BC, retains several of its cyclopean walls (4C BC). The **acropolis**★ can be reached on foot from the Porta di Cività and is laid out on a trapezoidal plan. One of the best preserved examples in Italy, it affords a fine **view**★★ of Alatri and the Frosinone Valley.

A maze of steep stairways and alleyways is lined with Gothic houses. The Palazzo **Gottifredi** (Largo Luigi di Persiis)

is 13C and the church of **Santa Maria Maggiore**★ in the transitional Romanesque-Gothic style has a façade with three porches. Inside there is interesting 12C-15C **carved woodwork**★.

Subiaco
37km/23mi northwest of Alatri on S 155 and S 411 (scenic route).

St Benedict, founder of the Benedictine Order, and his twin sister Scolastica retired to this spot at the end of the 5C and built 12 little monasteries before moving to Monte Cassino.

▶ *Access to the monasteries of Santa Scolastica and San Benedetto is 3km/2mi before Subiaco, shortly after the Aniene Bridge.*

Monastero di Santa Scolastica
⏱ *Open 9.30am-12.30pm and 3.30-6.30pm, Sun and public holidays, 9-10am, 11.15am-12.30pm and 3.30-6.30pm.* 👣 *Guided tours only.* 💰*Donations welcome.* ☎*0774 82 421; www.benedettini-subiaco.it.*

Standing on a fine site overlooking the Aniene Gorges, the monastery has preserved a majestic 11C *campanile*, its remodelled 18C church has three cloisters. The third, the work of the Cosmati, is admirable in its simplicity.

Monastero di San Benedetto★
⏱*Open 8.30am-12.30pm and 3-6.30pm.* 📖 *Book in advance.* 💰*Donations welcome.* ☎*0774 85 039.*

This 14C monastery clings to the rock face above an earlier one. The **upper church** has frescoes of the 14C Sienese school and 15C Umbrian school. The **lower church** is frescoed by Magister Consolus, of the 13C Roman school.

Visitors are admitted to the Sacred Cave (Sacro Speco) where St Benedict lived as a hermit for three years. A spiral staircase then leads up to a chapel, which contains the earliest portrait of St Francis (without Stigmata or halo). The Holy Staircase (Scala Santa) leads down to the Chapel of the Virgin, the Shepherd's Cave and the rose garden where St Benedict threw himself into brambles to resist temptation.

ANCONA

POPULATION 101 000

MICHELIN MAP 563 L 22.

TOWN PLAN IN THE MICHELIN ATLAS ITALY – MARCHES.

Ancona is a busy port and the main embarkation point for Croatia (Zara, Split and Dubrovnik) and Greece (Corfu, Igoumenitsa, Patras and Cephallonia). The town takes its name from the shape of the rocky promontory on which it is situated, forming as it does an acute angle (Greek ankon – elbow). Often ignored by tourists in a hurry to get to the port, Ancona offers a wealth of attractions, its historic centre packed with churches and museums.

- **Information:** (Jul-Aug) Stazione Marittima. ☎071 20 11 83.
- ▶ **Orient Yourself:** Ancona is accessible via the A 14.
- **Don't Miss:** The Riviera del Conero to the south of the city.
- **Organizing Your Time:** Start your tour of Ancona in the north of the city, where the monuments of greatest interest are clustered.
- **Especially for Kids:** Boat trips along the Riviera from Sirolo and Numana.
- **Also See:** *FERMO.*

Visit

Duomo★

During the summer open daily 8am-noon and 3-6pm, rest of the year 9am-noon and 3-5pm. ☎071 56 288.
The cathedral was dedicated to St Cyriacus, 4C martyr and patron saint of Ancona. The Romanesque building combines Byzantine (the Greek cross plan) and Lombard (mouldings and arcades on the outside walls) architectural features.

Museo Archeologico Nazionale delle Marche

Via Ferretti 1, at the southern end of Piazza del Senato. (&) Open daily 8.30am-7.30pm. Closed Mon, 1 Jan, 1 May, 25 Dec. 4 €. ☎071 20 26 02; www.archeomarche.it.
The museum has interesting prehistoric and archaeological collections, particularly **Roman bronzes from Cartoeto.**

Galleria Comunale Podesti

Via Pizzecolli, 17. Open daily 9am-7pm, Mon 9am-1pm, Sat 8.30am-6.30pm, Sun 3-7pm. Closed public holidays and 4 May. 4.40 €. ☎071 22 25 041; www.comune.ancona.it.
Works by Crivelli, Titian, Lorenzo Lotto, C Maratta and Guercino hang in the public gallery. Works by Luigi Bartolini, Massimo Campigli, Bruno Cassinari

and Tamburini hand in the gallery of modern art.

▶ At the far end of the street, turn right towards the port.

Chiesa di Santa Maria della Piazza★

Open Apr-Oct, daily 8am-noon and 3-7pm, Nov-Mar, daily 8am-noon and 3-6pm. ☎071 52 688.
This 10C Romanesque church has a charming façade (1210) adorned with amusing figures. It was built over the site of two 5C and 6C churches, and retains mosaic pavement fragments.

Loggia dei Mercanti★

This 15C hall for merchants' meetings has a Venetian gothic façade that was the work of Giorgio Orsini

Arco di Traiano

The arch was erected in honour of Trajan who built the port in AD 115.

Excursions

Jesi

30km/18mi southwest of Ancona.
The ancient Roman settlement of Aesis became a prosperous free commune in the 12C and then part of the Papal

Address Book

WHERE TO STAY

☁☁ **Hotel City** *Via Matteotti 112/114 – ☎071 20 70 949 – Fax 071 20 70 372 – Closed 24-26 Dec – P Kids – 39 rm– .* A good solution for those travelling by car and looking for accommodation in the centre of town. Rooms are on the small side, but pleasant enough. Furnishings are modern and functional. In summer breakfast is served on the terrace.

WHERE TO EAT

☁☁ **La Moretta**
Piazza Plebiscito 52 – ☎071 20 23 17 –www.trattoriamoretta.com. Closed Sun,

1-10 Jan, 13-18 Aug – price +10% service charge. Run by the same family since 1897. Serves traditional, local cooking – both meat and fish dishes. Pleasant rustic-style interior, but for atmosphere (lunchtime and evening) try and get a table outside – the terrace looks out on to the square and the church of San Domenico.

EVENTS AND FESTIVALS

During the period following Easter Loreto houses the annual Rassegna Internazionale di Musica Sacra Virgo Lauretana. 🅸 *For information, contact* ☎071 75 01 596.

states, until the unification of Italy. Jesi's medieval and Renaissance nucleus is surrounded by fine **city walls**★★ (13C-16C), gates and towers. The theatre (18C) is dedicated to Jesi's celebrated composer, Giovan Battista Pergolese. The main artery of **Corso Matteotti** is lined with palaces and churches.

Pinacoteca comunale★

♿⏱*Open mid-Jun to mid-Sep, 10am-8pm, rest of the year 10am-1pm and 4-7pm, Sun and public holidays 10am-1pm and 5-8pm.* ⏱*Closed Mon* ☜*5.50 €.* ☎*0731 53 83 42; www.comune.jesi.an.it.* The municipal picture gallery is housed in Palazzo Pianetti, with a Rococo **gallery**★ on the first floor. The collection includes a considerable body of work by the Venetian artist **Lorenzo Lotto** (🕯*see LORETO).* The **Pala di Santa Lucia** is one of his masterpieces.

La Riviera del Conero Driving Tour★

45km

Portonovo★

12km/8mi southeast of Ancona. 🚶*Guided tours only (🅸 for information and to make a booking contact Portonovo Srl, c/o Hotel La Fonte, Loc. Portonovo, Ancona).* ☎*071 80 12 57.* Portonovo lies in a picturesque setting formed by the coastline of the **Conero**

Massif. A private woodland path leads to the 11C **Church of Santa Maria**★. Offering **panoramic views** the road winds south for 20 kilometres passing through pretty villages including **Sirolo** and **Numana**, from where there are Kids boat trips to nearby coves.

▶ *Just before Porto Recanati, turn from the coast and follow signs to Loreto.*

Loreto★

The small city of Loreto is grouped around its well-known church which is the scene of a famous pilgrimage to the "House of Mary". It is said that the Santa Casa (Holy House) or House of Mary was miraculously carried from Nazareth in stages by angels and set down in a wood of laurels, which gave its name to Loreto. In fact three walls of the House of Mary were transported in 1294 by the Angeli (angels in Italian), a noble family which ruled over Epiros.

Piazza della Madonna★

The front of the **basilica**★, is lined by the unfinished portico of the Palazzo Apostolico, which now houses a picture gallery, the **Pinacoteca**★. This contains a remarkable **collection of works**★ by Lorenzo Lotto, and paintings by Simon Vouet and Pomarancio. The Flemish tapestries were woven to designs by Raphael and there is a superb collection of Urbino faience vessels. ♿⏱*Open Apr to Oct, daily except Mon, 9am-1pm and*

4-7pm, rest of year 10am-1pm and 3.30-5.30pm (ticket office closes 30min early). ⏰Closed 1 Jan, Easter, 1 May, 15 Aug, 25 Dec. ✉Donations welcome. ☎071 97 01 04; www.santuarioloreto.it.

Il Santuario della Santa Casa★★

⏰Open daily, Apr to Sep 6.15am-8pm, rest of year 6.45am-7pm (⏰Santa Casa closed 12.30-2.30pm). ☎071 97 01 04; www.santuarioloreto.it
Many famous architects, painters and sculptors contributed to the building and decoration of this church, including Giuliano da Sangallo, Bramante and Vanvitelli. Admire the triple **apse**★ and Sangallo's dome from the outside.
The **three bronze doors**★★ are adorned with fine late-16C and early-17C statues. In the **Sacristy of St John**★ (San Giovanni) is a lavabo designed by Benedetto da Maiano under a vault painted with frescoes by Luca Signorelli. At the transept crossing is the **Santa Casa**★★ carved in the 16C by Antonio Sansovino and other sculptors.

▷ *Continue along the SS 77 for a further 7km/4mi.*

Recanati

This little town, perched on a hill, was the birthplace of the poet **Giacomo Leopardi** (1798-1837), the most perceptive but melancholy of Italian poets whose work was very melodious. The Palazzo Leopardi contains mementoes of the writer. (♿) ⏰Open daily, mid-Mar to mid-Sep, 9am-6pm; mid-Sep to mid-Mar, 9.30am-12.30pm and 2.30-5.30pm (Sat, Sun and public holidays 9.30am-1pm and 3-8pm). ⏰Closed 1 Jan, 25 Dec. ✉6.50€ (museum and library combined ticket). ☎071 75 73 380; www.giacomo-leopardi.it

AREZZO★★

POPULATION 94 675
MICHELIN MAP 563 L 17
SEE ALSO THE GREEN GUIDE TUSCANY.

Arezzo is surrounded by a fertile basin planted with cereal crops, fruit trees and vines. The town is renowned for being the birthplace of many an artistic genius including Guido d'Arezzo (997-c1050) the Benedictine monk and inventor of the musical scale, Petrarch the poet (1304-74), Pietro Aretino the author, (1492-1556) and Giorgio Vasari the painter and art historian (1511-74) 'The Aretine'. But it is to Piero della Francesca that Arezzo owes its greatest artistic heritage although the artist was born in Sansepolcro, 40km/24mi down the road.

- **Information:** Piazza della Repubblica 28, ☎0575 37 76 78.
- ▷ **Orient Yourself:** Arezzo is 11km/7mi from the Florence-Rome motorway, 81km/49mi from Florence.
- **Don't Miss:** The masterpiece of the Affreschi di Piero della Francesca.
- ⏰ **Organizing Your Time:** Allow a day to explore Arezzo fully.
- **Especially for Kids:** Picnics in the park around the Duomo.
- **Also See:** ANSEPOLCRO, SIENA.

Special Features

Chiesa di San Francesco

⏰Audioguided visits. Mon-Fri 9am-6.30pm, Sat-Sun 9am-5.30pm. ⏰Closed 1 Jan, 25 Dec. ✉6 € with prebooking. ☎0575 352 727, www.pierodellafrancesca.it. 🔭Binoculars recommended.

This is a vast church, designed for the preaching of sermons and built in the Gothic style in the 14C for the Franciscan Order. It was altered in the 17C and 18C but restoration work has now returned it to its original austerity. The Franciscan friars, as custodians of the Holy Places, showed particular devotion to the True

Cross and they commissioned Piero della Francesca to decorate the chancel of the church around this theme.

Affreschi di Piero della Francesca★★★
This fresco cycle (1452-1466) is a Renaissance masterpiece. The frescoes depict the Legend of the True Cross, a theme revered by the Franciscans in the Middle Ages. The cycle is based on Jacopo da Varagine's Legenda Aurea (13C).

Walking About

Piazza Grande★
The main square is surrounded by medieval houses and the Romanesque galleried apse of the church of Santa Maria della Pieve.

Chiesa di Santa Maria della Pieve★
This superb Romanesque parish church is crowned by a lofty campanile, which, owing to its numerous double bays (there are 40 of them in all), is referred to as the "Hundred Holes." Construction of the church began in the mid-12C and was completed in the 14C. In the 16C alterations were made, notably under the direction of **Giorgio Vasari**. The

façade★★, which was inspired by the Romanesque style used in Pisa, is very ornate with three tiers of arcades supported by colonnettes.

Duomo
The cathedral was built from 1278 to 1511 and contains some **fine works of art**★ including the fresco by Piero della Francesca depicting Mary Magdalen.

▶ Via Sasso Verde From Via Ricasoli.

Chiesa di San Domenico
This 13C church, built in the Gothic style but since restored, contains frescoes by the Duccio School and Spinello Aretino and his school. On the High Altar the **Crucifix**★★ is by Cimabue.

Worth a Visit

Museo d'Arte Medievale e Modern★★
🕐Open daily except Mon, 8.30am-7pm. 🕐Closed 1 Jan, 1 May, 25 Dec. ☞4€, 10€ combined ticket with Casa Vasari, Museo Archeologico, and Chiesa di San Francesco (frescoes of Piero della Francesca), valid for two days. ☎0575 40 90 50.
The museum of medieval and modern art contains sculptures, gold and sil-

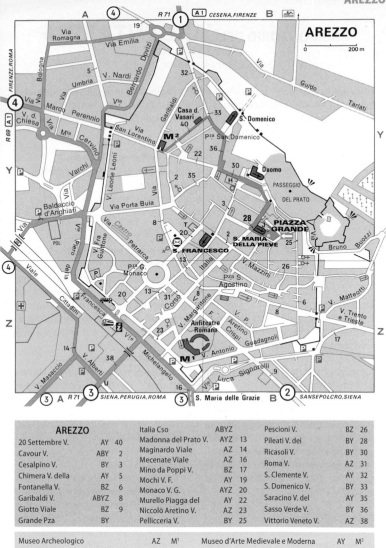

AREZZO			Italia Cso	ABYZ		Pescioni V.	BZ	26
20 Settembre V.	AY	40	Madonna del Prato V.	AYZ	13	Pileati V. dei	BY	28
Cavour V.	ABY	2	Maginardo Viale	AZ	14	Ricasoli V.	BY	30
Cesalpino V.	BY	3	Mecenate Viale	AZ	16	Roma V.	AZ	31
Chimera V. della	AY	5	Mino da Poppi V.	BZ	17	S. Clemente V.	AY	32
Fontanella V.	BZ	6	Mochi V. F.	AY	19	S. Domenico V.	BY	33
Garibaldi V.	ABYZ	8	Monaco V. G.	AYZ	20	Saracino V. del	AY	35
Giotto Viale	BZ	9	Murello Piagga del	AY	22	Sasso Verde V.	BY	36
Grande Pza	BY		Niccolò Aretino V.	AZ	23	Vittorio Veneto V.	AZ	38
			Pellicceria V.	BY	25			

Museo Archeologico	AZ	M¹	Museo d'Arte Medievale e Moderna	AY	M²

verware and paintings from the Middle Ages to the 19C. The 19C is represented by Macchiaioli artists such as Fattori and Signorini. Look out for the outstanding collection of Umbrian Renaisssance **maiolica**★★.

Museo Archeologico

&. ○ *Open daily except Mon 8.30am-7.30pm.* ○ *Closed 1 Jan, 1 May, 25 Dec.* ∞ *4 €, 10 € combined ticket with Casa Vasari, Museo d'Arte Medievale e Moderna, and Chiesa di San Francesco, valid for two days.* ☎ *0575 20 882.*

The archaeological museum stands adjacent to the oval 1C **Roman amphitheatre**, with collections of Etruscan and Roman bronze statuettes (6C BC to 3C AD), Greek vases (Euphronios' krater), Aretine vases, and ceramics.

Chiesa di Santa Maria delle Grazie

1km/0.6mi to the south via Viale Mecenate.

A graceful **portico**★ by the Florentine, Benedetto da Maiano (15C) crowns the front, while inside is a marble **altarpiece**★ by Andrea della Robbia.

PROMONTORIO DELL'**ARGENTARIO**★

MICHELIN MAP 563 O 15
SEE ALSO THE GREEN GUIDE TUSCANY.

This ancient promontory, now linked to the mainland by three ancient causeways formed by a build-up of sand (tomboli), consists of the small limestone hill called Monte Argentario, which rises to a height of 635m/2 083ft and is skirted by a road which affords fine views.

- **Information:** Piazza della Repubblica, 1, Orbetello. ☎0564 86 04 47.
- ▶ **Orient Yourself:** Take the Via Aurelia and exit at either Albinia or Orbetello.
- **Don't Miss:** Harbour views at Porto Santo Stefano.
- **Organizing Your Time:** A tour of the promontory takes around 2 hours.
- **Also See:** *GROSSETO.*

Promontory Tour

▶ *43km/26mi. Leave from Orbetello.*

Ortobello

Built on the central dike in the lagoon, it is situated at the end of the main access road to the peninsula (SS 440). The town was originally called Urbis Tellus, literally the territory of the city (Rome), probably because it was given in AD 805 to the Abbazia delle Tre Fontane in Rome by Charlemagne. The **fortifications** are a reminder of the influence of the Sienese and, later, the Spaniards (16C-17C) who made the town the capital of a small State. The **cathedral** was built on the site of an ancient Etruscan-Roman temple.

Porto Santo Stefano ♙♙

This is the peninsula's main town and the embarkation point for trips to the island of Giglio. Its houses are built up the hillside beside a 17C Aragon-style fort from which there is a superb **view**★ over the Talamone Gulf.

Head north out of Porto Santo Stefano, taking the scenic route. As the road ascends there are fine **views**★★ along the southwest coast, over the island of Rossa and Argentario promontory.

Porto Ercole ♙♙

This seaside resort has a tiny old urban district with machicolations linked to the fortress by crenelated walls.

Excursion

Rovine di Cosa★

11km/7mi south of Orbetello, at the far end of the southernmost bar, Tombolo di Feniglia. ⏱*Open daily 8am-1hr before dusk.* ☜*Archaeological site is free. Museum: 2€.* ☎*0564 88 14 21.*
The ruins of Cosa, a 3C-4C AD Roman colony have been found near the Via Aurelia, including an acropolis.

Address Book

⚃*For coin ranges see the Legend on the cover flap.*

WHERE TO STAY

⊜⊜ **Azienda Agraria Grazia**
Località Provincaccia 110 – 58016 Orbetello Scalo – 7km/4mi east of Orbetello, 140km/84mi along Via Aurelia in the direction of Rome – ☎0564 88 11 82 – Fax 0564 88 11 82 – www.agrituris

mograzia.com – ⤢ – 3 studio. Light, airy studios; well equipped and comfortable, in modern-rustic style. Tucked away in an oasis of flora and fauna where deer, *mouflon* (wild sheep) and wild boar roam free.
⊜⊜⊜ **Antica Fattoria La Parrina**
Località Parrina – 58010 Albinia – 5km/3mi north of Orbetello Scalo,

146km/88mi from the Via Aurelia in the direction of Firenze – ☎0564 86 26 36 – Fax 0564 86 26 36 – www.parrina.it – Closed Thursdays in winter 🅿 – 16 rooms.
Housed in a 19C villa that is now a working farm and guesthouse, set in parkland. Elegantly decorated with antique furniture. Breakfast and dinner served on the terrace in summer. A stylish, rural retreat. Produces its own cheeses, wines and olive oil.

WHERE TO EAT

🍽 Il Moresco
Via Panoramica 156, Cala Moresca – 58019 Porto Santo Stefano – 5.5km/3.4mi southwest of Porto Santo Stefano – ☎0564 82 41 58 – Closed Tue, Jun-Sep and Wed lunchtime, Feb. Pleasantly situated in a quiet spot looking out to sea and the island of Giglio. A magical combination of good home cooking (fish and meat dishes) and fine views.

🍽🍽 Il Cavaliere
Via G. Pantini 3 – 58010 Orbetello Scalo – At the exit from the station underpass ☎0564 86 43 42 – Closed Wed, 10-25 Nov – 🍽 – 🅰 Advanced booking recommended. Situated off the beaten

track, away from the hordes of tourists, this restaurant is popular with the locals for its antipasti, as well as its fish-based starters and main courses. A simple, family-run restaurant (albeit a little noisy when the trains pass by).

TAKING A BREAK

Bar Bagianni
Piazza Eroe dei 2 Mondi – 58015 Orbetello – ☎0564 86 81 34 – Mon-Sat 7am-1am, Sun 7am-1pm and 3pm-1am.
Ice cream bar, cocktail bar, internet café and tea room – all rolled into one establishment. Housed in an attractive building overlooking the main square. Popular with the locals from early in the morning until late into the night.

Baretto
Lungomare Andrea Doria 53/54 – 58018 Porto Ercole – ☎0564 83 26 54 – Open daily Jul-Aug 8am-3am; rest of the year; closed Wed and one month in winter.
Of all the bars overlooking the harbour, the Baretto boasts the best location – right in the centre. Very popular with the locals (mainly young clientele) on account of its warm welcome and delicious cocktails made with fresh fruit.

ASCOLI PICENO★★
POPULATION 52 000
MICHELIN MAP 563 N 22 – MARCHES.

A city of travertine and towers, known as piccola Siena (little Siena) for the harmony and elegance of its medieval and Renaissance buildings, Ascoli lies in a valley where the Tronto and Castellano rivers meet.

- **Information:** Piazza del Popolo 17, ☎0736 25 30 45.
- **Orient Yourself:** Ascoli Piceno is on Via Salaria, 30km/18mi from the Adriatic.
- **Don't Miss:** Piazza del Popolo and a stop for coffee at Cafe Meletti.
- **Organizing Your Time:** Allow a day.
- **Also See:** FERMO.

A Bit of History

Several traces of the thriving Roman town of Asculum remain, although these are often incorporated into structures of a later date. In the Middle Ages and the Renaissance, the city saw bitter conflicts between opposing factions; in spite of

this the town flourished and constructed many civic and religious buildings. Its economic and artistic vigour also attracted important figures from other parts of Italy. Notables include the Venetian painter **Carlo Crivelli** (1430-94), who elected to settle in Ascoli permanently. Initially influenced by Mantegna and

Bellini, Crivelli developed a highly original style that fused the solidity of Renaissance geometry with late Gothic decorative opulence. He had a profound effect on painters throughout the region.

Walking Tour

Piazza del Popolo★★

The well-proportioned main square is the city's public drawing room, paved with large flagstones and framed by Gothic and Renaissance buildings and elegant arcades.

The **Palazzo dei Capitani del Popolo★**, (People's Captains' Palace) erected in the 13C, owes its current appearance to additions made in the 16C by Cola dell'Amatrice, among others, who also designed the austere rear façade. Inside there is an attractive arcaded courtyard (16C).

The 13C-16C **Church of San Francesco★** has several Lombard features. On the south side there is a fine 16C portal above which stands a monument to Julius II and the **Loggia dei Mercanti★** (Merchants' Loggia), a graceful early-16C building showing Tuscan influence, particularly in the capitals. On the left-hand side there are cloisters: the principal **Chiostro Maggiore**, 16C-17C, which shelters a colourful fruit and vegetable market, and the more intimate 14C **Chiostro Minore** (*access from Via Ceci*). There is an elegant structure of double belltowers in the apse.

▸ *Cross the square away from San Francesco and turn left into Via XX Settembre.*

Duomo

🕐*Open 8am-12.30pm and 4-7.30pm.* 🎫*Donations welcome.* ☎*0736 25 97 74.* The grandiose Renaissance façade of this 12C cathedral was the work of Cola dell'Amatrice. On the north side stands the **Porta della Musa**, a fine late Renaissance construction. Inside, in the Cappella del Sacramento (Eucharist Chapel – south aisle) there is a superb **polyptych★** by **Carlo Crivelli** in which the late Gothic grace of the Madonna and Child

contrasts with the dramatic Pietà which derives from Mantegna.

To the left of the Duomo stands the 11C **Baptistery★**, a fine square structure crowned by an octagonal lantern with graceful trefoil openings. The entrance is surmounted by a triangular pediment. The draining channels carved into the stonework above the portal are typical of the local architecture.

Corso Mazzinia

This is the grand street of the city and is lined with old palaces of varying epochs, embellished with Latin and Italian inscriptions. At no 224 the 16C **Malaspina Palace** has an original loggia with columns shaped like tree trunks. At the beginning of Via delle Torri is the Renaissance **Church of Sant'Agostino**, which has a fresco of Christ by Colla dell'Amatrice and a Madonna dell'Umilta of the Fabriano school.

Via delle Torri

This street owes its name to the many towers that once stood here; of these two 12C towers remain. At the end of the street stands the 14C **Church of San Pietro Martire.**

S.S. Vincenzo e Anastasio★

☎*0736 25 52 14.*
This church of early Christian origin is a fine example of Romanesque architecture. Its 14C **façade★** is divided into 64 sections which were originally covered in frescoes. The strikingly simple interior houses a crypt of the 6C with remains of 14C frescoes.

Ponte romano di Solestà★

For information call ☎0736 29 82 04.
Heralded by a 14C gateway, this bridge is a bold construction of the Augustan Age supported by only one arch of 25m/82ft in height. From the far end there is an attractive view of the 16C public washtub (*lavatoio pubblico*).

Via dei Soderini

This street was once the main artery of the medieval city; this can be seen in its numerous mansions, feudal towers and picturesque side streets. The most interesting building is the **Palazzetto**

Longobardo (11C-12C), a Lombard mansion which is flanked by the ele-gant Ercolani Tower (Torre Ercolani), more than 40m/130ft high. A typical Ascoli architrave stands above its doorway.

Visit

Pinacoteca★
♿ⓇOpen daily 9am-1pm and 3-7pm. ⓇClosed 1 Jan, 25 Dec ⊜5 €. ☎0736 29 82 13.

The picture gallery is housed on the main floor of the town hall (Palazzo Comunale) has a notable collection of figurative arts from the 16C-19C (Guido Reni, Titian, Luca Giordano, Carlo Maratta). Most notable among the paintings of the Marches region are the works by **Carlo Crivelli, Cola dell'Amatrice** and, of Crivelli's circle, Pietro Alamanno. A precious, delicately worked 13C English relic **(piviale★)**, the cope, donated in 1288 by Nicholas IV to the cathedral chapter, is a particularly prized exhibit.

Opposite the town hall, in Palazzo Panichi, the **Museo Archeologico** displays relics of the Piceno age (9-6C BC) and 1C AD Roman mosaics. ♿ⓇOpen daily except Mon 8.30am-7.30pm. ⓇClosed 1 Jan, 1 May, 25 Dec. ⊜2 €. ☎0736 25 35 62.

On nearby Via Bonaparte, at no 24, **Palazzo Bonaparte** is one of the best examples of domestic Renaissance architecture.

Excursion

Civitella del Tronto★
24km/15mi southeast. This charming village perched on a travertine mountain 645m/2 116ft above sea level, enjoys a splendid **setting★★**. Its picturesque winding streets are lined with fine religious and civic architecture of the 16C-17C. The imposing structure of the16C **Fortress★** was the last Bourbon stronghold to surrender to the Sardinian-Piedmontese armies in 1861. ♿ⓇOpen daily Mar-Sep, 10am-7pm, public holidays 10am-8pm; Oct-Feb 10am-1pm and 3-6pm. ⓇClosed 25 Dec. ⊜4 €. ☎333 90 30 360 (mobile); www.fortezzacivitella.it.

ASSISI★★★

POPULATION 26 196

MICHELIN MAP 563 M 19 – UMBRIA.

The walled city of Assisi is closely associated with St Francis, as related in the numerous accounts of his life and work. Under the influence of the Franciscan Order of Minors founded by St Francis, a new, essentially religious, artistic movement developed which marked a turning-point in Italian art. The son of a rich Assisi draper, Francis preached poverty, humility and mysticism, and his teachings gave rise to a new artistic vision expressed in the purity of Gothic art. During the 13C the stark, austere churches, which were designed for preaching, were embellished with a new splendour to reflect the tender love of St Francis for nature and its creatures, as described in the tales of St Bonaventure. From the end of the 14C famous masters came from Rome and Venice to Assisi to work on the Basilica of St Francis. These artists abandoned the rigid traditions of Byzantine art in favour of a more dramatic art imbued with a spiritual atmosphere. Cimabue and later Giotto were its most powerful exponents.

- **Information:** Piazza del Comune 12, ☎075 81 25 34.
- ▶ **Orient Yourself:** Assisi is prettily spread across the slopes of Monte Subasiphrase and lies between Perugia and Foligno, on S 75.
- **Don't Miss:** Frescoes in the Basilica di San Francesco, enchanting Spello.
- **Organizing Your Time:** Take a day to explore Assisi, and add a half day for trips out to Spello, Foglino and Bevagna.
- **Also See:** *PERUGIA*.

Basilica di San Francesco★★★

From the green esplanade or from the road that winds up to Assisi from the flat countryside, the basilica is an imposing and striking vision at all hours of the day. The simple façade has a Cosmati work rose window.

The group of buildings consists of two churches, resting on a series of immense arches. The whole building, erected after the death of St Francis to the

Spectacular view of Assisi from the valley

R. Mattes/MICHELIN

plans of Brother Elias, was consecrated in 1253. It was this monk who influenced the Franciscans to use more splendour and decoration.

Basilica Inferiore – Beyond the long narthex, the walls of the dark, sombre four-bay nave of the lower church are covered with 13C and 14C **frescoes★★★**. From the nave, enter the first chapel on the left with **frescoes★★** by Simone Martini (c 1284-1344) illustrating the life of St Martin. These are remarkable for their delicate drawing, graceful composition and bright colours. Further along, above the pulpit is a fresco of the *Coronation of the Virgin* attributed to Maso, a pupil of Giotto (14C). The choir **vaulting★★** is painted with scenes symbolising the Triumph of St Francis and the virtues practised by him. They are the work of one of Giotto's pupils.

The north transept is decorated with **frescoes★★** of the Passion. Those on the ceiling, attributed to pupils of Pietro Lorenzetti, are valued for their narrative design and charm of detail; those on the walls, probably by Lorenzetti himself,

Address Book

🥤 *For coin ranges see the Legend on the cover flap.*

WHERE TO STAY

🍽 **Casa di Santa Brigida** –*Via Moiano 1 – ☎075 81 26 93 – Fax 075 81 32 16 – s.brigida.assisi@libero.it –* 📺📶🅿 *– 18 rm – ⌁.* With its flower-filled garden and shady trees this is a haven of peace and quiet. The interior is equally relaxing with rooms redolent of monastic calm. The half-board and full-board rates are good value. Light meals served, traditional cooking.

🍽 **Hotel Berti** – *Piazza San Pietro 24 – ☎075 81 34 66 – Fax 075 81 68 70 – www.hotelberti.it – Closed 10 Jan-1 Mar – 10 rm– ⌁.* Former stable block used as a hostel by pilgrims heading for the Eremo delle Carceri. Small, family-run hotel with clean, pleasant rooms. Warm welcome. Close to the Da Cecco restaurant, run by the same family.

WHERE TO EAT

🍽 **Da Erminio** – *Via Montecavallo 19 – ☎075 81 25 06 – www.trattoriadaerminio.it – Closed Thu, 15 Jan-3 Mar, 1-15 Jul.* Situated in a quiet, residential area beyond San Rufino, this small restaurant is well worth the climb! Serves traditional Umbrian dishes including *strangozzi al tartufo* (pasta dish with truffles). The open fire is an added attraction.

🍽 **Da Cecco** – *Piazza San Pietro 8 – ☎075 81 24 37. Closed Wed, 18 Dec-Feb.* A smart restaurant with a friendly ambience. The cuisine is traditional, but has a distinctive personal touch. Specialities include salami and strangozzi alla boscaiola (pasta with mushrooms, argula/rocket and walnuts), along with meat grilled in the open fireplace. Simple decor with rustic and medieval elements.

---

are striking for their dramatic expression **(Descent from the Cross)**. In the south transept is the majestic work by Cimabue, a **Madonna with Four Angels and St Francis**★★.

From the Sixtus IV cloisters make for the **treasury**★★ with its many valuable items and the **Perkins collection** of 14C to 16C paintings.

At the bottom of the steps, beneath the centre of the transept crossing, is **St Francis' Tomb** which is both spare and evocative.

Basilica Superiore – This accomplished Gothic work with its tall and graceful nave bathed in light, contrasts with the lower church. The apse and transept were decorated with frescoes (many have since been damaged) by Cimabue and his school. In the north transept Cimabue painted an intensely dramatic **Crucifixion**★★★.

Between 1296 and 1304 **Giotto** and his assistants depicted the life of St Francis in a famous cycle of **frescoes**★★★. There are 28 clearly defined scenes, each showing a greater search for realism. They mark a new dawning in the figurative traditions of Italian art, which was to reach its apogee during the Renaissance.

Walking About

Via S. Francesco★

This picturesque street is lined by medieval and Renaissance houses. At No 13a the Pilgrims' Chapel (Oratorio dei Pellegrini) is decorated inside with 15C frescoes, notably by Matteo da Gualdo (🕐*open daily, 10am-noon and 4-6pm.;*🕐*closed Sun* ☎075 81 22 67).

Piazza del Comune★

This square occupies the site of the forum: note the **Tempio di Minerva**★ (1C BC), a temple converted into a church, and, to the left, the People's Captains' Palace (13C).

Duomo di San Rufino★

The cathedral was built in the 12C and its Romanesque **façade**★★ has a harmonious arrangement of its openings and ornamentation.

ASSISI		
Brizi V.	B	2
Comune Pza del	B	3
Fontebella V.	B	
Fortini V. A.	B	4
Fosso Cupo V. del	AB	6
Frate Elia V.	A	7
Galeazzo Alessi V.	C	8
Garibaldi Piazzetta	B	9
Giotto V.	B	10
Mazzini Cso	B	12
Merry del Val V.	A	13
Porta Perlici V.	C	14
Portica V.	B	16
S. Apollinare V.	B	17
S. Chiara Pza	BC	19
S. Francesco Pza	A	20
S. Gabriele della Addolorata V.	BC	21
S. Giacomo V.	A	23
S. Pietro Pza	A	24
S. Rufino V.	B	26
Seminario V. del	B	28
Torrione V. del	C	30
Villamena V.	C	31
Oratorio dei Pellegrini	B	B

The interior, on a basilical plan, was rebuilt in 1571. To the right at the entrance is the baptismal font used for the baptism of St Francis, St Clare and Frederick II.

Chiesa di Santa Chiara★★

From the terrace in front of the church of St Clare there is a pretty view of the Umbrian countryside. The church was built from 1257 to 1265 and resembles the Gothic upper basilica of St Francis. The Byzantine crucifix brought here from St Damian's Monastery, which is said to have spoken to St Francis and caused his conversion to the Christian faith, can be seen in the small church of St George, which adjoins the south aisle. The crypt enshrines the remains of St Clare.
*See Rocca Maggiore★★ (**view★★★**); S. Pietro★*

Excursions

Eremo delle Carceri★★

4km/2.5mi east.
The hermitage stands in a beautiful site at the heart of a forest of age-old green oaks. It is said that, having been blessed by St Francis, a huge flock of birds flew out of one of the trees, symbolising the spread of the Franciscan Order throughout the world. The hermitage was founded here by St Bernardino of Siena (1380-1444). The spot derives its name from the fact that Francis and his followers liked to retire from the world here as if they had been put into prison (*carcere* in Italian) in order, according to one of his biographers, to chase out "from the soul the tiniest speck of dust left in it by contact with mankind." Narrow passageways clearly indicating the structure of the monastery (built around the outline of the rock) lead to St Francis' Cave and the old refectory with its 15C tables.

Convento di San Damiano★

2km/1mi south of the gateway, Porta Nuova. Open daily, summer 10am-noon and 2-6pm; winter 10am-noon and 2-4.30pm. ☎075 81 22 73.
St Damian's Monastery and a small adjoining church stand alone amid olive and cypress trees and are closely associated with St Francis, who received his

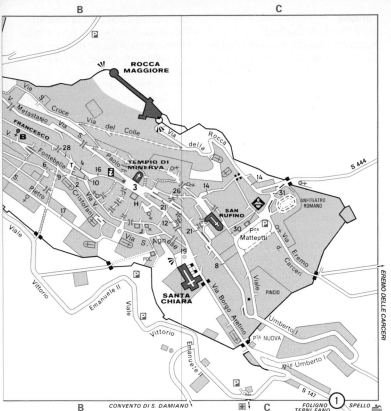

calling here and composed his *Canticle of the Creatures*, and also with St Clare who died here in 1253.

Basilica di Santa Maria degli Angeli★

5km/3mi southwest.

The basilica of St Mary of the Angels was built in the 16C around the **Porziuncola**, a small chapel named after the small plot (*piccola porzione* in Italian) of land on which it was built before the year AD 1000. It was in the Porziuncola that St Francis named Clare the "Bride of Christ." It contains a **fresco**★ (1393) representing episodes from the history of the Franciscan Order *(above the altar)*. It was in the adjacent chapel, Cappella del Transito, that Francis died on 3 October 1226. The St Mary Major Crypt contains an enamelled terracotta **polyptych**★ by Andrea della Robbia (c 1490). Near the church is the rose bush said to have lost its thorns when the saint threw

himself onto it to escape temptation, and the cave in which he used to pray. In the corridor leading to the rose bush is a statue of the saint holding a nest where doves roost.

Spello★

12km/8mi southeast.

A picturesque little town in which the bastions and gateways bear witness to its past as a Roman settlement. The **Church of Santa Maria Maggiore** contains **frescoes**★★ *(chapel on the left)* by **Pinturicchio** depicting the Annunciation, the Nativity, the Preaching in the Temple *(on the walls)* and the Sibyls *(on the vaulting)*. By the high altar are frescoes by Perugino. Nearby, in the **Church of Sant'Andrea**, which was built in 1025, is a painting by Pinturicchio and a crucifix attributed to Giotto. The village is also famous for its Flower Festival *(Le Infiorate del Corpus Domini)* held on the Feast of Corpus Christi.

Foligno

18km/11mi to the southeast.
Piazza della Republica is overlooked by the 14C Palazzo Trinci, built by the local overlords, and the cathedral (Duomo) with its fine doorway decorated with Lombard-style geometric decoration.

Palazzo Trinci

(&) ⏱Open daily, 10am-7pm. ⏱Closed Mon, 1 Jan, 25 Dec ☎5 €. ☎0742 35 76 97.
The focal point in this palazzo are the **frescoes**★, executed with an almost perfect technical grasp of perspective. The frescoes in the Loggia depict the legend of Romulus and Remus and seem almost three-dimensional. In the Studio (referred to as the "Rose room" as roses were presented to apostolic vicars such as the Trinci) there are depictions of the Trivium arts (Grammar, Rhetoric, Dialect) and the Quadrivium arts (Arithmetic, Geometry, Music, Astronomy). Hours of the day are portrayed in relation to the ages of man and the planets. The Gothic thrones would suggest a northern attribution to these frescoes.

The frescoes and decorations along the corridor that leads to the cathedral represent great figures of Antiquity on one wall, and the seven ages of man on the other.
Only the frescoes in the chapel, relating the life of Mary, are signed. They were completed by Otta Viano Nelli in 1424.

Bevagna★

24km/14mi south of Assisi.
Bevagna is a typical medieval town, divided up into four *guaite*, or quarters. Remains of various buildings bear witness to its Roman past, particularly from the 2C AD: ambulatory of the Roman theatre, temple and the **terme di Mevania** (thermal baths).

Piazza Silvestri

The square is typically medieval, overlooked by two churches – the late-11C church of San Michele and the late-12C church of San Silvestro (note the epigraph on the façade) – as well as the 13C **Palazzo dei Consoli**, which houses the charming **Teatro Torti**.

BARI

POPULATION 328 458
MICHELIN MAP 564 D 32 – PUGLIA.

An agricultural and industrial centre, Bari is first and foremost a port. The Levantine Fair (Fiera del Levante), held in September, is an important trade fair, which was inaugurated in 1930 to encourage trade with other Mediterranean countries. Bari comprises the old town, clustered on its promontory, and the modern town with wide avenues, laid out on a grid plan in the 19C.

- 🏢 **Information:** Piazza Aldo Moro 32/A, ☎080 52 42 244.
- ▶ **Orient Yourself:** The capital of Puglia, Bari overlooks the Adriatic. To get there, take either A 14 or S 16 motorway.
- 🐾 **Don't Miss:** A wander through the treasures of the Basilica di San Nicola and Cattedrale.
- 🕐 **Organizing Your Time:** The Old Town can be enjoyed in half a day, or allow a day to explore the modern town as well.
- 🕯 **Also See:** *PROMONTORIO DEL GARGANO, PUGLIA.*

Visit

Basilica di San Nicola★★

The basilica in the heart of the old town (*città vecchia*), also known as the Nicho-

las "stronghold (*citadella*)", was begun in 1087 and consecrated in 1197 to St Nicholas, Bishop of Myra in Asia Minor, who achieved fame by resurrecting three children, whom a butcher had

cut up and put in brine. The building is one of the most remarkable examples of Romanesque architecture and the model for many local churches. On the north side there is the richly decorated 12C Lions' Doorway. Inside, the nave and two aisles with a triforium were re-roofed in the 17C with a coffered ceiling. A 12C *ciborium* (canopy) surmounts the high altar behind which is an 11C marble **episcopal throne**★. The tomb of St Nicholas lies in the crypt.

Cattedrale★
This 11C-12C Romanesque cathedral was added to and then altered at a later date. The works of art include a pulpit made up of 11C and 12C fragments, and a baldachin rebuilt from 13C fragments.

A copy of the **Exultet** is displayed in the north aisle (the original is kept in the sacristy just outside the church), a precious 11C Byzantine parchment scroll in Beneventan script, typical of medieval southern Italy. The illustrations are on the reverse side so that the congregation could see them as the parchment was unrolled.

Castello★
(♿) ⏱Open daily except Wed, 8.30am-7.30pm. ⏱Closed 1 Jan, 1 May, 25 Dec ⏱2 €. ☎080 52 86 225. wwwpuglia.beniculturali.it. The Emperor Frederick II of Hohenstaufen built the castle in 1233 over the foundations of earlier Byzantine and Norman buildings. The irregular courtyard and two towers date from the Swabian period.

Pinacoteca
On Lungomare Nazario Sauro. ♿⏱Open daily, 9.30am-1pm and 4-7pm, Sun 9am-1pm. ⏱Closed Mon, public holidays. ⏱2.58 €. ☎080 54 12 422.

WHERE TO EAT

⌐Al Sorso Preferito 1 *Via Vito Nicola De Nicolò 40, 70122 Bari – ☎080 52 35 747 – Closed Wed, Sun evening* ▤
A popular restaurant and surprisingly good value. The management prides itself on the quality of its cooking and raw ingredients. Hearty, traditional cooking. Menu includes meat and fish dishes, and includes regional specialities.
Booking recommended.

The gallery, on the fourth floor (lift) of the Palazzo della Provincia, comprises Byzantine works of art (sculpture and paintings), a 12C-13C painted wood statue of **Christ**★, *The Martyrdom of St Peter* by Giovanni Bellini and canvases by the 17C-18C Neapolitan school.

Museo Archeologico
First floor of the university. ⛔ *Closed for restoration at publication.* ☎080 52 35 786 or 080 52 10 484.
The archaeological museum displays Greco-Roman collections from excavations made throughout Puglia.

Coast Excursion

The road from Bari to Barletta passes through many attractive coastal towns that were fortified against invasion by the Saracens during the Middle Ages and the Turks at the end of the 15C. These include **Giovinazzo** with its small 12C cathedral dominating the fishing harbour; **Molfetta** pinpointed by the square towers of its Apulian Romanesque cathedral; and **Bisceglie**, a picturesque fishing village.

A Bit of History
Legend has it that Bari was founded by the Illiri and then colonised by the Greeks. Between the 9C and 11C Bari was the capital of Byzantium's domain in Italy. In its role as a pilgrimage centre to St Nicholas' shrine and as a port of embarkation for the Crusades, Bari was a very prosperous city in the Middle Ages. It declined under the Sforza of Milan and Spanish rule in the 16C.

BARI

BASSANO DEL GRAPPA★

POPULATION 41 752
MICHELIN MAP 562 E 17 – VENETO.

Bassano del Grappa, a pottery town that also produces brandy (grappa), is built on the banks of the Brenta River. The town is attractive, with painted houses and squares bordered by arcades. At the centre is Piazza Garibaldi. The covered bridge (Ponte Coperto) is well known in Italy and was built in the 13C.

- **Information:** Largo Corona d'Italia, 35. ☎0424 52 43 51.
- ▶ **Orient Yourself:** The town with its famous bridge lies on S 47 linking Bassano del Grappa with Padua.
- **Don't Miss:** Views from Monte Grappa, Ponte Coperto and a taste of grappa itself.
- **Organizing Your Time:** Bassano can be explored in half a day.
- **Also See:** *PADOVA, TREVISO and VICENZA.*

Visit

Museo Civico★
Open Tue-Sat 9am-6.30pm, Sun 3.30-6.30pm. Closed Mon, 1 and 19 Jan, Easter and 25 Dec. 4.50 €. ☎0424 52 22 35; www.museobassano.it.
The municipal museum is housed in the monastery next to the church of St Francis. The first floor **picture gallery** has works by the local Da Ponte family. Jacopo da Ponte, otherwise called **Jacopo Bassano** (1510-92), was the best-known. His works were marked by a picturesque realism and contrasts of light and shade. **St Valentine baptising St Lucilla** is his masterpiece.
Other Venetian painters include Guariento, Vivarini, Giambono (14C and 15C), Pietro Longhi, Giamattista Tiepolo and Marco Ricci (18C). There are also works by Magnasco (18C) and Canova.

Piazza Garibaldi
The square is dominated by the 13C square tower, **Torre di Ezzelino**, and overlooked by the church of San Francesco. The church, which dates from the 12C-14C, has an elegant porch (1306). Inside, the 14C Christ is by Guariento.

Excursions

Monte Grappa★★★
32km/20mi north – alt 1 775m/5 823ft.
The road heads up through forests and mountain pastures to the summit, from where there is a magnificent **panorama** out to Venice and Trieste.

Asolo★
14km/9mi east.
The streets of this attractive little town, dominated by its castle, are lined with palaces painted with frescoes. The town is closely associated with Robert Browning and Eleonora Duse, the famous Italian tragic actress who interpreted the works of Gabriele D'Annunzio. Duse is buried in the peaceful cemetery of Sant'Anna.

Marostica★
7km/4mi west.
Piazza Castello★, the main square of this charming small medieval city serves as a giant chessboard for a highly original game of chess – **Partita a Scacchi** – with costumed people as the chessmen.

Cittadella
13km/8mi south.
This 12C stronghold was built by the Paduans and has fine brick **walls**★.

Possagno
18km/11mi northwest.
This was the birthplace of the sculptor **Antonio Canova** (1757-1822), known for his neo-Classical works. Visit the **house** where he was born and a **sculpture gallery** (Gipsoteca) nearby. (♿) *Open*

daily except Mon 9am-12.30pm and 3-6pm. ◐*Closed 1 Jan, Easter, 25 Dec.* ⊜*5 €.* ☎*0423 54 43 23; www.museocanova.it.* The **Tempio di Canova**, a temple designed by the master himself, crowns an eminence. Inside are the sculptor's tomb and his last sculpture, a **Descent from the Cross**★. ◐*Open summer 9am-noon and 3-6pm, rest of the year 9am-noon and 2-5pm. For admission to the dome, contact the custodian.* ◐*Closed Mon.* ⊜*No charge to enter temple, cupola 1.30 €.* ☎*339 65 48 00 (mobile).*

Castelfranco Veneto★
26km/16mi southeast.
Castelfranco is a pleasant citadel surrounded by moats and the birthplace of the artist **Giorgione** (1478-1510). The cathedral contains his masterpiece, the **Madonna and Child with Saints**★★. The artist's birthplace, (Casa natale di Giorgione) in *Piazza del Duomo* is now a museum. ◐*Open daily except Mon, 10am-12.30pm and 3-6.30pm.* ◐*Closed 1 Jan, Easter, 15 Aug, 25, 26 and 31 Dec.* ⊜*2.50 €.* ☎*0423 72 50 22.*

BELLUNO★

POPULATION 35 077

MICHELIN MAP 562 D 18 – VENETO.

This pleasant town stands on a spur at the confluence of the River Piave and River Ardo rivers and is surrounded by high mountains. To the north are the Dolomites with the Belluno Pre-Alps in the south. An independent commune in the Middle Ages, Belluno came under the aegis of the Venetian Republic from 1404.

- **Information:** Piazza dei Martiri 8, ☎0437 94 00 83.
- ▶ **Orient Yourself:** Belluno lies on the A 27 to Venice.
- **Don't Miss:** Pretty Piazza Maggiore in Feltre.
- **Organizing Your Time:** Leave half a day to vist Belluno.
- **Also See:** *DOLOMITI.*

Walking About

Walk along via Rialto through the 13C gateway, Porta Dojona (remodelled in the 16C), across **Piazza del Mercato**★, bordered with arcaded Renaissance houses and adorned with a 1409 fountain, along via Mezzaterra and Via Santa Croce to the gateway, Porta Rugo. Via del Piave offers an extensive **view**★ of the Piave Valley.
Piazza del Duomo★ is surrounded by the late-15C Venetian-style **Rectors' Palace**★ (palazzo dei Rettori), the Episcopal Palace (palazzo dei Vescovi) and the **cathedral** (Duomo), dating from the 16C with its Baroque campanile by Juvara. In the crypt there is a 15C **polyptych**★ by the Rimini school. The Jurists' Palace (Palazzo dei Giuristi) houses the municipal museum (Museo civico). ◐*Open May-Sep 10am-1pm and 4-7pm; Oct-Apr, Mon-Wed 9am-1pm, Thu, Sun and public holidays 9am-1pm and 3-6pm.* ◐*Closed Mon (summer), 1 May, 15 Aug and 1 Nov.* ⊜*2.30 €.* ☎*0437 94 48 36; www.comune.belluno.it.*

Excursion

Feltre
31km/19mi southwest. Feltre, grouped around its castle, has kept part of its ramparts and in **Via Mezzaterra**★, old houses, adorned with frescoes in the Venetian manner. **Piazza Maggiore**★ is a beautiful square with its noble buildings, arcades, stairways and balustrades. The **Municipal Museum** (*23 Via Lorenzo Luzzo, near the Porta Oria*) displays works by Lorenzo Luzzo, a local artist, Marescalchi, Bellini, Cima da Conegliano, Ricci and Jan Massys (♿◐*open 10.30am-12.30pm and 4-7pm (3-6pm in winter);* ◐ *closed Mon, 1 Jan and 25/26 Dec;* ⊜*4 €;* ☎*0439 88 52 42; www. comune. feltre.bl.it.*

BENEVENTO

POPULATION 63 000

MICHELIN MAP 564 D 26 – CAMPANIA.

This was the ancient capital of the Samnites, who hindered the Roman expansion for some time. In 321 BC they trapped the Roman army in a defile known as the Caudine Forks (Forche Caudine) between Capua and ancient Beneventum. The Romans occupied the town following the defeat in 275 BC of Pyrrhus (transforming the old name **Maleventum** into **Beneventum**) and his Samnite allies. During the reign of Trajan, the town was designated as the starting point for the Appian Trajan Way (Via Appia Traiana) leading to Brindisi. Under Lombard rule it became the seat of a duchy in 571 and later a powerful principality. Following the Battle of Benevento in 1266, Charles of Anjou, supported by Pope Urban IV, claimed the kingship.

- **Information:** Via Nicola Sala 31, ☎0824 31 99 11.
- **Orient Yourself:** To get to Benevento take S 88, which links the town with Isernia and A 16, or the Via Appia, which goes to Caserta.
- **Don't Miss:** Opera and theatre at the Teatro Romano.
- **Organizing Your Time:** Allow for a half a day to explore this compact town.
- **Also See:** *REGGIA DI CASERTA*.

Worth a Visit

Teatro Romano

Access from Via Port'Arsa, to the left of S. Maria della Verità church. ⚐☾*Open May-Aug daily 9am-1h before sunset.* ☾*Closed 1 Jan, 1 May, 25 Dec.* ✑*2€.* ☎*0824 47 213. www.comune.benevento.it.*
This is one of the largest Roman theatres still in existence; it was built in the 2C by the Emperor Hadrian and enlarged by the Emperor Caracalla. In the summer it hosts theatre, dance and opera performances.
From Piazza Duomo, dominated by the imposing cathedral, turn into Corso Garibald, lined with the city's most significant buildings. Note the Egyptian obelisk from Isis' Temple (AD 88).

Arco di Traiano★★

From Corso Garibaldi; left on Via Traiano.
The "Porta Aurea," erected in AD 114 to commemorate the emperor who had turned Benevento into an obligatory stopover on the journey to Apulia, is Italy's best-preserved triumphal arch, with low reliefs depicting scenes of peace on the side facing the city and scenes of war facing the countryside.

Chiesa di Santa Sofia

Piazza Matteotti.
An 8C building which was rebuilt in the 17C. The interior has an unusual layout consisting of a central hexagon enclosed by a decagonal structure. Adjacent to the 12C cloisters★ with their Moorish style arches, the **Museo del Sannioa** houses an important archaeological collection.

The Witches of Egypt

In the 1C AD, Benevento was one of the principal centres of the cult of the Egyptian goddess Isis, which flourished until the 6C. With the invasion of the Lombards, the practice of magic and mystic rites was considered incompatible with Christianity. Believers continued to conduct rites outside the city walls, near a walnut tree, in the valley of the River Sabato. This gave rise to the myth of witches' Sabbaths and the witches of Benevento. According to legend, St Barbato ended these activities in the 7C by cutting down the trunk. The myth lives on, however, in the famous liqueur *Strega* (witch), created in 1861 by Giuseppe Alberti; the Società Strega now finances the prestigious literary prize that bears this name.

BERGAMO★★

POPULATION 116 510

MICHELIN MAP 561 E 10-11 – LOMBARDY.

Bergamo, one of the principal towns of Lombardy, is situated on the northern edge of the Lombardy plain at the confluence of the Brembana and Seriana valleys. It has a strong artistic heritage, and is also a thriving business and industrial centre. The modern lower town is pleasant, while the old upper town is quiet, picturesque and evocative of the past. It also has many delightful, old cake shops whose windows are filled with the small yellow cakes that are a local speciality, the "polenta e osei."

- **Information:** Viale Vittorio Emanuele II, ☎035 21 02 04; www.comune.bergamo. it. Città Alta: vicolo Aquila Nera, 2, ☎035 24 22 26.
- ▶ **Orient Yourself:** Bergamo is crowned by the old town of Bergamo Alta, and can be seen from the A4 motorway. The town is 50km/30mi from Milan.
- **Parking:** Parking outside the walls of the Citta Alta.
- **Don't Miss:** Piazza Vecchia in the Citta Alta.
- **Organizing Your Time:** Allow a day for Bergamo. It is also an ideal base for excursions into mountain valleys nearby and visits to Lakes Como, d'Iseo and Garda.
- **Especially for Kids:** Exquisite nativity scenes at the Museo del Presepio and Commedia dell'Arte performances.
- **Also See:** BRESCIA, MILANO, REGIONE DEI LAGHI.

A Bit of History

The Gauls seized the settlement in 550 BC and called it Berghem. The Romans renamed it Bergomum when they took over in 196 BC. The city was destroyed by the barbarians, before enjoying a period of peace under the Lombards and, in particular, Queen Theodolinda. An independent commune from the 11C to the 13C, it then joined the Lombard League against the Emperor Frederick Barbarossa. The town suffered during the struggles between the Guelphs (followers of the pope) and the Ghibellines (followers of the emperor). Under the rule of **Bartolomeo Colleoni** (1400-75), the town fell first to the Visconti family from Milan and then to the Republic of Venice, which the mercenary leader served successively. Bergamo came under Austrian rule in 1814 and was liberated by Garibaldi in 1859.

Masques and Bergamasques – In addition to a large group of local artists, namely Previtali, Moroni, Cariani,

---

Address Book

WHERE TO EAT

☺ **Osteria D'Ambrosio** –
Via Broseta 58/A, Bergamo città bassa –
☎035 40 29 26 – Closed Sat lunchtime,
Sun and public holidays, 5-25 Aug,
25 Dec, Easter – ☐ – Reseverations
recommended. An authentic, rustic-style osteria (tavern). Warm welcome assured by the rather eccentric but friendly proprietor. Communal-style eating, at basic tables, but with truly old-fashioned prices. Regional cuisine.

☺☺ **Baretto di San Vigilio** –
Via Castello 1, San Vigilio – 5min
from the funicular in the città alta –
☎035 25 31 91 – www.baretto.it – Closed
Mon, Jan, Feb and Nov. This cosy café-restaurant is right at the funicular stop. The food is both traditional and imaginative. The menu includes some regional and local specialities, as well as delicious pastries. Seating outside in summer, with the added attraction of wonderful views over the town.

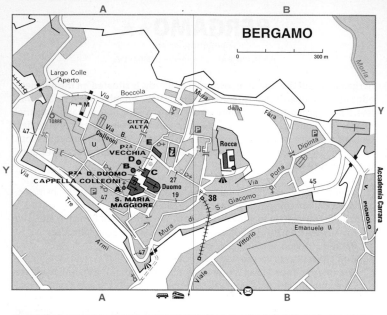

BERGAMO

0   300 m

BERGAMO		Gombito V.	AY	27	Viale delle	BY	45
Colleoni V. B.	AY	Mercato delle Scarpe Pza	BY	38	Mura di S. Grata	AY	47
Donizetti V. G.	AY 19	Mura di S. Agostino					

Battistero	AY	B	Palazzo della Ragione	AY	C	Torre	AY	D
Palazzo Scamozziano	AY	E	Tempietto di Santa Croce	AY	A			

Baschenis and Fra Galgario, numerous others worked in the town, including **Lorenzo Lotto**, Giovanni da Campione and Amadeo. Bergamo is also the home of the composer Donizetti (1797-1848). The vivacity of the people is displayed in the local musical folklore: the Bergamasque, a lively dance, is accompanied by pipers playing their *pifferi*.

Kids The **Commedia dell'Arte** originated at Bergamo in the 16C. The comedy consists of an improvisation *(imbroglio)* based on a pre-arranged theme *(scenario)*, with gags *(lazzi)* uttered by masked actors representing stock characters: the valet (Harlequin), a stubborn but wily peasant from the Brembana Valley, the braggart (Pulcinella) the lady's maid (Columbine), the lover (Pierrot), the knave (Scapino), the old fox (Scaramouch), the clown (Pantaloon) and the musician (Mezzetino). This form of theatre was popular in France in the 17C and 18C.

Visit

Città Alta★★★
You can either drive or take the funicular *(station in Viale Vittorio Emanuele II)*, which ends in **Piazza del Mercato delle Scarpe** (Square of the Shoe Market). ⓟOutside the walls.

Piazza Vecchia★
The writer Stendhal once called this historic center "the most beautiful place on earth." The **Palazzo della Ragione**, Italy's oldest town hall, dates from 1199, but was rebuilt in the 16C. It has graceful arcades, trefoil openings and a central balcony surmounted by the Lion of St Mark, symbolising Venetian rule. A 14C covered stairway leads to the majestic 12C tower with its 15C clock. ⓞ*Open Apr-Oct Tue-Fri, 9.30am-7pm, Sat-Sun and public holidays 9.30am-9.30pm; Nov-Mar by appointment only (minimum of 5 people), Sat-Sun and public holidays 9.30am-4.30pm.* ⓞ*Closed Mon.* ⌂*3 €, combined*

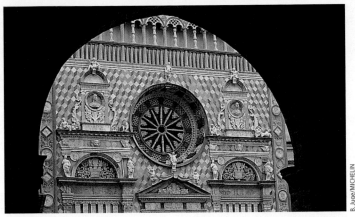

Cappella Colleoni, delicate Renaissance trefoil work.

B. Juge/MICHELIN

ticket with other museums in the town. ☎035 24 71 16; www.bergamoestoria.it. The **Palazzo Scamozziano** opposite is in the Palladian style. The Doge of Venice, Alvise Contarini, offered the central fountain to Genoa in 1780.

▶ Through Palazzo della Ragione head toward **Piazza del Duomo,**★★ bordered by the chief monuments of the upper town.

Cappella Colleoni★★

&. ○Open daily except Mon, Mar-Oct 9am-12.30pm and 2-6.30pm; Nov-Feb 9.30am-12.30pm and 2-4.30pm. ○Closed 1 Jan, 25 Dec. ⊛ Donations welcome. ☎035 21 00 61.

The architect of the Carthusian monastery at Pavia, **Amadeo**, designed the chapel (1470-76), a jewel of Lombard-Renaissance architecture. Bartolomeo Colleoni asked that this mausoleum stand on the sacristy site of the basilica of St Mary Major. The funerary chapel opens into the basilica's northern side.

The elegant **façade** is faced with precious multicoloured marble. Its delicate sculptures include figures of children *(putti)*, fluted and wreathed columns, pilasters, vases and candelabra.

The **interior** is sumptuously decorated with low reliefs of extraordinary delicacy: frescoes by Tiepolo and Renaissance stalls with intarsia work. The **Colleoni monument**, also by Amadeo, is surmounted by an equestrian statue of the leader in gilded wood. The low reliefs of the sarcophagi show scenes from the New Testament, separated by niches housing statues of the Virtues. Between the two crypts are portraits of the leader's children. His favourite daughter, Medea, who died at the age of 15, lies near him *(to the left)*, in a delicate tomb by Amadeo.

Basilica di Santa Maria Maggiore★

○Open daily, summer 9am-12.30pm and 2.30-6pm (winter 5pm). ⊛ Donations welcome. ☎035 22 33 27; www.lombardiacultura.it.

This church, dedicated to St Mary Major, is 12C. However, the two lovely north and south **porches** – with loggias and supported by lions in the Lombard Romanesque style – were added in the 14C by Giovanni da Campione. The interior, remodelled in the Baroque style (late 16C-early 17C), features stucco and gilding. The walls of the aisles and the chancel are hung with nine splendid Florentine **tapestries**★★ (1580-86), beautifully designed after cartoons by Alessandro Allori, which relate the Life of the Virgin. On the nave's west wall hangs a sumptuous Flemish tapestry depicting the **Crucifixion**★★. The tapestry was woven in Antwerp from 1696-8 after cartoons by L Van Schoor. This part of the church also contains Donizetti's tomb (1797-1848). Incorporated in the chancel screen are four superb panels of 16C **intarsia work**★★ depicting Old Testament scenes.

▶ Leave by the door giving onto Piazza di Santa Maria Maggiore to admire the 14C south porch, as well as the charming **Tempietto Santa Croce,** which was built on the quatrefoil plan in the early-Romanesque style. To return to Piazza del Duomo, walk round the basilica's **east end**★, where radiating chapels are decorated with graceful arcading

Battistero★

This charming octagonal baptistery is encircled by a red Verona marble gallery and 14C statues representing the Virtues. It is a reconstruction of Giovanni da Campione's original 13C work. It originally graced the east end of the nave of St Mary Major but was deemed too cumbersome and was demolished in 1660 and rebuilt in 1898.

♿ *Duomo; Via Bartolomeo Colleoni (Luogo Pio Colleoni); Rocca (views★).*

Città Bassa★

Piazza Matteotti is at the centre of the present-day business and shopping district in the lower town. Market days are Monday and Saturday.

Accademia Carrara★★

♿⏱*Open 10am-1pm and 2.30-5.30pm (last admission 30min before closing time).* ⏱*Closed Mon (except festivals).* ✎ *2.60 €, no charge Sun.* ☎*035 39 96 77; www.accademiacarrara.bergamo.it.*

This collection of 15C-18C Italian and foreign paintings is housed in a neo-Classical palace.

Beyond the early-15C works, hang two important portraits of **Giuliano de'Medici** by Botticelli and the refined one of **Lionello d'Este** by Pisanello. These are followed by works of the Venetian school: by the Vivarini family, Carlo Crivelli, Giovanni Bellini, Carpaccio and Lorenzo Lotto.

Next come the late-15C and early-16C works represented by Cosmè Tura, master of the Ferrarese school (a very realistic *Virgin and Child* showing the influence of Flemish art), by the Lombard Bergognone (soft light), and by the local artist,

Previtali.The 16C covers works by the Venetian masters, Titian and Tintoretto, and a particularly rich group of 16C **portraits** from the Ferrarese school, which specialised in this art.

Foreign artists include Clouet *(Portrait of Louis de Clèves)* and Dürer. The 17C-18C Bergamo school is represented by Baschenis (1617-77) and excellent portraits by Fra Galgario (1655-1743). The 17C Flemish and Dutch section is dominated by a Van Goyen seascape.

Old Quarter★

The main street of this quarter is **Via Pignolo**★ which winds among old palaces, mostly 16C and 18C and churches containing numerous works of art. Among these are the **church of San Bernardino,** which has in the chancel a **Virgin Enthroned and Saints**★ (1521) by Lorenzo Lotto. Another highlight is **Santo Spirito**, which contains a *St John the Baptist Surrounded by Saints* and a polyptych by Previtali and a *Virgin and Child* by Lorenzo Lotto.

Piazza Matteotti★

This immense square is in the centre of the modern town. It is flanked by the **Sentierone**, the favourite promenade of the citizens of Bergamo. In the square stand the **Donizetti Theatre** and the **Church of San Bartolomeo,** which houses the **Martinengo Altarpiece** by Lorenzo Lotto depicting the enthroned Virgin surrounded by saints.

Excursions

San Pellegrino Terme⚱⚱

(8km/5mi southwest. 4km/2.5mi from the Dalmine motorway exit. Follow directions for the museum.) **Museo del Presepio**★

Kids ⏱*Open Dec-Jan Mon-Fri 2-6pm, Sun and public holidays 9am-noon and, 2–7pm, Feb-Nov, Sun and public holidays 2-6pm.* ✎ *3.50 €.* ☎*035 56 33 83; www. museodelpresepio.com.*

Over 800 nativity scenes are on display at the Museo del Presepio. The smallest fits in a nutshell, the largest is a 17-minute animatronic spectacle that sprawls over 80 sq m/262 sq ft.

BOLOGNA★★

POPULATION 374 500
MICHELIN MAP 562 AND 563 I 15-16
(TOGETHER WITH TOWN PLAN) – EMILIA-ROMAGNA.

Bologna often is portrayed as being *dotta, grassa e rossa* (learned, self-indulgent and "red"). The city is indeed wise, thanks to its university: Europe's oldest, alongside its peer in Paris. The self-indulgence associated with "Bologna the Fat" – its Italian nickname – refers to the agricultural abundance and its gastronomic opulence, which has enshrined it as the country's food capital. Its "redness," which over time has acquired political connotations, refers to the colour of its masonry. Its buildings, towers and 37km/23mi of arcades all buzz with activity, which helped earn the "Cultural Capital of Europe" title in 2000.

- **Information:** Piazza Maggiore 6, ☎051 24 65 41.
- **Orient Yourself:** Bologna is well placed for access to the Adriatic and Tuscan coasts, as well as the Dolomites. The city is situated at an important motorway interchange, with access to A 1, A 14 to the Adriatic and A 13. It is also near the beginning of A 22, the Brenner transalpine route.
- **Parking:** Driving in Bologna can be difficult. ⚠ Private traffic is forbidden downtown from 7am–8pm.There are car parks located near public transport interchanges or stations.
- **Don't Miss:** Piazza Maggiore, the Torre pendenti, Basilica di Santo Stefano and the Maestà by Cimabue in Santa Maria dei Servi.
- **Organizing Your Time:** Scratch the surface of Bologna in a day, but allow two for a fuller experience.
- **Especially for Kids:** The city hosts the world's largest fair of children's books each April, so bookstores here are always well-stocked. Families also enjoy the Torri pendenti.
- **Also See:** *DELTA DEL PO, FAENZA, FERRARA, MODENA, PARMA.*

A Bit of History

The Etruscan settlement of *Felsina* was conquered in the 4C BC by the Boïan Gauls, whom the Romans then drove out in 190 BC. Their settlement, *Bononia,* fell under the sway of the barbarians until the 12C. In the subsequent century, the city enjoyed the status of an independent commune and developed rapidly. A fortified city was built, and the university flourished.

Against the Ghibellines and the emperor, Bologna supported the Guelphs, partisans of communal independence. The latter won, defeating the Imperial Army of Frederick II at Fossalta in 1249. The emperor's son, Enzo, was taken prisoner and remained at Bologna until his death 23 years later.

In the 15C, following violent clan struggles, the city fell to the **Bentivoglio** family whose rule continued until 1506.

The city then remained under papal control, until the arrival of Napoleon Bonaparte. The Austrians severly repressed several insurrections in the early 19C. Bologna was united with Piedmont in 1860.

Famous citizens include the Popes Gregory XIII, who established our present Gregorian calendar (1582).

The Bologna School of Painting was an artistic movement founded by the brothers Agostino (1557-1602) and Annibale (1560-1609) with their cousin Ludovico (1555-1619) **Carracci**. They reacted against Mannerism with more "classical" compositions that tried to express a simple spirituality. Numerous artists –in particular the Bolognese painters **Francesco Albani**, **Guercino**, **Domenichino** and **Guido Reni** – followed this movement, known as the **Accademia degli Incamminati** (Academy of the Eclectic), stressing the study of nature. In 1595 Annibale Carracci

Address Book

GETTING ABOUT

By car – Situated 100km/62mi from Florence, 200km/125mi from Milan and 150km/93mi from Venice, Bologna is at a key intersection of a busy motorway network. ▣Those intending to stay in the city for a while, should park and use public transport to get around.

By train – The railway station is in Piazza Medaglie d'Oro, at the end of Via dell'Indipendenza. Buses nos 17 and 25 go to Piazza Maggiore.

By plane – Guglielmo Marconi airport is situated 6km/4mi northwest of the city in Borgo Panigale. It is served by major national and international airline companies, which connect it to major Italian and European cities.

The Aerobus – The Airbus offers a fast connection between the airport and the city centre, the railway station and the exhibition hall (*fiera*) district. Journey time between the railway station and airport is 15min. It runs from 5.20am to midnight (departures every 30min) and costs 5 € (including luggage transport) for a full journey; 2.50 € for intermediate stops. Purchase tickets at ATC offices, automated machines or on board. For information contact ☎051 29 02 90, www.atc.bo.it

Public transport – Bologna has a wide network of public transport. For information call ☎051 29 02 90. Purchase tickets at ATC offices, authorised vendors and automated machines. There are various types of tickets: the City pass (6.50 €) provides 8 journeys, no more than 60min long in the daytime, no more than 70min from 8.30pm to 6.30am, and can be used by one or more people at the same time; one-day tickets (3 €) are valid for 24hr from the moment they are validated; one-hour tickets (1 €) are valid for 60min in the daytime and for 70min between 8.30pm and 6.30am.

Taxis – CO.TA.BO. (Cooperativa Taxisti Bolognesi) radiotaxi ☎051 37 27 27 and C.A.T. (Consorzio Autonomo Taxisti) radiotaxi ☎051 53 41 41.

VISITING

Visitors can obtain a pass *(La Carta Bologna dei Musei)* to all the municipal museums in the city. Purchase tickets at the museums (marked with a diamond symbol) or the ATC offices. *Tariff:* ⊜ *6 € (valid for one day) or 8P (valid for 3 days). For coin ranges see Legend at the back of the guide.*

WHERE TO EAT

⊜ **Da Bertino** – *Via delle Lame 55 – ☎051 52 22 30 – Closed Sun, Sat pm (summer), Mon pm (winter), August, 1 Jan, 25 Dec –* ▤. An old-fashioned, traditional trattoria with a loyal following. Typical Bolognese dishes. Mouthwatering starters and home-made pasta dishes.

⊜ **Gigina** – *Via Henri Beyle Stendhal 1 – 4018 Bologna – 4km/2.4mi northeast of the centre – ☎051 32 23 00 – Closed 23 Dec-2 Jan and two weeks in Aug. – Reservations recommended.* Located just outside the city, this family-run trattoria has a good reputation for traditional food including regional specialities. The cooking is homely and the atmosphere cosy. Warm welcome.

⊜⊜ **Teresina** – *Via Oberdan 4 – 41026 Bologna – ☎051 22 89 85 –Closed Sun, 10-30 Aug –* ▱ - *Reservations recommended. Busy trattoria*, with a menu featuring a little of everything. Simple surroundings inside, if a little cramped. Alfresco dining in the summer.

⊜⊜ **Conte Bistrot** – *Via Rolandino 1/2 – 40122 Bologna –☎051 22 55 05 – www. ilcontebistrot.com – Closed Sat and Sun, 10-20 Aug.* Located within the precincts of the church of San Domenico, this fashionable bistro-restaurant is popular with the locals. Eclectic menu which recommends fish and seafood dishes to start with, followed by foie gras.

WHERE TO STAY

Note that most hotels have higher tariffs when exhibitions are being held at the *fiera* (exhibition hall). Check prices by telephone beforehand and book well in advance.

⊜⊜ **Albergo Accademia** – *Via delle Belle Arti 6 – 40126 Bologna – ☎051 23 23 18 – Fax 051 56 35 –* ▱ ▣ *– 28 rm –* ⊟. An unpretentious but comfortable hotel in the historic centre. Modern and functional rooms, some without bath (these are cheaper). The hotel also has a garage (at a charge) which is a rare luxury in the historic centre of Bologna.

⊖⊜ **Albergo San Vitale** – *Via San Vitale 94 – 40125 Bologna – ☎051 22 59 66 – Fax 051 23 93 96 –* ⊠ *– 17 rm.* This pleasant, well-kept hotel was originally an old convent (of which the garden remains). The rooms are simple but comfortable. Excellent value for money.

⊖⊜ **Albergo Villa Azzurra** – *Viale Felsina 49 – 5km/3mi east of the historic centre, take Strada Maggiore – 40139 Bologna (5km/3mi east of the historic centre, take Strada Maggiore) – ☎051 53 54 60 – Fax 051 53 13 46 – Closed 10-20 Aug –* ⊠ *– 15 rm.* This is a peaceful hotel located in an attractive old villa with a pretty garden. Rooms are large and tastefully decorated. No credit cards. Very convenient for those arriving in Bologna by car who don't require accommodation in the city centre and are looking for a little peace and quiet.

⊖⊜ **Albergo Centrale** – *Via della Zecca 2 – 40121 Bologna – ☎051 22 51 14 – Fax 051 23 51 62 – Closed 10 days in Aug – 25 rm.* Housed in a fine old building, the hotel is light and airy. Rooms are spacious and pleasantly simple. Room 9 has preserved its original Art Deco furnishings. Rooms with a shared bathroom are cheaper.

⊖⊜⊜ **Hotel Roma** – *Via Massimo d'Azeglio 9 – 40123 Bologna – ☎051 22 63 22 – Fax 051 23 99 09 – www.hotel-roma.biz –* [P] ⊟ *– 82 rm* ⊠ *– Restaurant.* Situated in a quiet pedestrianised street, a stone's throw from the Basilica di S. Petronio. The hotel is of a high standard, although the public areas and rooms are a little cramped. Look out for the kitsch touches, including the floral upholstery and bright red armchairs in the dining room.

⊖⊜⊜ **Hotel Corona d'Oro 1890** – *Via Oberdan 12 – ☎051 74 57 611 – Fax 051 74 57 622 – www.bolognarthotels.it –* ⊟ *– 35 rm.* ⊠. With many of the original features tastefully preserved, this elegant hotel exudes style. The wooden columns on the first floor are a testament to its 14C

structure, there are 15C-16C caisson ceilings along with a stunning Art Nouveau reception hall.

TAKING A BREAK

Osteria dell'Orsa – *Via Mentana 1/F – ☎/Fax 051 23 15 76 – www.osteriadellorsa.com – Open daily 12.30-1.30am.* Something of an institution and popular with staff and students from the University, this is a large bar where some of the best jazz musicians come and play live.

Paolo Atti & Figli – *Via Caprarie 7 – ☎051 22 04 25 – www.paoloatti.com – Open Mon-Wed, Fri 8.30am-1pm and 4.30-7.15pm, Sat 8.30am-1pm. Closed Thu and Sat afternoon, Sun (except Dec) and Aug.* Famous Art-Nouveau style bakery founded in 1880 that has numbered Giosuè Carducci and the painter Morandi among its frequenters. Also an excellent delicatessen. Specialities include the tortellini.

Tamburini – *Via Caprarie 1 – ☎051 23 47 26 – Fax 051 23 22 26 – www.tamburini.com. Open Mon-Sat 8am-7pm.* This is the smartest eatery in the area. It also serves as a delicatessen, producing and selling all the local culinary specialities. There are hams, a variety of home-made pastas and cheeses which can all be sampled there and then or, if you can bear to wait, ordered for later.

Enoteca Regionale Emilia-Romagna – *Chiesa Santa Maria dell'Assunta, Rocca Sforzesca – 45050 Dozza – 29km/17mi southeast of Bologna. – ☎0542 67 80 89 – Fax 0542 67 80 73 – www.enotecaemiliaromagna.it – Open Tue-Fri 9.30am-1pm and 2.30-6pm, Sat 10.30am-1pm and 2.3--6pm, Sun and holidays 10am-1pm and 3-6.45pm, wine bar open on Sun from 2.30-5.30pm.* Located within the fort, this large cantina has a wide selection of wines from the Emilia-Romagna region.

GOING OUT

Bottega del Vino Olindo Faccioli – *Via Altabella 15/B – ☎051 22 31 71 – Open in the evenings, daily. Closed 20 days Jul-Aug.* Handed down from father to son in 1924, this wine shop stocks more than 500 different wines Italy. A great place for discovering some of the many wines that this country produces.

Tastings at the bar or in the main reception area.

Cantina Bentivoglio – *Via Mascarella 4/B* – ☎*051 26 54 16* – *www.cantinabentivoglio.it* – *Open every evening* – *Closed Sun (in summer)*. The elegant antique furnishings make an excellent backdrop for wine tastings. The wine cellar has more than 400 wines in stock, including some very rare vintages. Live jazz in the evenings.

Enoteca des Arts – *Via San Felice 9/A* – ☎*051 23 64 22* – *Mon-Sat 4.30pm-3am. Closed Thu, Sat mornings, Sun, Aug.* A

wine bar-cantina, tucked away in a long "corridor" with vaulted ceilings, the walls feature old bottles. Popular with students at the University in Bologna who have made friends with the proprietor who is passionate about his choice of wines, Italian or otherwise.

Il Circolo Pickwick – *Via San Felice 77/A* – ☎*051 55 51 04* – *Open daily 7pm-2am* – *Closed Tues (winter) and Sun (summer)*. The pub's location, in an old pharmacy makes this a good venue for meeting friends. Serves a mix of Italian wines, English beer and Cuban cocktails.

moved to Rome to execute a commission for the Farnese family. His frescoes at Palazzo Farnese veer towards an illusionism that heralds Baroque art.

City Centre★★★

The two adjoining squares, **Piazza Maggiore** and **Piazza del Nettuno**★★★, together with **Piazza di Porta Ravegnana**★★, the heart of Bologna, form a harmonious ensemble.

Fontana del Nettuno★★
This vigorous fountain is the work of the Flemish sculptor known as Giambologna or Giovanni Bologna (1529-1608). The gigantic muscular bronze Neptune (Nettuno), is surrounded by four sirens spouting water from their breasts.

Palazzo Comunale★
♿🕐*Open only if rooms not in use (Sala Rossa, Sala del Consiglio, Cappella and Sala Farnese, Cappella Palatina).* ✎ *No charge.* ☎*051 21 93 629; www.comune. bologna.itit/bolognaturismo.*
The façade of the town hall is composed of buildings from 13C, through 15C to 16C and is surmounted by a statue of Pope Gregory XIII. Above and to the left of the doorway is a statue of the *Virgin and Child* (1478) in terracotta by Niccolò dell'Arca. At the far end of the courtyard, under a gallery on the left, rises a great ramp, the so-called *Scala dei cavalli* (for horse-drawn carriages) leading to the first-floor rooms. Open-

ing off the vast Farnese Gallery with 17C frescoes are the splendid rooms, at one time Cardinal Legato's rooms, now the **Collezioni comunali d'arte**, the town's art collections, with sections on furniture, the decorative arts and a selection of Emilian **paintings**★ (14C-19C). They also house the **Museo Morandi**★, which boasts the largest collection of works by the painter and engraver from Bologna as well as a reconstruction of the artist's studio. *Exhibitions:* ♿🕐*Open 9am-3pm, Sun and public holidays 10am-6.30pm.* 🕐*Closed Mon, 1 Jan, 25 Dec. Donations welcome.* ☎*051 21 93 629; www.comune. bologna.it. Museum:* ♿🕐*Open 10am-3pm, Sat, Sun and public holidays 10am-6.30pm.* 🕐*Closed Mon, 1 Jan, 1 May, 25 Dec* ✎*Donations welcome.* ☎*051 21 93 332; www.museomorandi.it.*

Palazzo del Podestà★
The Palazzo del Podestà and the Palazzo di re Enzo are open during exhibitions and special events. ☎*051 20 30 40.*
The Renaissance façade of the Governor's Palace facing Piazza Maggiore has arcades separated by Corinthian columns on the ground floor. The 13C **King Enzo's Palace** (Palazzo di Re Enzo) stands next to it, with a fine courtyard.

Basilica di San Petronio★★
Building on the basilica, dedicated to St Petronius, began in 1390 to the plans of Antonio di Vincenzo (1340-1402) and completed in the 17C. The façade is remarkable chiefly for the expressive

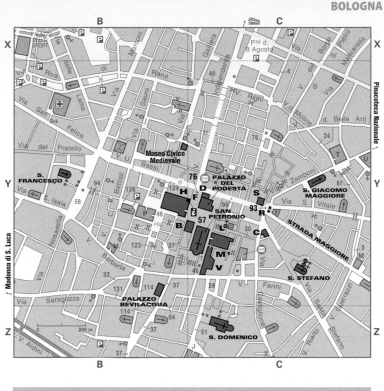

reliefs on its **doorway**★★ created by Jacopo della Quercia.

The immense **interior** has many **works of art**★ including frescoes by Giovanni da Modena (15C) in the first and the fourth chapels. Particularly striking is the fourth chapel, the right wall of which depicts the *Journey of the Kings* and the left wall an impressive *Inferno* and *Paradise*. Additional works include a *Martyrdom of St Sebastian* by the late-15C Ferrara school in the fifth chapel and the tomb of Elisa Baciocchi, Napoleon's sister, in the seventh chapel.

Near the basilica is the Museo Civico Archeologico (*see below*) and the 16C Bishop's Palace (Palazzo dell'-Archiginnasio), the home of an extensive library (10 000 manuscripts) and the 17C-18C Anatomy Theatre (Teatro Anatomico). ⚹⊙*Open 9am-1.45pm.* ⊙*Closed Sun and public holidays.* ⊛ *Donations welcome.* ☏*051 27 68 11. Fax 051 26 11 60; www.comune.bologna.it/ archiginnasio.*

⚹In the nearby **Santa Maria della Vita**, note the dramatic **Mourning of Christ**★, a terracotta by Nicolò dell'Arca (15C).

An Exceptional Talent

The still-life painter **Giorgio Morandi** (1890-1964) lived most of his life in his native Bologna. Morandi used a limited palette of ochre, blue, white, ivory, brown and grey to portray a rigorous world, characterised by the absence of the human figure and by a restrained intensity. Bottles, vases, carafes, fruit bowls, all skilfully composed and re-composed in a myriad of variations, make up pictograms, while his geometric, subtle landscapes show the influence of Cézanne.

To the left of the Palazzo Comunale stands the austere 14C-15C Notaries' Palace (Palazzo dei Notari).

Torri pendenti★★

These two leaning towers in Piazza di Porta Ravegnana belonged to noble families and are symbols of the continual conflict between the rival Guelphs and Ghibellines in the Middle Ages. The taller, **Torre degli Asinelli**, nearly 100m/330ft high, dates from 1109. It is worth climbing the 486 steps that lead to the top in order to admire a **panorama**★★ of the city. The second, **Torre Garisenda**, is 50m/165ft high and has a tilt of over 3m/10ft. *Torre degli Asinelli:* ○*Open daily summer 9am-6pm, rest of the year 9am-5pm.* ⊘ *3 €. www.comune. bologna.it/bolognaturismo.*
The 14C Mercanzia or Merchants' House, in the next square, bears the coats of arms of the various guilds.

Outside the Centre

Chiesa di San Giacomo Maggiore★

○*Open daily 7am-noon and 3.30-6pm.* ⊘*Donations welcome.* ☎*051 22 59 70; http://web.tiscalinet.it/agostiniani/* ⊘**Cappella Bentivoglio**
The church, dedicated to St James the Great, was founded in 1267. On the north side is a fine Renaissance portico. Inside is the magnificent **Cappella Bentivoglio★**. Its frescoes depict *The Triumph of Fame and Death* and the beautiful *Madonna Enthroned with the Bentivoglio Family*, both by the Ferrarese painter Lorenzo Costa. The chapel also houses a masterpiece of Francesco Francia, the *Madonna Enthroned and Saints* (c 1494). Opposite the chapel, in the ambulatory, stands the **tomb**★ (c 1433) of the jurist, Antonio Bentivoglio, by Jacopo della Quercia.
St Cecilia's Chapel *(entrance on Via Zamboni 15)* is a small church, founded in the 13C with additions made in the 15C. Inside there are remarkable **frescoes**★ depicting St Cecilia (1506) by F Francia, L Costa and A Aspertini.

▷ *Further along via Zamboni is the Pinacoteca Nazionale (⊘see below).*

Strada Maggiore★

Along this elegant street, lined with some fine palaces (note Casa Isolani at no 19, a rare example of 13C architecture with a wooden portico) is the **Museo d'Arte industriale e Galleria**

B. Juge/MICHELIN

The composite façade of the Palazzo Comunale with the statue of Pope Gregorio XIII

Davia Bargellini, housed in an attractive palace dating from 1658 (at no 44), which has collections of "industrial art" (applied and decorative arts) and paintings from the 14C-18C. ○*Open 9am-2pm, Sun and public holidays 9am-1pm.* ○*Closed Mon, 1 Jan, 1 May, 25 Dec.* ⊜ *No charge.* ☏*051 23 67 08.* A little further down, on the right, is the church of **Santa Maria dei Servi** (founded in the 14C) which is heralded by a Renaissance quadrisection **portico**★. Inside, in the third chapel on the right, there is a **Maestà**★★ by Cimabue.

Basilica di Santo Stefano★

○*Open daily, 9am-12.15pm and 3.30-6.15pm.* ⊜ *Donations welcome.* ☏*051 22 32 56; www.abbaziasantostefano.it.* The basilica comprises a group of buildings (originally seven) overlooking the square with its Renaissance mansions. Entrance is through the **Church of the Crucifix** (Crocifisso), an old Lombard cathedral restored in the 11C and remodelled in the 19C. Turning left make for the atmospheric 12C **Church of the Holy Sepulchre** (Santo Sepolcro) and the shrine of Bologna's patron saint, St Petronius. The black cipolin marble columns were originally part of the ancient Temple of Isis (AD 100), which was turned into a baptistery and later into a church. The font, originally consecrated with water from the Nile, was re-consecrated with water from the Jordan River. Go through the Church of the Holy Sepulchre to reach the charming **Court of Pilate** (11C-12C) and, from there, through to the **Church of the Trinity** (Trinità), 13C, the old *Martyrium* (4C-5C) where the bodies of martyrs were brought.

Chiesa di San Domenico★

The church, dedicated to St Dominic, was built at the beginning of the 13C and remodelled in the 18C. It houses the beautiful **tomb**★★★ (*arca*): the fine sarcophagus is by Nicola Pisano (1267), while the arch with statues (1468-73) crowning it was executed by Niccolò da Bari, who was afterwards known as Niccolò dell'Arca, and completed by Michelangelo in 1494 with the two missing saints (Saint Procolo and Saint

Petronius) and the angel on the right. The finial by Niccolò celebrates the creation, symbolised by *putti* (sky), garlands (earth) and dolphins (sea).

The chapel to the right of the presbytery has a fine painting by Filippino Lippi, the **Mystic Marriage of St Catherine** (1501).

○In Via D'Azeglio, is **Palazzo Bevilacqua**★, a Renaissance palace.

Chiesa di San Francesco★

This church was erected in the 13C and is one of the first examples of Gothic architecture in Italy. Inside, at the high altar, is a marble **altarpiece**★ (1392), by the Venetian sculptor Paolo dalle Masegne. The Museo Civico Medievale is nearby (○*see below*).

Museums

Pinacoteca Nazionale★★

Via Belle Arti 56, entrance on Via Zamboni. ○**St Cecilia** by Raphael and the **Carracci Room**. ○○*Open daily 9am-7pm.* ○*Closed Mon.* ⊜ *4 €.* ☏*051 42 09 411; www.pinacotecabologna.it.*

An important collection, predominantly of the Bolognese school (13C to 18C). Among the works are the energetic **St George and the Dragon**★ by Vitale da Bologna and Giotto's *Madonna Enthroned and Child*. The section on Renaissance painting boasts Perugino's **Virgin and Child**★ – a profound

---

The Lord's Dogs

St Dominic was born in Spain in 1170. His mother was Blessed Joan de Aza de Guzmán who, when pregnant, had a vision that her unborn child was a dog bearing a torch, symbolising truth and the flame of faith. In 1216, St Dominic founded the Order of Preachers, more commonly known as the Dominicans. This name came from the Latin name for the legend (*Domini canes*, the Lord's dogs), and the dog and torch sometimes appear in representations of St Dominic. He established a friary in Bologna and died there in 1221.

influence on the Bolognese school – and **St Cecilia**★★ by Raphael, who portrays renunciation with symbolic instruments abandoned on the ground.

The **Carracci Room**★★ contains numerous masterpieces by Ludovico, one of the great interpreters of the new spirituality of the Counter-Reformation with his blend of quiet intimacy and high emotion: the graceful *Annunciation*, the *Bargellini Madonna*, the *Madonna degli Scalzi* and the dramatic *Conversion of St Paul,* which heralds Baroque painting. Of Agostino Carracci note the *Communion of St Jerome* and of Annibale Carracci's work, the *Assumption of the Virgin*, a masterpiece and early example of Baroque painting. The **Guido Reni Room** houses some stunning work by this painter. In the famous **Massacre of the Innocents,** the eternal moment is captured in the balance of architecture and figures forming a reversed triangle. The intense **Portrait of a Widow**, generally thought to be a portrait of the artist's mother – is considered one of the finest portraits in Italian 17C painting. In the **Baroque corridor** is **St William**★, an early masterpiece of Baroque art by Guercino. Of 18C painting note the

works by Giuseppe Maria Crespi, one of the major painters of 18C Italy including the **Courtyard Scene**★.

Museo Civico Medievale

&.🕐*Open Apr-Dec, Tue-Fri 9am-3pm, Sat, Sun and public holidays 10am-6.30pm, rest of the year 9am-6.30pm (closed Sun).* 🕐*Closed 1 Jan, 1 May, 25 Dec.* ✉ *Free entry.* ☎*051 21 93 930; www.comune.bologna.it*

The Medieval Civic Museum is housed in the **Palazzo Fava-Ghisilardia** (late 15C) which stands on the site of the Imperial Roman palace. The collections relate the development of art in Bologna from the Middle Ages to the Renaissance.

Excursion

Madonna di San Luca
5km/3mi southwest. Leave the city centre by Via Saragozza.

The 18C church is linked to the city by a **portico**★ (4km/2.5mi long) of 666 arches. In the chancel is the Madonna of St Luke, a painting in the 12C Byzantine style. There is a lovely **view**★ of Bologna and the Apennines.

BOLZANO★
BOZEN
POPULATION 97 236
MICHELIN MAP 562 C 15-16, TOWN PLAN IN THE MICHELIN ATLAS ITALY –
TRENTINO-ALTO ADIGE.

Nestling in a valley covered with orchards and vineyards, the industrial and commercial town of Bologna is now also a busy tourist centre. The architecture of the town shows a marked Austrian influence, which was exercised between the 16C and 1918. At the centre of the town are Piazza Walther and the delightful Via dei Portici★.

- 🛈 **Information:** Piazza Walther 8, 39100 Bolzano. ☎*0471 30 70 00. www.bolzano-bozen.it.*
- ▶ **Orient Yourself:** Capital of the Alto Adige, Bolzano lies on A 22, the Brenner transalpine route, at the confluence of the Adige and the Isarco. Bolzano anchors one end of the wine road (*Stada di Vino*).
- 🅿 **Parking:** Park at the bottom of the furnicular at Soprabolzano to travel up to the Renon Plateau.
- ☺ **Don't Miss:** Museo Archeologico dell'Alto and The Renon Plateau.
- 🕐 **Organizing Your Time:** Allow a day, with an extra half day for Renon Plateau.
- Kids **Especially for Kids:** "Ötzi" at the archaeological museum.
- ☝ **Also See:** *DOLOMITI, TRENTO*

Address Book

WHERE TO STAY
Albergo Belvedere-Schönblick – 39050 San Genesio – ☎0471 35 41 27 – Fax 0471 35 42 77 – www.schoenblick-belvedere.com – Closed 1 Jan – 🅿🖥 – 30 rm – 🛏. A short drive from Bolzano, this hotel has fine views over the city. An oasis of calm with cheerful, Tyrolean-style interior decor. High standard of cooking, local fare.

WHERE TO EAT
Vögele – Via Goethe 3 – ☎0471 97 39 38 – Fax 0471 32 57 50 – www.voegele.it – 🍽. A rustic-style eatery, situated near Piazza delle Erbe. Warm and friendly atmosphere, if a little on the noisy side. Regional cooking, wooden tables, no tablecloths. On the first floor, the dining facilities are more stylish and reserved for non-smokers.

Visit

Duomo★
Construction work on the pink sandstone cathedral was carried out between 5C and 13C. On the north side is the "Small Wine Portal" (porticina del vino) on which all the decorative features have a connection with grape harvesting. It indicates the privilege enjoyed by this church to sell wine at this doorway. Inside, there is a fine Late Gothic sandstone **pulpit★** (1514).

Museo Archeologico dell'Alto Adige, "Il Museo di Ötzi"★
♿ ⏱Open daily except Mon, 10am-5pm. ⏱Closed Mon (except Dec), 1 Jan, 1 May, 25 Dec. ⚶8 €. In order to avoid a long wait, book your tickets in advance: ☎0471 32 01 00; www.iceman.it.
This museum illustrates the chronology of the Alto-Adige region from the last Ice Age (15000 BC) to the Carolingian age (AD 800) and houses the "Iceman," known as "Ötzi," whose ice-preserved remains were found by German mountain climbers in the Ötzi Alps, in 1991. Ötzi lived in the Copper Age and is 5 300 years old. A study in 2001 concluded that his death at about 45 years old was due to an arrow wound.

Chiesa dei Francescani
Via Francescani 1. ⏱Open Mon-Sat 10am-noon and 2.30-6pm, Sun and public holidays 3-6pm. ⚶Donations welcome. ⓘThe Nativity altar. ☎0471 97 72 93.
Burnt down in 1291, the Franciscan church was rebuilt in the 14C and the Gothic vaulting added in the 15C. The **Nativity altar★** is a remarkable wooden altarpiece carved by Hans Klocker (16C).

Antica Parrocchiale di Gries
Access via Corso Libertà. Beyond Sant'Agostino.
The original Romanesque building was replaced by a 15C Gothic parish church containing a side altar with an **altarpiece★** carved by Michael Pacher (1430-98), an Austrian sculptor depicitng the Crowning of the Virgin between Archangel Gabriel, about to strike the devil, and St Erasmus, holding a winch with which to tear out his guts.

Excursions

The Renon Plateau★ (Ritten)
The Renon (Ritten in German) is the dazzlingly green fertile plateau that dominates the Isarco Valley (Eisacktal) between Bolzano and Ponte Gardena. It can be reached by car from Bolzano north or the funicular at Soprabolzano in Bolzano. ⓘRomantics may prefer to take the electric train from Maria Assunta (Maria Himmelfahrt) to Collalbo (Klobenstein).
The Renon overlooks the Dolomites, best seen from the funicular to Corno del Renon. 🅿 Parking is available at bottom of the funicular. The plateau is full of charming villages and curious erosion caused by a natural phenomenon called "earth pillars" at Soprabolzano, Monte di Mezzo and Auna di Sotto.

RIVIERA DEL **BRENTA**★★
MICHELIN MAP 562 F 18 –
35KM/22MI EAST OF PADUA – VENETO.

The Riviera del Brenta is a bucolic strip of land favoured by the Venetian nobility for summer residences. For visitors to the area, whether they arrive by water, bicycle or car, these grandiose **villas**★ – their reflections sparkling in the river that meanders from Padua to the lagoon – still exude an aristocratic quality.

- **Information:** Via Nazionale, 420 Villa Widmann Foscari, 30034 Mira Porte, ☎041 424 973, www.riviera-brenta.it.
- ▶ **Orient Yourself:** The Brenta Riviera runs along the ancient course of a river linking Padova to Venice. Standing alongside the Brenta canal between Strà and Fusina are numerous Classical villas by Palladio (*see Index*).By car take the road that follows the Brenta passing through Strà, Dolo, Mira and Malcontenta.
- **Don't Miss:** A walk around the stunning gardens at Villa Pisani.
- **Organizing Your Time:** The timing of a visit will depend on the method of getting to the Riviera (car or boat) and villas visited. For a first visit two days are recommended.
- **Also See:** *PADOVA, VENEZIA.*

Visit

Strà

The **Villa Pisani**★has a majestic garden with a delightful vista. The spacious **apartments**★of this 18C palace were decorated by artists, including Giovanni Battista Tiepolo, who painted his masterpiece, **The Apotheosis of the Pisani Family**★★. *Open Apr-Sep 8.30am-7pm, Oct-Mar 9am-4pm. Closed Mon (Tue, if Mon is a public holiday), 1 Jan, 1 May, 25 Dec. Park 2.50€, park and villa 5€.* ☎049 50 20 74.

Mira

The **Palazzo Foscarini** and **Villa Widmann-Foscari** are both 18C. The **ballroom**★of the latter is entirely decorated with frescoes. *Villa Widmann: Open daily May-Sep 10am-6pm (Apr &Oct 5pm), Nov-Mar Sat, Sun and public holidays only 10am-5pm. Closed Mon, 1 Jan, 25 Dec. 5€.* ☎041 56 00 690.

Malcontenta

Palladio built the Villa Toscari in 1574. Giovanni Battista Zelotti and Battista Franco were responsible for the frescoes. The villa was named after the wife of a Foscari, who was ill-pleased (*malcontenta*) at being consigned there. *Open May-Oct, Tue and Sat 9am-noon; other days by appointment only. Closed Mon, Nov-Apr. 7 € (Tue and Sat), 8€ (Wed-Fri).* ☎041 54 70 012; www.lamalcontenta.com.

A River Trip with a Difference…

Experience life on the "Burchiello" in the 18C – if only for a day. A modern boat follows the old 18C transport route. (if accompanied). *The "Burchiello" excursion runs from Mar to Oct. Departure from Padua (Piazzale Boschetti) on Wed, Fri and Sun at 8.15am and arrival in Venice (Pontile della Pietà 9 – Piazza degli Schiavoni) in late pm including visits to Villa Pisani, Villa Widmann (also known as Barchessa Valmerana) and Villa Foscari (known as La Malcontenta). Departure from Venice (Pontile della Pietà 9 – Piazza degli Schiavoni) on Tue, Thu and Sat at 9am; same programme but visits in reverse order. Arrival in Padua in late pm. Closed Mon. 62 €. Reservations required – contact: Il Burchiello di Sita Spa* ☎049 82 06 910; www.ilburchiello.it.

Villa Pisani, the residence of the doge Alvise Pisani

L. Pessina/MICHELIN

BRESCIA★

POPULATION 192 164

MICHELIN MAP 561 2 – LOMBARDY

The important industrial town of Brescia lies at the foot of the Lombard Pre-Alps, and has retained the regular street plan of the Roman camp (*castrum*) of Brixia. The town is dominated to the north by a medieval castle (Castello) and its bustling centre has many fine buildings from all periods: Antiquity, Romanesque, Renaissance and Baroque.

- **Information:** Piazza Loggia 6. ☎030 24 00 357; www.comune.brescia.it; for Lake Garda www.lagodigarda.it.
- ▶ **Orient Yourself:** Brescia lies on A 4, not far from Lake Garda. Four piazzas anchor downtown, just beyond the main Corso Palestro.
- **Don't Miss:** The Brescia School at the Pinacoteca Tosio Martinengo.
- **Organizing Your Time:** Allow half a day to see all the main sights.
- **Especially for Kids:** The charming clockwork figures on the clocktower opposite the Loggia and collections of armour at the Museo delle Armi Luigi Marzoli.
- **Also See:** *BERGAMO, REGIONE DEI LAGHI, VERONA*.

Visit

Piazza della Loggia★

The **Loggia**, now the town hall, dates from the end of the 15C to the beginning of the 16C. Sansovino and Palladio were among those involved in building the upper storey. **Kids** The **Clock Tower** opposite the Loggia is topped by two clockwork figures (Jacks) that strike the hours.

On the square's south side stand the palaces, **Monte di Pietà Vecchio** (1484) and **Monte di Pietà Nuovo** (1497).

Piazza Paolo VI

The 17C **Duomo Nuovo** (New Cathedral) in white marble seems to crush the **Duomo Vecchio**★(Old Cathedral), a late 11C Romanesque building that

BRESCIA		
10 Giornate V. delle	BY	22
Castellini V. N.	CZ	3
Fratelli Porcellaga V.	BY	7
Loggia Pza della	BY	9
Martiri della		
Libertà Cso	AZ	13
Mercato Pza del	BY	15
Palestro Cso	BY	
Paolo VI Pza	BY	16
Pastrengo V.	AY	17
S. Crocifissa di Rosa V.	CY	18
Vittoria Pza	BY	20
Zanardelli Cso	BZ	21

Broletto	BY	P
Loggia	BY	H
Palazzo del Monte di		
Pietà Vecchio e del		
Monte di Pietà Nuovo	BY	B
Santa Maria dei Miracoli	AZ	A

succeeded an earlier sanctuary, known as the rotunda after its shape.

Inside, there is a magnificent sarcophagus in rose-coloured marble, surmounted by a recumbent figure of a bishop, and in the chancel paintings by local artists, Moretto and Romanino. The organ was built in 1536 by Antegnati.

Pinacoteca Tosio Martinengo★

&. ⟟Open daily, Jun-Sep, 10am-1pm and 2.30-6pm; Oct-May 9.30am-1pm and 2.30-5pm. ⟟Closed Mon, 1 Jan and 25 Dec. ⟟3€. ☎030 37 74 999; www. bresciamusei.com.

The art gallery displays works of the **Brescia School**, characterised by richness of colour and well-balanced composition: religious scenes and portraits by Moretto, more sumptuous religious scenes in the Venetian manner by Romanino and other works, as well as canvases by Vincenzo Foppa and Savoldo. The works of Clouet, Raphael, the Master of Utrecht, Lorenzo Lotto and Tintoretto are also on view.

Via dei Musei★

This picturesque street has some interesting sites: the ruins of the **Capitoline Temple**★(AD 73), with the remains of the cells, the tribunal and the adjacent Roman theatre **(Teatro Romano)**. Beyond the remains of the forum is the monastery founded in AD 753 by Ansa, the wife of the last king of the Lombards, Desiderio. Legend has it that Desiderio's daughter, Ermengarda, wife of Charlemagne (who later repudiated her) died here. Included in the monastery complex were the basilica of **San Salvatore**, the Romanesque church of **Santa Maria** in Solario and the **Church of Santa Giulia**, which dates back to the

Renaissance. The complex is now the **Museo della Città**★ (city museum). The Church of Santa Giulia has a dome decorated with a fresco of God the Father giving his blessing against a star-studded sky and **Desiderio's Cross**★★ (8C-9C). 🔥🕐 *Open daily Jun-Sep 10am-6pm; Oct-May 9.30am-5.30pm.* 🕐 *Closed Mon, 1 Jan and 25 Dec.* 🎫8€. ☎030 29 78 834; www.bresciamusei.com.

Castello

Built in 1343 for the Visconti over the remains of a Roman temple, the castle was given additional bastions in the 16C and its entrance is decorated with the lion representing St Mark. It now

houses the **Museo delle Armi Luigi Marzoli**, a collection of 14C-18C arms and armour. Roman remains can be seen inside the museum. 🕐 *Open daily Jun-Sep 10am-5pm; Oct-May 9.30am-1pm and 2.30-5pm.* 🕐 *Closed Mon, 1 Jan and 25 Dec.* 🎫3 €. ☎030 29 32 92; www.bresciamusei.com.

🔥 S. Francesco★ (8C); S. Maria dei Miracoli (façade★); S.S. Nazaro e Celso (*Coronation of the Virgina* by Moretto); S. Alessandro (*Annunciation*★ by Jacopo Bellini, *Descent from the Cross*★ by Civerchio); S. Agata (*Virgin of Pity*★ by the 16C Brescian School and the *Virgin with Coral*★).

BRINDISI

POPULATION 87 935

MICHELIN MAP 564 F 35 – PUGLIA.

Its name probably derives from the Greek Brenteséion (stag head), evoking the shape of the old city, which was enclosed by two "seni" (breasts) of water surrounding it from east and west. Trajan replaced the old Appian Way beyond Benevento with the new Via Traiana, increasing Brindisi's importance from AD 109 onwards. After the Norman conquest, the town became a port of embarkation for the Crusades to the Holy Land, and in particular the Sixth Crusade (1228).

- **Information:** Via XXIV Maggio 26, 72100 Lecce. ☎0832 230 033. www.pugliaturismo.com.
- **Orient Yourself:** This important naval and trading port lies on the Adriatic side of the 'boot's heel'. By car it is on S 379. Corso Umberto and Corso Garibaldi pierce through the centre, where the most interesting monuments are located.
- **Don't Miss:** A visit to the imposing Chiesa di Santa Maria del Casale.
- **Organizing Your Time:** The city centre and its churches and monuments can be seen in half a day.
- **Also See:** *LECCE, PUGLIA, TARANTO.*

Visit

The centre contains the most interesting monuments. Principal access to the old city was through the 13C **Porta Mesagne**, which was opened in the 13C. The 13C **Swabian Castle** (Castello Svevo) guards the Seno di Ponente; the castle was built on the iniative of Frederick II and today houses the Navy. The two marble **Roman columns** that stand on the cape probably denoted the end of the Appian Way.

Piazza Duomo

The square is overlooked by the Balsamo Loggia (at the corner of Tarantini), which dates from the 14C, the Portico of the Knights Templar (14C) and the Romanesque cathedral (Duomo), rebuilt in the 18C. Inside, at the end of the north aisle and around the high altar are remains of the old mosaic flooring.

The piazza also houses the **Museo Archeologico F. Ribezzo.** Note in particular the collection of Apulian, Messapici and Attic vases. *Tour: Open Mon-Fri, 9am-1pm, also Tue, Thu and Sat 3.30-6.30pm. Closed Sun and public holidays. No charge.* ☎0831 56 55 08; www.museo.brindisi.it.

Chiese

The historic centre contains numerous churches. The church of **San Giovanni al Sepolcro** is a Templar church erected in the 11C. The small Romanesque church of **Santa Lucia** has 13C fresco remains in its interior (unfortunately these are very patchy). Underneath the church stands the old Basilian structure with its vaulted ceiling. The walls are covered with fine **frescoes** (12C), such as the Virgin and Child and, on the right, the *Maddalena Mirrofora* (Magdalene bearing Myrrh).

Excursion

Chiesa di Santa Maria del Casale★

www.santamariadelcasale.net.

This is a splendid 14C Romanesque-Gothic building built by Philip d'Anjou and his wife Catherine of Flanders. The exterior, enlivened by bi-coloured geometric patterns, is characterised by a porch crowned by an embellishment consisting of Lombard arches that mirror the recurring motif of the eaves. The interior has an interesting cycle of frescoes from the same period in the Byzantine style, of which the superb *Day of Judgement* and the *Tree of the Cross* stand out.

CALABRIA

MICHELIN MAP 564 G-N 28-33.

Greeks colonized the southernmost tip of Italy over 2,800 years ago. The coast rivalled Athens as a cosmopolitan centre in 8 BC; the mystic philosopher Pythagoras preached vegetarianism there alongside the decadent Sybarites and Homer set part of *The Odyssey* on the Strait of Messina.

Invaders plundered this land throughout history; Byzantines, Germanic warriors, Saracens, Normans, Turks and Bourbons. Infamous for bandits and Mafia bloodshed, Calabria also has a gentle side. The sea–often purple-hued–between Gioia Tauro and Villa San Giovanni–washes the base of this craggy coast. Ionian ruins and Roman mosaics dot the farmland, rich with agritourism B&Bs. High in the crumbling mountains, five villages retain a bilingual Greek-Italian culture. In season, mushroom hunters search the slopes here among the ski chalets.

The backbone of Calabria is formed by the Pollino Massif (Pollino Mountain has an altitude of 2248m/7375ft), which is a national park, and by the Sila and Aspromonte massifs. Here, the olive groves produce excellent oil – Rossano's has a very low level of acidity – and the citrus harvest includes clementines and blond and bergamot oranges.

- **Information:** Parco Nazionale del Pollino: Via delle Freece Tricolori 6, 85048 Rotonda (Potenza), ☎0973 66 93 11, www.parcopollino.it; Parco Nazionale dell'Aspromonte: Via Aurora, 89050 Gambarie di Santo Stefano, ☎0965 74 30 60, www.parcoaspromonte.it.
- **Orient Yourself:** Calabria is in the extreme south of the Italian peninsula, covering the narrow stretch of land between the Gulf of Policastro and the Gulf of Taranto. The main access road is A 3, the Salerno-Reggio Calabria motorway.
- **Don't Miss:** The mythology and history of the town of Scilla.
- **Organizing Your Time:** Allow half a day to explore the Tyrrhenian Coast and two days for the "Toe" and along the Ionian Coast.
- **Especially for Kids:** Wolf and deer enclosures at Parco Nazionale della Calabri.
- **Also See:** *Parco Nazionale del CILENTO.*

A Bit of History

The first colonies on the Ionian coast were founded by the Greeks in the 8C BC and they, together with the Byzantines and Basilian monks (**St Basil**, father of the Greek Church, lived from c AD 330-379) shaped the early art and history of this region. In the 3C BC, Rome undertook the conquest of southern Italy, but did not establish a complete and peaceful domination until Sulla reorganised the administration of these provinces in the 1C BC. After the fall of the Roman Empire, Calabria and the neighbouring regions fell under the sway of the Lombards, Saracens and Byzantines before being reunited with the Norman kingdom of the Two Sicilies and

finally becoming part of a unified Italy in 1860. Natural disasters, such as the powerful earthquakes which struck in 1783 and 1908, famine, poverty, banditry, social and emigration problems have plagued Calabria which, thanks to agrarian reform and commitment to tourism and cultural activities, finally has occasion for real hope of a rebirth.

Features

Massiccio della Sila★★
www.paarcosila.it.
Sila has an ancient name which signifies "primordial forest": the Greek version of the word is *hyla*, the Latin *silva*. This plateau measures 1 700km2/656sq mi,

Address Book

🪙 *For coin ranges see the Legend at the back of the guide.*

WHERE TO STAY

🛏**Hotel Punta Faro** – *Località Grotticelle, Capo Vaticano – 89685 San Nicolò di Ricardi – 10km/6mi southwest of Tropea –* ☎*0963 66 31 39 - Closed 23 Sep-May –* 🅿🍴 *– 19 rm* 🛏🗝. This well-situated hotel is a stone's throw from the sea. Good parking facilities. Rooms are modern and functional. Lovely balcony with views of the Aeolian Islands and Sicily. Free umbrella.

🛏🛏**Hotel Aquila-Edelweiss** – *Via Stazione 11 – 87052 Camigliatello Silano – 31km/19mi northeast of Cosenza on S 107 –* ☎*0984 57 80 44 – Fax 0984 57 87 53 – haquila@fidad.it. – Closed Nov and Dec – 48 rm* 🛏 *–* 🗝 *€5.* A comfortable hotel, with a warm and friendly atmosphere, tucked away in the conifer woods up in the Sita. Worth a detour for the restaurant's regional specialities.

🛏🛏**Hotel Annibale** – *Via Duomo 35 – 88841 Isola di Caporizzuto – 10 km southwest of Caporizzuto –* ☎*0962 79 50 04 – Fax 0962 79 53 84 –* 🅿🍽 *– 20 rm –* 🛏. *Restaurant €27/37.* This rather rustic-style hotel is situated in the heart of an old fishing village. Rooms furnished in heavy-duty pine. The dining room boasts a large fireplace and a profusion of pans and meats hanging from the wooden ceiling. Meals served in the garden in summer, under the pergola.

WHERE TO EAT

🍽**Hostaria de Mendoza** – *Piazza degli Eroi 3 – 87036 Rende – 10km/6mi northwest of Cosenza –* ☎*0984 44 40 22 – Closed Wed, Sun (Jul and Aug), 10-18 Aug –* 🍴 *– Booking advisable –* 🛏. An unpretentious restaurant with rustic ambience, heavy wooden furnishings and a multitude of objects hanging from the walls. Genuine home cooking. During the summer, meals are served under a large wooden gazebo.

🍽**Il Normanno** – *Via Duomo 12 – 89852 Mileto – 30km/18mi southeast of Tropea on S18 –* ☎*0963 33 63 98 – www.ilnormanno.com. – Closed Mon (except Aug), 1-20 Sep –* 🍴 🛏. Attractive trattoria in the centre. Rustic-style interior with wood panelled walls. Small terraced area for dining in summer. Good, traditional home cooking.

🍽**Trattoria del Sole** – *Via Piave 14 bis – 87075 Trebisacce – 15km/9mi north of Sibari on S 106 –* ☎*0981 51 797 – Closed Sun (except 15 Jun-15 Sep).* This simple eatery is tucked away in the maze of little streets in the historic centre. Warm and friendly atmosphere. Mouthwatering selection of fish (and a few meat) dishes prepared with the freshest ingredients. Ask the proprieter for his recommendations. In summer meals are served on the terrace.

🍽🍽**Gambero Rosso** – *Via Montezemolo 65 – 89046 Marina di Gioiosa Ionica – 10km/6mi north of Locri on S 106 –* ☎*0964 41 58 06 – rist.gamberorosso@tiscali.it. – Closed Mon –* 🍽 *–* 🛏. A traditional restaurant located on the main thoroughfare. Good selection of antipasti, laid out on a large table in the entrance of the main dining room. Variety of delicious fish dishes, prepared with super fresh ingredients.

alternating prairies and forests of larch pine and beech trees.

On the Sila Grande are the two towns of Camigliatello and Lorica. About ten kilometers away from Camigliatello is the visitors' centre of the **Parco Nazionale della Calabria.** Fauna enclosures display deer and wolves in their natural habitat, viewed from wooden hides with windows. The centre also offers botanical and geological walks for visitors.

The wooden houses that dot the landscape contribute to the northern-country atmosphere, particularly along the lakes Cecita, **Arvo**★and Ampolino.

Aspromonte★

The Aspromonte Massif forms Calabria's southern tip and culminates in a peak of 1 955m/6 414ft. Fabled mushrooms sprout on this misty crag, known as "the Cloud Gatherer" or the "harsh mountain" and celebrated by Homer: "piercing the sky, with storm cloud round the peak dissolving never...No mortal man could scale it, nor as much land there, not with twenty hands and feet, so sheer are the cliffs."

Italy's most recently established national park protects chestnut trees, oaks and beeches. The massif serves as a catchment area from which radiate deep valleys eroded by fast-flowing torrents (fiumare). The wide riverbeds are dry in summer but may fill up rapidly and the waters become destructive. S 183 between S 112 and Melito di Porto Salvo runs through attractive scenery and affords numerous and often spectacular **panoramas**★★★. Watch out for shattered asphalt roads and hairpin turns in Parco Nazionale dell'Aspromonte. 0965 74 30 60, www.parcoaspromonte.it.

The Tyrrhenian Coast

Paola

St Francis of Paola was born here around 1416. A **monastery** (santuario) visited by numerous pilgrims stands 2km/1mi away up the hillside. This large group of buildings includes the basilica with a lovely Baroque exterior that enshrines the relics of the saint, cloisters and a hermitage hewn out of the rock, which contains striking votive offerings. ⏱ Open daily, summer 6.30am-1pm and 2-8pm, winter 6.30am-1pm and 2-5.30pm. 0982 58 25 18; www.sanfrancescodipaolalamezia.it/link.htm.

Tropea

Tropea is built on a sandy clifftop. Opposite stands the solitary church of **Santa Maria dell'Isola**, which clings to a rock. The most evocative reference to the past is the Romanesque-Norman **cathedral** and its original façade. The Swabian portico, grafted onto it, links the church to the bishop's residence. www.tropea.biz.

Palmi

This town perched high above the sea has a fishing harbour and a lovely sandy beach. The **Museo comunale** (Casa della Cultura, Via San Giorgio) has an **ethnographic section**★evoking the life and traditions of Calabria: local costumes, handicrafts, ceramics etc. ⏱Open daily,

8am-2pm (Thu also 3-6pm). Closed Sat, Sun and public holidays. 1.55 €. 0966 26 22 50.

Scilla★

This town, like a perfect cameo carved from the rock, has a bloody mythology. Here Ulysses confronted the monster Scilla, a woman with dog-headed tentacles, who ate six of his sailors, as well as the Sirens "on their sweet meadow lolling... bones of dead men rotting in a pile beside them and flayed skins shrivel around the spot." Opposite Scilla, near Messina, lurked Charybdis, whom Jupiter turned into a sea monster for her voracity. Three times daily she engulfed the surrounding waves. Subsequently Charybdis spurted the water out, creating a strong current. Ulysses vessel rowed past her once. During their second encounter, the epic narrowly escaped her clutches by grabbing a fig tree at the entrance of the monster's grotto.

The fisherman's district, the Chinalèa, is comprised of an intricate maze of houses and alleys going down to the water's edge. Higher up, Ruffo Castle (1255) gazes nobly over the town, while in the waters around Scilla, like the waters of Bagnara Calabra, contain numerous swordfish.

Around the "Toe" and along the Ionian Coast

Around 500km/300mi. Allow 2 days. The Graecanico mountain villages, as their ancient Greek-Italian culture is fading quickly.

Pentedattilo★

Pentedattilo is a striking ghost town, totally abandoned by its inhabitants. Once the site of a grisly ambush in the 17th century, the bloody hand prints of the slaughtered Alberti family are said to be visible, pressed in stone. Legend has it that the menacing rock resembling a hand that stands above it (in Greek pentedaktylos signifies 'five fingers') put an end to men's violence. There is some truth to this: no voices have echoed in the narrow alleyways of the town since

The Cattolica church in Stilo, a delicate expression of 10C Greek-Byzantine art

the mid-1960s as the crumbling rock was deemed unsafe.

Gerace

Gerace rises up on a hill of 480m/1 575ft. The Graecanico town has a more commercial veneer – the vast 11C Romanesque cathedral – crowned by Greek domes, courtyards and ornate pillars (pirated from ancient buildings) charges admission, which destroys the remote aura. The town's symbol is a hawk, reflected in its Greek name, hierax. Byzantines and Normans lived there together, and it was subjected to invasions by the Swabians, French and Aragonese. It was also an illustrious episcopal seat. At one time Gerace had so many churches it was known as "the city of a hundred bells".

In the Largo delle Tre Chiese (square of three churches) the **Church of San Francesco** has a polychrome marble **high altar**★. ☎0964 35 61 40; www.locride.net/gerace.htm.

Stilo

The native town of philosopher **Tommaso Campanella** (1568-1639), filled with hermitages and Basilian monasteries, clings to a mountain at an altitude of 400m/1 312ft. Further up, almost camouflaged, is the Byzantine jewel of a church, **La Cattolica**★. This 10C structure has a square plan and is roofed with five cylindrical domes. The elegant external decoration consists

of brickwork, a traced central dome and roof tiles. Inside, the Greek cross is composed of nine domed and barrel-vaulted sections, each held up by four marble columns. Unfortunately one cannot admire the mosaics, which are very damaged. ♿ ⏱Open daily, 21 Mar-21 Oct, 8am-8pm, rest of the year 8am-6pm. ✆No charge. ☎0964 77 60 06; www.comune.stilo.rc.it.

Capo Colonna

This cape was once called Capo Lacinio. From the last decades of the 8C BC, one of Magna Graecia's most famous temples stood here, that of of Hera Lacinia. It had a golden age in the 5C BC, but began to decline in 173 BC, when the Consul Fulvio Flacco removed part of the marble roof. The rennovation failed due to the complexity of the original design. It was then plundered by pirates and became a quarry for the Aragonese foundations of Crotone in the 16C. The temple was finally destroyed by an earthquake in 1683. Now only 48 columns remain of this Doric temple, which was dedicated to the most important goddess of Olympus. In 1964 Pier Paolo Pasolini (1922-75) shot some scenes of his film The Gospel According to St Matthew here.

Crotone

The ancient town of Croton was an Achaean colony of Magna Graecia, founded in 710 BC. It was celebrated in Antiquity for its riches, the beauty of its women

Citrons for Sukkoth

The Feast of the Tabernacles, *Sukkoth*, is the Jewish Festival of Tents, commemorating Exodus, when Jews slept in the wilderness. The fruit traditionally used for this feast, chosen with painstaking care, is the citron. Every summer rabbis come to *Santa Maria del Cedro* (which has ideal growing conditions for this fruit) in the province of Cosenza, to select citrons for their communities all over the world.

Leviticus 23, 39-40: On the fifteenth day of the seventh month, when you have gathered up the produce of the land, you shall keep the festival of the Lord, lasting seven days; a complete rest on the first day, and a complete rest on the eighth day. On the first day you shall take the fruit of majestic trees, branches of palm trees, boughs of leafy trees, and willows of the brook: and you shall rejoice before the Lord your God for seven days.

and the prowess of athletes such as Milo of Croton, so admired by Virgil. Around 532 BC Pythagoras founded several religious communities devoted to the study of mathematics. When they became too powerful, these scholars were expelled northwards toward Metapontum (present-day Metaponto). The rival city of Locari defeated Croton in the mid-6C BC, which in turn defeated its other rival, Sybaris. The city welcomed Hannibal during the Second Punic War, before being conquered by Rome. Crotone is today a prosperous seaport and industrial centre as well as a popular holiday resort. The town also houses a Museo Archeologico. ◑*Open daily 9am-8pm (last admission 7.30pm). Closed Mon, 1 Jan and 25 Dec.* ⬤*2€.* ☎*0962 23 082.*

Rossano

The town spreads over a hillside clad in olive groves. In the Middle Ages Rossano was the capital of Greek monasticism in the west, where expelled or persecuted Basilian monks came for refuge, living in the cells , which can still be seen today. The perfect little church of San Marco dates from this period. The flat east end has three projecting semi-circular apses with graceful openings. To the right of the cathedral, the **Museo Diocesano** has a valuable **Purpureus Codex**★, a 6C evangelistary with brightly coloured illuminations. ◑*Open Tue-Sat 9.30am-12.30pm and 4.30-7pm, Sun and public holidays, 10am-noon and 5-7pm.* ◑ *Closed Mon.* ⬤ *3.10 €.* ☎*0983 52 52 63.*

Touring Calabria

Cosenza

Town plan in the Michelin Atlas Italy.
The modern town is overlooked by the old town, where streets and palaces recall the prosperity of the Angevin and Aragonese periods. Consenza was then considered the artistic and religious capital of Calabria. The 12C-13C **cathedral** (Duomo) has recently been restored to its original aspect. It has a **mausoleum**★that contains the heart of Isabella of Aragon, wife of Philip III, King of France. She died in 1271 outside Consenza on the way back from Tunis with the sainted king's body and was buried in France's St-Denis Basilica.

Altomonte

The large market town is dominated by an imposing 14C Angevin cathedral dedicated to **Santa Maria della Consolazione**. which boasts a fine rose window. Inside there are no aisles and the east end is flat. the fine **tomb**★is that of Filippa Sangineto. The small **museo civico** beside the church has several precious works of art in addition to a statue of **St Ladislas**★attributed to Simone Martini. *Tour* ◑*Open daily.* ⬤*3€.* ☎*0981 94 80 4116.; www.altomonte.com.*

Serra San Bruno

Between the Sila and Aspromonte Massifs, amid the Calabrian mountains covered with oak and pine **forests**★, this small market town grew up around a **hermitage** founded by St Bruno, who died in 1101.

ISOLA DI **CAPRI**★★★

POPULATION 7 200

MICHELIN MAP 564 F 24 – CAMPANIA.

This island's enchantment owes much to its ideal position off the Sorrento Peninsula, beautiful rugged landscape, mild climate and luxuriant vegetation. It has captivated everyone from Roman emperors Augustus and Tiberius to luminaries such as D. H. Lawrence, George Bernard Shaw and Lenin and today the swathes of tourists that wander the fashionable lanes of Capri town.

- **Information:** Piazza Umberto I 1, 80073 Capri (NA), ☎081 83 70 686; Fax 081 83 70 918; www.capritourism.com; touristoffice@capri.it and Via Orlandi 19/a, 80071 Anacapri (NA), ☎081 83 71 524.
- ▶ **Orient Yourself:** Capri can be reached by ferry from Naples, Sorrento and other towns along the Amalfi Coast. **Marina Grande**★ is the main port where boats arrive on the northern side of the isle. A funicular railway connects Marina Grande to Capri, where there is a bus service to Anacapri
- P **Parking:** Much of Capri Town is pedestrianised. Parking can be difficult.
- **Don't Miss:** The azure waters of Grotta Azzurra and island boat trips.
- **Organizing Your Time:** Allow for a couple of days on the island.
- **Kids Especially for Kids:** The Marina Grande-Capri funicular and Anacapri-Monte Solaro chair lift.
- **Also See:** *COSTIERA AMALFITANA, ISCHIA, NAPOLI, Golfo di NAPOLI.*

Capri★★★

Capri is like a stage setting for an operetta with its small squares, little white houses and Moorish-looking alleyways. Here wild and lonely spots can still be found near crowded and lively scenes. Capri is expensive; expect big-city prices, especially in outdoor bars.

Piazza Umberto I★

This famous *piazzetta* is the centre of town and the spot where fashionable crowds gather. The narrow side streets, such as **Via Le Botteghe**★, are lined with souvenir shops and boutiques.

Belvedere Cannone★★

To reach the belvedere take **Via Madre Serafina**★. The promenade presents the mysterious aspect of Capri with its covered and winding stepped alleys.

Belvedere di Tragara★★

▶ *Access by Via Camerelle and Via Tragara.*

Certosa di San Giacomo e Giardini d'Augusto

Closed for restoration. For information ☎081 83 76 218.
This 14C Carthusian Monastery has two cloisters, with Roman statues taken from the Blue Grotto on one.
From Augustus' Gardens there is a beautiful **view**★★ of Punta di Tragara and the Faraglioni (sea stacks). Lower down, **Via Krupp**★, clinging to the rock face, leads to Marina Piccola.

Marina Piccola★

At the foot of Monte Solaro is a fishing harbour and beautiful small beaches.

One of many delightful viewpoints on Capri

B. Morandi/MICHELIN

Address Book

For coin ranges, see the Legend on the cover flap.

WHERE TO STAY

Hotel Florida – *Via Fuorlovado 34 – 80073 Capri – ☏081 83 70 710 – Closed Nov-Feb – 19 rm –* ☐. A small hotel, centrally located and just two minutes from the funicular down to the beach, but for all that an oasis of calm. 1950s-style, simple interior with a lacquer finish. Breakfast is served on the terrace in the garden. Very reasonably priced.

Hotel Villa Eva – *Via La Fabbrica 8 – 80073 Anacapri – 100m from the bus-stop for the Grotta Azzurra – ☏081 83 71 549 – Fax 081 83 72 040 – www.villaeva.com – Closed Nov-1 Mar – ⚲ ☒ – Booking advisable – 10 rm –* ☐. An oasis of peace and quiet situated near the le–gendary Grotta Azzurra. Surrounded by luxuriant greenery are a number of small-scale buildings – predominantly Mediterranean in style. You can doze off in a hammock or head to the swimming pool.

Capri Palace Hotel – *Via Capodimonte 2 – 80071 Anacapri – ☏081 79 78 01 11 – Fax 081 83 73 191 – www.capripalace.com – Closed Nov-Mar – ☒ ☐ – 80 rm –* ☐. For sheer elegance, exquisite taste and attention to detail, look no further than this hotel. Facilities include suites and rooms with private pool. And if this isn't enough, indulge yourself with a treatment at the spa.

WHERE TO EAT

Le Arcate – *Viale T. De Tommaso 24 – 80071 Anacapri – ☏081 83 73 325 – Closed Mon, 15 Jan-1 Mar.* A simple eatery, just a stone's throw from the centre. This place is popular for a quick bite at lunchtime. During the evening it is quieter and more relaxing. Good for both pizzas and pasta.

Pulalli Wine Bar – *Piazza Umberto I – 80073 Capri – ☏081 83 74 108 – Closed Tue –* ☐. A pleasant wine bar, situated up the steps by the tourist office. Head for the much sought-after tables on the little terrace where there is a good view over the piazza. Inside dining area is modern and elegant. Some excellent wines and a good choice of first and second courses. Also good for snacks.

Verginiello – *Via Lo Palazzo 25/A – 80073 Capri – ☏081 83 70 944 – Closed 10-25 Nov –* ☐. This unpretentious, family-run restaurant is situated just as you enter Capri. From the large terrace and dining room there are fine views out to sea and over the Marina Grande. Cooking is of a high quality. Specialises in fish and seafood dishes. Value for money.

La Savardina – *Da Eduardo – Via lo Capo 8 – 80073 Capri   About 40min on foot from Capri on the road to Villa Jovis – ☏081 83 76 300 – www.caprilasavardina.com – Closed Tue in Apr –* ☐. If you decide to visit Villa Jovis or are in the mood for a walk, make sure you leave enough time for lunch en route. The mouth-watering flavours, shady citrus grove and unforgettable view will linger on in your memory.

Da Giorgio – *Via Roma 34 – 80073 Capri – ☏081 83 75 777 – www.dagiorgiocapri.com – Closed Tue, 8 Jan-Easter.* A pleasant, unpretentious restaurant with a wonderful veranda and huge windows with splendid views over the gulf of Capri. Traditional cuisine. Also serves pizzas. Near the centre of Capri.

Da Paolino – *Via Palazzo a Mare 11, 80073 Marina Grande – ☏081 83 76 102 – Closed at lunchtime, Nov-Easter.* This restaurant is best described as the Mediterranean equivalent of the Garden of Eden, deliciously scented with the aroma of lemons. Warm and friendly ambience. The wrought-iron tables are a nice touch. Serves both meat and fish dishes.

Aurora – *Via Fuorlovado 18 – 80073 Capri – ☏081 83 70 181 – Closed Jan-Mar – www.auroracapri.com.* Pleasant eatery, well-established and family run. Popular with celebrities. In-formal atmosphere but elegant ambien-ce. Good selection of wines to accompany both fish and meat dishes. Small dining area outside – very sought after.

Villa Jovis★★

🚶The steep walk from Piazza Umberto – along the Via Botteghe and Via Tiberio – takes 30-40 min 🕐Open 9am-1hr before dusk. 🕐Closed public holidays. 🎫2 €. ☎081 83 74 549.

Jupiter's Villa was the residence of the Emperor Tiberius. Excavations have uncovered servants' quarters, the cisterns and the Imperial apartments. From the esplanade there is a **panorama**★★ of the whole island. Take the stairway behind the church for **Tiberius' Leap**★ (Salto di Tiberio), from which his victims were allegedly thrown.

Arco naturale★

▶ A 25-minute walk from Capri, along the Via Sopramonte and Via Croce.

Coastal erosion created this gigantic natural rock arch. Lower down is the **Grotta di Matromania**, a cave where the Romans venerated the fertility goddess *Mater Magna* (Great Mother).

Anacapri★★★

Take Via Roma to reach Anacapri, a delightful village with shady streets and fewer crowds than Capri.

Villa San Michele

▶Access from Piazza della Vittoria. 🕐Open May-Sept 9am-6pm; rest of the year 9am-1hr before dusk. 🎫5 €. ☎081 83 71 401; www.sanmichele.org.
The villa was built at the end of the 19C

for the Swedish doctor-writer, Axel Munthe (d 1949), who lived here up to 1910 and described the atmosphere of the island in his *Story of San Michele*. The house contains 17C and 18C furniture and Roman sculptures. The pergola at the end of the **garden** provides a splendid **panorama**★★★ of Capri, Marina Grande, Mount Tiberius and the Faraglioni.

Just below the villa is a stairway, **Scala Fenicia**, of nearly 800 steps down to the harbour. For a long time, this was the only link between the town and its port. Here Munthe met the old Maria "Porta-Lettere" depicted in his book.

Chiesa di San Michele

🕐Open Apr-Oct 10am-7pm; rest of the year telephone for opening times. 🎫1 €. ☎081 83 72 396. From the organ gallery note the majolica **floor**★ (1761) representing the Garden of Eden.

Monte Solaro★★★

♿ 🕐The chairlift operates from Apr to Oct, 9.30am-5pm, Nov-Mar, 9.30am-3.30pm. 🎫7 € return. ☎081 83 71 428; www.seggioviamontesolaro.it.
The chairlift swings above gardens and terraces brimming with luxuriant vegetation. From the summit there is an unforgettable **panorama**★★★ of the Bay of Naples as far as the island of Ponza, the Apennines and the mountains of Calabria to the south.

Belvedere di Migliara★

▶1hr on foot there and back. Pass under the chairlift to take Via Caposcuro. There

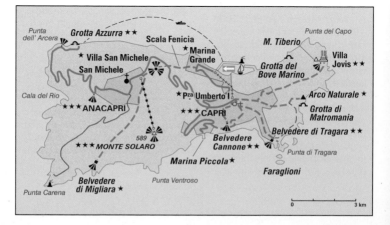

is a remarkable **view**★ of the lighthouse on the headland, Punta Carena.

Excursions

Grotta Azzurra★★

Boats leave from Marina Grande. It is also possible to go by road (8km/5mi from Capri). Boat trip and visit to the cave all year, daily (except at high tide and when the sea is rough), 9am-1hr before dusk. Duration: 1hr. ➡ 8.50 € (rowing boat + entrance fee). Excursion from Marina Grande with the following companies: Laser Capri (☎081 83 75 208, info@laser-capri.com) ➡ 11 €; Gruppo Motoscafisti (☎081 83 75 646, www.motoscafisticapri. com) ➡ 10 €; includes trip by fast or small boat and grotto.

The Blue Grotto is the most famous among the many marine caves on the island. The light enters, not directly, but by refraction through the water, giving it a beautiful blue color.

Trip around the island★★★

Leave from Marina Grande. Boat trip all year (except when the sea is rough), departing from Marina Grande at regular intervals with the following companies: Gruppo Motoscafisti (☎081 83 75 646, www.motoscafisticapri.com), Laser Capri (☎081 83 75 208, info@lasercapri.com).

Duration: about 2hr. ➡ 10-11 € + 8.50 € for a trip to the Grotta Azzurra. People swim in the cave, but the current is dangerously strong.

Visitors will discover a rugged coastline, pierced with caves and small peaceful creeks, fringed with fantastically shaped reefs and lined with sheer cliffs dipping vertically into the sea.

The island is barely 6km/4mi long and 3km/2mi wide with a particularly mild climate favouring the growth of a varied flora: pine, lentisk, juniper, arbutus, asphodel, myrtle and acanthus.

The boats go in a clockwise direction and the first sight is the **Grotta del Bove Marino** (Sea Ox Cave), which derives its name from the roar of the sea rushing into the cave in stormy weather. Beyond is the headland (Punta del Capo) dominated by Mount Tiberius (Monte Tiberio). Once past the impressive cliff known as Tiberius' Leap (see above), the headland to the south, Punta di Tragara, is fringed by the famous **Faraglioni**, rocky islets eroded into fantastic shapes by the waves. The **Grotta dell'Arsenale** (Arsenal Cave) was used as a nymphaeum during the reign of Tiberius.

Continue past the small port of Marina Piccola to reach the more gentle west coast. The last part of the trip covers the north coast and includes the visit to the Blue Grotto.

REGGIA DI **CASERTA**★★

MICHELIN MAP 564 D 25 – CAMPANIA.

As a sensible precaution, Charles III of Bourbon chose Caserta, far from the vulnerable Neapolitan coast, to host a magnificent edifice that could compete with other European courts. The Royal Palace of Caserta – together with Vanvitelli's Aqueduct and the San Leucio buildings (which housed the silk factory founded in 1789 by Ferdinand IV of Bourbon) – have been included in UNESCO's World Heritage List.

- **Information:** Palazzo Reale, 81100 Caserta, ☎0823 32 22 33; www.comune.caserta.it.
- **Orient Yourself:** Reggia di Caserta lies off A 1 (exit Caserta Nord), about 20km/12mi from Naples.
- **Don't Miss:** The Palazzo and the treasures of the Museo Archeologico dell'Antica Capua.
- **Organizing Your Time:** Allow half a day to see all the major sights.
- **Especially for Kids:** The Roman amphitheatre at Santa Maria Capua Vetere.
- **Also See:** BENEVENTO, COSTIERA AMALFITANA, NAPOLI, GOLFO DI NAPOLI.

Visit

Palazzo

&♿⌖Vanvitelli's *materpiece staircase.*
🕐*Open daily except Mon, 8.30am-
dusk.*🕐*Closed Tue, 1 Jan, 25 Dec.*
✎*Apartments: 4.20 €, park and gardens
2 €, park and apartments 6 €.* ☎*0823 44
80 84; www.arethusa.net.*

In 1752 Charles III of Bourbon commissioned the architect **Luigi Vanvitelli**
to erect a palace *(reggia)*. Compared to
the grand royal residences of the period,
Caserta has a more geometric, severe
layout that reflects the personality of
the architect. If its purity of line seems
almost to anticipate the neo-Classical
style, the theatrical design of its interior
is still typically Rococo.

The building consists of a vast rectangle (249m/273yd long and 190m/208yd
wide) containing four internal courtyards interconnected by a magnificent
entrance hall★. The façade first seen
by the visitor is adorned by a projecting
colonnade and a double row of windows
supported by a rusticated base. The principal façade, facing the garden, reproduces this motif, but embellishes it with
pilaster strips bordering each window.

The sumptuous **grand staircase**★★
(scalone d'onore) a masterpiece of
Vanvitelli, leads to the Palatine Chapel
(not open to visitors) and to the luxurious
royal apartments decorated in the neo-
Classical style. The **Eighteenth Century
Apartment** (Appartamento Settecen-
tesco) is particularly interesting with its
vaulted frescoed ceilings depicting the
seasons and some wonderful views of
ports by JP Hackert. The pretty **Queen's
Apartment** (Apartamento della Regina)
has some curious pieces include a chan-
delier adorned with little tomatoes and
a cage containing a clock and a stuffed
bird. In the Sala Ellittica, there is an 18C
Neapolitan **crib**★ *(presepe)*.

Park

This park epitomises the ideal grand
Baroque garden. Its seemingly infinite
expanse is arranged around a central
canal. The fountains and fish-ponds are
powered by the Aqueduct. This monu-
mentally ambitious work by Vanvitelli
spans five mountains and three valleys with a total length of 40km/25mi.
Notable mythological sculptures
include the group of *Diana and Actaeon,*
which stands at the foot of the great
cascade★★ (78m/256ft high) and
depicts hounds attacking a stag.

To the right of the cascade lies a picturesque English garden (**giardino
inglese**★★) created for Maria-Carolina
of Austria.

Excursions

Caserta Vecchia★

10km/6mi north. ⌖*This small town is
dominated by the ruins of its 9C castle.*
🕐*Castle tours daily, Mar-Nov 9am-
1pm and 3.30-8pm; Dec-Feb, 9am-1pm
and 3.30-6pm.* ✎*Donations welccome.*
☎*0823 37 13 18.*

The town has a certain charm with its
narrow alleyways lined by old buildings
with brown tufa walls. The 12C **Cathedral** combines Sicilian-Arab, Apulian and
Lombard motifs.

Basilica di Sant'Angelo
in Formis★★

▶*15km/9mi northwest of Caserta Vecchia (take SS 87 to S. Iorio).* 🕐*Open daily,
9.30am-12.30pm and 3.30-6.30pm.* ▯ *If it is
closed, contact Don Franco Duonnolo* ☎*0823
96 08 17.*

One of the most beautiful medieval
buildings in Campania. Erected in the
11C on the initiative of Desiderio, Abbot
of Monte Cassino, the basilica combines
a rudimentary architectural structure
with one of the richest Romanesque
cycle of frescoes. The interior is covered
in **frescoes**: the Last Judgement (east
wall), the Life of Christ (nave), the Old
Testament (north and south aisle) and
Maestà (apse). Although of local production, these frescoes have a strong Byzantine influence (owing to the intervention
of Greek painters who had worked at
Monte Cassino), tempered by local culture as can be seen in the crude use of
colour and liveliness of some images.
In the apse there is a representation of
the Abbot Desiderio offering the church
to God (the square halo indicates that
the Abbot was still alive when the fresco
was painted).

Lara Pessina/MICHELIN

Mysterious mythological figures adorn the park of the royal palace at Caserta

Capua

6km/4mi southwest of S. Angelo in Formis.
www.cittadicapua.it.
This walled city, founded by the Lombards, is the native town of Ettore Fieramosca, Captain of the 13 Italian knights who vanquished the French in the Defeat of Barletta (1503).

Duomo – *Open daily, 8.30am-noon and 3-6pm. 0823 96 10 81.*
The cathedral, which dates from the 9C, has been rebuilt several times since. The columns of the atrium have lovely 3C **Corinthian capitals**, while the interior houses a 13C paschal candelabrum, an *Assumption* by F Solimena.

Museo Campano★ – *At the corner of Via Duomo and Via Roma.* The earth-goddess figurines *Open 9am-1.30pm, Sun 9am-1pm. Closed Mon, public holidays. 4.13 €. 0823 62 00 76; www.capuaonline.it.*
This museum is housed in a 15C building with a fine lava stone Catalan **doorway**. The archaeological section has an astonishing collection of 6C to 1C BC **Matres Matutae,** Italic earth goddesses holding their newborn children; and a charming imposing gateway built by the Emperor Frederick II of Hohenstaufen around 1239. Note the head of a woman known as *Capua Fidelis*.
Southeast of the museum there is an area with an interesting series of Lombard churches (San Giovanni a Corte, San Salvatore Maggiore a Corte, San Michele a Corte, San Marcello).

Santa Maria Capua Vetere

5km/3mi southeast of Capua. The second largest Roman amphitheatre, where Spartacus revolted.
This is the famous Roman Capua where the downfall of Hannibal was brought about by the temptations that were cast his way. Capua was considered one of the most opulent cities of the Roman Empire. After Saracen attacks in the 9C, the inhabitants of the city moved to the banks of the River Volturno where they founded the present Capua. The **Anfiteatro Campano★**, restored in the 2C AD, was the seat of the famous gladiator school in which the revolt headed by Spartacus erupted in 73 BC. *Open Tues-Sun, 9am-6.30pm. Closed Mon, 1 Jan, 1 May, 25 Dec. 2.50 € including the Mitreo and the Museo dell'Antica Capua. 0823 84 42 06; www.comune. santa-maria-capua-vetere.ce.it.*
The **Mitreo** (2C AD) is an underground chamber boasting a rare **fresco★** of the Persian god Mithras sacrificing a bull.
The pleasant **Museo Archeologico dell'Antica Capua** *(Via R. d'Angiò)* has interesting artefacts relating local history from the Bronze Age to the Imperial Age. These include three *Matres Matutae.* *Open daily except Mon, 9am-6.30pm. Closed 1 Jan,1 May, 25 Dec. 2.50 € including the Anfiteatro and the Mitreo. 0823 84 42 06; www.archeona. arti.beniculturali.it.*

PARCO NAZIONALE DEL **CILENTO**★

MICHELIN MAP 564 F-G 26-28 – CAMPANIA.

The Cilento nature reserve was founded in 1991 and is on UNESCO's World Nature Reserve List. This superlative Mediterranean park is situated at the crossroads of the most diverse cultural influences, from the basin of the Mediterranean to the Apennines, and has some gorgeous coastline with lovely beaches, interesting caves and rocky outcrops.

- **Information:** Via Palumbo 18, 84078 Vallo della Lucania ☎0974 71 99 11, www. parks.it/parco.nazionale.cilento.
- ▶ **Orient Yourself:** The Parco Nazionale del Cilento extends from the Tyrrhenian coast to the Diano Valley. It lies off A 3 between Salerno and Reggio Calabria
- **Don't Miss:** The natural wonders of the Oasi WWF di Persano.
- **Organizing Your Time:** Enjoy the beaches in the morning and visit shady caves in the hot afternoon.
- **Kids Especially for Kids:** Room of Sponges at the Grotte di Pertos.
- **Also See:** *CALABRIA, COSTIERA AMALFITANA, PAESTUM, Golfo di POLICASTRO*

A Bit of History

The vast variety of landscapes is the result of the twofold nature of the rocks. The *flysch* variety of the Cilento is to be found in the western part of the park and along the coast (Stella and Gelbison mountains) with its gentle landscape and Mediterranean vegetation. The calcareous rock of the interior (Alburni mountains and Mount Cerviati) and the southern coast (from Cape Palinuro to Scario) produces a barren landscape with spectacular karst formations. The most interesting floral species is the Palinuro primrose, the park's symbol, while fauna includes otters, wolves and royal eagles.

Tour

Sights are listed based on an ideal itinerary which descends from Vella towards the coast and then up to the northwest. 170km/102mi. ⏱Allow at least 1 day.

Velia★

40km/25mi southeast of Paestum on S 18 and S 267. 🛈 www.velia.it. This colony was founded in 535 BC by Phoenician Greek refugees who had been expelled by the Persians. A prosperous port, Velia (known as Elea to the Greeks) became a Roman territory in 88 BC. The city was famous for its Eleatic school of philosophy in the 6C-5C BC, including Parmenides and his pupil Zeno.

▶ *Pass under the railway line to reach the ruins.*

Ruins

⏱*Open daily, 9am-1hr before dusk.* ⏱*Closed 1 Jan and 25 Dec.* ☜ *2 €.* ☎*0974 97 23 96.*

From the entrance there is an interesting view of the archaeological site of the **città bassa** (lower town) with its lighthouse, 4C BC city wall, the south sea-gateway and Roman baths from the Imperial era (mosaic and marble floor remains). From the baths, Via di Porta Rosa borders the marketplace and climbs up to the ancient gateway (6C BC) and the **Porta Rosa**★ (4C BC), a fine example of a cuneiform arch and the most important Greek civic monument in *Magna Graecia*.

The **acropolis** on the promontory above the lower town has remains of the medieval castle erected on the foundations of a Greek temple, and the Palatine Chapel, which houses epigraphic material. Slightly below are the remains of the Greek theatre, remodelled in the Roman era. Halfway down, towards the lower town, a Hellenistic villa with fresco remains has been discovered.

Address Book

WHERE TO STAY

Bed & Breakfast Iscairia –
Via Isacia 7 –84058 Marina di Ascea –
☎0974 97 22 41 – Fax 0974 97 23 72
– iscairia@cilento.it – 11rm 70/90 €.
Situated at the foot of the Greek ruins
at Velia, this unusual B&B has something of the seaside guesthouse and
rural retreat about it. Guests sleep on
wrought-iron beds and breakfast under
a wooden gazebo, amongst
the olive trees. Facilities for fitness
enthusiasts. Meals with a regional
flavour on request.

Hotel Giacaranda – *Contrada
Cenito – 84071 San Marco – 30km/18mi
northwest of Velia on S 267 (1km/0.6mi
south of San Marco) - ☎0974 96 61 30
– Fax 0974 96 68 00 – Closed 23-26 Dec –
8 rm 110/240 €.* Wrought-iron beds,
linen sheets, 19C chests of drawers all
add to the atmosphere. Guests can
even get a newspaper in the morning.
The lovely airy sitting room also serves
as a dining area. Otherwise meals are
served under the shade of a jacaranda.
Can arrange cultural and gastronomic
programmes for guests.

Capo Palinuro★★

30km/18mi southeast of Velia on S 447.
Kids *Boat trip to the Grotta Azzurra.*
♿☼*Open daily, mid-Mar to Dec 9am-
6pm, (tour takes about 1hr 30min including a short break on one of the beaches).*
☼ *Closed Jan to mid-Mar.* ☜ *12 €.*
☎0974 93 16 04; www.capopalinuro.com.
The name Palinuro refers to Aeneas'
mythical steersman, who was killed
here. From Palinuro there are **boat
trips** to the **Grotta Azzurra**★ and other
caves on the promontory.
From S 562 head toward the beautiful beaches on the coast (☼*see Gulf of
POLICASTRO).*

▸ *66km/40mi northeast on SS 562, SS
447 (passing through Poderia and following signs for Policastro Busentino),
SS 517 and SS 19.*

Certosa di Padula★

♿ ☼ *Open daily, 9am-8pm (last admission 7pm).* ☜ *4.13 €.* ☎0975 77 745
The charterhouse of San Lorenzo,
founded in 1306, is one of the largest
architectural complexes in southern
Italy. From the cloisters, a 14C cedarwood doorway leads to the Baroque
church that houses the **Padri**★. The
Great Cloisters (104x149m/341x488ft)
are surrounded by monks' cells, while
the left arcade leads to a dramatic 18C
staircase★.

▸ *35km/21mi northwest on SS 19.*

Grotte di Pertos★

Kids *Room of the Sponges* ♿ ☼*Guided
tours only (1hr), Mar-Oct, daily, 9am-7pm,
Nov-Feb 9am-4pm.* ☜ *10-15 € (depending on tour).* ☎0975 39 70 37; www.grottedipertosa.it
These caves, which extend over an area
of about 2.5km/1.5mi, lie in the natural
amphitheatre of the Alburni mountains
and are reached via a small lake. Inhabited since Neolithic times, the caves have
fine concretions, mainly of sodium carbonate; the most interesting area is the
Sponge Room (Sala delle Spugne)
The S 166 leads up to the Sentinella Pass
(932m/3 057ft) crossing **landscapes**★
dotted with yellow broom.

▸ *42km/25mi northeast on SS 19.*

Oasi WWF di Persano

♿ ⬙*Guided tours only (2hr); Jun-Sep
9am and 5pm; Oct-May 10am, 11am and
3pm (book at least one week in advance).*
☜ *5 €.* ☎0828 97 46 84; www.wwf.it.
The "oasis" extends over 110ha/271 acres
of alluvial plains formed by the River
Sele between the Alburni and Picentini
mountains. The most interesting flora
can be found in the marshland, one of
the last refuges of the otter.

CORTONA★★

POPULATION 22 008
MICHELIN MAP 563 M 17
SEE ALSO THE GREEN GUIDE TUSCANY.

Cortona occupies a remarkable spot on the steep slope overlooking the Chiana Valley, close to Lake Trasimeno. It was part of the League of Twelve Etruscan Towns before coming under the control of Rome. It has retained its medieval town walls, commanded by a huge citadel (fortezza) that replaced the Etruscan precinct. The town, annexed to Florence in 1411, has barely changed since the Renaissance period.

- **Information:** Via Nazionale 42, 52044. ☎0575 63 03 52; www.cortonaweb.net.
- ▶ **Orient Yourself:** Cortona lies off S 71, linking Arezzo with Lake Trasimeno.
- **Don't Miss:** The Museo Diocesano.
- **Organizing Your Time:** Allow half a day.
- **Also See:** *AREZZO*

Worth a Visit

Piazza del Duomo, against the ramparts, affords a lovely valley view. The Romanesque cathedral (Duomo) was remodelled at the Renaissance.

Museo Diocesano★★

Opposite the Duomo. ⚬Open Apr-Oct 10am-7pm, Nov-Mar 10am-5pm. Closed Mon (in winter). ⚬ 5 €. ☎0575 63 72 35; www.cortonaweb.net. This former church houses a beautiful **Annunciation** and *Madonna and Saints* by Fra Angelico; works from the Sienese school by Duccio, Pietro Lorenzetti and Sassetta; and a remarkable **Ecstasy of St Margaret** by the Bolognese artist Giuseppe Maria Crespi (1665-1747). Note the fine 2C Roman sarcophagus.

Palazzo Pretorio★

The Etruscan oil lamp ⚬Open Apr-Oct 10am-7pm, Nov-Mar 10am-5pm. Closed Mon (in winter), 1 Jan, 25 Dec. ⚬ 7€. ☎0575 63 72 35; www.accademia-etrusca.org. The Praetorian Palace houses the **Museo dell'Accademia Etrusca★** with Etruscan exhibits including a 5C BC bronze **oil lamp★★** with 16 burners shaped like human figures.

Santuario di Santa Margherita

This enshrines the Gothic **tomb**★ (1362) of St Margaret. Via Santa Margherita leads off to the south of the church. Severini decorated the street with mosaics of the *Stations of the Cross*.

Chiesa di San Domenico

This church has a fine *Madonna with angels and saints* by Luca Signorelli and a fresco by Fra Angelico.

Chiesa di Santa Maria del Calcinaio★

3km/2mi west. Santa Maria, built from 1485 to 1513 by **Francesco di Giorgio Martini,** strongly resembles the work of Brunelleschi. The church is remarkable for the grace and harmony of its design and its well-balanced proportions. The

Town of Artists and Saints

Cortona began to attract artists in the 14C and it was the Sienese School which predominated, until the arrival of Fra Angelico (c 1400-55). The town's main claim to fame, however, is that it was the birthplace of a number of famous old masters including **Luca Signorelli** (c 1450-1523) and **Pietro da Cortona** (1596-1669). **Gino Severini** (1883-1966) who was linked to the Futurist movement was also born here.

Address Book

WHERE TO STAY

Albergo Italia – Via Ghibellina 5 – ☎0575 63 02 54 – Fax 0575 60 57 63 – Closed 26 Nov-15 Dec, Restaurant closed Thu (excluding Apr-Oct) – ▦ – 26 rm – ☐. The hotel is right in the historic centre. Wonderful views over the Val di Chiana from the terrace. Comfortable rooms, some with antiques. Delightful restaurant in an old cave, with a 16C well.

WHERE TO EAT

Osteria del Teatro – Via Maffei 5 – ☎0575 63 05 56 – www.osteria-del-teatro.it – Closed Wed, 2 weeks in Nov. Small, intimate eatery with a theatrical theme enhanced by the black and white photos on the wall. The ambience is very informal with the chefs making an occasional appearance at the table. Delicious, traditional cooking.

TAKING A BREAK

Caffè degli Artisti – Via Nazionale 18 – ☎0575 60 12 37 – Summer, open daily, 7am-2am; rest of the year closed Thu and Nov. This café gets its name from the numerous American celebrities who have paid this establishment a visit over the years. A warm, cosy atmosphere, lots of laughter and delicious cocktails! **Pasticceria Banchelli** – Via Nazionale 64 – ☎0575 60 31 78 – Summer, open daily, 7am-midnight; rest of the year 7am-9pm. Sugar reigns supreme in this pasticceria which is as famous for its pan pepato (spicy bread) as it is for its homemade ice cream. Lovely little tea room for those special treats!

---

domed church is built on the Latin cross plan and the lofty interior is well lit. In the oculus of the façade is a remarkable stained-glass window designed by a French artist, Guillaume de Marcillat (1467-1529).

COSTIERA AMALFITANA★★★
AMALFI COAST
MICHELIN MAP 564 F 25 – CAMPANIA.

With its charming fishing villages and luxuriant vegetation – a mixture of orange, lemon, olive and almond trees, as well as vines and bougainvillea – the Amalfi Coast has long been popular with travellers and artists. The wild and rugged landscape contrasts with its glamorous reputation. The international jet set of the 1950s and 1960s came aboard fabulous yachts in search of La Dolce Vita, and although these days the "Costiera" attracts tourists from all walks of life, it maintains its reputation as a hot spot for the rich and famous.

- **Information:** Corso delle Repubbliche Marinare 27/29, 84011 Amalfi (Salerno), ☎089 87 11 07; www.touristbureau.com.
- **Orient Yourself:** Arguably the most stunning coastline in Italy, the Amalfi Coast runs between Sorrento and Salerno. The artistic and natural beauty of this area earned it a place in UNESCO's 1997 World Heritage List.
- **Parking:** There is plenty of parking by the beach at Amalfi. Visitors to Salerno can park in the carpark at Via Alveraz.
- **Don't Miss:** Jaunty Amalfi or Ravello's dramatic stairways and roof passages.
- **Organizing Your Time:** Allow a day for a leisurely coastal drive.
- **Especially for Kids:** Grotte Dello Smeraldo, or fun on the beach at Amalfi.
- **Also See:** CASERTA, Parco Nazionale del CILENTO, ERCOLANO, Golfo di NAPOLI, PAESTUM, POMPEI. The first 4 itineraries are included in Golfo di NAPOLI, which is the ideal point of departure or end to this journey.

5 Along the Coast

80km/49mi – allow 1 day. The route below constitutes the continuation of itinerary E, as described in Golfo di NAPOLI. For exploring the "Costiera" alone, the best point of departure is Positano.

Positano☆☆☆

🏛 Via del Saracino 4, ☎089 87 50 67, *www.aziendaturismopositano.it* The white cubic houses of this old fishing village reveal a strong Moorish influence; lush gardens dotted on terraced slopes go down to the sea. Positano is "the only place in the world designed on a vertical axis" (Paul Klee). Much loved and frequented in the past by artists and intellectuals (Picasso, Cocteau, Steinbeck, Moravia and Nureyev who bought Li Galli island) and by the trend-setters of *La Dolce Vita* who used to meet up at the *Buca di Bacco* nightclub, today Positano is one of the most popular resorts of the Amalfi coast. "Positano fashion" was born here in the 1950s, with its brightly coloured materials and equally famous sandals that were desperately sought after by women of the jet set during their trips here.

Vettica Maggiore

Its houses are scattered over the slopes. From the esplanade there is a fine **view**★★ of the coast and sea.

Vallone di Furore★★

The Furore Valley, between two road tunnels, is the most impressive section of the coast owing to the dark depths of its steep, rocky walls and, in stormy weather, the thunder of wild, rough seas. A fishermen's village has, nevertheless, been built where a small torrent gushes into the sea. The houses clinging to the slopes and vividly coloured boats are drawn up on the shore. Those who wish to explore the spot on foot should take the path that goes along one side of the gorge. Note the **"Art walls"** (Muri d'autore), outdoor contemporary paintings and sculptures that relate local history.

Grotta dello Smeraldo★★

Access to cave by lift from street above 9am-4pm. ☞ 5 €. Visit also possible by boat

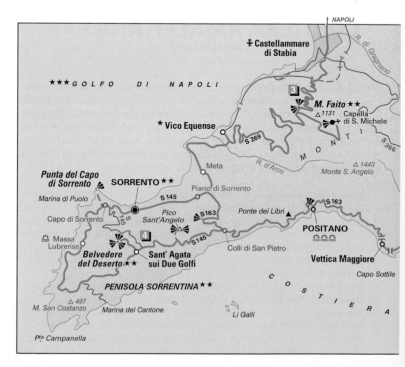

A Bit of History

Amalfi is Italy's oldest republic founded in 840; by the end of the 9C it came under the rule of a doge. It enjoyed its greatest prosperity in the 11C, when shipping in the Mediterranean was regulated by the Tavole Amalfitane (Amalfi codex), the oldest maritime code in the world. Amalfi traded regularly with the Orient, in particular Constantinople, and the Republic had an **arsenal** *(to the left of Porta della Marina)* where many large galleys were built. This fleet of galleys played a large part in carrying Crusaders to the Levant.

from Amalfi harbour, 🚐 *10 € round trip (admission not included).* ☎089 87 11 07; *www.amalfitouristoffice.it*

The exceptionally clear water of this marine cave is illuminated indirectly by rays of light which give it a beautiful emerald *(smeraldo)* colour. The bottom looks quite near, though the water is 10m/33ft deep. Fine stalactites add to the interest of the trip. The cave became submerged as a result of variations in ground level caused by the volcanic activity that affects the whole region.

Amalfi★★

Set in a steep valley, Amalfi is centered on the beach. The main street, Via Genova, leads to a wild gorge with mill-ruins.

🅿 *By the beach.* 🛈 *Via delle Repubblica 27 Marinare* ☎089 87 11 07; *www.amalfitouristoffice.it.*

Amalfi is a Spanish-looking little town with tall white houses built on slopes facing the sea in a wonderful **setting** ★★★. Amalfi enjoys a mild climate, making it a popular holiday resort.

Starting at Piazza Duomo, Via Genova, Via Capuano (its continuation) and **Via dei Mercanti** (parallel on the right) make up the **historic centre**★ and business heart of the city with its picturesque variety of façades, flowering balconies and niches. The Islamic-looking layout of the town is characterised by winding alleyways, staircases and vaulted passages which open out onto

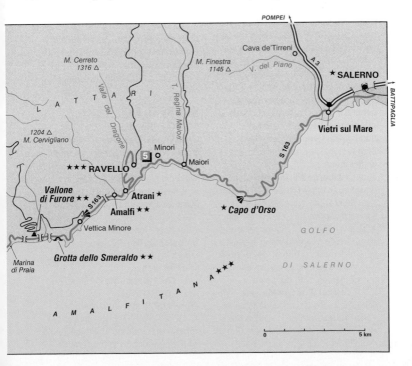

Address Book

For coin ranges, see the Legend on the cover flap.

WHERE TO STAY

⬲⬳ **Albergo Hostaria di Bacco** – *Via Lama 9 – 84110 Furore –* ☎*089 83 03 60 – Fax 089 83 03 52 – www.baccofurore.it – Closed 25 Dec (restaurant closed out of season) –* 🅿 *– 18 rm 70/80 –* 🍽 *7 €.*
A comfortable, family-run hotel and restaurant with fine views out to sea. Good location, at the top end of the charming village of Furore, not far from the Amalfi coast. Represents value for money

⬲⬳ **Hotel Le Fioriere** – *Via G. Capriglione 138 – 84010 Praiano – 11km/7mi southwest of Amalfi –* ☎*089 87 42 03 – www.lefloriere.it –* 🅿▤ *– 14 rm –* 🍽.
A chance to live it up without breaking the bank. Simple, spacious rooms, modern in style. Some benefit from a pretty little terrace area overlooking the sea where breakfast (generous servings) can be taken in summer. A little on the noisy side.

⬲⬳ **Hotel Santa Lucia** – *Via Nazionale 44 – 84010 Minori – 5km/3mi northeast of Amalfi on S 163 –* ☎*/Fax 089 87 71 42/Fax 089 85 36 36 – www.hotelsantalucia.it –* 🅿▤ *(charge) – 30 rm –* 🍽 *– Restaurant.* A well-established, family-run hotel. Although it dates back to the 1960s there is a modern feel to the furnishings and general ambience. The beach (part of which has been reserved for hotel guests) is only 100m away. Both regional and national dishes on the menu.

⬲⬳⬳ **Albergo Marincanto** – *Via Cristoforo Colombo 50 – 84017 Positano –* ☎*089 87 51 30 – Fax 089 87 55 95 – www.marincanto.it – Closed Nov-Mar –* 🅿▤ *– 25 rm –* 🍽. Rather retro and simple in style. Large parking area (charge) which makes the hotel very popular with visitors arriving by car. Lovely terrace-garden, with sea views.

⬲⬳⬳ **Hotel Villa San Michele** – *Via Carusiello 2 – 84010 Castiglione di Ravello – 5km/3mi south of Ravello –* ☎*/Fax 089 87 22 37 – www.amalfi.it/smichele – Closed 7 Jan-10 Feb –* 🅿▤ *– 12 rm –* 🍽 *–*

Restaurant. Situated at the top of the cliff face, the hotel boasts magnificent views over the Gulf and the Capo d'Orso. Delightful setting with its luscious garden and the steps down to the beach. Decorated in blue and white with tiled floors, the rooms are beautifully sunny.

⬲⬳⬳ **Hotel Aurora** – *Piazza dei Protontini 7 – 84011 Amalfi –* ☎*089 87 12 09 – Fax 089 87 29 80 – www.aurora-hotel.it – Closed Nov-Mar (open 25 Dec) – 29 rm –* 🍽. A charming hotel, situated right on the seafront and a stone's throw from the hustle and bustle of the quayside. Light, airy rooms with modern furnishings. The majolica ware is a nice touch. Lovely terrace-garden, pleasantly shaded by the bougainvillea.

⬲⬳⬳ **Hotel Palazzo Murat** – *Via dei Mulini 23 – 84017 Positano –* ☎*089 87 51 77 – Fax 089 81 14 19 – www.palazzomurat.it – Closed 4 Nov-20 Mar –* ▤ *– 31 rm –* 🍽 *– Restaurant.*
A throwback to 18C Neapolitan Baroque architecture and the Vanvitelli school which so enthralled Joachim Murat (King of Naples) that he took it on as his summer residence. With their original features some of the rooms are particularly atmospheric. Surrounded by a botanical garden with a variety of exotic plants and brightly coloured flowers.

WHERE TO EAT

⬲⬳ **Giardiniello** – *Corso Vittorio Emanuele 17 – 84010 Minori – 5km/3mi northeast of Amalfi on S 163 –* ☎*089 87 70 50 – www.amalfinet.it/giardiniello – Closed Wed (except Jun-Sep).* Restaurant situated in the heart of the village with large airy dining room. Meals served under the pergola in summer. Delicious regional cooking. Specialises in fish. Pizzas also served in the evening. Very good value for money.

⬲⬳ **Chez Black** – *Via del Brigantino 19/21 – 84017 Positano –* ☎*089 87 50 36 – Fax 089 87 57 89 – www.chezblack.it – Closed 7 Jan-7 Feb.* Ideally located right on the seafront. The large dining room opens out on to the veranda and diners are assured of a sea view wherever they are seated. There is no pressure to have a three-course meal – the staff are equally happy for diners to order one dish, even a pizza.

Buca di Bacco – *Via Rampa Teglia 4 – 84017 Positano – ☎089 87 56 99 – Fax 089 87 57 31 – www.bucadibacco.it – Closed Nov-Mar.* This restaurant is part of the hotel of the same name, situated in the centre of town. Specialises in fish dishes. Lovely terrace area with views out to sea. Popular with the artistic and intellectual jet set in the early 20C.

Palazzo della Marra – *Via della Marra 7/9 – 84010 Ravello – ☎089 85 83 02 – www.palazzodellamarra.com – Closed Tue (except Apr-Oct), mid-Jan-mid-Feb – Booking recommended.* A charming restaurant housed in a splendid townhouse with noble pretensions, dating back to the 12C. Rather sombre interior with high vaulted ceilings. Medieval-style cuisine.

La Caravella – *Via Matteo Camera 12 – 84011 Amalfi – ☎089 87 10 29 – www.ristorantelacaravella.it –Closed Tue, 10 Nov-25 Dec – – Booking recommended.* Comprises three small elegant dining rooms – white walls and simple furnishings, much of it 1940s in style. Mouth-watering fish dishes, good wines and excellent service.

little squares. Famous for its lemons, Amalfi produces a sweet-and-sour liqueur called *limoncello*.

Duomo di Sant'Andrea★

Chiostro del Paradiso and Museo Diocesano: Open Jul-Sept 9am-8pm, Mar-Jun & Oct 9am-7pm, rest of the year 10am-1pm and 2.30pm-4.15pm. Closed 7 Jan-Feb. 2.50 €. ☎089 87 13 24.

Founded in the 9C and subsequently altered numerous times, the cathedral is a good example of the Oriental splendour favoured by maritime cities. The façade, rebuilt in the 19C on the original model, is the focal point at the top of a stairway, with striking varied geometrical designs in multicoloured stone. The campanile, on the left, is all that remains of the original church. A beautiful 11C bronze **door**★, cast in Constantinople, opens onto the vast atrium that precedes the church.

The atrium leads into the **Cloisters of Paradise**★★ (Chiostro del Paradiso) which date from 1268 where the architecture combines Romanesque austerity and Arab fantasy. The Museo Diocesano is housed in the **Basilica del Crocefisso,** which used to be the site of the old 9C cathedral. From the basilica make for the crypt which holds the relics of St Andrew the Apostle, brought to Amalfi from Constantinople in 1206.

Atrani★

This pleasant fishermen's village at the mouth of the Dragon Valley (Valle del

A. Targat/MICHELIN

Positano

Dragone) has two old churches: Santa Maria Maddalena and San Salvatore. The latter was founded in the 10C and has a fine bronze door similar to the one in Amalfi Cathedral. The road winds up the narrow valley, planted with vines and olive groves, to Ravello.

Ravello★★★

Most attractions cluster around the Piazza Vescovado. The **Villa Rufolo and Villa Cimbrone.** *Via Roma 18, ☎089 85 70 96; www.ravellotime.it*

Ravello's stairways and roofed passages cling to the steep slopes of the Dragon Hill. The **site**★★★, suspended between sea and sky, is unforgettable. The town's aristocratic restraint has, over the centuries, beguiled artists, musicians and writers such as members of the Bloomsbury Group led by Virginia and Leonard Woolf (*see Villa Cimbrone below*), DH Lawrence, Graham Greene, Gore Vidal, Hans Escher and Joan Mirò.

Villa Rufolo★★★ – *Piazza Vescovado, next to the Duomo.* *Open daily 9am-1 hr before sunset.* *Closed 1 Jan, 25 Dec.* *5 €. ☎089 85 76 57.*

The villa was built in the 13C by the rich Rufolo family of Ravello (cited in Boccaccio's *Decameron*) and was the residence of several popes, Charles of Anjou and more recently, in 1880, of **Richard Wagner**. When the German composer, in search of inspiration for *Parsifal*, laid eyes on the villa's splendid garden he exclaimed, "the garden of Klingsor is found". A well-shaded avenue leads to a Gothic entrance tower. Beyond is a Moorish-style courtyard with sharply-pointed arches in the Sicilian-Norman style.

From the terraces there is a splendid **panorama**★★★ of the jagged peaks as far as Cape Orso, the Bay of Maiori and the Gulf of Salerno. Summer **concerts** in the gardens are held against a backdrop of trees, flowers and sea. *Società dei Concerti di Ravello, ☎089 85 81 49; Fax 089 85 82 49; www.ravello.info*

Duomo

Open daily 9am-1pm and 4.30-7pm, museum 9am-7pm. *2 € (museum).* *☎089 85 83 11; www.chiesaravello.com*

The cathedral, founded in 1086, was remodelled in the 18C. The campanile is 13C. The splendid **bronze door**★ with its panels of reliefs was cast in 1179 by Barisanus da Trani. There is a magnificent mosaic-covered **pulpit**★★ with a remarkable variety of motifs and fantastic animals (1272). On the left is an elegant 12C **ambo** adorned with green mosaics representing Jonah and the Whale. The small **museum** in the crypt has mosaics and a silver head-reliquary with the relics of St Barbara.

To the left of the Duomo, the Cameo Factory houses a tiny **Coral museum** displaying some prized pieces, including a snuffbox encrusted with cameos.

Chiesa di San Giovanni del Toro

Closed for rennovation. *☎089 85 83 11; www.chiesaravello.com*

Via S. Giovanni del Toro, with its stunning **belvedere**★★, leads to this 11C church with its 11C **pulpit**★, a Roman sarcophagus (south aisle) and 14C frescoes in the apses and the crypt.

Villa Cimbrone★★

Via Santa Chiara 26. *Open daily, 9.30am-dusk.* *5 €. ☎089 85 74 59, Fax 089 85 77 77; www.villacimbrone.com.*

A charming **alley**★ leads from Piazza Vescovado to the 19C villa, passing on the way through the Gothic porch of the convent of St Francis. Villa Cimbrone is a homage to the history of Ravello and a point of reference for the **Bloomsbury Group** for whom the garden embodied the ideal aesthetic of clarity, order and harmony. A wide alley leads through the garden to the belvedere, adorned with marble busts. There is an immense **panorama**★★★ over the terraced hillsides, Maiori, Cape Orso and the Gulf of Salerno.

Capo d'Orso★

The cape with its jagged rocks affords an interesting view of Maiori Bay.

Vietri sul Mare

At the eastern end of this stretch of coastline, this pretty town is known for its ceramic ware. It affords magnificent **views**★★ of the Amalfi coast.

Salerno★

The medieval quarter starts at Corso Vittorio Emanuele and stretches along the Via dei Mercanti. ⓘ *The largest lot is on Via Alvarez.* ⓘ *Lungomare Trieste 7/9.* ☎089 22 47 44; www.aziendaturismo.sa.it

Salerno, lying along the graceful curve of its gulf, has retained a medieval quarter on the slopes of a hill crowned by a castle. From the Lungomare Triestea promenade, planted with palm trees and tamarinds, there is a wide view of the Gulf of Salerno. The picturesque via Mercantia, which crosses the old town, is lined with shops, old houses and oratories. At its west end stands an arch, Arco di Arechi, built by the Lombards in the 8C.

Duomo★★

ⓘ*Open daily 7am–12pm and 4-7.30pm.* ⓘ*No charge.*

The cathedral is dedicated to St Matthew the Evangelist, who is buried in the crypt. It was built on the orders of Robert Guiscard and consecrated by Pope Gregory VII in 1085. The Norman-style building was remodelled in the 18C and suffered considerable damage in the 1980 earthquake. The church is preceded by an arcaded atrium of multicoloured stone with ancient columns. The square tower to the right is 12C. The central doorway has 11C **bronze doors★** cast in Constantinople.

The spacious interior contains two **ambosa★** encrusted with decorative mosaics and on columns with marvellously carved capitals, along with the paschal candelabrum and the elegant iconostasis, which encloses the chancel. The Crusaders' Chapel at the end of the south aisle is where the Crusaders had their arms blessed. Under the altar is the tomb of Pope Gregory VII who died in exile at Salerno (1085). In the north aisle is the tomb of Margaret of Durazzo, wife of Charles III of Anjou.

Museo Archeologico

ⓘ ⓘ*For information on opening times* ☎089 23 11 35 ⓘ *No charge. www.musei-biblioteche.provincia.salerno.it.*

Housed in the attractive St Benedict monastery complex, the museum has artefacts dating from prehistory to the late Imperial era. Of particular note is the **bronze Head of Apollo★** (1C BC) and a fine collection of pre-Roman amber.

CREMONA★

POPULATION 70 944

MICHELIN MAP 561 OR 562 G 11/12 – LOMBARDY.

The original Gallic settlement became a Latin city before emerging as an independent commune in the Middle Ages. It suffered from the Guelph and Ghibelline troubles of the period. In 1334 the town came under Visconti rule and was united with the Duchy of Milan in the 15C. During the Renaissance the town was the centre of a brilliant artistic movement. In the 18C and 19C the French and Austrians fought for supremacy over Cremona until the Risorgimento. Cremona is the birthplace of the composer Claudio Monteverdi (1567-1643) who created modern opera with his *Orfeo* and *The Coronation of Poppea*.

- ⓘ **Information:** Piazza del Comune 5, 26100 Cremona. ☎0372 23 233; www.comune. cremona.it.
- ▶ **Orient Yourself:** Cremona is an important agricultural market town in the heart of a fertile agricultural region, the Pianura Padana, on the banks of the River Po. It is easily reached from A 21 which links Brescia with Piacenza
- ⓘ **Don't Miss:** Zodiac illustrations in the Torrazzo's tower and the Duomo.
- ⓘ **Organizing Your Time:** A tour of the town will take half a day.
- ⓘ **Also See:** *BRESCIA, PIACENZA*

The Violins of Cremona

From the late 16C the stringed-instrument makers of Cremona gained a reputation as violin and cello makers. The town was the birthplace of the greatest violin makers of all time and their instruments are still highly sought after by famous violinists today. The sound they produce is quite extraordinary, almost supernatural in tone and incredibly close to the human voice. The International School of Violin Making carries on this tradition. The first of the famous violin makers of Cremona was Andrea Amati, from whom King Charles IX of France commissioned instruments in the 16C. His work was continued by his sons and his nephew, Nicolò, master of Andrea Guarneri and the most famous of all of them, Antonio Stradivarius (c 1644-1737), who made more than 1 000 instruments including the "Cremonese" which was made in 1715. Andrea Guarneri was the first of another renowned dynasty in which the most skilled violin maker of them all was Giuseppe Guarneri (1698-1744), better known as Guarneri del Gesù because of the three letters IHS (Jesus, Saviour of Mankind) inscribed on all his violins. Knowledgeable music lovers will find it easy to distinguish between the crystal-clear tones of a Stradivarius and the deeper, powerful tones of a Guarneri del Gesù. A discourse on violin making must include reference to Niccoló Paganini (1782-1840), the violinist whose genius of interpretation, virtuosity and pyrotechnics were legendary. Paganini played a number of violins made in Cremona and these include the Guarneri (1743), known as "Il Cannone", which is now owned by the Comune of Genoa.

G. Bludzin/MICHELIN

Visit

Torrazzo★★★

🕓 Open 10am-1pm and 2.30-6pm. 🕓Closed Mon (except public holidays), 1 Jan, 25 Dec. ▰4 €. ☎0372 27 386.

The remarkable late-13C campanile is linked to the cathedral by a Renaissance gallery. Its massive form is elegantly crowned by an octagonal 14C storey. From the top (112m/367ft), there is a lovely view★ over the town. The astronomical clock, which dates from 1471, has undergone a number of alterations in its history, the last being in the 1970s. It is notable for its illustrations of the stars and the constellations of the zodiac.

Duomo★★

This magnificent Lombard cathedral was begun in the Romanesque and completed in the Gothic style (1107-1332). The richly decorated white marble façade is preceded by a porch. Numerous decorative features were later additions, namely the frieze by the followers of Antelami, the large 13C rose window and the four statue-columns of the central doorway.

The spacious **interior** is decorated with **frescoes**★ by the Cremona School (Boccaccino, the Campi, the Bembo, Romanino da Brescia, Pordenone and Gatti). Also of interest, at the entrance to the chancel, are the **high reliefs**★★ by Amadeo, the architect-sculptor of the Carthusian Monastery at Pavia.

Battistero★

This harmonious octagonal baptistery, preceded by a Lombard porch and decorated with a gallery, was remodelled during the Renaissance.

Palazzo Comunale

♿🕓Open Tue-Sat 10am-1pm and 2.30-6pm 🕓Closed Mon (apart from Bank Holidays), 1 Jan, 1 May, 25 Dec. ▰4 €. ☎0372 27 386.

This 13C palace was remodelled at a later date. Inside are displayed the most famous violins in the world: the *Charles IX of France* (Amati), the *Hammerle* (Amati), the *Quarestani* (Guarneri), the *Cremonese* 1715 (Antonio Stradivarius) and the *Stauffer* (Guarneri del Gesù).

To the left of the palace is the lovely 13C **Loggia dei Militi**.

Museo Civico Ala Ponzone

&. ○*Open Mon-Sat 9am-6pm, Sun and public holidays 10am-6pm.* ○*Closed Mon (except Easter Mon), 1 Jan, 1 May, 25 Dec.* ◎*7 € combined ticket with Museo Stradivariano.* ☎*0372 40 77 70; www.cremonamostre.it*

Installed in a 16C palace, this municipal museum has a **picture gallery** with works of the Cremona School. Note the dramatic **St Frances in Meditation** by **Caravaggio**, the *Vegetable Gardener* by **Arcimboldo**.

Museo Stradivariano

&. ○*Open Mon-Sat 9am-6pm, Sun and public holidays 10am-6pm.* ○*Closed*

TRATTORIA

Alba – *Via Persico 40* – ☎*0372 43 37 00* – ○*Closed Sun, Mon, 24 Dec-7 Jan, Aug* – ▤ – *Book* – *15/23 €.* Typical trattoria with a family atmosphere. Simple interior with panelled walls. Hearty home cooking, traditional dishes with a regional flavour – at its best during the winter months. The cotechino (pork sausage) baked in a bread crust is particularly good

Mon (except Easter Mon), 1 Jan, 1 May, 25 Dec. ◎*7 € combined ticket with Museo Civico.* ☎*0372 40 77 70; www. cremonamostre.it*

This museum has displays of wooden models and tools belonging to Stradivarius, as well as stringed instruments from the 17C-20C.

🕯 Palazzo Fodri★, Palazzo Stanga, Palazzo Raimondi, S. Agostino, S. Sigismondo.

DELTA DEL PO★
PO DELTA

MICHELIN MAP 562 H 18 – EMILIA-ROMAGNA, VENETO.

This area around the Po Delta was once a malaria-infested marshy district. Land reclamation and drainage have since turned it into a fertile agricultural area and a designated nature reserve. The Chioggia to Ravenna road (90km/56mi) traverses these flat expanses stretching away to the horizon. Clumps of poplars and umbrella pines add touches of colour to the monotony of this countryside where eel fishing is still common on the canals that criss-cross the area. To the south the Valli di Comacchio, Italy's most important zone of lagoons, has a melancholy beauty. The Polesine is the strip of the Pianura Veneta that stretches from Rovigo to the delta, taking in the ancient cities of Adria and Porto Tolle, the last town on the map before the River Po flows out to sea. What you see today is the result of the combined action of the Po, the Adige and man.

▪ **Information:** For the Emilia-Romagna region: Castello Estense, 44100 Ferrara, ☎0532 29 93 03; www.emiliaromagnaturismo.it, Consorzio Parco del Delta, Via Cavour 11, 44022 Comacchio (FE), ☎0533 31 40 03; For the Veneto region: Via Dunant 10, 45100 Rovigo, ☎0425 36 14 81; Via dei Pini 4, 45010 Rosolina Mare, ☎0426 68 012; www.regione.veneto.it.

▶ **Orient Yourself:** The Po Delta is the region between Venice and Ravenna, which takes in the provinces of Rovigo and Ferrara.

👁 **Don't Miss:** Colourful Comacchio and the imposing Abbazia di Pomposa.

🕐 **Organizing Your Time:** Allow half a day.

🕯 **Also See:** *FERRARA, LAGUNA VENETA, RAVENNA, VENEZIA*

Visit

Comacchio

🗐 Comacchio Tourist Information Office, Piazza Folegatti 28 , 44022 Comacchio. ☏ 0533 31 01 11; www.comune.comacchio.fe.it

Comacchio is built on sand and water and in many ways it resembles Chioggia. The main activity here is eel fishing. Its brightly-coloured fishermen's houses, its canals spanned by curious bridges and the fishing boats lend it a special charm.

Abbazia di Pomposa★★

🕐 Open daily, 9.30am-1pm and 2.30-5.30pm. 🕐 Closed 1 Jan, 1 May, 25 Dec. ☜ Donations welcome. ☏ 0533 99 95 23; www.pomposa.info.

This Benedictine abbey was founded in the 6C and enjoyed fame in the Middle Ages when it was distinguished by its abbot, St Guy (Guido) of Ravenna, and by another monk, **Guido d'Arezzo**, the inventor of the musical scale and note system. In July and August the abbey hosts classical music concerts.

The fine pre-Romanesque **church** in the style typical of Ravenna is preceded by a narthex whose decoration exemplifies the Byzantine style. The nave has some magnificent **mosaic flooring** and two holy water stoups, one in the Romanesque style and the other in the Byzantine style. The walls bear an exceptional cycle of 14C **frescoes** based on the illuminator's art. From right to left the upper band is devoted to the Old Testament while the lower band has scenes from the Life of Christ; the corner pieces of the arches depict the *Apocalypse*. On the west wall are a *Last Judgement* and in the apsidal chapel *Christ in Majesty*. Opposite the church stands the Palazzo della Ragione, where the abbot dispensed justice.

The melancholy charm of the Po Delta near Ferrara

L. Pessina/MICHELIN

DOLOMITI★★★
THE DOLOMITES
MICHELIN MAP 562 C 16-19 – VENETO – TRENTINO-ALTO ADIGE.

Situated between the Veneto and Trentino-Alto Adige, the fan of so-called "Pale Mountains" (Monti Pallidi) take on red tints at sunset. Their harsh, rocky contours embrace crystalline lakes and mysteries, which have become the very stuff of numerous poetic legends.

- **Information:** Azienda di Promozione Turistica Dolomiti, Piazzetta S. Francesco 8, 32043 Cortina d'Ampezzo (Belluno), ☎0436 32 31, www.apt-dolomiti-cortina.it; Consorzio Turistico Alta Badia, Strada Col Alt 36, 39033 Corvara, ☎0471 83 61 76, www.altabadia.org; Consorzio Turistico Val Gardena, Via Dursan 78/bis, 39047 S. Cristina, ☎0471 79 22 77, www.valgardena.it; Consorzio Turistico Rosengarten-Latemar, 39050 Ponte Nova, ☎0471 61 03 10, www.rosengarten-latemar.com; Comitato Turistico Sciliar-Alpe di Siusi, Via Sciliar 16, 39040 Siusi, ☎0471 70 70 24, www.alpe-di-siusi.info. Website for the whole of the Alto-Adige: www.hallo.com.
- **Orient Yourself:** In the Trentino-Alto Adige region, the Dolomites are reached by A 22 off the Brennero transalpine route. From the Veneto region take A 27.
- **Parking:** Leave your car in the car park north of Chiusa if visiting the Convento di Sabiona.
- **Don't Miss:** Val Gardena and panoramas from Tofana di Mezzo.
- **Organizing Your Time:** Allow for 3-4 days of skiing or walking.
- **Especially for Kids:** Vigo di Fassa, and the furnicular railway at Sesto.
- **Also See:** *BELLUNO, BOLZANO, TRENTO.*

A Bit of History

The Dolomites are made of a white calcareous rock, dolomite, which takes its name from the French geologist Déodat de Dolomieu, who studied its composition in the 18C. Some 150 million years ago this land was submerged by the Tethys sea. On its sandy depths coral reefs and limestone began to shape the "Pale Mountains".

About 70 million years ago, during the Alpine orogenis (the corrugation of the earth's crust) the layers were violently compressed and forced to the surface. The Dolomites were nearly completed in the Quaternary Era (about 2 million years ago) when glaciers softened and hollowed out the valleys.

The massifs – To the southeast rise the Pelmo (3 168m/10 393ft) and the Civetta (3 220m/10 564ft) massifs. To the south, near the peak of the Vezzana, the Pale di San Martino, streaked by fissures, divide into three chains separated by a plateau. The Latemar

(2 842m/9 324ft) and the Catinaccio (2 981m/9 780ft) massifs, together with the Torri del Vaiolet (Towers of Vaiolet), frame the Costalunga Pass. To the north of the pass rise the Sasso Lungo and the vast Sella Massif (Gruppo di Sella).

To the east, the chief summits in the Cortina Dolomites are the Tofane, the Sorapis and the Cristallo. Finally, in the heart of the range, stands the **Marmolada Massif** (Gruppo della Marmolada, 3 342m/10 964ft).

Between Cortina and the Piave Valley the wooded region of **Cadore** boasts the Antelao (3 263m/10 705ft) and the triple peak, Tre Cime di Lavaredo (Drei Zinnen), which it shares with the Parco delle Dolomiti di Sesto in Alto Adige.

Flora and fauna – The Dolomite landscape is coloured by coniferous forests, crocuses, edelweiss, rhododendron, lilies and alpine bluebells. Tourist activity drives away wild animals, but the Dolomites are still a refuge for many, including royal eagles and woodcock.

Excursions

1 Strada delle Dolomiti★★★

From Bolzano to Cortina – 210km/131mi –allow two days.
The main touring route is the great Dolomite Road, a world-famous example of road engineering.

Bolzano★   *see BOLZANO*

Gola della Val d'Ega★
This narrow gorge, the Ega Valley, with pink sandstone walls, is guarded by the **Castel Cornedo**.

Passo di Costalunga★
From this pass on the Dolomite Road there is a **view**★ over the Catinaccio on one side and the Latemar on the other

Vigo di Fassa❋❋
Kids *School and kinderpark for young skiiers. Via Rezia, 38039 Vigo di Fassa. ☎0462 76 31 25; www.scuolascivigo. com* 🄸 *Piaz G. Marconi, 5, 38032 Canazei. ☎0462 60 96 00; www.fassa.com* This resort, in a picturesque site★in the Val di Farsa, is a mountaineering centre in the Catinaccio Massif (cable car).

Canazei❋❋❋
🄸 *Piaz G. Marconi, 5, 38032 Canazei. ☎0462 60 96 00; www.fassa.com* Canazei lies in the heart of the massif, between the Catinaccio, the Towers of Vaiolet (Torri del Vaiolet), the Sella Massif and the Marmolada. This is the usual base for excursions in the Marmolada range.

Tre Cime di Lavaredo

L. Pessina/MICHELIN

▶ *At Canazei turn right onto S 641.*

This road affords very fine **views**★★ of the Marmolada range and its glacier. As one comes out of a long tunnel a lake, **Lago di Fedaia**★, suddenly appears.

Marmolada★★★
🄸 *www.marmolada.com* This is the highest massif in the Dolomites, famous for its glacier and very fast ski-runs. The **cable car** from Malga Ciapela goes up to 3 265m/10 712ft offering admirable **panoramas**★★★ of the Cortina peaks (Tofana and Cristallo), the Sasso Lungo, the enormous tabular mass of the Sella Massif and in the background the summits of the Austrian Alps including the Grossglockner.

▶ *Return to Canazei then after 5.5km/3mi turn left.*

Passo di Sella★★★
Linking the Val di Fassa and Val Gardena this pass offers one of the most extensive **panoramas**★★★ in the Dolomites, including the Sella, Sasso Lungo and Marmolada massifs.

Val Gardena★★★
🄸 *www.val-gardena.com* One of the most famous valleys in the Dolomites both for its beauty and crowds of tourists. The inhabitants still speak a language which was born during the Roman occupation: the Ladin dialect.
Skilful local woodwork can be seen in shops in Selva (Wolkenstein), Santa Cristina and Ortisei (St Ulrich).
Selva di Val Gardena❋❋❋ – 🄸 *www.val-gardena.com*. This resort lies at the Sella Massif base and is a craft centre.
Ortisei❋❋❋ – 🄸 *www.ortisei.com* From Ortisei a cable car climbs up to **Alpe di Siusi**❋ (Seiser Alm), a 60km2/23sq mi plateau in a delightful **setting**★★ overlooking the Sasso Lungo and the Sciliar. This base for excursions suits all tastes and abilities.

▶ *Return to the Dolomite Road.*

Passo Pordoi★★★
The highest pass (2 239m/7 346ft) on the Dolomite Road lies between huge

Address Book

For coin ranges see the Legend on the cover flap.

WHERE TO STAY

Hotel Gran Ancëi – *39030 San Cassiano – 26.5km/16mi west of Cortina d'Ampezzo – ☎0471 84 95 40 – Fax 0471 84 92 10 – www.granancei.com – Closed mid-Apr-mid-Jun and mid-Oct-beg-Dec – ▣ – 29 rm – ☞ – Restaurant.* Surrounded by woodland and located near the ski slopes, this is very much a mountain-style hotel. Furniture and decor in the rooms and public areas are mostly in wood. Relaxing, peaceful ambience. Spacious and airy with wonderful views over the Dolomites.

Hotel Erika – *Via Braies di Fuori 66 – 39030 Braies – 5km/3mi north of Lago di Braies – ☎0474 74 86 84 – Fax 0474 74 87 55 – www.hotelerika.net – Closed mid-Apr-mid-Jun, Nov-mid -Dec – ▣ ✕◈ – 28 rm P78/146 – ☞ 7.75 € – Restaurant.* Friendly and enthusiastic staff on hand to ensure you get the best out of your stay in the Dolomites – whatever the season. Comfortable rooms with chunky wooden furniture – the rooms on the third floor are particularly attractive. Rates for half-board and full-board accommodation.

Hotel Cavallino d'Oro – *Piazza Kraus – 39040 Castelrotto – 26km/16mi northeast of Bolzano – ☎0471 70 63 37 – Fax 0471 70 71 72 – www.cavallino.it – Closed 10 Nov-5 Dec – 23 rm – ☞ – Restaurant.* Would suit those looking for a romantic ambience – complete with four-poster beds and elegant antique Tyrolean-style furniture. The dining area has an equally intimate atmosphere, housed in the 17C "stuben" which are characteristic of the local architecture.

Monika Hotel – *Via del Parco 2 – 39030 Sesto – ☎0474 71 03 84 – Fax 0474 71 01 77 – www.monika.it – Closed 3 Apr-19 May, 15 Oct-15 Dec – ✕ ▣ – 27 rm – ☞ – Restaurant.* This hotel has a "chocolate-box" appeal – Tyrolean in style, stylish wooden interior, set in verdant, peaceful surroundings. The rooms are simple but comfortable. In contrast, the dining room is more elegant.

Hotel Lavaredo – *Via M. Piana 11 – 32040 Misurina – ☎0435 39 227 – Fax 0435 39 127 – www.lavaredohotel.it – Closed mid-Apr-mid-May and Nov-20 Dec – ▣ – 31 rm – ☞ 8 € – Restaurant.* Lakeside setting overlooked by the magnificent mountain peaks of the Cime di Lavaredo. Family-run hotel with comfortable rooms and spacious public areas (lots of wood!). Cooking has a national rather than regional flavour: some international dishes.

Hotel Colfosco-Kolfusch-gerhof – *Via Ronn 7 – 39030 Corvara in Badia – 2km/1.2mi east of Passo Gardena on S 244 – ☎0471 83 61 88 – Fax 0471 83 63 51 – www.kolfuschgerhof.com – Closed Oct-2 Dec, Apr to mid-Jun – ▣◈◈ – 44 rm – ☞ – Restaurant. 30/33 €.* Situated near the lifts, this hotel would appeal to both summer and winter mountain sports enthusiasts. The hotel also has squash courts and table tennis tables: other facilities include the sauna, Turkish baths and massage rooms. The ambience is typically Tyrolean. Friendly atmosphere. Good for anyone in search of some peace and quiet.

WHERE TO EAT

Concordia – *Via Roma 41 – 39046 Ortisei – ☎0471 79 62 76 – www.restaurantconcordia.com – Closed Nov-May.* One of the few restaurants in the region to merit the definition. Tasty, carefully-prepared dishes with a regional flavour. Attractive surroundings and informal, friendly atmosphere.

Gérard – *Via Plan de Gralba 37 – 39048 Selva di Val Gardena – ☎0471 79 52 74 – www.chalet-gerard.com – ◷Closed Apr, May and part of Oct and Nov – ✍.* If the cooking is typical of the region, with the ubiquitous polenta served alongside a variety of local products, the wonderful views that this kind of refuge affords (altitude 2 000m/6 560ft!) is unique: the Sella and Sasso Lungo mountain ranges are stunning. Overnight stays possible.

Rifugio Larin – *Località Senes – 32046 San Vito di Cadore – 9km/5mi south of Cortina d'Ampezzo on S 51 – ☎0436 91 12 – Closed Oct-May.*

A classic mountain hut-restaurant with lots of atmosphere. Hearty but carefully prepared food. Also accessible by car – although it would be a shame to miss out on a pleasant stroll. Wonderful views.

🍴🍴 **Unterwirt** – *Località Gudon – 39043 Chiusa d'Isarco – 34km/20mi northeast of Bolzano on S 12 – ☎0472 84 40 00 – www.unterwirt-gufidaun. com – Closed Sun and Mon, Jan-Mar and 10 days in June and July – 🅿️ – 7 rm.* Although the cooking has a traditional slant, it is imaginative and the dishes are beautifully presented. Lovely surroundings – take a stroll in the garden or lounge by the swimming pool after your meal. There are some "ecologically friendly" rooms for overnight stays. Charming village location.

GOING OUT

Enoteca – *Via Mercato 5 – 32043 Cortina d'Ampezzo – ☎0436 86 20 40 – Mon-Sat 10.30am-1pm and 4.30-9pm, open throughout the day in high season. Closed mid-May to mid-Jun.* A beautiful old door opens onto this lovely little wine bar with its wooden ceiling. A great place for tasting the local wines.

SPORT AND LEISURE

MOUNTAIN FOOTPATHS

The Dolomites have a dense network of footpaths. Whether you are an expert climber or simply want to take a peaceful walk, there is a vast choice of routes for those wishing to get a better look at the Monti Pallidi. Maps and guides listing paths, mountain huts and bivouacs are on sale just about everywhere.

Some mountain pathways include:

No 2 (Bressanone-Feltre): This path crosses the Plose, the Puez Group, the Gardenaccia, the Sella and the Marmolada massif.

No 3 (Villabassa-Longarone): This path winds its way through Val Pusteria, the Croda Rossa, Misurina, the Cristallo, the Sorapis and the Antelao.

No 4 (San Candido-Pieve di Cadore): This track goes through the Sesto Dolomites, the Cadini di Misurina and the Marmarole.

To be fully prepared for a mountain excursion it is advisable to contact the tourist offices listed above.

Scuola di Volo Fly Ten – *Via Dolomiti 75 – 38031 Campitello di Fassa – ☎335 67 57 667 (mobile phone) – Open 8.45am-noon.* No physical training is required before undertaking paragliding. For those brave enough the sensation is absolutely exhilarating.

Gruppo Guide Alpine Scuola di Alpinismo – *Corso Italia 69/A – 32043 Cortina d'Ampezzo – ☎0436 86 85 05 – guidecortina@mnet-climb.com – Open Mon-Sat 8am-noon and 4-8pm, Sun 4-8pm. Closed mid-Sep to last week in Jun.* Waterfalls, lakes, caves, routes with ropes (open to everybody) – a wide variety of organised excursions on offer.

---

blocks of rock with sheer sides and shorn-off tops.

Passo del Falzarego

Nearing Cortina the pass cuts through the Tofane and skirts the barren landscape of the Cinque Torri, which inspired Tolkein when he wrote The Lord of the Rings.

Cortina d'Ampezzo★★★

🔲 *www.cortina.dolomiti.com* Cortina, the capital of the Dolomites, is a winter sports and summer resort with a worldwide reputation. Set in the heart of the Dolomites at an altitude of 1 210m/ 4 000ft Cortina makes a good excursion centre for discovering the magnificent **mountain scenery**★★★.

Tondi di Faloria★★★

🚠 *Cable car service to Faloria from Via Ria di Zeto. From Cortina d'Ampezzo to Tondi di Faloria: in winter, "Tondi," "Girilada," "Vitelli," "Rio Gere" and "Bigontina" chairlifts* 🎿*. ☎0436 32 31; www.dolomiti.org.* From the summit a grand panorama may be enjoyed. Excellent ski slopes.

Tofana di Mezzo★★★ – *"Freccia del Cielo" cable car: for information telephone the tourist office (*🔎*see above).* A cable car

The Legend of the Pale Mountains

Legend has it that a prince who lived at the foot of the Alps married the daughter of the King of the Moon. The young girl loved flowers and meadows but was disturbed by the dark colour of the rocks. She so desperately missed the pale mountains of her home that she felt compelled to return to the Moon. Some dwarfs came to the disconsolate prince's aid and made some skeins of thread from the moon's rays, weaving them into nets which they placed on the mountains. The princess was thus able to return and the dwarfs were allowed to live in the kingdom.

At sunset, however, the Monti Pallidi assumed fiery hues, probably caused by the beautiful rose garden situated on one of the mountains where the King of the Dwarfs lived. One day, attracted by the rose garden, some foreign warriors arrived in the kingdom and imprisoned the king, who cursed the plant and ordered that roses would never be seen again, by day or night. The curse did not, however, mention sunset, a moment suspended between day and night. Thus for those few minutes the Catinaccio mountain, which the Germans refer to as Rosengarten (rose garden), is still inflamed and throws light onto every rock of the Dolomites.

climbs to 3 244m/10 743ft, for superb panorama of the mountain.

Belvedere Pocol★★ – ○*Open Dec-Easter and 15 Jul-15 Sep. For information on ☎0436 86 79 21. Hourly bus service from Piazza Roma, Cortina.*

Lying to the southwest, this viewpoint affords a lovely sunset view of Cortina.

②Val Pusteria and surrounding area

Val Pusteria, or Pustertal, is bordered to the south by the Dolomites and by the central Alps to the north. From the end of the 13C until the 16C it belonged to the County of Gorizia and formed part of the Strada d'Alemagna, a road which linked Venice and Germany. This itinerary begins in Bressanone and continues into the Pusteria Valley.

Bressanone★★

🛈 *Associazione Turistica di Bressanone, Bahnhofstrasse 9, 39042 Bressanone. ☎0472 83 64 01; www.brixen.org .*

Set at the confluence of the Rienza and Isarco rivers, Bressanone is an elegant Tyrolean town that enjoys an exceptionally high number of sunshine hours. Conquered by the Romans in 15 BC, it then belonged to Bavaria and Austria, until 1919 when it became Italian.

Duomo – This Baroque cathedral has a neo-Classical west front, luminous interior decorated with golf leaf frescoes and Romanesque **cloisters.**★

Palazzo vescovile – Commissioned by Prince-Bishop Bruno de Kirchberg after 1250, the palace underwent numerous alterations but retained its superb **courtyard**★. It now houses the vast **Museo diocesano**★ containing a wonderful set of polychrome **wood carvings**★★ (Romanesque and Gothic Tyrolean), **altarpieces**★ carved in the round dating from the Renaissance, the cathedral **treasure**★ and **Nativity scenes**★ dating from the 18C to 20C. ○*Open mid-Mar to Oct 10am-5pm, rest of the year 2-5pm.* ○*Closed Mon (in summer), Feb to mid-Mar, Nov and 24-25 Dec. 6 € combined ticket, 4 € museum only. ☎0472 83 05 05; www.hofburg.it.*

▸ *Head south towards Chiusa.*

Convento di Sabiona

🅿*Leave the car in the car park north of Chiusa.* ▸*To get to the convent from the village, go on foot (30min).* This convent of Benedictine nuns dates back to the 17C. It was built on the rock where the bishop's palace had stood, the palace having burnt down after being struck by lightning in 1535.

▸ *Turn around and head in the direction of Bressanone, turning right onto the road for Plose.*

Plose★★

To the southeast. Alt 2 446 m/8 031ft. Cable car: from Sant'Andrea, southeast

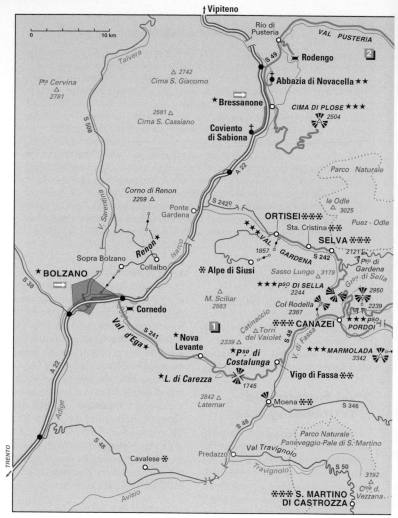

↑ Vipiteno

VAL PUSTERIA

Rio di Pusteria

■ Rodengo

● Abbazia di Novacella ★★

★ Bressanone

CIMA DI PLOSE ★★★
✳ 2504

Coviento di Sabiona

2742
Cima S. Giacomo

2581
Cima S. Cassiano

Parco Naturale

le Odle
3025

Puez - Odle

ORTISEI ★★★
Sta. Cristina ★★

SELVA ★★★

Corno di Renon
2259

Ponte Gardena

2121

VAL
1857

Pso di Gardena

Alpe di Siusi

GARDENA

S 242

Sasso Lungo
3179

Sopra Bolzano

Renon

★ BOLZANO

Collalbo

M. Sciliar
2563

★★★ Pso DI SELLA
2244

✳ 2950
2239

Col Rodella
2387

★★★ Pso
PORDOI

■ Cornedo

CANAZEI

Cetinaccio
Torri
del Vaiolet
2339

★ Nova Levante ★

Val d'Ega

V. di Fassa

★★★ MARMOLADA
3342

Pso di
Costalunga

✳ 1745

Vigo di Fassa ★★

★ L. di Carezza

2842
Latemar

Moena ★★

S 346

Parco Naturale
Paneveggio-Pale di S. Martino

Cavalese ✳

Predazzo

Val Travignolo

S 50

3192

Travignolo

Cima d.
Vezzana

★★★ S. MARTINO
DI CASTROZZA

of Bressanone, cable car to Valcroce (winter and Jul-Sep), then chairlift to Plose (in winter only). ℹ Bressanone tourist office ☎ 0472 83 64 01, www.brixen.org or Società Funivia Plose ☎ 0472 20 04 33. The cable car from Valcroce and then another from Plose enable visitors to enjoy a wonderful **panorama**★★★ of the Dolomites and the Austrian mountains.

▶ Retrace your steps and continue along SS 49. The Abbazia di Novacella is 3km/2mi north of Bressanone.

Abbazia di Novacella★★

3km/2mi north. 🚶Guided tours by appointment only, ⬦ 5 €. ☎ 0472 83 61 89; www.abbazianovacella.it

The abbey was founded in 1142 and run by Augustinian monks. The courtyard contains the **Well of Wonders** decorated with "eight" wonders of the world, one of which is the abbey itself. The Bavarian Baroque **church** has an ornate interior and **Rococo** library of 76 000 rare books, and manuscripts. The first village encountered when arriving on the State road is Rio di Pusteria. Close by stands the **Castello di Rodengo**, decorated with the oldest

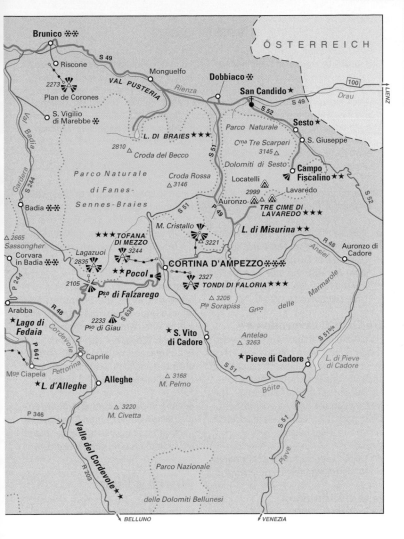

cycle of Romanesque frescoes (13C) with a profane theme: the epic poem *Iwein* by Hartmann von Aue. *Open mid-May to mid-Oct. Guided tours only (1hr) at 11am and 3pm (also at 4pm mid-Jul to mid-Aug). Closed Mon. 4 €. For information contact: 0472 45 40 56.*

Brunico✳✳

♿ *Open Tue-Sat 9.30am-5.30pm; Sun and public holidays 2-6pm. Closed Nov-Easter. 5 €. 0474 55 20 87; www.provinz.bz.it/volkskundemuseen* This is the main town in the Pusteria Valley. The interesting **Ethnography Museum**★ (♿ *Open Tue-Sat 9.30am-*

5.30pm; Sun and public holidays 2-6pm. *Closed Nov-Easter. 5 €. 0474 55 20 87; www.provinz.bz.it/volkskunde-museen*) in **Teodone** covers an area of 3ha/7 acres, and includes various types of rural building: country manor, hayloft, farm, grain store, oven, mill.

▶ *From Brunico go in the direction of Dobbiaco. After Monguelfo turn right where Lago di Braies is signposted.*

Lago di Braies★★★

Alt 1 495m/4 905ft. This shimmering lake (called Pragser Wildsee in German) can be circumnavigated in one hour. It is also

The Ladin Culture

Ladin is a curious ancient language which has its roots in the Latin language and is spoken by around 30 000 people in and around the Dolomites. It had emerged by the 5C as a direct result of the earlier Roman expansion into the mountainous regions. At Ciastel de Tor, in San Martino in Badia, there is the Museumladina, which has an impressive exhibition on the Ladin culture. The artistic displays and the creative use of the latest technology (projectors, computers, interactive exhibitions) make for an interesting visit. ◷*Open Apr-Oct, Tue-Sat 10am-6pm, Sun 2-6pm, rest of the year Wed-Fri 2-6pm only.* ◷*Closed Mon, Nov, 25 Dec.* ⊜*5.50 €.* ☎*0474 52 40 20; www.museumladin.it.*

the starting point of some rather arduous mountain footpaths.

▷ *Proceed through the Pusteria Valley. Turn right before Dubbiaco in the direction of Cortina. Follow directions for Misurina and then for Tre Cime di Lavaredo. The last stretch is a toll-road. ☎0435 39 109.*

Tre Cime di Lavaredo★★★

From the refuge at Auronza the Lavaredo shelter is reached in half an hour. From there the Locatelli shelter is reached in an hour. This last stretch offers spectacular views of the Tre Cime range. The Tre Cime can also be reached from Sesto, along path 102, which leads to Locatelli in two and a half hours.

▷ *On the way back from Tre Cime a stop at Lago di Misurina is recommended.*

Lago di Misurina★★

Alt 1 759m/5 770ft. This lake is set among a plantation of fir trees and is an excellent starting point for excursions to the surrounding mountains, from the Tre Cime di Lavaredo to the Cristallo.

Dobbiaco⁕

Dobbiaco (Toblach in German) was an important town in the Middle Ages as it was at a crossroads with the Strada dell'Alemagna.

San Candido★

This pretty village has the most important Romanesque church in the Alto Adige. The **collegiata**⁕ dates from the 13C. Most striking is the *Crucifixion*, a 13C

wood sculptural group with Christ's feet resting on Adam's head.

▷ *At San Candido turn right for Sesto leaving the Pusteria, which eventually leads to Austria.*

Sesto★

Sesto overlooks the Dolomites and offers a huge variety of footpaths and alpine excursions. The Monte Elmo funicular ᴷⁱᵈˢ makes distances shorter. For a peaceful walk, path 4D crosses the forest and high pastures and affords views of the Meridiana del Sesto.

▷ *At San Giuseppe (Moos) the Val Fiscalino leads to* **Campo Fiscalinoa**⁕ *for stunning views of the Meridiana di Sesto and Cima dei Tre Scarperi.*

Worth a Visit

Valle del Cordevole★★

The road from Caprile to Belluno is lined with hilltop villages. **Alleghe** on the **lake**⁕ is a good excursion centre.

San Martino di Castrozza⁕⁕⁕

A good starting point for excursions.

Pieve di Cadore★

◷*Open Jun-Sep 10am-12.30pm and 3-7pm, Oct-May by appointment only.* ◷*Closed Sun and holidays (winter).* ⊜*2 €.* ☎*0435 32 262; www.magnifica-comunitadicadore.it*

The birthplace of the artist, **Titian**, the town church holds one of his works and his family house is now a **museum**.

ISOLA D'**ELBA**★★

MICHELIN MAP 563 N 12/13
SEE ALSO THE GREEN GUIDE TUSCANY.

The Allied Governments exiled Napoleon Bonaparte here in 1814. Though given the title "Emperor of Elba", he escaped after nine months and began the 100 Days Campaign –his last hurrah – in France. It's the largest island in the **Tuscan Archipelago**★★, which includes Pianosa, Capraia, Giglio, Giannutri and Montecristo. The capital is Portoferraio.

Elba is more of a holiday resort than a place for a day excursion, but it is possible to tour the island in two days, either in one's own car or in a hire car available in Portoferraio.

- **Information:** Calata Italia, 26, 57037 Portoferraio (LI), ☎0565 91 46 71, www.arcipelago.turismo.toscana.it. Ferry crossings are operated by Navarma-Moby Lines: Via Giuseppe Ninci 1, 57037 Portoferraio (LI), ☎0565 91 81 01, www.mobylines.it; Toremar: Calata Italia 22, 57037 Portoferraio (LI), ☎0565 91 80 80, www.toremar.it.
- ▶ **Orient Yourself:** The Isle of Elba lies in the Tuscan Archipelago and is easily reached from Piombino, from where there are crossings to Portoferraio and Rio Marina.
- **Don't Miss:** The beach at Biodola and panorama at Monte Capanne.
- **Organizing Your Time:** To tour the island set aside at least two days.

A Bit of History

Elba is closely associated with Napoleon who was exiled here following his abdication. Between 3 May 1814 and 26 February 1815 the fallen emperor ruled over his small court and the island, which was garrisoned by about 1 000 soldiers.

In the distant geological past Elba was part of the vanished continent of Tyrrhenia.

Like Corsica, Sardinia, the Balearics and the Maures and Estérel Massifs on the French Riviera coast, Elba has an indented coastline with small creeks, caves and beaches.

The vegetation is typically Mediterranean with palms, eucalyptus, cedars, magnolias and, in great quantity, olives and vines. The wines produced (white Moscato and red Aleatico) are heady with a strong bouquet.

The granitic relief culminates in Monte Capane. To the east of the island the iron mines worked by the Etruscans are no longer exploited.

Excursions

Start from Portoferraio and follow one of the two itineraries indicated on the map below: **western Elba** *(about 70km/44mi, about 5hr)* and **eastern Elba** *(68km/42mi, about 3hr)*.

Portoferraio

Tour: Open daily except Tue, 9am-7pm, Sun and public holidays 9am-1pm. Closed Tue, 1 Jan, 1 May. 3 €, 5 € combined ticket with Museo S. Martino (closed Mon). ☎0565 91 58 46; http://portoferraio.e-unico.it

This island capital, guarded by ruined walls and two forts, lies at the head of a beautiful bay. In the upper part of the town is the **Museo Napoleonico** housed in the **Villa dei Mulini**, a simple house, with a terraced garden, which Napoleon sometimes occupied. His personal library and various mementoes are kept here.

Beyond the great sandy beach at **Biodola**, the road goes towards **Marciana Marina**, a small port protected by

Address Book

For coin ranges see the Legend on the cover flap.

WHERE TO EAT

Da Pilade – *Località Marina di Mola – 57031 Capoliveri – On the road to Capoliveri – ☎0565 96 86 35 – www. hoteldapilade.it – Closed mid-Oct to Easter.* This restaurant is not too far from the coast. Specialities include mouth-watering Aberdeen Angus steak alla griglia (grilled) and a wide range of unusual antipasti. Also has rooms and self-catering apartments, with a little garden or a terrace with sea view.

Affrichella – *Via S. Chiara 10 – 57033 Marciana Marina – ☎0565 99 68 44 – Closed Wed.* This little restaurant, which is renowned for its seafood dishes, is situated just behind the Duomo. Boasts a variety of both hot and cold antipasti, and an interesting wine list. In summer meals are served at candlelit tables on the adjacent piazzetta.

La Lanterna Magica – *Via Vitaliani 5 – 57036 Porto Azzurro – ☎0565 95 83 94 – Closed Mon (except Jun-Sep), Dec and Jan –.* With its huge windows looking out over the sea in the direction of Porto Azzurro, it is almost as if this restaurant has been erected on stilts sunk into the seabed. The menu has a regional flavour and features some local specialities. The wine and oil are produced on the family farm and are of an excellent quality.

WHERE TO STAY

Hotel Residence Villa Giulia – *Località Lido di Capoliveri – 57036 Porto Azzurro – 7.5km/4.5mi northwest of Capoliveri, heading towards Portoferraio – ☎ 0565 94 01 67 – Fax 0565 94 01 10 – www.villagiuliahotel.it – Closed mid-Oct to Easter – 35 rm.* The hotel is divided into four small buildings.

The rooms are comfortable and well appointed, with rattan furniture, all with a balcony or a small terrace garden. During the summer months meals (only for guests) are served on the terrace which has lovely views out to sea.

Da Giacomino – *57030 Sant'Andrea – 6km/4mi northwest of Marciana – ☎0565 90 80 10 – Fax 0565 90 82 94 – www.hoteldagiacomino.it – Closed Nov-Easter – 33 rm – 13 € – Restaurant.* An ideal location for a holiday. The hotel rises up behind the cliffs and there is a wonderful garden which runs to the edge of the sheer cliff-face with stunning views down to the sea. The rooms are light and airy… and the staff are friendly.

GOING OUT

Calata Mazzini – *Calata Mazzini – 57037 Portoferraio.* There are various cafés and tea rooms along this (somewhat noisy) street. A good place to watch the boats coming and going in the busy little harbour.

SPORT AND LEISURE

Centro Velico Naregno – *Spiaggia di Naregno, northwest of Capoliveri – 57031 Capoliveri – ☎ 0565 96 87 64 – www.centroveliconaregno.it.* The Naregno sailing club runs various courses and hires out equipment including sailboards, catamarans, dinghies, scooters etc.

Nautilus Bagni Lacona – *Spiaggia Grande – 57031 Capoliveri – ☎ 0565 96 43 64.* For anyone who is not keen on scuba diving, this underwater vehicle is a very pleasant way of finding out about the multicoloured marine fauna and flora in the area. Sports enthusiasts can also hire motorboats, canoes, sailing boats and hang-gliders.

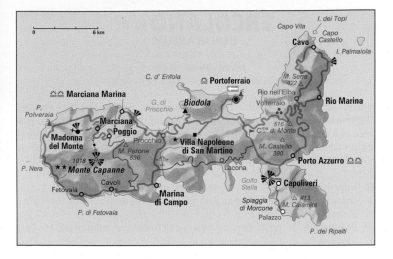

two piers, one of which is dominated by a round tower, and climbs the wooded slopes of Monte Capanne.

Monte Capanne★★
Cable cars leave from Marciana. Alt 1 018m/3 339ft. ◷ *Open daily Jul-Oct 10am-12.15pm and 2.30-6pm, Easter-Jun 10am-12.15pm and 2.30-5.30pm.* ◷ *Closed Nov-Easter.* ☞ *12 € (round trip).* ☏*0565 90 10 20.*
From the summit not far from the terminus there is a splendid **panorama**★★ of Elba, the Tuscan coast to the east and the coast of Corsica to the west.

Marciana
◷*Open daily Jul-Aug, 9.30am-12.30pm and 6-11pm, Sept 9.30am-12.30pm and 4.30-7.30pm; rest of the year telephone for opening hours, call* ☏*0565 90 12 15.*
From this attractive village there is a lovely view★ of Poggio, perched on its rocky spur, Marciana Marina and the Bay of Procchio.

Madonna del Monte
Take the road up to the castle that dominates Marciana and from there a rocky path leads up to this sanctuary, on the northern slope of Monte Giove. Beside the 16C chapel there is a semicircular fountain and a "hermitage" where Napoleon and his lover Maria Walewska spent time in the summer of 1814.

Marina di Campo
This small fishing port lies at the head of a lovely bay backed by a hinterland plain of olive groves and vineyards.

Museo Nazionale di Villa Napoleone di San Martino★
◷ *Open daily except Mon, 9am-7pm, Sun and public holidays 9am-1pm. Rest of the year telephone for opening times.* ◷ *Closed 1 Jan, 1 May.* ☞ *3 €, 5 € combined ticket with Museo dei Mulini.* ☏*0565 91 46 88.*
Nestling in a setting of silent hills, planted with evergreen oaks and vineyards, this modest house was the ex-emperor's summer residence.

Capoliveri
Not far from this village there is a **panorama**★★ of three bays: Portoferraio, Porto Azzurro and Golfo Stella.

Porto Azzurro
This pretty port is overlooked by a fort, which now serves as a prison.

Rio Marina
A pleasant port and mining village protected by a crenellated tower. Beyond Cavo, the return journey to Portoferraio is by a high altitude **road**★★ affording remarkable views of the ruins of Volterraio, the Bay of Portoferraio and the sea.

ERCOLANO★★
HERCULANEUM
POPULATION 57 638
MICHELIN MAP 564 E 25 –
SEE ALSO THE LOCAL MAP IN GOLFO DI NAPOLI.

Herculaneum was founded, according to tradition, by Hercules. Like Pompeii the Roman town was buried during the AD 79 eruption of Vesuvius. Many craftsmen and rich and cultured patricians were drawn to Herculaneum because of its beautiful setting, overlooking the Bay of Naples. In 1997 Herculaneum was included in UNESCO's World Heritage List.

- **Information:** ☎081 73 24 333; www.pompeiisites.org.
- ▶ **Orient Yourself:** Herculaneum lies at the foot of Vesuvius, off A 3, the Naples-Pompeii-Salerno road.
- **Don't Miss:** The baths, Casa del Mosaico di Nettuno e Anfitrite and the Casa dei Cervi.
- **Organizing Your Time:** Avoid visiting Herculaneum at the height of the midday sun, as there is very little shade in the ruins.
- **Also See:** *COSTIERA AMALFITANA, NAPOLI, Golfo di NAPOLI, POMPEI.*

Visit

Villa dei Papiri. Entrance in Corso Resina. Access from Porta Marina (Via Villa dei Misteri or Piazza Esedra) or from Piazza Anfiteatro. ◐2hr. NB: Some of the houses listed below may be closed for maintenance and restoration. Open Apr-Oct 8.30am-7.30pm (last admission 6pm); Nov-Mar 8.30am-5pm (last admission 3.30pm). ◐ Closed 1 Jan, 1 May, 25 Dec. ◐11€; 20€ (3 days) combined ticket for Pompeii, Herculaneum, Oplontis, Stabia and Boscoreale.

Herculaneum is broadly divided into four sections, delineated by the two main streets *(decumani)* and three other thoroughfares *(cardi)*. All timber structures (frameworks, beams, doors, stairs and partitions) were preserved by a hard shell of solidified mud, whereas at Pompeii they were consumed by fire. Most of the houses were empty, but many inhabitants died as they tried to flee the city or make for the sea.

▶ *The following itinerary starts at the bottom of Cardo III.*

The **Casa dell'Albergo** was about to be converted into apartments for letting, hence its name. This vast patrician villa was one of the most badly damaged by the eruption.

The **Casa dell'Atrio a mosaico**★★ takes its name from the chequered mosaic on the floor in the atrium. The garden on the right is surrounded by a peristyle. On the left are the bedrooms and at the far end, a pleasant *triclinium* (dining room). The terrace, flanked by two small rest rooms, offers an attractive view of the sea.

In the **Casa a graticcio**★★ the framework *(graticcio)* of the walls was formed by a wooden trellis. It is a unique example of this type of house from Antiquity.

With its façade remarkably well preserved, the **Casa del Tramezzo carbonizzato**★ is a good example of a patrician dwelling that housed several families. The atrium is separated from the *tablinium* (living room) by the remains of a wooden partition.

Next door is the **Bottega del tintore** (A), the dyer's shop, which contains an interesting wooden clothes press.

The **Casa Sannitica**★★, was built on the very simple plan typical of the Samnites (an Italic people of the Sabine race). The **atrium** is surrounded by a gallery with Ionic columns.

The **baths**★★★ of Herculaneum, which are in excellent condition, were built at the time of Augustus and show a remarkable degree of practical planning. In the **men's baths** visit the *palestra*, the cloakroom, the *frigidarium* with frescoes on the ceiling, the *tepidarium* and the *caldarium*. The **women's baths** include the waiting-room, the cloakroom *(apodyterium)*, adorned with a mosaic pavement depicting the sea god Triton, the tepidarium with a fine floor mosaic representing a labyrinth, and the *caldarium*.

The **Casa del Mobilio carbonizzato**★ (**B**) has the remains of a charred *(carbonizzato)* bed in one room.

The **Casa del Mosaico di Nettuno e Anfitrite**★★ is equipped with a **shop**★; its counter opened onto the street. Mosaics depicting Neptune and Amphitrite adorn the nymphaeum.

Nearby is one of the most original houses in Herculaneum, the **Casa del Bel Cortile**★ (**C**), with its courtyard *(cortile)*, stone staircase and balcony.

The **Casa del Bicentenario**★ was unearthed in 1938, 200 years after digging officially started. The house has fresco decorations and a small cross incorporated in a stucco panel. This is one of the oldest Christian relics brought to light in the Roman Empire.

An inscription states that the **Pistrinum**★★ (bakery) belonged to Sextus Patulus Felix. In the shop are flour mills, storage jars and a large oven.

The **Casa dei Cervi**★★ was probably the most grandiose patrician villa overlooking the bay. It is adorned by works of art, including a sculptured group of stags *(cervi)* being attacked by dogs.

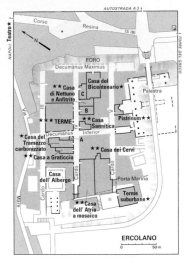

The tour concludes with a visit to the **Terme Suburbane**★, elegantly decorated baths, and the **teatro**★ *(entrance at Via Mare 123)*, with a 2 000 capacity.

Villa dei Papiri

Approximately 250m/300yd west of the archaeological area, below the modern town. ⏱*Visits by appointment only Sat-Sun 9am-noon.* ☎*081 85 75 347; www.villadeipapiri.it.*

This large country villa takes its name from the collection of 1000 Greek papyrus manuscripts that were discovered here. Although excavation work is still taking place, visitors are admitted to the frescoed lower floor and the upper floor, with its atrium and mosaics, Natatium and Nympheum - and to other ruins to the north-west of the site.

FAENZA

POPULATION 54 700

MICHELIN MAP 562, 563, 430 J 17 – EMILIA-ROMAGNA.

Having given its name to the ceramics known as faience, Faenza is synonymous with its glazed and painted ceramics, which have been produced here since the 15C.

- 🛈 **Information:** Piazza del Popolo 1. ☎0546 25 231; www.racine.ra.it/faenza.
- ▶ **Orient Yourself:** Faenza is off SS 9, the Via Emilia, linking Bologna with Rimini
- 👁 **Don't Miss:** The Museo Internazionale delle Ceramiche.
- 🕐 **Organizing Your Time:** Set aside a day to see the town fully.
- 👣 **Also See:** *BOLOGNA, DELTA DEL PO, RAVENNA, RIMINI*

Late-15C plate

Museo Internazionale delle Ceramiche, Faenza

Visit

Pinacoteca Comunale★
Via S. Maria dell'Angelo 1. ⏰ *Open Jun-Sept , Sat, Sun and public holidays 10am-1pm and 3-7pm, rest of the year 10am-6pm. Free entry.* ☎0546 68 02 51, www.racine.ra.it/pinacotecafaenza.
This important art collection includes works by Giovanni da Rimini, Palmezzano, Dosso Dossi, Rossellino.

Cattedrale
The 15C cathedral was built by Giuliano da Maiano but the façade is unfinished. It contains the tomb (1471) of Bishop St Savinus by Benedetto da Maiano.

Piazza del Popolo
The elongated square is bordered by the 12C Palazzo del Podestà (governor's house) and the 13C-15C Palazzo del Municipio (town hall).

Ceramics

In Italy faience is also known as majolica, because during the Renaissance Faenza potters were inspired by ceramics which were imported from Majorca in the Balearic Isles. Faenza ceramics feature fine clay, remarkable glaze, brilliant colours and a great variety of decoration. An international competition and biennial of art ceramics celebrate a vocation that is still strongly felt by artists and artisans.

Museum

Museo Internazionale delle Ceramiche★★
Viale Baccarini 19. ♿⏰ *Open Apr-Oct 9.30am-7pm, rest of the year Tue-Thu 9.30am-1.30pm, Fri, Sat and Sun 9.30am-5.30pm.* ⏰ *Closed Mon, 1 Jan, 1 May, 15 Aug and 25 Dec.* ☞ *6 €.* ☎0546 69 73 11; www.micfaenza.org.
These vast collections present the development of ceramic work throughout the world. On the first floor is a collection of Italian Renaissance majolica, examples of the local ware and an Oriental section. On the ground floor there are fine works by Matisse, Picasso, Chagall, Léger, Lurçat and the V allauris School.

Excursions

Forlì
17km/10mi southeast. Situated on the Via Emilia, Forlì was an independent commune ruled by an overlord in the 13C and 14C. The citadel was heroically defended against Cesare Borgia in 1500 by Caterina Sforza.
The **basilica of San Mercuriale** *(Piazza Aurelio Saffi)* is dominated by an imposing Romanesque campanile. The lunette of the doorway to the basilica is adorned with a 13C low relief. Numerous works of art inside include several paintings by Marco Palmezzano and the tomb of Barbara Manfredi by Francesco di Simone Ferrucci.
At 72 Corso della Repubblica is the **pinacoteca**. The art gallery includes works by local 13C-15C artists. There is a delicate **Portrait of a Young Girl** by Lorenzo di Credi. ⏰ *Telephone for opening times.* ⏰ *Closed Mon, 4 Feb.* ☞ *No charge.* ☎0543 71 26 09,i; www.turismoforlivese.it.

Cesena
20km/12mi southeast of Forlì. Tourist Office, Piazza del Popolo 11, 47023 Cesena, ☎0547 35 62 35, Fax 0547 35 63 29; www.comune.cesena.fc.it
The town lies at the foot of a hill on which stands the great 15C castle of the Malatestas. It contains the Renaissance library, **Biblioteca Malatestiana**★

(Piazza Bufalini). The interior of the library comprises three long aisles with vaulting supported on fluted columns capped with fine capitals. On display are valuable manuscripts, including some from the famous school of miniaturists at Ferrara, as well as the Missorium, a great silver-gilt plate probably dating from the 4C. *Open for guided tours 9am-12.30pm and 2.30-5.30pm (summer 4-7pm).* Closed Sun afternoon 1 Jan, 25 Dec. *Advance booking necessary for groups.* 2.50 €. 0547 61 08 92.

Bertinoro
12km/7mi west of Cesena. Piazza della Libertà 3. 0543 46 92 13, www.comune. bertinoro.fo.it.
This small town is famous for its panorama and its yellow wine (Albana). In the middle of the town is a "hospitality column" fitted with rings, each corresponding to a local home. The ring to which the traveller tethered his horse would determine which family should be his hosts. From the nearby terrace there is a wide **view**★ of Romagna.

FERMO ★

POPULATON 35 781
MICHELIN MAP 563 M 23 – MARCHES.

Fermo is a lovely town, enhanced by its hillside setting★, overlooking the surrounding countryside and sea. At the heart of the historic centre is the elegant Piazza del Popolo.

- **Information:** Piazza del Popolo 6, 0734 22 87 38 ; www.fermo.net.
- ▶ **Orient Yourself:** Fermo is close to the Adriatic coast. Take A 14, exiting at Porto San Giorgio.
- **Don't Miss:** Views from Piazza del Duomo, the Crivelli polyptych at Montifiore dell'Aso.
- **Organizing Your Time:** Allow a day for the town and excursions.
- **Also See:** *ASCOLI PICENO.*

Visit

Piazza del Popolo★
This square in the town centre is surrounded by arcades,16C porticoes and bordered by palaces including the 15C-16C **Palazzo dei Priori** (Prior's Palace) with a statue of Sixtus V (former Bishop of Fermo) on its façade, the Palazzo degli Studi, now the municipal library, and opposite, Palazzo Apostolico.

Pinacoteca Civica
Open 10am-1pm and 3.30pm-7pm (11.30pm Thu in Aug). Closed Mon. 3 €. 0734 21 71 40; www.fermo.net
The municipal art gallery is housed on the first floor of the Palazzo dei Priori and boasts a fine collection, mainly of art from the Veneto and Marches. The most notable works include **Lu Margutta** (16C), a Saracen wood sculpture used as a target in knights' tournaments, the elegant Late Gothic **Scenes from the Life of Saint Lucy**★ by Jacobello del Fiore (fl 1394-1439) and the **Adoration of the Shepherds**★★ by Rubens (1577-1640), one of the finest works produced by the artist during his sojourn in Italy. In the Map Room there is an 18C **terraqueous globe**.
Near the Piazza, in Via degli Aceti, are the **Roman cisterns**, dating from the 1C AD comprised of 30 interconnecting chambers making up a total surface area of more than 2 000m2/21 528sq ft. *Same admission times and charges as the Pinacoteca.*
Off Piazza del Popolo is **Corso Cefalonia**, the main street, lined with Renaissance buildings (Palazzo Azzolino, Palazzi Vitali Rosati) and the 13C Matteucci Tower.

Piazza del Duomo

From this esplanade in front of the cathedral there are splendid views★★ of the Ascoli area, the Apennines, the Adriatic and Conero Peninsula.

Duomo★

🕐 *Open daily, mid-Jun to mid-Sep 10am-12.30pm and 4-7pm; mid-Sep to mid-Jun 9.30am-noon and 3.30-5.30pm (telephone to confirm opening times).* ⬛ *2 € (⬛ guided tour).* ☎️*0734 22 09 232.*
The Romanesque-Gothic cathedral (1227), built by the Maestri Comacini has a majestic **façade**★ in white Istrian stone. A carved doorway shows Christ with the Apostles on the lintel, and symbolic scenes on the uprights. In the atrium, part of the old church, note the sarcophagus of Giovanni Visconti, 14C lord of the city. The 18C **interior** has a fine Byzantine **icon** and a 5C AD **mosaic**★ in which a peacock drinking from a vase symbolises Christ's resurrection.

Excursions

Montefiore dell'Aso

20km/12mi south. 🕐 *Open Mon-Sat, 9am-noon and 3.30-6pm; Sun and public holidays, 10-11am and 3.30-6pm.* ☎️*0734 93 91 18.*
The collegiate church in this pretty town possesses a masterpiece of **Carlo Crivelli**, a **polyptych**★★, which although incomplete, is finely chiselled and highlighted with gold representing six saints. The depiction of Mary Magdalene represents a high point in the career of this artist. The saint, richly cloaked in gold and silk brocade with a scarlet mantle symbolising the passion of Christ, holds the vessel of ointment.

Chiesa di Santa Maria a piè di Chienti★

24km/14mi northwest. 🕐 *Open 8am-6pm, Sun and public holidays 9.30-10.30am and 11.30am-6pm.* ⬛ *Donations welcome.* ☎️*0733 86 52 41.*
This important Romanesque monument was founded in the 12C and subsequently remodelled. The atmospheric **interior** is divided into three aisles that open into an **ambulatory** with surrounding chapels of Cluniac influence. At the end of the 15C the raising of the presbytery created a second church with a frescoed apse.

Tolentino

50km/31mi NW. In 1961 a group of artists from Tolentino founded the Biennale Internazionale dell'Umorismo nell'arte (The International Biennial of humour in art). The success of this exhibition led to the creation of the quirky Museo dell'Umorismo dell'arte, housed in Palazzo Sangallo, in Piazza della Libertà. ♿ 🕐 *Open Tue to Sun 10am-1pm and 3-6pm.* 🕐 *Closed 1 Jan, 1 May, 25 Dec.* ⬛ *3 €.* ☎️*0733 96 97 97; www.biennaleumorismo.org*

Basilica di San Nicola★★

Basilica: 🕐 *Open 7am-noon and 3-7.30pm.* ⬛ *Museum closed for restoration at time of publication.* ☎️*0733 97 63 11; www.sannicoladatolentino.it*
The basilica is dedicated to the Augustine monk who was venerated for his magic powers. St Nicholas died in Tolentino in 1305 and was buried in the basilica's crypt. Building began in 1305 and the façade, remodelled in the 17C, has an elegant late-Gothic doorway by the Florentine sculptor Nino di Bartolo (15C), a pupil of Donatello.
The interior is striking for its opulent marble, gold and stucco decoration and the grand coffered ceiling (1628).

Cappellone di San Nicola

The chapel serves as south transept and is the most famous part of this pilgrimage church, owing to its cycle of 14C **frescoes**★★ by an unknown master of the Rimini school.

Museums

These include the Museo delle Ceramiche (Ceramics Museum) and the Museo dell'Opera, with its 14C wood nativity.

San Severino Marche

▶ *65km/40mi northeast of Fermo and 11km/7mi northwest of Tolentino.*
The medieval and Renaissance heart of this town clusters around Piazza del Popolo. There is a delightful view★ of

the town from the hill where the cathedral stands *(go up Via della Pitturetta)*.

Pinacoteca Civica
Palazzo Tacchi-Venturi, via Salimbeni 39.
🕐 *Open daily except Mon, summer 9am-1pm and 4.30-6.30pm, rest of year 9am-1pm.* 🕐 *Closed 2nd and 4th Sun of month in winter.* 👝 *2 €.* ☎*0733 63 80 95; www.comune.sanseverinomarche.mc.it*

This gallery has an interesting collection of local paintings: **Lorenzo Salimbeni** and his brother Jacopo revolutionised the idiom of 15C painting, adding vivid realism to Gothic Style.
Nearby *(turn left at the end of Via Salimbeni)* is the church of San Lorenzo in Doliolo (11C) whose beautiful **crypt**★ is covered in frescoes attributed to the Salimbeni brothers and their school.

FERRARA★★

POPULATION 132 000
MICHELIN MAP 562 H 16 – EMILIA-ROMAGNA.

Ferrara is a tranquil town which is best explored in a leisurely manner. The streets lined with red-brick houses and austere palaces, and its charming squares – which were a source of inspiration to the 20C metaphysical painters De Chirico and Carrà – are easily accessible on foot or by bicycle. A splendid cultural centre during the Renaissance, these days Ferrara is a young and vibrant town and remains one of the major artistic and cultural centres in Italy.

- 🛈 **Information:** Castello Estense, 44100 Ferrara, 0532 20 93 70; www.ferrarainfo.com.
- ▸ **Orient Yourself:** Ferrara rises up near the Po Delta, off A 13, which links Bologna with Padua.
- 🔎 **Don't Miss:** The cathedral, Corso Ercole I d'Este, the salons of Palazzo Schifanoia and Rosetti works in Palazzo dei Diamanti.
- 🕐 **Organizing Your Time:** Allow two days for the whole city.
- 🕖 **Also See:** *BOLOGNA, DELTA DEL PO.*

A Bit of History

Patrons of the Arts
Initially an independent commune, Ferrara belonged to the **Este** family from 1208 to 1598, and despite numerous family dramas, often bloody, the Estes embellished their native city with fine buildings and patronised both men of letters and artists. **Niccolò III** (1393-1441) murdered his wife Parisina and her lover but he begat **Lionello** and **Borso**, moulding them into efficient administrators and enlightened patrons. **Ercole I** (1431-1505), who was responsible for his nephew's murder encouraged artists, as did his two famous daughters, Beatrice and Isabella d'Este. **Alfonso I** (1475-1534), the son of Ercole, became the third husband of Lucrezia Borgia, and **Ercole II** (1508-59) married Renée of France, the protector of the Calvinists.

After the demise of **Alfonso II** (1533-97) who left no heirs, Ferrara came under the rule of the Papacy and the Estes retired to the Duchy of Modena. The arts flourished with the secular university (founded in 1391) and the patronage of the Este dynasty. Three poets benefitted from the Este's largesse: **Matteo Maria Boiardo** (1441-94), **Ludovico Ariosto** and **Torquato Tasso** (1544-95).

The Ferrarese school
The leader of the Ferrarese school of painting *(known as the officina ferrarese)* was **Cosmè (Cosimo) Tura** (c 1430-95), a man of strong personality; the school's main characteristic was a meticulous realism, borrowed from the Northern schools. This was combined with a rather grim expressionism which derived from Mantegna, and powerful modelling reminiscent of Donatello.

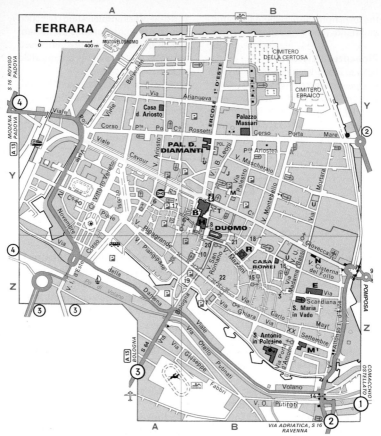

FERRARA

FERRARA			Porta Reno Cso	BZ	10	Travaglio Pza del	BZ	19
Borgo di Sotto V.	BZ	3	S. Maurelio V.	BZ	14	Trento Trieste Pza	BZ	20
Cavour Viale	AY		Saraceno V.	BZ	15	Voltapaletto V.	BZ	21
Garibaldi V.	ABY	6	Savonarola V.	BZ	16	Volte V. delle	BZ	22
Martiri d. Libertà Cso	BY	8	Spadari V.	AY	17			
Pomposa V.	BZ	9	Terranuova V.	BZ	18			

Castello Estense	BY	B	Palazzo del Municipio	BY	H
Palazzina di Marfisa d'Este	BZ	N	Palazzo di Ludovico il Moro	BZ	M¹
Palazzo Schifanoia	BZ	E	Sinagoghe	BZ	R

The main members were **Francesco del Cossa** (1435-77), who tempered the severity and the metallic sense of form of Tura and whose free and luminous style is evocative of Piero della Francesca; **Ercole de' Roberti** (1450-96), who conversely adopted Tura's strong modelling tradition; and **Lorenzo Costa** (1460-1535) who moved his studio to Bologna where the dark tones of the Umbrian and Tuscan schools prevailed. In the 16C the colourist **Dosso Dossi** (c 1490-1542) and **Benvenuto Garofalo** (1481-1559) favoured a greater harmony of colour in line with the Venetian style and allied themselves to the classical tradition of Raphael and the Roman school.

Old Town

Castello Estense★

🔥 ⏱ *For information on admission times and charges, call ☎0532 29 93 03; www.castelloestense.it.*

This massive castle, guarded by moats and four fortified gateways with drawbridges, was the seat of the Este family.

The ground floor houses the spartan prison where Parisina and her lover were locked away. On the *piano nobile*, where the orangery is, visitors may view the Ducal Chapel collection and the apartments decorated with frescoes by the Filippi, active in Ferrara in the second half of the 16C.

Duomo★★

The cathedral was built in the 12C in the Romanesque-Gothic Lombard style and presents a triple **façade**★★ with a splendid porch. On the tympanum is depicted the Last Judgement recalling the decoration of French Gothic cathedrals. In the lunette above the central door, the sculpture of St George is by Nicholaus, an artist of the school led by the Romanesque master, Wiligelmo, who was responsible for the carved decoration of Modena cathedral. On the south side there are two tiers of galleries on the upper section; below is the Loggia dei Merciai, a portico occupied by shops in the 15C. Here stood the Portal of the Months; the panels are kept in the cathedral museum. The belltower which was never completed was designed by Leon Battista Alberti. The semicircular apse with its decorative brickwork is by Biagio Rossetti.

The In the south arm of the transept note The Martyrdom of St Lawrence by Guercino and two 15C bronze statues (St Maurelius and St George) and The Last Judgement by Bastianino on the vaulting in the apse.

Museo della Cattedrale – *Housed in the old church and monastery of San Romano, in the street of the same name.* ◷ *Open all year 9am-1pm and 3-6pm.* ◷ *Closed Mon, public holidays.* ✉ *Donations welcome. 4.50 €. ☎0532 20 99 88; www. ferrarainfo.com*

The museum contains two statues by Jacopo della Quercia, the **panels**★★ of an organ painted by **Cosmè Tura** representing *St George slaying the Dragon and The Annunciation* and the admirable **12C sculptures**★ from the Portal of the Months, admirable in their immediacy and close observation of reality (the finest example is the month of September). The 13C town hall, **Palazzo del Municipio**, facing the cathedral, was once the ducal palace.

Medieval streets

Via San Romano, which is still a commercial artery, linked the market square (Piazza Trento e Trieste) and the port (now Via Ripagrande). It is lined with several houses with porticoes, an unusual feature in Ferrara. **Via delle Volte** has become one of the symbols of the town. Covered alleyways *(volte)* linked the houses of the merchants and their warehouses, thus making more habitable space available. Along Via Mazzini are the **Sinagoghe** (synagogue complex) which comprise three temples for different rites: the Italian and German traditions and that from Fano in the Marches. ◷ *Guided tours at 10am, 11am and noon.* ◷ *Closed Fri, Sat, Jewish feasts, Aug.* ✉ *4 €. ☎0532 21 02 28; www.comune.fe.it/museoe braico.*

Casa Romei★

◷*Open all year 8.30am-7.30pm (last admission 7pm).* ◷ *Closed Mon, 1 Jan, 1 May, 25 Dec.* ✉ *2 €. ☎0533 24 03 41.* This rare example of a 15C bourgeois residence combines late-Gothic decorative features (Room of the Sibyls) and Renaissance elements such as the courtyard portico.

Palazzina di Marfisa d'Este★

◷ *Open 9am-1pm and 3-6pm.* ◷ *Closed Mon, public holidays.* ✉2 €. *☎0532 20 99 88; www.ferrarainfo.com.* This elegant single-storey residence (1559) is where Marfisa d'Este entertained her friends, among them the poet Tasso. The interior is remarkable for the ornate ceiling decoration including grotesques, and elegant 16C-17C furniture. Pass into the garden to visit the Orangery (Loggia degli Aranci); the vault features a mock pergola complete with vine shoots and animals.

Palazzo Schifanoia★

◷ *Open all year 9am-6pm.* ◷ *Closed Mon.* ✉ *4.50 €. ☎ 0532 20 99 88; www.ferrarainfo.com* This 14C palace is where the Estes used to come to relax (*schifanoia* means carefree). There are splendid frescoes in the Room of the Months **(Salone dei Mesi**★★**)**. This complex cycle to the glory of Borso d'Este unfortunately retains

Address Book

🍴 *For coin ranges, see the Legend on the cover flap.*

WHERE TO EAT

⊖⊖ **Antica Trattoria Volano** – *Viale Volano 20 – ☎0532 76 14 21 – 44100 Ferrara – ⏱ Closed Fri – 🍽.*
A simple trattoria that has been around a long time (reportedly as far back as the 18C). The cooking has a regional flavour, based around local produce. Unpretentious ambience but pleasant, comfortable surroundings. Family run.

⊖⊖ **Tassi** – *Viale Repubblica 23 – 44012 Bondeno – 20km/12mi northwest of Ferrara on S 496 – ☎0532 89 30 30 – ⏱ Closed Mon, 1-4 Jan, 14 Jul-12 Aug. – 🍽. 10rm.* A long-established feature of the restaurant scene in Ferrara, this trattoria has a pleasantly retro feel about it. With a number of delicious meat dishes on the menu, this is a good place to sample some of the region's cuisine and specialities. Look out for the trolley of bolliti (boiled meats). Ask the staff for their recommendations. Also has rooms.

WHERE TO STAY

⊖⊖ **Locanda Borgonuovo** – *Via Cairoli 29 – 44100 Ferrara – ☎0532 21 11 00 – Fax 0532 24 800 – www.borgonuovo.com – 🍽 – 4 rm – 🍽.* A delightful B&B in the heart of the historic centre. Very homely – less of a hotel and more of a private house that has been opened to the public. Warm welcome. The breakfasts are excellent with generous portions and served on a lovely terrace area in summer.

⊖⊖ **Bed & Breakfast Corte Arcangeli** – *Via Pontegradella 503 – 44030 Pontegradella – 3km/1mi northeast towards Pomposa Mare – ☎0532 70 50 52 – Fax 0532 70 50 52 – www.cortearcangeli.it – 🍽 – 6 rm – 🍽.* English-style B&B in a lovely old farm-house in a verdant setting but only a few minutes from the centre. Rooms have been tastefully decorated: features include antique beds with painted headboard. The other rooms, which guests share with the owners, are large and spacious. Huge breakfasts and bicycles available for leisurely rides in the countryside! Animals welcome.

only some of the 12 months. The three levels illustrate three different themes, notably everyday life at court, astrology and mythology. The frescoes, which demonstrate an extraordinary delicacy, attest to Ferrara's cultural achievements during the Renaissance.

The palace houses a museum, the **Museo Civico di Arte Antica**, which displays archaeological collections, medals, bronzes and marquetry. The museum is part of the **Lapidario**.

The nearby Palazzo di Ludovico il Moro, situated in Via XX Settembre, houses the Museo Archeologico (*see Worth a Visit below*).

Monastero di San Antonio in Polesine

⏱ *Open all year 9.30-11.30am and 3-5pm; Sat 9.30-11.15am and 3-4pm.* ⏱ *Closed Sun and public holidays.* 🪙 *Donations welcome. For information ☎0532 64 068; www.ferrarainfo.com*

The convent founded in 1257 by Beatrice II d'Este, who joined the Benedictine order, stands in an isolated and peaceful setting.

The **church** has three chapels decorated with fine 14C-16C **frescoes**★ by the Giotto and Emilian schools.

The Renaissance Town

In 1490 Ercole I d'Este commissioned **Biagio Rossetti** to extend the town to the north. The extension (**Addizione Erculea**) built around two main axes – Corso Ercole I d'Este and Corso Porta Pia, Bragio Rossetti and Porta Mare – is a great Renaissance town featuring parks and gardens. With this grandiose town-planning scheme Ferrara became the first modern city in Europe, according

The Jewish Community of Ferrara

The Jewish community flourished in the 14C and 15C owing to the policy of the Estes, who welcomed Jews from Rome, Spain and Germany. The ghetto was instituted under Papal rule in 1624: five gates closed at dusk sealing off the area bounded by Via Mazzini, Vignatagliata and Vittoria. The gates were taken down under the new Italian Kingdom in 1859.

The Jewish community of Ferrara is portrayed in the novel, *Garden of the Finzi-Contini*, by Giorgio Bassani, which was turned into an Oscar-winning film in 1970 by Vittorio De Sica.

to the art historian Jacob Burckhardt, and in 1995 was included in UNESCO's World Heritage List.

Corso Ercole I d'Este★

The street lined with splendid Renaissance palaces but lacking any shops retains its original residential aspect. The focal point is the **Quadrivio degli Angeli** at the intersection with the other main axis, emphasised by three palaces with a rich angular decoration, including the Palazzo dei Diamanti.

Palazzo dei Diamanti★★

The most distinctive of all the works by **Biagio Rossetti**, the palace takes its name from the marble façade of 8 500 diamond bosses; the different angles at which they have been placed creates a curious optical effect. The palace was designed for a diagonal view: the central feature is therefore the corner embellished with pilasters and a balcony. On the first floor is the art gallery (&see Worth a Visit below).

Visit

Pinacoteca Nazionale★

Corso Ercole I 21. & ○ *Open all year 9am-7pm.* ⊚ *4 €.* ☎ *0532 20 58 44; www.ferrarainfo.com.*
The gallery displays paintings showing the development of the Ferrarese, Emilian and Venetian Schools from the 13C to 18C. Among the masterpieces are two tondi dedicated to San Maurelio by Cosmè Tura, a Death of the Virgin by the Venetian Carpaccio, a Descent from the Cross by Ortolano, an altarpiece by Garofalo and frescoes from churches in

Ferrara. The Sacrati Strozzi Collection includes paintings of the Muses Erato and Urania from Leonello d'Este's Studiolo in Palazzo di Belfiore which was situated near the present Corso Ercole I d'Este and was later dismantled when the town was under Papal rule.

Museo Archeologico Nazionale

Via XX Settembre. & ○ *Open all year 9am-2pm (last admission 1.30pm).* ○ *Closed Mon, 1 Jan, 1 May and 25 Dec.* ⊚ *4 €.* ☎ *0532 66 299.*
The archaeological museum is housed in the Palazzo di Ludovico il Moroa, designed in the 15C by Biagio Rossetti. The museum displays an important collection of 5C-4C BC **Attic vases**★ and burial accoutrements found at Spina, once one of the most important commercial ports in the Mediterranean.
& Casa dell'Ariosto, Palazzo Massari (Museo Boldini).

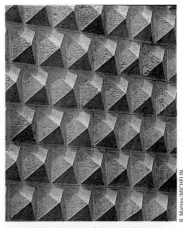

Some of the "diamonds" on the Palazzo dei Diamanti... a sort of optical illusion

FIESOLE★

POPULATION 14,278
MICHELIN MAP 563 K 15
SEE ALSO THE MICHELIN ATLAS ITALY, THE RED GUIDE ITALIA
AND THE GREEN GUIDE TUSCANY

The road from Florence winds uphill to Fiesole through olive-clad slopes, past luxuriant gardens and cypress trees, and affords views of this incomparable countryside★★★, so often depicted by the masters of the Italian Renaissance. The Etruscans founded this city in the 7C or 6C BC, strategically built high in the hills. Fiesole was the most important city in northern Etruria and dominated its neighbour and rival Florence until the 12C.

- **Information:** Via Portigiani 3. ☎055 59 87 20; www.comune.fiesole.fi.it
- ▶ **Orient Yourself:** Fiesole is 8km/5mi northeast of Florence.
- **Don't Miss:** Performances in the Roman theatre at the Zona Archeologica.
- **Organizing Your Time:** Climb up to the Convento di San Francesco at sunset for Florentine views.

Worth a Visit

Convento di San Francesco★

🕐 *Open May-Sept daily 9am-noon and 3-7pm (6pm in winter), Sun and public holidays 9-11am and 3-6pm; Sat-Sun and public holidays 3-6pm only (5pm Oct-Apr). Free entry.* ☎*055 59 175.*

The climb up to this Franciscan convent starts in front of the Duomo and offers a splendid **view**★★ over Florence (from a small terrace about halfway up).

Duomo★

Founded in the 11C and enlarged in the 13C and 14C, the cathedral was extensively restored in the late 19C. The austere **interior**★ has columns supporting Antique capitals. There are two handsome **works**★ by the sculptor Mino da Fiesole.

Zona archeologica

♿ 🕐 *Open summer 9.30am-7pm; rest of the year 9.30am-5pm.* 🕐 *Closed Tue (winter), 1 Jan and 25 Dec.* ⊜ *6.50 € including admission to Museo Bandini; 14.50 € family ticket.* ☎*055 59 477; www.fiesolemusei.it.* This archaeological site, in its enchanting **setting**★, comprises a **Roman theatre**★ (c 80 BC) that is still used for performances, a small **Etruscan temple** and the remains of Roman baths. The **museo archeologico**★ exhibits finds from the Etruscan to the medieval period.

Museo Bandini

Opposite the entrance to the archaeological site. 🕐 *Open Apr-Sep 9.30am-7pm, Mar and Oct 9.30am-6pm, winter 9.30am-5pm.* 🕐 *Closed Tue (winter).* ⊜ *6.50 €, including Museo Archeologico.* ☎*055 59 477; www.fiesolemusei.it.*

The museum houses a collection of 14C and 15C Tuscan paintings. Note Petrarch's masterpiece Triumphs illustrated by Jacopo del Sellaio.

Chiesa di San Domenico di Fiesole

2.5km/1.5m southwest (see also the plan of Florence on Michelin map 430). 🛈 *www.sandomenicodifiesole.op.org.*

It was in this 15C church that Fra Angelico took his vows. In the first chapel on the north side is a **Madonna and Saints**★ by the artist.

Badia Fiesolana

3km/2mi southwest (♿see also the plan of Florence on Michelin map 430).

This former Benedictine convent was rebuilt in the 15C. The original Romanesque **façade**★ with its green and white marble geometrical motifs, was incorporated into the new building.

FIRENZE★★★
FLORENCE
POPULATION 368 059
MICHELIN MAP 563 K 15
SEE ALSO THE GREEN GUIDE TUSCANY.

Acknowledged as one of Italy's most beautiful cities and one of the world's greatest artistic capitals, Florence is a testament to the Italian capacity for genius. The birthplace of Dante and the model for the Italian language, the city was the cradle of civilisation which nurtured the humanist movement and the Renaissance in the first half of the 15C.

- **Information:** Via Cavour 1, 50129 Firenze, ☎055 29 08 32/3; www.comune.firenze.it, www.firenze.net.
- **Orient Yourself:** Florence lies at the foot of the Apennines in the Arno valley. The city is situated at an important motorway interchange, at the point where A 1 and A 11 (Florence-coast route) meet.
- **Parking:** There are car parks at Fortezza da Basso and S.Maria Novella station.
- **Don't Miss:** Piazza del Duomo, the Uffizi Gallery, Palazzo Vecchio, Museo del Bargello, Chiesa di S. Lorenzo and the Medici tombs, Galleria Palatina in the Palazzo Pitti, Museo di S. Marco, frescoes by Ghirlandaio in Chiesa di S. Maria Novella.
- **Organizing Your Time:** With such a density of art and culture, you will need at least four days to see all the main sights. Many of Florence's treasures are clustered in the compact city centre, which can be easily traversed on foot.
- **Especially for Kids:** Il Museo dei Ragazzi, il Giardino di Boboli.
- **Also See:** *FIESOLE, PRATO.*

A Bit of History

Florence is without doubt the city where the Italian genius has flourished with the greatest display of brilliance and purity. For three centuries, from the 13C to the 16C, the city was the cradle of an exceptional artistic and intellectual activity from which evolved the precepts which were to dictate the appearance of Italy at that time and also the aspect of modern civilisation throughout Europe. The main characteristics of this movement, which was

B. Juge/MICHELIN

later to be known as the Renaissance, were partly a receptivity to the outside world, a dynamic open-minded attitude which encouraged inventors and men of science to base their research on the reinterpretation of the achievements of ancient Rome, and on the expanding of the known horizons. The desire to achieve universality resulted in a multiplication of the fields of interest.

Dante was not only a great poet but also a grammarian and historian who did much research on the origins and versatility of his own language. He was one of Florence's most active polemicists. **Giotto** was not only a painter but also an architect. **Lorenzo the Magnificent** was the prince who best incarnated the spirit of the Renaissance. An able diplomat, a realistic politician, a patron of the arts as well as a poet himself, he regularly attended the Platonic Academy in the Medici villa at Careggi, where philosophers such as Marsilio Ficino and Pico della Mirandola and men of letters like Politian and others established the principles of a new humanism. This quest to achieve a balance between nature and order had its most brilliant exponent in **Michelangelo**, painter, architect, sculptor and scholar whose work typifies a purely Florentine preoccupation.

Florence is set in the heart of a serenely beautiful **countryside**★★★ bathed by a soft, amber light. The low surrounding hills are clad with olive groves, vineyards and cypresses which appear to have been harmoniously landscaped to please the human eye. Florentine architects and artists have variously striven to recreate this natural harmony in their works, whether it be the campanile of La Badia by Arnolfo di Cambio, or that of the cathedral by Giotto, the façade of Santa Maria Novella by Alberti or the dome of Santa Maria del Fiore by Brunelleschi. The pure and elegant lines of all these works of art would seem to be a response to the beauty of the landscape and the intensity of the light. The Florentine preoccupation with perspective throughout the Quattrocento (15C) is in part the result of this fascination for the countryside and that other great concern of the period, the desire to recreate what the eye could see.

This communion of great minds, with their varied facets and fields of interest, expressed a common desire to push their knowledge to the limits, and found in the flourishing city of Florence an ideal centre for their artistic and intellectual development. The city's artists, merchants, able administrators and princely patrons of the arts, all contributed to the creation of just the right conditions for nurturing such an intellectual and artistic community, which for centuries was to influence human creativity.

In the beginning…

The colony of Florentia was founded in the 1C BC by Julius Caesar on the north bank of the Arno at a spot level with the Ponte Vecchio. The veteran soldiers who garrisoned the colony controlled the Via Flaminia linking Rome to northern Italy and Gaul.

The Middle Ages

It was only in the early 11C that the city became an important Tuscan centre when Count Ugo, Marquis of Tuscany, took up residence here, and again towards the end of the same century when the Countess Matilda affirmed its independence. During the 12C Florence prospered under the influence of the new class of merchants who built such fine buildings as the baptistery and San Miniato. This period saw the rise of trades organised in powerful guilds (arti), which soon became the ruling class when Florence became an independent commune. In the 13C one third of Florence's population was engaged in either the wool or the silk trades, both of which exported their products to the four corners of Europe and were responsible for a period of extraordinary prosperity. These tradesmen were ably supported by the Florentine money houses which succeeded the Lombard and Jewish institutions, and themselves acquired a great reputation by issuing the first-ever bills of exchange and the famous florin, struck with the Florentine coat of arms. The latter was replaced in

Brunelleschi's dome – a familiar landmark in Florence

B. Pérousse/MICHELIN

the late 15C by the Venetian ducat. The main banking families were the Bardi-Peruzzi who advanced huge sums to England at the beginning of the Hundred Years War; they were soon to be joined in the forefront by the Pitti, Strozzi, Pazzi and of course the Medici.

The Guelph cause

Despite its prosperity, Florence did not escape the internal strife between the Ghibellines who were partisans of the Holy Roman Emperor and the Guelphs who supported the Pope. The Guelphs at first had the advantage; but the Ghibellines on being driven out of Florence, having allied themselves with other enemies of Florence, notably Siena, regained power after the Battle of Montaperti in 1260. The Guelphs counter-attacked and retook Florence in 1266. Under their rule the physical aspect of the city changed considerably, notably with the destruction of the fortified tower houses built by the Ghibelline nobility. They created the system of government known as the *signoria* which was made up of the *priori* (masters of the city's Guilds). There then occurred a split between the Black Guelphs and the White Guelphs who opposed the Papacy. During the split, Dante, who supported the White Guelphs, was exiled for life in 1302. In 1348 the Black Death killed more than

half the population and put an end to the period of internal strife.

A glorious era (15C)

Among the numerous wealthy families in Florence, it was the **Medici** who gave the city several leaders who exercised their patronage both in the sphere of fine arts and finance. The founder of this illustrious dynasty was Giovanni di Bicci, a prosperous banker who left his fortune in 1429 to his son **Cosimo the Elder**, who in turn transformed his heritage into the city's most flourishing business. He discreetly exercised his personal power through intermediaries, and astutely juggled his own personal interests with those of the city, which assured Florence a kind of peaceful hegemony. His chief quality was his ability to gather around him both scholars and artists, whom he commissioned for numerous projects. Cosimo the Elder was a passionate builder and Florence owes many of her great monuments to this "Father of the Land". His son, Piero II Gottoso (the gouty) survived him by five years only and he in turn bequeathed all to his son **Lorenzo the Magnificent** (1449-92). Having escaped the Pazzi Conspiracy, Lorenzo reigned like a true Renaissance prince, although it was always unofficially. He distinguished himself by his skilful politics and managed to retain

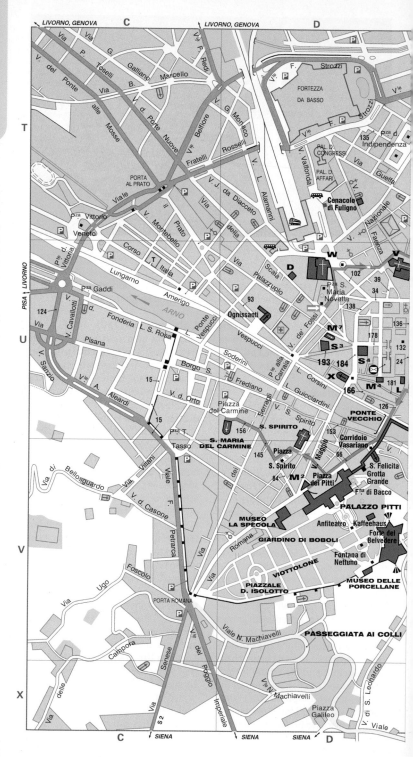

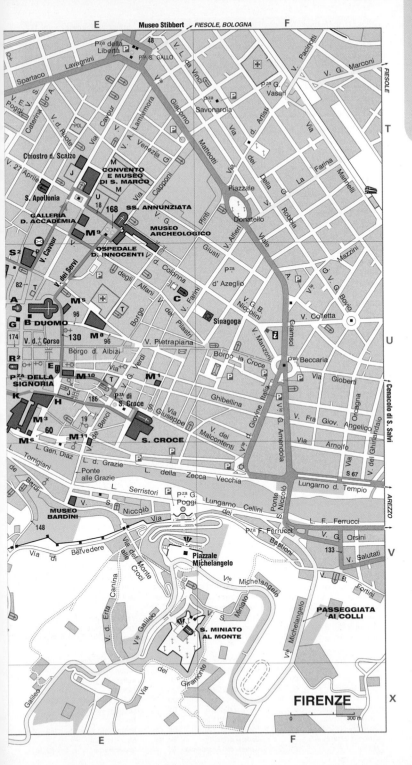

Museo Stibbert FIESOLE, BOLOGNA

FIESOLE

Pza della Libertà
48
PTA S. GALLO
Spartaco
Lavagnini
V. L. da Vinci
V. Pacinotti
V. G. Marconi
Poggi
V. E. V.
S.
Caterina
Gd' A.
V. d. Ruote
Cavour
Lamarmora
Giacomo
Pza G. Vasari
Pza
Savonarola
Matteotti
Via
d. Artisti
La
Farina
Mantelli
POL
Via
A. Venezia
Via
dei
Della
T
Chiostro d. Scalzo
M
J
V. 27 Aprile
CONVENTO E MUSEO DI S. MARCO
M
Caponi
Piazzale
Donatello
Robbia
S. Apollonia
U
18
168
SS. ANNUNZIATA
Pinti
GALLERIA D. ACCADEMIA
Mª
MUSEO ARCHEOLOGICO
V. Alfieri
Viale
Mazzini
S²
V. Cavour
V. dei Servi
OSPEDALE D. INNOCENTI
d. Colonna
Giusti
Pza d'Azeglio
V. G. B. Niccolini
V.ª
G.
V. G. Boyio
82
T
P
degli
Alfani
V. dei
Pilastri
Farini
Borgo
A
G
B DUOMO
Mⁱ
96
C
Sinagoga
V. Colletta
174
V. d. Corso
130
Mª
96
V. Pietrapiana
V. Manzoni
Pza Beccaria
R²
Borgo d. Albizi
Borgo la Croce
Via
Gioberti
Pᶻᴬ DELLA SIGNORIA
M¹⁰
Via
M¹
Ghibellina
P
V. Fra Giov. Angelico
Ocagna
K
H
J
186
Pza di S. Croce
S. Giuseppe
Via
V. Giovine Italia
V.le G. Amendola
M³
60
de Benci
V. dei Malcontenti
Via
Arnolfo
V. dei Ghirlandaio
M⁶
M¹¹
S. CROCE
V. dei
L. Gen. Diaz
Torrigiani
L. d. Grazie
L. della Zecca Vecchia
S 67
Lungarno d. Tempio
de Bardi
Ponte alle Grazie
Serristori
Pza G. Poggi
Lungarno Cellini
Ponte Niccolò
L. F. Ferrucci
AREZZO
MUSEO BARDINI
148
V.
S.
Niccolò
Via
dei
Pza F. Ferrucci
Bastioni
V. G. Orsini
133
V. Salutati
Via
di
Belvedere
V. d. Monte alle Croci
Erta Canina
Piazzale Michelangelo
V.le Michelangelo
V. B. Fortini
V.le
Galileo
S
Miniato
PASSEGGIATA AI COLLI
S. MINIATO AL MONTE
V.le Michelangelo
Galileo
Via
dei
Giramonte
FIRENZE

0   300 m

Cenacolo di S. Salvi

X

211

FIRENZE

Museo Marino Marini	DU	M[7]	Ognissanti	DU		Ponte Vecchio	DU	
Museo Stibbert	ET		Opificio delle Pietre dure	ET	M[9]	San Lorenzo	DU	V
Museo archeologico	ET		Orsanmichele	EU	R[2]	San Miniato al Monte	EFV	
Museo dell'Opera del Duomo	EU	M[5]	Ospedale degli Innocenti	ETU		Sant'Apollonia	ET	
Museo della Casa Fiorentina Antica	DU	M[4]	Palazzo Medici-Riccardi	EU	S[2]	Santa Croce	EU	
Museo delle Porcellane	DV		Palazzo Pitti	DV		Santa Felicita	DV	
Museo di Storia della Scienza	EU	M[6]	Palazzo Rucellai	DU	S[3]	Santa Maria Novella	DU	W
Museo storico topografico Firenze com'era»	EU	M[8]	Palazzo Strozzi	DU	S[4]	Santa Maria del Carmine	DUV	
Museo«La Specola»	DV		Palazzo Vecchio	EU	H	Santa Trinita	DU	X
			Palazzo e museo del Bargello	EU	M[10]	Santissima Annunziata	ET	
			Passeggiata ai colli	DFVX		Santo Spirito	DU	
						Sinagoga	FU	

the prestige of Florence among its contemporaries while ruining the Medici financial empire. This humanist and man of great sensitivity was a great patron of the arts, and he gathered around him poets and philosophers, who all contributed to make Florence the capital of the early Renaissance.

A turbulent period

On Lorenzo's death, which had repercussions throughout Europe, the Dominican monk **Girolamo Savonarola**, taking advantage of a period of confusion, provoked the fall of the Medici. This fanatical and ascetic monk, who became the Prior of the Monastery of St Mark, preached against the pleasures of the senses and of the arts, and drove the citizens of Florence to make a "bonfire of vanities" in 1497 in Piazza della Signoria, on which musical instruments, paintings and books of poetry were burnt. A year later Savonarola himself was burnt at the stake on the same spot.

The Medici family returned to power with the help of the Emperor Charles V and they reigned until the mid-18C. **Cosimo I** (1519-74) brought some lost splendour back to Florence, conquered Siena and he himself became Grand Duke of Tuscany. He continued the tradition of patron of the arts.

Francesco I (1541-87), whose daughter Maria was to marry Henri IV King of France, took as his second wife the beautiful Venetian Bianca Cappello. The last prominent Medici was Ferdinand I (1549-1609) who married French princess, Christine de Lorraine. After the Medici, the Grand Duchy passed to the House of Lorraine, then to Napoleon Bonaparte until 1814, before returning to the House of Lorraine until 1859. As part of the Italian Kingdom, Florence was capital from 1865 to 1870.

Florence, Capital of the Arts

The relatively late emergence of Florence in the 11C as a cultural centre and its insignificant Roman heritage no doubt contributed to the growth of an independent art movement, which developed vigorously for several centuries. One of its principal characteristics was its preoccupation with clarity and harmony which influenced writers as well as architects, painters and sculptors.

Dante Alighieri (1265-1321) established the use of the Italian vernacular in several of his works, thus superseding Latin as the literary language. He made an admirable demonstration with his *New Life (Vita Nuova)*, recounting his meeting with a young girl, Beatrice Portinari, who was to be the inspiration for his **Divine Comedy** *(Divina Commedia)*, in which Dante, led by Virgil and then by Beatrice, visits the Inferno, Purgatory and Paradise. In the 14C Dante was responsible for creating a versatile literary language to which Petrarch (👉 *see Index*) added his sense of lyricism and Boccaccio (👉 *see Index*) the art of irony.

Niccolò Machiavelli (1469-1527), born in Florence, was the statesman on whose account Machiavellism became a synonym for cunning. He was the author of **The Prince** *(Il Principe* – 1513), an essay on political science and government in which he counselled that in politics the end justifies the means.

Francesco Guicciardini (1483-1540) wrote an important history of Florence and Italy, while **Giorgio Vasari** (1511-74), much later, with his work *The Lives of the Most Eminent Italian Architects,*

Painters and Sculptors, was the first real art historian. He studied and classified local schools of painting, tracing their development from the 13C.

The Florentine school had its origins in the work of **Cimabue** (1240-1302) and slowly it freed itself from the Byzantine tradition with its decorative convolutions, while **Giotto** (1266-1337) in his search for truth gave priority to movement and expression. Later **Masaccio** (1401-28) studied spatial dimension and modelling. From then on perspective became the principal preoccupation of Florentine painters, sculptors, architects and theorists.

The Quattrocento (15C) saw the emergence of a group of artists such as **Paolo Uccello** (1397-1475), **Andrea del Castagno** (1423-57), **Piero della Francesca** (see Index) a native of the Marches, who were all ardent exponents in the matters of foreshortening and the geometrical construction of space; while others such as **Fra Angelico** (1387-1455), and later **Filippo Lippi** (1406-69) and **Benozzo Gozzoli** (1420-97) were imbued with the traditions of International Gothic and were more concerned with the visual effects of arabesques and the appeal of luminous colours. These opposing tendencies were reconciled in the harmonious balance of the work of **Sandro Botticelli** (1444-1510). Alongside Botticelli, the **Pollaiuolo** brothers, **Domenico Ghirlandaio** (1449-94) and **Filippino Lippi** (1457-1504) ensure the continuity and diversity of Florentine art.

The High Renaissance with its main centres in Rome and other northern towns reached Florence in the 16C. **Leonardo da Vinci**, **Michelangelo** and **Raphael**, all made their debut at Florence, and inspired younger Mannerist artists such as **Jacopo Pontormo, Rosso Fiorentino, Andrea del Sarto** (1486-1530) and the curious portraitist of the Medici, **Agnolo Bronzino** (1503-72).

The emergence of a Florentine school of painting is, however, indissociable from the contemporary movement of the architects who were creating a style, also inspired by Antiquity, which united the classical traditions of rhythm, a respect for proportion and geometric decoration. The constant preoccupation was with perspective in the arrangement of interiors and the design of façades. **Leon Battista Alberti** (1404-72) was the theorist and grand master of such a movement. However it was **Filippo Brunelleschi** (1377-1446) who best represented the Florentine spirit, and he gave the city buildings which combined both rigour and grace, as in the magnificent dome of the cathedral of Santa Maria del Fiore.

Throughout the Quattrocento (15C), buildings were embellished with admirable sculptures. The doors of the baptistery were the object of a competition in which the very best took part. If **Lorenzo Ghiberti** (1378-1455) was finally victorious, **Donatello** (1386-1466) was later to provide ample demonstration of the genius of his art, so full of realism and style, as did **Luca della Robbia** (1400-82) and his dynasty who specialised in glazed terracotta decoration, **Andrea del Verrocchio** (1435-88) and numerous other artists who adorned the ecclesiastical and secular buildings of Florence. In the 16C **Michelangelo**, who was part of this tradition, confirmed his origins with his New Sacristy (1520-55) of San Lorenzo, which he both designed and decorated with sculpture. Later **Benvenuto Cellini** (1500-71), Giambologna or **Giovanni Bologna** (1529-1608) and **Bartolomeo Ammannati** (1511-92) maintained this unity of style which was responsible for the exceptional beauty of Florence.

Piazza del Duomo★★★

In the city centre, the cathedral, campanile and baptistery form an admirable group, demonstrating the traditions of Florentine art from the Middle Ages to the Renaissance.

Duomo (Santa Maria del Fiore)★★

🕐*Open Mon, Tue, Wed and Fri 10am-5pm, Thu 10am-4.30pm, Sat 10am-4.45pm, Sun and public holidays 1.30-4.45pm. Crypt, 10am-5pm. ☎ 055 23 02 885; www. operaduomo.firenze.it.*

One of the largest cathedrals in the Christian world, the Duomo is a symbol

Address Book

GETTING ABOUT

Walking is by far the best way to explore the city. Florence has an ancient urban structure with narrow streets full of innumerable scooters and cars driven by Florentines who tend to be rather fast drivers. The one-way systems can be daunting if one doesn't know the city, traffic is often restricted to residents only and some car parks are also open to residents only. It's therefore a good idea to leave your car at the car parks at Fortezza da Basso or S. Maria Novella station and then walk or take a bus.

R. Mattes/MICHELIN

BUSES

A guideline to the main routes:
Lines 12 and 13 go to the Colli and Piazzale Michelangiolo.
Line 7 goes from the station to Fiesole.
Line 10 goes from the station to Settignano.
Line 17 goes from the station to the youth hostel.
Tickets with 75min validity cost 1.20€ and a booklet of four tickets valid for 75min costs 4.50€. Tourist tickets: valid for 24hr (4.50€), 3 days (12€) and 7 days (16€). The "carta agile" is valid for 12 journeys and costs 10€.
For further information consult the ATAF website: www.ataf.net; ☎800 42 45 00.

TAXIS

Dial either ☎055 4242, 055 4390, or ☎055 4798.

CAR RENTAL

Cars can be rented at the airport or at offices in the city:

AVIS, Borgo Ognissanti 128r, ☎055 21 36 29, 055 28 90 10; www.avis.com
EUROPCAR, Borgo Ognissanti 53r, ☎055 29 04 37; www.europecar.com
HERTZ, Via Maso Finiguerra 33r, ☎055 28 22 60; www.hertz.com

GETTING AROUND BY BICYCLE

This is by far the best way of getting around Florence which is always beleaguered by traffic.
Some hotels rent out bicycles but to meet the needs of all cyclists there is an association in Via S. Zanobi 120r/122r, called Florence by bike (www.florenceby-bike.it). Various types of bicycles can be rented and organised tours of the city by bike, with commentary on the sights by a tour leader, are also available.

SIGHTSEEING

To avoid the queues (of anything up to an hour) visitors are advised to book their tour of the Uffizi in advance. Booking office: ☎055 29 48 83; www. polomuseale.firenze.it/musei/uffizi
For coin ranges, see the Legend at the back of the guide.

WHERE TO EAT

In Florence, there is no shortage of bars selling sandwiches and ready cooked food as well as restaurants catering for tourists – but few of them are good. The best places to head for are the little *trattorie* which serve traditional Florentine dishes including tripe (*trippa and lampredotto),* vegetable soup (*ribollita*), bread cooked with tomatoes (*pappa al pomodoro),* various pasta dishes including rigatoni strascicati,

J. Malburet/MICHELIN

steak (bistecca), stewed meatloaf (polpettone in umido), sausages with beans (salsiccia con i fagioli all'uccelletto) and the sweetened loaf schiacciata dolce fiorentina.

Cantinetta dei Verrazzano – *Via dei Tavolini 18/20r, Firenze – ☎055 26 85 90 – www.verrazzano.com – Closed Sun.* A charming little establishment with a winning formula which combines wonderful breads and pastries with good wines – open 24 hours a day!

Palle d'Oro – *Via Sant'Antonino 43/45r, Firenze – ☎055 28 83 83 – Closed Sun, Aug – ▭ – Reservation recommended.* Situated a few minutes' walk from the market in San Lorenzo, this establishment dates back to the early 20C when the great-grandfather of the present owners set up a wine shop here. The menu features a number of Tuscan specialities and first courses. If you are short of time, there is a selection of sandwiches and rolls which can be consumed at the bar.

Vini e Vecchi Sapori – *Via dei Magazzini 3r, Firenze – ☎055 29 30 45 – www.vinievecchisapori.it – Closed Mon, Sun evening, Aug – ▭ – Reservation recommended.* A small, but very pleasant establishment tucked away behind the Palazzo Vecchio. Local specialities include vegetable soup (ribollita) and tripe (including the lam-predotto version) as well as crostini, sliced ham and salami (affettati) and cheeses (formaggi). It can get very busy so be patient.

Del Fagioli – *Corso Tintori 47r, Firenze ☎055 24 42 85 – Closed Sat and Sun, Aug ; ▭.* A typical Tuscan trattoria with a relaxed, family atmosphere. Authentic home cooking and traditional Florentine dishes. A good place for a leisurely lunch.

Osteria de' Benci – *Via de' Benci 11/13r, Firenze ☎055 23 44 923 – Closed Sun ▭ – Reservation recommended.* A traditional Tuscan trattoria with plenty of atmosphere and rustic ambience, wooden tables included. Traditional dishes with a regional flavour, based around seasonal produce. Good wine list – Tuscan wines only.

Trattoria-Cibre Cibreino – *Via dei Macci 122r, Firenze – ☎055 23 41 100 – Closed Sun, Mon, 26 Jul-6 Sep, 31 Dec-6 Jan – ▭ – Reservation recommended.* This wine bar is located in the vicinity of the market in Sant'Ambrogio, adjacent to its sister restaurant. With its informal, friendly and trendy ambience it is one of the most popular establishments in the city. Delicious food and quality wines.

Trattoria 13 Gobbi – *Via del Porcellana 9r, Firenze – ☎055 28 40 15 – ▭ – Reservation recommended.* A well-known trattoria in Florence, popular for its authentic cooking and cheerful atmosphere. Rustic-style decor and furnishings in the two rooms which make up the dining area. During the summer meals are served in the lovely little courtyard.

Il Latini – *Via dei Palchetti 6r, Firenze – ☎055 21 09 16 – torlatin@tin.it – Closed Mon, 24 Dec-5 Jan.* Popular with Florentines and tourists alike this is a lively establishment, the wooden tables always heaving with diners. Lots of witty banter and Tuscan cooking.

Cibreo – *Via A. del Verrocchio 118r, Firenze – ☎055 23 41 100 – cibreo.fi@tin.it – Closed Mon, Sun, 31 Dec-6 Jan and 26 Jul-6 Sep – ▭ – Reservation recommended.* An informal but stylish establishment in the vicinity of the market in Sant'Ambrogio. The menu is based on traditional Tuscan cooking and the dishes are beautifully presented. The service is attentive and there is a good choice of wines.

WHERE TO STAY

The accommodation listed below also includes information on religious orders (addresses with no description) which offer reasonably priced rooms to visitors.

Sette Santi Fondatori – *Via dei Mille 11, Firenze – ☎055 50 48 452 – Fax 055 50 57 085 – 7santi@eidinet.com – ▭ – 65 rooms.*

Residenza Hannah e Johanna – *Via Bonifacio Lupi 14, Firenze – ☎055 48 18 96 – www.johanna.it – ▭ – 11 rooms.* A pleasant hotel where great attention has been paid to detail, to the extent that in some rooms there are niches full of books and magazines. Breakfast is served in a do-it-yourself formula: everything you need is set out on a tray in your room. This is an excellent address (near Piazza S. Marco), atmosphere and reasonable prices.

Hotel Orchidea – *Borgo degli Albizi 11, Firenze – ☎055 24 80 346 – www. hotelorchideaflorence.it – ✂ – 7 rooms.* This little pensione is housed on the first floor of a palazzo in the historic centre. The English lady who owns it has created a pleasantly relaxing, family atmosphere. The rooms are reasonably spacious, have high ceilings and are simply decorated. Shared bathrooms.

Albergo Scoti – *Via Tornabuoni 7, Firenze – ☎055 29 21 28 – www.hotelscoti. com – ♿ – 11 rooms – ☐.* An eclectic residence on Via Tornabuoni. The Renaissance palazzo with its richly frescoed salon creates a charming atmosphere of genteel aristocratic decline. Tiny, shared bathrooms.

Casa della Madonna del Rosario – *Via Capo di Mondo 44, Firenze – ☎055 67 96 21 – Fax 055 67 71 33 – ✂ – 32 rooms – ☐.*

Hotel Cimabue – *Via B. Lupi 7, Firenze – ☎ 055 47 56 01 – www.hotelci mabue.it – Closed for 3 weeks in Dec – 16 rooms – ☐.* Even if you do not have the good fortune to stay in one of the rooms with a frescoed ceiling or one of the suites, you will not be disappointed – the rooms are spacious and tastefully furnished.

Residenza Johanna – *Via Cinque Giornate 12, Firenze – ☎055 47 33 77 – www.johanna.it – ✂ P – 6 double rooms – ☐.* This small hotel is clean and in a pleasantly secluded position, if a little far from the city centre (half an hour on foot). There is also the advantage of a gravel courtyard where you can park your car. Breakfast is served in a do-it-yourself formula: everything you need is set out on a tray in your room.

Villa I Cancelli – *Via Incontri 21, Firenze – ☎055 42 26 001 – Fax 055 42 26 001 – ✂ – 31 rooms – ☐.*

Oasi del Sacro Cuore – *Via della Piazzola 4, Firenze – ☎055 57 75 88 – Fax 055 57 48 87 – oasifirenze@.it – 58 rooms – ☐.*

Residenze Johlea I e II – *Via San Gallo 76/80, Firenze – ☎055 46 33 292 – Fax 055 46 34 552 –Closed 1-5 Jan and 1-27 Aug – ✂ – 12 rooms – ☐.* The latest addition to a rather charming chain of

B&Bs housed in two small buildings. Stylish interior, comfortable rooms. Very relaxed and cosy family atmosphere. Highly recommended. Check in by 7pm.

Locanda di Firenze – *Via Faenza 12, Firenze – ☎055 28 43 40 – Fax 055 28 43 52 – ☐ – 6 double rooms – ☐.* This guesthouse is situated on the third floor of a historic palazzo, a stone's throw from the market in San Lorenzo. It is run by an ex-University professor who has opened his home to tourists and is a hospitable host. Comfortable with great attention to detail.

Hotel La Scaletta – *Via Guicciardini 13, Firenze – ☎055 28 30 28 – www.lascaletta.com – ☐ – 14 rooms – ☐.* This hotel has a pleasant, homely feel – lovely antique furniture in the breakfast and reading rooms. Wonderful roof terrace which overlooks the whole of the historic centre. Rooms are bright and airy.

Convitto Ecclesiastico della Calza – *Piazza della Calza 6, Firenze – ☎055 22 22 87 – www.calza.it – ✂ – 50 rooms – ☐.*

Relais Uffizi – *Chiasso de' Baroncelli-chiasso del Buco 16, Firenze – ☎055 26 76 239 – Fax 055 26 57 909 – www.relaisuffizi.it – ☐ – ☐.* An elegant, convivial hotel housed in a fine medieval Florentine palazzo. Splendid lounge and breakfast area which overlook Piazza della Signoria – a very stylish start to the day.

TAKING A BREAK

Caffè Ricchi e Ristorante – *Piazza Santo Spirito 8/9r – ☎055 21 58 64 – enzo.ricchi@libero.it – Mon-Sat 7.30am-11pm – Closed Sun and for two weeks in Aug.* This is one of most celebrated gelaterie in Florence and its ice creams are all home-made. The café has a lovely outdoor terrace for the summer months. Very busy on market days.

Enoteca Bonatti – *Via Gioberti 66/68r – ☎055 66 00 50 – erbonatti@tin.it –Closed Sun, Mon and for one week in Aug.* The Bonatti family's reputation as premium wine specialists goes back to 1934. The collection comprises more than 1 000 wines from all over Italy.

Rivoire – *Via Vacchereccia 4r –* ☎*055 21 44 12 – Closed Mon and for two weeks in Jan.* Founded in 1862, the Rivoire is a well-established feature of Florentine café life. Its greatest attraction is its location in Piazza della Signoria, overlooked by the Palazzo Vecchio and Cellini's statue of Perseus. Not so attractive are the prices (the coffee is Florence's most expensive!).

Vip Bar – *Viale Giuseppe Poggi 5r –* ☎*0335 54 17 544 (mobile) – Closed when it rains.* This bar has one of the finest views in Florence!

Vivoli Piero il Gelato – *Via Isola delle Stinche 7r –* ☎*055 29 23 34 – vivoli@mail. cosmos.it – Closed Mon and for three weeks in Jan and Aug.* There is no shortage of gelaterie in Florence but ice cream connoisseurs attest to this historic establishment (it dates back to 1930) being one of the very best.

GOING OUT

Antico Caffè del Moro "Café des artistes" – *Via del Moro 4r –* ☎*055 28 76 61 – Closed for three weeks in Aug.* In the 1950s artists who frequented this establishment would often pay for their drinks with paintings. which now decorate the walls of this cheerful bar.

Caffè Storico Letterario Giubbe Rosse – *Piazza della Repubblica 13/14r –* ☎*055 21 22 80 – www.giubberosse.it.* The waiters here wear their red gilets with great pride – this café has long been popular with writers and artists. It is celebrated for its connections with the early Italian Futurist movement.

Il Rifrullo – *Via San Niccolo 55r –* ☎*055 23 42 621.* Situated off the beaten tourist track, one of the attractions of this bar is the covered open-air area. It is popular with Florence's late-night revellers for chatting into the early hours while sipping house cocktails.

Jazz Club – *Via Nuova dei Caccini 3 –* ☎*055 24 79 700 – Closed Mon.* This is the jazz club of all jazz clubs in Florence! It is incredibly popular and you can see why – there are live concerts every evening with a different group (usually Italian) performing. Membership charge.

CONCERTS AND THEATRE

Florence is an art and music lover's city even at night, when plays and concerts animate its theatres. To find out what's on look in *La Nazione* and the pages on Florence in national daily newspapers or contact the theatres directly:

Box Office – *Via Alamanni 39r –* ☎*055 21 08 04 – Mon 3.30-7.30pm, Tue-Sat 10am-7.30pm.* Tickets on sale for a number of different theatres. To find out what's on, buy a copy of *Firenze Spettacolo.*

ETI – *Teatro della Pergola – Via della Pergola 18 –* ☎*055 22 641 – www.pergola. firenze.it. Ticket office closes 2hr before the concert begins.* ♿*See Teatro Comunale.*

Teatro Comunale – Corso Italia 12 – ☎*055 27 791 – www.maggiofiorentino. com – Open Tue-Fri 10am-4.30pm, Sat 10am-1pm.* Classical music is very much a feature of the cultural life of the city. Throughout the year concerts, operas and recitals are held at various different venues including Teatro Verdi, Teatro Comunale and Teatro della Pergola.

Teatro Verdi – *Via Ghibellina 99 –* ☎*055 21 23 20 – www.teatroverdifirenze. it – Open Mon-Fri 10am-2pm, 4-7pm, Sat 10am-1pm.* Ticket office closes 1hr before the performance begins. ♿*See Teatro Comunale.*

SHOPPING

Dolci e Dolcezze – *Piazza Beccaria 8r –* ☎*055 23 45 458 – Tue-Sun 8.30am-9.30pm – Closed Mon and Aug.* This tiny shop has a kitsch feel about it and a reputation as one of the best pasticcerie. The celebrated lemon tart (torta al limone) and chocolate tart (torta al cioccolato) are among the best.

Gilli – *Piazza della Repubblica 39r –* ☎*055 21 38 96 – www.gilli.it.* The Gilli establishments have been in existence for 250 years and have changed address several times before eventually settling, in 1910, in their current premises.

Procacci – *Via Tornabuoni 64r –* ☎*055 21 16 56 – Open Tue-Sat 10.30am-8pm – Closed Aug.* Founded in 1885, this delicatessen is an institution in Florence, celebrated for its white truffles (on sale from Nov to May).

of the city's 13C and 14C power and wealth. It was begun in 1296 by Arnolfo di Cambio and consecrated in 1436.

Exterior – Walk round the cathedral starting from the south side to admire the marble mosaic decoration and the sheer size of the **east end**★★★. The harmonious domeaaa by Brunelleschi took 14 years to build. To counteract the excessive thrust he built two concentric domes, linked by props. The façade dates from the late 19C.

Top of the dome: Mon-Fri 8.30am-6.50pm, Sat 8.30am-5pm, (last admission 40min before closing). *Closed Sun, from Maundy Thu to Easter Sun, 24 Jun, public holidays.* €6. 055 23 02 885; www.operaduomo.firenze.it.

Interior – The bareness of the interior contrasts sharply with the exterior's sumptuous decoration. The great octagonal **chancel** under the dome is surrounded by a delicate 16C marble balustrade. The dome is painted with a huge fresco of the Last Judgement. It is possible to go up to the inner gallery, which offers an impressive view of the nave, and then climb to the top of the dome (464 steps) for a magnificent **panorama**★★of Florence.

The sacristy doors on either side of the high altar have tympana adorned with pale blue terracottas by Luca della Robbia representing the Resurrection and the Ascension. In the new sacristy *(left)*, there are inlaid armorial bearings by the Maiano brothers (15C).

A dramatic episode of the **Pazzi Conspiracy** took place in the chancel. The Pazzi, who were rivals of the Medici, tried to assassinate Lorenzo the Magnificent on 26 April 1478, during the Elevation of the Host. Lorenzo, though wounded by two monks, managed to take refuge in a sacristy, but his brother Giuliano fell to their daggers.

The axial chapel contains a masterpiece by Ghiberti, the sarcophagus of St Zanobi, the first Bishop of Florence. One of the low reliefs shows the saint resurrecting a child. The frescoes in the north aisle include one showing Dante explaining the *Divine Comedy* to the city of Florence (1465).

A stairway on the other side of the nave, between the first and second pillars,

leads to the **Crypt of Santa Reparata**, the only remaining part of a Romanesque basilica that was demolished when the present cathedral was built. The basilica itself was formerly an early Christian church (5C-6C). Excavations have revealed traces of mosaic paving belonging to the original building and Brunelleschi's tomb (behind the railing-enclosed chamber, at the bottom of the stairs, on the left).

Campanile★★★

Open daily 8.30am-7pm. Closed 1 Jan, Easter, 8 Sep, 25 Dec. 6€. 055 23 02 885; www.operaduomo.firenze.it

The tall slender belltower (82m/269ft) is the perfect complement to Brunelleschi's dome, the straight lines of the former balancing the curves of the latter. Giotto drew plans for it and began building in 1334, but died in 1337.

The Gothic campanile was completed at the end of the 14C; its geometric decoration is unusual. The admirable low reliefs at the base of the campanile have been replaced by copies.The originals, designed by Giotto, are in the Cathedral Museum.

From the top of the campanile (414 steps) there is a fine **panorama**★★ of the cathedral and town.

Battistero★★★

Open Mon-Sat noon-6.30pm, Sun and public holidays 8.30am-1.30pm. Closed 1 Jan, Easter, 8 Sep, 24/25 Dec. 3€ 055 23 02 885; www.operaduomo.firenze.it

The baptistery is faced in white and green marble. The **bronze doors**★★★ are world-famous.

The south door *(entrance)* by Andrea Pisano (1330) is Gothic and portrays scenes from the life of St John the Baptist *(above)*, as well as the Theological Virtues (Faith, Hope, Charity) and the Cardinal Virtues *(below)*. The door frames are by Vittorio Ghiberti, son of the designer of the other doors.

The north door (1403-24) was the first done by Lorenzo Ghiberti. He was the winner of a competition in which Brunelleschi, Donatello and Jacopo della Quercia also took part.

The east door (1425-52), facing the cathedral, is the one that Michelangelo declared worthy to be the **Gate of Paradise**, the name by which it is known. In it Ghiberti recalled the Old Testament; prophets and sibyls adorn the niches. The artist portrayed himself, bald and cunning-looking, in one medallion.

Interior – With its 25m/82ft diameter, its green and white marble and its paving decorated with oriental motifs, the interior is grand and majestic. The dome is covered with magnificent 13C **mosaics★★★**. The Last Judgement is depicted on either side of a large picture of Christ the King; on the five concentric bands that cover the other five panels of the dome, starting from the top towards the base, are the Heavenly Hierarchies, Genesis, the Life of Joseph, scenes from the Life of the Virgin and of Christ, and St John the Baptist.

On the right of the apse is the tomb of the antipope John XXIII, a work executed in 1427 by Donatello assisted by Michelozzo.

Museo dell'Opera del Duomo★★

♿ ⏱ *Open Mon-Sat 9am-7pm, Sun and public hols 9am-1.30pm.* ⏱*Closed 1 Jan, Easter, 8 Sep, 24/25 Dec.* ⬤6€ ☎ 055 23 02 885; www.operaduomo. firenze.it

The museum contains items from the cathedral, campanile and baptistery; note models of Brunelleschi's dome on the ground floor. On the mezzanine is the famous **Pietà★★** which Michelangelo left unfinished. In the large room on the first floor are two statues by **Donatello** – a repentant **Magdalene★** carved in wood, and the prophets Jeremiah and Habakkuk, the latter nicknamed Zuccone (vegetable marrow) because of the shape of his head.

In the same room are the famous **Cantorie★★**, choristers' tribunes from the cathedral, by Luca della Robbia and Donatello. The museum also houses the famous silver **altarpiece★★** depicting the life of St John the Baptist, a 14C-15C masterpiece, and the admirable **low reliefs★★** from the campanile.

Piazza della Signoria★★★

Piazza★★★

Allow 1 day. This was, and still is, the political stage of Florence, with a wonderful backdrop formed by the Palazzo Vecchio, the Loggia della Signoria and, in the wings, the Uffizi Museum. The many statues make it virtually an open-air museum of sculpture: near the centre of the square, the equestrian statue of Cosimo I, after Giovanni Bologna, and at the corner of the Palazzo Vecchio, the Fountain of Neptune (1576) by Ammannati. In front of the Palazzo Vecchio are copies of the proud *Marzocco* or *Lion of Florence* by Donatello and Michelangelo's David.

Loggia della Signoria★★

The Loggia, built at the end of the 14C, was the assembly hall and later the guardroom of the Lanzi (foot soldiers) of Cosimo I. It contains ancient (Classical) and Renaissance statues: the *Rape of a Sabine* (1583), Hercules and the centaur Nessus by Giovanni Bologna and the wonderful Perseus★★★ holding up the severed head of Medusa, a masterpiece executed by Benvenuto Cellini from 1545 to 1553.

Palazzo Vecchio★★

♿ ⏱*Open 9am-7pm; Thu 9am-2pm.* ⏱*Closed 1 Jan, Easter, 1 May, 15 Aug, 25 Dec. Restaurant. Bookshop.* ⬤6€, 8€ combined ticket with Cappella Brancacci (reservation required) and Museo dei Ragazzi. ☎055 27 68 465; www.muse oragazzi.it.

The Old Palace's powerful mass is dominated by a lofty belltower, 94m/308ft high. Built from 1299 to 1314, probably to plans by Arnolfo di Cambio, it is in a severe Gothic style.

The refinement and splendour of the Renaissance interior is a complete contrast. The **courtyard★** was restored by Michelozzo in the 15C and decorated in the following century by Vasari. The 16C fountain is surmounted by a delightful winged goblin, a copy of a work by Verrocchio (the original is in the palace).

B. Pérousse/MICHELIN

Linking the Uffizi with the Palazzo Pitti: the Ponte Vecchio with its little shops

Initially the seat of government (Palazzo della Signoria), the palace was then taken over in the 16C by Cosimo I as his private residence, as it was better suited to accommodating his large court. Most of the redecoration done by Vasari dates from this period. When Cosimo I abandoned the palace in favour of the Pitti Palace it was renamed Palazzo Vecchio. The apartments were decorated with sculptures by Benedetto and Giuliano da Maiano (15C) and paintings by Vasari and Bronzino (16C).

On the first floor the great Sala dei Cinquecento, painted with frescoes by several artists including Vasari, contains a group carved by Michelangelo, The Genius of Victory. The walls of the magnificent **studiolo**★★ or study of Francesco de' Medici, which was designed by Vasari, were painted by Bronzino, who was responsible for the portraits of *Cosimo I* and *Eleanora of Toledo*.

On the second floor, Cosimo I's apartments are known as the Apartment of the Elements because of the allegories decorating the first chamber, designed by Vasari.

Beyond these chambers are Eleonora of Toledo's apartments, again designed by Vasari. Finally, in the apartments of the *Priori*, the best-known chamber is the **Sala degli Gigli**★ (Chamber of Lilies) which has a magnificent coffered ceiling by Guiliano da Maiano and the **Sala del Guardaroba**★ (dressing-room) lined with 16C maps.

Galleria degli Uffizi★★★

♿🕑*Open daily 8.15am-6pm.* 🕑*Closed Mon, 1 Jan, 1 May, 25 Dec.* Ⓜ*6.50€ (9.50€ during exhibitions). Book in advance to avoid the long queues.* ☎*055 29 48 83 (booking office and information); www.uffizi.firenze.it.*

This is one of the finest art museums in the world. These collections were assembled by generations of Medici and follow the evolution of Italian art from its beginnings to the 17C.

The early nucleus was gathered together by Francesco I (1541-87) to which were added the collections of the Grand Dukes Ferdinand I and II, and Cosimo III. In 1737 the last member of the Medici dynasty, Anna Maria Luisa, Electress Palatine, bequeathed the collection to her native city of Florence. It was then housed in the Renaissance palace, designed by Vasari in 1560, which contained the offices *(uffizi)* of the Medici administration.

Galleries

The first gallery *(east)* is essentially dedicated to Florentine and Tuscan artists: there are works by Cimabue, Giotto, Duccio, Simone Martini (the **Annuncia-**

tion, a masterpiece of Gothic art), Paolo Uccello (**Battle of San Romano**) and Filippo Lippi. **The Botticelli Room**★★★ houses the artist's major works: the allegories of the **Birth of Venus** and **Spring** and the *Madonna with Pomegranate*. Other exhibits in the gallery include the **Adoration of the Magi** and the **Annunciation** by Leonardo da Vinci and a series of Italian and foreign paintings from the 15C and 16C (Perugino, Cranach, Dürer, Bellini, Giorgione, Correggio).

The first 11 rooms of the second gallery (west) contain works from the Italian Cinquecento (16C): **Tondo Doni** by Michelangelo, *Madonna and the Goldfinch* and **Leo X** by Raphael, **Madonna and the Harpies** by Andrea del Sarto, **Urbino Venus** by Titian and **Leda and the Swan** by Tintoretto. The other rooms are dedicated to both Italian and foreign paintings from the 17C and 18C: included in the collection are **Isabella Brandt** by Rubens, **Caravaggio's Adolescent Bacchus** and works by **Claude Lorrain** and **Rembrandt**.

Ponte Vecchio★★

As its name suggests, this is the oldest bridge in Florence. It has been rebuilt several times and spans the narrowest point of the Arno. Its original design includes a line of jewellers' shops and the **Corridoio Vasariano**, a passageway which was built by Vasari to link the Palazzo Vecchio to the Pitti Palace and which passes overhead.

Palazzo Pitti★★

This 15C Renaissance building, of rugged but imposing appearance, with pronounced rustication and many windows, was built to the plans of Brunelleschi for the Pitti family, the rivals of the Medici. It was Cosimo I's wife, Eleanora di Toledo, who enlarged the palace by the addition of two wings. The court moved to the palace in 1560.

Galleria Palatina★★★

&. ⊙*Open daily except Mon, 8.15am-6pm.* ⊙*Closed 1 Jan, 1 May, 25 Dec.* ⊛ *6.50€ (gallery and apartments).* ☎*055 29 48 83; www.sbas.firenze.it.*

This gallery houses a marvellous collection of paintings: **groups**★★★ of works by Raphael (*Portrait of a Lady* or **La Velata, Madonna del Granduca** and **Madonna della Seggiola**) and Titian (**La Bella, The Aretino, The Concert** and the **Grey-eyed Nobleman**).

On the first floor are the **Appartamenti reali**★ (State Apartments).

The building also houses the **Galleria d'Arte Moderna,**★ which mainly displays Tuscan works from the 19C and 20C. The section devoted to the **Macchiaioli** movement is represented by an exceptional seriesaa by Fattori, Lega, Signorini, Cecioni. &. ⊙*Open daily, 8.15am-1pm.* ⊙*Closed 1st, 3rd and 5th Mon of the month, 2nd and 4th Sun of the month, 1 Jan, 1 May, 25 Dec.* ⊛*5€.* ☎*055 23 88 760; www.sbas.firenze.it*

In the other wing is the Silver Museum (**Museo degli Argenti**★★) presenting items largely from the Medici collections. ☎*055 29 48 83; www.sbas.firenze. it/argenti.*

Giardino di Boboli★

☎*055 29 48 83; www.sbas.firenze.it.*

This Italian-style terraced garden, behind the Pitti Palace, was designed in 1549 by Tribolo. At one end of an avenue to the left of the palace is the **grotta grande**, a grotto created in the main by Buontalenti (1587-97). Cross the amphitheatre to reach the highest point, from which, on the right, the **Viottolone**★, an avenue of pines and cypresses, runs down to **Piazzale dell'Isolotto**★, a circular pool with a small island with citrus trees and a fountain by Giovanni Bologna. A pavilion houses a porcelain museum, the **Museo delle Porcelane**★.

The Forte del Belvedere, at the top of the hill, affords a splendid panoramaa of Florence. ⌖ *The panorama from the Forte del Belvedere*

Palazzo e Museo Nazionale del Bargello★★★

&. ⊙*Open daily 8.15am-6pm.* ⊙*Closed 2nd and 4th Mon of the month, 1 Jan, 1 May and 25 Dec.* ⊛*4€.* ☎*055 23 88 606; www.polomuseale.firenze.it/musei/bargello.*

This austere palace was formerly the residence of the governing magistrate *(podestà)*, then becoming a police headquarters *(bargello)*. It is a fine example of 13C-14C medieval architecture planned round a majestic **courtyard**★★ with a portico and loggia. The Volognona tower (57m/188ft) towers above. The palace is now a museum of sculpture and decorative arts.

The rooms on the ground floor are devoted to the works of 16C Florentine sculptors: **Brutus** and the **Pitti Tondo** (a marble medallion depicting the Virgin and Child with St John) by Michelangelo; **low reliefs** from the pedestal of the Perseus bronze by Benvenuto Cellini.

There is an exceptional collection (first floor) of **sculpture**★★★ by **Donatello** which includes his **Marzocco** (the Florentine heraldic lion), the bronze **David**, as well as the low relief of **St George** from Orsanmichele.

The rooms on the second floor display works by **Verrocchio**, including the famous bronze of **David**.

Chiesa di San Lorenzo★★★

This was the Medici family parish church, and most of the family were buried here. The **church**★★ was begun by Brunelleschi c 1420.

His great achievement is the **Old Sacristy**★★ *(at the far end of the north transept)*. Donatello was responsible for part of the decoration of this and also the two **pulpits**★★ in the nave.

Biblioteca Medicea Laurenziana★★

○*Open daily 8am-2pm.* ○*Closed two weeks in Sept, public holidays.* ☎*055 21 07 60; www.bml.firenze.sbn.it.*

Cosimo the Elder's library was added to by Lorenzo the Magnificent. Access is from the north aisle of the church or through the charming 15C **cloisters**★ *(entrance to the left of the church).* The vestibule was designed as an exterior and is occupied by a magnificent **staircase**★★. The staircase was built by Ammannati to Michelangelo's designs. The **library**, also by Michelangelo, displays 10 000 manuscripts in rotation.

Cappelle Medicee★★

Entrance on Piazza Madonna degli Aldobrandini. ○*Open daily 8.15am-5pm.* ○*Closed 1st, 3rd and 5th Mon of the month, 2nd and 4th Sun of the month, 1 Jan, 1 May, 25 Dec.* ⊛*4€.* ☎ *055 29 48 83; www.polomuseale. firenze.it/musei/cappellemedicee.*

The **Princes' Chapel** (17C-18C), grandiose but gloomy, is faced with semi-precious stones and is the funerary chapel for Cosimo I and his descendants.

The **New Sacristy** was Michelangelo's first architectural work and despite its name was always intended as a funerary chapel. Begun in 1520, it was left unfinished when the artist left Florence in 1534. Michelangelo achieved rhythm and solemnity by using contrasting materials, dark grey sandstone (pietra serena) and the white of the marbles.

The famous **Medici tombs**★★★ were also the work of Michelangelo. Giuliano, Duke of Nemours (d 1516), is portrayed as Action, surrounded by allegorical figures of Day and Night; and Lorenzo II, Duke of Urbino (d 1519), as a Thinker with Dawn and Dusk at his feet. Of the plans for Lorenzo the Magnificent's tomb only the admirable group of the Madonna and Child flanked by saints was completed. In the plain tomb underneath lie Lorenzo the Magnificent and his brother Giuliano. ⊚ *Don't miss the Medici tombs by Michelangelo.*

Palazzo Medici-Ricardi★★

&○ *Open daily 9am-7pm.* ○ *Closed Wed. 4€.* ☎*055 27 60 340; www.palazzo-medici.it.*

This noble but austere building is typical of the Florentine Renaissance with its mathematical plan and rustication. The palace was begun in 1444 by Michelozzo on the orders of Cosimo the Elder. From 1459 to 1540 it was a Medici residence, and Lorenzo the Magnificent held court here. In the second half of the 17C the palace passed to the Riccardi.

Cappella★★★

First floor: entrance by the first stairway on the right in the courtyard. This tiny chapel was decorated with admirable **frescoes** (1459) by **Benozzo Gozzoli**.

The Procession of the Magi is a vivid picture of Florentine life with portraits of the Medici and of famous dignitaries from the east who had assembled for the Council of Florence in 1439.

Sala di Luca Giordano★★

First floor: entrance by the second stairway on the right in the courtyard. The entire roof of this gallery built by the Riccardi at the end of the 17C and splendidly decorated with gold stucco, carved panels and great painted mirrors, is covered by a brightly-coloured Baroque fresco of the Apotheosis of the second Medici dynasty, masterfully painted by Luca Giordano in 1683.

San Marco★★

♿ 🕐 *Open Mon-Fri 8.15am-1.30pm, Sat, Sun and public holidays 8.15am-6.30pm.* 🕐 *Closed 1st, 3rd and 5th Sun of the month, 2nd and 4th Mon of the month, 1 Jan, 1 May, 25 Dec.* 🎫 *4€.* ☎ *055 23 88 608; www.polomuseale.firenze.it/english/ musei/sanmarco.*

The museum in a former Dominican monastery, rebuilt c 1436 in a very plain style by Michelozzo, is virtually the **Fra Angelico Museum**★★★. Fra Angelico took orders in Fiesole before coming to St Mark's, where he decorated the walls of the monks' cells with edifying scenes. Humility, gentleness and mysticism were the qualities expressed by this artistic monk in a technique influenced by the Gothic tradition. His refined use of colour, delicate draughtsmanship and gentle handling imbued these frescoes with a suitably pacifying power.

The former guest hall, opening off the cloisters on the right, contain many of the artist's works on wood, especially the triptych depicting the **Descent from the Cross**, the famous **Last Judgement** and other religious scenes. The chapter house has a severe *Crucifixion* while the refectory contains an admirable **Last Supper**★ by Ghirlandaio.

The staircase leading to the first floor is dominated by Fra Angelico's masterpiece, the **Annunciation**. The monks' cells open off corridors, with lovely timber ceilings. Along the corridor to

the left of the stairs are the *Apparition of Christ to the Penitent Magdalene (1st cell on the left)*, the *Transfiguration (6th cell on the left)* and the *Coronation of the Virgin (9th cell on the left).*

Off the corridor on the right is the **library**★, one of Michelozzo's finest achievements.

Galleria dell'Accademia★★

♿ 🕐 *Open daily except Mon, 8.15am-6.50pm.* 🕐 *Closed 1 Jan, 1 May, 25 Dec.* 🎫 *9.50€.* ☎ *055 29 48 83; www.sbas. firenze.it/accademia/.*

The museum gives the visitor some idea of the extraordinary personality of **Michelangelo** and the conflict between the nature of his raw materials and his idealistic vision. The **main gallery**★★★ contains the powerful figures of **Four Slaves** (1513-20) and **St Matthew** (all unfinished) who would seem to be trying to struggle free from the marble. At the far end of the gallery, in a specially designed apse (1873), is the monumental figure of **David** (1501-04), the symbol of youthful but well-mastered force and a perfect example of the sculptor's humanism. The **picture gallery**★ has works by 13C-15C Tuscan masters, including a painted chest by Adimari and two Botticellis.

Chiesa di Santa Maria Novella★★

🕐 *Open Mon-Thu, Sat 9.30am-5pm; Fri and Sun and public hols 1-5pm.* 🎫 *2.50€.*

The Church of Santa Maria Novella and the adjoining monastery were founded in the 13C by the Dominicans. The church overlooks a square that was originally the setting for chariot races.

The **church**★★, begun in 1279, was completed only in 1360, except for the **façade**, with geometric patterns in white and green marble, designed by Alberti (upper section) in the 15C.

On the wall of the third bay in the north aisle is a famous **fresco**★★ of the Trinity with the Virgin, St John and the donors in which Masaccio, adopting the new Renaissance theories, shows great mastery of perspective. At the far end of the north transept, the Strozzi di Mantora

Chapel (raised) is decorated with **frescoes**★ (1357) by the Florentine Nardo di Cione depicting the Last Judgement on a grand scale. The **polyptych**★ on the altar is by Nardo's brother, Orcagna di Cione. The sacristy contains a fine **Crucifix**★ *(above the entrance)* by Giotto and a delicate glazed terracotta **niche**★ by Giovanni della Robbia.

In the Gondi Chapel *(first on the left of the high altar)* hangs a **Crucifix**★★ by Brunelleschi, which so struck Donatello that he is said, on first seeing it, to have dropped the eggs he was carrying.

The chancel is ornamented with admirable **frescoes**★★★ by **Domenico Ghirlandaio** who, on the theme of the Lives of the Virgin and of St John the Baptist, painted a dazzling picture of Florentine life in the Renaissance era.

The church is flanked by two cloisters. The finest are the **Chiostro Verde**★ (Green Cloisters), so-called after the dominant colour of the frescoes painted by Paolo Uccello and his school (scenes from the Old Testament). Opening off these to the north is the **Cappellone degli Spagnoli** (Spaniards' Chapel) with late-14C **frescoes**★★ by **Andrea di Bonaiuto** (also known as Andrea da Firenze). With intricate symbolism the frescoes depict the Church Triumphant and the glorification of the deeds of the Dominicans.

Museum and cloisters: &. ©*Open Mon-Thu and Sat 9am-4.30pm (public holidays 1.30pm).* © *Closed Fri Sun, 1 Jan, Easter, 1 May, 15 Aug and 25 Dec.* ✎*Guided tours available.* ©*2.70 €.* ☎*055 28 21 87; www.comune.fi.it.*

Chiesa di Santa Croce★★

©✎*Tour: Open Mon-Sat 9.30am-5pm, Sun and public holidays 1-5pm.* ©*5€ combined ticket with Cappella dei Pazzi and museum.* ☎*055 24 66 105.*

The church and cloisters of 13-14C Santa Croce look onto one of the town's oldest squares. The **interior** is vast (140m x 40m/460ft x 130ft) as the church was designed for preaching and is paved with 276 tombstones.

South aisle: By the first pillar, a *Virgin and Child* by Antonio Rossellino (15C); opposite, the tomb of Michelangelo (d

1564) by Vasari; opposite the second pillar, the funerary monument (19C) to Dante (d 1321, buried at Ravenna); by the third pillar, a fine **pulpit**★ (1476) by Benedetto da Maiano and facing it the monument to V Alfieri (d 1803) by Canova; opposite the fourth pillar, the 18C monument to Machiavelli (d 1527); facing the fifth pillar, a low relief of the **Annunciation**★★ carved in stone and embellished with gold by Donatello; opposite the sixth pillar, the **tomb of Leonardo Bruni**★★ humanist and chancellor of the Republic, (d 1444) by Bernardo Rossellino, and next to it the tomb of the composer Rossini (d 1868).

South transept: At the far end, the Baroncelli Chapel with **frescoes**★ (1338) depicting the Life of the Virgin by Taddeo Gaddi and at the altar, the **polyptych**★ of the Coronation of the Virgin from Giotto's studio.

Sacristy★ *(access by the corridor on the right of the chancel)*: This dates from the 14C and is adorned with **frescoes**★ including a Crucifixion by Taddeo Gaddi and, in the fine Rinuccini Chapel, with scenes from the Life of the Virgin and of Mary Magdalene by Giovanni da Milano (14C). At the far end of the corridor is the Medici Chapel (1434) built by Michelozzo, with an **altarpiece**★ in glazed terracotta by Andrea della Robbia.

Chancel: The first chapel to the right of the altar contains evocative **frescoes**★★ (c 1320) by Giotto depicting the life of St Francis. The chancel is covered with **frescoes**★ (1380) by Agnolo Gaddi.

North transept: At the far end is a famous **Crucifixion**★★ by Donatello, which Brunelleschi tried to surpass at Santa Maria Novella.

North aisle *(coming back)*: Beyond the second pillar, a fine **monument to Carlo Marsuppini**★ by Desiderio da Settignano (15C); facing the fourth pillar the tombstone of L. Ghiberti (d 1455); the last tomb (18C) is that of Galileo (d 1642).

Cappella dei Pazzi★★

&.©*Open Mon-Sat 9.30am-5pm, Sun and public holidays 1-5pm.* ©*4€ combined ticket with museum.* ☎*055 24 46 19.*

This chapel by Brunelleschi is a Florentine Renaissance masterpiece, remarkable for the harmony of its decoration (glazed Della Robbia terracotta).

Chiostro Grande

Entrance at the end of the first cloisters, on the right. These cloisters designed by Brunelleschi shortly before his death (1446) were completed in 1453.

Museo dell'Opera di Santa Croce

♿⏱*Open Mon-Sat 9.30am-5pm, Sun and public holidays 1-5pm.* 🎫*4€ combined ticket with Cappella dei Pazzi.* ☎*055 24 46 19.*

The museum contains a famous **Crucifixion**★ by Cimabue that was seriously damaged by the 1966 floods.

Passeggiata ai Colli★★

2hr on foot or 1hr by car.

For a drive to the hills take the road to the east along the south bank of the Arno to the medieval tower in Piazza Giuseppe Poggi. Take the winding pedestrian street to Piazzale Michelangiolo for a splendid city **view**★★★.

Not far from here, in a splendid **setting** ★★ overlooking the town, the church of **San Miniato al Monte**★★ is a remarkable example of Florentine Romanesque architecture. The **Chapel of Cardinal James of Portugal**★ opening out of the north aisle is a fine Renaissance structure. The pulpit and chancel screen (*transenna*) form a remarkable **ensemble**★★ inlaid with marble (early 13C). The **frescoes**★ (1387) in the **sacristy** are by Spinello Aretino.

Other Museums and Monuments

Chiesa di Santa Maria del Carmine★★★

⏱*Open by appointment only: 10am-4.30pm, Sun and public holidays 1-4.430pm.* ⏱*Closed Tue.* 🚶*Guided tours available.* 🎫*4€.* ☎ *055 27 68 224.*
Cappella Brancacci: fresco cycle (1427) by Masolino, **Masaccio** and Filippino Lippi depicting Original Sin and the Life of St Peter.

La Badia

10C church of a former abbey (badia) with an elegant **campanile**★. The interior has a coffered **ceiling**★★ and houses works of art including Filippino Lippi's **Virgin appearing to St Bernard**★, a delicate **relief**★★ sculpture in marble by Mino da Fiesole and the **tombs**★ carved by the same artist.

Museo Archeologico★★

♿⏱*Open Wed, Fri, Sat and Sun 8.30am-2pm, Mon 2-7pm, Tue and Thu 8.30am-7pm.* ⏱*Closed 1 Jan, 1 May, 25 Dec.* 🎫*4€.* ☎*055 23 575; www.sbat.it/*
The museum has an important collection of Egyptian, Greek (**François vase**★★), Etruscan (**Arezzo Chimera**★★) and Roman art.

Opificio delle Pietre Dure★

♿⏱*For admission times and charges, call.* ☎ *055 26 511; www.opificio.arti.beniculturali.it/ita/home.htm.*
Lorenzo the Magnificent was responsible for reviving the ancient tradition of decorating with semi-precious stones in the form of mosaics (pietre dure). This workshop now specialises in restoration work. There is a small **museum**.

Orsanmichele★

Originally a grain storehouse, Orsanmichele was rebuilt in the 14C. There are works by Donatello, Ghiberti and Verrocchio and a splendid Gothic **tabernacle**★★ by Orcagna.

Palazzo Rucellai★★

This 15C palace was designed by Leon Battista Alberti. The façade is the first cohesive example of the three ancient orders placed one on top of the other.

Palazzo Strozzi★★

This 15C building has rusticated stonework, cornice and arcaded courtyard.

Piazza della SS. Annunziata★

This fine piazza is enhanced by Giambologna's statue of Ferdinando I de' Medici and two Baroque fountains.

Chiesa Santissima Annunziata

In the chancel of this 15C church are some fine **frescoes**★ by Rosso Fiorentino and Pontormo that were completed by Franciabigio. The interior is in the Baroque style; the north arm of the transept gives access to the Renaissance Cloisters of the Dead (Chiostro dei Morti). The vault by the door is adorned with the **Madonna with the Sack**★ by Andrea del Sarto (16C).

Ospedale degli Innocenti★

Open daily 8.15am-2pm (Thurs 7pm). Closed Sun, 1 Jan, Easter, 1 May, 15 Aug, 25 Dec. 4€. 055 20 37 308; www. istitutodeglinnocenti.it.

Brunelleschi's **portico**★★ has terracotta **medallions**★★ by Andrea della Robbia. The Foundlings' Hospital houses a **gallery** of Florentine works.

Casa Buonarroti★, Cenacolo di S. Apollonia (*Last Supper*★ by Andrea del Castagno), Cenacolo di S. Salvia (fresco★★ by Andrea del Sarto of the Last Supper), Ognissanti (*Last Supper*★ in the church refectory), S. Spirito★ (works of art★), S. Trinità (Cappella dell'Annunciazione★ decorated with frescoes by Lorenzo Monaco and the frescoes in the Cappella Sassetti★★ by Ghirlandaio), Loggia del Mercato Nuovoa, Museo della Casa Fiorentina Antica★ (housed in the Palazzo Davanzati★), Museo Marino Marini, Museo di Storia della Scienza★.

Excursions

See the plan of the sutrounding area on Michelin map 430.

Villa di Castello★

5km/3mi north of Castello near the airport. For admission times and charges, call 055 29 48 83; www.polomuseale.firenze.it/musei/villacastello. This villa was restored in the 18C, it has a fine garden.

Villa La Petraia★

Near Villa di Castello, at the end of Via della Petraia. Open daily 8.15am-2hr before dusk. Closed 2nd and 3rd Mon of month, 1 Jan, 1 May, 25 Dec. 2€. 055 49 48 83; www.polomuseale. firenze.it/english/musei/petraia.

In 1576 Cardinal Ferdinand de' Medici commissioned Buontalenti to convert this castle into a villa. In the **garden**, there is a fine fountain by Tribolo.

Villa di Poggio a Caiano★★

17km/11mi north by the Pistoia road, S 66. Open 8.15am-1hr before dusk. Closed 2nd and 3rd Mon of the month, 1 Jan, 1 May, 25 Dec. 2€. 055 87 70 12; www.polomuseale.firenze. it/musei/poggiocaiano.

Sangallo designed this villa for Lorenzo the Magnificent. The drawing room has **frescoes** by Pontormo of Vertumnus and Pomona, gods of orchards.

Villa La Ferdinanda★★

26km/16mi west of Artimino.

This 16C villa has a double spiral stairway and a magnificent setting overlooking the Arno valley. It houses a **museum of Etruscan archaeology**. Open daily except Wed, 9.30am-12.30pm. Closed public holidays. 4€. 055 87 50 210; www.po-net.prato.it/artestoria/fuori/eng/ferdi.htm

Certosa del Galluzzo★★

6km/4mi south by the Siena road. Open daily except Mon 9am-noon and 3-6pm (5pm in winter). Donations welcome. 055 20 49 226; www.cistercensi.info/certosadifirenze.

The grandiose 14C Carthusian monastery has an adjoining palace containing frescoes by Pontormo.

GAETA

POPULATION 21 500
MICHELIN MAP 563 S 22 – LAZIO.

Gaeta is a fomer fortress, still partly walled. The last bastion of the Bourbons, it now hosts an American base. A handsome castle crowns the medieval quarter. South of Gaeta, Serapo Beach is a pleasant stretch of sugar-fine sand.

- **Information:** Via Canada 10. ☎0771 71 24 84; www.catturismo.it.
- ▶ **Orient Yourself:** Gaeta is in the south of Lazio, on the point of a promontory bounding a beautiful **bay**★. The coastal road affords magnificent views.
- **Don't Miss:** A tour along the coast of the Arcipelago Ponziano, pretty Sperlonga and its beaches and the Abbazia di Fossanova.
- 🕐 **Organizing Your Time:** Allow half a day to see Gaeta, and a day for excursions along the coast and inland.
- **Especially for Kids:** Grotta di Tiberio and the Museo Archeologico, and the sandy beach that stretches from the grotto to Sperlonga.
- 💧 **Also See:** Abbazia di MONTECASSINO, ANAGNI.

Walking About

Duomo
The cathedral is interesting for its 10C and 15C Romanesque Moorish campanile adorned with glazed earthenware and resembling the Sicilian or Amalfi belltowers. Inside, the late-13C **paschal candelabrum**★is remarkable for its 48 low reliefs depicting scenes from the Lives of Christ and St Erasmus, protector of sailors.
A picturesque medieval quarter lies near the cathedral.

Castello
The castle, dating from the 8C, has been altered many times. The lower castle was built by the Angevins, and the upper one by the Aragonese.

Monte Orlando
🕐 Open Jun-Sep 9am-8pm, Oct-May 9am-6pm. ≈1.03 €. For guided excursions apply to Parco Regionale Urbano Monte Orlando, Comune di Gaeta, Piazza XIX Maggio, ☎0771 45 00 93; www.parks. it/parco.monte.orlando.
A legend claims that this sea-cliff split when Jesus died. At the summit is the tomb of the Roman Consul Munatius Plancus, who founded the colonies of Lugdunum (Lyon) and Augusta Raurica (Augst near Basle).

Ponza★ and Arcipelago Ponziano★

This volcanic island, lying beyond the Gulf of Gaeta, has a verdant ridge and white or blue-grey cliffs, bordered by narrow beaches or dropping abruptly into the sea. At the southeast end of the island is the village of Ponza★★ with its serried ranks of gaily painted houses around a small harbour. The latter is busy with fishing boats, coasting vessels and the ferries that ply back and forth to the mainland. The island is popular with underwater fishermen.

For information on ferries to Ponza contact: Agenzia Regine, molo Musco, Ponza, ☎0771 80 565; Libera Navigazione Mazzella, via S. Maria, Ponza, ☎0771 80 99 65.

From the Golfo di Gaeta to Agro Pontino

75km/47mi from Gaeta to Sabaudia, with a stop inland to visit the Abbazia di Fossanova. Allow one day.

Grotta di Tiberio and Museo Archeologico★
Follow the SS 213 to Terracina. Before Sperlonga, a sign on the left leads to the grotto and museum (below the Gaeta-Terracina

road - left after the last tunnel) ♿ ⊕*Open daily, 8.30am-7.30pm.* ⊘*Closed 1 Jan and 25 Dec.* ⊜*2€.* ☎*0771 54 80 28.*
This cave (grotta) contains a large ornamental pool. Here the Emperor Tiberius narrowly escaped death, when part of the roof crumbled. In the superb museum, there are 4C-2C BC statues, busts and realistic theatrical masks. The excavation's most famous find was a colossal group depicting Ulysses punishing Cyclops Polyphemus.
Kids A pleasant sandy beach –dotted with bars – stretches between the grotto and Sperlonga. Should you stroll down, cut inland to purchase tickets at the museum: the grotto is fenced off.

Sperlonga ⌂
North of Gaeta and the Villa of Tiberius.
🛈*www.archeologia.beniculturali.it.*
The village stands on a rocky spur, pitted with caves, between the sea and the Aurunci mountains. Italian tourists cram its narrow white-washed alleys in summer, diminishing its charm. The free beach is south of the upper town.

Terracina ⌂
🛈*www.terracinaonline.it.*
At the foot of Monti Ausoni, this seaside town has been a popular retreat since Roman times, but is best known for the dramatic clifftop Temple of Jupiter.

Duomo★
The cathedral overlooks the attractive Piazza del Municipio, which still has the paving of the Roman forum. It was consecrated in 1075 and is fronted by a portico on ancient columns which support a 12C mosaic frieze. Inside, note the pulpit and *paschal candelabruma*, a lovely 13C work by the Cosmati.

Tempio di Giove Anxur
3km/2mi east of the historical centre.
⊕*Allow 45 minutes to climb from Piazza Municipio up the Via Anxur on foot.*
🛈*www.parks.it/z.tempio.giove.anxur/index.html.*
Although there are few remains other than the foundations, a vaulted gallery and an underground passage (cryptoporticus), it is worth visiting the site of

the Temple of Jupiter for the extensive panorama★★ of the town, the canals and port, Monte Circeo and the Pontine marshes, Fondi with its lakes, and the coast as far as Gaeta.

▷ *Continue to San Felice Circeo.*

Parco Nazionale del Circeo★
Behind the local museum, a road winds up to the summit and ancient temple. ⊕*The witch's grotto and views from Monte Circeo.* 🛈*Piazza Municipio has a tourist office,* ☎*0773 54 73 36; www.circeoprimo.it. The visitors' centre is at Via C. Alberto 107, Sabaudia,* ☎*0773 51 13 85; www.parcocirceo.it.*
Designated in 1934, this park covers a narrow coastal strip between Anzio and Terracina and includes part of the former Pontine marshes. Beauty spots include Monte Circeo, the refuge of the witch Circe who transformed Ulysses' companions into a herd of pigs and Lago di Sabaudia, a lake that can be reached by a bridge leading to the town of **Sabaudia** ⌂; the scenic route *(5km/3mi from the San Felice – Torre Cervia road)* is lined with luxury villas. The park is a UNESCO nature reserve.

Abbazia di Fossanova★★
⊕*Open Apr-Sept 9am-noon and 4-6pm. Rest of the year 9am-noon and 3-5.30pm.* ⌚*Guided tours by appointment.* ☎*0773 93 90 61.*
Standing, as the rule prescribes, in a lonely site, the Cistercian abbey of Fossanova is the oldest of the Order in Italy. Monks from Cîteaux in France settled here in 1133. In 1163 they began to build their abbey church, which was to serve as a model for many Italian churches. Although restored, Fossanova has kept its original architecture and plan, designed along the rules of austerity laid down by St Bernard.

Chiesa
The 13C church is in the Burgundian style; its exterior is built to a Latin cross plan, with flat east end, octagonal transept crossing tower, rose windows and a triple-bayed window at the east end in a typically Cistercian style.

Chiostro

The picturesque cloisters have three Romanesque sides and a fourth or south side in the late-13C pre-Gothic style. It was in the separate guest house that teacher and scholar St Thomas Aquinas died in 1274.

PROMONTORIO DEL **GARGANO**★★★
GARGANO PROMONTORY
MICHELIN MAP 564 B-C 28-30 – PUGLIA.

The Gargano Promontory is one of Italy's most attractive natural regions, with its wide horizons, mysterious forests and rugged coastline. This sun and sea paradise is marred by one drawback: most of the beaches and bays belong to camping sites and hotels, and are not easily accessible.

🛈 **Information:** Parco Nazionale del Gargano, Largo R.il Guiscardo 2, 71037 Monte Sant'Angelo, ☎0884 56 89 11, www.parcogargano.it.

▶ **Orient Yourself:** The Gargano Promontory projects like a spur from the "boot" of Italy. The nearest main road is A 14.

🚘 **Don't Miss:** Foresta Umbra, views from Monte Sant'Angelo.

🕐 **Organizing Your Time:** The promontory is a good place to stay for a few days holiday, but for a short visit allow a day.

👝 **Also See:** PUGLIA, Isole TREMITI.

A Bit of History

Geologically, Gargano is independent from the Apennine Mountains; it is a limestone plateau fissured with crevices. Originally an island, Gargano was connected to the mainland by accumulated deposits brought down by the rivers from the Apennines. Today the massif is riven by high-altitude valleys and heavily forested in the east. The plateaux supports sheep, goats and black pigs. The Tremiti Islands belong to the same geological formation.

Sights

Monte Sant'Angelo★

www.comune.monte-sant-angelo.fg.it
Monte Sant'Angelo stands in a wonderful **site**★★. The town is built on a spur (803m/2 634ft) dominated by its castle and overlooks both the Gargano Promontory and the sea. It was in a nearby cave between 490 and 493 that the Archangel Michael, chief of the Heavenly Host, appeared three times to the bishop of Siponto. After a further apparition in the 8C, an abbey was founded. During the Middle Ages Crusaders came to pray to the Archangel Michael, the saintly warrior, before embarking at Manfredonia. On 29 September the annual feast day includes the procession of the Archangel's Sword.

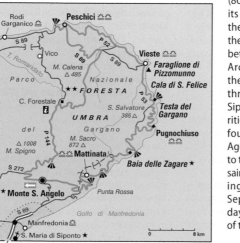

Address Book

WHERE TO STAY

⊜ **Hotel Peschici** – *Via San Martino 31 – 71010 Peschici – ☎0884 96 41 95 – Fax 0884 96 41 95 – Closed Nov-mid Mar –* 🅿 *– 40 rm – ⌂*. One of the main attractions of this pension is its location – it is situated right in the heart of the village and yet overlooks the sea. Rustic-style ambience enhanced by the vaulted ceiling. Rooms are simple but well maintained. Family-style guesthouse with a warm and friendly welcome.

⊜⊜ **Hotel Solemar** – *Località San Nicola – 71010 Peschici – 3km/2mi east of Peschici – ☎0884 96 41 86 – Fax 0884 96 41 88 – Closed 21 Sep-19 May –* 🅿🏊 *– 66 rm – Restaurant*. An ideal location for a relaxing seaside vacation, this lovely hotel overlooks the bay (private) and is surrounded by greenery. The rooms are light and airy and all of them have a sea view. Guests can make their way down to the sea along the pleasantly shaded paths.

⊜⊜ **Park Hotel Paglianza e Paradiso** – *Località Manacore – 71010 Peschici – 10.5km/6.5mi east of Peschici – ☎0884 91 11 18 – www.grupposaccia.it – Closed 15 Oct-Mar –* 🅿🏊 *– 133 rm ⌂ – Restaurant*. Situated a few minutes walk from the sea, deep in a dense forest of pine trees, this establishment is the ideal solution for anyone looking for a comfortable, relaxing hotel with sporting facilities.

⊜⊜⊜ **Hotel Svevo** – *Via Fratelli Bandiera 10 – 71019 Vieste – ☎0884 70 88 30 – Fax 0884 70 88 30 – www.hotel-svevo.com – Closed 16 Oct-29 May –* 🅿🏊 *– 30 rm ⌂*.

A charming hotel not far from the castle of the same name. Family run – the owners are very enthusiastic. Rooms are simple but well maintained. Wonderful terrace-solarium with swimming pool looking down over the sea and a fantastic panorama.

WHERE TO EAT

⊜ **Medioevo** – *Via Castello 21 – 71037 Monte Sant'Angelo – ☎0884 56 53 56 – www.ristorantemedioevo.it – Closed Mon (except Jul-Sep)*. Diners are given a warm welcome in this little trattoria which is tucked away up in the heart of the historic centre. Simple, modern-style dining room with a vaulted ceiling. Regional cuisine with some personal touches, dishes are lovingly prepared using the freshest ingredients – wonderful aromas.

⊜ **Taverna al Cantinone** – *Via Mafrolla 26 – 71019 Vieste – ☎0884 70 77 53 – Closed Fri (until May) and Nov-Easter –* 🗐. Simple, cheerful trattoria in the heart of the historic centre. Traditional home cooking. Recommended for its use of fresh, local produce and value for money.

⊜⊜ **La Collinetta** – *Località Madonna di Loreto – 71010 Peschici – 2km/1mi southeast of Peschici – ☎0884 96 41 51 – lacollinetta@yahoo.it – Closed lunchtime, Oct-15 Mar – Book*. Wonderful views over the coast from the terrace and excellent seafood dishes (prepared with super fresh ingredients) – a great combination. Friendly, enthusiastic staff. Overnight stays possible – pleasant rooms.

Santuario di San Michele★

🔲 *www.gargano.it/sanmichele*. The church dedicated to St Michael, designed in the transitional Romanesque-Gothic style, is flanked by a detached octagonal campanile dating from the late 13C. Opposite the entrance a stairway leads to the richly worked 11C **bronze door**★. It gives access to the nave with pointed vaulting, which opens onto the cave (to the right) in which St Michael is said to have appeared. The marble statue of the saint is by Andrea Sansovino (16C) and the 11C episcopal throne is decorated in characteristic Apulian style.

Tomba di Rotaria

Go down the stairs opposite the campanile. 🕐 *Open 8.30am-1pm and 2.30-7.30pm.* The tomb is to the left of the apse of the ruined church of San Pietro. Inside, the tower rises in stages through a square, an octagon and finally a triangle to the dome. The tomb was supposed to contain the remains of Rotharis, a 7C Lombard king, but is really a 12C baptistery.

Chiesa di Santa Maria Maggiore
Right of Tomba di Rotari. The church, built in the Apulian Romanesque style boasts a fine doorway. Inside there are traces of the Byzantine frescoes.

Foresta Umbra★★
www.parcogargano.it.
Forests are rare in Puglia and this vast expanse of beeches, elders, pines, oaks, chestnuts and ancient yews, covers over 11 000ha/27 000 acres. The forest is well equipped with recreational facilities. Shortly after the turning to Vieste there is a forestry lodge (Casa Forestale), which is now a **visitor centre**.

Peschici ⌂⌂
www.peschicionline.it.
Well situated on a spur jutting out into the sea, this fishing town is now a seaside resort.

Vieste ⌂⌂
&⏰*Open Jun-Sep 9.30am-1pm and 5pm-midnight; Oct-May, contact the museum for opening times. ⌦No charge.* ☏*0884 70 76 88.; www.comunedivieste.it.*
This town, dominated by its 13C cathedral, has an interesting shell museum, **Museo Malacologico**. To the south is a vast beach with a limestone sea-stack, **Faraglione di Pizzomunno**, standing offshore. Between Vieste and Mattinata there is a fine **scenic stretch**★★ of corniche road. After 8km/5mi the square tower in **Testa del Gargano** marks the massif's easternmost extremity; there's a fine **view**★ of the inlet, **Cala di San Felice**. Beyond the resort of **Pugnochiuso**⌂⌂ lies the pretty **Baia delle Zagare**★ (Bay of Zagare).

Mattinata ⌂⌂
www.comune.mattinata.fg.it
From the road to Mattinata there is a fine **view**★★of this market town, encircled by olive groves and mountains.

GENOVA★★
GENOA
POPULATION 605 000
MICHELIN MAP 561 I 8

The capital of Liguria, Italy's greatest seaport and the birthplace of Christopher Colombus, Genoa "la Superba" boasts a spectacular **location**★★. Sprawled across the slopes of a sort of mountainous amphitheatre, the port is overlooked by the colourful façades of a host of buildings. It is a city of surprises, where the most splendid palaces stand side by side with the humblest alleyways, known as carruggi, interspersed with picturesque squares. As a centre for the arts, the city has a vibrant cultural life, which earned it the title of European Capital of Culture (Capitale Europea della Cultura) in 2004.

- **Information:** Via Sottoripa 5. ☏010 55 74 372, Stazione Principe, ☏010 24 62 633; www.apt.genova.it ; www.genova-2004.it.
- **Orient Yourself:** The city is enclosed by a mountain range curving around 30km/18mi of coastline. The historic centre around the port is a maze of alleyways (carruggi), the modern part of the city is crossed by wide avenues.
- **Parking:** There's a pay lot in Piazza della Vittoria or at the Porto Antico.
- **Don't Miss:** The bustling port and aquarium, the Baroque palaces of the Musei di Strada Nuova, the "Holy Grail" in the Museo del Tesoro di San Lorenzo, Galleria di Palazzo Spinola and the Palazzo del Principe.
- **Organizing Your Time:** Allow 2-3 days to really explore all that the city has to offer.
- **Especially for Kids: The** Wonders of the deep at the Acquario, Città dei Bambini at Antichi Magazzini del Cotone.
- **Also See:** *Promontorio di PORTOFINO, RIVIERA LIGURE.*

A Bit of History

Genoese expansion was based on a fleet, which, by the 11C ruled supreme over the Tyrrhenian Sea, having vanquished the Saracens. By 1104 the fleet already comprised 70 ships, all built in the famous dockyards, making it a formidable power much coveted by foreign rulers such as the French kings, Philip the Fair and Philip of Valois.

The Crusaders offered the Genoese an opportunity of establishing trading posts on the shores of the Eastern Mediterranean and following the creation of the Republic of St George in 1100, seamen, merchants, bankers and moneylenders united their efforts to establish the maritime supremacy of Genoa.

Initially, Genoa allied itself with Pisa in the struggle against the Saracens (11C) and then became her enemy during a conflict over Corsica (13C). Finally it became the most persistent rival of that other great maritime republic, Venice (14C) for the trading rights of the Mediterranean. At this time, Genoa's colonies were as far afield as the Black Sea.

In the 14C the Genoese merchant seamen controlled the trade in precious cargoes from the Orient; in particular they had the monopoly in the trading of alum, used to to fix dye colours.

Limited partnership companies flourished. Founded in 1408, the famous Bank of St George, grouping the maritime state's lending houses, administered the finances of the trading posts. The merchants became ingenious moneylenders and instituted such modern methods as bills of credit, cheques and insurance to increase their profits.

Following continual struggles between rival Genoan families, the decision was taken in 1339 to elect a doge for life and then to seek, essentially in the 15C, foreign protection.

In 1528 the great admiral **Andrea Doria** (1466-1560) gave Genoa its aristocratic constitution, which confered on it the status of a mercantile republic. The enterprising and independent Andrea was one of Genoa's most famous sons: an admiral, a legislator and an intrepid and wise leader who distinguished himself against the Turks in 1519 and, while serving François I, by covering the French retreat after their defeat at Pavia (1525). In 1528, indignant at François I's unjust treatment of him, he entered the service of Charles V, who plied him with honours and favours. Following his death and the development of ports on the Atlantic coast, Genoa declined as a port and it was Louis XIV who destroyed the harbour in 1684. In 1768, by the Treaty of Versailles, Genoa surrendered Corsica to France. In 1848, under Giuseppe Mazzini, it became one of the cradles of the Risorgimento.

Fine Arts in Genoa – As in many countries, the decline of commercial prosperity in the 16C and 17C coincided with intense artistic activity, evidenced in the building of innumerable palaces and the arrival at Genoa of foreign artists, especially the Flemish. In 1607 Rubens published a work on the *Palazzi di Genova (Palaces of Genoa)* and from 1621 to 1627 Van Dyck painted the Genoese nobility. Puget lived at Genoa from 1661 to 1667, working for patrician families such as the Doria and the Spinola.

The art of the Genoese school, characterised by dramatic intensity and the use of muted colours, is represented by Luca Cambiaso (16C), Bernardo Strozzi (1581-1644), the fine engraver Castiglione, and especially **Alessandro Magnasco** (1667-1749) whose sharp and colourful brushwork marks him out as a precursor of modern art.

In the field of architecture, Galeazzo Alessi (1512-72), when at his best, was the equal of Sansovino and Palladio in the nobility and ingenuity of his designs when integrating isolated buildings in the existing urban landscape.

Features

Port★★★

Boat tour departures daily from Aquarium. Hours vary depending on number of passengers: Duration: 45min. May to Sep mini-cruises for San Fruttuoso, Portofino, Cinque Terre, Porto Venere, and nature excursions for cetacean sightings in collaboration with WWF. ⓞDepartures from 9am, and 10.30am from Savona. ☎010 26 57 12; www.battellierigenova.it,

Address Book

GETTING ABOUT

INFORMATION

☎010 55 81 14, www.amt.genova.it

TOURS

Circonvallazione a monte – For a "tour of the avenues" take bus no 33 (from Piazza Corvetto or the railway station) which takes in this panoramic route. The road is flanked by some fine 19C buildings.

A "passeggiata" by train – This is one of the locals' favourite Sunday outings. A trip into the country on a small, painted train (that runs on a narrow gauge line) up into the hills and little villages between Genoa and Casella. Frequent departures on a daily basis from the Genova-Casella station. For information contact ☎010 83 73 21; www.ferroviagenovacasella.it.

Giro Tour – Daily departure, leaving Piazza Caricamento (in front of the Acquario) at 3pm. A guided tour (multilingual) of the historic and cultural hotspots of the city (about 2hr). The ticket costs around €13. For information, contact: Macramè Viaggi ☎010 59 59 779.

Volabus Linea 100 – This bus links the airport with the city centre, departing every 30min. 3 €. For information contact: ☎010 55 82 41, www.amt. genova.it.

SIGHTSEEING

Card Musei – Includes entry to 20 museums in Genoa as well as discounts on certain attractions including the Acquario and exhibitions at the Palazzo Ducale. It costs 16 € for a 48hr pass – www.museigenova.it.

Libreria Ducale – In the Palazzo Ducale. ☎010 59 41 12 – www.palazzo-ducale.genova.it. A specialist bookshop with a wide range of art books. Also stocks books on and maps of Genoa.

WHERE TO EAT

🍽 **Antica Osteria della Foce** – *Via Ruspoli 72/74r – ☎010 55 33 155 – Closed Sun, lunchtime on Sat and public holidays, 24 Dec-2 Jan, Aug, Easter – Book.* A pleasant, friendly establishment, the atmosphere enhanced by the

two large wood-burning ovens and the old bar. Cooking is based on traditional Ligurian specialities but the focaccia and savoury tarts (torte salate) are also good. Very speedy service and reasonable prices.

🍽 **Cantine Squarciafico** – *Piazza Invrea 3r – 16123 Genova – ☎010 24 70 823 – www.squarciafico. it – Closed Aug – 🚭.* Located near the church of S. Lorenzo, this charming eatery is housed in the old cisterns of the 15C palazzo of the same name. Authentic Genovese cuisine.

🍽 **Sul Fronte del Porto – Bar & Restaurants** – *Calata Cattaneo, 3rd floor, Palazzo Millo – Porto Antico – ☎010 25 18 384 – www.sulfrontedel-porto.it – Closed Mon, Sat lunchtime, 15-30 Jan – 🍴.* An innovative and highly original establishment which provides three restaurants, a cocktail bar and a snack bar all in one premises. There is the "Irifune," an authentic Japanese sushi bar, the rather eccentric "Compagnia delle Aragoste" and lastly the "Portocarlo" brasserie, which is a typical French bistro complete with oyster sellers outside. Located near the Acquario with all its hustle and bustle.

🍽 **I Tre Merli** – *Edificio Millo – Calata Mandraccio – Porto Antico – ☎010 24 64 416 – www.itremerli.it – Closed Mon – 🍴 – Book.* An unusual wine bar which is housed in an old coffee warehouse in the Porto Antico near the Acquario. Elegant but curious interior decor which contrasts rough stone walls with coloured marble columns. Serves delicious fish dishes (the cuisine has a national rather than local feel to it) as well as the more traditional focacce and farinate.

🍽 **Pintori** – *Via San Bernardo 68/r – 16123 Genova – ☎010 27 57 507 – Closed Sun, Mon 24, Dec-7 Jan, 10-31 Aug – Book.* Even if it is difficult to find, located in a narrow "carruggio" in the old town, this trattoria is definitely worth hunting down. Meals are served at rustic-style tables in a lovely vaulted dining room. Authentic Ligurian cuisine with the odd Sardinian dish thrown in for good measure. Excellent wine cellar with more than 700 different wines. Very reasonably priced.

Antica Osteria del Bai – *Via Quarto 12, Quarto dei Mille – 16148 Ge-nova – ☎010 38 74 78 – www.osteri-adelbai.it – Closed Mon, 10-20 Jan, 1-20 Aug –*

🍽 ✕– *Book.* A restaurant with a history. It is housed in an old fort which overlooks the beach from where Garibaldi set off with his "Thousand" men. The elegant, cheerful interior has a maritime feel to it as does the cooking. Dishes are cooked with super fresh ingredients.

WHERE TO STAY

It is worth noting that during the trade fairs, and in particular the international boat show **(Salone Nautico Internazionale)** which lasts for 10 days in October, the hotels tend to raise their prices. Enquire about this when you make your booking.

Albergo Soana – *Via XX Settembre 23-8, (4th floor) – 16121 Genova – ☎010 56 28 14 – Fax 010 56 14 86 – www.hotelsoana.it – Closed 23-28 Dec – 19 rm – ☐.* A small hotel with simple, modern rooms housed in an early 20C palazzo. Located in front of the Ponte Monumentale. A good hotel if you want to stay in the centre of town.

Albergo Cairoli – *Via Cairoli 14/4 – 16124 Genova – ☎010 24 61 454 – Fax 010 24 67 512 – www.hotelcairoli-genova.com – 12 rm – ☐.* This small hotel is situated right in the heart of the city centre but has a cosy, homely ambience. The rooms are rather cramped but the terrace, with its mass of flowering plants, is attractive.

Hotel Galles – *Via Bersaglieri d'Italia 13 – 16126 Genova – ☎010 24 62 820 – Fax 010 24 62 822 – www.hotelgallesgenova.com – ☐ – 20 rm. ☐.* A comfortable hotel stra-tegically situated between the Porta Principe railway station and the Ponte dei Mille seaport. Large, airy reception area – the vases of flowers are a nice touch. The rooms are spacious and welcoming with modern furnishings. Competitive prices.

Hotel Bristol – *Via 20 Settembre 35 – 16121 Genova – ☎010 59 25 41 – Fax 010 56 17 56 – www.hotelbristolpalace.com – ☐ – 128 rm. ☐ –* Restaurant. A luxurious, if rather austere hotel housed in a late 19C palazzo. The splendid entrance hall with its wonderful staircase sets the scene. The public areas and the rooms are all elegantly furnished with antiques. Very attentive service.

TAKING A BREAK

Mangini – *Via Roma 91 r – Genova – ☎010 56 40 13 – Open daily, 7.30am-8.30pm.* Founded in 1876, this famous café-pasticceria, with its olde worlde charm, has long been popular with journalists and writers.

Romanengo – *Via Soziglia 74/76r – ☎010 24 74 574 – Open Tue-Sat 9am-1pm, 3.15-7.15pm – Closed Aug.* Founded in 1780, this is one of the most famous confectionery shops in Italy. A cornucopia of sweet delights including candied fruit, pralines, chocolates, caramels and other sweets.

Caffè degli Specchi – *Salita Pollaiuoli 43r – ☎010 24 68 193 – Open Mon-Sat 7am-8.30pm.* This rather elegant but cosy café with its Art Nouveau interior has a reputation for being popular with the locals. Situated near the Palazzo Ducale.

Caffè del Barbarossa – *Piano di S. Andrea, 21/23r – ☎010 24 5 097 – Open Mon 7.30am-2.30pm, Tue-Fri 7.30am-2.30am, Sat-Sun 4.30pm-2.30am.* A small, friendly café/bar on two levels. Very popular with the locals and always heaving with people, particularly in the early evening.

www.porto.genova.it, www.acquario.ge.it, www.whalewatchliguria.it. From the raised road *(Strada Soprael-evata)* which skirts the port, there are good views of Italy's principal port. To the east the **Porto Vecchio** (old port) includes a pleasure boat harbour, ship-yards, and quays for ferries leaving for the islands or Africa. It is dominated by the **Bigo**, a metallic structure resembling a crane, designed by **Renzo Piano** (b 1937), which has a lift affording an excellent bird's-eye **view**★.

Porticciolo di Sturla

Ph. Orain/MICHELIN

To the west of the historical centre, the entrance to the Porto Nuovo di Sampierdarena is marked by Genoa's lighthouse, La Lanterna, symbol of the city. *The Museo della Genovesità was under construction near the Lanterna at the time of going to press; for information on visits to the lighthouse, call ☎010 24 65 346.*

Acquario★★★

Kids & Open Jul and Aug, 9am-11pm; rest of the year 9.30am-7.30pm, Sat, Sun and public hols 9.30am-8.30pm (ticket office always closes 1hr 30min early). 14 €. Guided tours available and audioguides in various languages. ☎010 23 45 678; www.acquariodigenova.it.

The aquarium has a modern, instructive layout. Illuminated panels describe (in Italian and English) the species and explain the varied habitats.

The visit begins with a film that provides an introduction to the underwater world. Then, a computerised system offers an opportunity for a "hands-on" experience and various observation points give visitors the impression that they are in amid the fish and marine mammals. There are also reconstructions of the underwater environments of the Mediterranean, the Red Sea, Madagascar, a tropical forest and a coral reef. Of interest are the seals, reptiles with striking camouflage, dolphins, sharks, penguins, and the tank filled with species that can be touched.

Antichi Magazzini del Cotone

Built in the 19C, the former cotton warehouse was restored by Renzo Piano to mark the celebrations honouring Christopher Columbus. On the first floor is the **Città dei Bambini**★, a space devoted to children between the ages of 3 and 14. Through a series of interactive games, young visitors are encouraged to explore their senses, the natural world, basic technological and scientific principles and to develop their social skills and the concepts of respect, tolerance and diversity. *Kids Children only admitted if accompanied by one or two adults. Open Jul-Sep 11.30am-7.30pm; Oct-Jun 10am-6pm. Last entry 1hr 15min before closing time. Closed Mon. 7 €. ☎010 24 75 702; www.cittadeibambini.net.*

To the west of the Porto Antico, the Galata della Darsena district is home to the new Museo del Marea, which, together with the Commenda di Pré and the Museo Navale delle Riviere di Pegli, forms part of the city's maritime museums (Musei del Mare di Genova). Through interactive and multimedia displays the museum gives an overview of the maritime trading traditions of the city (*Calata De Mari 1, Darsena, Porto Antico; Open 10am-6.30pm (Nov-Feb 10am-5pm), Closed Mon (except Aug). 10 €. ☎010 23 45 655; www.galatamuseodelmare.it.*

Sailors' quarter★

At the centre of this district is the 13C **Palazzo San Giorgio,** which was the headquarters of the famous Bank of St George. The building was remodelled in the 16C. Behind the palace on **Piazza Banchi** (of the banks) is the Loggia dei Mercanti, which houses a fruit and vegetable market and a flea market.

Renaissance and Baroque Tour★★

Set off from Piazza Fontane Marose, which is overlooked by a number of splendid palaces. Allow 2hrs.
Note the frescoes on the façade of the Palazzo Interiano Pallavicini (1565).

Strada Nuova (Via Garibaldi)★★

Tours by reservation only, Mon-Fri, 9am-6pm. Closed Sat, Sun and public holidays. No charge. 010 24 76 351; www.stradanuova.it
In the middle of the 16C a number of patrician families decided to build their residences on a street away from the historic centre. Once known as Via Aurea, this street of palaces was built to designs by Alessi in the 16C and is one of the loveliest streets in Italy. Alessi was also responsible for the designs of many of the actual palaces among which are No 1 **Palazzo Cambiaso** (1565) and no 4 the **Palazzo Carrega-Cataldi** (1588-61) which has preserved a delightful entrance hall decorated with grotesques. This leads into a large reception room that used to open onto the garden, which was sacrificed to create more space for the building itself. In this new wing, on an upper floor, is a dazzling gilded **gallery**★ in the Rococo style.
At no 7, the ornate façade of **Palazzo Lomellino**★ (1565-67) hides a fine nymphaeum that opens onto a courtyard (*4.50 €. 010 59 57 060; www.palazzolomellino.org*).

▷ *Return to Piazza Fossatello and take Via Lomellini.*

No 11 Via Lomellini, flanked by beautiful palazzi, was the birthplace of Giuseppe Mazzini and now houses the Museo del Risorgimento (*open Tue-Fri 9am-7pm, Sat 10am-7pm. closed Sun and Mon. 4€. 010 24 65 843, www.istitutomazziniano.it*). The Palazzo Municipale (Town Hall), the former Palazzo Doria Tursi, at no 9, has a lovely arcaded courtyard. The collections include manuscripts by Christopher Columbus (normally not on view) and Paganini's violin (to view ask at the mayor's office on the first floor). *For information 010 55 72 274.*
Palazzo Bianco (no 11) and **Palazzo Rosso** (no 18) house a very fine **art gallery**★ and **picture gallery**★ (*see "Worth a Visit" below*).

▷ *Take Via Cairoli and Via della Zecca to get to Piazza del Carmine and the church of the Santissima Annunziata (17C).*

The sumptuous decoration inside this 17C church is a mixture of gilding, stucco and frescoes, and a good example of the Genoese Baroque style.

Via Balbi

This street is lined with palaces. The **Palazzo Reale** (Royal Palace), formerly the Balbi Durazzo, at no 10, dates from 1650 and the principal floor has period furnishings of the 18C and 19C. There are frescoes on the ceiling by Domenico Parodi (1668-1740) who also designed the stunning **Mirrored Gallery**★ styled on the Gallery in the Doria Pamphili palace in Rome and the more famous one at Versailles. Beyond the sumptuous throne room, in the audience room is the Portrait of *Caterina Balbi Durazzo* by Van Dyck. The imposing 17C University building, **Palazzo dell'Universita**★, at no 5 has a court and a majestic staircase. The 17C Palazzo Durazzo Pallavicini is at no 1.

Palazzo Reale (Balbi-Durazzo)★★

Open Tue-Wed, 9am-1.30pm; Sun-Thu 9am-7pm. Closed Mon and holidays. 4€; €6.50 including Palazzo Spinola.

☎010 27 10 272; www.palazzorealegenova.it
From Via Balbi head back to Via Lomellini in the direction of the church of **San Siro,** its **interior**★ decorated with 17C frescoes by GB Carlone. The high altar, in marble and bronze, is the work of P Puget (1670).

Beyond Palazzo Spinola (&for a description, see under "Worth a Visit"), is the church of **Santa Maria Maddalena**, the **interior**★ of which is one of the most characteristic examples of the local Baroque style.

Proceed along Vico Casana as far as the Piazza de Ferrari with its prestigious **Teatro Carlo Felice** and various other buildings, including the Accademia Ligustica di Belle Arti. Piazza G. Matteotti is dominated by the monumental façade of the **Palazzo Ducale** (1778). Of note inside is the lovely **chapel**★ with frescoes by GB Carlone that illustrate scenes from the history of the city.

The **church of Gesù**, erected by Tibaldi in 1597, houses in its sumptuous interior the Assumption by Guido Reni and two paintings by Rubens: *The Circumcision and The Healing by St Ignatius.*

Old Town★★ *allow 2hr*

Heading east out of Porto Antico you wind your way up charming, narrow alleyways.

▶ *The stroll described below is a continuation of the one above. Skirt along the left side of the Palazzo Ducale as far as Piazza S. Matteo.*

Piazza S. Matteo★

In the city centre, this small but harmonious square is lined with 13C-15C palaces that belonged to the Doria family. No 17 is a Renaissance building presented to Andrea Doria by a grateful republic. The **church of San Matteo** has a Genoese-style façade with courses of black and white stone. The tomb of Andrea Doria is in the crypt.

Cattedrale di San Lorenzo★★

The cathedral, originally built in the 12C, with additions made through to the 16C,

has a splendid Gothic **façade**★★, typical of the Genoese style. French influence appears in the placing of the 13C doorways and the large rose window. The carving on the central doorway represents a Tree of Jesse and scenes from the Life of Christ *(on the piers)* and the Martyrdom of St Lawrence and Christ between the Symbols of the Evangelists *(on the tympanum)*. The early-13C knifegrinder, at the right corner of the façade, resembles the angel of the sundial at Chartres. The transept crossing is crowned with a dome designed by Alessi.

The severe and majestic **interior**★ has marble columns in the nave and a false gallery above The **Chapel of St John the Baptist**★ *(at the end of the north aisle)* once held the remains of St John.

Museo del Tesoro di San Lorenzo★

🕐Open daily 9am-noon and 3-6pm; 1st Sun of month 3-6pm only. 🖼The alleged Holy Grail. ☞5.50 €. ☎010 24 71 831; www.museosanlorenzo.it.
Access from the left aisle. The treasury museum includes the famous 9C Sacro Catino, a hexagonal cup in emerald green blown glass, which, according to legend, is said to be the Holy Grail. It also houses the reliquary for St John the Baptist (14C) in the International Gothic style, and a precious chalcedony plate (whose colour changes according to the light) of the 1C AD with the head of St John the Baptist in the center (added in the 15C).

Museo Diocesano★

Via Tommaso Reggio 20 r. ♿🕐Open 3-7pm, Tue and Sat 10am-1pm also. 🕐Closed Mon. ☞5.50 €. ☎010 25 41 250; www.diocesi.genova.it/museodiocesano.
This museum is housed in the beautiful **cloisters**★ of the Cathedral Canons' residence (12C). It displays archaeological finds from the Domus Romana (1C BC) and a collection of sculptures and paintings, many of which are the work of artists from Genoa.

▶ *Head along Via di Scurreria and turn right into Vico S. Matteo.*

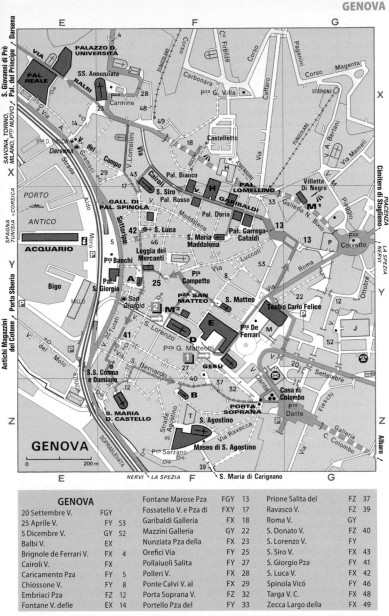

GENOVA

Chiesa di Santa Maria di Castello★

🕐 *Open daily, 9am-noon and 3.30-6pm. For reservations and information* ☎ *010 25 49 511.*

Three cloisters surround this Roman-esque church, the nave of which is flanked by chapels added in the 15C and 17C. In the Grimaldi chapel, note the Polyptych of the *Annunciation* by Maz-zone (1469). The second cloister (15C), the loggia of which overlooks the port, houses the fresco of the Annunciation by Giusto di Ravensburg.

Chiesa di San Donato★

Built in the 12C and 13C, this church has its original doorway and a delightful Romanesque octagonal **campanile**★. The Romanesque interior is also alluring: note the Madonna and Child (1401) in the south apse and the sumptuous **Adoration of the Magi**★★ polyptych by Joos Van Cleve.

Via S. Donato leads into Piazza delle Erbe where the youth of Genoa gather in the evening. The Salita del Priore leads to **Porta Soprana**, one of the oldest entrances to the city (12C), characterised by twin towers. Just beyond Porta Soprana are the ruins of the so-called **Casa di Colombo**, with the elegant cloister of the church of Sant'Andrea (12C) adjacent to it.

Worth a Visit

Musei di Strada Nuova★★

Ticket office on Via Garibaldi 9. &.◯*Open Tue-Fri 9am-7pm, Sat-Sun and public holidays 10am-7pm.* ◯*Closed Mon, 1 Jan, 1 May, 25 Dec.* ⊗*7 €.* ☎*010 24 76 351; www. museigenova.it.*

This group of museums includes three of the palazzi on Via Garibaldi: Palazzo Rosso, Bianco and Tursi.

Palazzo Rosso

Via Garibaldi 18. www.museopalazzorosso.it.

On display are works by Palma il Vecchio, Guido Reni, Guercino (The Eternal Father with an Angel), 1620, Mattia Preti and paintings of the Genoese school such as Guidobono. On the second floor (note the frescoed ceilings by the Genoese painters De Ferrari, Piola and Viviano) are some remarkable **portraits**★ by Van Dyck. In addition there are collections of wooden sculpture of the Baroque era.

Palazzo Bianco★

▶ *Via Garibaldi 11.* 🔲*www.museigenova. it, www.museopalazzobianco.it.*

The exquisite Altarpiece with Scenes from the Lives of Saints Lawrence, Sixtus and Hippolitus (13C), a gift from the Byzantine Emperor to the Genoese Republic to commemorate a treaty made in 1261, opens the collection. Numerous Flemish and Dutch paintings from the 15C to the 17C bear witness to the close commercial ties that linked Genoa to the Low Countries. Among these are the intense **Christ Blessing**★ by Hans Memling, works by Jan Matsys, Van Dyck *(Christ of the Coin)* and Rubens *(Venus and Mars)*. Genoa also welcomed Italian artists such as Veronese *(Crucifixion)* and Palma il Giovane *(Christ and the Samaritan Woman)*. Finally, there are works by Spanish (Murillo, 17C) and Genoese painters, among whom are Bernardo Strozzi (1581-1644), Domenico Piola (1627-1703) with *Charity* and Gregorio de Ferrari (1647-1726).

Palazzo Tursi

www.museigenova.it

This palazzo houses an extension of the Palazzo Bianco gallery, with works by Genoese artists such as Magnasco (1720). The Sala Paganini is home to the famous "Cannone", the violin donated by Paganini to his native city. The main floor of the palazzo exhibits a collection of tapestries, furniture and ceramics, as well as coins and weights from the Genoese Republic.

Galleria Nazionale di Palazzo Spinola★

Piazza Pellicceria 1. &.◯*Open Tue-Sat, 8.30am-7.30pm, Sun and public holidays 1.30-7.30pm.* ◯*Closed Mon, 1 Jan, 1 May, 25 Dec.* ⊗*4 €. 6.50 € includes Palazzo Reale.* ☎*010 25 30 454; www.palazzospinola.it.*

This palace, built at the end of the 16C by the Grimaldi family and then acquired by the Spinola family, has preserved its original interior decoration. The paintings and period furniture make for an atmospheric setting. The two principal floors are fine examples of 17C (first floor) and 18C (second floor) interior styles. It is thus possible to identify the evolution of fashions not just in furnishings but also in fresco painting of **ceilings**★. Tavarone's ceiling (17C) is richly Baroque, while those by L Ferrari and S Galeotti (18C) are more light and airy. The kitchen between the first and second floors can also be viewed. The **art collection**★ comprises works by painters of the Italian and Flemish Renaissance among which an enchanting **Portrait of Ansaldo Pallavicino** by Van Dyck, a Portrait of a Nun by the Genoese painter Strozzi, *Sacred and Profane Love* by Guido Reni and, on the third floor, a moving **Ecce Homo**★ by Antonello da Messina.

Palazzo del Principe★

Piazza Principe 4 (not on the map). Take either Via Balbi or Via Gramsci. ♿ ⏰ *Open Tue-Sun, 10am-5pm (last admission 4pm).* ⏰ *Closed Mon, 1 Jan, Easter, 1 May, 25 Dec and Aug.* ✎ *7€.* ☎*010 25 55 09; www.palazzodelprincipe.it* This is the 16C residence of Andrea Doria who was granted the title of prince in 1531. **Perin del Vaga** (1501-47), a pupil of Raphael in Rome, was responsible for the **frescoes**★ in the entrance hall, the Loggia degli Eroi and the symmetrical apartments of the prince and his wife, accessible from the loggia. The fresco in the Salone della Caduta dei Giganti (which takes its name from the subject) is particularly well preserved and contains a **Portrait of Andrea Doria**★ by **Sebastiano del Piombo** (1526) and another portrait of Doria at 92.

Villetta Di Negro-Museo Chiossone★

Piazzale Mazzini 4 n. ⏰ *Open Tue-Fri 9am-1pm, Sat-Sun and public holidays 10am-7pm.* ⏰*Closed Mon, 1 Jan, 25 Dec.* ✎*4€.* ☎*010 54 22 85; www.museochiossonegenova.it.*
On higher ground to the northwest of Piazza Corvetto, this is a sort of belvedere-labyrinth with palm trees, cascades and artificial grottoes. From the terrace there is a lovely **view**★ over the town and the sea. Standing on the summit is the Museo Chiossone di Arti Orientalia, which houses the collection of the Genoese engraver Chiossone, who was passionate about Oriental art after living in Japan for 23 years. The collection includes sculptures, buddhas, objets d'art, armoury and a remarkable assortment of prints, ivories and lacquerwork.

Museo di Sant' Agostino

Piazza Sarzano 35 r. ♿ ⏰ *Open Tue-Sat, 9am-7pm, Sun 10am-7pm.* ⏰*Closed Mon and public holidays.* ✎*4€.* ☎*010 25 11 263; www.museosatagostino.it.*
This convent building complex, with its adjacent 13C church (today an auditorium), houses a collection of fragments and sculptures salvaged from destroyed churches and private houses. Of particular interest are the 13C tombstone of Simonetta Percivalle Lercari, which has the appearance of a stone illuminated manuscript, the Monument to Margaret of Brabant by Giovanni Pisano (14C) and, on the second floor, sculptures by Pierre Puget (Rape of Helen) and Antonio Canova (Penitent Magdalen).

Chiesa di Santo Stefano

From its elevation on the Via XX Settembre, the church overlooks the town's arterial road, flanked by elegant, Art Nouveau-style buildings. The Romanesque church has a fine Lombardy-style apse. Inside note the splendid painting by Giulio Romano, the Martyrdom of St Stephena (c 1524).

Chiesa di Santa Maria di Carignano

▶ *Take Via Ravasco.* This vast church was built in the 16C to plans by Alessi. Inside, there is a fine statue of **St Sebastian**★ by Puget.

Excursions

Cimitero di Staglieno★

▶*1.5km/1mi north. From Piazza Corvetto take Via Assarotti (off the map) and then turn left into Via Montaldo.* In this curious cemetery there are ornate tombs and simple clay tumuli.

Albaroe

This is the location of the lido, which has been built around avenues shaded with trees and is flanked by elegant buildings. Albara has been a holiday resort since the end of the 14C and it retains some fine 16C villas, including the **villa Cambiaso Giustiniania,** designed by Alessi. **Corso Itali**, where the locals head for their early evening "passeggiata", is flanked by art nouveau-style villas.

The little **porto di Boccadasse**★, over-looked by the multicoloured fishermen's houses, has retained its charm. From the top of Santa Chiara is a wonderful **view**★★ over the Riviera as far as Portofino. The little streets, which are shaded by tree canopies, lead to the **porticciolo di Sturla**.

Pegli

15km/9mi west of Genova. Parco Durazzo Pallavicina – Via Pallavicini 13 (next to the railway station). ♿◷*Open daily except Mon, Apr-Sep 9am-6pm (last admission 6pm); Oct-Mar 9am-5pm (last admission 4pm).* ◷*Closed 1 Jan, 25 Dec, 31 Dec.* ☜*3.62 €.* ☎*010 69 82 776.*

This is the most beautiful **park**★ in Genoa. It was designed around the middle of the 19C by Michele Canzio, the set designer at the Carlo Felice theatre. He arranged the garden in a series of theatrical scenes marked by little buildings, lakes, grottoes and waterfalls.

GUBBIO★★

POPULATION 32 563
MICHELIN MAP 563 L 19 – UMBRIA.

The small town of Gubbio, spread out over the steep slopes of Monte Ingino, has preserved almost intact its rich cultural and artistic heritage. Encircling ramparts, buildings of warm yellow stone roofed with Roman tiles, and towers and palaces outlined against a burnt, austere landscape make it one of the Italian towns where the harsh atmosphere of the Middle Ages is most easily imagined.

- **Information:** Via della Repubblica 15, ☎075 92 20 693; www.comune.gubbio.pg.it, www.comune.perugia.it
- **Orient Yourself:** Gubbio lies off S 298, 40km/24mi from Perugia.
- **Don't Miss:** The Old Town and pretty Fabriano.
- **Organizing Your Time:** Allow half a day to day, with excursions.
- **Especially for Kids:** Papermaking at the Museo della Carta e della Filigrana and stalagtites and stalagmites at Grotte di Frasassi.
- **Also See:** *ASSISI, PERUGIA.*

Old Town★★

Piazza Grande stands at the heart of this charming but austere area of the old town with its steep, narrow streets, spanned by arches. The houses, flanked by palaces and towers, are often used as ceramic artists' workshops. The façades, sometimes have two doors; the narrower one known as the Door of Death through which coffins were brought out. The most picturesque streets are Via Piccardi, Baldassini, dei Consoli, 20 Settembre, Galeotti and those along the river, leading to Piazza 40 Martiri.

Palazzo dei Consoli★★

◷*Open daily, Apr-Oct, 10am-1pm and 3-6pm, Nov-Mar 10am-1pm and 2-5pm.* ◷*Closed 1 Jan, 14-15 May, 25 Dec.* ☜*5 €.* ☎*075 92 74 298; www.comune.gubbio.pg.it*

Overlooking Piazza Grande, this imposing Gothic building, supported by great arches rising above Via Baldassini, has a majestic façade which reflects the palace's internal plan. The stairway leads up to the vast hall (Salone) where assemblies were held and which contains statues and stonework.

Next is a museum, Museo Civico, where the **Tavole eugubine** have pride of place. The bronze tablets (2C-1C BC) are inscribed in Umbria's ancient language. The tablets are unique in linguistic and epigraphic terms – they record the region's political organisation and religious practices in Antiquity.

G. Bludzin/MICHELIN

The splendid Palazzo dei Consoli

Palazzo Ducale★

♿🕐*Open daily except Mon, 8.30am-7.30pm.* 🕐*Closed 1 Jan, 25 Dec.* 🎫*2 €.* ☎*075 92 75 872.*

The Ducal Palace, which dominates the town, was built from 1470 onwards for Federico de Montefeltro. The design is attributed to Laurana, although it was probably finished by Francesco di Giorgio Martini, who was inspired by the ducal palace at Urbino. The elegant courtyard is delicately decorated. The rooms are adorned with frescoes and lovely chimney pieces.

Churches

Duomo – The cathedral's plain façade has low reliefs showing the Symbols of the Evangelists. Off the single nave, the **Episcopal Chapel** to the right, is the room where the bishop would follow the services.

Chiesa di San Francesco – The walls of the north apse are covered with early-15C **frescoes**★by Ottaviano Nelli.

Chiesa di Santa Maria Nuova – houses a fine **fresco**★by Ottaviano Nelli.

Teatro romano

This Roman theatre dates from the reign of Augustus.

Excursions

Fabriano

38km/24mi east.

Famous since the 13C for paper manufacture, Fabriano is a tranquil town, and the birthplace of two artists; Allegretto

---

Address Book

WHERE TO EAT

🍽🍽 **Fabiani** – *Piazza 40 Martiri 26A/B – Gubbio* – ☎*075 92 74 639* – 🕐*Closed Tue, Jan.* An elegant restaurant that has retained the style and ambience of the 15C palazzo in which it is housed. Umbrian specialities on the menu. Meals served outside in the courtyard in the summer. Car park nearby.

EVENTS AND FESTIVALS

Gubbio has its traditional festivals; the most spectacular is the Candle Race. Three "candles", or *ceri*, strange wooden poles 4m/13ft tall, each topped with the statue of a saint (including St Ubald, patron saint of the town), are carried through the crowded streets in a frenzied race covering a distance of 5km/3mi, from the historical town centre to the basilica of Sant'Ubaldo situated at an altitude of 820m/2 665ft. During the race the "candle"-carriers, dressed in medieval costumes, demonstrate their skill by attempting not to drop their "candles" and carrying St Ubald into the church first, before the doors are slammed shut after the other two statues have arrived. These three strange *ceri*, whose origins date back to the pre-Christian era, grace Umbria's coat of arms.

GUBBIO

Baldassini V.	2	Grande Pza	17
Barbi V.	3	Nelli V.	18
Bruno Pza		Parruccini	
Giordano	4	Viale U.	19
Camignano		Piccardi V.	20
V. del		Popolo V. del	
Consoli V. dei	7	Repubblica	
Dante V.	8	V. della	21
Fabiani V.	9	S. Lucia Borgo	23
Falcucci V.	12	Tifernate V.	27
Galeotti V.	13	Vantaggi V. H.	28
Palazzo dei Consoli			B

Nuzi (1320-73), the main exponent of the Fabriano School, and **Gentile da Fabriano** (c 1370-1427), one of the principal exponents of the International Gothic style.

Piazza del Comune★

Characterised by its odd trapezoidal shape, the square is overlooked by the grim 13C Governor's Residence (Palazzo del Podestà), the Bishop's Palace (Palazzo Vescovile) and by the town hall (Palazzo Comunale) with its adjacent Loggia of St Francis. At the centre, is the Sturinalto, a fine Gothic fountain.

Piazza del Duomo

This peaceful square is overlooked by the Cathedral, decorated with frescoes by Allegretto Nuzi inside.

Museo della Carta e della Filigrana★★

Largo Fratelli Spacca. Kids *Learn to make paper and experiment with origami.*

Open 10am-6pm, Sun and public holidays 10am-noon and 4-7pm (2-5pm in winter). Closed Mon, 1 Jan, Easter, 1 May, 1 Nov, 25 Dec. 5.30 €. 0732 70 92 97; www.museodellacarta.com

Housed in the ex-Convent of St Damian (15C) this lively museum illustrates the manufacture of paper through the reconstruction of an operative medieval workshop. The museum also has displays of antique Fabriano paper and international watermarked paper.

Grotte di Frasassi★★

55km/34mi northeast. Kids *Open 9.30am-12.30pm and 3-6pm, but call to confirm. Closed 1 Jan, 10-30 Jan, Dec. 12 €. For information on opening times, call 0732 90 080; www.frasassi.com.*

A tributary of the River Sentino has formed a vast network of caves (grotte). The largest, the Grotta del Vento, is full of stalagmites and stalactites.

ISOLA D'**ISCHIA**★★★
POPULATION 17 883
MICHELIN MAP 564 E 23 – CAMPANIA.

Ischia, known as the Emerald Island because of its luxuriant vegetation, is the largest island in the Bay of Naples and one of its major attractions. A clear, sparkling light plays over a varied landscape: a coast covered with pinewoods, indented with bays and creeks sheltering villages with their colourful cubic houses; the slopes covered with olive trees and vineyards (producing the white or red Epomeo wine); and an occasional crumbling tower. The cottages, sometimes roofed with a dome and with an outside staircase, often have vine-swathed walls.

- **Information:** Via Lasolino 1. ☎081 333 32 20/22. www.comuneischia.it.
- **Orient Yourself:** Capri's lesser-known neighbour takes up 47-square kilometres of the Bay of Naples.
- **Parking:** Only pedestrians, mules and mopeds are allowed inside the village of Sant'Angelo. Park and walk in, or catch a three-wheeled minicab.
- **Don't Miss:** A walk around the Castello Aragonese, and a step back in time in the secluded fishing village of Sant'Angelo.
- **Organizing Your Time:** A tour of the island, which is fairly small, can be done in a matter of hours.
- **Also See:** *Isola di CAPRI, COSTERIA AMALFITANA, NAPOLI, Golfo di NAPOI.*

A Bit of History

The island rose out of the sea during the Tertiary Era at the time of a volcanic eruption. The soil is volcanic and there are many hot springs with various medicinal properties.

Celebrities from Michelangelo to Elizabeth Taylor have sought refuge here. Norwegian playwright Henrik Ibsen once pottered about in Casamicciola, the town where Guiseppe Garibaldi recovered from his war wounds. Gods and mythological heroes rested

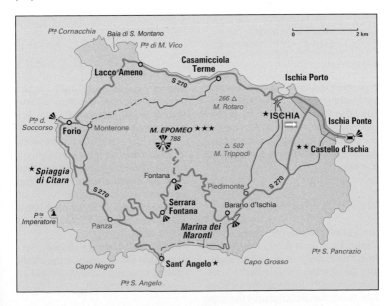

Address Book

For coin ranges, see the Legend on the cover flap.

WHERE TO STAY

Hotel Providence Terme – *Via Giovanni Mazzella 1 – 80075 Citara – ☎081 99 74 77 – www.providence.it – Closed Nov-Mar – ⊠📄 (payment) ⬜ – 69 rm – ⬜ – Restaurant.* This hotel boasts a splendid setting, near the famous "Poseidon" gardens and the beach at Citara, as well as some excellent spa facilities. Modern-style rooms and a pleasant terrace area with a swimming pool. Everything you need for a relaxing, restorative holiday.

Villa Angelica – *Via 4 Novembre 28 – 80076 Lacco Ameno – ☎081 99 45 24 – www.villaangelica.it – Closed Nov-15 Mar – ⬜ – 20 rm ⬜ – Restaurant.* A charming hotel with enthusiastic, friendly staff. At the centre of the light and airy public areas is a lovely, little garden. The rooms are spacious and modern in style. The spa facilities including a swimming pool (half indoors/half outdoors). Half- and full-board rates on request. One of our favourites.

Hotel San Giorgio Terme – *Spiaggia dei Maronti – 80070 Barano d'Ischia – Southeast of Serrara Fontana – ☎081 99 00 98 – www.hotelsangiorgio. com – Closed 29 Oct- 6 Apr – 📄⬜ – 81 rm ⬜.* From the large terrace – where drinks are served – or the swimming pool (thermal water) guests can enjoy fine views over one of the most beautiful beaches on the island. The public areas are light and spacious, the rooms are all very individual in style. An ideal base for a relaxing holiday.

WHERE TO EAT

Da "Peppina" di Renato – *Via Montecorvo 42 – 80075 Forio – ☎081 99 83 12 – Closed lunchtime, Tue (except Jun-Sep), Nov-Feb – Book.* The climb up the narrow, winding path is worth it for the great view over the sea and the coastline. If you're looking for good home cooking, packed with flavour, this is the place to come. Meals are served under the shady pergola with unusual wrought-iron benches that have been constructed from the headboards of antique beds.

Il Melograno – *Via Giovanni Mazzella 110 – 80075 Citara – 2.5km/ 1mi south of Forio – ☎081 99 84 50 – Closed Mon (Oct) 7 Jan-15 Mar – Book –10% service charge.* This restaurant specialises in fish dishes which are cooked with great skill and attention to detail. The menu varies on a daily basis depending on the availability of the "raw materials". Meals are served in two very cheerful dining rooms complete with a splendid fireplace, or, weather permitting, in the garden under the shade of the olive trees.

---

on Ischia too. Ulysses visited the king on Castiglione hill, while Aphrodite soaked in the thermal waters. Aeneas beached his boat in Lacco Ameno and the archangel Michael gave the picturesque fishing village of Sant'Angelo its name.

Getting There

Ischia and Procida can be reached from Naples, Capri and Pozzuoli. For Ischia: from Naples there are daily ferry crossings (1hr 25min); from Capri there are daily hovercraft crossings (40min) from April to October; from Pozzuoli there are daily ferry crossings (1hr); from Procida there are daily ferry crossings (30min) and hovercraft crossings (15min). For Procida: from Naples there are daily ferry crossings (1hr) and hovercraft crossings (35min); from Ischia there are daily ferry crossings (25min); from Pozzuoli there are daily ferry crossings (30min) and hovercraft crossings (15min).

Caremar (Naples and Pozzuoli to Ischia and Casamicciola), ☎892 123 or 081 01 71 998; www.caremar.it.

Alilauro Volaviamare (Naples, Sorrento, Capri and locations on the Amalfi Coast to Ischia and Forio), ☎081 497 22 22; www.volaviamare.it.

Medmar (Naples and Pozzuoli to Ischia and Casamicciola), 081 55 13 352; www.medmargroup.it.
SNAV (Naples and Procida for Casamicciola), ☎081 42 85 555; www.snav.it.

Sights

▷ *40km/25mi: follow the itinerary on the map.* The narrow road offers numerous viewpoints of the coast.

Ischia★

The capital is divided into two settlements, **Ischia Porto** and **Ischia Ponte**. The Corso Vittoria Colonna, an avenue lined with cafés and smart shops, links the port, in a former crater, and Ischia Ponte. The latter owes its name to the dike built by the Aragonese to link the coast with the rocky islet on the summit of which stands the **Castello Aragonese★★**, a beautiful group of buildings comprising a castle and several churches. ○*Open daily 9.30am-dusk.* ○*Closed 7 Jan-Feb.* ◉8€. ☎081 99 19 59; www.castelloaragonese.it
There is an enchanting **view★★** from the terrace of the bar of the same name. On the outskirts are a large pinewood and a fine sandy beach.

Monte Epomeo★★★

Access is by a path which branches off in a bend of the road once level with the public gardens. ○*1hr 30min on foot there and back.* The dramatic landscape was the cinematic backdrop for *The Talented Mr Ripley.* Cliffs swoop down to sandy beaches, with Mount Epomeo towering 788m/ 2 585ft above. Its name means *to see from a height panoramically* – visitors can do just that after a steep hike. Footsore tourists may prefer to rent a mule in Fontana. From the summit of this tufa peak there is a vast panorama of the entire island and the Bay of Naples.

Serrara Fontana

Not far from this settlement a belvedere offers a plunging **view★★** of the site of Sant'Angelo with its beach and peninsula.

Sant'Angelo★

This peaceful fishing village clusters around a small harbour. Artists, such as painter Wernes Gilles, flocked there in the 1950s, declaring it "the most beautiful place in the world".
A narrow isthmus stretches to one of the Tyrrhenian Sea's most distinctive landmarks. The *Roja* – otherwise known as the *Isolotto Di Sant'Angelo* – is a volcanic cone, capped with the remains of a tower and Benedictine monastery (both destroyed when Nelson's English fleet shelled the area in 1809).
Visitors can clamber onto the islet's eroded lower slopes or catch a water taxi on the isthmus. The Maronti Beach *fumarole* (steam plume) and the ancient Roman baths at Cava Scura are popular destinations *(access by footpaths).*
P*Only pedestrians, mules and mopeds are allowed inside the village. Park and stroll – or catch an "ape," a three-wheeled minicab.*

Spiaggia di Citara★

This fine beach is sheltered by the majestic headland, Punta Imperatore. Another thermal establishment, Giardini di Poseidone, is laid out with numerous warm-water swimming pools amid flowers and statues.

Forio and La Mortella

Via F. Calise 39, Forio. ○*Open April-Oct Tues, Thurs, Sat and Sun 9am–7pm.* ○*Closed Mon, Wed, Fri and Nov–March.*

Procida: Mediterranean colours and light

B. Morandi/MICHELIN

🎵10€, weekend concert tickets 15€.
☎081 98 62 20; www.lamortella.it.
Landscaper Russell Page transformed a rough valley, dismissed as a quarry, into a tropical paradise. Built by the British composer William Walton, La Mortella (meaning myrtle) includes a small museum housing photographs, many snapped by scene-setter Cecil Beaton.

Lacco Ameno and Museo Archeologico di Pithecusae

Corso Angelo Rizzoli, Lacco Ameno.
🕐*9.30am–1pm & 3–7pm winter; 9.30am–1pm & 4–8pm summer,* ☎*081 90 03 56; www.pithecusae.it*
In 770 BC, Greeks established their first colony in the West here, called Pithecusa. Scholars once thought the name was connected to *pithêkos* (monkey), but now believe it derives from *pithos* (pitcher).
The **Pithecusae Archaeological Museum** in Lacco Ameno houses artefacts, including the Cup of Nestor. The vessel, created in Rhodes, is inscribed with a quotation from the Iliad: "I am

the delicious cup… of Nestor. Whoever drinks from this cup, straightaway that man the desire of beautiful-crowned Aphrodite will seize."
It is now a holiday resort. The church of Santa Restituta (Piazza Santa Restituta) was built on the remains of an early-Christian basilica and a necropolis. There is a small archaeological museum. The tour of the island ends with the important thermal spa of **Casamicciola Terme.**

Excursion

Procida★

▶ *Procida is a 15/30min boat ride from Ischia; see Address Book for further information.*
Procida was formed by craters levelled by erosion and remains the wildest island in the Bay of Naples. The fishermen, gardeners and winegrowers live in a setting of colourful houses with domes, arcades and terraces.

REGIONE DEI **LAGHI**★★★
LAKE DISTRICT
MICHELIN MAP 561 AND 562 D-F 7-14
PIEDMONT – LOMBARDY – TRENTINO-ALTO ADIGE – VENETO.

Narrow and long, these lakes are all of glacial origin and their banks are covered with luxuriant vegetation that flourishes in the particularly mild climate. This fairyland of blue waters at the foot of shapely mountains has always been a favourite haunt of artists and travellers. The charm of these Pre-Alpine lakes is due to the juxtaposition of Alpine and southern scenery, the numerous villas with lakeside gardens, the great variety of flowers throughout the year and the small sailing villages, where fresh fish is the speciality. Each lake has its own specific character, making it quite different from its neighbour.

- **Information:** Corso Italia 18 – 28838 Stresa. ☎0323 30 416; www.distrettolaghi.it.
- **Orient Yourself:** The Lake District extends from Piedmont to Veneto and from Switzerland to Trentino in the north.
- **Parking:** At the Parco Giardino Sigurtà, park in one of the thirteen car parks at the bottom of the 7km/4m route and walk up.
- **Don't Miss:** Lago Maggiore, Isole Borromee, Lago di Como, Bellagio, Lago di Garda and vast panoramas from Limone and the Tremosine plateau.
- **Organizing Your Time:** Allow 2-3 days to explore the lake district.
- **Especially for Kids:** The Doll Museum (Museo della bambola) at Angera, the puppet theatre on Isole Borromee, Villa Pallavicino's wildlife park and the funicular railway to the top of Monte Baldo.

Lago Maggiore★★★

Lake Maggiore is the most famous of the Italian lakes, in part for its legendary beauty at times both majestic and wild, and also for the Borromean Islands. It is fed by the River Ticino, which rises in Switzerland, and its waters change from a jade green in the north to a deep blue in the south. The mountains of the Alps and Pre-Alps shelter the lake which enjoys a constantly mild climate in which a luxuriant and exotic vegetation flourishes.

Angera★

This wonderful holiday resort stands in the shadow of the **Rocca Borromeo**. There is a vast panoramic view from a tower, the **Torre Castellana**. Known since the days of the Lombards (8C), the Rocca still has Law Courts decorated with admirable 14C **frescoes**★★ depicting the life of Archbishop Ottone Visconti. The fortress also houses the Kids**Museo della bambola**★ (Doll Museum) with an extensive collection of exhibits detailing doll-design since the early 19C. *Museum: Open daily, 9am-5.30pm. Closed mid-Oct to mid-Mar. 7.50 €. 0331 93 13 00; www.borromeoturismo.it.*

Arona

The chief town on Lago Maggiore is overlooked by the gigantic statue, **Colosso di San Carlone**★, of **St Charles Borromeo**, the Cardinal Archbishop of Milan who distinguished himself by the authority he showed in re-establishing discipline in the Church and by his heroic conduct during the plague of 1576. *Open daily, mid-Mar-Sept 8.30am-12.30pm and 2-6.30pm; Oct-4 Nov 8.30am-12.30pm and 2-5pm; rest of the year Sat, Sun and festivals only 9am-12.30pm and 2-5pm. 3.50€. 0322 24 96 69; www.comune.arona.no.it.*
At the summit of the old town the church of **Santa Maria** contains a lovely **polyptych**★ (1511) by Gaudenzio Ferrari. From the **Rocca**, the ruined castle, there is a **view**★ of Lake Maggiore, Angera and its mountain setting.

Baveno★

This quiet holiday resort, once visited by Queen Victoria, has a Romanesque church and an octagonal Renaissance baptistery.

Isole Borromee★★★

www.borromeoturismo.it.
A large area of the lake was given to the princely Borromeo family in the 15C, but only gradually did they purchase all the islands in the tiny archipelago. In the 17C, Charles III established a residence on **Isola Bella**, named after his wife, Isabella. The palace, built in the Lombard Baroque style, has several state rooms – medals room, state hall, music room, Napoleon's room, ballroom and Hall of Mirrors. The most unusual feature is the caves where those living in the palace could find cooler air on very hot days. The gardens, filled with exotic plants, form an amazing Baroque composition, a truncated pyramid of ten terraces ornamented with statues, basins, fountains and architectural perspectives simulating stage sets. At the top of the garden is the shell-shaped "amphitheatre".
Boat trips are available to the **Isola dei Pescatori**, which has retained its original charm, and the **Isola Madre**, an island totally covered with a splendid garden of flowers and rare or exotic plants. In the palazzo, note the Puppet Theatre Kids that once belonged to the House of Borromeo. ▶ *Town plan in the Michelin Atlas Italy, under Stresa. Take a boat trip to the lush Isola Madre.*

Cannero Riviera★★

The houses of this resort rise in tiers above the lake amid olive trees, vineyards, and orange and lemon groves.

Cannobio★

www.cannobio.net.
Cannobio is a small resort near the Swiss border with a Renaissance church of the Madonna della Pietà. Out of town *(on the Malesco road)* is the **Orrido di S. Anna**★, a precipice formed by the torrent.

Cerro★

This peaceful lakeside village has a fishing port and a **ceramics museum.**

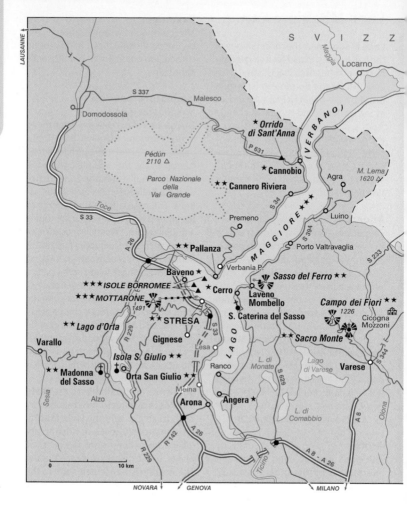

Laveno Mombello

www.comune.laveno.va.it.
A cable car climbs up to the summit of
Sasso del Ferro★★ for a fine **pano-
rama**.

Pallanza★★

Flowers deck and scent this wonderful resort. Its **quays★★**, sheltered by
magnolias and oleanders, offer lovely
views of the lake. On the outskirts of
the town on the Intra road is the **Villa
Taranto★★** with its gardens of azaleas,
heather, rhododendrons, camellias
and maples. ♿ ⏰*Open daily, 8.30am-
6.30pm.* ⏰*Closed Nov-Mar.* 🎫*8.50€.*
☎*0323 55 66 67; www.villataranto.it.*

Eremo di Santa Caterina
del Sasso

About 500m/550yd from Leggiuno.
⏰*Open daily, Apr to Oct 8.30am-noon
and 2.30-6pm, Nov-Mar 9am-noon and
2-5pm (Nov to Feb, Sat-Sun and public
holidays only).* 🎫*Donation welcome.*
☎*0332 64 71 72; www.provincia.va.it/
santacaterina.*
This 13C hermitage was founded by an
anchorite, Alberto Besozzo, and clings
to a rock overlooking the lake.

Stresa★★

This pleasant resort, which attracts many
artists and writers, enjoys a magnificent
situation on the west bank of Lago Mag-

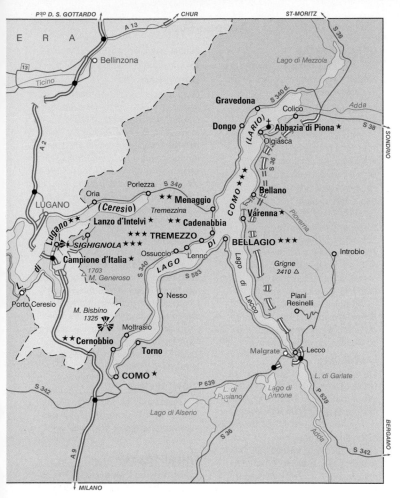

giore facing the Borromean Islands, and is a delightful place with all the amenities of a spring, summer, autumn and winter holiday resort. The ski slopes are on **Mottarone**★★★ *(take the Armeno road: 29km/18mi; the scenic toll-road from Alpino: 18km/11mi; or the cablecar)*, whose summit provides a magnificent **panorama** of the lake, Alps and Monte Rosa massif. *Funivia Stresa-Alpino-Mottarone. ☎0323 30 295; www.stresa-mottarone.it.* ▶*Town plan in the Michelin Atlas Italy.* Kids On the outskirts of the town sits the **Villa Pallavicino**★ and its wildlife park. ♿ ⏰*Open daily, 9am-6pm.* ⏰*Closed Nov-Feb.* ◉*8€.* ☎*0323 31 533; www.parcozoopallavicino.it.*

▶ *From Stresa, follow the Vezzo Gignese direction.*

Museo dell'Ombrello e del Parasole

8km/5mi southwest. ♿ ⏰*Open Tue-Sun, 10am-noon and 3-6pm.* ⏰*Closed Mon (except Jul and Aug), Oct-Mar.* ◉*2€.* ☎*0323 20 80 64; www.gignese.it/museo/ombrello.*

At **Gignese**, this interesting museum illustrates the history of the umbrella, particularly around Lago Maggiore with its celebrated umbrella-making tradition.

Address Book

GETTING THERE

One of the most pleasant ways to get around the lakes is to take a boat trip. See below for details.

LAGO MAGGIORE

Boat from Arona and/or Angera to Locarno, lunch available on board. From Stresa and/or Laveno for the Borromee Islands and Villa Taranto. Car ferry between Laveno and Intra. All-day tickets also available. Discounts for groups and senior citizens. Night cruise in summer. For information ☎800 55 18 01; www.navigazionelaghi.it.

The delightful **Borromee Islands** are situated in the middle of the lake. *All-day ticket valid for the islands: 6€ (2 islands round trip); 8€ (3 islands round trip); 10€ (3 islands and Villa Taranto round trip). For information, contact Ufficio Navigazione Lago Maggiore of the Ufficio del Turismo di Stresa ☎0323 30 416; www.borromeoturismo.it*

LAGO D'ORTA

Departures from Orta San Giulio: Easter-Oct, daily, every 30min, rest of year, only Sun and hols, every 45min. (Oct, Nov and Mar also Sat). Duration 5min. Price varies during the season. ☎0322 84 48 62. There is also a motor boat service. For information, contact Sig. Urani ☎338 30 34 904 (mobile) or Sig. Fabris ☎330 87 98 39 (mobile); www.www.lagodorta.com

LAGO DI LUGANO

"Grande Giro del lago" cruise daily from Apr to mid-Oct, dep Lugano 2.40pm, return 5.15pm. Restaurant on board. Explanations in four languages. Other boat excursions possible year-round in Italian and Swiss waters. For information contact Società Navigazione del Lago di Lugano. ☎0041 91 97 15 223; www.lakelugano.ch

LAGO DI COMO

Boat from Como to Colico, Tremezzo, Bellagio or Menaggio. From Tremezzo to Dongo, Domaso and Colico. Hydrofoil from Como to Tremezzo, Bellagio and Menaggio. Car ferries: between Bellagio, Varenna, Menaggio and Cadenabbia. All-day ticket valid for Lago Crociere, Sat night, in the summer. Discounts for groups and senior citizens. For infor-mation: ☎800 55 18 01; www.navigazionelaghi.it

LAGO D'ISEO

Departures in high season: from Sarnico, Iseo or Lovere around the lake, return in late pm, lunch available on board, stop at Monte Isola. Duration approx 7hr. From Iseo, afternoon excursion for the three islands, duration 2hr. From Sarnico, Iseo, Lovere or Monte Isola: tour of lake, afternoon departure and return in evening. For information contact I.A.T. in Iseo, Lungolago Marconi 2/C. ☎030 98 02 09; iat.iseo@tiscali.it.

LAGO DI GARDA

Boat tour from Desenzano and/or Peschiera to Riva del Garda, lunch available on board. Boat excursion across the lake taking in Sirmione, Gardone, Salò, Limone. Car ferry between Maderno and Torri. All-day tickets also available. Discounts for groups and senior citizens. Night cruise in summer. For information ☎800 55 18 01; www.navigazionelaghi.it, www.lagodigarda.it

SIGHTSEEING

The towns and sights for each lake are listed in alphabetical order. For places in Switzerland ℓ see *The Green Guide Switzerland.*

WHERE TO STAY

⌐**Agriturismo Il Monterosso** – Local-ità Cima Monterosso – 28922 Verbania (L. Maggiore) – 6km/3.6mi from Pallanza on the road which winds its way up to the top of Colle Monterosso – ☎0323 55 65 10 – www.ilmonterosso.it. Closed Jan, Feb; restaurant closed Mon and Tue – 8 double rm – ⌐ – Restaurant. What a setting to this little turreted farmhouse situated at the top of Colle Monterosso! It is surrounded by chestnut, pine and beech woods and boasts breathtaking views over the four surrounding lakes below as well as the Monte Rosa massif. This agriturismo combines good taste with simplicity and authentic home cooking. A good spot for walking and horse riding.

⌐**Hotel Il Chiostro** – Via F.lli Cervi 14 – 28921 Verbania Intra (L. Maggiore) – ☎0323 40 40 77 – www.chiostrovb.it – 🅿 ♿ – 108 rm ⌐. This lovely hotel is housed in what was a 17C convent and an old cotton factory that have been nicely converted. The hotel has also managed to retain some of the monastic calm while offering all modern conveniences – a rare achievement. The frescoed reading room and the charming cloisters are particularly lovely. The rooms, some of which look out onto the cloister, are simple in style. Highly recommended.

⊜⊜**Hotel Miravalle** – *Via Monte Oro 9 – 38066 Riva del Garda* – ☎*0464 55 23 35 – Fax 0464 52 17 07 – Closed Nov-Mar* – 🅿️ 🛟 *– 29 rm* 🍴 *– Restaurant*. The main attractions here are the location (not far from the centre), the lovely garden and the swimming pool. The rooms are pleasantly old-fashioned and the buffet-style breakfast is particularly good.

⊜⊜**Albergo Silvio** – *Via Carcano 10 / 12 – 22021 Bellagio (L. di Como) – 2km/1.2mi southwest of Bellagio –* ☎*031 95 03 22 – www.bellagiosilvio.com – Closed 10 Jan-20 Feb.* – 🗝️🅿️ *– 21 rm* 🍴 *– Restaurant*. Quiet, simply decorated rooms (particularly those in the roof which are very attractive). However, the main attraction is the cooking. Fish from the lake – caught by the owner himself – feature large on the menu. Meals served in a lovely dining room with fine views or under the large pergola. Situated very near the centre of town.

⊜⊜**Hotel Palazzina** – *Via Libertà 10 – 25084 Gargnano (L. di Garda) –* ☎*0365 71 118 – www.hotelpalazzina.it – Closed Oct-mid-Apr –* 🅿️ 🛟 *– 25 rm –* 🍴*8.01€ – Restaurant*. This popular, family-run hotel has a very easy-going, 1960s feel about it and its loyal clientele return year after year. The two large panoramic terraces, one of which has a swimming pool, are particularly lovely.

⊜⊜**Hotel Cangrande** – *Corso Cangrande 16 – 37017 Lazise (L. di Garda) – 5km/3mi south of Bardolino on N 249 –* ☎*045 64 70 410 – www.cangrandehotel.it – Closed 20 Dec-10 Feb –* 🅿️🛏️ *– 17 rm* 🍴. This hotel is housed in a 1930s building, close to the medieval walls, which also serves as the offices for the Girasole winery. The elegant rooms are modern in style. The huge barrels in the public areas add to the atmosphere.

Wine enthusiasts might like to visit the extensive cellar.

⊜⊜**Hotel La Fontana** – *Strada statale del Sempione 1 – 28838 Stresa (L. Maggiore) –* ☎*0323 32 707– www.lafontanahotel.com – Closed Dec and Jan –* 🅿️ *– 20 rm –* 🍴*7€*. The 1940s villa which houses this hotel is surrounded by lovely gardens. All the rooms have a little terrace with a view of lake. Decor is slightly retro in style. Centrally located and reasonably priced.

⊜⊜**Hotel Rigoli** – *Via Piave 48 – 28831 Baveno (L. Maggiore) –* ☎*0323 92 47 56 – www.hotelrigoli.com – Closed Nov-Easter –* 🅿️ *– 31 rm P70/110 –* 🍴*9.30€ – Restaurant*. The rooms are spacious, with modern pale-coloured furnishings, and the public areas are sunny and pleasant. This hotel exudes a real holiday atmosphere, nowhere more than the lakeside terrace-garden area which has lovely views out to the Borromee Islands. Half-board rates available.

⊜⊜**Hotel Desirée** – *Via San Pietro 2 – 25019 Sirmione (L. di Garda) –* ☎*030 99 05 244 – Fax 030 91 62 41 – Closed mid-Nov-mid-Mar –* 🅿️🛏️ *(payment) – 34 rm -* 🍴 *– Restaurant*. A simple, unpretentious hotel in a quiet location, not far from the beach and the thermal baths. The furnishings in the public areas are a little old-fashioned but the rooms have their own balcony. The dining room is lovely and light, with windows on three sides.

⊜⊜**Hotel Garni La Contrada dei Monti** – *Via Contrada dei Monti 10 – 28016 Orta S. Giulio (L. d'Orta) –* ☎*0322 90 51 14 – www.orta.net/lacontrada-deimonti/ – Closed 3-31 Jan –* ♿ *– 17 rm –* 🍴*7.75€*. A jewel of light and harmony, this charming little hotel is housed in an 18C palazzo which has been lovingly restored. Great attention to detail in the rooms: mirrors with hand-painted frames in the bathrooms, a frescoed vaulted ceiling in the hall. Would appeal to couples looking for romance!

WHERE TO EAT

⊜**Café delle Rose** – *Via Ruga 36 – 28922 Verbania Pallanza (L. Maggiore) –* ☎*0323 55 81 01 – Closed Sun and one week in June and Sept*. Fin de siècle ambience, enhanced by the furniture and furnishings which are mostly antique. At lunchtime, the café serves a variety of dishes and offers a very reasonably priced menu. In the evening the place transforms itself into a wine bar offering panini and other snacks late into the night. Excellent choice of music.

⌐**Al Porto** – *Via Zanitello 3 – 28922 Verbania Pallanza (L. Maggiore) – ☎0323 55 71 24 – Closed Nov, Mon and lunchtime – Book.* An unusual rustic-style establishment, which resembles the galley of an old sailing ship. Open late into the night for drinks as well as food, from simple home-made snacks to meals. Different menu every day. There is a wonderful view of the lake from the terrace on the first floor.

⌐**Papa** – *Via Bell'Italia 40 – 37010 San Benedetto di Lugana (L. di Garda) – 2.5km/1mi west of Peschiera del Garda – ☎045 75 50 476 – alb.papa@peschiera. com – Closed Nov-mid-Dec – ▭.* A traditional establishment with a loyal clientele who come back year after year to spend their holidays here. Regional cuisine, reasonable prices. Meals served under a lovely wisteria-covered per-gola. Pleasantly decorated rooms.

⌐**Ristoro Antico** – *Via Bottelli 46 – 28041 Arona (L. Maggiore) – ☎0322 46 482 – Closed Sun evening, Mon, Jul – ▭ – Book.* This family-style restaurant serves authentic home cooking. Great attention to detail and a menu that changes on a daily basis. Rustic-style interior with roof tiles exposed. Offers excellent value for money.

⌐**Il Gabbiano** – *Via I Maggio 19 – 28831 Baveno (L. Maggiore) – ☎0323 92 44 96 – Closed Mon, Tues and lunchtimes (except 15 Jun-15 Sep), rest of the year closed Mon – Book – ▭.* Housed in an old farmhouse just outside Baveno, this is a traditional restaurant with a difference. The menu is a wonderful mixture of simplicity and creativity and the dishes are imaginatively presented. Rustic-style ambience.

⌐**Italia** – *Via Ugo Ara 58, Isola dei Pesca-tori – 28838 Stresa (L. Maggiore) – ☎0323 30 188 – Closed Jan.* The establishment comprises a bar area complete with an old coloured cement floor – you might just be able to get a snack here – and a large terrace area overlooking the lake which is closed off and heated in winter. Fish from the lake is its staple fare, simply and traditionally prepared. Private moorings at night.

⌐**Aurora** – *Via Ciucani 1/7 – 25080 Soiano del Lago (L. di Garda) – 10km/6mi north of Desenzano on S 572 – ☎0365 67 41 01 – Closed Wed – ▭.* A rare combi-nation of quality and value for money. The cuisine is traditional and regional in style but has a very distinctive touch, and the dishes are stylishly presented. The dining room is light and airy, with elegant rustic-style furnishings.

⌐**Le Oche di Bracchio** – *Via Brac-chio 46 – 28802 Mergozzo (L. Maggiore) – 10km/6mi northwest of Pallanza – ☎0323 80 122 – www.leochedibracchio.it – Closed Wed, 10 Jan-15 Feb – Book.* A simple, rather alternative establishment which caters for vegetarians and those following a macrobiotic diet. The building is rather basic but is well maintained. The setting is enhanced by the fruit trees. Also offers facilities for various Eastern disciplines. A great place if you're look-ing to "find yourself" or simply looking for a bit of peace and quiet.

⌐⌐**Agriturismo Il Bagnolo** – *Località Bagnolo – 25087 Serniga (L. di Garda) – 1km/0.6mi northwest of Gardone Riviera – ☎0365 20 290 – Closed Tue, Oct-Apr open only Fri evening-Sun – Book – 9rm.* This farm guesthouse is an excel-lent example of its kind, and boasts a wonderfully verdant setting. In keeping with the agriturismo concept, the cook-ing is based on the farm's own produce and is delicious. Elegant rooms with a romantic feel about them and all very individual in style.

⌐⌐**Gatto Nero** – *Via Monte Santo 69 – 22012 Rovenna (L. di Como) – North of Cernobbio – ☎031 51 20 42 – Closed Mon, Tue lunchtime – Book.* A very popular establishment where people come to enjoy the panoramic setting complete with views of the lake and the mountains. Traditional cooking with a number of fish dishes on the menu. Warm and cosy inside, with rustic-style decor. The view from the summer ter-race is breathtaking. Would appeal to couples looking for romance!

TAKING A BREAK

Bar di Lago – *Via Mazzini 13 – 28832 Feriolo (L. Maggiore) – ☎0323 28 101 – Open daily in summer, 7am-midnight; rest of the year, Thu-Tue.* Located off the beaten track in a quiet, little marina between Stresa and Baveno. The bar has wonderful views over the lake and is a great spot for savouring an ice cream or a granita, while dangling your feet in the water!

Caffè Broletto – *Piazza del Popolo 24 – 28041 Arona (L. Maggiore) – ☎0322 46 640 – Tue-Sun 10am-2am, closed 10 days in winter.* From one of the loveliest outdoor terraces in Arona you get a view of this traffic-free piazza, a small church and the blue water of the lake. Try one of the fruit cocktails (with or without alcohol).

Gardesana – *Piazza Calderini 20 – 37010 Torri del Benaco (L. di Garda) – ☎045 72 25 411 – www.hotel-gardesana. com – Open Summer, 9am-midnight; rest of the year, Wed-Mon, closed 10 Nov-Jan.* Nestling between the splendid tower which overlooks the port and the old houses with their wrought-iron balconies, is an elegant hotel and tea room. Try and get a seat under the little portico which is covered in flowers. In summer, musicians come to play classical music every evening.

Gelateria Cremeria Fantasy – *Via Principessa Margherita 38 – 28838 Stresa (L. Maggiore) – ☎0349 35 64 327 – 9-24, Closed Nov-Jan except public holidays.* While it is not easy to find a gelateria which stands out from the rest, try this little parlour. The 32 flavours of ice cream and *semifreddi* – all home-made – are exceptionally good.

Gelateria Oasi – *Via Ruga 15 – 28922 Verbania Pallanza (L. Maggiore) – ☎0323 50 19 02 –Open Mon-Sat 10am-9.30pm, Sun 9.30am-24.30am.* Pistacchio, walnut, vanilla, carrot, basil... just some of the numerous and unusual flavours produced by this artisanal ice cream parlour, which was established four years ago. Very popular.

LEISURE

Garda Yachting Charter – *Lungolago Zanardelli – 25088 Maderno (L. di Garda) – In the port, beyond the landing stage – ☎030 294 32 99 – www.gyc.it – Book ahead.* Motorboats (with or without a licence) and sailing boats (3.65m/12ft to 8.50m/26ft) for hire.

Lago d'Orta★★

www.lagomaggiore.net.
Lake Orta, one of the smallest Italian lakes, is separated from Lake Maggiore by the peak "Il Mottarone" in the northeast. It is a delightful, with wooded hills and an islet, Isola San Giulio.
The lakesides have been inhabited since earliest times and in the 4C the people were converted to Christianity by St Julius.

Chiesa della Madonna dal Sasso★★
From the church terrace there is a magnificent view of the lake in its verdant mountain setting.

Orta San Giulio★★
This small resort on the tip of a peninsula has alleyways lined with old houses adorned with elegant wrought-iron balconies. The **Palazzotto**★or 16C town hall is decorated with frescoes.

Sacro Monte d'Orta★
*1.5km/1mi from Orta.*This sanctuary dedicated to St Francis of Assisi and set on a hilltop comprises 20 chapels, decorated in the Baroque style, with frescoes that serve as background to lifelike terracotta statues.

Isola di San Giulio★★
▶*Boats leave from Orta.*
On this jewel of an island, 300m/330yds long and 160m/175yds wide, stands the **basilica di San Giulio**, said to date from the 4C, when St Julius came to the island. Inside there is a lovely 12C amboa decorated with frescoes by the school of Gaudenzio Ferrari (16C). Note also the shrine containing relics of St Julius. ⏱*Open 9.30am-12.15pm (Mon 11am-12.30pm) and 2-5.45pm.*

Orta San Giulio

Varallo
▶ *About 20km/12mi west.*
This industrial and commercial town in the Val Sesia is famous for its pilgrimage to the **Sacro Monte**★★ with its 43 chapels. Again these are decorated with frescoes and groups of life-size terracotta figures (16C-18C). They were the work of several artists including Gaudenzio Ferrari (1480-1546), a local painter, a pupil of Leonardo da Vinci.

Lago di Lugano★★

Most of **Lake Lugano**, also known as Lake Ceresio by the Italians, is in Swiss territory. Lugano is wilder than Lakes Maggiore and Como and with its irregular outline has none of the grandeur or majesty of the others. Its mild climate and its steep mountain countryside make it an ideal place for a holiday.

Campione d'Italia★
An Italian enclave in Switzerland, Campione is a colourful village, popular on account of its casino. A chapel, the oratory of San Pietro, is a graceful building dating from 1326. It was the work of the famous **Maestri Campionesi** who vied with the Maestri Comacini in spreading the Lombard style throughout Italy (👓 *see Italian Art in the Introduction*).

Lanzo d'Intelvi★
Set in the heart of a pine and larch forest, this resort (alt 907m/2 976ft) is also a ski centre in winter. Some 6km/4mi away is the **belvedere di Sighignola**★★★, also

known as the "balcony of Italy" because of its extensive view of Lugano, the Alps as far as Monte Rosa and on a clear day Mont Blanc.

Varese
13km/8mi southwest of Porto Ceresio. Town plan in the Michelin Atlas Italy www. comune.varese.it.
This busy modern town stands close to the lake of the same name. One of its advantages is a mild climate due to its proximity to the Italian lakes.

▶ At 8km/5mi to the west rises the hilltop known as **Sacro Monte**★★, with its pilgrimage church dedicated to the Virgin. The road up to the basilica is lined with 14 chapels decorated with frescoes in *trompe l'oeil* and groups of life-size terracotta figures. From the summit there is a magnificent **view**★★ of the lakes and surrounding mountains.

▶ At a distance of 10km/6mi to the northwest is the long mountainous ridge, **Campo dei Fiori**★★, which raises its forest-clad slopes above the plain. There is a vast **panorama**★★ of the Lake District.

▶ About 10km/6mi to the south, on the road to Tradate, is **Castiglione Olona**, with fine **frescoes**★ by **Masolino da Panicale** (c 1383-1440) in the Collegiata (*Story of the Virgin Mary*) and in the Baptistery (*Story of St John the Baptist*).

Villa Cicogna Mozzoni a Bisuschio
▶ *8km/5mi northeast of Varese on the road to Porto Ceresio.* ♿ 🕐 *Open 9.30am-noon and 2.30-7pm.* 🕐 *Closed Dec-Mar and Easter.* 🎫 *6 €.* ☎ *0332 47 11 34; www. villacicognamozzoni.it.*
The villa, set in fine Italian terraced gardens, was originally a hunting lodge in the 15C, which was extended in the 16C with the addition of a residence. In the first floor rooms, complete with furnishings, the ceilings are adorned with fine frescoes in the Renaissance style.

Lago di Como★★★

Set entirely within Lombardy, **Lake Como**, of all the Italian lakes, has the most variety. Pretty villages, ports and villas in exotic gardens succeed one another along this Pre-Alpine lake.

Bellagio★★★

Bellagio occupies a magnificent site on a promontory dividing Lake Lecco from the southern arm of Lake Como. The gracious resort town has a worldwide reputation for friendliness and excellent amenities. The splendid lakeside **gardens**★★ of **Villa Serbelloni** (*Guided tours daily at 11am and 4pm from Uff. Promobellagio, Piazza della Chiesa 14. €7. Closed Mon and Nov-Mar. 031 95 15 55; www.bellagiolakecomo.com)* and **Villa Melzi** (*Open daily, 9am-6pm. Closed Nov-Mar. 6 €. 031 95 02 04)*, with their fragrant and luxuriant vegetation, are the main sights in Bellagio.

Bellano

This small industrial town stands on the River Pioverna at the mouth of the valley (Valsassina), with the Grigne towering behind. The attractive 14C **church** with a facade by Giovanni da Campione is in the Lombard Gothic style.

Cadenabbia★★

This delightful resort occupies an admirable site opposite Bellagio. A handsome avenue of plane trees, Via del Paradiso, links the resort with the Villa Carlotta and Tremezzo. From a chapel, **Capella di San Martino** (1hr30min on foot there and back), there is a good **view**★★ of Bellagio, Lakes Como and Lecco and of the Grigne.

Cernobbio★★

This location is famous for the **Villa d'Este**, the opulent 16C residence now transformed into a hotel and surrounded by fine parkland *(access to both the villa and the park is limited to hotel guests)*. The best view of the villa (from the ground) is from Piazza del Risorgimento, near the landing stage.

Chiavenna

Ancient Chiavenna owes its name to its key (*clavis* in Latin) position in the Splügen and Maloja transalpine passes between Italy and Switzerland. Chi-

avenna is also famous for its **crotti**, restaurants housed in natural caves and serving local specialities (found only in Valtellina) such as *pizzoccheri* (buckwheat pasta served with melted cheese) and *bresaola* (dried meat).

Nearby, above the Palazzo Balbini (15C) is **Il Paradiso**, a rock that was once a fortified site and is now set out as a pleasant garden, the **Giardino botanico e archeologico**. *Open daily except Mon, 10am-noon and 2-5pm. Closed mornings Mon-Fri in winter. Call to confirm opening times and costs. 0343 33 795.*

See also the strange frescoes decorating the exterior of the Palazzo Pretorio and the doorways in the Via Dolzino on which the inscriptions date back to the days of the Reformation.

Collegiata di San Lorenzo

Open daily except Mon, 3-6pm (2-4pm in winter), Sat also 10am-noon, Sun to 5pm. 3.10€. Call in advance for Baptistery 0343 37 485.

The Collegiate Church of St Lawrence, built during the Romanesque period and reconstructed in the 16C after a fire, contains two paintings, one by Pietro Ligari (1738) (2nd chapel on the right) and one by Giuseppe Nuvoloni (1657) (1st chapel on the left).

The **Baptistery** has a Romanesque **font**★ (1156) in *ollare* stone: the name of the stone being a reference to its being used to make *olle* (urns and vases). The low reliefs illustrate a baptismal scene depicting various social classes (nobleman hunting with his falcon, soldier and craftsman), a child with his godfather, a priest and acolyte, and members of the clergy. The inscription reveals the sponsors of the work.

The treasury houses a wonderful 12C binding for an evangelistary.

Strada del passo dello Spluga★★

▶ *30km/19mi from Chiavenna to the pass.*

The Splügen Pass Road is one of the boldest and most spectacular in the Alps. The **Campodolcino-Pianazzo section**★★★ is grandiose as it climbs the mountainside in hairpin bends.

Como

www.comolake.com.

Already prosperous under the Romans, the town was the birthplace of the naturalist Pliny the Elder and his nephew, the writer Pliny the Younger. Como reached its zenith in the 11C. It was destroyed by the Milanese in 1127, rebuilt by the Emperor Frederick Barbarossa and from 1355 onwards shared the fortunes of Milan. The **Maestri Comacini** known as early as the 7C, were masons, builders and sculptors who spread the Lombard style (*see Italian Art in the Introduction*) throughout Italy and Europe.

Duomo★★

Begun in the late 14C the cathedral was completed during the Renaissance and crowned in the 18C with an elegant dome by the architect, Juvarra. It has a remarkable **façade★★** that was richly decorated from 1484 onwards by the **Rodari brothers**, who also worked on the **north door**, known as the Porta della Rana because of the frog *(rana)* carved on one of the pillars. They were also responsible for the exquisitely delicate **south door.**

The **interior★**, full of solemn splendour, combines Gothic architecture and Renaissance decoration. In addition to the curious banners, hung between the pillars, and the magnificent 16C-17C **tapestries★**, there are canvases by B Luini **(Adoration of the Magi, Virgin and Child with Saints★)**, and G Ferrari **(Flight into Egypt)**, in the south aisle as well as a **Descent from the Cross★** (1489) carved by Tommaso Rodari in the north aisle. Note the organ in five parts, comprising 96 registers and 6 000 pipes. Various 17C artists were involved in its construction although its current form is by organ-makers Balbiani and Vegezzi-Bossi.

Adjoining the façade is the **Broletto★★**, or 13C town hall, with a lovely storey of triple-arched windows.

Chiesa di San Fedele★

In the heart of the old quarter, lies this church in the Romanesque Lombard style. The nave and two aisles are terminated by a polygonal Romanesque **chancel★** with radiating chapels.

Basilica di Sant'Abbondio★

This masterpiece of Romanesque Lombard architecture was consecrated in 1093. The noble façade★ has a lovely doorway. The remarkable 14C **frescos★** evoke the Life of Christ.

Villa Olmo

▶*3km/2mi north by S 35 and then S 340 to the right.* ☎*031 24 25 43; www.centro-volta.it.*

This large neo-Classical building is now a scientific institute. The gardens contain a small theater and a lovely **view★** of Como in its lakeside setting.

Dongo

It was in this village that Mussolini and his mistress, Clara Petacci, were captured on 27 April 1945.

Gravedona

This fishing village has an attractive Romanesque church, **Santa Maria del Tiglio★**. The 5C baptistery was remodelled in the Lombard style in the 12C.

Menaggio★★

Favoured by a cool summer breeze, this is one of the lake's smart resorts.

Abbazia di Pion★★

▶*2km/1mi from Olgiasca.*

This monastery adopted Cistercian under St Bernard of Clairvaux (1090-1153) and features Lombard Romanesque **cloisters★** (1252).

Torno

On the outskirts of this attractive port, the 14C church of San Giovanni has a fine Lombard Renaissance **doorway★**.

Tremezzo★★★

A mild climate and a beautiful site combine to make Tremezzo a favourite place for a stay. The terraced gardens, **Parco comunale★**, are peaceful.

The 18C **Villa Carlotta★★★** *(entrance beside the Grand Hotel Tremezzo)* occupies an admirable site facing the Grigne Massif. (*Open Apr to Sep, daily, 9am-6pm, Mar and Oct, 9am-noon and 2-5pm. Closed Nov to Feb.* 7.50€. ☎*0344 40 405; www.villacarlotta.it).* Statues include a copy by Tadolini of the famous group of Cupid and Psyche by Canova. The main attraction is, however, the beautiful terraced **garden**.

Santuario della Madonna di Tirano

69km/43mi east of Colico, at the northernmost point of the lake.
The church of the **Madonna di Tirano** was built from 1505 onwards on the spot where the Virgin Mary had appeared in a vision. It has a nave and side aisles. The west front dates from 1676 and is enhanced with highly ornate Baroque decoration, including frescoes by Cipriano Valorsa di Grosio (1575-78), nicknamed the "Raphael of La Valtellina" *(nave)*, a fresco of the Apparition dating from 1513 *(left, above the confessional)*, paintings by a pupil of Morazzone *(chancel)* and a highly ornate, grandiose 17C **organ**. The loft was made by Giuseppe Bulgarini and the panels on the gallery representing the Birth of the Infant Jesus, The Adoration of the Magi and The Circumcision were painted by Giuseppe Bulgarini Salmoiraghi (1638).

Varenna★

🕐 *Open Apr-Oct, daily, 9am-7pm.* 🕐*Closed Nov-Mar (gardens).* 🎫*2€.* ☎*0341 29 54 50; www.villamonastero.it*
This town with its many gardens stands on a promontory. The 16C **Villa Monastero** also has beautiful **gardens**★★.

Lago d'Iseo★

Though **Lake Iseo** is not very well known, its wild scenery, high mountain fringe and peaceful villages all lend charm to this small lake. From the midst of the waters emerges the island of Monte Isola (alt 600m/1 970ft).

Iseo★

The church, Pieve di Sant'Andrea, faces a charming square.

Lovere

In this small industrial town, the **Galleria Tadini** has a collection of arms, paintings (Bellini and Parmigianino), porcelain and sculpture by Canova. ♿🕐*Open Tue-Sat 3-7pm, Sun and holi-*

The enchanting Villa Carlotta, Tremezzo

B. Juge/MICHELIN

days 10am-noon and 3-7pm. 🕐*Closed Mon, mid-Oct to mid-Apr.* 🎫*5€.* ☎*035 96 27 80; www.accademiatadini.it.*

Monte Isola★★

Iseo, Lungolago Marconi 2c. ☎*030 98 02 09; Frequent connections from Iseo. From Sulzano, departure every 15-20min.* 🎫*3€ round trip. Access also from other locations on the lake and from Sale Marasino.*
From the church of the Madonna della Ceriola, crowning this green island, there is a vast **panorama**★★ of the lake and the Alps near Bergamo.

Pisogne★

This small port has an attractive lakeside setting. The church of **Santa Maria della Neve** is adorned with 16C **frescoes**★ by Romanino du Brescia.

Valcamonica

The Valcamonica follows the course of the River Oglio as far as Lago d'Iseo. The main access road from Bergamo is S 42. The valley which stretches from Lovere to Edolo, and is linked to the Valtellina by the **Passo di Gavia**, may be given over to industry at the lower level, but the higher you climb the more picturesque it is, dotted with castle ruins. Over a stretch of 60km/36mi are UNESCO World Hertiage prehistoric and early Roman rock carvings.

Rock carvings★★

Eroded by the alpine glaciers, the rocks of the Valcamonica became a highly polished surface which lent itself to figurative engravings, by the people of the region. Created by tapping or scratching away at the stone, the carvings are a testament to the daily life of the people who inhabited the region. Having dedicated themselves to hunting during the Palaeolithic era (c 8000-5000 BC), they adopted agricultural farming methods during the Neolithic era and then metallurgy during the Bronze Age (from 1800 BC) and the Iron Age (from 900 BC). There are four basic types of representation: deer (hunting scenes); ploughs and other agricultural machinery; weaponry and warriors; religious representations: prayers, symbols, idols. The carvings can be seen in the Parco Nazionale delle Incisioni Rupestri di Naquane. *Access from Capo di Ponte.* ⏰*Open Mar-Oct 8.30am-7pm; Nov-Feb 8.30am-5pm.* ⏰*Closed Mon except holidays, 1 Jan, 1 May, 25 Dec.* ☎*0364 320 489; www.valcamonicambiente.it*

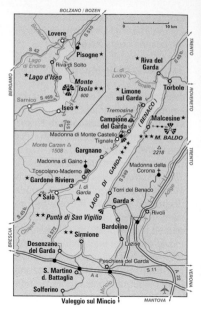

Riserva Naturale Regionale di Ceto, *Cimbergo e Paspardo (contact the Museo di Nadro di Ceto):* ♿⏰*Open summer 9am-6pm, winter 9am-noon and 1.30pm-5pm.* ⏰*Closed 1 Jan, 25 Dec.* ☜*3€ with entry to the Museo di Nadro.* ☎*0364 43 34 465; www. arterupestre.it*
♨**Breno**: 10C castle, church of S. Antonio (14C-15C), church of S. Salvatore.

Lago di Garda★★★

Lake Garda, the largest lake, is also considered one of the most beautiful. Its many assets include low-lying banks which are alluvial in the south, steep slopes on the west bank, and the mountain chain of Monte Baldo to the east.
The Dolomites to the north shelter the lake from the cold north winds, creating a very mild climate which had already earned it the name of "beneficent" lake *(Il Benaco)* in ancient times. It had both strategic and commercial importance and throughout history has been coveted by neighbouring powers. Artistically, the region was influenced by the Venetian Republic which ruled the region from the 15C to the 18C. Even in Roman times the lakes werepopular for holidays, and today there are many resorts to choose from.

Bardolino
www.comune.bardolino.vr.it.
This village, famous for its red wine, has an elegant 11C Romanesque **church**★ dedicated to St Severinus.

Campione del Garda
The Bishops of Trent, Brescia and Verona met here to bless the lake.

Desenzano del Garda
The old port, the picturesque Piazza Malvezzi and the neighbouring old quarter are all good places for a stroll. The 16C parish church, the **Parrocchiale Santa Maria Maddalena**, has a very intense **Last Supper**★ by Tiepolo. To the north of the town in Via Scavi Romani, the **Villa Romana** boasts remarkable multicoloured **mosaics**★ dating from the Roman period. ♿⏰*Open daily except Mon, Mar-Oct 8.30am-7pm, Nov-Feb 8.30am-4.30pm.* ⏰*Closed Mon, 1 Jan, 1 May, 25 Dec.* ☜*2€.* ☎*030 91 43 547.*

Garda★

This popular resort which gave its name to the lake shows a strong Venetian influence. Both the Palazzo dei Capitani and the Palazzo Fregoso are 15C.

Gardone Riviera★★

This small resort enjoys many hours of sunshine and offers the visitor a wide choice of hotels. At 1km/0.6mi from the town is the **Vittoriale**★ estate, which belonged to the poet **Gabriele D'Annunzio** (1863-1938), buried here. The neo-Classical villa, La Priora, is full of the solemn atmosphere which this writer-aesthete so cultivated. The museum and park display mementoes of his turbulent life. *Gardens: Open Apr-Sep, 8.30am-8pm, Oct-Mar 9am-5pm. Villa and museum: Apr-Sep, 9.30am-7pm, Oct-Mar 9am-1pm and 2-5pm. Closed Mon (villa), Wed (museum), 1 Jan, 24-25 Dec. 7€ (gardens), 11€ villa or museum, 16€ villa and museum. 0365 29 65 11; www.vittoriale.it.*

Gargnano

www.comune.gargnano.brescia.it.
This charming resort is surrounded by great expanses of glasshouses filled with lemon and citron trees. The church of **San Francesco** has 15C cloisters with curious Moorish-style galleries featuring capitals carved with oranges and lemons, recalling the fact that it was probably the Franciscan monks who introduced citrus fruits to the area. The lakeside promenade leads to **Villa Feltrinelli** *(not open)* that served as Mussolini's headquarters during the Fascist Republic (1943-45).

Limone sul Garda★

www.limone.com.
This is one of the lake's most attractive villages. Terraced lemon groves stretch along the shores. From Limone a **panoramic route**★★ climbs up to the Tremosine plateau before descending to Tignale, offering superb lake **views**★★★.

Malcesine★

Departures from 8am-5pm, 6pm or 7pm depending on the season. Closed at the end of the skiing season and the end of the summer season. *16€ round trip. 045 74 00 206*
This attractive town stands on a promontory at the foot of **Monte Baldo** and is dominated by the crenellated outline of the Castello Scaligeroa. This 13-14C castle belonged to the Scalider family of Verona.
The 15C Palazzo dei Capitani in the Venetian style stands on the edge of the lake. From the summit of Monte Baldo (cable car) there is a splendid **panorama**★★★ of the lake, the Brenta and Adamello Massifs. Kids *Take a ride on the funicular railway.*

Punta di San Viglio★★

This headland is in a romantic setting. Sanmicheli planned this 16C Villa Guarienti (not open) for the Veronese humanist, Agostino Brenzoni.

Riva del Garda★

Once a trading centre between Verona and the Aloday, today the old town★ is a maze of shopping streets. *Open 10.30am-dusk. Closed Mon (except Jul and Aug). 3€. 0464 57 38 69; www.comune.rivadelgarda.tn.it/cultura.*

Salò★

www.comune.salo.bs.it.
This was the seat of the Venetian Captain under the Venetian Empire. Inside the 15C **Duomo** are a large gilt **polyptych**★ (1510) and works by Moretto da Brescia and Romanino.

San Martino della Battaglia

Open daily 9am-12.30pm and 2.30-7pm (5.30pm Oct-Feb). 4€ combined ticket with Rocca and museum. 030 99 10 370. An ossuary-chapel, a museum and a tall tower commemorate the battle of 24 June 1859 at Solferino, (*see Solferino*), and the wars of the Risorgimento that were waged by the Italians for independence from Austria.

Sirmione★★

This important resort has been well known since the beginning of the century as a spa, and is said to be particularly effective in the treatment of resporatory disorders. The houses cluster around the

13C castle, **Rocca Scaliger**★★, at the tip of the Sirmione peninsula, as it stretches out into the lake. ©*Open daily except Mon, 8.30am-7.30pm.* ©*Closed 1 Jan, 25 Dec.* ☞*4€.* ☎*030 91 64 68; www.sirmione.com.*

On the peninsula tip are the remains of a vast Roman villa belonging to the poet Catullus, the **Grotte di Catullo**★★. ♿©*Open Tue-Sun, 8.30am-7pm (4.30pm in winter).* ©*Closed 1 Jan, 1 May, 25 Dec.* ☞*4€.* ☎*030 91 61 57.*

Solferino

An ossuary chapel and a **museum** recall the battle of 24 June 1859 (the field of battle extended to San Martino, ♿*see above*) when the French and Piedmontese troops defeated the Austrians and brought about Italy's independence (♿*see Towards Italian Unity*). The heavy casualties led to the founding of the **Red Cross** by Henri Dunant. *Museum:* (♿) ©*Open daily, Apr-Oct 9am-noon and 2.30-6.30pm.* ©*Closed Mon, Nov-Mar.* *1.55€.* ☎*0376 85 40 19.*

Torbole

This pleasant resort was the venue for a most unusal event in 1439. Venice in an attempt to rescue the town of Brescia, under seige by the Visconti of Milan, armed a fleet that sailed up the Adige and crossed the moutnains towards Tor-bole on Lake Garda. From there the fleet set sail to occupy Maderno on the west bank. The following year Venice was able to capture Riva and finally achieve suzerainty over the lake.

Valeggio sul Mincio

▶*Exit the Milan-Venice motorway at Peschiera. Follow signs for Parco Giardino Sigurtà, 10km/6mi south of Peschiera.* 🅿*Thirteen car parks lie along the 7km/4mi route.* ♿©*Open Mar-Oct, daily, 9am-6pm.* ©*Closed Nov-Feb. 8.50€. Park can be visited by mini-train 2, bike rental available.* ☎*045 63 71 033; www.sigurta.it.*

Having been granted the right to pump up spring water from the Minicio, Carlo Sigurtà (1898-1983), an industrial pharmacist who spent 40 years of his life working on the properties of thermal springs, completely transformed the 17C villa used by Napoleon III as his headquarters in 1859. Now this beautifully maintained park (50ha/123 acres), **Parco Giardino Sigurtà**★★, can only be visited by car, though footpaths wind up from each parking lot. In addition to its magnificent location on the Mincio, the park has a wonderful range of Mediterranean flora, cast grassy swards, architectural and natural features, and, in certain areas, the gentle sound of classical music.

LAGUNA VENETA �ీ☀☆
VENETIAN LAGOON

MICHELIN MAP 562 E, F, G 18-22
T SEE ALSO THE GREEN GUIDE VENICE.
VENETO – FRIULI-VENEZIA GIULIA.

The Venetian lagoon is the largest in Italy. It was formed at the end of the Ice Age by the convergence of flooded rivers, swollen by melted snow from the Alps and Apennines.

- 🛈 **Information:** Lungomare Adriatico 101, Sottomarina Lido Venezia. ☎041 40 10 68. www.choggiatourism.it.
- ▶ **Orient Yourself:** The Venetian lagoon is bordered to the south by Chioggia and to the north by Trieste. The main access road is A 4.
- 👁 **Don't Miss:** The Basilica at Aquileia.
- ⊙ **Organizing Your Time:** Allow a day to explore the area.
- 🧒 **Especially for Kids:** The Parco zoo Punta Verde and family-friendly beaches at Lignano.
- 👁 **Also See:** *TRIESTE, UDINE, VENEZIA.*

L. Pessina/MICHELIN

The haunting beauty of the Venetian lagoon

A Bit of History

In the 12C, Europe enjoyed a long period of mild weather followed by a noticeable rise in temperature; then came torrential rains that caused high tides and flooding. The River Brenta broke its banks and water flooded a large part of the lagoon, depositing silt, mud and detritus. Malaria broke out. The Republic of Venice tried to defend itself by placing palisades along the coast, diverting the course of the rivers and building great dikes, but the lagoon continued to pose a threat. Over the ensuing centuries (15C-17C), major drainage programmes were implemented that affected the Brenta, Piave, Livenza and Sile rivers. In 1896 the operation aimed at diverting the waters of the Brenta was finally completed, channelling them into the mouth of the Bacchiglione. Despite these measures, as water levels continue to rise and fall, the sand deposited into the lagoon by the rivers is buffeted back inland by the sea and the wind. Thus the sandbanks are formed and strengthened. All the while, caught between marine erosion and the rebuilding action of the rivers, the fate of Venice itself is at stake: after more than 1 000 years of existence, it is slowly sinking.

Nature of the Lagoon

The Venetian lagoon can be likened to a sophisticated system that has achieved a subtle balance between excessive sedimentation (leading to the emergence of "new" land) and erosion (in which the deposits carried by the sea and rivers are so scarce that a stretch of lagoon can turn into a stretch of sea). This is precisely the risk which is currently threatening the lagoon.

The tide, lifeblood of the lagoon

Tidal changes occur every six hours, fluctuating between two high points per day. Sea water is drawn into the lagoon through the three ports, flushing "new" water in and "old" water out – assisted by a current from the rivers on the opposite side. Parts affected by these tides are thereby known as the **laguna viva** (living lagoon), whereas the sections little affected by this lifeline are referred to as the **laguna morta** (dead lagoon). These outlying parts tend towards marsh, channelled with canals, fishing banks and diked lakes built by and for the fishing industry.

The tide, destroyer of the lagoon

The health of the lagoon is totally dependent upon the influx of "new" water brought by the tides: however, the inflow of fresh water provided by the rivers that once maintained saline levels has been greatly reduced as the rivers have progressively been diverted. This has also reduced the strength of current across the lagoon and allowed vast quantities of polluting material to be deposited.

In the 20C the problem was exacerbated by the growth of industrial sites around

Mestre and Porto Maghera accommodating petrol-tankers with obvious implications on the environment of the lagoon. The reduction in oxygenated water flowing through the canals of Venice is gradually eroding the ability of plant and marine life to survive.

Tidal flooding

The tide along these coasts can fluctuate wildly; for it to be classified as tidal flooding its level has to reach or exceed 1.10m/3ft 6in. The last such occurrence happened on 4 November 1966 when consequences were felt way beyond the shores of Venice – the Arno overflowed in Florence with tragic results. That year an alarming prediction was rumoured that Venice might possibly disappear – fortunately, radical action against further subsidence, including the closure of artesian wells on the mainland, have proved the prophecy false.

Similar crises of this kind are documented as far back as 589. Contemporary personal accounts are terrifying. **Paolo Diacono** (c 720-99) wrote of the first flood tide: "non in terra neque in aqua sumus viventes" (neither on earth nor in water were we alive). Records from 1410 state that "almost one thousand people coming from the fair at Mestre and other places drowned".

Since the 17C the water level of the Venetian lagoon has dropped by 60cm/24in. In past centuries, once every five years, the tide would rise above the dampproof foundations made of Istrian stone that were built to protect the houses against salt deposits. Nowadays, in the lower areas, these foundations are immersed in water more than 40 times in a single year and the buildings can do very little to stall the degradation.

Flora and fauna

The fish are the lagoon's real treasure, in their distinctive shoals on the sandbanks. At the lower end of the food chain are a variety of molluscs and at at the other end is man, seeking to exploit such rich resources.

Crab and **shrimp** are central to the fishing industry and to Venetian cuisine.

From a boat it soon becomes obvious where the fishing banks are situated as these attract various species of aquatic birds: **wild duck** (mallard and teal), tens of thousands of **coots**, **herons** and **marsh harriers**. The very rich bird life of the lagoon also includes the little **egret**, recognisable by its elegant carriage and startlingly white feathers with which ladies adorned themselves at the beginning of the 20C.

Among the mammals **rodents** provides a somewhat harmful presence. The rat, the so-called *pantagena*, is at home anywhere, on the city squares as well as in rubbish dumps and attics.

The sandbanks are abundantly cloaked in vegetation: **glasswort, sea lavender** and **asters** turn the mounds first green, then red, then blue, then grey. Rooted in the water are various **reeds** and **rushes** with long stalks and colourful spiky flowers.

Visit

▶ *Following the coastline, departing from Grado and finishing in Chioggia. 220km/132mi.*

Grado ▩ ▩

At the time of the barbarian invasions the inhabitants of Aquileia founded Grado which was from the 5C to the 9C the residence of the Patriarchs of Aquileia. Today Grado is a busy little fishing port and seaside resort with a growing reputation. The town situated in the middle of the lagoon is an imposing sight.

Quartiere vecchio★

This is a picturesque district with a network of narrow alleys (*calli*) running between the canal port and the cathedral. The Duomo di Santa Eufemia, is on the basilical plan and dates from the 6C. It has marble columns with Byzantine capitals, a 6C mosaic pavement, a 10C ambo and a valuable silver-gilt **altarpiece**★, a Venetian work of the 14C. Beside the cathedral a row of sarcophagi and tombs leads up to the 6C basilica of Santa Maria delle Grazie which has some original mosaics and fine capitals.

Address Book

&For coin ranges see the Legend on the cover flap.

WHERE TO EAT

⌐Al Bragosso del Bepi el Ciosoto – Via Romea 120 – 30010 Sant'Anna di Chioggia – 8km/5mi south of Chioggia on S 309 Romea – ☎041 49 50 395 – Closed Wed, Jan – ▤. The counter and bar made out of an old boat set the scene in this lovely trattoria which specialises in fish. The dishes are prepared with the freshest of ingredients, all of an excellent quality. The prices are very reasonable. Also has accommodation.

⌐Da Luigi – Via Dante 25 – 30020 Torre di Fine – 40km/24mi northeast of Venice – ☎0421 23 74 07 – Closed Wed (except Jun-Aug), Oct – ▤ – 10 rm. This trattoria is renowned for its traditional, homely cooking. Great care is taken to use produce of a high quality. The seafood dishes alla griglia are excellent. Also has rooms which are simply furnished but comfortable.

⌐La Colombara – Via Zilli 42 – 33051 Aquileia – 2km/1mi northwest of Aquileia – ☎0431 91 513 – www.lacolombara. it – Closed Mon. Although it is off the beaten track, this fish restaurant is well worth the detour. Cooked with great attention to detail and a lightness of touch, the dishes are always prepared with the freshest ingredients. Rustic-style decor and a welcoming atmosphere. Pleasant outside dining area.

WHERE TO STAY

⌐Hotel Cristina – Viale Martiri della Libertà 11 – 34073 Grado – ☎0431 87 64 48 – www.hotelcristinagrado.com – Closed Oct-May – ℗ – 26 rm ⌷ – Restaurant. More of a guesthouse than a hotel, in a panoramic setting. The 1970s feel extends to the public areas as well as the rooms. Lots of outdoor areas for lounging around. Meals served outside in summer. Authentic, homely cooking.

⌐⌐Hotel Park – Lungomare Adriatico 74 – 30019 Lido di Sottomarina – 10km/6mi east of Chioggia – ☎041 49 07 40– Fax 041 49 01 11 – ℗▤ – 41 rm – ⌷ – Restaurant. A simple, family-run establishment situated right on the beach. It has a restaurant, a private bathing area, spacious, simple rooms.

⌐⌐Eurotel – Calle Mendelssohn 13, at Lignano Riviera – 33054 Lignano Sabbiadoro – 7km/4mi southwest of Lignano Sabbiadoro – ☎0431 42 89 92 – Fax 0431 42 87 31 – ⌧ – 70 rm ⌷. One of the main attractions of this 1970s-style hotel is its peaceful, verdant setting. The rooms are spacious and most of them have a small cooking area. Private beach and swimming pool. Free lounger and umbrella for guests staying on a weekly basis.

Aquileia

www.aquileia.it.
While the town site was being outlined with a plough (181 BC), according to Roman custom, an eagle (aquila) hovered overhead: hence its name. Aquileia was a flourishing market, used as general headquarters by Augustus during his conquest of the Germanic tribes. The town then became one of Italy's most important patriarchates (554-1751), ruled by bishops.

Basilica★★

🕙Open Apr-Sep 9am-7pm, Oct-Mar 9am-1pm and 2.30-5.30pm. ⌐Crypts: 2.60€; bell tower 1€. ☎0431 91 19 (office).

The Romanesque church was built in the 11C on the foundations of a 4C building and restored in the 14C. Preceded by a porch, it is flanked by a campanile.

The interior with its nave and two aisles is in the form of a Latin cross. The splendid 4C mosaic **paving**★★, which is one of the largest and richest in western Christendom, depicts religious scenes. The timber ceiling and the arcades are both 14C, the capitals are Romanesque and the decoration of the transept Renaissance. The 9C Carolingian crypt known as **Cripta degli affreschi** is decorated with fine Romanesque **frescoes**★★.

The **Cripta degli Scavi** is reached from the north aisle. Finds from the excavations are assembled here, notably admirable 4C mosaic **paving**★★.

Aree archeologiche★

&⊙*Open daily, 8.30am to 1hr before dusk.* ⊙*Closed 1 Jan, 25 Dec.* ⊗*No charge.* ☎*0431 91 016; www.museoarcheo-aquileia.it Museo Paleocristiano:* ⊙*Open daily 8.30am-1.45pm.* ⊙*Closed 1 Jan, 25 Dec.* ☎*0431 91 131; www.museoarcheo-aquileia.it.*

Excavations have uncovered the remains of Roman Aquileia: behind the basilica, the Via Sacra leading to the river port, houses and the forum. The **Musei Archeologico e Paleocristiano** (Archaeological and Early-Christian Museums) contain an important collection of finds from local excavations.

Lignano♨♨

▶*Stretching east from the mouth of the Tagliamento, it closes off part of the Marano Lagoon, an angling reserve. www.lignano.it*

Lignano, the largest seaside resort on the coastline of Friuli, lies on a long, sandy peninsula covered with pine woods. Its **beach**★★, facing Grado, the Trieste Gulf and the coastline of Istria (which is often visible), is popular for its 8km/5mi of fine, golden sand; it is a nice Kids **holiday resort for families** with children.

Lignano Riviera gets its name from the nearby Tagliamento. Inland, holidaymakers can enjoy the 18-hole golf course and visit the zoo, the Kids **Parco zoo Punta Verde**, which presents animals from all over the world. &⊙*Open Feb-Oct.* ⊗*9€. For information on opening times, call* ☎*0431 42 87 75; www.parcozoopuntaverde.it*

Venezia★★★ &*see VENEZIA.*

Chioggia

www.chioggiatourism.it

Strictly speaking, Chioggia is not one of the lagoon islands, resting as it does on two parallel islands, linked to terra firma by a long bridge.

La città

The main street, the **Corso del Popolo**, runs parallel to the Canale della Vena – the Fossa Clodia of ancient times – rendered more colourful and lively by its fish market, to terminate in Piazzetta Vigo. The column bearing a winged lion marks the end of the Fossa Clodia. To cross the canal, walk over the stone bridge, the Ponte Vigo built in 1685.

The corso is dotted with the **Duomo**★, dedicated to Santa Maria Assunta, which was founded in the 11C, and several of the Chioggia churches.

The **Isola di San Domenico** (promontory) extends at the far end of Chioggia and is reached by following Calle di San Croce.

L'AQUILA★

POPULATION 69 161
MICHELIN MAP 563 O 22 – L
LOCAL MAP IN THE MICHELIN ATLAS ITALY – ABRUZZI.

Overlooked by Gran Sasso, the highest massif in the Abruzzi region, this rather austere town boasts both a long history and a wealth of artistic treasures. Equally enticing are its charming buildings and the intriguing legends surrounding its mysterious past.

- **Information:** Piazza Santa Maria di Paganica 5. ☎0862 41 08 08. www.comune laquila.it, www.abruzzoturismo.it.
- **Orient Yourself:** L'Aquila lies at the heart of the Abruzzi, off A 24.
- **Don't Miss:** Basilica di Santa Maria di Collemaggio, Chiesa di San Bernardino.
- **Organizing Your Time:** The town can be comfortably seen in half a day.
- **Also See:** *ABRUZZO.*

A Bit of History

According to legend, L'Aquila was founded in the 13C when the inhabitants of 99 castles in the valley at the foot of the Gran Sasso joined forces to form a city in which each castle had a corresponding church, square and fountain. Caught up in the vicissitudes of the Kingdom of Naples, L'Aquila was besieged, destroyed and rebuilt several times until it became the second most important city of the Kingdom in the 15C. Rich in splendid monuments, it also had a resurgence thanks to the commerce all over Europe of saffron, "red gold", which grows on the plateaux of Navelli. This was the period in which St Bernardino of Siena (who died in L'Aquila in 1444) resided in the city; the initials IHS (Iesus Hominum Salvator – Jesus Saviour of Mankind) marked on several doorways, bear witness to his presence.

Visit

Basilica di Santa Maria di Collemaggio★★

⏱*Open daily, 8am-12.30pm and 3.30-7.30pm.* ☎*0862 42 08 84; www.aquila. infn.it/aquila.*
Begun in 1287, the basilica was constructed in the Romanesque style on the initiative of Pietro da Morrone, the future Pope **Celestine V**, who was crowned there in 1294. The ample, horizontally crenellated **façade**★★, beautifully adorned with geometrical patterns in white and pink stone, is pierced with

---

Abdication

Pietro da Morrone (1215-96), hermit and founder of the Celestine order of the Morronese Abbey near Sulmona, was unexpectedly elected pope in September of 1294. Overwhelmed by the intrigues and plots of the pontifical court, Pope Celestine V abdicated after only a few months and was banished to the castle of Fumone by his successor, Boniface VIII. He died there shortly afterwards and in 1313 was canonised by Pope Clement V.

---

rose windows and doorways added in the 15C. On the left side of the basilica stands the **Porta Santa**, a beautiful richly decorated Romanesque doorway. The interior contains the 16C Lombard Renaissance-style tomb of Pope Saint Celestine V.

Chiesa di San Bernardino★★

⏱*Open daily, 6.30-11.45am and 3.30-6.30pm (7.30pm in summer).* ✏*No charge.* ☎*0862 22 255.*
This superb church, a masterpiece of **Cola dell'Amatrice** (1527), has a majestic and rich **façade**★★ which is articulated by entablatures that give definition to the three orders of double columns (Ionic, Doric and Corinthian). The spacious and well-lit interior, in the form of a Latin cross, is roofed with a lovely Baroque wooden ceiling and contains the **mausoleum of St Bernardino**★ which is adorned with figures by the local sculptor, Silvestro dell'Aquila, as is the elegant **tomb**★ of Maria Pereira.

Castello★

♿ ⏱ *Museum: Open daily except Mon 9am-8pm. Closed 1 Jan, 1 May, 25 Dec.* ✏*4€.* ☎*0862 63 32 39.*
Built in the 16C to by Pirro Luigi Escribà who also designed Castel Sant'Elmo in Naples, this square castle, reinforced with powerful bastions, is a good example of 16C military architecture. The great rooms now house a museum, the **Museo Nazionale d'Abruzzo**★★. On display on the ground floor are the **Archidiskodon Meridionalis Vestinus**, the fossil remains of an ancestor of the elephant that lived about one million years ago, and some interesting exhibits from Abruzzi in Roman times, including the **Calendario Amiterno.** On the first floor the section on **Sacred Art** (12C-17C) constitutes the core of the museum and displays some significant examples of painting, sculpture and decorative arts of the Abruzzi region. Among these it is worth noting the polychrome wooden sculptures, the **Croce processionale-**★by Nicola di Guardiagrele, a masterpiece of workmanship in gold, and the wooden statue depicting St Sebastian by Silvestro d'Aquila.

LECCE★★

POPULATION 83 137
MICHELIN MAP 564 F 36 – PUGLIA.

Nicknamed "the Baroque Florence", the town boasts a profusion of incredibly decorative buildings. At night, decked in lights, it resembles a sumptuous theatrical set. Lecce was in Roman times the prosperous town of Lupiae. The Normans greatly favoured the town and made it the capital of the region known as Terra d'Otranto. From the 16C to the 18C, Lecce knew a period of great splendour during which it was embellished with Renaissance, Rococo and Baroque monuments. The local finely grained limestone was particularly easy to work, and the town's numerous Baroque buildings are remarkable for the abundance of decorative work. The most inventive artists came from the Zimbalo family: their work is to be found in both churches and palaces and is widespread throughout the Salentina Peninsula.

- **Information:** Corso Vittorio Emanuele 43. ☎0832 24 80 92. www.comune.lecce.it; www.pugliaturismo.com.
- **Orient Yourself:** Lecce is set in the very heart of the Salento region, off S 613.
- **Don't Miss:** The historic Baroque centre and the sumptuously decoration of the Basilica di Santa Croce.
- **Organizing Your Time:** Allow a day for the town and excursions.
- **Also See:** *PUGLIA*.

Baroque Lecce★★

The historic centre, once surrounded by ramparts (16C), of which only traces remain, and a **castle** (built by Charles V on an existing Angevin fort), is now delineated by a ring of avenues. The heart of the city is the lively **Piazza S. Oronzo** which is dominated by a statue of the patron saint on top of one of the two columns that mark the end of the

Address Book

WHERE TO STAY

Hotel Delle Palme – *Via di Leuca 90* – ☎*0832 34 71 71* – *www.hoteldellepalmelecce.it* – – *96 rm* – *Restaurant*. A stone's throw from the historic town centre, this hotel has a Spanish feel to it – lots of wood and leather fixtures and fittings. The rooms are spacious, with wrought-iron beds and painted furniture.

Hotel Cristal – *Via Marinosci 16* – ☎*0832 37 23 14* – *www.hotelcristal. it* – – *65 rm* . An ultra-modern establishment – all glass and cement. The rooms are large and the public areas are very spacious and comfortable with brightly coloured decor and furnishings. The hotel is located not far from the historic centre.

WHERE TO EAT

Trattoria Casareccia-Le Zie – *Via Costadura 19* – ☎*0832 24 51 78* – *Closed Sun evening and Mon, 24 Dec-6 Jan, 30 Aug-15 Sep*. A simple, old-fashioned trattoria. Well run with a welcoming, family atmosphere. Delicious, authentic home cooking. All dishes are freshly prepared on the premises. Represents value for money.

Villa G.C. della Monica – *Via SS. Giacomo e Filippo 40* – – ☎*0832 45 84 32* – *Closed Tue, 10-30 Jan, 30 Jul-6 Aug* – . Housed in a 16C palazzo in the historic centre, this is one of the town's most renowned restaurants, as famous for its architectural features as its cuisine – the elegant dining rooms have vaulted ceilings and marble fireplaces. Traditional-style dishes.

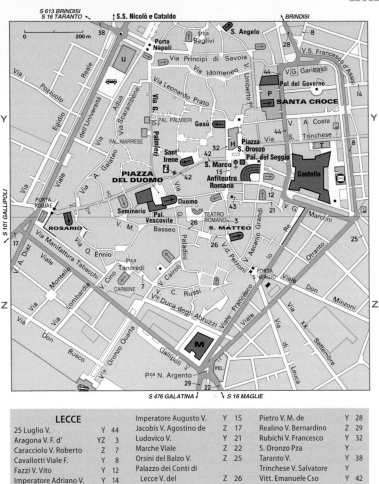

Appian Way, the other being in Brindisi (see BRINDISI).

To the south side of the square, parts of a **Roman amphitheatre** (2C), originally double tiered, have been unearthed. Also in the piazza are the small church of **San Marco**, attributed to Gabriele Riccardi and built by the Venetian colony, and the very old **palazzo del Seggio** which temporarily houses a papier mâché statue of San Giuseppe Patriarca (19C).

Basilica di Santa Croce★★

Several architects worked on this basilica in the 16C and 17C and it constitutes the best example of the Baroque style of Lecce. The façade is sumptuously decorated without being overbearing (the lower part is Renaissance in structure). The upper storey is almost without doubt the work of Zimbalo and is richly ornamented. The two storeys are linked by a long balcony held up by animal atlantes and caryatids while the parapet is adorned with cherubs holding mitres and books. The central rose window above seems as if it were fashioned by an expert lace-maker. The **interior** is light and airy and reminiscent of the Florentine Renaissance idiom. There is also abundant Baroque decoration of great delicacy. The side chapel at the end of the north aisle contains a fine **high altar** with low reliefs by Francesco Antonio Zimbalo and depicts scenes from the life of Francesco da Paola.

Palazzo del Governo

Adjoining the basilica the Governor's residence, a former Celestine monastery, has a rusticated façade with a frieze above and intricately decorated window surrounds, especially at first-floor level, designed by Zimbalo (ground floor) and Cino.

Chiesa del Gesù (or del Buon Consiglio)

The austere style of this church, built by the Jesuits (1575-79), makes a stark contrast to the other churches in Lecce. Inside is an ornate **Baroque altar**★.

Chiesa di Sant'Irene

Built by Francesco Grimaldi for the monks of the Theatine order, this church has lavish **Baroque altars** that are attributed to Francesco Antonio Zimbalo.

Piazza del Duomo★★

Enclosed in a homogeneous body of Baroque buildings and heralded by an arch facing Corso Vittorio Emanuele, this is one of the most remarkable squares in southern Italy. To the left, the **campanile** (1661-82) and the adjacent **Duomo** (1659-82) are by Giuseppe Zimbalo, the 17C **Palazzo Vescovile** and the **Seminario**, dating from 1709, by Giuseppe Cino. In the courtyard of the latter there is an ornately decorated **well**★ by the same sculptor.

Duomo

The first sighting of the Duomo is in fact of the north side. It is the most ornate façade of the church with its imposing entrance and arcade with a statue of St Oronzo. The main façade (visible from the square) is more restrained. Inside, the **crypt**, rebuilt in the 16C on an existing medieval structure, is held up by 92 columns with capitals adorned by figures of animals.

Chiesa del Rosario (or di San Giovanni Battista)★

This church was Giuseppe Zimbalo's last work and the façade features an abundance of decoration.

The **interior**★ is adorned with richly-embellised Baroque altars and some fine 17C altarpieces.

Via Palmieri

Several elegant buildings border this street; particularly noteworthy are the ones at Piazza Falconieri, Palazzo Marrese and Palazzo Palmieri (18C). At the end of the street, **Porta Napoli** (or Arco di Trionfo) was built in the 16C in honour of Charles V.

Chiesa di Sant'Angelo

Although unfinished, this façade is typical of Zimbalo's style (1663), with garlands, cherubs and angels.

Chiesa di San Matteo★

This church with its harmonious façade by Achille Carducci (1667-1700) shows the distinct influence of Borromini and his Roman work, the church of San Carlo alle Quattro Fontane.

Visit

Museo Provinciale Sigismondo Castromediano★

&⟳*Open 9am-1.30pm and 2.30-7.30pm, Sun and public holidays 9am-1.30pm only.* ☎*0832 68 35 03; www.musei.it.*

Housed in a modern building, the museum has a rich archaeological section (*ground floor*) and a very important **ceramics collection**★★ (*first floor*). Of particular interest are the Attic vases decorated with red figures. There is also a collection of epigraphs of various origins and two beautiful bronze statues (a figure of a woman and a priest). There is an art gallery on the third floor.

Excursion

Abbazia di Santa Maria di Cerrate★

14km/9mi north on the road to Brindisi, then turn right. &⟳*Open daily 9am-1.30pm and 2.30-7.30pm, Sun and public holidays 9am-1.30pm only.* ⟳*Closed Mon, 1 and 6 Jan, 1 May, 25 Apr, 25 Dec.* ☎*0832 36 11 76.*

This enchanting Benedictine abbey, in its isolated country setting, dates back to the 12C. The **church**★ enclosed on the north side by a fine portico with capitals embellished with figurative scenes (13C) has an elegant doorway whose vault is decorated with scenes from the New Testament. The interior retains part of the frescoes that probably once covered its entire surface. Some fresco fragments are conserved in the **Museo delle Tradizioni Popolari**. The museum also has displays of traditional wares such as oil-presses (the abbey has an underground olive-press).

LUCCA★★★

POPULATION 82 605

MICHELIN MAP 563 K 13 –

SEE ALSO THE GREEN GUIDE TUSCANY.

Situated in the centre of a fertile plain, Lucca has preserved within its girdle of ramparts a rich heritage of churches, palaces, squares and streets that give the town a charming air, unscathed by contemporary developments.

▸ The ramparts (4km/2.5mi long) extend all the way round the old town. They were built in the 16C and 17C and include 11 bastions, linked by curtain walls, and four gateways.

▸ **Information:** Piazza S. Maria 35. ☏0583 91 99 31. www.lucca.turismo.toscana.it; www.comune.lucca.it. Piazza S. Maria 35. b0583 91 99 31.

▸ **Orient Yourself:** Lucca is situated 74km/44mi from Florence and 20km/12mi from Viareggio.

▸ **Parking:** Lucca has a number of car parks located just inside the ramparts.

▸ **Don't Miss:** An atmospheric walk through old Lucca, a visit to the Duomo and Chiesa di San Michele in Foro and the magnificent 17C gardens at Villa Reale di Marlia.

▸ **Organizing Your Time:** Take half a day to explore Lucca, and a day to visit the villas.

▸ **Also See:** *COLLODI, GARFAGNANA, MONTECATINI TERME, PESCIA, PISA, PISTOIA, VERSILIA.*

A Bit of History

Lucca was colonised by the Romans in the 2C BC and it has retained the plan of a Roman military camp, with the two principal streets perpendicular to one another

During the Middle Ages a complicated system of narrow alleys and oddly shaped squares was added to the original network. The town became an independent commune at the beginning of the 12C and flourished until the mid-14C with the silk trade as its main activity. In the early 14C the town enjoyed a great period of prosperity and prestige under the control of the mercenary soldier and leader Castruccio Castracani (d 1328). Lucca's finest religious and secular buildings date from this period. Luccan architects adopted the Pisan style to which they added their own characteristic refinement and fantasy.

From 1550 onwards the town became an important agricultural centre and with this new prosperity came a renewed interest in building. The countryside was dotted with villas, the town encircled by ramparts and most of the houses were either rebuilt or remodelled.

In the early 19C, Elisa Bonaparte ruled the city for a brief period from 1805 to 1813. Following Napoleon's Italian campaigns he bestowed the titles of Princess of Lucca and Piombino on his sister. She showed a remarkable aptitude for public affairs and ruled her fief with wisdom and intelligence, encouraging the development of the town and the arts.

The Legend of the Holy Cross

The Volto Santo (Holy Visage) is a miraculous Crucifix kept in the cathedral. It is said that after Christ had been taken down from the Cross, Nicodemus saw the image of his face on it. The Italian Bishop Gualfredo, when on pilgrimage in the Holy Land, succeeded in tracing the Volto Santo and embarked in a boat without a crew or sails which drifted ashore on the beach at Luni, near La Spezia. As the worshippers at Luni and Lucca disputed possession of the Holy Image, the Bishop of Lucca had it placed on a cart drawn by two oxen; they immediately set off towards Lucca.

The fame of the Volto Santo, spread by merchants from Lucca, gained ground throughout Europe.

Walking About

Città vecchia

The streets and squares of old Lucca are full of atmosphere with their Gothic and Renaissance palaces, the towers of the nobility, old shops, sculptured doorways and coats of arms, wrought-iron railings and balconies. Starting from **Piazza San Michele**, follow Via Roma and Villa Fillungo to **Piazza del Anfiteatro** situated inside the Roman amphitheatre. From here go towards Piazza San Pietro (12C-13C church) and then take Via Guinigi where at No 29 stands Casa dei Guinigi with its **tower** (**panorama**★ of the town from the top) crowned with trees, which rises above the great façade with its Gothic windows. The houses opposite at Nos 20 and 22 also belonged to the Guinigi family. *For opening times, call.* ☎*0583 31 68 46.*

Continue to the Romanesque church of **Santa Maria Forisportam**, so-called because it stood outside the Roman walls. Via Santa Croce, Piazza dei Servi and Piazza dei Bernardin lead back to Piazza San Michele.

Visit

Duomo★★

The cathedral, dedicated to St Martin, was rebuilt in the 11C. The exterior was remodelled almost entirely in the 13C, as was the interior in the 14C and 15C. The strength and balance of the green and white marble **façade**★★, designed by the architect Guidetto da Como, is striking despite its asymmetry. The upper section with its three superimposed galleries is the first example of the

Piazza dell'Anfiteatro

Address Book

WHERE TO STAY

⊜**Ostello San Frediano** – *Via della Cavallerizza 12 – Lucca* – ☎*0583 46 99 57* – *www.ostellolucca.it* – ⊠♿ – *140 rm* – ⊡. This hotel is part of the former Real Collegio and is adjacent to the church of San Frediano. With all the comforts of a hotel but at guesthouse prices. The public areas are comfortable and spacious, and there is also a lovely garden area. Perfect for relaxing and winding down after a tiring day tramping round the historic centre.

⊜⊜**Piccolo Hotel Puccini** – *Via di Poggio 9* – ☎*0583 55 421* – *www. hotelpuccini.com* – *14 rm* – ⊡. Not far from the church of San Michele in Foro, is this little hotel which prides itself on its Puccini memorabilia. A great place for soaking up the magical atmosphere of this historic town. The management and the staff are friendly and enthusiastic, and also extremely knowledgeable! Very clean.

⊜⊜**Albergo San Martino** – *Via Della Dogana 9* – ☎*0583 46 91 81* – *Fax 0583 99 19 40* – *www.albergosanmartino.it* – ▤♿ – *9 rm* – ⊡. A stone's throw from the Duomo, this hotel is ideally situated. The other main attraction are the spacious, airy rooms. The hotel has all modern amenities, with pleasant, modern furnishings. The staff are young and dynamic, just what you need to put a spring in your step. Guided tours of the town can be arranged.

WHERE TO EAT

⊜**Osteria Baralla** – *Via Anfiteatro 5/7/9* – ☎*0583 44 02 40* – *www.osteriabaralla. it* – *Closed Sun, mid-Jan to mid-Feb* – *Book*. A charming restaurant housed in what was the entrance to the servants' quarters in a medieval palazzo. There are two dining areas, one of which has a vaulted ceiling. The other room is smaller and more intimate. The menu changes daily and features typical Tuscan dishes.

⊜**Da Giulio-in Pelleria** – *Via delle Conce 45, Piazza S. Donato* – ☎*0583 55 948* – *Closed Mon, Sun (except May, Sep, Dec, 20-31 Dec* – *Book*. Historic trattoria where the large number of covers does not impact on the quality of the food. Regional cooking, and reasonable prices. Despite all the comings and goings, the atmosphere is pleasant and the service attentive.

TAKING A BREAK

Antico Caffè Di Simo – *Via Fillungo 58* – *– Open Apr-Oct 8-24; Nov-Mar, Tue-Sun 8am-8.30pm*. With origins dating back to 1846, this café has seen a number of great Italian artists pass through its doors, among them Puccini, Verdi and Leopardi. The perfect place for immersing yourself in the history and cultural life of Lucca, while sipping one of the house cocktails.

Gelateria Sergio Santini – *Piazza Cittadella 1 – Open Summer 9am-midnight; rest of the year, Tue-Sun 9am-8pm*. This is the place to head for if you fancy sitting out in the sun enjoying one of the best chocolate ice creams in town, listening to Puccini. The ice cream is all home-made. Other specialities include paciugo and panettone gelato.

EVENTS AND FESTIVALS

Every year, a most unusual commemorative procession, **Luminara di Santa Croce**, passes through the illuminated town after dark (⟲*see under Events and Festivals in the Practical Points section*).

Pisan Romanesque style (⟲*see PISA)* as it developed in Lucca; the idiom is characterised by lighter, less rigid lines and by inventive ornamentation. The ornate sculpture and marble-inlaid designs are of great interest.

The slim and powerful campanile harmoniously combines the use of brick and marble, and the number of openings increases with height.

The sculptural decoration of the porch is extremely rich: pillars with simply

carved columns, arcading, friezes and a variety of scenes.

The Gothic **interior** has elevations where the round-headed main arches with their robust piers contrast with the delicacy of the elegant triforium.

On the west wall of the Gothic **interior** is an unusual Romanesque sculpture of St Martin dividing his cloak. The classical and sober lines of this sculpture herald the style of Nicola Pisano. In the north aisle is the lovely shrine (*tempietto*) built by the local artisan Matteo Civitali (1436-1501) to house the Volto Santo. The great 12C **figure**★ of Christ in wood blackened through time shows a distinctly Oriental influence because of its hieratic aspect. It is said to be a copy of the legendary holy image.

In the sacristy is one of the masterpieces of Italian funerary sculpture by the Sienese artist, Jacopo della Quercia (1406): the **tomb of Ilaria del Carretto**★★, wife of Paolo Guinigi, lord of Lucca in the early 15C. The recumbent figure wears a long, draped robe and at her feet lies a dog, a symbol of fidelity.

Other works of art include a *Presentation of the Virgin in the Temple* by Bronzino *(north aisle)* and the large-scale **Last Supper**★ with its subtle lighting by Tintoretto *(south aisle)*.

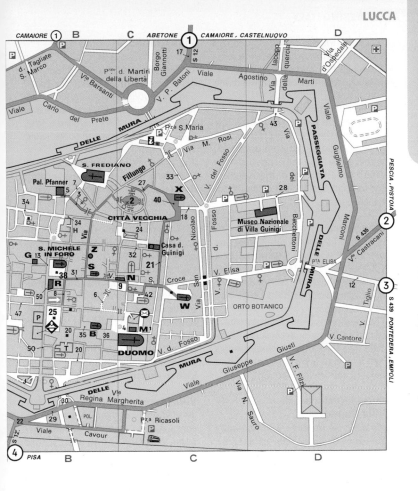

Chiesa di San Michele in Foro★★

The white mass of the 12C-14C church on the site of the Roman forum dominates the adjoining square which is lined by old mansions and the Palazzo Pretorio.

The exceptionally tall **façade**★★ (the nave itself was to have been taller) is a good example of Lucca-Pisan style, despite the fact that the lower part was remodelled in the last century.

The four superimposed galleries surmount blind arcarding and are decorated with varied motifs. At the top, two instrument-playing angels flank a statue of the Archangel Michael slaying the dragon.

The simplicity of the Romanesque **interior** is a direct contrast to the ornate exterior. On the first altar of the south aisle is a **Madonna**★ by Andrea della Robbia. The south transept is adorned with a lovely **painting**★ with brilliant colours by Filippino Lippi.

Chiesa di San Frediano★

This great church, dedicated to St Frigidian, was rebuilt in the original Lucca-Romanesque style in the 12C before the influence of the Pisan school was felt. The sober façade is faced with marble from the Roman amphitheatre. The upper middle section, remodelled in the 13C, is dominated by a Byzantine-style mosaic of the Ascension by local artists.

The interior comprises a nave and two aisles with wooden ceilings (flanked by lovely Renaissance and Baroque side chapels) on the plan of the Early-Christian basilicas: the nave, which ends in a semi-circular apse, is articulated by a number of antique columns that are crowned with fine capitals.

To the right on entering is a curious Romanesque **font**★ (12C) with low reliefs depicting the story of Moses. The Chapel of Sant'Agostino is decorated with frescoes by the Ferraran painter Amico Aspertini: one of these depicts the translation of the Volto Santo from Luni to Lucca.

Pinacoteca

Open Tue-Sat 8.30am-7.30pm, Sun and public holidays 8.30am-1.30pm. Closed Mon, 1 Jan, 1 May, 25 Dec. 4€; 6.50 € combined ticket with Museo Nazionale Villa Guinigi. ☎0583 55 570; www.comune.lucca.it.

The apartments of this 17C palace have remarkable interior decoration★ (17C-18C). The Pinacoteca includes works by 17C Italian artists (Salimbeni and Barocci) and foreign paintings.

Museo Nazionale di Villa Guinigi

Via della Quarquonia. *Open daily 9am-2pm.* *Closed Mon, 1 Jan, 1 May, 15 Aug, 25 Dec.* 4€; *6.50€ combined ticket with Palazzo Mansi.* ☎0583 46 033; www.comune.lucca.it.

The villa which once belonged to Paolo Guinigi now contains archaeological, sculpture (Romanesque, Gothic and Renaissance) and painting (Lucca and Tuscany) sections. There are remarkable panels of intarsia work.

Excursions

Villa Reale di Marlia

▶*8km/5mi north.* *Garden only.* *Open Mar-Nov for guided visits only.* *Closed Mon.* 6€. *For information* ☎0583 30 108; www.parcovillareale.it.

The Villa Reale is surrounded by 17C **gardens**★★ modified by Elisa Bonaparte. Unusual features include a lemon grove, a 17C nymphaeum and an open-air theatre.

Villa Grabau

▶*Near the Villa di Marlia.* *Open Easter-July and Sept-Nov 10am-1pm and 2-6pm (July-Aug 3-7pm), Nov-Easter, Sun and public holidays 11.30am-1pm and 2.30-5.30pm .* *Closed Mon and Tue morning.* *Park and villa 6.50€, park only 5€.* ☎0583 40 60 98, www.villagrabau.it.

The villa stands in the centre of a particularly magnificent perspective which draws the eye from the entrance avenue to the Italian garden, and beyond.

Fountains with bronze mascarons and white marble statues add to the elegant appearance of the **park**★★, which covers an area of 9ha/22 acres and is, in reality, a botanical garden. The layout includes an outdoor theatre, an informal English garden with large trees and exotic plants, and an Italian garden, decorated with old 18C and 19C lemon trees in their original containers.

Other features include a winter greenhouse and an unusual 17C-18C **Lemon House.**

Villa Mansi

▶*At Segromigno, 11km/7mi to the northeast.* *Open 10am-7pm (summer) and 10am-1pm and 3-5pm (winter).* *Closed Mon, 24 Dec-6 Jan.* 7€. ☎0583 92 02 34; www.villamansi.it.

This 16C villa has a façade covered with statues and a park★ where statue-lined alleys lead to a lovely pool.

Villa Torrigiani (or di Camigliano)★

▶ *12km/8mi to the northeast. For admission times and charges, call* ☎0583 92 80 41; www.villelucchesi.net.

This 16C villa was converted in the 17C into a summer residence by Marques Nicolao Santini, ambassador of the Lucca republic to the Papal Court and the Court of Louis XIV. The gardens designed by Le Nôtre, are adorned with fountains, grottoes and nymphaea. The villa, which has a delightful Rococo facade, contains rooms adorned with frescoes.

MANTOVA★★
MANTUA
POPULATION 48 103
MICHELIN MAP 561 OR 562 G 14.

Mantua is set in a flat fertile plain, which was formerly marshland, on the south-eastern border of Lombardy. It is encircled to the north by three lakes formed by the slow-flowing River Mincio. This active and prosperous town has important mechanical and petrochemical industries. This region is also the number one hosiery producer worldwide.

- **Information:** Piazza Andrea Mantegna 6. ☎0376 32 82 53; www.comune.mantova.it.
- ▶ **Orient Yourself:** Mantua lies at the southeast corner of Lombardy. The main access roads are the A 22 Brennero pass and S 236 from Brescia
- **Don't Miss:** The lavish apartments of Palazzo Ducale and the dramatic Palazzo Te.
- **Organizing Your Time:** Allow a day.
- **Also See:** *VERONA*.

A Bit of History

Although, according to a legend quoted by Virgil, Mantua was founded by Monto, daughter of the divine Tiresias, its origins would seem to be Etruscan dating back to the 6C or 5C BC. It passed to the Gauls before becoming Roman in the 3C BC. In 70 BC **Virgil** (Publius Virgilius Maro), the great poet and author was born in the Mantua area. Author of the Aeneid, in which he recounts the wanderings of Aeneas, the exiled Trojan prince, and the foundation of the earliest settlement from which Rome was to spring, Virgil describes his beloved Mantuan countryside, with its soft, misty light, and the pleasures of rural life in his harmonious but melancholy style in the *Eclogues* or *Bucolica* and in the *Georgics*.

In the Middle Ages Mantua was the theatre for numerous struggles between rival factions that successively sacked the town, before it became an independent commune in the 13C and finally the domain of Luigi Gonzaga, nominated Captain General of the People. Under the **Gonzaga** family, who were enlightened rulers and patrons of the arts and letters, Mantua became an important intellec-

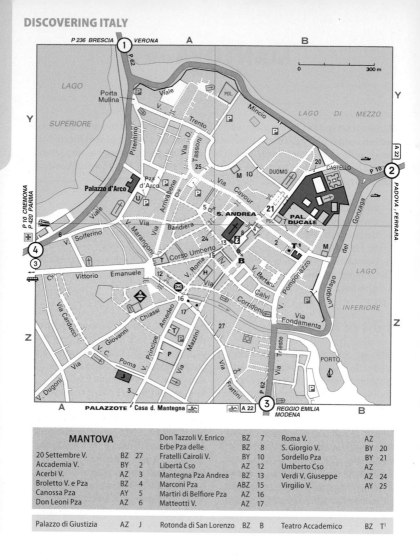

MANTOVA			Don Tazzoli V. Enrico	BZ	7	Roma V.	AZ	
			Erbe Pza delle	BZ	8	S. Giorgio V.	BY	20
20 Settembre V.	BZ	27	Fratelli Cairoli V.	BY	10	Sordello Pza	BY	21
Accademia V.	BY	2	Libertà Cso	AZ	12	Umberto Cso	AZ	
Acerbi V.	AZ	3	Mantegna Pza Andrea	BZ	13	Verdi V. Giuseppe	AZ	24
Broletto V. e Pza	BZ	4	Marconi Pza	ABZ	15	Virgilio V.	AY	25
Canossa Pza	AY	5	Martiri di Belfiore Pza	AZ	16			
Don Leoni Pza	AZ	6	Matteotti V.	AZ	17			

| Palazzo di Giustizia | AZ | J | Rotonda di San Lorenzo | BZ | B | Teatro Accademico | BZ | T¹ |

tual and artistic centre in northern Italy of the 15C and 16C. Thus Gian Francesco Gonzaga (ruled 1407-44) placed his children in the charge of the famous humanist Vittorio da Feltre (1379-1446) and commissioned the Veronese artist **Pisanello** (1395-1455) to decorate his ducal palace.

His son Ludovico III (1444-78), a mercenary army leader by profession, was a typical Renaissance patron: he gave land to the poor, built bridges and favoured artists. The Sienese humanist Politian (1454-94), the Florentine architect Leon Battista Alberti (1404-72) and the Pad-

uan painter **Andrea Mantegna** (1431-1506) all belonged to his court. Francesco II (1484-1519) married Isabella d'Este, a beautiful and wise woman who contributed to the fame of Mantua. Their son Federico II was made duke by the Emperor Charles V in 1530 and he commissioned the architect and artist **Giulio Romano** (1499-1546), Raphael's pupil, to embellish his native town; the artist worked on the ducal palace and cathedral and the Palazzo Te.

In 1627 Vicenzo II died without heirs and the succession passed to the Gonzaga-Nevers family, the cadet line.

The Habsburg Emperor Ferdinand II opposed the French succession, and in 1630 sent an army which sacked the town and then deserted it following a plague which decimated Milan and Lombardy (the background to these dramatic events is described in the novel I Promessi Sposi by Manzoni). The Gonzaga-Nevers, however, restored the fortunes of the town until 1707 when they were deposed. Mantua became part of the Austrian Empire which ruled until 1866, except for a period under Napoleonic rule (1787-1814), when it joined the Kingdom of Italy.

Visit

Palazzo Ducale★★★

Allow 1hr 30min. Open daily except Mon, 8.45am-6.30pm. Closed 1 Jan, 1 May, 25 Dec. 6.50€. 0376 35 21 00; www.mantovaducale.it.
The imposing Ducal Palace comprises buildings from various periods: the Magna Domus and the Palazzo del Capitano erected in the late 13C by the Bonacolsi, Lords of Mantua from 1272 to 1328; the Castello di San Giorgio, a 14C fortress, and other inner sections built by the Gonzaga in the 15C-16C, including the 15C Palatine chapel of Santa Barbara.

Apartments★★★

Start from the 17C Ducal Stairway, which gives access to the first floor. One of the first rooms displays *The Expulsion of the Bonacolsi and the Triumph of the Gonzaga on 16 August 1328* by Domenico Morone (1442-1517). The painting shows the medieval aspect of Piazza Sordello with the old façade of the cathedral. The **Pisanello rooms** on the first floor have fragments of frescoes and remarkable **sinopie**★★ (preparatory sketches using a red earth pigment), that were discovered in 1969 and are a good example of the refined and penetrating work of Pisanello. These lyrical scenes draw inspiration from the feats of the Knights of the Round Table and the fantastic and timeless world of medieval chivalry. The

Tapestry Room (Appartamento degli Arazzi), formerly known as the **Green Apartment** (Appartamento Verde), in the neo-Classical style, is hung with nine splendid Brussels tapestries after Raphael. The **Room of the Zodiac** (Camera dello Zodiaco) leads to the **Room of the Moors** (Stanzino dei Mori), in the Venetian style, and to the **Hall of the Rivers** (Sala dei Fiumi), which overlooks the **Hanging Garden** (Giardino Pensile). The giants depicted on the walls represents the rivers of Mantua. The **Corridor of the Moors** (Corridoio dei Mori) leads into the famous **Hall of Mirrors** (Sala degli Specchi) used for dancing and music. In the elegant **Room of the Archers** (Sala degli Arcieri), the antechamber to the ducal apartments, hang paintings by Rubens and Domenico Fetti. The **Ducal Apartments** (Appartamento Ducale) comprise a suite of rooms remodelled for Vincenzi I in the early 17C by Antonio Maria Viani, and including the Paradise Room (Appartamento del Paradiso) and the tiny Room of the Dwarfs (Appartamento dei Nani). The building known as the **Rustica** and the **Equestrian Court** (Cortile della Cavallerizza) are by Giulio Romano; the courtyard is lined by a **gallery**, Galleria della Mostra, built in the late 16C by Antonio Maria Viani to house Vicenzo I's art collection, and by the **Hall of the Months** (Galleria dei Mesi) erected by Giulio Romano.
In the **Castello di San Giorgio** you can see the **Room of the Spouses**★★★ (Camera degli Sposi) –so-called because this is where marriages were recorded – executed from 1465 to 1474 by **Andrea Mantegna**. The walls are covered with a celebrated cycle of frescoes that glorify the superb and refined world of the Gonzaga court. Mantegna creates an illusion of space with his knowledge of foreshortening and perspective and his skilful use of volume and materials. The painted *trompe l'oeil* and carved stucco decorations and garlands of foliage and fruits are also admirable.
On the north wall look for Ludovico II turned towards his secretary, and his wife Barbara seated full-face. The children cluster around their parents, as do

other members of the court, including an enigmatic dwarf.

On the west wall the fresco presents Ludovico with his son, Cardinal Francesco, against the background of a town with splendid monuments, which could well be Rome as imagined by Mantegna. Mantegna has portrayed himself as the figure in purple which can be glimpsed on the right of the dedication. His great mastery of trompe l'oeil culminates in the ceiling oculus from which gaze cupids and servants. This invention introduces a note of wry humour to this otherwise rather solemn ensemble.

Piazza Sordello★

This square, which was the centre of old Mantua, has retained its medieval aspect. To the west is the 13C Palazzo Bonacolsi – the tall Tower of the Cage (Torre della Gabbia) still bears on its façade the cage (gabbia) in which wrongdoers were exhibited – and the 18C Palazzo Vescovile where telamones adorn the 18C façade. To the east are the oldest buildings of the Palazzo Ducale: the Magna Domus and the crenellated Palazzo del Capitano.

On the north side stands the **Cathedral** (Duomo), which features varied elements and styles: the neo-Classical façade, the late-Gothic right wing and a Romanesque campanile. The 16C interior was designed by Giulio Romano.

Piazza Broletto

This was the centre of public life at the time of the commune (13C), when the Palazzo Broletto, a 13C communal palace was also built. On its façade it has a seated statue of Virgil (1225). At the right corner rises the Torre Comunale, a tower that was later converted into a prison.

Piazza delle Erbe★

&. ◑Open daily in summer 10am-1pm and 3-7 pm (Sat, Sun and public holiday 10am-7pm), rest of the year 10am-1pm and 2-6pm (Sat, Sun and public holidays 10am-6pm). ✆Donation recommended. ☎0376 32 22 97.

The Square of Herbs derives its name from a fruit and vegetable market. It is lined to the north by the rear façade of the Palazzo Broletto and to the east by the 13C Palazzo della Ragione, flanked by the 15C Clock Tower and the Romanesque church, the **Rotonda di San Lorenzo★**. Sober and elegant, this circular building has a colonnaded ambulatory with a loggia above and a dome crowning all.

Basilica di Sant'Andrea★

The basilica dedicated to St Andrew, built in the 15C to the plans of Alberti, is a masterpiece of the Italian Renaissance. The façade retains Classical architectural features: the tympanum, the triumphal arch, the niches between the pilasters. The **interior** has a single nave. The barrel vaulting and walls are painted in trompe-l'œil. The first chapel on the left contains the tomb of Mantegna. In the crypt two urns housed in a reliquary contain a relic of the Blood of Christ brought to Mantua by the Roman soldier Longinus.

Teatro Accademico

&. ◑Open daily 9.30am-12.30pm and 3-6pm. ◑Closed Mon, 1 Jan, 1 May, 15 Aug, 25 Dec. ✆3€. ☎0376 32 76 53; www.comune.mantova.it.

This pretty 18C theatre by Bibiena has a stage set in imitation marble with four architectural orders in pasteboard and a monochrome decor. The theatre welcomed the 13-year old Mozart on 13 December 1769, and is still used for concerts.

Palazzo d'Arco

◑Open Mar-Oct daily 10am-12.30pm and 2.30-6pm (rest of the year Sat, Sun and public holidays only, 10am-12.30pm and 2-5pm). ◑Closed Mon. ✆3€. ☎0376 32 22 42; www.museodarco.it.

This neo-Classical palace in the Palladian tradition (& see VICENZA) contains interesting collections of 18C and 19C furniture, paintings and ceramics.

Palazzo di Giustizia

The monumental façade of the Law Courts with caryatids is early 17C. At no 18 in the same street is Giulio Romano's house built in 1544 to his own designs.

Casa del Mantegna
47 Via Acerbi.
This rather severe-looking brick building was probably built to designs by Mantegna himself in 1476. It has a delightful courtyard.

Palazzo Te★★
&⊘*Open daily 9am-5.30pm, except Mon mornings.* ⊘*Closed 1 Jan, 1 May, 25 Dec.* ☞*8€.* ☎*0376 32 32 66.*
This large country mansion was built on the plan of a Roman house by Giulio Romano for Federico II from 1525 to 1535. It combines Classical features and melodramatic invention, such as the amazing "broken" entablature in the main courtyard, and is a major achievement of the Mannerist style.

The **interior** was ornately decorated by Giulio Romano and his pupils. In the **Room of the Horses** (Salone dei Cavalli), used for receptions, some of the finest horses from the Gonzaga stables are depicted. In the **Room of Psyche** (Sala di Psiche), used for banquets, the sensual and lively style of Guilio Romano is the best illustration of the hedonistic character of the palace. The frescoes in the **Room of the Giants** (Sala dei Giganti), the most celebrated room of the palace, depict the wrath of Jupiter against the Titans.

The overall decoration that covers the walls and vaulted ceiling creates an indefinite spatial illusion and the dome above gives a sense of artificiality in sharp contrast to the effect sought by Mantegna in the Camera degli Sposi in the Palazzo Ducale.

Excursions

Sabbioneta★
▶ *34km/20mi southwest of Mantua.*
⤏*Guided tours daily. For information on opening times for the Palazzo del Giardino, Teatro, Palazzo Ducale contact the tourist office* ☎*0375 22 10 44. For the*
Chiesa dell'Incoronata, contact the parish office at Via dell'Assunta 3, ☎*0375 52 035 or* ☎*0375 22 02 99; www.comune. sabbioneta.mn.it.*

The town was built from 1558 by Vespasiano Gonzaga (1531-91), a mercenary leader in the service of Philip II of Spain who conferred on his loyal servants the glorious order of The Golden Fleece. The order was created in 1429 by Phillip the Good, Duke of Burgundy. Vespasiano was a cultured man and he wanted to take personal charge of the construction of his ideal town. Its hexagonal walls and star plan and monuments make Sabbioneta a jewel of Italian Mannerism.

The **Garden Palace** (Palazzo del Giardino) was designed for festivities and its walls and ceilings were richly painted with frescoes by Bernardino Campi (1522-1591) and his school. The great **Galleria** (96m/315ft long) is one of the longest Renaissance galleries.

The **Olympic Theatre** (Teatro Olimpico), a masterpiece by Vicentino Scamozzi (1552-1616), was built from 1588 to 1590 and is one of the oldest covered theatres in Europe. The interior is decorated with frescoes by the school of Veronese and there is a ducal box adorned with statues of the gods.

The **Ducal Palace** (Palazzo Ducale), has finely carved wooden and coffered ceilings. There are interesting equestrian statues of the Gonzaga family. The Galleria degli Antenati is also noteworthy. Vespasiano Gonzaga is buried in the **church of the Incoronata** with its octagonal plan and dome. Vespasiano's mausoleum is adorned with a bronze statue by Leone Leoni (1509-90); he is depicted as Marcus Aurelius.

The **Museo d'Arte Sacra** displays the order of the **Golden Fleece** discovered in 1988 in Vespasiano's tomb (&*see above*) in the church.

The 19C **Synagogue** (Sinagoga) traces the story of the town's Jewish community whose legacy was the elegant printworks also used by Vespasiano.

MASSA MARITTIMA★★

POPULATION 8 810

MICHELIN MAP 563 M 14

SEE ALSO THE GREEN GUIDE TUSCANY.

The name Massa Marittima is believed by some to indicate that the territory formerly extended as far as the sea; others think it refers to the nearby Maremma region. This old medieval town stands in rolling countryside and blends harmoniously with the activities – mining, farming and craftwork – on which its prosperity has been based since its beginnings.

- **Information:** Via Todini 3/5. ☎0566 90 27 56. www.comune.massamarittima.gr.it.
- ▶ **Orient Yourself:** Massa Marittima is on the road that links Follonica with Siena.
- **Don't Miss:** The Duomo and the Abbazia and ermo di San Galgano.
- **Organizing Your Time:** Allow half a day.
- **Also See:** *SIENA.*

Visit

Piazza Garibaldi★★

This square is lined by fine medieval buildings, three of which are of Romanesque origin – Palazzo del Podestà with its many double-windowed bays, the crenellated Palazzo Comunale and the cathedral.

Duomo★★

The cathedral was probably built in the early 11C, and Gothic-style features were added in 1287 by **Giovanni Pisano**. The majestic building is adorned with blind arcades in the lower part and dominated by a fine campanile.

The interior, in the form of a Latin cross, comprises three aisles which are divided by two rows of columns crowned with capitals of different styles. The inside wall of the façade is decorated with striking pre-Romanesque low reliefs revealing the Byzantine influence (10C). There

is an unusual baptismal font (1267). In the chapel to the left of the choir stalls is the panel of the *Virgin of the Graces*, attributed to **Duccio di Buoninsegna** and the remains of the *Presentation of Christ at the Temple* by Sano di Pietro (1406-81).

Palazzo del Podestà

The 13C palace was the residence of the town's most eminent magistrate (*podestà*). The exterior is decorated with the cost of arms of the *podestà*. The building now houses the **Museo archeologico**, whose exhibits include an interesting stele by Vado dell'Arancio. The palace also houses the splendid Virgin in Majesty by Ambrogio Lorenzetti (1285-c 1348). ⏱*Open daily except Mon, Apr-Oct 10am-12.30pm and 3.30-7pm, Nov-Mar 10am-12.30pm and 3-5pm.* ⏱*Closed Mon, 1 Jan, 25 Dec.* ⊛*3€.* ☎*0566 90 22 89; www.coopcollinemet allifere.it.*

Museo della miniera

⚑*Guided tours only.* ⏱*Closed Mon, 1 Jan, 25 Dec.* ⊛*5€. For information on opening times, call*☎*0566 90 22 89; www. coopcollinemetallifere.it.*

The museum, which is situated near Piazza Garibaldi, evokes the mining activities in 700m/770yds of tunnels in the surrounding area; note the supporting timberwork and extraction techniques.

⊜⊜**Osteria da Tronca** – *Vicolo Porte 5 –* ☎*0566 90 19 91 – Closed Wed, 29 Dec-Feb –* ▤ *. The motto Amo talmente il vino che maledico chi mangia l'uva ("I love wine so much that damned be those who eat the grapes") leaves guests in no doubt as to what kind of establishment this is. Regional cooking, rustic-style interior and plenty to drink!*

Massa Marittima, a medieval jewel in the country

G. Bludzin/MICHELIN

Excursions

Abbazia and eremo di San Galgano★★

32km/20mi NE. www.sangalgano.info.
This ruined Gothic Cistercian Abbey, the first Gothic church in Tuscany, was built by monks from 1224 to 1288, and dedicated to **St Galgan** (1148-81). The monastery remains include cloisters, chapter house and scriptorium.

Grosseto

52km/31mi southeast.
This modern-looking provincial capital is situated in the fertile Ombrone Plain.

The old town is encircled with late-16C ramparts and their powerful bastions built by the Medici. There is an interesting **Museo Archeologico** (♿ 🕐 *open May-Oct, daily 10am-1pm and 5-8pm; Mar and Apr, daily 9.30am-1pm and 4.30-/pm; rest of year, Tue-Fri 9am-1pm, Sat-Sun and public holidays 9.30am-1pm and 4-7pm;* 🚫 *closed Mon, 1 Jan, 1 May, 25 Dec;* 💶 *5€;* ☎ *0564 48 87 50; www.archeologia-toscana.it).* The 13C abbey church of **San Francesco** contains small frescoes by the 14C Sienese school and a lovely painted 13C crucifix.

MATERA★★

POPULATION 59 144
MICHELIN MAP 564 E 31 – BASILICATA.

Matera overlooks a ravine separating it from the Murge Hills in Puglia. This provincial capital stands in the heart of a region dissected by deeply eroded gorges – a desolate landscape with wide horizons. Modern Matera, the town's centre of activity overlooks the lower town with its rock dwellings (sassi), now mostly abandoned. In the town and surrounding area there are some 130 churches hewn out of the rock. These date back to the 8C BC and the arrival of non-Latin monastic communities who settled locally. They were adept in this form of underground architecture which shows a Byzantine influence.

- 🅸 **Information:** Via De Viti de Marco 9. ☎ 0835 33 19 83. www.comune.matera.it, www.sassiweb.it.
- ▶ **Orient Yourself:** Matera lies in Basilicata, on S 7, Via Appia.
- 🙂 **Don't Miss:** A stroll down the panoramic Strada dei Sassi.
- 🕐 **Organizing Your Time:** Allow half a day.
- 🖐 **Also See:** *CALABRIA, PUGLIA.*

Visit

The Sassi★★

The two main cave-like quarters are on either side of the rock crowned by the cathedral. The roofs on some houses serve as walkways while the lower storeys are hewn out of the rock. Limwashed houses and stairways overhang one another in a labyrinth.

Strada dei Sassi★★

This panoramic street skirts the wild gorge and runs round the cathedral rock. The rock walls are riddled with both natural and man-made caves.

Duomo★

The cathedral was built in the 13C Apulian-Romanesque style; the façade has a lovely rose window and a projecting gallery above the single doorway. The walls are embellished with blind arcades. On the south side are two richly sculpted doorways. The interior was remodelled in the 17C and 18C. The Byzantine fresco portraying the Madonna dates from the 12C-13C and the Neapolitan crib is 16C. The **Chapel of the Annunciation**★ has a beautiful Renaissance decoration.

Chiesa di San Pietro Caveoso

For admission times and charges, call ☎0835 33 19 83; www.sassiweb.it.
This Baroque church stands at the foot of Monte Errone, which has several churches hewn out of the rock and decorated with frescoes.

Museo Nazionale Ridola

♿🕐*Open daily 9am-8pm.* 🕐*Closed Mon mornings, 1 Jan, 25 Dec.* ⌁*2.50€.* ☎*0835 31 00 58.*
This museum in a former monastery has an interesting collection of local archaeological finds.
👁 Views of Matera★★ from the two belvederes *(4km/2.4mi by the Altamura road, then take the Taranto road and finally turn right and follow the "chiese rupestri" – rock churches – signpost).*

MERANO★★
MERAN

POPULATION 35 119
MICHELIN MAP 562 B-C 15 – TRENTINO-ALTO ADIGE.

Merano is an important tourist centre and spa, whose thermal waters attract people seeking relief from respiratory problems, rheumatism and other conditions. Other attractions include the Gran Premio Ippico, the most famous steeplechase race in Italy. Cable cars and chairlifts rise up to Merano 2000, a winter sports centre, also popular for summer excursions into the mountains.

🄳 **Information:** Corso della Libertà 45. ☎0473 27 20 00. www.comune.merano.bz.it.
▸ **Orient Yourself:** Merano lies at the start of the upper valley of the Adige, the Val Venosta. There is a motorway link with Bolzano.
☺ **Don't Miss:** Views from Passeggiate Tappeiner and a drive through the pretty Val Venosta.
🕐 **Organizing Your Time:** Allow a day, and enjoy views and promenades along the Passeggiate d'Inverno and d'Estate at sunset.
👁 **Also See:** *BOLZANO.*

Visit

Passeggiate d'Inverno and d'Estate★★

These winter and summer promenades run along the Passirio River. The winter one, facing south, is lined with shops, cafés and terraces and is by far the busier. It is prolonged by the Passeggiata Gilf, which ends near a waterfall. The summer promenade, on the opposite bank, meanders through a park planted with pines.

Passeggiata Tappeiner★★

This promenade (4km/2.4mi long) winds above Merano with views to the Tyrol.

Duomo di San Nicolò

This Gothic cathedral has a huge belfry and a west front with a crenellated gable. The interior, roofed with beautiful ribbed **Gothic vaulting**★, includes two 15C stained-glass windows and two painted wooden **Gothic polyptychs**★(16C) by Knoller, a native of the Tyrol. In the neighbouring **Cappella di Santa Barbara** standing at the start of the old footpath leading to Tirolo is a 16C high relief of the Last Supper.

Via Portici (Laubengasse)★

This street is overlooked by houses with painted façades and oriel windows.

Castello Principesco★

&.&. ⊙*Open daily 10am-5pm.* ⊙*Closed Mon, Jan, Feb, 25 Dec.* ◎*2€; combined ticket with Museo Civico 3€.* ☎*0473 25 03 29; www.comune.merano.bz.it.*
This 14C castle was used by the Princes of Tyrol when they stayed in the town.

Excursions

Avelengo★

10km/6mi to the southeast.
A scenic road leads to the Avelengo Plateau, dominating the Merano valley.

Merano 2000※

Access by cable car from Val di Nova, 3km/1.9mi east. ⊙*Open Jun to 7 Nov*

and 8 Dec-30 Mar, daily, 8.30am-5pm. ☎*0473 23 48 21.*
This plateau is a winter sports centre. It also makes a good base for excursions into the mountains in summer.

Tirolo★

4km/2mi north. It can also be reached by ski lift from Merano.
This charming Tyrolean village is dominated by **Castel Tirolo,** built in the 12C by the Counts of Val Venosta. ⊙*Open May-Nov, daily except Mon, 10am-5pm.* ⊙*Closed in winter.* ◎*6€.* ☎*0473 22 02 21; www.schloss-tirol.it.*
Castel Fontana (also known as the **Brunnenburg**) is a strange set of 13C fortifications rebuilt at a later date. The American poet Ezra Pound worked on his *Cantos* here from 1958, when the accusation of Nazi collaboration, based on his radio programmes, was lifted.

Val Passiria★

50km/31mi to the Rombo Pass; 40km/25mi to the Monte Giovo Pass. The road follows the Passiria Valley as far as the Tyrolean village of **San Leonard**. The steep **Rombo Pass Road**★ (Timmelsjoch) offers impressive views of the mountain peaks on the frontier. The **Monte Giovo Pass Road**★ (Jaufenpass) climbs amid conifers. On the way down, there are splendid **views**★★ of the snow-capped summits of Austria.

Val Venosta★★

From Merano, take S 38 in the direction of Resia. Val Venosta is a long, sunny valley covered in orchard, which gradually widens as it climbs towards the Resia pass. It can be reached from Merano, just after the Birreria Forst. It is bordered by the Valtellina at the **Stelvio Pass**, Switzerland at the Tubre mountain pass and Austria at the Resia pass.
Val Venosta's most famous inhabitant, Ötzi, lived 5 300 years ago and his body was preserved by the ice in the spot where he died, in Val Senales. (*Ötzi is now in the Archaeological Museum of Bolzano.* &*see BOLZANO*).

WHERE TO EAT

⊜⊜⊜**Sissi** – *Via Galilei 44 – Merano – ☎0473 23 10 62 – Closed Mon, mid Jan-Feb –* ⊁ ▤ *– Book.* A quiet, elegant establishment. Lovely public lounge with picture windows and Art Nouveau lamps – very atmospheric in the evening. More intimate "snugs" on the first floor. Innovative cuisine using seasonal produce.

Naturno

From Merano take the road in the direction of the Resia pass for 15km/9mi. The road leads to Naturno at the crossroads of the Val Venosta and the Val Senales. This "junction" is dominated by the 13C **Juval Castle**, now owned by the mountain climber Reinhold Messner. ☞*Guided tours.* ⊜*7€. For opening times. call* ☎*348 44 33 871.*

Before entering the town, the slightly hidden church of **San Procolo**★, surrounded by fruit orchards, can be seen. The structure houses the oldest frescoes in the German-speaking part of the Alto Adige (8C). The most notable fresco is

An enchanting sight: the old campanile rising up from the Lago di Resia

the **Saint on a Swing**, thought to portray Procolo, the Bishop of Verona who fled the city. ♿☻*Open daily except Mon, 9.30am-noon and 2.30-5.30pm.* ☻*Closed Mon, 5 Nov to mid-Mar.* ⊜*Donation welcome.* ☎*0473 66 73 12.*

Sluderno

Sluderno's 13C **Coira Castle** has a renowned armoury. ☻*Open daily except Mon, 20 Mar to Oct 10am-noon and 2-4.30pm.* ☞*Guided tours.* ⊜*6€.* ☎*0473 61 52 41; www.churburg.com*

Glorenza

This old city counts less than 1 000 inhabitants. Glorenza was already, documented in 1178 and is well worth a visit as it is the only fortified town in the Alto Adige where time has stood still. Entirely surrounded by ramparts, it has the only arcading in the whole valley. The parish church, situated outside the city walls, has a frescoed exterior (1496) depicting *The Last Judgement.*

Malles

Malles is home to a jewel of Romanesque architecture, the 9C Church of **San Benedetto**★. Note the frescoes the depict a Frankish nobleman holding a sword and an ecclesiastic holding a model of the church, ☞*Guided tours.* ⊜ *2€. For opening times call* ☎*0473 83 11 90.*

Burgusio

Those en route to the Resia pass cannot miss the huge white abbey of **Montemaria**. Even when it is snowing the sloping roof and the bulbous towers of the campanile are still visible.

A visit to the **crypt** reveals Romanesque frescoes dating from the 12C. The paintings are based on the Apocalypse and show a clear Byzantine influence. ☞*Guided tours May-Oct; Nov-Apr by reservation only.* ☻*Closed Sun and public holidays.* ⊜*3€. For opening times, call* ☎*0473 83 13 06.*

Lago di Resia

A campanile mysteriously appears out of the waters of the lake: originally part of the church of Curono Vecchia, it was submerged by the waters of this artificial basin in 1950.

L.Pessina/MICHELIN

MILANO★★★
MILAN
POPULATION 1 271 898
MICHELIN MAP 561 F 9
AND THE MICHELIN CITY MAP 46 OF MILAN.

Milan is Italy's second city in terms of population, politics and cultural affairs. But the real spirit of Lombardy's capital lies in its commercial, industrial and banking activities which have made Milan, set in the heart of northern Italy at the foot of the Alps, the country's financial heartland. The enterprising spirit of its people has built upon the city's history to make Milan one of the country's most dynamic towns.

- **Information:** Via Marconi 1, ☎02 72 52 41; www.milanoinfotourist.com.
- ▶ **Orient Yourself:** Milan lies at the heart of a network of motorways that includes A 4 (Turin-Venice), A 7 (Milan-Genoa), A 1 (Milan-Florence) and A 8 (the Lake District). The town is bounded by two concentric boulevards: the shorter, enclosing the medieval centre, the outer marking the town's expansion during the Renaissance.
- **Parking:** Parking in the city centre and the Fiera (exhibition centre) district is by payment only.
- **Don't Miss:** The Duomo, *The Last Supper* by Leonardo Da Vinci in the Cenacolo, the Pinacoteca di Brera, Cappella Portinari and the Museo della Scienza e della Technologia Leonardo da Vinci.
- **Organizing Your Time:** Allow two days to see the city.
- **Especially for Kids:** Models of the gadgets of Leonardo da Vinci at the Museo della Scienza e della Technologia Leonardo da Vinci.
- **Also See:** *BERGAMO, Regione dei LAGHI, PAVIA.*

Milan's Duomo

B. Juge/MICHELIN

Address Book

GETTING THERE

By car and train – A good network of motorways serves the city (A 4 Turin-Venice, A 8/A 9 Milan-Lakes, A 7 Milan-Genoa, A 1 Autostrada del Sole which heads south).

By air – A train connects Malpensa airport with Cadorna station (every half-hour; journey time 40min) which in turn connects to the underground system. Tickets cost €11 (single). Information: ☎02 20 222; www.malpensaexpress.it.

There are also buses from the airport which leave approximately every 20 minutes (journey time 55min/1hr depending on traffic). They stop at both the Stazione Centrale and the Stazione Cadorna (in this case the bus serves as a substitute when the train doesn't run: before 6.50am and after 8.20pm). Tickets cost €5. www.malpensashuttle.it. Note that taxis are rather expensive as the airport is about 40km/25mi away from the city.

For flights landing at Linate airport there are buses which go to San Babila (line 73). Tickets cost 1€.

GETTING ABOUT

By public transport – It is highly advisable to use public transport: in general it is punctual and quick (especially the three underground lines). It also avoids problems like getting stuck in heavy traffic, losing one's way (particularly in the city centre with its obligatory traffic systems that frequently result in leading you far away from your required destination) and wandering around looking for parking spaces which often seem like mirages.

By car – If you do use a car bear in mind that parking in the city centre and the Fiera (exhibition centre) district is by payment only and subject to regulations. Yellow lines indicate parking for residents only, blue lines allow parking for up to 2 hours as long as pre-paid cards, purchased from parking attendants or at tobacconists, are displayed (1hr 1.50€, 2hr 3€). It is advisable to park in designated car parks (look out for blue signposts) or just outside the central zone of the city, but only where blue lines are displayed. Prices here are slightly lower than in the city centre and sometimes flat rates are charged (before you leave your car find out from the parking attendant what the charges are).

🕭 For coin ranges, see Legend on the cover flap.

WHERE TO STAY

It is worth noting that during trade fairs and exhibitions the hotels tend to put their prices up. Do enquire about this when you make your booking. The better hotels tend to be very expensive and in view of this, travellers on a tight budget might want to try and find accommodation outside the city (🕭 see PAVIA).

⊜⊜**Hotel Garden** – Via Rutilia 6, zona urbana Sud-Est – ☎02 55 21 28 38 – Fax 02 57 30 06 78 – Closed Aug – [P] – 23 rm. For value for money, this is a real find. An unpretentious hotel, with functional, comfortable rooms. Quiet situation, with good links to the city centre. There is also a lovely garden shaded by a large plane tree. Breakfast not included.

⊜⊜**Albergo Città Studi** – Via Saldini 24, zona Città Studi – ☎02 74 46 66 – www.hotelcittastudi.it – ▤ – 45 rm – ⌷. Located in one of the busiest University areas in town. Quiet, simple hotel, with adequate facilities. Most importantly it represents excellent value for money.

⊜⊜**Hotel des Etrangers** – Via Sirte 9, zona Navigli – ☎02 48 95 53 25 – Fax 02

Panettone

L. Pessina/MICHELIN

48 95 53 25 – 🖥 *– 96 rm* 🅿. This hotel is situated near the trade fair district and is well served by public transport. It is reasonably quiet with functional, modern rooms. Represents extremely good value for money.

🍴🛏**Hotel Gala** – *Viale Zara 89, zona urbana Nord-Est – ☎02 66 80 08 91 – Fax 02 66 80 04 63 – Closed Aug –* 🅿🖥 *– 22 rm –* 🅿. This family-run hotel
is particularly well situated for anyone arriving by car. Other attractions include easy access to the centre, quiet location and lovely garden. Definitely one for the address book.

🍴🛏**Hotel Regina** – *Via Cesare Correnti 13, zona Centro Storico – ☎02 58 10 69 13 – www.hotelregina.it – Closed 23 Dec-7 Jan, Aug. –* 🖥♿ *– 43 rm* 🅿. A rather grand and elegant hotel with 18C overtones. The internal courtyard, the vaulting supported by columns, has been covered over with glass creating a very atmospheric entrance hall. Highly recommended.

🍴🛏**Hotel Cavour** – *Via Fatebenefratelli 21, zona Centro Direzionale - ☎02 62 00 01 – www.hotelcavour.it – Closed 24 Dec-6 Jan, Aug –* 🖥 *– 113 rm* 🅿. There is an understated elegance about this hotel which extends to both the public areas and the rooms which are functional but comfortable. Efficiently and professionally managed by one of Milan's oldest family of hoteliers.

🍴🛏**Hotel Spadari al Duomo** – *Via Spadari 11, zona Centro Storico – ☎02 72 00 23 71 – www.spadarihotel.com –* 🖥 *– 40 rm* 🅿. A stylish, comfortable hotel with a very contemporary feel overlooking the spires of the Duomo. On display are various pieces of modern art and sculpture, the work of some of the city's more avant-garde artists, along with a collection of original designer furniture.

WHERE TO EAT

Milanese cooking is best known for its *costoletta di vitello fritta* (fillet of veal fried in breadcrumbs with cheese), *l'ossobuco* (a knuckle of veal with the marrowbone), *risotto allo zafferano* (rice cooked with saffron) and *minestrone* (a soup of green vegetables, rice and bacon). In terms of wine, look out for the Valtellina and Oltrepò Pavese labels, which are local to the region.

🍴**Premiata Pizzeria** – *Alzaia Naviglio Grande, zona Navigli – Milano – ☎02 89 40 06 48 –* 🍴. Tasty pizza in a setting where everything from the signboard to the covered courtyard is pleasant. Very crowded (on arrival leave your name and you will be told how long you will have to wait, then go and have a walk in the neighbouring vicolo dei Lavandai until your table is ready).

🍴 **Rino Vecchia Napoli** – *Via G. Chavez 4, zona Piazzale Loreto – Milano – ☎02 26 19 056 –* 🍴. Excellent pizzas that deserve manifold awards. Go there armed with patience (it's always very crowded) and be prepared to make way for the next customers. Needless to say service is speedy. Don't forget to book!

🍴**Pizzeria Geppo** – *Via G. B. Morgagni 37, zona Piazzale Loreto – Milano – pizza. geppo@tiscali.it – ☎02 29 51 48 62 – Closed Sun, 3-20 Aug –* 🍴 *– Book.* Practically a broom cupboard that serves delicious, large but thin pizza. As everyone knows about this place, be sure to book.

🍴**Dulcis in Fundo** – *Via Zuretti 55, zona Stazione Centrale – Milano – ☎02 66 71 25 03 – dulcissimi@libero.it – Closed Mon, Sun evenings (except Thu) –* 🍴 🖥. Post-Modern meets 1970s: a rather extraordinary establishment housed in an old industrial building which has been painted in pastel colours and decked out with an eclectic jumble of tables and chairs. On the menu is a vast selection of tarts, puddings and savouries as well as a limited number of unusual main courses. Thursday evening is a complete riot. Children very welcome.

🍴**Mykonos** – *Via Tofane 5, zona Naviglio Martesana – Milano – ☎02 26 10 209 – Closed Tue, lunchtime, 9am-midnight Aug –* 🍴 *– Book.* A simple, rustic-style Greek restaurant housed in a pretty building. The cuisine draws on tradition but the proprietor, who hails from Greece, also brings a personal touch to a number of typically Greek dishes.

🍴🛏**Trattoria all'Antica** – *Via Montevideo 4, zona Navigli – ☎02 58 10 48 60 – Closed Sat lunchtime, Sun, Aug, 26 Dec-7 Jan –* 🖥. A great combination

– authentic regional cooking, a cheerful ambience and an eccentric proprietor. Not for the fainthearted or those on a diet – the portions are very generous. The *risotto allo zafferano* (rice cooked with saffron) and *cotechini fumanti* (Italian pork sausage) are excellent as are the *affettati* (sliced cold meats and salami). More varied menu in the evening.

Al Mercante – *Piazza Mercanti 17, zona Centro Storico – Milano – ☎02 80 52 198 – Closed Sun, 1-7 Jan, 3-28 Aug –* ▤. A busy restaurant focusing on traditional, regional cooking. Smart interior with lovely outside dining area over-looking the little square. Specialities include risotto and ossobuco. Despite all the comings and goings, the staff are polite, friendly and efficient.

Masuelli San Marco – *Viale Umbria 80, zona Porta Romana-Porta Vittoria – Milano – ☎02 55 18 41 38 – Closed Sun and Mon lunchtime, 25 Dec-6 Jan, 16 Aug-10 Sep –* ▤ *– Book.* A popular restaurant which has been in the same family for eight generations. Classic, regional cooking which is closely linked to the seasons and the tradition of serving certain dishes on certain days, for example, "Cassoela" on Thursdays.

Savini – *Galleria Vittorio Emanuele II, zona Centro Storico – ☎02 72 00 34 33 – Closed Sun, 1-6 Jan, 6-27 Aug –* ▤ *– Book – 12% service charge.* One of the city's most historic establishments situated in one of the most atmospheric arcades in Italy. Would appeal to those looking for a gastronomic (but unpretentious) experience and a decadent fin de siècle atmosphere. The excellent cuisine draws on tradition but is also innovative.

TAKING A BREAK

Bar Basso – *Via Plinio 39, zona Stazione Centrale – ☎02 29 40 05 80 –Open Tue-Sun 7.30am-8.30pm.* This is where the "wrong" Negroni cocktail was invented, using champagne instead of gin.

Bar Bianco – *Giardini di Palestro, zona Porta Venezia.* Establishment specialising in milk-based drinks and other such products.

Bar Magenta – *Via Carducci 13, zona S. Ambrogio –* ☎02 80 53 808 *– 8-2.30am.* This is one of the most famous bars in Milan, frequented by people of different generations and ideological extractions, according to the fashion of the moment. It is worth tasting the very rich aperitivo while taking a look around: the counter is typical of the decor of this Art Nouveau style bar.

Bar della Crocetta – *Corso di Porta Romana 67 –* ☎02 54 50 228 *– 8-1.30am.* The perfect place for sandwich enthusiasts. They come in an impressive array of shapes and sizes and with a wide variety of fillings. Well located for anyone heading for the Teatro Carcano.

Crota piemunteisa – *Piazza Cesare Beccaria 10, zona Centro Storico –* ☎02 80 52 707 *– Tue-Sun 7am-2am, Mon 5pm-2am.* This tiny space behind the Duomo is just big enough to hold tables and wooden stools, a jukebox, two counters (one for beer, one for sandwiches – be sure to try the excellent frankfurters and sauerkraut). Over the decades this establishment has attracted a mixed bag of people who seem to have no common denominator.

Gattullo – *Piazzale Porta Lodovica 2.* One of the best places for a freshly baked brioche and a good cappuccino.

Gelateria Marghera – *Via Marghera 33, zona Fiera – ☎02 46 86 41 – 8am-midnight.* Not far from the Teatro Nazionale and the Fiera district. Excellent selection of creamy ice creams.

Moscatelli – *Corso Garibaldi 93, zona Brera – 10-1am.* The perfect place to taste Italian wines accompanied by something to nibble on.

Taveggia – *Via Visconti di Modrone 2, zona S. Babila – ☎02 76 02 12 57.* This establishment serves one of the best hot chocolates – dark and syrupy – in Milan.

Viel – *Corso Buenos Aires 15 – ☎02 29 51 61 23 – 9-1am – Viale Abruzzi 23 – ☎02 20 40 43 9.* Famous for its milkshakes, this bar has been a student hang-out for decades.

LIFE IN MILAN

The most frequented parts of Milan are around Piazza del Duomo, Via Dante and Via Manzoni. At the *Galleria Vittorio*

Emanuele II, the Milanese come to talk, read their *Corriere della Sera* or drink coffee side by side with the tourists. For visitors looking for luxury items or just wanting to stroll through the most fashionable districts in the city, the Corso Vittorio Emanuele II, the Piazza San Babila, the Corso Venezia, and the Via Monte Napoleone and Via della Spiga – where the couture houses are – are pleasant areas to explore. The Corso Magenta and the streets around Sant'Ambrogio have retained all the charm of the Milan of another age with old houses and winding, narrow streets lined with old cafés and antique shops.

GOING OUT

Head for the picturesque Brera District, which is popular with artists and full of art galleries, and buzzing with life in the evening.
Le Scimmie – *Via A. Sforza 49, zona Navigli* – ☎*02 89 40 28 74* – *www. scimmie.it* – *9-1am*. A large trattoria with four rooms in total and live music (mostly jazz).

ENTERTAINMENT

Milan has a very lively cultural and artistic scene. The city hosts a number of musical events – classical, jazz, klezmer – where some of the world's most famous stars come to perform. There are also a number of theatres.

MUSIC

La Scala – *Piazza Scala, zona Centro Storico* – ☎*02 72 00 37 44* – *www.teatroallascala.org* – Stages opera and ballet. The season traditionally starts on St Ambrose's day.
Auditorium di Milano – *Corso S. Gottardo, zona Navigli* – ☎*02 83 38 92 01* – *www.auditoriumdimilano.org* – Performances of classical, jazz, klezmer and other types of music. Also hosts literary evenings, events for children as well as audiences with well-known artistes.
Conservatorio – *Via Conservatorio 12, zona S. Babila* – ☎*02 76 21 101* – *www. consmilano.it* – Varied programme of chamber and orchestral music.

DRAMA

Teatro Dal Verme – Via San Giovanni sul Muro 5, zona Centro Storico. Box office: via Rovello – ☎*02 72 33 32 22; www.dalverme.org*.
Piccolo Teatro – The Piccolo Teatro di Strehler comprises three theatres, all of which are centrally located: *Teatro Strehler, Largo Greppi; Teatro Grassi, via Rovello 2; Teatro Studio, via Rivoli 6* – ☎*02 72 33 32 22; info@piccoloteatro.org; www.piccoloteatro.org*.
Teatro Carcano – *Corso di Porta Romana 63* – ☎*02 55 18 13 77; www.piccoloteatro.org*.
Teatro Manzoni – *Via Manzoni 40, zona Centro Storico* – ☎*02 76 36 901; www.teatromanzoni.it*.

A Bit of History

Milan is probably Gallic (Celtic) in origin, but it was the Romans who subdued the city of Mediolanum in 222 BC and ensured its expansion. At the end of the 3C Diocletian made Milan the seat of the rulers of the Western Empire, and in 313 Constantine published the **Edict of Milan,** which gave freedom of worship to the Christians. In 375 **St Ambrose** (340-96), a Doctor of the Church, became bishop of the town, thus adding to its prestige.
The barbarian invasions of the 5C and 6C were followed by the creation of a Lombard kingdom with Pavia as capital. In 756 Pepin, King of the Franks, conquered the area, and his son Charlemagne was to wear the Iron Crown of the Kings of Lombardy from 774. In 962 Milan again became Italy's capital.
In the 12C Milan allied itself to other cities to form the Lombard League (1167) to thwart the attempts of the Emperor Frederick Barbarossa to conquer the region. With victory at **Legnano** the cities of the league achieved independence. In the 13C the **Visconti**, Ghibellines and leaders of the local aristocracy, seized power. The most famous member was **Gian Galeazzo** (1347-1402), a man of letters, assassin and pious builder of Milan's Cathedral and the Monastery of Pavia. His daughter, Valentina, married Louis, Duke of Orleans, the grandfather

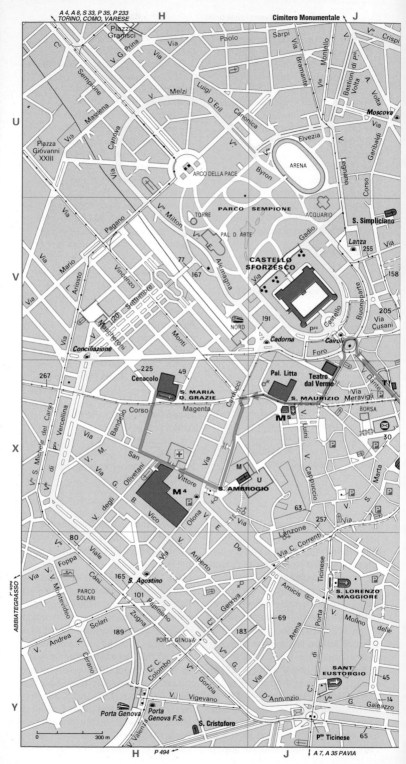

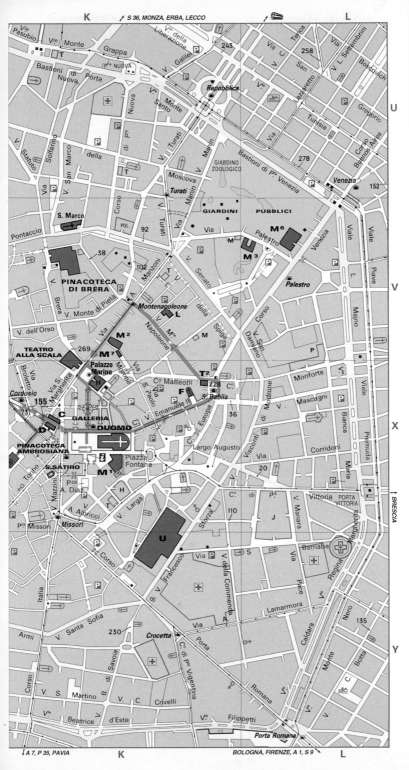

S. Chirol/MICHELIN

Galleria Vittorio Emanuele

of Louis XII of France. This family connection was the reason for later French expeditions into Italy.

After the death of the last Visconti, Filippo-Maria (d 1447) the Sforza took over the rule of Milan. The most famous figure in the **Sforza** family, **Ludovico il Moro** (1452-1508) made Milan a new Athens by attracting to his court the geniuses of the time, Leonardo da Vinci and Bramante. However, Louis XII of France proclaimed himself the legitimate heir to the Duchy of Milan and set out to conquer the territory in 1500. His successor François I renewed the offensive but was thwarted at Pavia by the troops of the Emperor Charles V. From 1535 to 1713 Milan was under Spanish rule. During the plague, from 1576 to 1630, members of the Borromeo family, St Charles (1538-84) and Cardinal Federico (1564-1631) distinguished themselves by their humanitarian work.

Under Napoleon, Milan became the capital of the Cisalpine Republic (1797) and later of the Kingdom of Italy (1805). In 1815 Milan assumed the role of capital of the Venetian-Lombard Kingdom.

Art and Architecture

The Cathedral (Duomo) marks the climax of architecture of the Gothic period. Prominent architects during the Renaissance were the Florentine Michelozzo (1396-1472) and especially **Donato Bramante** (1444-1514), master mason of Ludovico il Moro before he left for Rome. An admirer of Classical art, he invented the **rhythmic articulation** (a façade with alternating bays, pilasters and niches) which imparted harmony to Renaissance façades.

The Lombard school of painting sought beauty and grace above all else. Its principal exponents were Vincenzo Foppa (1427-1515), Bergognone (1450-1523) and Bramantino (between 1450 and 1465-1536). The works of Andrea Solario (1473-c 1520), Boltraffio (1467-1516) and especially the delicate canvases of

Saint Of Milan

Ambrose (c 337/339-397), an Imperial civil servant born in Treviri, was one of the key figures in the later Roman Empire. He brought peace to the Christians of Milan who were divided following the death of the Arian bishop Aussenzio (Arianism was a heresy which denied the divine nature of Christ) and by public acclaim was declared Bishop of Milan before having even been baptised. He was authoritative with emperors and even imposed a public penitence on Emperor Theodosius who had been responsible for the massacre of Thessalonicans. The power of his sermons proved crucial in the conversion of St Augustine. Ambrose also renewed the liturgy and calendar of the Milanese Church which even today follows the "Ambrosian" rite.

Bernardino Luini (c 1480-1532) attest to the influence of **Leonardo da Vinci** who stayed in Milan for some time.
Today Milan is Italy's publishing capital and an important centre, with numerous contemporary art galleries.

Piazza Duomo and Surrounding Area

Duomo★★★

Exterior
This Gothic marvel of white marble, bristling with belfries, gables, pinnacles and statues, stands at one end of an esplanade teeming with pigeons – largely responsible for the building's deterioration. The Duomo's recent restoration was a lengthy, technical process, and it ideally should be seen by the light of the setting sun. Building began in 1386 on the orders of Gian Galeazzo Visconti, continued in the 15C and 16C under Italian, French and German master masons and finished between 1805 and 1809, on Napoleon's orders.
Walk round the cathedral to view the **east end** with three bays of curved and counter-curved tracery and wonderful rose windows. The design is the work of a French architect, Nicolas de Bonaventure, and of a Modenese architect, Filippino degli Organi.
From the 7th floor of the Rinascente store in Corso Vittorio Emanuele there is a close-up view of the architectural and sculptural features of the roofs.

Interior
The imposing nave and aisles are separated by 52 high pillars (148m/486ft).
The mausoleum of Gian Giacomo Medici in the south arm of the transept is a fine work by Leoni (16C). In the north arm is the curious statue of St Bartholomew (who was flayed alive), by the sculptor Marco d'Agrate. In the crypt (cripta) and treasury (tesoro) the silver urn containing the remains of St Charles Borromeo, Bishop of Milan, who died in 1584, is on display.
On the way out, you can see the entrance to the Early-Christian baptistery (battistero) and the 4C basilica of Santa Tecla

whose outline has been marked out on the parvis. *Crypt and treasury ◷Open daily 9am-noon and 2-6pm. Baptistery, ◷Open daily, 9.45am-5.45pm.* ◉1.50 €. ☎02 72 02 26 56

Visit to the roof★★★
◷ *Open daily Feb-Oct 9am-5.45pm, Nov-Jan 9am-4.45pm.* ◷*Closed 1 Jan, 1 May, 25 Dec.* ◉*Lift 6€, on foot 4€.* ☎02 72 02 26 56; www.duomomilano.com
Take a walk on the roof to view the 135 pinnacles, numerous white marble statues (2 245 in all) and the Tiburio or central tower (108m/354ft), surmounted by a gilt statue, the Madonnina (1774).

Museo del Duomo★★
⌐*Closed for restoration at the time of going to press.* ☎02 86 03 58; www.duomomilano.com
Housed in the royal palace built in the 18C by Piermarini, the cathedral museum shows the various stages in the building and restoration of the cathedral. Also of note are the splendid **Aribert Crucifix**★ (1040), the original support for the Madonnina (1772-73), and the wooden **model**★ of the cathedral made to a scale of 1:20 in the 16C-19C.
Cross over to the **Galleria Vittorio Emanuele II**★, laid out in 1877. The far end opens on to Piazza della Scala.

Teatro alla Scala★★
www.teatroallascala.it.
Traditionally recognised as being the most famous opera house in the world, La Scala surprises people seeing it for the first time because of the simplicity of its exterior, which gives no hint of the magnificence of its auditorium. Built from 1776 to 1778 with six levels of boxes, it can seat 2 000 people.
The **Museo teatrale alla Scala**★ presents Toscanini and Verdi memorabilia. From the museum, you can visit boxes and see the auditorium.

▷ *Turn into via S. Margherita.*

Via and Piazza dei Mercanti★
In Via Mercanti stands the Palace of Jurisconsults (Palazzo dei Giureconsulti), built in 1564 with a statue of St Ambrose teaching on the façade. The

Piazza dei Mercanti is quiet and pictur-esque. The charming Loggia degli Osii (1316) is decorated with heraldic shields, statues of saints and the balcony from which penal sentences were proclaimed. Opposite is the town hall, the **Palazzo della Ragione** or Broletto Nuovo, built in the 13C and extended in the 18C.

Churches and Basilicas

Chiesa di San Maurizio Monastero Maggiore★★
This is a monastery church built in the Lombard-Renaissance style (early 16C). The bare façade, which often goes unnoticed on Corso Magenta, con-ceals an interior entirely decorated with **frescoes**★ by Bernardino Luini. To reach the chancel (where concerts are held), take the passageway to the left at the back of the church.

Basilica di Sant'Ambrogio★★
The basilica was founded at the end of the 4C by St Ambrose and it is a magnificent example of the 11C-12C Lombard-Romanesque style with its pure lines and fine **atrium**★ adorned with capitals. The façade pierced by arcading is flanked by a 9C campanile to the right and a 12C one to the left. The doorway was renewed in the 18C and has 9C bronze panels. In the crypt, behind the chancel, lie the remains of St Ambrose, St Gervase and St Protase. Inside the basilica there is a magnificent Byzantine-Romanesque **ambo**★ (12C) to the left of the nave, and at the high altar a precious gold-plated **altar front**★★, a masterpiece of the Carolingian period (9C). In the chapel of San Vittore in Ciel d'Oro *(at the end of the south transept)* there are remarkable 5C **mosaics**★. From the far end of the north transept one can gain access to Bramante's por-tico.

Chiesa di Santa Maria delle Grazie★
This Renaissance church erected by the Dominicans from 1465 to 1490 was finished by Bramante. The interior (restored), is adorned with frescoes by Gaudenzio Ferrari in the fourth chapel

on the right, and with the impressive **dome**★, gallery and cloisters all by Bra-mante. The best view of the **east end**★ is to be had from Via Caradosso.

Cenacolo
◷*Open daily 8.15am-6.45pm, by reserva-tion only.*◷*Closed Mon, 1 Jan and 25 Dec.* ☞*6.50€ +€1.50 reservation.*☏*02 89 42 11 46; www.cenacolovinciano.it.*

In the former refectory (cenacolo) of the monastery is the portrayal of **The Last Supper**★★★ by **Leonardo da Vinci**, painted between 1495 and 1497 at the request of Ludovico il Moro. It is a skil-ful composition that creates the illusion that the painted space is a continuation of the room itself.

Christ is depicted at the moment of the institution of the Eucharist: His half-open mouth suggests that he has just finished speaking. Around Him there is a tangi-ble sense of shock and premonition of imminent disaster with its intimation of Judas' betrayal.

The technique used (Leonardo chose egg tempera, possibly mixed with oil and placed the image on the coldest wall in the room), dust, the ravages caused by a bomb falling on the refec-tory in 1943 and, more recently, smog have all contributed to the necessity for considerable restoration work (it has been documented that the paint-ing has undergone restoration 10 times). In fact the condition of the painting was already compromised in 1517, and in 1901 Gabriele D'Annunzio wrote an ode: *On the Death of a Masterpiece.*

In May 1999, after 21 years of restoration work, the Cenacolo was finally unveiled and its original colours and use of chi-aroscuro admired.

Opposite the fresco is a **Crucifixion**★ (1495) by Montorfano, somewhat over-shadowed by *The Last Supper.*
⊚*The Last Supper by Leonardo da Vinci.*

Chiesa di Sant'Eustorgio★
This church was used by the inquisition prior to moving to Santa Maria delle Gra-zie, and is dedicated to St Peter Martyr, the inquisitor, murdered by a blow to the head in 1252.

Cappella Portinari★★

&⏱Open daily 10am-6pm. ⏱Closed Mon, Aug. ≋6€. ☎02 89 40 26 71; www.santeustorgio.it

This chapel, a jewel of the Lombard-Renaissance style, houses the finest cycle of paintings by the Milanese artist **Vincenzo Foppa** (c 1427-1515). Facing the entrance, the *Annunciation* provides a background to the balcony connecting two Renaissance palaces. Above the entrance is the *Assumption*.

On the right hand wall St Peter is depicted preaching from the pulpit.

The adjacent scene represents the devil assuming the guise of the Madonna and Child, his true identity revealed at the sight of the Host (note his horns).

On the wall in front, the saint is reattaching the foot to a boy's leg – cut off as punishment for striking his mother.

The final scene takes place in the Barlassina woods where Peter's earthly story reaches its conclusion.

Next to **Sant'Eustorgio the Museo Diocesano** houses works belonging to the diocese. ⏱Open daily 10am-6pm. ⏱Closed Mon, 1 Jan, 25-26 Dec. ≋Price of admission varies by exhibition. ☎02 89 40 47 14; www.museodiocesano.it.

Basilica di San Satiro★

With the exception of the 9C square campanile and the west front, which dates from 1871, the basilica, like the baptistery, was designed by Bramante. The architect adopted a Classical idiom to overcome the lack of space, integrating gilded stucco and *trompe l'oeil* work to create the impression of a chancel. The **dome**★ is also remarkable. The basilica also includes a small Oriental-style chapel on the plan of a Greek cross, decorated with a 15C terracotta statue of the *Descent from the Cross* and fragments of 9C-12C frescoes.

Basilica di San Lorenzo Maggiore★

The basilica was founded in the 4C and rebuilt in the 12C and 16C. It has kept its original octagonal plan. In front of the façade is a majestic **portico**★ of 16 columns, all that remains of the Roman town of Mediolanum. The interior is in the Byzantine-Romanesque style and has galleries exclusively reserved for women. From the south side of the chancel pass through the atrium and then a 1C Roman doorway to a chapel, the **Cappella di Sant'Aquilino**★dating from the 4C. It has retained its original plan and the palaeo-Christian mosaics. *Cappella:* ⏱Open Mon-Sat, 8.30am-12.30pm and 2.30-6.30pm; Sun and public holidays 10.30-11.30am and 12.30-6pm. ≋2€. ☎02 89 40 41 29; www.sanlorenzomaggiore.com.

Further on, the **Porta Ticinese**, a vestige of the 14C ramparts, leads to the artists quarter, the Naviglio Grande.

Chiesa di San Marco

Rebuilt in 1286 over much older foundations, this church houses an interesting black and white fresco painted by the Leonardo da Vinci School (north aisle) representing a **Madonna and Child with St John the Baptist** that was discovered in 1975.

Basilica di San Simpliciano

This was built in AD 385 on the orders of St Ambrose, Bishop of Milan. Extensions were made to the early-Christian basilica during the early Middle Ages and the Romanesque period. On the apse vaulting is a **Coronation of the Virgin** by Bergognone (1481-1522).

Both these churches host excellent concerts.

Museums

Pinacoteca di Brera★★★

⏱Open daily 8.30am-7.15pm. ⏱Closed Mon, 1 Jan, 1 May, 25 Dec. ≋5€. ☎02 72 26 31; www.brera.beniculturali.it.

The Brera Art Gallery forms part of a series of institutes – the Accademia di Belle Arti (Fine Arts Academy), the Biblioteca (library), the Osservatorio Astronomico (observatory) and the Istituto Lombardo di Scienze, Lettere ed Arti (The Lombardy Institute of Science, Arts and Letters) – all housed in a fine 17C building. In the courtyard a statue of Napoleon (1809) by Canova depicts him as a victorious Roman emperor.

The tour of the gallery starts with the Jesi collection which introduces the main artistic movements of the first half of the 20C: note the sense of movement and dynamism of the Futurist painters (Boccioni's **La Rissa in galleria**) and the clean geometry of the metaphysical works by Carrà (**The metaphysical muse**) and Morandi (**Still Life**). The sculpture collection is dominated by three artists: Medardo Rosso, Arturo Marini and Marino Marini. Along the passage to the left, it is possible to admire the Maria Theresa Room and the library, Biblioteca Braidense.

The Cappella Mocchirolo gives a brief review of Italian painting from the 13C to 15C (*Polyptych of Valle Romita* by Gentile da Fabriano).

The Brera holding of **Venetian paintings** is the largest and most important one outside Venice. Masterpieces include the **Pietà**★★ by Giovanni Bellini, in which the tragic event is echoed by the deserted landscape and metallic sky, and the famous **Dead Christ**★★★ by Mantegna, a meditation on death with a realism given added pathos by the artist's skill in foreshortening. In the Napoleon Rooms hang major works by Tintoretto (**Miracle of St Mark**★), Veronese (**Dinner at the house of Simon**) and Giovanni and Gentile Bellini *(St Mark preaching at Alexandria in Egypt)*.

The **Lombard school** is well represented and pride of place is given to a **polyptych with Madonna and saints**★ by Vicenzo Foppa, whose work shows the influence of the Paduan school and Mantegna in particular, and the Leonardesque **Madonna of the rose garden**★★ by Bernardino Luini.

One room contains two Renaissance masterpieces from **Central Italy**: the **Montefeltro altarpiece**★★★ by Piero della Francesca, in which the ostrich egg symbolises both the Immaculate Conception and the abstract and geometrical perfection of form sought by the artist, and the **Marriage of the Virgin**★★★ by Raphael, in which the graceful, delicate figures merge in the background with the circular Bramante-style building. Further along, Caravaggio's magnificent **Meal at Emmaus**★★★ is a fine example of the artist's use of strong contrast between light and shade and of his realism.

In the Room of 18C Venetian painting **Rebecca at the Well**★★ by Piazzetta is an exquisite portrayal of the girl's gaze of astonishment and innocence.

The last rooms are dedicated to 19C-20C painting. Paintings include the Carro rosso by Fattori and **The Kiss** by Hayez. Foreign artists include Van Dyck, Rubens and Reynolds.

Castello Sforzesco★★★

🕐*Open daily 9am-5.30pm.* 🕐*Closed Mon, 1 Jan, 1 May, 15 Aug, 25 Dec.* ⊗*3€.* ☎*02 88 46 37 03; www.milanocastello.it.* This huge brick quadrilateral building was the seat of the Sforza, Dukes of Milan. The **municipal art collections** are now on display in the castle.

Museo di Scultura★★

Ground floor. The museum's minimalist layout is particularly effective. Romanesque, Gothic and Renaissance works are mainly by Lombard sculptors. Interesting works include the **tomb of Bernabò Visconti**★★ (14C) ; and the **reclining figure of Gaston de Foix** and **statues**★★ (1523) by Bambaia, as well as the unfinished **Rondanini Pietà**★★★ by Michelangelo.

Pinacoteca★

1st floor. The gallery displays works by Mantegna, Giovanni Bellini, Crivelli, Bergognone, Luini, Moretto, Moroni, Magnasco, Tiepolo, Guardi, Lotto etc.

Museo degli strumenti musicali★

An extensive collection of stringed and wind instruments and keyboards.

Museo Archeologico

In the vault under the Rochetta courtyard. The museum includes prehistory, Egyptian art and lapidary collections. Another section of the museum is housed in the San Maurizio monastery *(👁see below).*

Pinacoteca Ambrosiana★★

🕐*Open daily 10am-5.30pm.* 🕐*Closed Mon, 1 Jan, Easter, 1 May, 25 Dec.* ⊗*7.50€.* ☎*02 80 69 21; www.ambrosiana.it.* This 17C palace, erected for Cardinal Federico Borromeo, was one of the first public libraries, and boasts Leonardo's **Codice Atlantico** drawings.

The gallery opens with an original body of work donated by the cardinal, and other acquisitions of the same period (15C and 16C). Note the **Portrait of a Lady** by De Predis and the delightful **Infant Jesus and the Lamb**★★ by Bernardino Luini. One of the most notable paintings of the Lombard School is the **Sacra Conversazione** by Bergognone (1453-1523), with its Madonna dominating the composition whose use of perspective is still very much anchored in the Middle Ages. The **Musician**★★ by Leonardo da Vinci has an unusually dark background for the artist who tended to create a strong relationship between the dominant figures and their surrounding space. In Room 3 the **Madonna Enthroned with Saints**★ by Bramantino is striking for the huge toad at the feet of St Michael (symbolising the dragon slain by the saint) contrasting with the grotesque swollen figure of Arius. The **Nativity**, a copy from Barocci, is pervaded by a glowing light which irradiates from the child. The splendid preparatory **cartoons**★★★ for Raphael's School of Athens (the fresco was painted in the Vatican *Stanze* in Rome) are the only surviving example of their kind. In Caravaggio's **Basket of Fruit**★★★ shrivelled leaves and rotten fruit render idea of life's transitory nature. The cardinal's collection also includes fine Flemish paintings by Paul Bril and Jan Brueghel's remarkable **Mouse with a Rose**★, painted on copper. Other rooms are mainly focused on painting from Lombardy. Of particular note are four **portraits**★ by Francesco Hayez.

Museo Poldi Pezzoli★★

Open daily 10am-6pm. Closed Mon, public holidays. 7€. 02 79 48 89; www.museopoldipezzoli.it.

Attractively set out in an old mansion, the museum displays collections of weapons, fabrics, paintings, **clocks**★, and bronzes. Among the paintings are works by the Lombard School (Bergognone, Luini, Foppa, Solario, Boltraffio), **portraits**★★ of Luther and his wife by Lucas Cranach and, in the Golden Hall decorated with a **Persian carpet**, the famous **Portrait of a Woman**★★★ by Piero del Pollaiolo, a **Descent from the Cross** and a **Madonna and Child**★★ by Botticelli, and a **Dead Christ**★ full of pathos by Giovanni Bellini. The other rooms are hung with works by Pinturicchio, Palma il Vecchio (Portrait of a Courtesan), Francesco Guardi, Canaletto, Tiepolo, Perugino and Lotto.

Palazzo Bagatti Valsecchia★

Open daily 1-5.45pm. Closed Mon, 1 Jan, Easter, 1 May, 25 Dec. 6€. 02 76 00 61 32, www.museobagattivalsecchi.org.

The palace façade is divided into two parts connected by a loggia (1st floor) surmounted by a balcony.

Museum

At the top of the stairs is the *piano nobile* of the residence of Fausto and Giuseppe Bagatti Valsecchi. Of particular interest are the **Fresco Room** (depicting the *Madonna of Mercy*, 1496), the **library** decorated with two 16C leather globes and objects including a 17C roulette set and Fausto's **bedroom**, dominated by a bed carved with *Christ's Ascent to Calvary* and battle scenes. The **Labyrinth Passage** leads to the **Domed Gallery**.

Access to the formal rooms is via the domed gallery: the huge **reception hall**, the **Arms Room** with its collection of bayonets and the **Dining Room** decorated with 14C Flemish tapestries.

Casa di Manzoni★

Via G. Morone 1. Open Tue-Fri, 9am-noon and 2-4pm. Closed Mon, Sat-Sun, public holidays, Aug, 25 Dec-6 Jan. 02 86 46 04 03; www.museidelcentro.milano.it.

Alessandro Manzoni lived in this mansion for 60 years. On the ground floor is the library, writer's books and desk. On the first floor are memorabilia and illustrations of his most famous novel, **The Betrothed**. The bedroom where he died still has its original furniture; *www.museidelcentro.mi.it/manzoni.htm.*

Museo della Scienza e della Tecnnologia Leonardo da Vinci★

&⃝*Open Tue-Fri 9.30am-5pm, Sat-Sun and public holidays 9.30am-6.30pm.* ⃝*Closed 1 Jan, 25 Dec.* ⊷*8€.* ☏*02 48 55 51, www.museoscienza.org.*

This vast museum exhibits interesting scientific documents. In the **Leonardo da Vinci Gallery** are models of the artist's inventions. The museum's other sections deal with acoustics, chemistry, telecommunications and astronomy. Large pavilions have displays relating to the railways, aircraft and shipping.

Kids *Look out for models of da Vinci's gadgets.*

Museo Civico di Archeologia★

⃝*Open daily 9am-1pm and 2-5.30pm.* ⃝*Closed Mon, 1 Jan, 1 May, 25 Dec.* ⊷*2€.* ☏*02 86 45 00 11; www.museidelcentro. mi.it.*

The museum housed in the extant buildings of the Benedictine monastery is divided into Roman and barbarian art on the ground floor and Greek, Etruscan and Indian (Gandhara) art in the basement. The most outstanding exhibits are the 4C **Trivulzio cup**★ cut from one piece of glass, and the **silver platter from Parabiago**★ (4C) featuring the festival of the goddess Cybele.

Opposite, stands **Palazzo Litta**.

Galleria d'Arte Moderna

Via Palestro 16. ⃝ *Open daily 9-11am.* ☏*02 76 34 08 09.*

The Modern Art Gallery has been set out in the 18C Villa Reale, which also houses the Marino Marini Museum and the Grassi Collection. It includes **The Fourth Estate** by Pelliza da Volpedo, works by Giovanni Segantini **(The Two Mothers, The Angel of Life)**, a Portrait of Alexander Manzoni by Francesco Hayez, and sculptures by Milanese sculptor, Medardo Rosso (1858-1928). The **Carlo Grassi Collection** includes works by Gaspare Van Wittel, Pietro Longhi, Cézanne, Van Gogh, Manet, Gauguin, Sisley, Toulouse-Lautrec, Boccioni and Balla. The **Marino Marini Museum** displays the artist's sculptures and paintings. The **Contemporary Art**

Pavilion (Via Palestro 14) has temporary exhibitions.

&⃝ Ca' Granda-Ex Ospedale Maggiore★ (University).

Excursions

Abbazia di Chiaravalle★

7km/4mi southeast. Leave by Porta Romana and head towards San Donato. Consult the plan of the built-up area on Michelin map 561. ⃝*Open daily 9am-noon and 3.30-5.30pm.* ⃝*Closed Mon, am on Sun and public holidays.* ⊷*Donation recommended.* ☏*02 57 40 34 04.*

The abbey, founded by St Bernard of Clairvaux in 1135, is dominated by a polygonal **bell tower**★. It is an early example of Gothic architecture in Italy. The small cloisters are delightful.

Monza

21km/13mi north.

Monza is a textile town, on the edge of the Brianza, a hilly area dotted with lakes and villas set in lovely gardens.

Duomo★

This 13-14C cathedral has a white, green and black marble Lombard **façade**★★ (1390-96), the work of Matteo da Campione, one of the *Maestri Campionesi*, who spread the Lombard style throughout Italy. The **interior**★ has a 14C silver gilt **altar front**★. To the left of the chancel is the Chapel of the Queen of the Longobards, Theodolinda (6C-7C), with 15C frescoes ★. The **treasury**★ *(tesoro)* has the famous 5C-9C **Iron Crown**★★ of the Kings of Lombardy, offered by Pope Gregory I the Great to the queen. *Treasury:* ⃝*Open daily 9-11.30am and 3-5.30pm* ⃝*Closed Mon and during religious ceremonies.* ⊷*4€.* ☏*039 32 34 04.*

Parco di Villa Reale★★

This neo-Classical royal villa was the residence of Eugène de Beauharnais (Napoleon's stepson) and Umberto I of Italy, who was assassinated at Monza in 1900. In the northern part of the park is the Monza racing circuit, the venue for the Grand Prix Formula One race.

MODENA★

POPULATION 180 000
MICHELIN MAP 561, 562 OR 563 I 14 –
TOWN PLAN IN THE MICHELIN ATLAS ITALY – EMILIA-ROMAGNA.

Modena, situated between the River Secchia and River Panaro, at the junction of the Via Emilia and the Brenner Autostrada, is a commercial and industrial centre (Modena is the home of the iconic Ferrari racing cars) and one of the most important towns in Emilia-Romagna. However, Modena with its archbishopric and university, remains a quiet town whose old quarter in the vicinity of the cathedral is adorned by several spacious squares lined with arcades. It is in this part of the town that one finds such gastronomic specialities as *zamponi* (stuffed pigs' trotters) and Lambrusco, a sparkling red wine which is produced locally.

- **Information:** Piazza Grande 17, 41100 Modena, ☎059 20 66 60; comune.modena.it.
- ▶ **Orient Yourself:** Modena is about 40km/24mi from Bologna. The main access road is A 1.
- **Don't Miss:** The Duomo and the Galleria Estense.
- **Organizing Your Time:** Allow a day.
- **Also See:** BOLOGNA, PARMA.

Visit

Duomo★★★

The cathedral, founded in 1099, is dedicated to St Geminian and is one of the best examples of Romanesque architecture in Italy. Here the Lombard architect, **Lanfranco**, gave vent to his sense of rhythm and proportion. The *Maestri Campionesi* put the finishing touches to his work. Most of the sculptural decoration is due to **Wiligelmo**, a 12C Lombard sculptor.

The façade is divided into three parts and is crowned by the Angel of Death carrying a fleur-de-lis, a work carried out by the "*Campionesi*" masters. The central portal is enhanced by a porch supported by two lions by Wiligelmo.

The south side overlooking the square is remarkable for its architectural rhythm. From left to right, are the Prince's Doorway carved by Wiligelmo, the Royal Entrance, a gem carved by the "Campionesi" masters in the 13C and a 16C pulpit decorated with the symbols of the four Evangelists.

To reach the other side of the church, walk under the Gothic arches linking the cathedral to the Romanesque campanile built of white marble (88m/286ft) known as **Ghirlandina** because of the

WHERE TO EAT

◖◖**Al Boschetto-da Loris** – *Via Due Canali Nord 202* – ☎*059 25 17 59* – *Closed Wed, and Tues and Sun evenings (Oct-Apr), Sat and Sun evenings (rest of the year).* This rustic but elegantly decorated restaurant is housed in what was the Duca d'Este's shooting lodge (18C). It is surrounded by some magnificent old trees that provide shade for diners eating alfresco. Delicious traditional, home cooking. The balsamic vinegar is made on the family estate.

Balsamic Vinegar

G. Bludzin/MICHELIN

bronze garland on its weather-vane. The recessed orders of the arches are decorated with episodes from the Breton cycle, one of the first examples of this subject matter in Italy.

The **interior** of the cathedral reveals the ebullience of Gothic churches and the simplicity of Romanesque architecture. In the north aisle beyond the 15C Altare delle Statuine (with small statues), is a 14C pulpit and, opposite, a wooden seat said to have been used by the public executioner. The **roodscreen**★★★, a Romanesque masterpiece, is supported by Lombardy lions and telamones and is the work of "*Campionesi*" masters dating from the 12C-13C. The atmospheric crypt contains a terracotta sculpture group of the **Holy Family**★ (15C) by Guido Mazzoni, and St Geminiano's tomb. In the south aisle is an exquisite 16C Nativity.

The **Museo del Duomo** contains the famous 12C **metopes**★★, low reliefs which used to surmount the flying buttresses. They represent wandering players or symbols incomprehensible today, but whose modelling, balance and style have an almost Classical air.

&♿ ◷*Open daily 9.30am-12.30pm and 3.30-7pm (6.30pm winter). ◷Closed Mon (except Easter Mon), 1 Jan, 25 Dec (am). ☞3€. ☏059 43 96 969; www.duomodi modena.it/musei/muse.html.*

Palazzo dei Musei

This 18C palace contains the two most important art collections gathered by the Este family.

Biblioteca Estense★

1st floor, staircase on the right. &♿◷*Open daily 9am-1pm. ◷Closed Sun and public holidays. ☞2.60€. ☏059 22 22 48; www. cedoc.mo.it/estense.*

This is one of the richest libraries in Italy, containing 600 000 books and 15 000 manuscripts. The prize exhibit is the **Bible of Borso d'Este**★★. It has 1020 pages illuminated by 15C Ferrara artists, including Taddeo Crivelli.

Galleria Estense★

&♿◷*Open daily 8.30am-7.30pm. ◷Closed Mon. ☞4€. ☏059 43 95 711; www.galle riaestense.it.*

This gallery opens with the **Marble bust of Francesco I d'Este** by Gian Lorenzo Bernini. The 15C Modena School is well represented (Bonascia, Francesco Bianchi Ferrari); it owes much to the Ferrarese School, represented by the powerfully modelled **St Anthony**★ by Cosmè Tura. There is also a fine collection of Venetian masters (Cima da Conegliano, Veronese, Tintoretto, Bassano), 16C Ferrarese painting (Dosso Dossi, Garofalo) and works linked to the Accademia degli Incamminati in Bologna (the Carracci, Guido Reni, Guercino). The foreign schools are also well represented; note the **Portrait of Francesco I d'Este** by Velasquez.

The gallery also has some fine terracotta figures, typical works by Modenese sculptors from the 15C-16C. (Nicolò dell'Arca, Guido Mazzoni, Antonio Begarelli). There are also collections of ceramics and musical intruments; note the splendid **Este harp** (1581).

Palazzo Ducale★

This noble and majestic building, the ducal palace, was begun in 1634 for Francesco I d'Este and has an elaborately elegant design. Today it is occupied by the Infantry and Cavalry schools.

Excursions

Abbazia di Nonantola

11km/7mi north. ◷Open 7am-8pm. ☏059 54 90 53; www.abbazia-nonantola.net.

The abbey was founded in the 8C and flourished during the Middle Ages. The 12C abbey church has some remarkable **Romanesque sculpture**★ carved by Wiligelmo's assistants in 1121.

Carpi

8km/11mi north.

This attractive small town has a 16C Renaissance cathedral by Peruzzi, overlooking **Piazza dei Martiri**★. The **Castello dei Pio**★ includes and a museum. ☍*Closed for restoration. ☏059 68 82 72; www.palazzodeipio.it.*

The 12C-16C Church of Sagra has a Romanesque campanile, **Torre della Sagra**.

Reggio Emilia

25km/15mi west on the SS 9 (Via Emilia).
This rich industrial and commercial centre on the Via Emilia, was the birthplace of the poet Ariosto (1474-1533) and the painter Antonio Fontanesi (1818-82). Like Modena and Ferrara, it belonged to the Este family (1409–1776).

The historic centre

Piazza Prampolini, the political, religious and economic centre of the town, is overlooked by the 15C cathedral, the Romanesque baptistery and the Town Hall with its 16C Bordello tower.
To the right of the cathedral is the lively Via Broletto, which leads into Piazza San Prospero. This square is dominated by the 18C façade of the church of San Prospero which has a cycle of frescoes in the apse by C. Procaccini and B. Campi as well as a fine wooden chancel. *Open 9am-11.45pm.* ⊚*Donation recommended.* ☎*0522 43 46 67.*

Chiesa della Madonna della Ghiara★

Corso Garibaldi. ⏱*Open 10am-noon and 4-5.30pm.* ☎*0522 43 97 07.*
This is a beautiful church, erected at the beginning of the 17C following a miracle. The interior contains splendid frescoes and paintings, an anthology of 17C Emilian painting; most significant of which is the *Crucifixion* by Guercino.
⚄Galleria Parmeggiani, Musei Civici.

MOLISE

MICHELIN MAP 564 A-C 24-27.

Molise is an ancient land of passage for seasonal movement of cattle, for armies and for travellers. Mountains dominate the territory and inhabitants of the region have always looked to them as a natural defence and refuge: strongholds, fortified castles and villages nestling on hillsides characterise its landscape.

- ▯ **Information:** Via Mazzini 94, 86100 Campobasso, ☎0874 42 91; www.regione.molise.it.
- ▶ **Orient Yourself:** Molise is shaped like a wedge inserted between the Apennines and the sea and the Abruzzi and Puglia. The main access road is A 14
- ☺ **Don't Miss:** Altilia Saepinum.
- ⏱ **Organizing Your Time:** Allow two days.
- ⚄ **Also See:** *ABRUZZO, PUGLIA.*

Visit

Agnone

▶*42km/26mi northeast of Isernia.*
This village owes its fame to the **Fonderia pontificia Marinelli**, the world's oldest bell factory, founded in the 10C. It now houses the **Museo Internazionale della Campana**. ⚄⏱*By reservation only, noon and 4pm.* ⏱*Closed Easter, 25 Dec.* ⊚*4.50€.* ☎*0865 78 235; www.campanemarinelli.com.*
The central street, Via Vittorio Emanuele, is bordered by the church of **Sant'Emidio** (15C) and the Italo-Argentinian theatre which was founded in the last century with funds raised from immigrants in South America. **Via Garibaldi**, lined with houses embellished by lions which bear witness to the community of Venetian merchants, leads to the **Ripa**★, a garden with a fine view over the Verrino Valley.

Altilia Saepinum★

▶*25km/15mi south of Campobasso on S 87.* ⏱*Open daily summer 9.30am-1.30pm and 3-6.30pm (rest of year 3-5pm).* ⏱*Closed Mon, 1 Jan, 1 May, 25 Dec.* ⊚*2€.* ☎*0874 79 02 07.*
The ruins of *Saepinum* rise in the middle of an attractive town on which construc-

tion began in the 17C using plundered stone. The Samnites founded the city, which was subsequently occupied by the Romans who built a city wall with fortified doors and 25 towers.

Access is through the Porta di Terravecchia gateway at the extreme south of the *cardo*, the city's principal street. At the crossroads of the *cardo* and the *decumanus* streets are the remains of the **basilica** to the left and, to the right, the **forum**. Turning right on the *decumanus* note the remains of the senate house (*curia*), the temple dedicated to Jupiter, Juno and Minerva, remains of mosaic flooring, a semicircular recess belonging to the "house of oil-presses" with four brick oil containers, and the *impluvium* of a Samnite house. To the extreme east of the *decumanus*, beyond the **Porta di Benevento** gateway, lies the **Mausoleum of Ennius Marsus**.

Returning to the main crossroads and continuing up the *decumano* cross the old residential and commercial quarters with remains of workshops and the *macellum* (market). At the eastern end of the street rises the **Porta di Boiano**★. Outside the fortifications is the **Mausoleum of Numisius Ligus**.

Against the inner face of the wall, the intimate **theatre**★ has preserved its monumental entrance. The adjacent buildings house a **museum**.

Pietrabbondante

28km/17mi northeast of Isernia. ○Open daily 8.30am to 1hr before dusk. ○Closed 1 Jan, 1 May, 25 Dec. 2€ 0865 76 129.

In an evocative natural setting stands the **Italic Sanctuary of Pietrabbondante**★. This was a sacred site for the Samnites who turned it into a political, as well as religious centre, and thus a symbol of anti-Roman resistance. All that remains are the foundations of the **high temple,** the minor temple and the **theatre**.

Monastero di Santa Maria di Canneto

36km/22mi southeast of Vasto.

This monastery, erected in the 8C, is a fine expression of Lombard-Cassinese culture. The **church** has two admirable works: the **pulpit**★ (8C) and the **altarpiece**★ portraying the refectory (10C).

Monastero di San Vincenzo al Volturno

28km/17mi northwest of Isernia. Guided tours (2hr) conducted by Associazione Culturale Atena. Reserve in advance. 3.50€. 0865 95 10 06.

In an enchanting setting with the backdrop of the Mainarde mountains stands this Benedictine monastery which was founded in the 8C and repeatedly destroyed by Saracen attacks.

Termoli

www.comune.termoli.cb.it.

Termoli is the departure point for the Tremiti islands. It has a fine **castle** (13C) and narrow alleyways that wind their way up to the **Cathedral**★★ (12C).

ABBAZIA DI MONTECASSINO★★
MONTE CASSINO ABBEY
MICHELIN MAP 563 R 23

The massive majestic abbey rising up over the summit of Monte Cassino is an awesome sight. The access road up to one of the holiest places of Roman Catholicism climbs in hairpin bends, affording wonderful valley views.

- **Information:** www.officine.it/montecassino
- **Orient Yourself:** Monte Cassino lies off A 1 which links Rome with Naples.
- **Don't Miss:** The Abbey and the Museo abbaziale.
- **Organizing Your Time:** Allow a couple of hours.
- **Also See:** *ANAGNI, GAETA, SPERLONGA.*

A Bit of History

The monastery of Monte Cassino, the mother house of the Benedictines, was founded in 529 by **St Benedict** (d 547). It was here that the saint drew up a complete and precise set of rules combining intellectual study and manual labour with the virtues of chastity, obedience and poverty. In the 11C under Abbot Didier the abbey's influence was at its height. The monks were skilled in the arts of miniatures, frescoes and mosaics and their work greatly influenced Cluniac art.

The abbey has been destroyed several times since its foundation and has since been rebuilt to the original plans.

Monte Cassino was the setting for one of the most terrible battles of the Second World War which resulted in the deaths of thousands of men and the destruction of one of the greatest centres of Christianity. After the Allies had taken Naples in 1944, the Germans made Cassino the key stronghold in the system of defences guarding the approaches to Rome. On 17 May the Allies launched their final assault, with the Polish corps as the spearhead. After a raging battle, the Germans abandoned Cassino on the following day, allowing the Allies to join forces and leaving open the road to Rome.

Visit

Abbey★★

Abbey: ⏱*Open daily 8.30am-12.30pm and 3.30-6pm (5.30pm winter). Museum:* ⏱*Open Apr-Oct 8.30am-noon and 3.30-6pm; Nov-Mar, Sun and public holidays only 8.30am-12.30pm and 3.30-5.30pm.* ✆*1.50€.* ☎*0776 31 15 29; www.officine. it/montecassino.*

It is preceded by a suitably solemn suite of four communicating cloisters. The bare façade of the basilica quite belies the sumptuousness of the **interior**★★ where marble, stucco, mosaics and gilding create a dazzling if somewhat austere ensemble in the 17C-18C style. The chancel has lovely 17C walnut stalls and the marble tomb enshrining the remains of St Benedict. *Don't miss the elegant tomb of St Benedict.*

Museo abbaziale

The museum presents documents on the abbey's history and works of art which survived the 1944 bombing.

On the way down to Cassino are a museum, the **Museo archeologico nazionale**, and the neighbouring excavation site (amphitheatre, theatre and tomb of Umidia Quadratilla). ⏱*Open daily 9am-7.30pm.* ⏱*Closed 1 Jan, 1 May, 25 Dec.* ✆*2€.* ☎*0776 30 11 68.*

MONTECATINI TERME♧♧♧

POPULATION 20 766

MICHELIN MAP 563 K 14

MAP IN THE MICHELIN GUIDE ITALIA

SEE ALSO THE GREEN GUIDE TUSCANY

The spring water at Montecatini has been famous for its medicinal properties for centuries. With its parks, wide variety of entertainment and racecourse the town provides the ideal setting for an enjoyable break.

- ℹ **Information:** Viale Verdi 66/68, 51016 Montecatini Terme (PT), ☎0572 77 22 44; www.comunemontecatini.com, www.termemontecatini.it.
- ▶ **Orient Yourself:** Montecatini Terme is situated between Florence and Lucca, off the motorway that links Florence to the coast.
- ☺ **Don't Miss:** A visit to a spa.
- ⏱ **Organizing Your Time:** Allow half a day.
- **Kids** **Especially for Kids:** The Parco di Pinocchio.
- ☝ **Also See:** *LUCCA, PISTOIA.*

A typical little square in Italy: Montecatini Alto

G. Bludzin/MICHELIN

Facilities

Elegant Montecatini is one of Italy's most popular spa resorts. The spring water here is used to treat metabolic disorders, liver, stomach and intestinal complaints and rheumatism, through drinking, mud baths and balneotherapy.

Museo dell'Accademia d'Arte (works by the Italian artists Guttuso, Primo Conti, Messina and some of the personal belongings of Verdi and Puccini).

Excursions

Collodi★★
▶*15km/9mi west.*
Collodi was the pen-name adopted by Carlo Lorenzini, the author of Pinocchio, whose mother was born in the village. Kids A park, **Parco di Pinocchio**, in the form of a maze is laid out on the banks of the River Pescia. ⓑⓞ*Open daily, 8.30am-dusk.* 8.50€. 0572 42 93 13; *www.pinocchio.it.*

Address Book

For coin ranges, see the Legend on the cover flap.

WHERE TO STAY
Hotel **La Pia** – *Via Montebello 30 – Montecatini Terme – 0572 78 600 – Fax 0572 77 13 82 – Closed Nov-9 Apr – P – 37 rm – – Restaurant.* An extremely well-run establishment, with simple, well-maintained rooms, centrally located in a quiet part of town. The young proprietors are very thoughtful – nothing is too much trouble. Excellent food (guests only).

WHERE TO EAT
La Torre – *Piazza Giusti 8/9, Montecatini Alto – 5km/3mi northeast of Montecatini Terme – 0572 70 650 – info@latorre-montecatinialto.it –* Closed Tue – 10% service charge. Well-established restaurant situated in the main piazza of this charming village. Combines gastronomic cuisine with top quality wines. Warm welcome. Has been in the same family for more than 40 years.

TAKING A BREAK
Caffè Giusti – *Piazza Giuseppe Giusti 24, Montecatini Alto – 5km/3mi north-east of Montecatini Terme – 0572 70 186 – Thu-Tue 9am-midnight.* With tables set out in the little piazza and a good view of the medieval tower, what better place to sit and watch the world go by? And if you're hungry, treat yourself to some of the delicious bruschette (toasted bread snacks).

Castello e Giardino Garzoni

🕐 *Open daily 9am-1hr before dusk* 🔒 *Castle closed for restoration at time of going to press, only garden open to vistors).* 🎫*5.20 €. For information* ☎*0572 42 95 90.*

The villa is an amazing building dating from the Baroque period. In the **gardens** are vistas, pools, clipped trees, grottoes, sculpture and mazes creating an imaginative spectacle.

MONTEFALCO ★

POPULATION 5 686
MICHELIN MAP 563 N 19 – UMBRIA.

Ramparts from the 14C still girdle this charming little town, which lies among vineyards and olive groves. It is perched – as its name suggests – like a falcon on its nest and has been called the Balcony of Umbria. Montefalco, won over to Christianity in 390 by St Fortunatus, has its own saint, Clara, not to be confused with the companion of St Francis of Assisi.

- 🛈 **Information:** Rivolgersi al Museo (si veda sotto) o all'Ufficio Cultura del Comune, ☎0742 37 90 22, www.montefalcodoc.com.
- ▶ **Orient Yourself:** Montefalco is near S 3, which links Foligno with Spoleto.
- 🞉 **Don't Miss:** L'antica chiesa di San Francesco.
- 🕐 **Organizing Your Time:** Allow a couple of hours.
- ⏱ **Also See:** *ASSISI, PERUGIA.*

Visit

Torre Comunale

🔒*Closed for restoration at time of going to press.* From the top (110 steps) of the communal Tower there is a beautiful **panorama**★★★ of nearly the whole of Umbria.

L'antica chiesa di San Francesco

🕐*Open daily 10.30am-1pm and 3-7pm (2.30-5pm in winter).* 🕐*Closed Mon.* ☎*0742 37 95 98.*

This historic Franciscan church, now deconsecrated, provides an enchanting setting for the **museum** which contains mid-15C **frescoes**★★ depicting scenes from the life of St Francis and St Jer-ome by Benozzo Gozzoli, a *Nativity* by Perugino and an awe-inspiring Crucifix by the Expressionist Master of Santa Chiara (active in Umbria from the end of the 13C to the beginning of the 14C. The museum also houses a gallery with works by Francesco Melanzio (c 1487-1526), a Montefalco native.

Chiesa di Sant'Illuminata

The church is Renaissance in style. The tympanum of the main doorway and several niches in the nave were painted by Francesco Melanzio.

⏱ S. Agostino (Gothic, with frescoes by Umbrian painters of the 14C, 15C and 16C), S. Fortunato *(1km/0.6mi south)* (fresco★ by Benozzo Gozzoli).

MONTEPULCIANO★★

POPULATION 14 107
MICHELIN MAP 563 M 17
SEE ALSO THE GREEN GUIDE TUSCANY.

Montepulciano is an attractive town typical of the Renaissance period. It occupies a remarkably picturesque setting★★on the top of a tufa hill separating two valleys. The town was founded in the 6C by people from Chiusi fleeing the barbarian invasions. They named it Mons Politianus, which explains why people from the town are known as Poliziani. Poets have long sung the praises of its ruby-red wine ("vino nobile").

🗎 **Information:** Piazza Don Minzoni 1, 53045 Montepulciano (SI).
☎0578 75 73 41; www.montepulciano.com.
▶ **Orient Yourself:** Montepulciano lies off S 146, which goes from San Quirico d'Orcia to Chiusi.
👁 **Don't Miss:** The old town.
🕐 **Organizing Your Time:** Allow half a day.
👜 **Also See:** *PIENZA.*

Walking About

Città antica★

Beyond the gateway, Porta al Prato, the high street, the first part of which bears the name Via Roma, loops through the monumental area in the old town. At no 91 Via Roma stands the 16C **Palazzo Avignonesi** attributed to Vignola; no 73, the palace of the antiquarian Bucelli, is decorated with stone from Etruscan and Roman buildings; further along, the **Renaissance façade★** of the church of **Sant'Agostino** was designed by Michelozzo (15C); a tower opposite has a Pulcinello as Jack o'the clock. At the Logge del Mercato (Grain Exchange) bear left into Via di Voltaia nel Corso: Palazzo Cervini (no 21) is a fine example of Florentine Renaissance architecture with its rusticated stonework and curvilinear

and triangular pediments designed by Antonio da Sangallo, a member of an illustrious family of architect-sculptors, who designed some of the most famous buildings in Montepulciano. Continue along Via dell'Opio nel Corso and Via Poliziano (no 1 is the poet's birthplace).

Piazza Grande★★

At the centre of the city this square with its irregular plan is lined by the **Palazzo Comunale★** (Town Hall). From the top of the square **torre** (tower) there is an immense **panorama★★★** of the town and its environs. *Tower:* 🕐*Open Apr-Oct, 10am-6pm.* ☜*1.55€.* ☎*0578 75 73 41.* The majestic Renaissance **Palazzo Nobili-Tarugia** facing the cathedral is attributed to Antonio da Sangallo the Elder. Inside the 16C-17C **Duomo**, to the left, lies the recumbent figure

Famous Inhabitants

This was the birthplace of **Angelo Poliziano** (1454-94), one of the most exquisite Renaissance poets. The poet was a great friend of Lorenzo de' Medici, whom he called Lauro (Laurel) and whom he saved from assassination during the Pazzi Conspiracy (👜 *see Duomo in FIRENZE*). The Stanzas, Poliziano's masterpiece, describe a sort of Garden of Delight haunted by attractive women. Parallels can be drawn between Poliziano's verse and the paintings of his friend Botticelli. **Antonio da Sangallo il Vecchio**, one of the two senior members of the famous family of Renaissance sculptors and architects, bequeathed some well-known works to Montepulciano.

Address Book

WHERE TO STAY

⌂**Agriturismo Relais Ai Battenti** – *Via dell'Antica Chiusina B3 – 1.5km/1mi south of Montepulciano – ☎0578 71 70 09 – Closed 10 Jan-20 Mar. –* ⌷ *– 4 rm* ⌂. This establishment has a great family atmosphere. Comfortable, country-style rooms.

⌂⌂**Albergo Meublé Il Riccio** – *Via Talosa 21 – Montepulciano – ☎0578 75 77 13 – www.ilriccio.net – Closed – 6 rm –* ⌂. Housed in a medieval palazzo, with views from the terrace areas. Rooms are simple.

WHERE TO EAT

⌂⌂**Borgo Buio** – *Via Borgo Buio – ☎0578 71 74 97 – www.borgobuio.it – Closed Thu*. With its wide selection of snacks and pasta dishes (all home-made) this is definitely one for the address book.

⌂⌂**La Grotta** – *Località San Biagio – 1km/0.6mi southwest of Montepulciano on S 146 – ☎0578 75 74 79 – ristorante. lagrotta.@tiscali.it – Closed Wed, Jan and Feb*. Housed in a fine 16C palazzo –this restaurant offers authentic Tuscan cooking. Alfresco dining.

TAKING A BREAK

Caffè Poliziano – *Via Voltaia nel Corso 27/29 – ☎0578 75 86 15 – Open 6.30am-1am*. First opened in 1868, this lovely café has long been popular with artists and writers – previous visitors have included the writer Luigi Pirandello and the film-maker Federico Fellini!

---

of Bartolomeo Aragazzi, secretary to Pope Martin V; the statue was part of a monument by Michelozzo (15C). The monumental **altarpiece**★(1401) is by the Sienese artist, Taddeo di Bartolo.

▸ *Continue along the high street to Piazza San Francesco for a fine view of the surrounding countryside and of the church of San Biagio.*

▸ *Walk down Via del Poggiolo and turn right into Via dell'Erbe to return to the Logge del Mercato.*

⌖ Museo Civico – Pinacoteca Crociani (glazed terracotta by Andrea della Robbia; 13-18C Etruscan remains and paintings).

Excursions

Chiesa della Madonna di San Biagio★★

1km/0.6mi. Leave by the Porta al Prato and then take the Chianciano road before turning right. This pale stone 16C church is an architectural masterpiece by **Antonio da Sangallo** and greatly influenced by Bramante's design for St Peter's in Rome. San Biagio's design is a Greek cross crowned by a dom, and with a south transept prolonged by a semi-circular sacristy. The interior gives the same impression of majesty. To the left of the west door is a 14C Annunciation. Opposite the church stands the elegant porticoed Canonica (canonry).

Chianciano Terme ⚐⚐

10km/6mi southeast. www.chiancianot-erme.com, www.termechianciano.it. The healing properties of the waters at this thermal spa (which can help relieve kidney and liver disorders) were known to the Etruscans and the Romans. ♿⏱*Open daily 10am-1pm and 4-7pm (Nov-Mar, Sat, Sun and public holidays only. ⏱Closed Mon.* ⌖4€. *☎0578 30 471.*

Chiusi

27km/16mi southwest. www.comune. chiusi-della-verna.ar.it. The little town of Chiusi was once one of the 12 sovereign cities of Etruria.

Museo Archeologico★

Via Porsenna. ♿⏱*Open daily 9am-8pm.* ⏱*Closed 1 Jan, 1 May, 25 Dec.* ⌖4 €. *☎0578 20 177; www.comune.firenze.it.* The museum presents finds from local Etruscan burial grounds: sarcophagi, rounded tombstones (*cippi*), alabaster funerary urns, burial urns (*canopae*) in the shape of heads, clay ex-votos as well as utensils, lamps and jewellery.

NAPOLI★★★
NAPLES
POPULATION 1 000 000
MICHELIN MAP 564 E 24 –CAMPANIA.

Naples is a universe of its own, imbued with fantasy and fatalism, superstition and splendour. It is a city of a thousand faces: chaotic and heaving with traffic, yet rich with history, art and culture, ready to surrender its mysteries to anyone who scratches the surface. Then there is the lovely bay with its horizon bounded by Posillipo, the islands, the Sorrento Peninsula and lofty Vesuvius; it is one of the most beautiful in the world. Craded within, its charms and architectural splendours have been praised by poets and writers. UNESCO included the historic centre of the city in its 1995 World Heritage List.

- ▪ **Information:** Via S.Carlo 9, ☎081 40 23 94, Piazza del Plebiscito (Palazzo Reale). ☎081 25 25 711. www.inaples.it.
- ▸ **Orient Yourself:** The main access roads to Naples include A 1, Autostrada del Sole, A 3 for those arriving from the south and A 16, linking Naples to the Adriatic.
- ▣ **Parking:** Proceed on foot and public transport, as Naples' traffic is among Italy's—and possibly the world's— fiercest.
- ⊚ **Don't Miss:** Spaccanapoli, the treasures of the Museo Archeologico Nazionale and the Galleria Nazionale di Capodimonte, the Carthusian monastery of Certosa di San Martino, Piazza del Plebiscito and the Porto di Santa Lucia and the pretty port and views of Mergellina.
- ⊙ **Organizing Your Time:** Dedicate at least three days to exploring the city. Allow around half a day for the Spaccanapoli and the Decumanus Maximus alone.
- **Kids** **Especially for Kids:** The bible illustrations in a nutshell at Chiesa di San Lorenzo Maggiore, the collections of cribs at the museum at Certosa di San Martino and the door knockers at Palazzo Reale.
- ⊛ **Also See:** *CAPRI, CASERTA, COSTIERA AMALFITANA, ERCOLANO, ISCHIA, Golfo di NAPOLI, POMPEI.*

A Bit of History

According to legend, the siren Parthenope gave her name to a town which had sprung up round her tomb, which is why Naples is called the Parthenopaean City. In fact, Naples originated as a Greek colony named Neapolis, conquered by the Romans in the 4C BC. Rich inhabitants of Rome such as Virgil, Augustus, Tiberius and Nero used to winter there, but the Neapolitans themselves retained the Greek language and customs until the Empire's decline.

Since the 12C, seven princely dynasties have reigned over Naples. The Normans, Hohenstaufens, Angevins, Aragonese, Spanish and Bourbons ruled successively until the end of the 18C. The French Revolution of 1789 brought in French troops, and in 1799 a **Parthenopaean Republic** was set up, followed

Inherent Artistic Talent

Neapolitans have always shown a great love of culture, be it **opera**, where great importance is placed on the virtuosity of the singer, or more popular music, sometimes joyful, sometimes melancholy, performed to the accompaniment of a guitar or a mandolin. Naples gave the character Scaramouch (old fox) to the Commedia dell' Arte (⊛ *see BERGAMO)* as well as **Pulcinella** who is the real face of Naples. The great theatrical tradition has continued to the present day with such prodigious exponents as the **De Filippo** brothers, particularly **Eduardo** (1900-84).

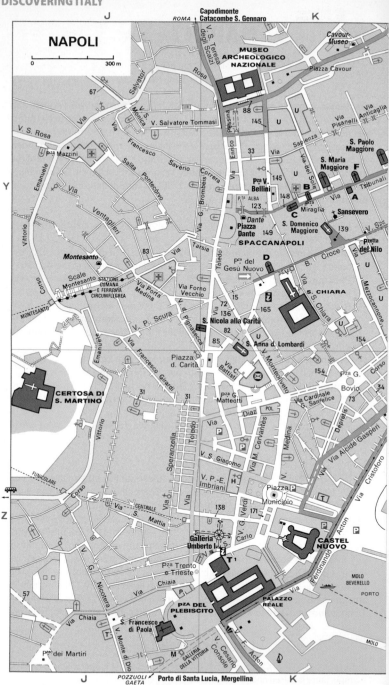

NAPOLI

NAPOLI

Acton V. F.	KZ	
Acton V. Ferdinando	KZ	
Anticaglia V.	KY	
Arte della Lana V.	LY	8
Bagio dei Librai V. S.	KLY	
Baldacchini V. S.	LY	
Battisti V. C.	KZ	
Bellini Pza V.	KY	
Bovio Pza G.	KZ	
Brombeis V. G.	JKY	
Capitelli V. D.	KY	15
Cardinale G. Sanfelice V.	KZ	
Carità Pza d.	JKZ	
Cavour Pza	KY	
Cervantes V. M.	KZ	
Chiaia V.	JZ	
Colombo V. C.	KLZ	
Concezione a Montecalvario V.	JZ	31
Console V. C.	KZ	
Conte di Ruvo V.	KY	32
Correra V. F. S.	JKY	
Cortese V. Giuio C.	KZ	34
Costa V. O.	LY	
Croce V. B.	KY	
Dante Pza	KY	
Depretis V.	KZ	
Diaz V.	KZ	
Donnaregina Largo	LY	
Duomo V. del	LY	
Filangieri V. G.	JZ	57
Forno Vecchio V.	JY	
Gasperi V. Alcide	KZ	
Gesù Nuovo Pza del	KY	
Girardi V. F.	JZ	
Grande Archivio Vico del	LY	
Imbriani V. E.	KZ	
Imbriani V. M. R.	JY	67
Maddaloni V.	KY	72
Marchese Campodisola V.	KZ	73
Marotta V. G.	LY	74
Martiri Pza dei	JZ	
Matteoti Pza G.	KZ	
Mattia V. S.	JZ	
Mazzini Pza	JY	
Medina V.	KZ	
Mezzocannone V.	KY	
Miraglia Pza	KY	
Miroballo al Pendino V.	LY	81
Monte di Dio V.	JZ	
Monteoliveto Pza	KY	82
Monteoliveto V.	KZ	
Montesanto Scale	JY	
Montesanto V.	KY	83
Morgantini V. M.	KY	85
Municipio Pza	KZ	
Museo Nazionale Pza	KY	88
Nicotera V. G.	JZ	
Nilo Piazzetta del	KY	
Pessina V. E.	KY	

Pignasecca V. d.	JY	
Pisanelli V.	KY	
Plebiscito Pza del	JKZ	
Pontecórvo Salita	JY	
Port' Alba V.	KY	123
Porta di Massa V.	LZ	
Porta Medina V.	JY	
Rosa V. S.	JY	
S. Anna dei Lombardi V.	KY	136
S. Apostoli V.	LY	
S. Brigida V.	KZ	138
S. Carlo V.	KZ	
S. Chiara V.	KY	
S. Domenico Pza	KY	139
S. Giacomo V.	KZ	
S. Gregorio Armeno V.	LY	142
S. Marcellino V.	LY	
S. Maria di Costantinopoli V.	KY	145
S. Monica V.	JY	
S. Pietro a Maiella V.	KY	148
S. Sebastiano V.	KY	149
S. Teresa degli Scalzi	KY	
Sapienza V.	KY	
Scura V. P.	JY	
Sedile di Porto V. del	KYZ	154
Sole V. del	KY	
Speranzella V.	JZ	
Tarsia V.	JKY	
Toledo V.	JKYZ	
Tommasi V. S.	JKY	
Tribunali V.	KLY	
Trieste e Trento Pza	JZ	
Trinità Maggiore Calata	KY	165
Umberto I Cso	KLY	
Ventaglieri V.	JY	
Verdi V. G.	KZ	
Vicaria Vecchia V.	LY	169
Vittoria Galleria della	JKZ	
Vittorio Emanuele Cso	JYZ	
Vittorio Emanuele III V.	KZ	171
Zite V. del	LY	

Porta Capuana	LV		
Porto di Santa Lucia	JZ		
Purgatorio ad Arco	KY	F	
Quadreria dei Girolamini	LY	L	
S. Anna dei Lombardi	KY		
S. Domenico Maggiore	KY		
S. Francesco di Paoloa	JZ		
S. Giovanni a Carbonera	LY		
S. Gregorio Armeno	LY		
S. Lorenzo Maggiore	LY		
S. Maria Donnaregina	LY		
S. Maria Maggiore	KY		
S. Nicola alla Carità	KY		
S. Paolo Maggiore	KY		
S. Pietro a Maiella	KY	C	
San Severo	KY		
Santa Chiara	KY		
Teatro S. Carlo	KZ	T¹

Address Book

GETTING ABOUT

It is preferable to get to Naples by train or plane as traffic in the city is chaotic and few hotels have garages. Capodichino Airport, ☎081 78 96 259; www.gesac.it/en (for general information), is 6km/4mi away from the city. Buses to Naples include no 14 (the terminus is in Piazza Garibaldi where the railway station is) and no 3 S which stops at the station and at Molo Beverello.

Naples has a generally good network of public transport although overground transport does fall prey to traffic which can be chock-a-block.

Information listed is intended for guidance only; for details check transport maps available from Tourist Offices.

Trains – The **Cumana** and **Circumflegrea** trains (terminus in Piazza Montesanto) connect Naples to Bagnoli and the Campi Flegrei district. The **Circumvesuviana** train (terminus in Corso Garibaldi) has swift connections to Herculaneum, Pompeii, Castellammare, Vico Equense and Sorrento.

Underground – The **Metropolitana FS** crosses the city vertically from Piazza Garibaldi to Pozzuoli, while the **metropolitana collinare** from Piazza Vanvitelli goes up to Piscinola/Secondigliano. The new link goes from Piazza Vanvitelli to the Museo Archeologico.

Funicular railway – Three routes offer swift connections to the Vomero: the **Funicolare centrale** (Via Toledo-Piazza Fuga), the **Funicolare di Chiaia** (Via del Parco Margherita-Via Cimarosa) and the **Funicolare di Montesanto** (Piazza Montesanto-Via Morghen). The **Funicolare di Mergellina** links Via Mergellina to Via Manzoni.

Tickets – "GiraNapoli" tickets allow travel on buses, trams, the funicular railway and the underground (both the Metropolitana FS and the Metropolitana collinare). There are two types of ticket: 90min tickets and 1-day tickets. Monthly passes are also available.

Radiotaxi – **Free** ☎081 55 15 151, **Blu** ☎081 55 64 444, , **Partenope** ☎081 55 60 202 and **Consor Taxi** ☎081 55 25 252.

Sea connections – Ferry and hovercraft crossings to Capri, Ischia, Procida, the Amalfi Coast and Sorrento leave from Molo Beverello and Mergellina port. Boats depart from Molo Angioino for Sardinia and Sicily.

Tirrenia (to Cagliari, Palermo, Isole Eolie, Capri, Ischia, Procida): ☎081 01 71 998; www.gruppotirrenia.it

Alilauro (to Ischia Porto, Forio, Capri, Positano, Sorrento, Isole Eolie): Via Caracciolo 11, Naples, ☎081 49 72 222; www.alilauro.it

Aliscafi SNAV (to Capri, Ischia, Procida, Palermo, Isole Eolie, Ponza e Ventotene): Stazione Marittima, Naples, ☎081 42 85 555; www.snav.it

Navigazione Libera del Golfo (to Capri and Amalfi Coast): Molo Beverello, Naples, ☎081 55 20 763; www.navlib.it

VISITING

The Campania Artecard is available for 3 (€25) or 7 days (€28), and gives free entry into many of the principal museums and archaeological sites in Naples and the Campania region, and discounts on other events and attractions. www.campaniartecard.it .

Bring your broken dolls to the Dolls' Hospital to be "cured".

B. Morandi/MICHELIN

WHERE TO STAY

For coin ranges see the Legend on the cover flap.

I Vicoletti – *Via S. Domenico Soriano 46, (4th floor, no lift) – 80135 Naples* – ☎081 56 41 156 – www.ivicoletti.it – – 5 rm .

The main attraction of this establishment is the vast terrace with views over the Castel Capuano. Other strong points include the rooms which are spacious, simply furnished but very colourful, and the friendly, enthusiastic staff. Situated in the heart of the historic centre, this hotel exudes a very Mediterranean atmosphere. Shared bathrooms and lots of stairs.

Bed & Breakfast Cappella Vecchia 11 – *V. Santa Maria a Cappella Vecchia 11 – 80121 Napoli – ☎081 24 05 117 – www.cappellavec chia11.it – 6rm* ⌐. Close to Piazza dei Matiri, this bright and cheerful bed and breakfast combines minimalist style with a great central location. Price includes internet connection.

Bed & Breakfast Napoli t'amo – *Via Toledo 148, (1st floor, no lift) – 80134 Naples – ☎/Fax081 55 23 626 – www. napolitamo.it – 12 rm.* A stylish setting for this B&B: it is housed on the first floor of a fine 16C palazzo (complete with coat of arms above the rather grandiose portal) in one of the smartest shopping streets in the city. The rooms and public areas are very spacious, with simple, functional furnishings. Pity about the cramped bathrooms.

Hotel Le Orchidee – *Corso Umberto I 7, (5th floor, with lift) – 80138 Naples – ☎081 55 10 721 – www.hotelorchidee. com – ⌐ ▭ – 7 rm* ⌐ *3.10 €.* This small hotel is very well situated, a stone's throw from the historic centre and not far from the embarkation point for the islands. Housed in an old palazzo, it offers comfortable accommodation. The rooms are spacious and well maintained with simple, modern furnishings.

Hotel Ausonia – *Via Francesco Caracciolo 11 – 80122 Naples – ☎081 68 22 78 – www.hotelausoniana poli.com – ▭ – 19 rm* ⌐. Very close to the Porto di Mergellina. The marine theme is carried through the hotel: from the bedsteads featuring rudders and portholes to a 17C barometer in the small entrance area. For a nautical experience without leaving terra firma.

Soggiorno Sansevero – *Vicolo S. Domenico Maggiore 9, (1st floor, with lift) – 80134 Naples – ☎081 79 01 000 – www.*

albergosansevero.it – ⌐ ▭ – 6 rm ⌐. The Sansevero group of hotels offers stylish accommodation in three 18C palazzi in the heart of Naples. Good-sized rooms have been attractively decorated, with wickerwork furniture and wrought-iron beds. Cheerful, sunny atmosphere makes for a very pleasant stay. The prices are reasonable and it is worth noting that the rooms with shared bathrooms are even cheaper.

Hotel Suite Esedra – *Via Cantani 12 –80133 Naples I – ☎/Fax 081 28 74 51 – ▭ – 16 rm* ⌐. A historic hotel in what was a rather fine patrician residence. Elegant interior with damask upholstery and a 19C table for breakfast. All the rooms have their own individual style and there is even a suite with a hydromassage bath for two. Facilities also include a small gym. Service is of a very high standard.

Bed & Breakfast Parteno – *Via Lungomare Partenope 1, (1st floor, with lift) – 80121 Naples – ☎081 24 52 095 – www.parteno.it – ▭ – 6 rm* ⌐. An elegant and rather stylish B&B with the decor and furnishings chosen by a well-known local artist. Warm, welcoming atmosphere enhanced by the setting: it is housed in a splendid nobleman's re–sidence that has been carefully resto–red. Facilities include a sauna and gym.

Hotel Villa Capodimonte – *Via Moiariello 66 – 80131 Naples – ☎081 45 90 00 – www.villacapodi monte.it – Fax 081 29 93 44 – P▭ – 57 rm* ⌐ *– Rest 31/44 €.* A little off the beaten track but easy to get to. Splendid setting with lovely parkland surrounding this villa-style hotel and wonderful views over the Bay of Naples. Spacious rooms with Art Nouveau-style decor and deluxe facilities. Most have a balcony.

WHERE TO EAT

Pizzeria Di Matteo – *Via Tribunali 93/94 – 80138 Naples – ☎081 45 52 62 – Closed Sun, 2nd and 3rd week of Aug – ⌐* Long a haunt of the rich and famous: previous visitors include the Italian film-star Marcello Mastroianni and more recently Bill Clinton. Simple surroundings, tasty pizzas. Excellent prices and quick service. Mind you don't bang your head going up the stairs to the first floor!

Trianon da Ciro – *Via Pietro Colletta 42/46 – 80100 Naples* – ☎*081 55 39 426* – *Closed 25 Dec, 1 Jan* – ▤. 1920s-style establishment with stucco ceilings and walls painted a splendid yellow ochre colour. Very traditional and atmospheric. Don't be surprised if your delicious pizza is accompanied by a few lines of poetry from the proprietor, who is passionate about both!

Antica pizzeria Da Michele – *Via Cesare Sersale 1/3/5/7 – 80100 Naples* – ☎*081 55 39 204 – www.damichele.net* – *Closed Sun, 3 weeks in Aug* – ▤. A very popular pizzeria: the decor is unpretentious and the main attraction is the excellent pizzas. Come armed with bags of patience – queuing is part of the experience and almost obligatory.

Antica pizzeria Gino Sorbillo – *Via Tribunali 32 – 80138 Naples* – ☎*081 44 66 43 – www.sorbillo.it* – *Closed Sun, 6-25 Aug* – ▤ *10% service charge.* One of the best pizzerias in town. As explained in the menu, the young and enthusiastic proprietor Gino comes from a long line of pizzaioli – 21 in all. Great ambience and fantastic pizzas.

Luigi Lombardi a S. Chiara – *Via Benedetto Croce 59, zona Piazza S. Domenico Maggiore* – ☎*081 52 20 780* – *Closed Mon, Aug* – ▤ *+ 13% service charge.* This pizzeria has been in the same family since the mid-19C – a veritable dynasty of pizzaioli. Over the years it has satisfied the hunger pangs of generations of students and Neapolitan intellectuals. Splendid dining room divided into smaller, more intimate alcoves behind brick-built arches. Excellent pizzas and various other traditional dishes.

Pizzeria Brandi – *Salita di S. Anna di Palazzo 1-2, zona Piazza de Plebiscito* – ☎*081 41 69 28 – www.brandi. it* ▤. Tradition has it that the mythical Margherita pizza was born here on 11 June 1889, so called in honour of Queen Margherita. One for the address book of all pizza connoisseurs, this is a good place to head for after a little light afternoon shopping.

Osteria della Mattonella – *Via Nicotera 13 – 80132 Naples* –

☎*081 41 65 41* – *Closed Sun evening* – ▤ ▤ – *Book.* If you're looking for traditional Neapolitan cooking and an authentic setting, you couldn't do better than this. Paper napkins and informal, friendly service. Limited menu but genuine home cooking and generous portions.

Beverino – *Via S. Sebastiano 62 – 80134 Naples* – ☎*081 29 03 13* –*Closed Mon, Sun evening, 15-22 Aug.* Situated near the atmospheric Piazza Bellini. Good for both lunch and informal dinners. Good wine list to accompany various pasta dishes and cold appetisers. Rustic ambience. Like any self-respecting wine bar it is housed in a vaulted cellar underground – perfect for getting away from the summer heat.

A Tiella – *Riviera di Chiaia 98/100 – 80122 Naples* – ☎*081 76 18 688* – *Closed Sun evening.* What better way to end a gentle stroll along the seafront than a meal at this lovely, little restaurant? The main focus of the menu is fish but other dishes are included. Another attraction is the Neapolitan-style homemade pasta. Charming surroundings complete with vaulted ceiling and small courtyard. Other nice touches include the lemon- and ivy-themed decor and lovely photographs of old Naples.

Taverna dell'Arte – *Rampe S. Giovanni Maggiore 1/A, (across Via Mezzocannone) – 80100 Naples* – ☎*081 55 27 558 – losed Sun, 4-25 Aug* – ▤ – *Book.* For a truly authentic gastronomic experience complete with wines from the Campania region, this is the place to come. Understated but elegant in its rusticity. It is a very popular restaurant and you are advised to book well in advance.

Marino – *Via Santa Lucia 118/120 – 80132 Naples* – ☎*081 76 40 280* – *Closed Mon, Aug* – ▤ *–15% service charge.* A typical Neapolitan trattoria, always crowded and noisy. Run by the same family for many years, with generation after generation faithfully adhering to the same gourmet recipes for both meat and fish dishes. A particularly mouth-watering and abundant display of antipasti.

L'Europeo di Mattozzi – *Via Campodisola 4/6/8 – 80133 Naples* – ☎*081 55 21 323* – *Closed Sun, evenings* *(except Thu-Sat and before public holidays), 15-31 Aug – ▤ – 12% service charge.* Authentic, home cooking inspired by regional traditions and seasonal ingredients which are always super-fresh. Friendly staff combine great courtesy with infectious enthusiasm for food. Simple surroundings and pleasantly noisy.

◛◛**La Chiacchierata** – *Piazzetta Matilde Serao 37 – 80132 Naples – ☎081 41 14 65 – Closed evenings (except Fri), Aug; from Jun-Sep also Sat and Sun – Book – 10% service charge.* Bijou, family-run restaurant with a loyal clientele. Simple, homely cooking with a choice of meat and fish dishes. You can even watch the chef at work: the kitchen is on view. Informal atmosphere. Very centrally located and very reasonably priced.

TAKING A BREAK

Gran Caffè Gambrinus – *Via Chiaia 1/2 – ☎081 41 75 82 – www.caffegambrinus.com – Open daily 8am-1am.* The most famous of all the Neapolitan cafés, it exudes an air of historical importance. Its sumptuously decorated rooms have witnessed 150 years of the most important events of Neapolitan history.

Intra Moenia – *Piazza Bellini Vincenzo 70 – ☎081 29 07 20 – www.intramoenia. it – Open daily 10am-3am.* Situated in the old heart of Naples, this establishment has long been popular with the city's intellectual élite. A café, bookshop and gelateria all rolled into one, the building also houses a publishing house, one of the few that is still in operation.

La Caffettiera – *Piazza dei Martiri 25/26 – ☎081 76 44 243 – Open daily 7.30am-11pm. Good coffee and delicious brioches.*

Scaturchio – *Piazza S. Domenico Maggiore 19 – ☎081 55 17 031 – Open daily 7.30am-8.40pm.* The place to try the sfogliatella riccia (a flaky pastry stuffed with ricotta and candied fruit, flavoured with orange oil) straight out of the oven or a baba, a cake of foreign origin but very much appreciated in the Kingdom of Naples.

GOING OUT

Dizzy Club – *Corso Vittorio Emanuele 19/20 – Open Thu-Tue 8pm-2am.* Over 150 cocktails to choose from here! Also the place to go if you fancy a game of cards or chess.

ENTERTAINMENT

Teatro San Carlo – *Via San Carlo 98 – ☎081 79 72 111 – www.teatrosancarlo. it –Opera season: Dec-May – Box office: Tue-Sun 10am-1pm and 4.30-6.30pm.* With its opera company permanently in residence, the San Carlo is one of the best opera houses in the world.

SHOPPING

The figurines from the Nativity scenes (head for Via San Gregorio Armeno) make lovely souvenirs and presents. The best place for cameos and coral pieces is the Napoletano (especially Torre del Greco).

EVENTS AND FESTIVALS

With all their pomp and circumstance and magnificent ceremonial trimmings, there are a number of well-known religious festivals. These include Madonna di Piedigrotta (8 Sep), Santa Maria del Carmine (16 Jul) and especially the Feast of the Miracle of St Januarius (1st Sun in May and 9 Sep). During the Christmas period (until 6 Jan), the churches are decorated with wonderful Nativity scenes.

USEFUL TELEPHONE NUMBERS

Carabinieri Police ☎081 54 81 111
State Police ☎081 79 41 111
Road Police ☎081 59 54 111
City Police ☎081 75 13 177
Emergency Ambulance ☎081 75 28 282 or 081 75 20 696
Railway Information ☎147 88 80 88

by a French kingdom (1806-15) under Joseph Bonaparte (Napoleon's brother) and afterwards Joachim Murat (Napoleon's brother-in-law), who promoted excellent reforms. From 1815 to 1860 the Bourbons remained in power in spite of two serious revolts.

Art in Naples

A Royal Patron of the Arts

Under the princes of the House of Anjou, Naples was endowed with many ecclesiastical buildings, influenced by the French Gothic style. **"Robert the Wise" of Anjou** (1309-43) attracted poets, scholars and artists from regions of Italy to his court in Naples. Boccaccio spent part of his youth in Naples where he fell in love with Fiammetta, whom some believe to have been the king's own daughter. His friend Petrarch also spent time in this city. In 1324 Robert the Wise brought the Sienese sculptor **Tino di Camaino** to adorn many of the churches with his monumental tombs. Other churches were embellished with frescoes by the Roman artist Pietro Cavallini, later by Giotto whose works have unfortunately disappeared.

The Neapolitan School of Painting (17C-early 18C)

The busiest period in Neapolitan painting was the 17C which began with the arrival in Naples in 1607 of the great innovator in painting, **Caravaggio**. The master's style was bold and realistic: he often used real people as models for his crowd scenes. He used chiaroscuro with dramatic effect with light playing a fundamental part. So a new school of painting flourished, its members greatly inspired by the master. The principal followers were Artemisia Gentileschi, the Spaniard **José de Ribera** alias Spagnoletto, **Giovanni Battista Caracciolo** and the Calabrian Mattia Preti. One pupil who differed greatly from the others was **Luca Giordano** whose spirited compositions were full of light. His decorative work heralds the painting of the 18C. **Francesco Solimena** perpetuated Giordano's style but he was also influenced by the more sombre style of Mattia Preti and by Classicism. His paintings are characterised by chiaroscuro effects which lend a strong balance to the use of space.

The Baroque period

Numerous architects built fine Baroque buildings in Naples and the surrounding area. **Ferdinando Sanfelice** (1675-1748) had a highly inventive and theatrical approach to staircases, which he placed at the far end of the courtyard where they became the palace's most important decorative feature. It was, however, **Luigi Vanvitelli** (1700-73) who was the great Neapolitan architect of the 18C. The Bourbon King Charles III entrusted Vanvitelli with the project to build another Versailles at Caserta (see CASERTA). It was in the 17C that Naples began to specialise in the marvellous **Christmas mangers** (presepi).

Spaccanapoli and the Decumanus Maximus★★

Enter Via Benedetto Croce. To get the most out of this itinerary, including access to all the buildings, set out in the morning. Open daily, 7am-1pm and 4-7.30pm. ☎081 55 18 613.

The main axis of old Naples, formed by the Via S. Benedetto Croce, Via S. Biagio dei Librai and Via Vicaria Vecchia is nicknamed 'Spaccanapoli', (the street that bisects Naples). It follows the course of a main road through ancient Naples, the **Decumanus Maximus**, which now traces the Via Tribunali.

In Piazza del Gesù Nuovo is the church of **Gesù Nuovo** whose façade is decorated inside with Solimena's *Expulsion of Heliodorus* from the Temple.

Chiesa di Santa Chiara★

Church: Open 7.30am-12.30pm and 4.30-8pm. Museum: Open 9.30am-5.30pm, Sun and public holidays, 9.30am-2pm. €4. ☎081 195 75 915; www.santachiara.info.

Sancia of Majorca, the wife of Robert the Wise of Anjou, had this Church of the Poor Clares built in the Provençal-

Gothic style. The interior was destroyed in the 1943 bombing and then rebuilt in its original form. A lofty nave, lit by narrow twin windows, opens onto nine chapels. At the end, memorials to the Anjou dynasty line the wall: including the **tomb**★★ of Robert the Wise and on the right the tomb of Charles of Anjou, attributed to **Tino di Camaino** who is also responsible for the **tomb**★ of Marie de Valois (near the south wall). To the right of the presbytery a vestibule leads to the 14C chancel★.

Cloisters★★

The current layout is the work of Domenico Antonio Vaccaro who, in the 18C, transformed the interior of the cloisters into a garden. He was also responsible for embellishing the wall of the portico, the seats and the columns lining the avenues with **majolica decoration**★.

Chiesa di San Domenico Maggiore

⏲Open daily, 8am-noon and 4.30-7pm. ☎081 45 91 88.
The interior of this church has both Gothic (**caryatids** by Tino di Camaino support a huge paschal candelabrum) and Baroque features. In the right side aisle, the second chapel has frescoes by Pietro Cavallini (1309). The 18C sacristy contains coffins of members of the court of Aragon (in the balustrade).

Cappella Sansevero

⏲Open daily 10am-5.40pm, Sun and public holidays 10am-1.10pm. ⏲Closed Tue. ◎6€. ☎081 55 18 470; www.museosansevero.it.
This 16C chapel was completely restored in the 18C by Raimondo de Sangro, an eccentric whose passion for alchemy and scientific study gave rise to a certain notoriety. There are even two skeletons complete with "petrified" circulatory system (in an underground chamber, access from the south aisle).
In the chapel there are fine marble **sculptures**★: on either side of the choir are Chastity (the veiled woman) and Despair (symbolised by a man struggling with a net); the central one depicts **Christ covered by a shroud**★, a masterpiece by **Giuseppe Sammartino**.

Just before Via S. Biagio dei Librai, is **Piazzetta del Nilo,** which derives its name from a statue of the Nile. Further along, to the left, is Via S. Gregorio Armeno, lined with shops and workshops where the figurines for the Nativity scenes (presepio) are produced. The skills have been handed down from father to son since the 19C. These days the statuettes include modern figures. The area is particularly charming around Christmas time. ⏲The petrified skeletons are particularly interesting.

Chiesa di San Gregorio Armeno

⏲Open daily, 9.30am-noon. ◎Donation recommended. ☎081 55 20 186.
This church is dedicated to St Gregory. A spacious atrium leads onto the **interior**★ of the church which is opulently Baroque in style. The frescoes along the nave and in the cupola are the work of Luca Giordano. At the end of the nave are two huge Baroque **organs**. Of particular interest in the presbytery is the high altar with intarsia work in polychrome marble and, to the right, the comunichino, a brass screen from behind which the nuns followed Mass. The **cloisters** (access via the steps in the monastery) have a splendid fountain (centre) decorated with statues of Christ and the Samaritan woman (late 18C).
At the end of Via S. Gregorio Armeno is Via dei Tribunali, which runs into the Decumamus Maximus that dates back to ancient Rome.

Chiesa di San Lorenzo Maggiore

Kids The Bible illustrations in a nutshell. ⏲Open 9.30am-5.30pm, Sun and public holidays 9.30am-1.30pm. ◎5€. ☎081 21 10 860; www.sanlorenzomaggiore.com.
The church of St Lawrence was built in the 14C over an early Christian church, the remains of which include the perimeter walls and columns from the nave. It is built on the plan of a Latin cross with an elegant **arch**★ that spans the transept crossing. The nave, a simple, austere rectangular space (except for a chapel on the west wall which has kept its splendid Baroque additions) is a testament to the Franciscan influence. The **polygonal apse**★ is an interesting specimen of French Gothic architecture

in southern Italy. It is surmounted by elegant arches crowned by twin bays and terminates in an ambulatory onto which open chapels with frescoes by disciples of Giotto. The north transept houses a large chapel dedicated to St Anthony and, on the altar, a painting of the saint surrounded by angels (1438), on a gold background. To the right of the high altar is the remarkable **tomb**★ of Catherine of Austria, attributed to Tino di Camaino.

From the cloisters of the church make for the **chapter house**, which houses a unique "illustrated Bible" – terracotta figurines placed inside nutshells which date from the 1950s. Access to the **ruins** is also from the cloisters. The ruins reveal a crucial part of Naples' Greco-Roman history: along with the forum there are traces of the treasury, bakery and macellum (large covered market). *Ruins: (⚲entrance from Vico dei Maiorani).* 🔊*Guided tours available (1hr).* ☎*081 45 49 48.*

Duomo★

🕐*Treasury of San Gennaro open to visitors Mon-Sat 9.30am-5pm, Sun and public holidays 9.30am-2.30pm.* ☎*081 29 49 80; www.museogennaro.com, www.duomo dinapoli.it.*

Built in the 14C, the cathedral was altered at a later date. Held in great veneration by the people, the **Tesoro di San Gennaro**★(Chapel of St Januarius), in a Baroque style, is preceded by a remarkable 17C bronze grille: behind the high altar are two glass phials containing the saint's blood which is supposed to liquefy, failing which disaster will befall the town. The Feast of the **Miracle of St Januarius** is held twice annually on the first Sunday in May and on 19 September. The dome is decorated with a Lanfranco fresco showing an admirable sense of movement.

The south transept houses an **Assumption** by Perugino and the Gothic **Minutolo Chapel** which has a beautiful 13C mosaic floor. The **succorpo** (crypt) is an elegant Renaissance structure.

A door in the north aisle gives access to the 4C **Basilica di Santa Restituta**, which was transformed in the Gothic period and again in the 17C. At the far end of the nave, the 5C **Baptistery of San Giovanni** is a fine structure containing mosaics★★of the same period.

Decumanus Maximus★★

Broadly takes the course of the Via dei Tribunali. 🔊*Tour of decumanus monuments, daily 9am-1.30pm. Pio Monte della Misericordia.* ☎*081 44 69 44. Quadreria dei Girolamini:* 🕐*9am-1pm (last admission 12.20pm);* 🕐*Closed Aug;* ☎*081 44 91 39. Library:* ⚲*Closed for restoration at the time of going to press. San Paolo Maggiore* ☎*081 45 40 48. Purgatorio ad Arco: also open Sun morning,* ☎*081 45 93 12. Croce di Lucca:* ☎*081 56 52 85. San Pietro a Maiella:* 🕐*Also open Sun morning,* ☎*081 45 90 08.*

Turn right to get to the 17C **Pio Monte della Misericordia** which houses six panels; the themes are linked to the charitable works carried out by the institute. Of particular interest are St Peter freed from Prison by Caracciolo and the **The Seven Works of Mercy**★★★ by Caravaggio.

▷ *Turn back and at the junction of Via Duomo turn right.*

Quadreria dei Girolamini

Entrance from Via Duomo 142.

On the first floor of a convent, this collection has a considerable body of work from the Neapolitan, Roman and Florentine schools of the 16C-18C. These include paintings by Luca Giordano, GB Caracciolo, José de Ribera **(Apostles)**, Guido Reni and Francesco Solimena *(Prophets)*. The convent also houses a Library with a splendid **18C room**★.

The **chiesa dei Girolamini** has works of art by Pietro Bernini (father of Lorenzo), Pietro da Cortona, Luca Giordano and Francesco Solimena.

A little further on is the church of **San Paolo Maggiore**, whose sacristy houses fine **frescoes**★by Solimena: 🕐*The Fall of Simon Magus* and the Conversion of St Paul *(on the side walls)* are among this artist's masterpieces.

Further along, to the right, is the church of **Purgatorio ad Arco** with its tiny underground cemetery **(cimitero sotterraneo)** where, until recently, the widespread practice of cleaning the bones was carried out for the purposes of receiving grace.

At no 362 is **Palazzo Spinelli di Laurino** with an elliptical courtyard embellished by one of Sanfelice's staircases.

On the parvis of the church of **Santa Maria Maggiore**, also known as Pietrasanta, with its beautiful brick and majolica (1764) flooring, rise the Renaissance chapel, Cappella Pontano, and, to the right, a fine 11C campanile.

Beyond **Croce di Lucca**, a 17C church with coffered ceiling of gilded wood, is the church of **San Pietro a Majella**.

The tour ends in Piazza Bellini which is a pleasant place to spend the evening. In the centre are the ruined Greek walls. A little further on is **Piazza Dante**, overlooked by a range of buildings, the work of Vanvitelli. *The beautiful Baptistry mosaics are worth visiting.*

City Centre★★★
Visit: 2hr 30min

Castel Nuovo (or Maschio Angioino)★★
Open Mon-Sat 9am-7pm (ticket office closes 6pm). Closed Sun and public holidays. 5€. 081 42 01 241.

This imposing castle, surrounded by deep moats, was built in 1282 by Pierre de Chaulnes and Pierre d'Agincourt, the architects of Charles I of Anjou. It was modelled on the castle at Angers. A remarkable **triumphal arch**★★ embellishes the entrance on the town side. This masterpiece bearing sculptures to the glory of the House of Aragon, was built to designs by Francesco Laurana in 1467. Access to the **Sala dei Baroni** is via the staircase in the inner courtyard (at the far end on the left). The fine vaulting is star shaped, formed by the tufa groins intersecting with other architectural features. The (14C) features an elegant Renaissance doorway is now kept in the sacristy.

Teatro San Carlo★
Guided tours only, 9am-6pm (depending on performance and rehearsal times). €5. For information, call 081 66 45 45; www.teatrosancarlo.it.

The theatre was built under Charles of Bourbon in 1737 and rebuilt in 1816 in the neo-Classical style, and is an institution in the Italian music world.

The auditorium, with boxes on six levels and a large stage, is built of wood and stucco to achieve perfect acoustics.

Piazza del Plebiscito★
This semicircular "square" (19C) is enclosed by the royal palace and the neo-Classical façade of the church of San Francesco di Paola, built on the model of the Pantheon in Rome. The equestrian statues of Ferdinand I and Charles III of Bourbon are by Canova.

Palazzo Reale★
Open daily 9am-6pm. Closed Wed and public holidays. 4€. 081 58 08 11.

The royal palace was built at the beginning of the 17C by the architect Domenico Fontana and has been remodelled several times. The façade retains more or less its original appearance. Since the late 19C the niches on the façade have contained eight statues of the most famous Kings of Naples. A huge staircase with twin ramps and crowned by a coffered dome leads to the **apartments**★ and the sumptuously decorated royal chapel. The richly ornamented rooms have retained their numerous works of art, tapestries, paintings, period furniture and fine porcelain. Of particular interest are the splendid **door knockers**★ Kids made of wood: *putti*, nymphs and animals are set off against a gilded background.

Porto di Santa Lucia★★
See plan of the built-up area on Michelin map 431.

Santa Lucia is the name of the small suburb that juts out towards the sea. It is best known as the name of a tiny port, immortalised by a famous Neapolitan song, nestling between a rocky islet and the jetty linking it to the shore. **Castel dell'Ovo** is a severe edifice built by the Normans and remodelled by the Angevins in 1274. Legend has it that Virgil hid a magic egg (uovo) within its walls and that the destruction of the egg would result in a similar fate for the castle.

From the jetty there is a splendid **view**★★of Vesuvius on the one hand and of the western side of the bay on the other. In the evening, go further along to Piazza Vittoria which offers a **view**★★★of the residential suburbs on the Vomero and Posillipo hillsides, brightly lit up by a myriad of twinkling lights.

The view of Vesuvius is particularly memorable from the jetty.

Museo Archeologico Nazionale★★★

Visit: 2hr. ⏱*Open daily 9am-7.45pm.* ⏱ *Closed Tue and public holidays.* 6.50€. ☎84 88 00 288; www.pierreci.it. The National Archaeological Museum collections comprise of art belonging to the Farnese family and treasures discovered at Pompeii and Herculaneum. It is one of the world's richest museums for Greco-Roman antiquities.

Look out for the Tazza Farnese, blue vase and Temple of Isis.

Ground floor

Greco-Roman sculpture★★★
The large atrium displays sculptures from Pompeii and Haerculaneum. At the front of the room a staircase on the right leads to the section in the basement dedicated to the **epigraphy section** (ancient inscriptions) and the **Egyptian collection**.

Galleria dei Tirannicidi – *Turn right on entering the Atrium.*
The Tyrant-Slayers' Gallery is devoted to Archaic art. The **Aphrodite Sosandra** with a fine, proud face and elegantly-draped robe is a splendid copy of a Greek bronze (5C BC), while the powerful marble group of the **Tyrant-Slayers**, a copy of a Greek bronze, represents Harmodios and Aristogiton who delivered Athens from the tyrant, Hipparchus, in the 6C BC.

Galleria dei Grandi Maestri – *Access from the Galleria dei Tirannicidi.*
The Great Masters' Gallery contains the statue of the Farnese Pallas (Athena), Orpheus and Eurydice bidding each other farewell, a low relief copied from an original by Phidias (5C BC), and the

Doryphorus, the spear-bearer, a copy of the famous bronze by Polyclitus.
At the end of the Galleria dei Tirannicidi, to the left, is a gallery displaying the famous **Callipygian Aphrodite** (Callipige signifies "with lovely buttocks", 1C) and the statue of **Artemis of Ephesus** (2C) in alabaster and bronze, representing the deity venerated at the temple by the Aegean Sea. She is represented with numerous breasts.

Galleria del Toro Farnese – *Access from the preceding gallery.*
This gallery houses the monumental sculptural groups found at the Baths of Caracalla in Rome in the 16C.
In the centre is the colossal *Flora farnese*. In the last room is the impressive sculptured group called the **Farnese Bull** depicting the death of Dirce, a legendary queen of Thebes. It was carved from a single block of marble. It is a 2C Roman copy, which like many works in the Farnese collection has undergone much restoration. In the right wing is the **Farnese Hercules**.
From this gallery visit the room dedicated to **engraved gemstones** that includes one of the museum's greatest masterpieces, the **Tazza Farnese**★★★, an enormous cameo in the shape of a cup made in Alexandria in the 2C BC.

Mosaics★★
To the left on the mezzanine.
Although most of these come from Pompeii, Herculaneum and Stabia, they offer a wide variety of styles and subject matter. There are two small works *(Visit to a Fortune-Teller and Roving Musicians)* by Dioscurides of Samos along with the Actors on stage in the Room of the Tragic Poet *(Room LIX)*. Mosaics including a Frieze with masks and the splendid mosaic of the Battle of Alexander and Darius *(Room LXI)*, which paved the floor of the House of the Faun at Pompeii, are found in Rooms LX and LXI. The collection ncludes examples of opus sectile.

First floor

Works from Villa di Pisone and dei Papiri★★★
At the beginning of the Salone della Meridiana, on the right.

The villa, which was discovered at Herculaneum in the 18C but was later reburied, is thought to have belonged to L Calpurnius Pison who was Julius Caesar's father-in-law. The owner had turned the house into a museum. The documents and splendid works of art from his collections are priceless. The Sala dei Papiri (Room CXIV) contains photographs of some of the 800 papyri from the library. In Room CXVI are exhibited **bronze statues** that adorned the peristyle of the villa: the **Drunken Faun** lost in euphoria, a **Sleeping Satyr** with a beautiful face in repose; the two **Wrestlers** are inspired from Lysippus (4C BC); the **Dancers from Herculaneum** are probably water-carriers; Hermes at Rest, reflects Lysippus' ideal.

In Room CXVII, is the **portrait** mistakenly identified as that of **Seneca**, one of Antiquity's most expressive works.

Silver, ivory, terracotta and glass gallery★

At the beginning of the Salone della Meridiana, on the left. These rooms are mostly devoted to finds brought back from Pompeii and Herculaneum. Exhibits include silver from the House of Menander in Pompeii, ivory ornaments, weapons, glass; note the stunning **Blue vase**★★ decorated with *putti* and harvest scenes. From here, head to the room with a **model of Pompeii**.

Sale del Tempio di Iside★★★

After the room above.
The room features objects and pictures from the Temple of Isis discovered behind the Great Theatre at Pompeii. Three areas have been partially reconstructed to evoke the original structure: the portico, the *ekklesiasterion* (the assembly room where the worshippers met) and the *sacrarium* (sanctuary). The frescoes illustrate a still life (figs, grapes, geese and doves are elements linked to the worship of this Egyptian goddess). Of particular interest are the large panels depicting rites and scenes illustrating the myths surrounding Io (Isis).

Sale degli affreschi★★★

At the far end of the Salone della Meridiana, on the left, or after the Sale del Tempio di Iside. The collection includes some splendid frescoes from Pompeii, Herculaneum and Stabia in particular. The diversity of style and colour is a testament to the richness of this form of decorative art practised by the Romans (see POMPEI). Exhibits include beautiful paintings with mythological subjects such as Heracles, Ariadne, and Medea and Iphigenia, and epic poems including episodes from the Trojan war that are inserted in architectural perspectives, friezes of cupids, satyrs and maenads.

Palazzo and Galleria Nazionale di Capodimonte★★

Visit: 2hr. North of the city. Open daily, 8.30am-7.30pm (ticket office closes 6.30pm). Closed Wed, 1 Jan, 1 May, 15 Aug, 25 Dec. 7.50€. 84 88 00 288 (Freephone); www.lineadarte.it.
This former **royal estate**★ extends to the north of the city and includes a palace, a park, the remains of the 18C porcelain factory and an art gallery.

Pinacoteca

The nucleus is the Farnese collection, inherited by the Bourbons, enriched subsequently and tracing main trends in the evolution of Italian painting.
The collections open with the Farnese Gallery, which displays famous portraits of the most important members of the Farnese family. Note the portrait of **Paolo III with his nephews**★★, a masterpiece by Titian.
In the **Crucifixion**★★★ by Masaccio, Mary Magdalene in a red dress with arms stretched towards the cross is a fine example of perspective that made Masaccio a key figure in the revolution of the Renaissance. Renaissance painting is represented by the works of Botticelli (*Madonna and Child with Saints*), Filippino Lippi and Raphael. A fine example of the Venetian school is the **Transfiguration**★★ by Giovanni Bellini; the soft colours and light convey serenity that suffuses the landscape.
In the Venetian section note the celebrated **Portrait of Fra Luca Pacioli**,

possibly by a Spanish artist. Among the main exponents of Mannerism are Sebastiano del Piombo (**Portrait of Clement VII**★), Pontormo and Rosso Fiorentino. Titian's study of light is exemplified in the sensual **Danae** and in the works of his pupil El Greco. Serenity and tenderness are evoked in a small canvas, **The Mystic Marriage of St Catherine**, by Correggio and in the Holy Family by Parmigianino, which stresses the essential role of the mother. Also note the Lucrezia and the **Antea**★. The section devoted to Flemish artists includes fine works by Peter Bruegel the Elder (*The Misanthrope* and **The Parable of the Blind**★★).

The second floor houses the "Neapolitan Gallery", a collection formed by Gioacchino Marat of works acquired from suppressed monastic orders. Masterpieces include **St Ludovic of Toulouse** by Simone Martini, **St Jerome in his studio** by Colantonio and the **Flagellation**★★ by Caravaggio. There are also works by Caracciolo, Ribera, Mattia Preti, Luca Giordano and Francesco Solimena. The third floor is devoted to contemporary art.

Royal apartments

The rooms on the first floor have fine furnishings. Of note is the **room**★ with walls faced in porcelain and decorated with chinoiserie flowers. Also on view are a fine porcelain collection including the 19C *Procession of Aurora* in biscuit porcelain, and an especially rich collection of royal armoury.

Certosa di San Martino★★

&. ⓒ *Visit: 1hr. Open daily 8.30am-6.30pm.* ⓒ *Closed Wed, 1 Jan, 25 Dec.* ⓔ *6€. For information call* ☎ *84 88 00 288 (Freephone); www.pierreci.it.*

This 14C Carthusian monastery founded by the Anjou dynasty is situated on the Vomero hill. The **Castel Sant'Elmo** was rebuilt by the Spaniards in the 16C and used as a prison. From the drill square *(access on foot or by lift)* there is a wonderful view over the city and the bay.

Church

The **interior**★★ is lavishly Baroque and adorned with paintings by Caracciolo, Guido Reni and Simon Vouet. Beyond the sacristy is the treasury decorated with frescoes by Luca Giordano and a painting by Ribera, *La Pietà*.

The **great cloisters** is the work of the architect-sculptor Cosimo Fanzago.

Museum★

The section devoted to festivals and costumes contains an exceptional collection of figurines and Neapolitan **cribs**★★ 📷 *(presepi)* in polychrome terracotta from the 18C and 19C. The tour concludes with a large, impressive crib from the late 19C.

Legend and mystery around Castel dell'Ovo

Elsewhere in the Historic Centre

Chiesa di Sant'Anna dei Lombardi

☞*Closed for restoration at the time of going to press.* ☏081 55 13 333.
This Renaissance church, dedicated to St Anne of the Lombards, is rich in contemporary Florentine **sculpture**★.

Palazzo Como★

☞*Closed for restoration at the time of going to press.* ☏081 20 31 75.
This late-15C palace contains the **Museo Civico Filangieri**, which displays collections of armour, ceramics and porcelain, furniture and paintings.

Porta Capuana★

This is one of the fortified gateways built in 1484 to the plans of Giuliano da Maiano. The **Castel Capuano** nearby was the former residence of the Norman princes and the Hohenstaufens.

Chiesa di San Giovanni a Carbonara★

This 14C church holds the tomb of Ladislas of Anjou (15C).

Chiesa di Santa Maria Donnaregina★

Go through cloisters adorned with 18C faience. A Baroque church of the same name precedes the 14C Gothic church. Inside is the **tomb**★of the founder, Mary of Hungary, widow of Charles II of Anjou, by **Tino di Camaino**. The chancel is decorated with 14C **frescoes**★.

Outside the Historic Centre

The following places of interest are not on the town plan. See the map of the built-up area on Michelin map 564.

Villa Floridiana★

▶*To the west of Naples.* ◷*Open daily except Mon, 8.30am-2pm.* ✆*2.50€.* ☏*848 800 288 or 081 57 88 418; www.beniculturali.it.*

This graceful small white palace (*palazzina*) in the neo-Classical style stands high up on the Vomero hillside. The façade overlooks the gardens, which afford a splendid **panorama**★★. The villa houses the **Museo Nazionale di Ceramica Duca di Martina**★, with fine displays of faience and porcelain.

Catacombe di San Gennaro★★

▶*North of the city.* ☚*Guided tours only (40min), daily 9am, 10am, 11am and noon.* ◷*Closed Mon, 1 Jan.* ✆*5€.* ☏*081 74 11 071.*
The catacombs dug in the volcanic rock extend over two floors. The tomb of St Januarius, whose remains were transferred here in the 6C, is decorated with frescoes of the saint. There are beautiful paintings in the niches (3C-10C). In the upper section and the atrium vault is adorned with early Christian work and portraits adorning family tombs.

Villa Comunale

Toward Mergellina, along the seafront.
Vanvitelli laid out these public gardens along the waterfront in 1780 and they are popular with Neapolitans for their evening stroll. At the centre of the gardens is the **Aquarium**. ♿◷*Open daily except Mon, Mar-Oct 9am-6pm, Sun and public holidays 9.30am-6.30pm, Nov-Feb 9am-5pm, Sun and public holidays 9am-2pm.* ✆*1.55€.* ☏*081 58 33 263.*

Museo Principe di Aragona Pignatelli Cortes

Riviera di Chiaia, opposite the Villa Comunale. ◷*Open daily 8.30am-1pm.* ◷*Closed Tue, 1 Jan, 1 May, 25 Dec.* ✆*2€.* ☏*081 41 07 066.*
The ground floor of the summer residence of the Princess Pignatelli (she lived here until the 1950s) is open to. The stables house a collection of English, French and Italian carriages.

Mergellina★

Mergellina, at the foot of the Posillipo hillside, affords a splendid bay **view**★★: the Vomero hillside, crowned by Castel Sant'Elmo, slopes down towards the Santa Lucia headland, with Castel dell'Ovo and Vesuvius in the distance.

GOLFO DI **NAPOLI**★★★
BAY OF NAPLES
MICHELIN MAP 564 E-F 24-26 – CAMPANIA.

The Bay of Naples, extending from Cumae to Sorrento, is one of the most beautiful Italian bays. Here, in close proximity, you will find isolated areas conducive to meditation, such as the archaeological sites, the bare slopes of Vesuvius, the Sibyl's Cave or Lake Averno, and others bustling with activity and crowded with traffic, further enlivened by the exuberance of the local people. Its legendary beauty is somewhat marred by the uncontrolled sprawl of industrial development that has reached the outskirts of Naples. However, its islands, capes and mountains are as lovely as they were two thousand years ago.

- **Information:** in Naples: Via S.Carlo 9, ☏081 40 23 94., Via Marino Turchi 16, ☏08124 00 911, Piazza del Plebiscito 1, ☏081 25 25 711; www.inaples.it.
- ▶ **Orient Yourself:** The main access roads to the Bay of Naples are A 1, the so-called Autostrada del Sole, A 3 if you are arriving from the south and A 16, which links Naples to the Adriatic
- **Don't Miss:** Campi Flegrei, Vesuvius, Sorrento and the Penisola Sorrentina.
- **Organizing Your Time:** Dedicate 4-5 days to exploring the region.
- **Especially for Kids:** Volcanic activity in Solftara and the Planetarim and Officina dei Piccoli in Bagnoli.
- **Also See:** *CAPRI, CASERTA, COSTIERA AMALFITANA, ERCOLANO, ISCHIA, NAPOLI, POMPEI.*

Excursions

Below are four itineraries (the first two departing from Naples), each of them a natural progression from the previous one. For itinerary 5, see COSTIERA AMALFITANA.

1 Campi Flegrei★★

From Naples to Cuma. 45km/28mi – 6hrs.

This volcanic area, the Phlegrean Fields, which received its name from the ancients ("phlegrean" is derived from a Greek word meaning "to blaze"), extends along the Gulf of Pozzuoli. Hot springs, steam-jets and sulphurous gases rise from the ground and sea, due to underground activity. Lakes have formed in the volcanic craters.

Naples★★★ see NAPOLI

Posillipo★

www.capriweb.com/Napoli/Posillipo. This famous hill forms a promontory and separates the Bay of Naples from the *Gulf of Pozzuoli*. Posillipo, dotted with villas, lovely gardens and modern buildings, is Naples' main residential area. It affords splendid bay views.

Marechiaro★

This small fishermen's village built high above the sea was made famous by a Neapolitan song *Marechiare*.

Parco Virgiliano

Also called the **Garden of Remembrance**, the park has splendid **views**★★over the Bay of Naples, from Cape Miseno to the Sorrento Peninsula, and the islands of Procida, Ischia and Capri.

Museo Vivo di Città della Scienza a Bagnoli★

Open Tue-Sat 9am-5pm, Sun and public holidays 10am-7pm (call ahead to confirm opening times). Closed Mon, 1 Jan, 25 Dec. 7€; Planetarium 1.50€, on reservation. ☏081 37 23 728; www.cittadellascienza.it.
A fine industrial building from the mid-19C now houses the innovative Science Center, divided up into various sections – each with a different theme (physics, classical world, nature, evolution,

Bay of Naples and Vesuvio

communications). Worth a visit are the Planetarium and the **Officina dei Piccoli** where children from one to 10 years of age can learn through play. Kids *Enjoy educational play at Officina dei Piccoli.*

Pozzuoli★

www.comune.pozzuoli.na.it.
Pozzuoli, which is of Greek origin, became an active trading port under the Romans. As the town is at the centre of the volcanic area known as the Phlegrean Fields and is constantly affected by changes in the ground level that occur in this region, the town centre has been evacuated. The town has given its name to *pozzolana*, a volcanic ash with a high silica content, which is used in the production of certain kinds of cement.

Anfiteatro Flavio★★

Corso Terracciano. &. ⏱*Open daily 9am-1hr before dusk.* ⏱*Closed Tues, 1 Jan, 1 May, 25 Dec.* ≈4€. ☎081 52 66 007.
This amphitheatre is one of the largest in Italy and dates from the reign of Vespasian, the founder of the Flavian dynasty. It could accommodate 40 000 spectators. Built of brick and stone, it is relatively well preserved: note the outer walls, the entrances and the particularly well-preserved **basements**★★.

Tempio di Serapide★
Set back from Via Roma.

The temple, dedicated to Serapis, which is situated near the sea, was really the ancient market place and was lined with shops. There is a sort of apse in the end wall that contained the statue of Serapis, the protecting god of traders. The central edifice shows the effects of variations in ground level: the columns reveal signs of marine erosion.

Tempio di Augusto★

The temple, dedicated to Augustus, dated from the early days of the Empire and was converted into a Christian church in the 11C. A recent fire has revealed a grandiose marble colonnade.

Solfatara★★

&. ⏱*Open daily, Apr-Sep 8.30am-7pm (Oct 6pm, Nov-Mar 4.30pm).* ≈5€. ☎081 52 62 341; www.solfatara.it.
Although extinct, this crater still has some of the features of an active volcano such as jets of steam charged with sulphurous fumes, strong smelling and with traces of yellow, miniature volcanoes spitting hot mud, and bubbling jets of sand. The ground gives a hollow sound and the surface is hot. The sulphurous vapours have been used for medicinal purposes since Roman times. Kids *The excitement of mild volcanic activity.*

Lago Lucrino

In Antiquity, oyster farming was practised here on the lake and the banks were lined with villas. One of these

Address Book

For coin ranges see the Legend on the cover flap.

WHERE TO STAY

Hotel Sant'Agata – *Via dei Campi 8/A – 80064 Sant'Agata sui due Golfi – ☎081 80 80 800 – www.hotelsantagata. com – Closed Nov-15 Mar –* P ▤ *(payment) – 33 rm* ᴗ *– Restaurant*. This hotel is ideally situated for a holiday touring the beautiful Amalfi coast and the sites of Pompeii and Herculaneum. The public areas are roomy and light; the rooms have been tastefully decorated. The attention to detail also extends to the cuisine. Very reasonably priced.

Hotel Désirée – *Via Capo 31/bis – 80067 Sorrento – ☎081 87 81 563 – Fax 081 87 81 563 – Closed Feb –* P *– 22 rm* ᴗ. A small, rather old-fashioned hotel with a charming family atmosphere and simple surroundings. Perched high above the sea, there are wonderful views taking in the Bay of Naples and Vesuvius. Facilities include a terrace-solarium and private beach (you take a lift to get down there!). Extremely reasonably priced.

Hotel Regina – *Via Marina Grande 10 – 80067 Sorrento – ☎081 87 82 722 – www.hotelreginasor rento.com – Closed Nov-Feb –* P *– 36 rm – Restaurant*. A stone's throw from the centre, yet lovely and quiet. Facilities at the hotel include a lovely citrus-grove garden and a terrace-solarium with wonderful views. Panoramic restaurant.

WHERE TO EAT

Taverna Azzurra-da Salvatore – *Via Marina Grande 166 – 80067 Sorrento – ☎081 87 72 510 – Closed Mon (Jan-May) –* ▤ *– Book*. This taverna is mainly frequented by the locals – they know where to head for some of the best sea-food in town! The fish is always of the best quality and super-fresh, and what the chef purchases depends on what is on sale at the daily fish market. Simple surroundings, with a marine theme to the decor. If you are lucky you might get a table right by the beach.

Zi'ntonio – *Via De Maio 11 – 80067 Sorrento – ☎081 87 81 623 – www.zinto nio.it – Closed Tue (except Mar-Oct) –* ▤. This establishment is popular with the locals and tourists alike. Charming majolica-tiled dining area. There is also an intermediate floor with a rustic-style wooden finish. Combines authentic regional cooking with some national dishes. Also serves delicious pizzas. One for the address book.

Taverna del Capitano – *Piazza delle Sirene 10/11, Località Nerano – 80068 Marina del Cantone – 5km/3mi southwest of Sant'Agata sui Due Golfi – ☎081 80 81 028 – www.tavernadelcap itano.it – Closed Mon (except Jun-Sep), 8 Jan-Feb –* ▤ *– Book – 12 rm*. A quiet, elegant restaurant with vast picture windows overlooking the sea. Typical Mediterranean cooking, with an emphasis on fish. Dishes prepared with excellent, super-fresh ingredients. Stylish well-maintained surroundings. Also has rooms (very pleasant).

TAKING A BREAK

Bar Ercolano – *Piazza Tasso 28 – 80067 Sorrento – ☎08 18 07 29 51 – Wed-Mon 6am-1am*. Situated right on the main square, this is the perfect spot for whiling away a summer's evening.

Circolo dei Forestieri – *Via L. De Maio 35 – 80067 Sorrento – ☎081 87 73 263 – Daily, 9.30am-1am*. Amazing views from the superb terrace area at the top. Live music almost every night.

belonged to Cicero; another was the scene of Agrippina's murder, on the orders of her son, Nero.

Baia

This Greek colony was in Roman times a fashionable beach resort, as well as a thermal spa *(terme)* with the most complete equipment in the world for hydrotherapy. The Roman emperors and patricians had immense villas, all of which disappeared under the sea after a change in ground level. An underwater archaeological park has recently been opened to allow visitors to explore these ruins. *For information on underwater visits, call ☎081 52 48 169, fax 081 52 49 850; www.baiasommersa.it.*

Parco archeologico★★

🕐 *Open daily 9am-1hr before dusk.* 🕐 *Closed Mon.* ✏*4€.* ☎*081 86 87 592; www.ulixes.it.*
Ruins of the famous baths remain on the hilltop overlooking the sea. Facing the hill, these include from left to right the baths of Venus, Sosandra and Mercury. The archaeological area also includes ruins of the Imperial palace of Baia and a late-Republican period villa.

Castello di Baia

Built in the 15C over the remains of a villa traditionally thought to belong to Caesar, this castle is now home to the Museo archeologico dei Campi Flegrei. The museum houses a collections of artefacts excavated in the area. 🕐*Open daily 9am-dusk.* 🕐*Closed Mon.* ✏*4.10€.* ☎*081 52 33 797.*

Bacoli

On the high ground in the old town rises the **Cento Camerelle**★*(Via Cento Camerelle, to the right of the church).* This huge reservoir, which belonged to a private villa, is built on two levels: the grandiose upper level built in the 1C AD has four sections and immense arches; the lower part, built much earlier, has a network of narrow galleries forming a cross, that emerge high above sea level. The famous **Piscina Mirabilea** *(at the church take the road to the left, Via Ambrogio Greco, and then Via Piscina Mirabile to the right)* was an immense cistern designed to supply water to the Roman fleet in the port of Miseno. It is 70m long, 25m wide and nearly 15m high (230ft x 82ft x 49ft) and is divided into five sections with 48 pillars supporting the roof. There are remarkable light effects. *Cento Camerelle:* 🕐*Open daily, 9am-1hr before dusk. Contact custodian on Via Cento Camerelle.* ✏*Donation recommended. For additional information* ☎*081 52 33 797 (Ufficio Beni Culturali del Comune di Bacoli); www.comune.bacoli. na.it.*

Miseno

This name is given to a lake, a port, a promontory, a cape and a village. Lake Miseno, a former volcanic crater, was believed by the ancients to be the Styx, across which Charon ferried the souls of the dead. Under the Emperor Augustus it was linked by a canal to the port of Miseno, which was the base of the Roman fleet. The village of Miseno is dominated by Monte Miseno, on which Misenus, the companion of Aeneas, is said to have been buried. The slopes of the promontory were studded with luxurious villas, including the one where in AD 37 the Emperor Tiberius choked to death.

Lago del Fusaro

A lagoon with a small island on which Vanvitelli built a hunting lodge for King Ferdinand IV of Bourbon in 1782.

Cuma★

Cumae, one of the oldest Greek colonies, was founded in the 8C BC. The city soon dominated the whole Phlegrean area including Naples, leaving an important Hellenic heritage. Its splendour was at its height under the tyrant Aristodemus. After its capture by the Romans in 334 BC, decline set in and continued until AD 915 when it was pillaged by the Saracens. The ancient city of Cumae stands in a serene and solemn setting near the sea. Visitors have access to the ruins of the acropolis, the upper town where most of the temples stood. In the lower town, excavations have revealed the remains of an amphitheatre, a temple dedicated to the Capitoline Triad (Jupiter, Juno and Minerva) and baths.

Parco Archeologico★★

♿ 🕐*Open daily, 9am-1hr before dusk.* ✏*4€ (combined ticket with Castello di Baia, Terme di Baia, Anfiteatro Flavio and excavations – valid for two days).* ☎*081 85 43 060 or 848 800 288 (Free phone); www.pierreci.it.*
The acropolis is built on a hill of volcanic material (lava and tufa) in a lonely site and is reached by an alley lined with laurels. After the vaulted passageway, the path to the left leads to the Sibyl's Cave, **Antro della Sibilla**★, one of the most venerated places of Antiquity. Here the Sibyl delivered her oracles. The cave was hollowed out of the rock by the Greeks in the 6C or 5C BC and it is rectangular in shape with three small niches.

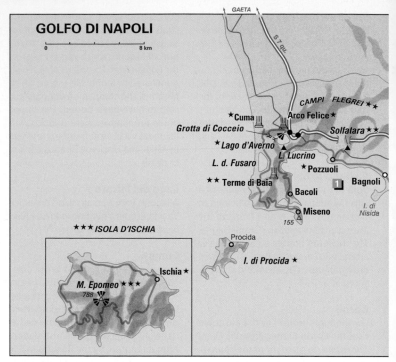

GOLFO DI NAPOLI

0 — 8 km

GAETA

CAMPI FLEGREI ★★

★Cuma Arco Felice★

Grotta di Cocceio Solfatara ★★★

★ *Lago d'Averno*

L. Lucrino

L. d. Fusaro ★ Pozzuoli

★★ Terme di Baia Bagnoli

Bacoli 1 I. di Nisida

Miseno 155

★★★ *ISOLA D'ISCHIA*

Procida

Ischia ★ I. di Procida ★

M. Epomeo ★★★

788

Take the stairway up to the sacred way (Via Sacra). From the belvedere there is a good **view**★of the sea. Some finds from the excavations are on display. On the right are the remains of the **Tempio di Apollo** (Temple of Apollo) which was later transformed into a Christian church. Further on is the **Tempio di Giove** (Temple of Jupiter) which was also converted by the early Christians. In the centre stands a large font and there are several Christian tombs near the sanctuary.

Arco Felice★

The minor road in the direction of Naples leads to this triumphal arch which was erected on the Via Domitiana; there are still traces of the paved Roman way.

Lago d'Averno★

The lake lies below the Cumae-Naples road: belvedere on the right approximately 1km/0.6mi beyond Arco Felice.

This lake within a crater is dark, still and silent and wrapped in an atmosphere of mystery, which was all the more intense in Antiquity as birds flying overhead were overcome by fumes and dropped

into it. Virgil regarded it as the entrance to the Underworld. Under the Roman Empire, Agrippa, a captain in the service of the Emperor Augustus, developed it as a naval base and linked it by canal with Lake Lucrino (*see above*), which in turn was linked to the open sea. An underground gallery 1km/0.6mi long, known as **Grotta di Cocceio** (Cocceio's Cave), connected Avernus with Cumae, and was used by chariots.

2 **Vesuvio★★★**

Naples to Torre Anunziata 45km/28mi. Allow one day.

The coast road relieves the Salerno motorway across a densely-populated industrial zone, once a favoured resort of the Neapolitan aristocracy (18C-19C). There are two important sites located a short distance from the road.

Portici

The road crosses the courtyard of the **royal palace** built in 1738 for the Bourbon King Charles III. Today the palace buildings are the home of the Naples

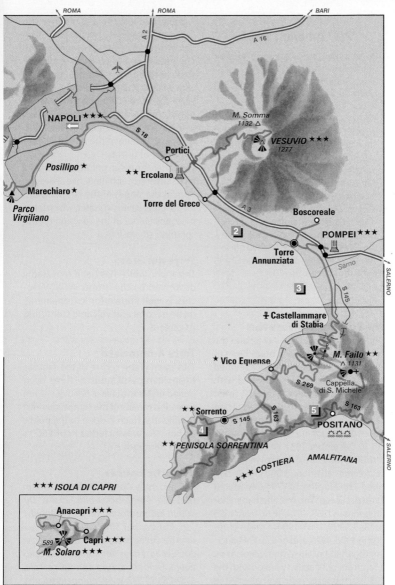

Faculty of Agronomy. In his opera *The Mute Girl of Portici (Muette de Portici)*, the French composer, Auber, features the 17C revolt against the Spaniards, instigated by **Masaniello**, a young fisherman from Portici.

Herculaneum★★ ⓖ *See ERCOLANO.*

Il Vesuvio★★★

The outline of Vesuvius, one of the few still active volcanoes in Europe, is an intrinsic feature of the Neapolitan landscape. It has two summits: to the north **Monte Somma** (alt 1 132m/3 714ft) and to the south Vesuvius proper (alt 1 277m/4 190ft). Over time the volcanic materials on the lower slopes have become fertile soil with orchards and vines producing the famous *Lacryma Christi* wine.

The Cumaean Sibyl

In Antiquity the Sibyls were virgin priestesses dedicated to the cult of Apollo and deemed to be semi-divine creatures with powers of divination. The Sibyl from Cumae (one of the main centres of Greek civilisation in Italy) was a famous prophetess. She is reputed to have sold the Sibylline Books, collections of the Sibyls' prophecies, to the Etruscan King of Rome, Tarquin the Elder or Tarquin the Superb (6C BC). The oracles were later used by the rulers to answer their subjects' petitions and expectations. One of the best-known depictions of the Cumaean Sibyl by Michelangelo adorns the ceiling of the Sistine Chapel in the Vatican.

The Eruptions of Vesuvius

Until the earthquake of AD 62 and the eruption of AD 79 which buried Herculaneum and Pompeii, Vesuvius seemed extinct; its slopes were clothed with famous vines and woods. By 1139, seven eruptions had been recorded. Then came a period of calm during which the slopes of the mountains were cultivated. On 16 December 1631 Vesuvius had a terrible awakening, destroying all the settlements at its foot: 3 000 people perished. The eruption of 1794 devastated Torre del Greco. The volcano had minor eruptions in 1858, 1871, 1872, from 1895 to 1899, 1900, 1903, 1904, a major eruption in 1906, 1929, and one in 1944 altering the shape of the crater. Since then, apart from brief activity linked with the 1980 earthquake, Vesuvius has emitted only a plume of smoke.

Climbing the Volcano

From Herculaneum and via Torre del Greco: 27km/17mi plus 45min on foot there and back. Wear good walking shoes. Paid parking, on street or in Herculaneum, bus service from railway station, Circumvesuviana line. ✆*Guide required to go to edge of crater 6.50€. Head guide: Sig. Pompilio ☎0335 24 71 54 (mobile), Collegio Regionale Guide Alpine, Via Panoramica 172, Ercolano, ☎081 77 75 720.*

A good road leads to a junction in the midst of lava flows. Take the left fork *(car park a few kilometres further on).* The path is an easy but most impressive climb up the volcano, scattered with cinders and lapilli.

From the summit there is an immense **panorama**★★★over the Bay of Naples with the Sorrento Peninsula in the south and Cape Miseno in the north. Beyond is the Gulf of Gaeta.

The crater affords an unforgettable sight for its sheer size and the sense of desolation on the slopes of the jagged walls, for the great yawning crater, which takes on a pink colour in the sun, and for the spouting steam-jets.

Torre del Greco

This town, which has been repeatedly destroyed by the eruptions of Vesuvius, is well known for its ornaments made of coral and volcanic stone, and its cameos.

Torre Annunziata

This town is the centre of the famous Neapolitan pasta industry. It has been buried under the lava of Vesuvius seven times. It is the site of the sumptuous Villa di Oplontis which is open to the public and in 1997 was included in UNESCO's World Heritage List.

Villa di Oplontis★★

🕐*Open daily Apr-Oct 8.30am-7.30pm (Nov-Mar 5pm). Ticket office closes 1hr 30min before closing time.* 🕐*Closed 1 Jan, 25 Dec.* ✆*5.50€ inclusive (valid 1 day) for Oplonti, Stabia and Boscoreale; 20€ (valid 3 days) for Pompeii, Herculaneum, Oplonti, Stabia and Boscoreale.* ☎*081 85 75 347; www.pompeiisites.org.*
This fine example of a Roman suburban villa is thought to have belonged to Poppea, wife of Nero. The vast building, in which can be identified the slaves' quarters (to the east) and the area given over to the imperial apartments (to the west), has many well-preserved examples of beautiful original **wall paintings**. In particular, there are landscape scenes featuring architectural elements, portrait medallions and still-life paintings, including a basket of figs and details of fruit (in the two recesses or *triclinia* to

the east and west of the atrium respectively). Of the various animals depicted, the peacock appears so frequently as to have supported the theory that the name of the villa was derived from it. Within the villa, the kitchens are easily identified (with ovens and sink), as are the latrines which represent an advanced drainage system. The area to the west of the piscina, perhaps used as a conservatory, has fine wall paintings with foreshortened flowers and fountains.

③ Vesuvius to the Penisola Sorrentina★★★

▶ 70km/42mi. Allow 1 day. The departure point for this itinerary is Torre Annunziata.

Pompeii★★★ ⑥ See POMPEI.

Castellammare di Stabia⚓

This was an ancient Roman spa town. Occupied successively by the Oscans, the Etruscans, the Samnites and finally the Romans in the 4C BC, Stabiae rebelled against Rome but was destroyed by Sulla in the 1C BC. The town was rebuilt in the form of small clusters of houses, while luxury villas for rich patricians spread over the high ground. In the AD 79 eruption of Vesuvius the new town was wiped out along with Herculaneum and Pompeii. The naturalist Pliny the Elder, who came by boat to observe the phenomenon at close range, perished by asphyxiation. In the 18C the Bourbons undertook excavations, repaired the port, and built shipyards which are still in use.

Antiquarium★

Via Marco no 2. ⑤ Same admission times and charges as Villa di Oplontis.
The finds from the excavations are displayed here and include a magnificent series of **mural paintings** from the villas and some fine stucco **low reliefs.**

Roman villas

▶2km/1mi to the east. Arriving from the north take S 145, follow directions for Agerola-Amalfi, take the flyover and after the tunnel turn left to reach the excavation

site. ⑤ Same admission times and charges as Villa di Oplontis.
Villa di Arianna (Ariadne's Villa) was one of the luxurious villas facing the sea with an incomparable view of the bay and of Vesuvius. The architectural refinement of **Villa San Marco** with its two storeys was enhanced by gardens and swimming pools. It was probably a sumptuous country residence.

Monte Faito★★

▶ Access is from Vico Equense via a scenic route; alternatively there is a cable car that departs from Piazza Circumvesuviana in Castellammare di Stabia. ⑤ The cableway (10min) operates from Apr to Oct, departures every 20-30min, 9.35am-4.25pm; mid-Jun to Aug, 7.25am-7.15pm. ⬬6.20€. For information ☎081 77 22 444.
Monte Faito is part of the **Lattari range**, a headland which separates the Bay of Naples from the Gulf of Salerno and forms the Sorrento Peninsula. Its name is derived from the beech trees (fagus in Latin), which offer shade in summer. From Belvedere dei Capi there is a splendid **panorama**★★★ of the Bay of Naples. From there the road continues up to a chapel, **Cappella San Michele**, which affords an especially enchanting **panorama**★★★ – the wild landscape of the Lattari mountains contrasts strongly with the smiling scenery of the Bay of Naples and the Sarno plain.

Vico Equense★

This is a small health and seaside resort on a picturesque rocky site.

④ Sorrento and the Penisola Sorrentina★★

▶30km/18mi. Allow half a day.
The innumerable bends on this road afford constantly changing views of enchanting landscapes, wild, fantastically shaped rocks plunging vertically into a crystal-clear sea, deep gorges spanned by dizzy bridges and Saracen towers perched on jagged rock stacks. The Amalfi coast, with its wild and rugged landscape, is formed by the jagged fringe of the Lattari Mountains, a deeply eroded limestone range. Contrasting with these awe-inspiring scenes are the

more charming views of fishing villages and the luxuriant vegetation, a mixture of orange, lemon, olive and almond trees, vines and all the Mediterranean flora. The region is very popular with foreigners and artists. A significant part of the attraction is the local cuisine with abundant seafood (fish, crustaceans and shellfish), and the local mozzarella cheese washed down with the red Gragnano or white Ravello and Positano wines.

Sorrento★★

This important resort, known for its many beautiful gardens, overlooks the bay of the same name. Orange and lemon groves are to be found in the surrounding countryside and even encroaching on the town. Local craftsmen produce various marquetry objects. The poet **Torquato Tasso** (&see FERRARA) was born in Sorrento in 1544.

Museo Correale di Terranova★

🕐Open daily except Tue, 9am-2pm. 🕐Closed for 10 days in Jan, public holidays. ≈6€. ☎081 87 81 846; www.museo correale.it.

Housed in an 18C palace, the museum has some splendid examples of local intarsia work (**secretaire**, 1910), a small archaeological section and, on the first floor, a collection of 17C and 18C furniture as well as an interesting collection of 17C-18C Neapolitan paintings. Two rooms are devoted to the landscape painters of the **Posillipo School** which flourished in the 1830s, including the main exponent of this school, **Giacinto Gigante** (1806-76). On the second floor there is a collection of porcelain and ceramics. From the terrace there is a fine **view**★★ over the Gulf of Sorrento.

The historic centre

Via S. Cesareo, the *decumanus* of the Roman city, leads to the **Sedile Dominova**, seat of city administration in the Angevin period. It consists of a loggia decorated with frescoes surmounted by a 17C ceramic dome. The steeply sloping street, Via San Giuliani, leads to the church di S. Francesco. This Baroque church has a bulbous campanile and is flanked by delightful 13C **cloisters**★ whose vegetable-motif capitals sustain interlaced arcades in the Sicilian-Arab style.

The nearby public gardens, **Villa Comunale**, offer a good **view**★★ of the Bay of Naples.

Penisola Sorrentina★★

▶ *Leave Sorrento to the west by S 145 and at the junction take the road to the right to Massa Lubrense.*

This winding road skirts the Sorrento Peninsula and affords fine views of the hillsides covered with olive groves, orange and lemon trees and vines.

From the headland (**Punta del Capo di Sorrento**) *(footpath: from the church in the village of Capo di Sorrento take the road to the right and after the college the paved path, 1hr there and back)* there is a superb **view**★★ of Sorrento.

At **Sant'Agata sui Due Golfi**, perched on a crest which dominates both the Gulf of Salerno and the Bay of Naples, the **Belvedere del Deserto** (a Benedictine monastery situated 1.5km/1mi west of the town) affords a splendid **panorama**★★. *Since this is a closed monastery, visits must be reserved in advance by calling the monastic community.* ☎081 87 80 199.

Beyond Sant'Agata, the road which descends steeply to Colli di San Pietro is spectacular. From here you could return to Sorrento by S 163 which offers some superb **views**★★ over the Bay of Naples, or you could head for Positano (&see itinerary F described in COSTIERA AMALFITANA).

The Islands★★★

Capri★★★ &see CAPRI.

Ischia★★★ &see ISCHIA.

Procida★ &see ISCHIA.

ORVIETO★★

POPULATION 20 841
MICHELIN MAP 563 N 18 – UMBRIA.

This important Etruscan centre later became a papal stronghold and it was here that Clement VII took refuge in 1527 when Rome was sacked by the troops of the French King Charles V. Orvieto enjoys a remarkable site★★★ on the top of a plug of volcanic rock. The area produces an excellent white wine, Orvieto.

- **Information:** Piazza del Duomo 24, 05018 Orvieto (TR), ☎0763 34 17 72; www.umbriatourism.com.
- **Orient Yourself:** Orvieto is situated in southern Umbria, near Lake Bolsena. The main access road is A 1.
- **Don't Miss:** Underground Orvieto, Signorelli's frescoes in Cappella della Madonna di San Brizio and a bottle of Montefiascone's legendary wine.
- **Organizing Your Time:** Allow half a day.
- **Also See:** *TODI, VITERBO.*

Duomo★★★

Cappella di S. Brizio: ⏰*Open 8am-12.45pm and 2.30-dusk.* ⏰*Closed Sun morning and during religious services.* ⏺*5€ (ticket office in Piazza Duomo 24).* ☎*0763 34 35 92; www.opsm.it.*
The cathedral, in the transitional Romanesque-Gothic style, was begun in 1290 to enshrine the relics of the Miracle of Bolsena. Over 100 architects, sculptors, painters and mosaicists took part in the building, completed in 1600. ⏺*Cappella della Madonna di San Brizio.*
The **Palazzo dei Papi**★now houses the **Museo dell'Opera.** ⏰*Open July and Aug 10am-1pm and 3-7pm (rest of the year 10am to dusk).* ⏺*5€ (combined ticket with cappella di S.Brizio)* ☎*0763 34 35 92.*

Façade★★★

This is the boldest structure and the richest in colour among Italian Gothic buildings. The original design, elaborated (c 1310-30) by the Sienese Lorenzo Maitani, was developed by Andrea Pisano, Andrea Orcagna and Sanmicheli. Maitani was also responsible for the **low reliefs**★★ adorning the pillars which, reading from left to right, portray: *Genesis, Jesse's Tree, Scenes from the New Testament, and the Last Judgement.*

Interior

The nave and aisles are roofed with timber, while Gothic vaulting covers the transepts and the chancel. In the north transept under the 16C organ is the entrance to a chapel, the **Cappella del Corporale**, which enshrines the linen cloth (corporal) in which the bleeding Host was wrapped. A tabernacle encloses the **Reliquary**★★ of the corporal, a masterpiece of medieval goldsmiths' work (1338).
A fine Gothic stained-glass **window**★ in the chancel illustrates the Gospel.
The south transept gives access, beyond a wrought-iron grille (1516), to the famous **Cappella della Madonna di San Brizio**, painted with admirable **frescoes**★★. These were begun in 1447 by Fra Angelico, and then taken up in 1490 by **Luca Signorelli** (c 1445-1523).

Marble, mosaics and intricate stone patterns enliven the façade of the Duomo

R. Mattes/MICHELIN

Address Book

Sights

Underground Orvieto

Guided tours only. *5.50€.* *For opening times and reservations 0763 34 06 88; www.orvietounderground.it.* Orvieto lies on a bed of volcanic earth., with underground chambers (already present in Etruscan times) dug out of the hill, now cellars. These caves (more than 1 000 are officially listed) hold medieval niches for funerary urns, the foundations of a 14C oil mill and a 6C BC well.

Pozzo di San Patrizio★★

Open daily 10am-6.45pm (rest of the year 5.45pm). *4.50€.* *0763 34 37 68.*

St Patrick's Well was dug by order of Pope Clement VII de' Medici to supply the town with water in case of siege. The well is over 62m/203ft deep.

Palazzo del Popolo★

The Romanesque-Gothic town hall has a majestic balcony, elegant windows and curious fluted merlons.

Quartiere Vecchio★

This quiet, unfrequented quarter has retained its old houses, medieval towers and churches, including **San Giovenale**, decorated by 13C-15C frescoes.

A Few Minutes in Front of Luca Signorelli's Frescoes

The atmosphere that permeates the Chapel of San Brizio is even more disturbing if one considers the images as the anticipation of an apocalyptic day which could strike at any time. Monsters, the torture of the damned and the corpse-like colour of the demons all contribute to a sense of anguish. Every detail is imbued with a monstrous quality, even the grotesques.

The frescoes should be read starting from the north wall. The first is a portrayal of the Preaching of the Antichrist; the Antichrist, who has the devil as his adviser, has taken on the appearance of Christ. Signorelli has portrayed himself in the noble dark figure on the extreme left. This image is followed by the Calling of the Elect to Heaven.

On the wall of the altar, on the left: the Angels leading the Elect to Paradise; on the right: Angels chasing out the Reprobates, with scenes of hell.

On the right wall: The Damned in Hell and the Resurrection of the Dead.

On the west wall, in the End of the World, the sun and moon have lost all traces of familiarity, the earth is in the throes of an earthquake. A sibyl, a prophet and demons are all represented in this scene.

Museo Archeologico Faina

 ⊙*Open daily, Apr-Sep 9.30am-6pm; Oct-Mar 10am-5pm.* ⊙*Closed Mon (Nov-Feb), 1 Jan, 25-26 Dec.* ✎*4.50€.* ☎*0763 34 15 11; www.museofaina.it.*
This important **Etruscan Collection**★ includes carved terracotta funerary urns and a rare 4C sarcophagus.

Piazza della Repubblica

It stands on the site of the ancient forum, dominated by the church of Sant'Andrea.

The Miracle of Bolsena

The famous miracle at the Bolsena Mass took place in 1263. A Bohemian priest had doubts about the doctrine of transubstantiation, that is, the incarnation of Christ in the Host at consecration. According to legend, as he was celebrating Mass in St Christina's church, the Host began to bleed profusely at the moment of consecration. The priest no longer doubted the mystery and the Feast of Corpus Christi was instituted.

 Etruscan Necropolis of Crocifisso.

Excursions

Bolsena

▶*22km/13mi southwest of Orvieto.* Bolsena, the ancient Etruscan city of Volsinii, stands on the banks of Italy's largest lake★ of volcanic origin; its level is continually changing owing to earth tremors. In the old part of the town, its sombre-coloured houses cling to the hillside. There is a good view from S 2, the Viterbo-Siena road. *For information on boat trips, call* ☎ *0761 87 07 60; www.navigabolsena.com (from Capodimonte).*

Chiesa di Santa Cristina★

⊙*Catacombs: guided tours every 30min 9.30am-noon and 3.30-6.30pm (summer) and 9.30-11.30am and 3-4.30pm (winter).* ✎*4€.* ☎*0761 79 90 67; www.basilicasan tacristina.it.*
The 3C Saint Christina was a victim of the persecutions of Diocletian. Although the church is 11C the façade is Renaissance. The columns inside are Roman. The

north aisle leads to the **Chapel of the Miracle**, where the pavement stained by the blood of the Host is revered.

Montefiascone

▶*17km/10.5mi northwest.Via Cassia Vecchia. www.bolsenalake.com.*
Montefiascone stands in the vineyard country that produces the delicious white wine Est! Est!! Est!!!
Opposite the church of San Flavianoa is the tombstone of Johann Fugger, a German prelate who died on his way to Rome. He sent one of his servants ahead of him with orders to mark the inns where the wine was the best, with the word est ("is," short for Vinum est bonum in Latin). When he arrived at Montefiascone the faithful servant found the wine so good that he wrote, in his enthusiasm, "Est, Est, Est". And his master, becoming enthusiastic in his turn, drank so much, much, much of it that he died.
☺Hear tales of the local wine with its colorful legend.

PADOVA★★
PADUA
POPULATION 210 821
MICHELIN MAP 562 F 17 – VENETO.

An art and pilgrimage centre, Padua revolves around historic Piazza Cavour. Caffè Pedrocchi, a meeting-place of the liberal elite in the Romantic period, is close by.

- **Information:** Stazione Ferrovie dello Stato. ☎049 87 52 077; www.turismopadova.it.
- ▶ **Orient Yourself:** Padua is off A 4,40km/24mi from Venice. It is linked to Bologna by A 13.
- **Don't Miss:** Giotto's frescoes in the Scrovegni Chapel, the Basilica del Santo and mud treatments at Abano Terme.
- **Organizing Your Time:** Allow one day to explore the town.
- **Also See:** *Riviera del BRENTA, LAGUNA VENETA, TREVISO, VENEZIA, VICENZA.*

A Bit of History

There are few traces of ancient *Patavium,* which was one of the most prosperous Roman cities in the Veneto during the 1C BC owing to its river trade, its agriculture and the sale of horses. In the 7C Padua was destroyed by the Lombards, and from the 11C to 13C it became an independent city-state. The city underwent its greatest period of economic and cultural prosperity under the enlightened rule of the lords of Carrara (1337-1405). In 1405 Padua came under the sway of the Venetian Republic and remained a loyal subject until 1797 when the Venetian Constitution was abolished by Napoleon.
The City of St Anthony the Hermit – This Franciscan monk was born in Lisbon in 1195 and died at the age of 36 in the environs of Padua. He was a forceful preacher and is generally represented holding a book and a lily.
A Famous University – The University of Padua, founded in 1222, is the second oldest in Italy after Bologna. Galileo was a professor and its students included Renaissance scholar Pico della Mirandola, the astronomer Copernicus and the poet Tasso.
Art in Padua – In 1304, **Giotto** came to Padua to decorate the Scrovegni Chapel, with a superlative cycle of frescoes.
In the 15C the Renaissance in Padua was marked by **Donatello**, another Florentine, who stayed in the city from 1444 to 1453. Also in the 15C, Paduan art flourished under the influence of the Paduan artist, **Andrea Mantegna** (1431-1506), a powerful painter and an innovator in the field of perspective.

Sights

Frescoes by Giotto in the Scrovegni Chapel★★★

&. ⓒOpen Mar-Dec 9am-9.45pm (rest of the year 7pm). ⓒClosed Mon (museum), 1 Jan, 1 May, 25 Dec. ⓢ12€ daytime, 8€ evening (Cappella degli Scrovegni and multimedia room only.) Phone to check evening times. ☎049 20 100 20; www.cappelladegliscrovegni.it.

The cycle of 39 frescoes was painted c 1305-10 by Giotto on the walls of the **Cappella degli Scrovegni**. The chapel, built in 1303, illustrates the lives of Joachim and Anna (the parents of the Virgin), Mary and Jesus: the *Flight into Egypt, Judas' Kiss* and the *Entombment* are among the most famous. On the lower register, the powerful monochrome figures depict the Vices (*left*) and Virtues (*right*). The *Last Judgement* on the west wall completes the cycle. On the altar stands a **Virgin**★ by the Tuscan sculptor Giovanni Pisano. ⓐDon't let Giotto's frescoes overshadow Pisano's Virgin★ on the altar

Frescoes in the Chiesa degli Eremitani★★

www.cappelladegliscrovegni.it.
In the Cappella Ovetari of the 13C church of the Hermits *(the second on the right of the Cappella Maggiore)* are fragments of frescoes by **Mantegna**; *Martyrdom of St James* on the north wall, *Assumption* in the apse and *Martyrdom of St Christoper* on the south wall. The Lady Chapel (Cappella Maggiore) has splendid frescoes by **Guariento**, Giotto's pupil.

Museo Civico agli Eremitani★

&. ⓒOpen daily 9am-7pm. ⓒClosed Mon, 1 Jan, 1 May, 25 Dec. ⓢ12€ including Cappella degli Scrovegni. ☎049 82 04 551; www.cappelladegliscrovegni.it.

The museum in the Hermitage of St Augustine (Sant'Agostino) comprises archaeology (Egyptian, Etruscan, Roman and pre-Roman), coins (Bottacin Bequest) and 15C-18C Venetian and Flemish paintings (Emo Capodilista collection). The museum contains the former Art Gallery's collection including **paintings**★★, mostly from the Venetian School (14C-18C). Note works by Giotto.

Basilica del Santo★★

This important pilgrimage church overlooks the square in which Donatello erected an **equestrian statue**★★ of the Venetian leader **Gattamelata** (nickname Erasmo di Nardi). This bronze was the first of its size to be cast in Italy.

The basilica was built from 1232 to 1300 in the transitional Romanesque-Gothic style. The **interior**★★ contains the **Cappella del Santo**★★, location of the tomb/altar of St Anthony (Arca di Sant'Antonio) by Tiziano Aspetti (1594). On the walls are 16C **high reliefs**★★. In the chancel the **high altar**★★ has bronze panels (1450) by Donatello. The third chapel has **frescoes**★ by Altichiero (14C), a Veronese artist.

There is a fine **view**★ of the building from the cloisters, to the south.

Oratorio di San Giorgio and Scuola di Sant'Antonio★

&. ⓒOpen daily, Apr-Sep 9am-12.30pm and 2.30-7pm (rest of the year 2.30-5pm). ⓒClosed 1 Jan, Easter, 25 Dec. ⓢ2€. ☎049 87 55 235; www.arciconfraternitasantantonio.org.

St George's oratory is decorated with 21 **frescoes**★ (1377) by Altichiero.
In the adjacent Scuola di Sant'Antonio, are 18 16C frescoes★ relating the life of St Anthony. Four of these are by Titian.

Palazzo della Ragione★

&. ⓒOpen daily Feb-Oct 9am-7pm (rest of the year 6pm). ⓒClosed Mon. ⓢ8€. ☎049 82 05 006; www.padovanet.it.

The Law Courts, between two **squares**★, the Piazza della Frutta and the Piazza delle Erbe, are remarkable for their roof in the form of an upturned ship's keel. The **salone**★★ is adorned with 15C frescoes depicting the *Labours of the Months, the Liberal Arts, the Trades* and the *Signs of the Zodiac.*

Piazza dei Signori

This square is overlooked by the clock tower, **Torre dell'Orologioa**.

Università

The University is housed in a palace known as the "Bo" from the name of an inn that once stood on the site. It has retained a lovely 16C courtyard and an

PADOVA

58 Fanteria V.	DZ	75
8 Febbraio V.	DZ	74
Altinate V.	DYZ	
Carmine V. del	DY	10
Cavour Pza e V.	DY	15
Cesarotti V. M.	DZ	17
Dante V.	CY	
Erbe Pza delle	DZ	20
Eremitani Pza	DY	21
Filiberto V. E.	DY	24
Frutta Pza della	DZ	25
Garibaldi Cso	DY	27
Garibaldi Pza	DY	28
Gasometro V. dell' ex	DY	29
Guariento V.	DY	35
Insurrezione Pza	DY	39
Monte di Pietà V. del	CZ	45
Petrarca V.	CY	50
Ponte Molino Vicolo	CY	52
Ponti Romani		
Riviera dei	DYZ	53
Roma V.	DZ	
S. Canziano V.	DZ	57
S. Fermo V.	DY	
S. Lucia V.	DY	59
Vandelli V. D.	CZ	66
Verdi V. G.	CY	67
Vittorio Emanuele II Cso	CZ	70

Battistero	CZ	D
Caffè Pedrocchi	DZ	N
Museo civico agli Eremitani	DY	M
Oratorio di San Giorgio e Scuola di Sant'Antonio	DZ	B
Palazzo del Capitano	CZ	E
Palazzo della Regione	DZ	J
Statua equestre del Gattamelata	DZ	A
Università	DZ	U

340

Address Book

For coin ranges see the Legend on the cover flap.

WHERE TO STAY

Hotel Al Fagiano – *Via Locatelli 45 – Padua – 049 87 53 396 – www.alfagiano.com – – 29 rm – .* Only 100m/110yd from the Basilica di Sant'Antonio. Attractive public areas with good-sized and functional rooms. Reasonably priced.

WHERE TO EAT

Trattoria la Ragnatela – *Via Caltana 79 – 30030 Scaltenigo – 13km/8mi northeast of Padua – 41 43 60 50 – Closed Wed – .* Simple, informal trattoria where the clientele ranges from decorators in their overalls to businessmen in suits. Authentic regional cooking, full of flavour and deliciously fragrant, benefits from the chef's personal touch.

---

anatomy theatre, **Teatro Anatomico** (1594). *Guided tours only: Mon, Wed and Fri 3.15pm, 4.15pm and 5.15pm, Tue, Thu and Sat 9.15am, 10.15am and 11.15am (rest of the year Mon, Wed and Fri 3.15pm and 4.15pm, Tue, Thur and Sat 10.15am and 11.15am). Closed Sun and public holidays. 5€. 049 82 75 111; www.unipd.it.*

Caffè Pedrocchi

This neo-Classical building is a café, and where the student rebellion against the Austrians was played out in 1848. *Open daily 9.30am-12.30pm and 3.30-6pm. Closed Mon, 1 Jan, 1 May, 25/26 Dec. 4€ combined ticket with Museo del Risorgimento. 049 87 81 231; www.caffepedrocchi.it.*

Chiesa Santa Giustina

This 16C church, dedicated to St Justina has an **altarpiece** by Veronese.

Orto Botanico

Open daily Apr-Oct 9am-1pm and 3-7pm, Nov-Mar 9am-1pm. Closed Sun (winter). 4 €. 049 82 72 119; www.ortobotanico.unipd.it.
The botanical gardens, laid out in 1545, contain many exotic species including the palm tree, which inspired Goethe's reflections on plant development.

Excursions

Montagnana★

47km/29mi southwest. www.montagnanaonline.com.

impressive 14C **ramparts**★★ reinforce this town. The **Duomo**, by Sansovino, contains a *Transfiguration* by Veronese.

Colli Euganei★

The Euganean hills, south of Padua, are of volcanic origin and were appreciated in Roman times for their hot springs and wines.

Abano Terme

www.abanomontegrotto.it.
This thermal spa, shaded by pines, is one of Italy's most famous spa towns.

Montegrotto Terme

This was the ancient *Mons Aegrotorum* (Mountain of the Sick).

Monselice★

www.comune.monselice.padova.it.
This town (Latin name *Mons Silicis*; granite mountain) was an ancient Roman mining community. The upper terrace of the Villa Balbi with its Italian garden affords a lovely **view**★ of the region.

Arquà Petrarca★

6.5km/4mi northwest of Monselice.
It was here that the poet **Petrarch** (1304-74) died. **Petrarch's house**★ is open to the public. Exhibits include memorabilia and autographs of visitors such as Carducci and Byron. *Open Mar-Oct daily 9am-noon and 3-6.30pm (Nov-Feb 2.30-5pm). Closed Mon, 1 Jan, 1 May, 25-26 Dec. 3€. 0429 71 82 94; www.arquapetrarca.com.*

Riviera del Brenta★★

see Riviera del BRENTA.

PAESTUM★★★

MICHELIN MAP 564 F 26-27 – CAMPANIA.

One of Italy's most important archaeological sites, Paestum was discovered by chance around 1750, when the Bourbons started to build the road that crosses the area today. The initial settlement was an ancient Greek colony founded around 600 BC under the name of Poseidonia by colonists from Sybaris. Around the year 400 BC the city fell to a local tribe, the Lucanians. It became Roman in the year 273 BC, but began to decline toward the end of the Empire due to malaria, which eventually drove out its inhabitants. The yellow limestone temples stand amid the ruins of dwellings, sheltered by cypresses and oleanders.

- **Information**: Via Magna Grecia 887, 84063 Capaccio-Paestum (SA), ☎0828 81 10 16; www.infopaestum.it.
- ▶ **Orient Yourself:** Paestum is on the coast, close to S 18, 48km/29mi south of Salerno.
- **Don't Miss:** The Tempio di Nettuno. The metopes and Tomba del Tuffatore in the Museo.
- **Organizing Your Time:** Allow half a day.
- **Also See:** *Parco Nazionale del CILENTO, COSTIERA AMALFITANA.*

Visit

The suggested itinerary (2hr) proceeds from south to north. Those wishing to visit the museum first should start from the north. Open daily, 9am-2hr before dusk. ⊙Closed 1 Jan, 25 Dec. ⊚4€; 6.50€ including museum. ☎0828 81 10 16; www. infopaestum.it.
Take the Porta della Giustizia through the 5km/3mi-long city wall, **Cinta Muraria★**, and follow the **Via Sacra**, the principal street of the ancient city.

Basilica★★

The rear of the "Basilica" stands to the right of the Via Sacra. This mid-6C BC temple, the oldest in the city, was dedicated to Hera, sister and bride of Zeus. The swelling at the centre of the columns (*entasis*) and the squashed *echini* (moulding above the capital) of the columns convey the way in which architectural structures were considered living entities that swell and squash when submitted to pressure. The porch (*pronaos*) leads into the central chamber divided into two aisles, indicating that two cults were practised here.

Tempio di Nettuno★★★

When Paestum was first discovered this well-preserved Doric temple was thought to have been dedicated to Neptune (or Poseidon in Greek, hence the town's name Poseidonia), but it has since been proved that it was dedicated to Hera. Dating from the mid-5C BC, one of the most impressive structural devices is the convexity (2cm) of the horizontal lines, which makes the numerous columns look straight. For this same reason the fluting on the corner columns veers slightly inwards.

In the centre of the city stands the **forum**, surrounded by a portico and shops, and overlooked by the **curia**, the adjacent *macellum* (covered market) and the *comitium* (3C BC), the most important public building where magistrates were elected. To the left of the *comitium* stands the **Temple of Peace** (2C-1C BC) constructed on a north-south plan according to Italic custom.

To the east of the forum stands the **amphitheatre**, constructed between the Republican and Imperial ages and divided by the main road. Unusually it is not located outside the city centre, a measure that was adopted to enable a flow of people to the amphitheatre.

The *gimnasium* (c 3C BC) was probably a sanctuary with a pool. During ritualistic celebrations the statue of the divinity was immersed in the pool and then placed on a platform. The pool was

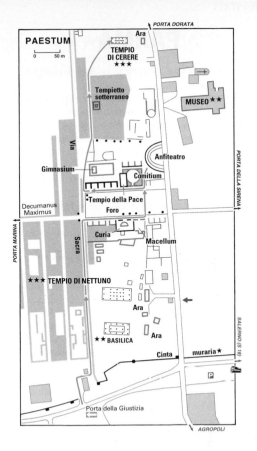

buried in the 1C AD and the structure subsequently housed the gymnasium. The **Tempietto Sotterraneo** (small underground temple, 6C BC) has been interpreted as being a *heroon*, a kind of cenotaph devoted to the cult of the city's founder who was made a hero after his death. Some bronze vases with traces of honey were also found here; these are housed at the museum.

Tempio di Cerere★★

Originally erected in the late 6C BC in honour of Athena, the Temple of Ceres combines an interesting mix of styles: the Doric colonnade is solid and massive whereas the internal Ionic columns are more graceful and decorative. Near the entrance of the temple, on the east side, is the sacrificial altar, the **ara**.

Museo★★

&. ⓒ *Open 9am-7pm.* ⓒ *Closed 1st and 3rd Mon of the month, 1 Jan, 25 Dec.* ✆*4€,*

6.50€ including archaeological site. ☎*0828 81 10 16; www.infopaestum.it.*
The masterpieces in this museum include the famous **metopes**★★, 6C BC low reliefs in the Doric style that adorned both the *Thesauròs*, or temple of Hera (scenes from the life of Heracles and the Trojan Wars), and the High Temple (Dancing Girls) of the Sanctuary of Hera at Sele *(10km/6mi north near the mouth of the River Sele)* as well as the Tomb of the Diver. The **Tomba del Tuffatore**★★ constitutes a rare example of Greek funerary painting with banquet scenes and the dive, symbol of the passage from life to death. The museum also houses **vases**★ (6C BC) from the underground temple, a true masterpiece of bronze sculpture, the painted Lucanian tombs (4C BC) and the representations of Hera Argiva with a pomegranate (symbol of fertility) and the flower-woman in terracotta, used as an incense burner.

PARMA★★

POPULATION 174 000

MICHELIN MAP 561, 562 H 12-13 – EMILIA-ROMAGNA.

Parma is an important market town with a rich musical heritage (the famous 20C conductor Arturo Toscanini was born here). The town has a refined charm and a gastronomic reputation that centres on two of the country's most prized culinary possessions: Parmesan cheese and dry-cured ham. At the heart of the town is Piazza Garibaldi, a popular meeting-place.

- **Information:** Via Melloni 1/B, 43100 Parma, ☎0521 21 88 89; http://turismo. comune.parma.it.
- **Orient Yourself:** Parma is situated near A 1, between the Po and the Apennines.
- **Don't Miss:** The Episcopal Centre, a taste of Parma ham and a visit to Castello di Torrechiara.
- **Organizing Your Time:** Allow two days to see Parma fully.
- **Also See:** *BOLOGNA, MODENA, PIACENZA.*

A Bit of History

A settlement was founded on this site by the Etruscans in 525 BC and it became a Roman station on the Via Emilia in 183 BC. It declined but revived in the 6C under the Ostrogoth king, Theodoric. After having been an independent commune from the 11C-13C, it became a member of the Lombard League. After the fall of the commune's government in 1335, Parma was governed in turn by the Visconti, the Sforza and, later, the French before being annexed by the Papacy in 1513. In 1545 Pope Paul III, Alessandro Farnese gave two papal territories, Parma and Piacenza, having made them a duchy, to his son Pier Luigi Farnese, who was assassinated in 1547. However, the **Farnese** dynasty reigned until 1731 and several members of the house were patrons of the arts and letters, collectors and great builders.

When it passed to the Bourbons, its first sovereign was Charles, successively King of Naples then King of Spain. When Don Philip, the son of Philip V of Spain and Elizabeth Farnese, married Louise Elizabeth, the favourite daughter of Louis XV, the town underwent a period (1748-1801) of great French influence in several domains (customs, administration and the arts).

Numerous Frenchmen came to work in Parma while others like Stendhal chose to live here; he made Parma the setting of his well-known novel, The *Charterhouse of Parma*. The Bourbons of Parma had their Versailles at Colorno, north of the town.

The Parma School

The school is represented by two main artists, Correggio and Il Parmigianino, whose works formed the transition between the Renaissance and Baroque art. Antonio Allegri (1489-1534), known as **Correggio**, was a master of light and chiaroscuro; his work shows a gracefully sensual and optimistic vision which seem to herald 18C French art. Francesco Mazzola (1503-40), or **Il Parmigianino** (The Parmesan) as he was commonly known, was a more troubling and melancholy personality. His elongated forms and cold colours were characteristic of Mannerism. His canon of feminine beauty influenced the Fontainebleau school and all the other European Mannerists of the 16C, through the intermediary of Niccolò dell'Abbate and Il Primaticcio.

Walking About

This historic core of the city comprises the Romanesque **Episcopal Centre**★★★ including the cathedral and baptistery, the Baroque church of San Giovanni and the surrounding palaces as well as the

Palazzo della Pilotta (16C-17C) and Correggio's Room.

Duomo★★

http://turismo.comune.parma.it.

The cathedral is in the Romanesque style and is flanked by an elegant Gothic *campanile*. The façade includes a Lombard porch supported by lions and surmounted by a loggia and three tiers of galleries with little columns. Inside, the dome is decorated with the famous **frescoes** painted by Correggio from 1522 to 1530. The ascending rhythm of the *Assumption of the Virgin* with the central figure amid a swirling group of cherubim is remarkable. The artist's mastery of perspective and movement is expressed in an original and exuberant style virtually Baroque in spirit. In the south transept the **Descent from the Cross** (1178) by the sculptor Antelami clearly shows the influence of the Provençal School, although the solemnity of the figures distinguishes it. In the nave, the frescoes are by Gambara (1530-74); on the vaulting they were painted by

Bedoli (16C). The gilded copper *Angel* (1284) that crowned the spire of the bell tower is now on the third pillar to the left of the nave.

Battistero★★★

www.battistero.it.

This is Italy's most harmonious medieval monument. The octagonal baptistery in Verona rose-coloured marble was started in 1196 and the architecture and carved decoration, which show great unity of style, date from the 13C. The baptistery is attributed to Antelami who was also responsible for the sculptures; his signature appears on the lintel of the north door, dedicated to the Virgin. Inside (the interior is a 16-sided polygon), the admirable 13C **frescoes** of Byzantine inspiration depict scenes from the *Life of Christ* and the *Golden Legend*.

Chiesa di San Giovanni Evangelista

This Renaissance church, dedicated to St John the Evangelist, has a Baroque

---

Address Book

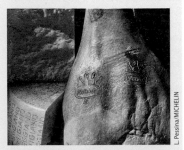

A label and a guarantee

L. Pessina/MICHELIN

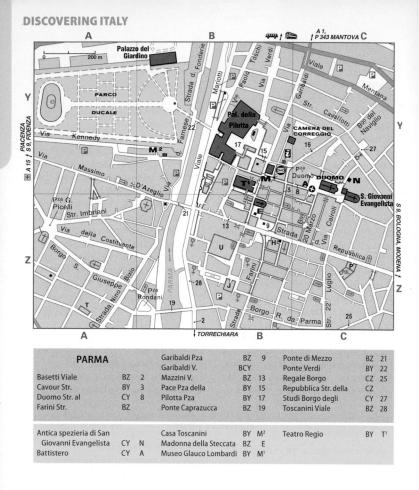

PARMA		Garibaldi Pza	BZ	9	Ponte di Mezzo	BZ	21
		Garibaldi V.	BCY		Ponte Verdi	BY	22
Basetti Viale	BZ 2	Mazzini V.	BZ	13	Regale Borgo	CZ	25
Cavour Str.	BY 3	Pace Pza della	BY	15	Repubblica Str. della	CZ	
Duomo Str. al	CY 8	Pilotta Pza	BY	17	Studi Borgo degli	CY	27
Farini Str.	BZ	Ponte Caprazucca	BZ	19	Toscanini Viale	BZ	28

Antica spezieria di		Casa Toscanini	BY M²	Teatro Regio	BY	T¹
Giovanni Evangelista	CY N	Madonna della Steccata	BZ E			
Battistero	CY A	Museo Glauco Lombardi	BY M¹			

façade. Inside, the **frescoes on the dome**★★, painted by Correggio (1520-24), depict the Vision of St John at Patmos and the *Translation of St John the Evangelist*. Those on the arches of the chapels to the north (1st, 2nd and 4th) were executed by Parmigianino.

In the convent next door are the **Renaissance cloisters**. ⏰*Open Mon-Sat 8.30am-noon and 3-6pm.* ⏳ *Donation recommended. Silence is requested in the monastery;* ⏰*Closed during church services.* ☎*0521 23 53 11; www.parma sangiovanni.com.*

Antica spezieria di San Giovanni Evangelista

♿⏰*Open daily except Mon, 8.30am-1.45pm.* ⏰*Closed Mon, 1 Jan, 25 Dec.* ⏳*2€.* ☎*0521 23 33 09; www.artipr.arti. beniculturali.it.*

This 13C pharmacy was started by the Benedictine monks. The furnishings date from the 16C.

Camera di San Paolo★

♿⏰*Open daily 8.30am-1.45pm.* ⏰*Closed Mon, 1 Jan, 25 Dec.* ⏳*2€.* ☎*0521 23 33 09; www.artipr.arti.beniculturali.it.*
Correggio's Room was the dining room of the Abbess of St Paul's Convent. The ceiling frescoes depicting mythological scenes with a luminous quality are Correggio's first major work (1519-20). The garlands of flowers and trellis-work and the reliefs and architectural detail at the base of the vault reveal the influence of Mantegna, whom he met in his youth in Mantua (⏳*see MANTOVA*). The next room was decorated by Araldi (1504).

Teatro Regio

www.teatroregioparma.org.
The Royal Theatre, built between 1821 and 1829 at the request of Marie-Louise of Habsburg, has a Classical frontage. The inaugural performance was of Bellini's opera, *Zaira*. The acoustics are excellent.

Chiesa di Madonna della Steccata

Call ahead for opening times. Donation recommended. 0521 23 49 37; www. museoconstantinianodellasteccata.it.
This 16C church, designed by the architects Bernardino and Zaccagni, contains fine **frescoes** by Parmigianino representing The Foolish and the Wise Virgins, placed between the figures of Adam and Moses, and Eve and Aaron. The mausoleum of Neipperg, husband of the former French Empress Marie-Louise who became Duchess of Parma, is on the left, and the tombs of the Farnese family and the Parma Bourbons are in the crypt.

Palazzo della Pilotta

The palace was so-called because the game of fives (*pilotta*) was played in its courtyards. This austere building houses the Palatine Library and the Farnese Theatre (*see below*).

Palazzo del Giardino

The **Parco Ducale** (ducal garden) was landscaped by the French architect Petitot and adorned with statues by another Frenchman, Boudard.

Visit

Musei del Palazzo della Pilotta

Museo Archeologico Nazionale★

Call for information on openings times and admission prices. Closed Mon. 0521 23 37 18.
The National Museum of Antiquities displays pre-Roman and Roman artefacts including the finds made in the excavation of Velleia, west of Parma.

Galleria Nazionale★★

Open daily 8.30am-1.45pm. Closed Mon, 1 Jan, 25 Dec. 6€ (combined ticket, Teatro Farnese). 0521 23 33 09; www.artipr.arti.beniculturali.it.
The gallery exhibits Emilian, Tuscan and Venetian paintings of the 14C, 15C and 16C by: Fra Angelico, Dosso Dossi, El Greco, Canaletto, Bellotto, Piazzetta and Tiepolo. Parmigianino is represented by his portrait **Turkish Slave**, and Correggio by one of his masterpieces, The **Virgin with St Jerome** (1528). The gallery also houses a sketch by Leonardo da Vinici, (*La Scapigliata*).

Teatro Farnese★★

Open daily 8.30am-2pm (last admission 1.30pm). Closed Mon, 1 Jan, 25 Dec. 2€, 6€ combined ticket with Galleria Nazionale. 0521 23 33 09; www.artipr.arti.beniculturali.it.
This imposing theatre was built in wood in 1619 by G B Aleotti, following the model of Palladio's Olympic Theatre in Vicenza (*see VICENZA*). Inaugurated for the marriage of Margaret de' Medici and Odoardo Farnese, the theatre was almost totally destroyed in 1944 and was rebuilt exactly as before in the 1950s.

Fondazione-Museo Glauco Lombardi★

Open Tue-Sat 9.30am-3.30pm; Sun and public holidays, Jul-Aug 9am-1.30pm, Sep-Jun 9am-6.30pm. Closed Mon, 1 Jan, 1 May, 15 Aug, 1 Nov,25 Dec. 4€. 0521 23 37 27; www.museolombardi.it.
The Glauco-Lombardi museum is chiefly devoted to life in the Duchy of Parma and Piacenza in the 18C and 19C. It contains paintings and mementoes of the former Empress Marie-Louise who governed the duchy. There are numerous works by French artists: Nattier, Mignard, Chardin, Watteau, Fragonard, Greuze, La Tour, Hubert Robert, Vigée-Lebrun, David and Millet.

Museo Casa Toscanini, Museo Multimediale Casa della Musica

Excursions

Castello di Torrechiara★

17km/11mi south by the Langhirano road. ♿🕐*Open daily May-Oct 8.30am-6.45pm, Nov-Apr 8am-3.15pm, Sat and Sun 9am-4.15pm.* 🕐*Closed Mon, 1 Jan, 1 May, 25 Dec.* 🎫*3€.* ☎*0521 35 52 55; www.torrechiara.it.*

This 15C fortress, built on a hilltop, is powerfully fortified by double ramparts, massive corner towers, a keep and machicolated curtain walls. The upper rooms (the Gaming and Gold Rooms) have remarkable **frescoes**★. From the terrace there is a superb **view**★ as far as the Apennines.

Castello di Canossa

32km/20mi southwest of Parma. From Torrechiara (23km/14mi), take the SS 513 and follow signs to San Polo d'Enza. www. castellimatildici.it.

Only the romantic ruins, perched on a rock, remain of the stronghold which belonged to the Countess of Tuscany, Matilda (1046-1115), who supported the Pope against the Emperor for 30 years during the quarrel over the investiture of bishops and abbots. The Emperor Heinrich IV of Germany came barefoot and in his shirtsleeves through the snow, to make amends to Pope Gregory VII in 1077. He had to wait three days for his absolution. This is the origin of the expression "to go to Canossa"; that is, to humble oneself after a quarrel.

Fidenza

23km/14mi west on the SS 9 (Via Emilia). Leave Parma by Via Massimo D'Azeglio. www.fidenzavillage.com.

This attractive agricultural town has a 11C Gothic-style Duomo★ completed in the 13C. The sculpture of the **central porch**★★ is most likely the work of the Parmesan sculptor, Antelami. The three fine **Romanesque doors** are adorned with lions, a typically Emilian feature.

Fontanellato

19km/12mi to the northwest by the Fidenza road and then the road to Soragna, to the right. ♿🕐*Open Tue-Sat Apr-Oct, 9.30am-11.30pm and 3-6pm, Sun 9.30am-noon and 2.30pm-6pm; Nov-Mar 9.30am-12.30pm and 2.30-5pm, Sun 9.30am-noon and 2.30pm-5pm.* 🕐*Closed Mon (winter), 1 Jan, 25 Dec.* 🎫*7€.* ☎*0521 82 32 20; www.fonta nellato.org.*

The vast moat-encircled castle, **Rocca Sanvitale**, stands in the centre of town. The ceiling of one of the rooms is decorated with a **fresco**★depicting Diana and Actaeon by Parmigianino.

Brescello

22km/13.5mi northwest.

The town owes its name (Brixellum) to the Celts who settled in the Po Plain and who, as they had moved along the plain, had already founded the settlements of Bressanone (Brixen) and Brescia (Brixia).

In spite of its ancient origins, Brescello nowadays is famous for being the setting of the films about Don Camillo and Peppone. The museum contains memorabilia and posters relating to the films and as well as objects used during the filming such as bicycles, a motorcycle and sidecar and even a tank. ♿🕐*Open Mon-Sat 10am-noon and 2.30-6pm, Sun and public holidays 9.30am-12.30pm and 2.30-7pm (book several days in advance: Sig. Carpi, 8am-1.30pm).* 🎫*Donation welcome.* ☎*0522 96 21 58; www.pragmanet. it/pro-loco.*

PAVIA★

POPULATION 71 366

MICHELIN MAP 561 G 9 – LOMBARDY.

This proud city is rich in buildings from the Romanesque and Renaissance periods. An important military camp under the Romans, it became, successively, the capital of the Lombard kings, rival of Milan in the 11C, famous intellectual and artistic centre during the 14C under the Visconti, a fortified town in the 16C and one of the most active centres of the 19C independence movements. The university, one of the oldest in Europe, was founded in the 11C and its students included Petrarch, Leonardo da Vinci and the poet Ugo Foscolo.

- **Information:** Via Fabio Filzi 2. ☎0382 22 156; www.comune.pv.it.
- ▶ **Orient Yourself:** On the banks of the River Ticino, Pavia linked to Milan by A 7 and S 35, around 38km/23mi away.
- **Don't Miss:** Masterpieces in the Pinacoteca, Chiesa di San Michele and Certosa di Pavia.
- **Organizing Your Time:** Allow half a day.
- **Also See:** *MILANO, PIACENZA.*

Visit

Castello Visconteo★

Open daily 10am-6pm; Jul-Aug and Dec-Jan 9am-1.30pm. Closed Mon and public holidays. 6€ (museums); 1€ for castle courtyard only. ☎0382 33 85.

This impressive brick building was built by the Visconti. It now houses the **Musei Civici**★, the municipal collections, which are rich in archaeological finds, medieval and Renaissance sculpture and, particularly, paintings. The **pina**coteca★, the picture gallery, on the first floor, has numerous masterpieces including a lovely altarpiece by the Brescian artist Vincenzo Foppa, a *Virgin and Child* by Giovanni Bellini and a very expressive *Christ bearing the Cross* by the Lombard artist, Bergognone. The last room contains a 16C model of the cathedral by Fugazza after plans by Bramante. *The pinacoteca has a collection of masterpieces.*

Address Book

For coin ranges see the Legend on the cover flap.

WHERE TO STAY

Agriturismo Tenuta Camillo – 27010 Bascapé – 23 km/14m north of Pavia – ☎0382 66 509 – www.agriturismo.com/tenutacamillo/ – Closed Sep-Oct – ⊟ P ⌧ – 6 rm – ⌧ 5 €. Nestling in a flower-filled "basin," between the rice fields and the lines of poplar trees, this is a lovely spot which is also well located for getting to Milan. The rooms and studios have been tastefully decorated with plain, country-style furnishings: the beds have painted headboards. Authentic, home-cooked food.

WHERE TO EAT

Enoteca Enotria – *Via dei Mille 160/162* – ☎0382 56 67 55 – enotria_pv@virgilio.it - Closed Sun, Mon and lunchtimes – Reservations recommended. This wine bar is situated on the far side of the river, in the charming Borgo Ticino. The enthusiastic proprietor has a flair for matching classical dishes with interesting wines. Informal, family atmosphere. Pleasant dining room with tiled floor and rose-tinted walls.

B. Juge/MICHELIN

The Certosa is a harmonious blend of late-Lombard Renaissance, Gothic and monastic spirituality

Duomo★

This vast cathedral, surmounted by one of Italy's largest domes, was begun in 1488: both Bramante and Leonardo da Vinci are said to have worked on the plan. The façade is 19C. To the left of the façade stood an 11C municipal tower, which fell down in March 1989, while opposite is the 16C Bishop's Palace. The adjoining Piazza Vittoria is overlooked by the 12C **Broletto** or town hall.

Chiesa di San Michele★★

This Romanesque church, dedicated to St Michael, has a sandstone **façade**★, including an impressive Romanesque doorway on the south side with a lintel on which Christ is seen giving a papyrus volume to St Paul and the Keys of the Church to St Peter. Inside, there are interesting architectural features (dome on squinches, the friezes and modillions beneath galleries, mosaics, capitals etc). The apse is decorated with a 15C **fresco**★ of the *Coronation of the Virgin*.

Chiesa di San Pietro in Ciel d'Oro★

This Lombard-Romanesque church, which was consecrated in 1132, has a richly decorated west **door**★. In the chancel is the Arca di Sant'Agostinoa (the Tomb of St Augustine – 354-430), the work of the Maestri Campionesi.

Chiesa di San Lanfranco

2km/1mi west. In the chancel is a **cenotaph**★ (late 15C) by Amadeo commemorates Lanfranc, who was born in Pavia and became Archbishop of Canterbury, where he is buried (d 1098).

Excursions

Certosa di Pavia★★★

10km/6mi to the north. ○*Open daily 9-11.30am and 2.30-5.30pm.* ·*Guided tours available (1hr).* ·*Donation recommended.* ☎*0382 92 56 13; www. certosadipavia.com.*

The 14C "Gratiarum Cartusia" (Charterhouse of the Graces), is a remarkable example of Lombard art and home to a community of **Cistercian monks**.

Façade

The ornate lower part (1473-99) was the work of the Mantegazza brothers, the architect and sculptor Amadeo, who worked also in Bergamo, and his pupil, Briosco. The upper part was completed in 1560 by Cristoforo Lombardo.

The façade is adorned with multicoloured marble sculptures, with statues of saints in the niches and foliage and ornaments. Round Amadeo's famous windows are scenes from the Bible and the life of Gian Galeazzo Visconti. The low reliefs round the central doorway by Briosco depict Carthusian history.

Interior and cloisters

The interior has a certain solemn grandeur and, although it is essentially Gothic, the beginnings of the Renais-

The Sad Story (with a Happy Ending) of a Masterpiece

In August 1984 the *Triptych* by Baldassare degli Embriachi was stolen and the thieves demanded a ransom for its return. To raise the ransom money, a concert was organised and the great flautist Severino Gazzelloni (1919-92) was invited to perform in the church. However, several panels and statuettes, which had been sold, were recovered and this eventually led to the arrest of the thieves. Restoration of the Triptych was carried out between 1986 and 1989 by the Istituto Centrale per il Restauro.

sance can be detected in the transept and the chancel.

Upon entering, look up: above the south chapels a painted Carthusian monk peeks out at visitors from a window with twin openings. From higher up, visitors are observed by stars which emblazon the intense blue of the vaulting.

The south arm of the transept is decorated with a *Virgin and Child* (1481-1522) by **Bergognone** who was also responsible for the *Madonna del Tappeto* above the entrance of the **small cloisters**, with their Lombard terracottas.

Adjacent to the small cloisters, the ceiling of the **refectory** is decorated with the *Madonna del Latte*, also by Bergognone.

The atmospheric **large cloisters** occupy a vast space; above the arcades, note the roofs and chimneys of the 24 monks' cells which until 1968 were inhabited by Carthusian brothers.

Enter one of the cells and observe the surprising interior: although spartan in the extreme, each cell is a veritable apartment which looks out on the garden.

Back in the church, on the vaulting of the right altar of the transept, note the *Virgin Enthroned* receiving the charterhouse from Gian Galeazzo Visconti. The latter's tomb dates from the late 15C.

In the **lavatorium** note the *Madonna del Garofano* (Virgin with Carnation) by Bernardino Luini (c 1480-1532).

The transept is separated from the chancel by a marble partition wall. The inlay work of the choir stalls was executed to plans by Bergognone.

The **old sacristy** houses a **triptych** by Baldassare degli Embriachi (late 14C), made from ivory and hippopotamus teeth, with scenes from the lives of the Virgin and Christ. In the middle of the sacristy note the *Virgin and Child*, a recurring theme in the monastery which attests to the profound gratitude felt by Gian Galeazzo's wife Catherine to the Virgin.

The north arm of the transept contains another work by Bergognone, the *Ecce Homo*, as well as the cenotaph of Ludovico il Moro and Beatrice d'Este, by Cristoforo Solari (1497).

Proceeding towards the exit, in the second chapel on the north side note Perugino's Eternal Father (c 1445 1523).

La Lomellina

The region between the Ticino and the Po, is Italy's great rice-growing area and a landscape of vast stretches of flooded land divided by long rows of willows and poplars. Towns of interest are: **Lomello** *(32km/20mi southwest of Pavia*; **Mortara** *(15km/9mi north of Lomello on S 211)* with its 14C church of San Lorenzo (paintings by Gaudenzio Ferrari) and **Vigevano** *(12km/7mi northeast of Mortara on S 494)* and Piazza Ducale. Bramante's tower dominates the square (which was possibly designed by Leonardo da Vinci).

Also of interest in the area is **Novara**, and industrial and commercial centre . Worth a visit is the 16-17C **basilica di San Gaudenzio**★ crowned with a slender **dome**★★ (1844-78), an audacious addition by a local architect, A Antonelli. Inside are several interesting works of art, including paintings by Morazzone (17C) and Gaudenzio Ferrari (16c), and the silver **sarcophagus**★ of the city's patron saint (St Gaudentius). The neo-Classical **Duomo** by Antonelli has a 6C-7C paleo-Christian baptistery.The chancel adorned with a black and white Byzantine-style mosaic **floor**★.

PERUGIA★★

POPULATION 157 842
MICHELIN MAP 563 M 19 – UMBRIA.

Perugia was one of the 12 Etruscan city-states known as lucumonies that comprised the federation of Etruria in the 7C and 6C BC. The massive Etruscan wall with its gateways gives some idea of the splendour of that age. The town also has numerous ecclesiastical and secular buildings from the Middle Ages. Today the capital of Umbria is an industrial and commercial centre and a vibrant university town.

- **Information:** Piazza IV Novembre 3, ☎075 57 23 327; www.provincia.perugia.it www.comune.perugia.it.
- **Orient Yourself:** Perugia is perched atop a hill, in the heart of Umbria. The main access road is E 45 which links the town with Emilia-Romagna.
- **Don't Miss:** The National Gallery of Umbria, Chiesa di San Pietro and the Oratorio di San Bernardino.
- **Organizing Your Time:** Allow a day to see the main sights.
- **Also See:** *ASSISI, GUBBIO.*

Features

Piazza IV Novembre★★
Allow 2hr.
This square in the heart of Perugia is one of the grandest in Italy. The chief buildings of the city's glorious period as an independent commune are grouped here: the Priors' Palace, the Great Fountain and the Cathedral. Leading off the square is **Via Maestà delle Volte★** with its medieval houses and passages.

Fontana Maggiore★★
The Great Fountain was built to the designs of Fra Bevignate (1278) and is admirably proportioned. The sculpted panels are the work of Nicola Pisano (lower basin) and his son Giovanni (upper basin). Copies replace some of the originals, which are on display in the National Gallery of Umbria.

Palazzo dei Priori★★
The Priors' Palace was begun in the 13C and enlarged in the following centuries.

View of Perugia

R. Mattes/MICHELIN

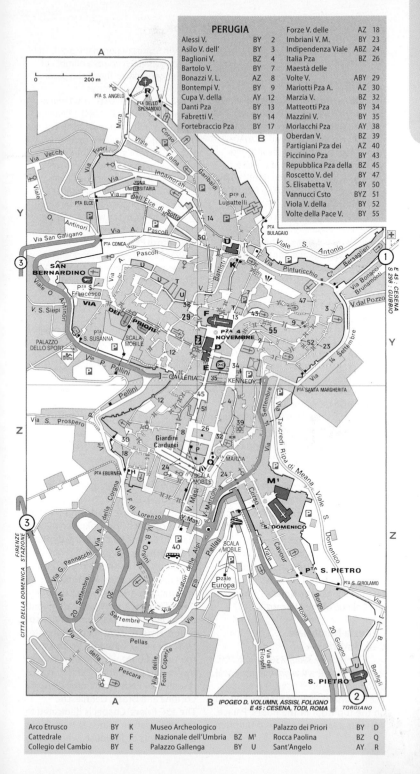

PERUGIA

Alessi V.	BY	2	Forze V. delle	AZ 18
Asilo V. dell'	BY	3	Imbriani V. M.	BY 23
Baglioni V.	BZ	4	Independenza Viale	ABZ 24
Bartolo V.	BY	7	Italia Pza	BZ 26
Bonazzi V. L.	AZ	8	Maestà delle	
Bontempi V.	BY	9	Volte V.	ABY 29
Cupa V. della	AY	12	Mariotti Pza A.	BZ 30
Danti Pza	BY	13	Marzia V.	BZ 32
Fabretti V.	BY	14	Matteotti Pza	BY 34
Fortebraccio Pza	BY	17	Mazzini V.	BY 35
			Morlacchi Pza	AY 38
			Oberdan V.	BZ 39
			Partigiani Pza dei	AZ 40
			Piccinino Pza	BY 43
			Repubblica Pza della	BZ 45
			Roscetto V. del	BY 47
			S. Elisabetta V.	BY 50
			Vannucci Csto	BYZ 51
			Viola V. della	BY 52
			Volte della Pace V.	BY 55

Arco Etrusco	BY	K	Museo Archeologico		Palazzo dei Priori	BY	D
Cattedrale	BY	F	Nazionale dell'Umbria	BZ M¹	Rocca Paolina	BZ	Q
Collegio del Cambio	BY	E	Palazzo Gallenga	BY U	Sant'Angelo	AY	R

Address Book

For coin ranges see the Legend on the cover flap.

WHERE TO STAY

Hotel Priori – *Via dei Priori – ☎075 57 23 378 – www.hotelpriori.it – 60 rm.* The main attraction of this pleasant, no-frills hotel is the splendid terrace which looks down over the little old alleyways and the roofs of the historic centre. Simple rooms, some with a view, furnished with dark wooden furniture.

Hotel La Rosetta – *Piazza Italia 19 – ☎075 57 20 841 – Fax 075 57 20 841 – www.perugiaonline.com/larosetta – 90 rm.* Whereas some of the rooms have frescoed ceilings and gorgeous antique furnishings, others, although pleasant and spacious, have a more cluttered feel and are not quite so elegant. Located in the vibrant heart of the city.

WHERE TO EAT

Dal Mi' Cocco – *Corso Garibaldi 12 – ☎075 57 32 511 – Closed Mon, 25 Jul-15 Aug – – Reservations recommended.* "Like going to stay with friends" is the motto and the reality of this rather alternative establishment housed in some old stables. Diners are welcomed with a glass of red wine and treated to some Vin Santo later on in the meal. The fixed-price menu features a number of Umbrian specialities. Bread and pasta are cooked on the premises.

Locanda degli Artisti – *Via Campo Battaglia 10 – ☎075 57 35 851 – Closed Tue, 10-20 Jan – .* This restaurant is housed in a brick-walled vault, in a medieval *palazzo* in the historic centre. Tasty regional cooking as well as some specialities from Lucania. The menu also includes some national dishes as well as various pizzas. Pictures by aspiring artists hang on the walls. Musical entertainment in the evenings.

Caffè di Perugia – *Via Mazzini 10 – ☎075 57 31 863 – www.caffediperugia. it –* Housed in what was a medieval palazzo that has been tastefully restored to its former glory, much to the joy of the locals. Choose from the grill-pizzeria in the old vault, or the elegant dining room with its frescoed ceiling, or the well-stocked wine bar. Imaginative menus.

EVENTS AND FESTIVALS

Perugia has been the backdrop for the **Umbria Jazz** festival for 30 years. *Piazza Danti 28, ☎075 57 32 432, Fax 075 57 22 656, www.umbriajazz.com.tg.*

It forms an ensemble of impressive grandeur. The façade overlooking the square has a majestic outside staircase leading up to a marble pulpit from which the priors harangued the people. The Corso Vannucci façade boasts a fine 14C doorway. Inside, the palace rooms are decorated with 14C frescoes or carved 15C panelling in the Notaries' Chamber and College of the Mercanzia.

Galleria Nazionale dell'Umbria★★

Open daily 8.30am-7.30pm. 6.50€. ☎075 57 21 009; www.gallerianazionale umbria.it.
The National Gallery of Umbria, housed on the top floor of the Priors' Palace, presents a large selection of Umbrian art showing its development from the 13C to the late 18C.

On display are: a **Madonna** by Duccio, a **Crucifix** by the unknown master, Maestro di San Francesco, a **polyptych of St Anthony** by Piero della Francesca and works by Fra Angelico, Boccati and Fiorenzo di Lorenzo. Masterpieces by Pinturicchio and Perugino include a **Dead Christ** with its black background and an admirable **Madonna of Consolation**. Note also the marble statuettes by Nicola and Giovanni Pisano from the Great Fountain, and other works by Arnolfo di Cambio. The 17C is represented by Federico Barocci, Pietro da Cortona and Orazio Gentileschi.

The 15C Priors' Chapel is dedicated to the city's patron saints: St Herculanus and St Louis of Toulouse, whose story

Artistic Heritage

In harmony with their peaceful countryside, the Umbrian painters had gentle, mystic souls. They loved landscapes with pure lines, punctuated with trees; and in their stylised compositions, the women are depicted with a tender gracefulness, sometimes too mannered. Their technique is characterised by extremely delicate draughtsmanship and soft colours. The masters were **Giovanni Boccati** (1410-c1485), **Fiorenzo di Lorenzo** (d 1520) and especially **Pietro Vannucci alias Perugino** (1445-1523), the teacher of Raphael. His favourite subjects were religious; in them he showed his sense of space, atmosphere and landscape, marred only by a touch of mannerism. The historical artist Pinturicchio (1454-1518) was influenced by Perugino but his charmingly realistic scenes were painted more naïvely than those of his predecessor.

is told by Benedetto Bonfigli (d 1496) in a remarkable cycle of **frescoes**. The museum also has some lovely 13C and 14C French enamels and ivories.

Cattedrale★
The cathedral is Gothic, but the Piazza Dante façade was completed with a Baroque doorway.
The south chapel contains an interesting **Descent from the Cross** by Barocci, which inspired Rubens in his *Antwerp Descent*. In the north chapel is a ring said to be the Virgin's wedding ring. In both these chapels, note the superb **stalls** with 16C marquetry work.

Visit

Chiesa di San Pietro★★
To reach the church, dedicated to St Peter, go through the **Porta San Pietro★**, a majestic but unfinished work of the Florentine Agostino di Duccio. The church was built at the end of the 10C and remodelled during the Renaissance. Inside are 11 excellent canvases by Vassilacchi, alias Aliense, a Greek contemporary of El Greco. Also of note are the **carved tabernacle** by Mino da Fiesole and the marvellous 16C **stalls★★**.

Chiesa di San Domenico★
The interior of this imposing Gothic church, dedicated to St Dominic, was altered in the 17C. To the right of the chancel is the 14C **funerary monument** of Pope Benedict XI.

Museo Archeologico Nazionale dell'Umbria★★
♿ ◷Open daily 8.30am-7.30pm (Mon 10am). ◷Closed 1 Jan, 1 May, 25 Dec. ◚4€. ☎075 57 27 141; www.archeopg.arti.beniculturali.it.
The National Archaeological Museum comprises prehistoric, Etruscan and Umbrian sections. The remarkable collections include funerary urns, sarcophagi and Etruscan bronzes.

Collegio del Cambio★
◷Open Mar-Oct, Tue-Sat 9am-12.30pm and 2.30-5.30pm, Sun and public holidays 9am-1pm. ◷Closed Mon, 1 Jan, 25 Dec. ◚2.60€. ☎075 57 28 599; www.perugiaonline.com/perugia_collegiodecambio.html.
The Exchange was built in the 15C for the money-changers. In the Audience Room are the famous **frescoes★★** of Perugino and his pupils. These frescoes display the humanist spirit of the age, which sought to combine Classical civilisation and Christian doctrine. The Justice statue is by Benedetto da Maiano (15C).

Oratorio di San Bernardino★★
To reach the oratory of St Bernardino, walk along the picturesque **Via dei Priori★**. This Renaissance jewel (1461) by Agostino di Duccio is exquisite in its harmonious lines, the delicacy of its multicoloured marbles and its sculptures. The low reliefs on the façade depict St Bernardine in glory on the tympanum, the life of the saint on the lintel and delightful angel musicians on the shafts. Inside the church, the altar consists of a 4C early-Christian sarcophagus.

Via delle Volte della Pace★

The picturesque medieval street is formed by a long 14C Gothic portico as it follows the Etruscan town wall.

Sant'Angelo★

The interior of this small 5C-6C circular church includes 16 ancient columns.

Rocca Paolina★

Access via Porta Marzia.

These are the remains of a fortress built in 1540 on the orders of Pope Paul III – hence the name "Pauline". The impressive interior still has huge walls, streets and wells dating from the 11C to 16C. Escalators have been built to facilitate access within the fortress.

Arco Etrusco★

This imposing Etruscan Arch is built of huge blocks of stone. A 16C loggia surmounts the tower on the left.
Alongside, the majestic 18C **Palazzo Gallenga** serves as a summer school for foreign students.

Giardini Carducci

There is a superb **view**★★ from the Carducci Gardens, which dominates the San Pietro quarter, over the Tiber Valley.

Excursions

Ipogeo dei Volumni★

6km/4mi southeast. ⊙*Open Jul-Aug, daily, 9am-1pm and 4.30-7pm, Sep-Jun 9am-1pm and 3.30-6.30pm.* ⊙*Closed 1 Jan, 1 May, 25 Dec.* ✆*3€.* ☎*075 39 33 29; www. archeopg.arti.beniculturali.it. (&also see LAGHI).*

This vast Etruscan hypogeum hewn out of the rock, comprises an atrium and nine burial chambers. The Volumnian tomb is the largest; it contains six rounded tombstones (cippi), the biggest being that of the head of the family (2C BC).

Torgiano

16km/10mi southeast. This village dominating the Tiber Valley has the interesting **Museo del Vino**★ (Lungarotti Foundation) describing wine-growing traditions in Umbria and Italy since the days of the Etruscans: excellent historical and photographic documents. (&) ⊙*Open daily, 9am-1pm and 3-7pm (6pm winter).* ⊙*Closed 25 Dec.* ✆*4€.* ☎*075 98 80 200; www.lungarotti.it.*

Panicale

32km/20mi southwest. ▶*Take S 220, turn right after Tavernelle and follow directions. www.comunepanicalepg.it*
Panicale is a medieval town perched on a hillside overlooking Lake Trasimeno. The church of San Sebastiano houses a Martyrdom of St Sebastian by Perugino.

Città della Pieve

42km/26mi southwest on S 220.

This warm ochre-coloured town, founded in about AD 7-8 and originally called *Castrum Plebis*, was the birthplace of Pietro Vannucci, better known as **Perugino**. Some of his works are housed in the cathedral *(Baptism of Christ. Virgin with St Peter, St Paul, St Gervase and St Protasius)*, in the oratory of Santa Maria dei Bianchi *(Adoration of the Magi*, an elegant composition balanced by the portrayal of the gentle Umbrian countryside) and in *Santa Maria dei Servi (Descent from the Cross)*. In the oratory of San Bartolomeo there are mid-14C frescoes by the Sienese artist, Jacopo di Mino del Pellicciaio *(Weeping of the Angels)*. Among the numerous monuments in the city, which date from the Middle Ages to the 18C, note the Palazzo della Corgna, built in the middle of the 16C by the Perugian architect Galeazzo Alessi and frescoed by Niccolò Pomarancio and Salvio Savini.

PIACENZA★

POPULATION 99 000

MICHELIN MAP 561 G 11

TOWN PLAN IN THE MICHELIN ATLAS ITALY – EMILIA-ROMAGNA.

Piacenza was originally built by the Romans at the end of the Via Emilia on the south bank of the Po. It flourished in the Middle Ages and was a member of the Lombard League. In 1545 Pope Paul III, Alessandro Farnese, gave the papal lands of Piacenza and its neighbour Parma to his son Pier Luigi along with a dukedom. After this the Farnese ruled Piacenza until 1731 when the dukedom passed to the Bourbons.

- **Information:** Corso Garibaldi 50. ☎0523 79 53 19; www.provincia.pc.it/turismo.
- **Orient Yourself:** Piacenza is situated on the banks of the River Po. It is the first city you reach as you enter Emilia from Lombardy on A 1. The main road connecting it to Turn and Brescia is A 21.
- **Don't Miss:** The Duomo and the Musei Civici di Palazzo Farnese.
- **Organizing Your Time:** The main sights can be seen in half a day.
- **Also See:** CREMONA, PARMA.

Walking Tours

Piazza dei Cavalli★

The old political and economic centre of the city, this square derives its name from the **equestrian statues**★★ of Dukes Alessandro and Ranuccio I Farnese, a Baroque masterpiece by Francesco Mochi (1580-1654).

The square is dominated by the imposing **"Gotico"**★★, the old town hall, a masterpiece of 13C Lombard-Gothic architecture. The building is both severe and harmonious and displays a notable contrast between the marble lower part and the brick upper storeys, the great openings and the elegantly decorated windows.

To the left of the square is the façade of the 13C **Church of San Francesco**, an interesting example of Franciscan Gothic architecture, embellished by a fine splayed doorway.

Duomo★

This remarkable Lombard-Romanesque cathedral dates from the 12C-13C. The façade is adorned with a rose window and a porch with three notable doorways. The two lateral doorways are influenced by the sculptural styles at Modena and Nonantola. The **interior** on the plan of a Latin cross is simple but enriched by the sweeping frescoes (Guercino, Morazzone, 17C) which adorn the dome, and by the canvases in the chancel (Camillo Procaccini and Ludovico Carracci).

Basilica di Sant'Antonino

This former palaeo-Christian basilica dedicated to St Anthony was remodelled in the 11C and has interesting features: an octagonal tower (40m/131ft high) and the north "Paradise" vestibule (1350) in the Gothic style.

Chiesa di San Savino

This 12C church, with its very pure architectural lines, contains priceless traces of the original construction, such as the fine capitals and the **mosaic flooring**★ in the chancel and in the crypt.

Palazzo Farnese

This imposing late-Renaissance palace, built to designs by Vignola but never completed, now houses the **Museo Civico**★ (*see Worth a Visit, below*).

Chiesa di San Sisto

This rather curious 16C building was designed by Alessio Tramello, an architect from Piacenza. The façade is preceded by a doorway, dated 1622, which opens onto a 16C atrium. The interior has an interesting Renaissance decoration and a splendid 16C wood chancel. Raphael painted the famous *Sistine Madonna* for this church, now replaced by a copy.

Chiesa della Madonna di Campagna★

This beautiful church, in the form of a Greek cross and built in the idiom of Bramante, constitutes one of the most important Renaissance buildings in Italy. The interior contains splendid **frescoes★** by Pordenone (1484-1539), an exponent of the Mannerist style.

Worth a Visit

Musei Civici di Palazzo Farnese★

Piazza Cittadella. &⊕*Open Tue-Thu, 8.45am-1pm, Fri-Sun 3-6pm also.* ⊕*Closed Mon, public holidays and 4 Jul.* ⊛*6€.* ☎*0523 49 26 58; www: musei. piacenza.it.*

On the ground floor the sumptuous **Fasti Farnesiani★** cycle of frescoes by Draghi and Ricci is richly framed in stuccowork. The images portray stories of Alessandro Farnese who became Pope Paul III. There are also collections of ceramics and glass, frescoes from local churches (14C-15C) and a series of Romanesque sculptures of the "Piacenza School" which combine influences both from the contemporary French school and Wiligelmo (**The Prophets David and Ezekiel**, 12C). Note also the bronze **Etruscan Divining Liver★★**, a soothsayer's device dating from the 2C-1C BC. The first floor, houses collections of paintings from the 16C-19C Emilian, Lombard and Ligurian schools, a **Virgin and Child with St John** by Botticelli and the Fasti Farnesiani dedicated to Elisabetta Farnese. There is also a Carriage Museum and a Risorgimento Museum. ⌂*Galleria Alberoni (Ecce Homo★★ by Antonello da Messina), Galleria d'Arte Moderna Ricci-Oddi.*

PIENZA★★

POPULATION 2 230
MICHELIN MAP 563 M 1
SEE ALSO THE GREEN GUIDE TUSCANY.

Pienza displays a remarkable unity of style, especially in its main square, and is a perfect example of Renaissance town planning. It was commissioned by Pope Pius II, the diplomat and humanist poet, who wanted to build the ideal town. The architectural unity was intended to reflect the utopian concepts of the "ideal city," as conceived by the 15C humanist movement.

- **Information:** Ufficio Turistico, corso Rossellino 59, 53026 Pienza (SI), ☎0578 74 90 71; www.comunedipienza.it.
- ▶ **Orient Yourself:** Pienza is off S 146, between San Quirico d'tOrcia and Montepulciano.
- ⌂ **Don't Miss:** The Abbazia di Sant'Antimo.
- ⊕ **Organizing Your Time:** Allow a day for the town and its surrounding areas.
- ⌚ **Also See:** *MONTEPULCIANO.*

Visit

The centre of Pienza is the work of the Florentine architect, **Bernardo Rossellino** (1409-82), a pupil of Alberti, whose design centred on lining the town's main axis with principal monuments.

The town hall is opposite the cathedral. The other sides of the square are framed by the Bishop's Palace and the Palazzo Piccolomini; enchanced by a pretty well outside. There is a fine **view★** over the Orcia Valley from behind the cathedral.

Cattedrale★

The cathedral, which was completed in 1462, has a Renaissance façade. The interior (restored) contains paintings by the Sienese school, including an **Assumption**★★ by Vecchietta.

Museo Diocesano

♿🕐*Open daily Mar-Oct 10am-1pm and 3-7pm (Sat and Sun 6pm).* 🕐*Closed Tue.* 🎫*4.10€. For information on opening times, call ☎0578 74 99 05; www.provincia.siena.it/musei.*

The Cathedral Museum contains pictures of the 14C and 15C Sienese school and a 14C English historiated cope.

Palazzo Piccolomini★

🕐*Open daily 10am-12.30pm and 3-6pm.* 🕐*Closed Mon, for two weeks in Feb and Nov.* 🎫*3€. ☎0578 74 85 03.*

Rossellino's masterpiece was greatly influenced by the Palazzo Rucellai in Florence (👈 *see FIRENZE)*. The three sides facing the town are similar; the fourth, overlooking the Orcia Valley looks onto hanging gardens, among the earliest to have been created. The palace still has its armoury, the incunabula and a Baroque bed from the papal bedchamber.

Excursions

Montalcino★

24km/15mi west. In addition to part of its 13C walls, this small hillside town still has its magnificent **fortress**★★★ built in 1361. It is shaped like a pentagon, with a parapet walk and five towers. Ordinary people would seek shelter within the outer walls. It was here that the Sienese government took refuge when the town was captured by Holy Roman Emperor Charles V in 1555. 🕐*Open daily 9am-8pm.* 🕐*Closed Mon.* 🎫*3.50€; 6€ combined ticket including Museo Civico. ☎0577 84 92 11; www.prolocomontalcino.it.*

Montalcino is also famous for its **Brunello**, an excellent red wine. The town is a labyrinth of medieval streets leading to a Romanesque and Gothic church, the 13C town hall, the **Palazzo Comunale**★, or the small **Museo Civico e Diocesano**. ♿🕐*Open daily 10am-1pm and 2-5.30pm.* 🕐*Closed Mon, 1 Jan and 25 Dec.* 🎫*4.50€, 6€ combined ticket with fortress. ☎0577 84 60 14; www.prolocomontalcino.it.*

Abbazia di Sant'Antimo★★

35km/22mi southwest. 🕐*Open Mon-Sat, 10.15am-12.30pm and 3-6.30pm, Sun and public holidays 9.15-10.45am and 3-6pm. Masses sung in Gregorian chant.* 🎫*Donation welcome. www.antimo.it.*

The 9C abbey stands in an isolated hill **site**★ amid cypress and olive groves. Its prosperity was at its peak in the 12C when the **church** was built. It is a fine example of Cistercian Romanesque architecture with Burgundian (ambulatory and apsidal chapels) and Lombard (porch, bell tower with Lombard bands and façades) influences. The interior is spacious and austere. Columns topped by fine alabaster capitals divide the nave from the aisles.

In the Monastery of Sant'Antimo silence is transformed into music as the small community sings Gregorian chants

PISA★★★

POPULATION 88 363

MICHELIN MAP 563 K 13 –

SEE ALSO THE GREEN GUIDE TUSCANY.

Pisa's superb buildings reflect past splendours. The city is more spacious than Florence and less austere thanks to its yellow, pink or yellow-ochre house fronts but, like Florence, it is bisected by the River Arno, which forms one of its most majestic meanders at this point. Pisa also owes its charm to its somewhat aristocratic air, the genteel lifestyle that this seems to encourage, and the special quality of the light, probably due to the proximity of the sea.

Almost totally encircled by walls, Pisa is traversed by a main street lined with shops; on the south bank this is the Corso Italia and on the north bank a narrow street flanked by arcades, Borgo Stretto. The winding, Via Santa Maria, linking Piazza del Duomo to the Arno, is one of the most characteristic streets in Pisa with its noble yet cheerful appearance. These two streets on the north bank flank the busiest district in the city, full of shops and restaurants.

- **Information:** Piazza dei Miracoli, 56126 Pisa, ☎050 56 04 64; www.pisa.turismo. toscana.it.
- **Orient Yourself:** Pisa is situated near the mouth of the River Arno, with the Parco Naturale di Migliarino-S. Rossore-Massaciùccoli between the town and the sea.
- **Don't Miss:** The Torre Pendente (Leaning Tower) and the rich decoration of the Duomo and Battistero.
- **Organizing Your Time:** Allow one day to see Pisa.
- **Especially for Kids:** Trying to "hold up" the Leaning Tower of Pisa.
- **Also See:** *LUCCA, VERSILIA.*

A Bit of History

Sheltered from raiding pirates, Pisa was a Roman naval base and commercial port until the end of the Empire (5C). It became an independent maritime republic at the end of the 9C and continued to benefit from its geographical location. Pisa became the rival of Genoa and Venice, and the Pisans waged war against the Saracens in the Mediterranean basin. It was in the 12C and the beginning of the 13C that Pisa reached the peak of its power and prosperity.

Piazza del Duomo

G. Bludzin/MICHELIN

Address Book

♿*For coin ranges see the Legend on the cover flap.*

WHERE TO STAY

◉**Hotel Galileo** – *Via S. Maria 12, (1st floor, no elevator)* – ☎050 40 621 – 9 rm. A good solution for anyone wanting to stay in the centre of town, within easy reach of the famous piazza, and at a reasonable price! The rooms are simple, with modern furnishings and have large windows. They all have private bathrooms but not always en suite.

◉◉◉**Hotel Francesco** – *Via S. Maria 129* – ☎050 55 54 53 – www. hotelfrancesco.com – 🛏 ♿. This comfortable hotel is situated in a quiet part of town, a stone's throw from the Leaning Tower. Modern-style, wooden furniture throughout. Spacious rooms and bathrooms. Breakfast al fresco in summer – there is a lovely terrace area to sit at outside.

WHERE TO EAT

◉**Osteria Dei Mille** – *Via dei Mille 32* – ☎050 55 62 63 – 🛏 🍴. This charming establishment is just five minutes from the hustle and bustle of the Piazza dei Miracoli. Authentic

Tuscan cooking with a wide selection of vegetarian dishes. The copper saucepans hanging on the walls are a nice touch.

◉**La Clessidra** – *Via Santa Cecilia 34* – ☎050 54 01 60 – *Closed Sat lunchtime, Sun, 24 Dec-7 Jan, 3 weeks in Aug* – 🛏 – *Reservations recommended.* A simple, pleasant restaurant with a very able and hard-working chef. The cuisine is typically Tuscan but with an innovative touch and a few variations on the traditional themes. Located in one of the smartest and best-preserved parts of town.

TAKING A BREAK

Caffè dell'Ussero – *Lungarno Pacinotti 27* – ☎050 58 11 00 – *Open Sun-Fri 7.30am-9pm. Closed Aug.* Situated on the ground floor of the Palazzo Rosso is this rather grand café, which dates back to the 18C. It has had an interesting past: initially the meeting-place for Pisa's intellectual elite, it has also been a cinema! These days it is a pleasant tea room which hosts some quite smart social gatherings. The cafe overlooks the River Arno.

This period was marked by the construction of some fine buildings and the foundation of the university.

During the 13C there were struggles between the Emperor and the Pope. Pisa supported the Ghibellines and thus opposed Genoa on the seas and Lucca and Florence on land. In 1284 the Pisan fleet was defeated at the naval **Battle of Meloria**. Ruined by internal strife, Pisa's maritime empire foundered; Corsica and Sardinia, which she had ruled since the 11C, were ceded to Genoa. Pisa herself passed under Florentine rule and the Medici took a special interest in the city, especially in the study of science there. Its most famous son was the astronomer and physicist **Galileo** (1564-1642). His patron was Cosimo II, Grand Duke of Tuscany. Nevertheless Galileo had to defend his theory of the rotation of the earth before the Inquisition and in fact renounced it.

The economic prosperity of the powerful maritime Pisan Republic from the 11C to the 13C fostered the development of a new art style, particularly evident in the fields of architecture and sculpture. The **Pisan-Romanesque style**, with the cathedral as the most rigorous example, is characterised by external decoration: the alternate use of different coloured marbles to create geometric patterns, a play of light and shade due to the tiers of loggias with small columns on the upper parts of the façade, and intarsia decoration showing the strong influence of the Islamic world and of Christian countries of the Near East that had relations with the maritime republic.

Alongside architects such as Buscheto, Rainaldo and Diotisalvi there were numerous sculptors to embellish the exteriors. Pisa became an important centre for Gothic sculpture in Italy, thanks to the work of **Nicola Pisano**

(1220–c 1280), originally from Puglia, and his son **Giovanni Pisano** (1250–c 1315).

Sights

Piazza del Duomo (Campo dei Miracoli)★★★

🕐Duomo: open Apr-Sep 10am-8pm (Sun 1-8pm); rest of the year phone ahead for admission times. Other monuments: 9am to late afternoon (times vary from month to month). ➭Duomo: 2€; Leaning Tower: 15€; single monument: 5€; all monuments except Leaning Tower: 10.50€. ☎050 38 72 210; www.opapisa.it.

In and around this famous square, also known as Campo dei Miracoli (Field of Miracles), are four buildings that form one of the finest architectural complexes in the world. It is advisable to approach on foot from the west through the Porta Santa Maria to enjoy the best view of the Leaning Tower.

Duomo★★

http://torre.duomo.pisa.it.

This splendid cathedral was built with the spoils captured during the expeditions against the Muslims. Building started in 1063 under Buscheto and was continued by Rainaldo, who designed the façade.

The **west front**★★★ is light and graceful with four tiers of small marble columns and a decorative facing of alternating light- and dark-coloured marble. The church itself is built on the plan of a Latin cross. The original doors were replaced by **bronze doors**★ cast in 1602 to designs by Giovanni Bologna. The south transept door has very fine Romanesque bronze **panels**★★ (late 12C) by Bonanno Pisano, depicting the Life of Christ in a free creative style.

The **interior**, with its nave and four aisles, is impressive for its length (100m/330ft), its deep apse, its three-aisled transept and the forest of piers which offer an astonishing variety of perspectives. Note in particular the beautiful **pulpit**★★★ of **Giovanni Pisano** on which he worked from 1302 to 1311. It is supported by six porphyry

columns and five pillars decorated with religious and allegorical statues.

The eight panels of the pulpit evoke the Life of Christ and group a multitude of personages with dramatic expressions. Near the pulpit is Galileo's lamp, which gave the scholar his original idea for his theory concerning the movement of the pendulum. *👁Don't miss Galileo's lamp, which hangs near the pulpit.*

Torre Pendente★★★

The **Leaning Tower of Pisa** is both a bell tower and belfry. This white marble tower (58m/189ft high) was begun in 1173 in a pure Romanesque style by Bonanno Pisano and completed in 1350. Built, like the towers of Byzantium, as a cylinder, the tower has six storeys of galleries with columns which seem to wind round in a spiral because of the slope of the building. On the lower level is the blind arcading decorated with lozenges that is specific to the architecture of Pisa. The tower slowly began leaning in 1178 and has continued to do so at a rate of between 1 and 2mm a year (or half an inch over a typical decade). The movement is caused by the alluvial soil on which the tower is built, soil that is insufficiently resistant to bear the weight of the building. Over the years, architects tried in vain to correct the unfortunate "lean." The tower was closed to the public in 1990 and a committee was formed to debate how best to find a long-term solution to the problem. In 1992 the tower was surrounded by two stainless steel cables at first-floor level and, in 1993, the base was strengthened by a reinforced concrete "corset", which included 670t of lead to counterbalance the lean; progression of the lean was effectively stopped for several years. Another restoration attempt in September 1995 ended in disaster when the tower shifted 2.5mm/1/8in in one night, double the annual rate. Engineers dumped lead on the base of the North side, and the tower was prevented from falling. No further restoration work took place until 1998, when steel-cable "braces" were attached to the tower. They were removed in 2001 when the tower had moved a further 40cm/16in towards the vertical, returning the tower to the

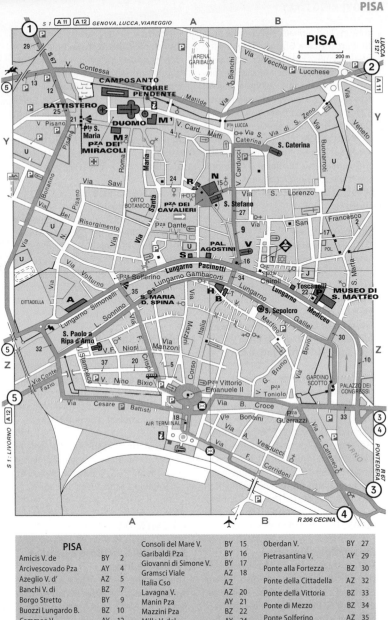

PISA

		Consoli del Mare V.	BY	15	Oberdan V.	BY	27
Amicis V. de	BY	2	Garibaldi Pza	BY	16	Pietrasantina V.	AY	29
Arcivescovado Pza	AY	4	Giovanni di Simone V.	BY	17	Ponte alla Fortezza	BZ	30
Azeglio V. d'	AZ	5	Gramsci Viale	AZ	18	Ponte della Cittadella	AZ	32
Banchi V. di	BZ	7	Italia Cso	AZ		Ponte della Vittoria	BZ	33
Borgo Stretto	BY	9	Lavagna V.	AZ	20	Ponte di Mezzo	BZ	34
Buozzi Lungardo B.	BZ	10	Manin Pza	AY	21	Ponte Solferino	AZ	35
Cammeo V.	AY	12	Mazzini Pza	BZ	22	Zerboglio V.	AZ	37
Cascine V. delle	AY	13	Mille V. del	AY	24			
			Niccolini V.	AY	25			

Arsenali Medicei	AZ	A	Palazzo Gambacorti			(Prefettura)	BZ	P
Loggia di Bianchi	BZ	B	(Municipio)	BZ	H	Palazzo della		
Museo dell'Opera			Palazzo Upezzinghi	AY	S	Gherardesca	AY	R
del Duomo	AY	M¹	Palazzo dei Cavalieri	BY	N	San Michele in Borgo	BY	V
Museo delle Sinopie	AY	M²	Palazzo dei Medici					

angle it was at in 1838. The tower was reopened to the public later that year. Kids *Children will love the curious leaning tower.*

Battistero★★★
Work on the Baptistery began in 1153 and the two lower storeys are in the Pisan-Romanesque style, while the

frontons and pinnacles above the first-floor arcades are Gothic. The majestic interior is full of light and has a diameter of 35m/115ft. The sober decoration consists of light- and dark-coloured marble; in the centre is a lovely octagonal **font**★ (1246) by an artist from Como, Guido Bigarelli. The masterpiece of the baptistery is the admirable **pulpit**★★ (1260) by Nicola Pisano. It is less ornate than the one done by his son for the cathedral and stands on simple columns. The five panels of the pulpit depict the Life of Christ.

Camposanto★★

This burial ground was begun in 1277 by Giovanni di Simone, an architect of the Leaning Tower. Work was interrupted by the naval Battle of Meloria (see above) and completed in the 15C. Inside, one of the most famous cycles comprising **The Triumph of Death**★★★ and the **Last Judgement**★★ and **Hell**★ by a 14C artist is displayed in the north gallery.

Museo dell'Opera del Duomo★★

The Cathedral Museum contains works of art from the monuments in Piazza del Duomo: 12C-16C sculptures (Romanesque period influenced by Islamic and Burgundian art, Gothic and Renaissance); cathedral treasure (ivory **Madonna and Child** by Giovanni Pisano) and silverware. The first floor has 15C-18C paintings and sculpture and 12C-13C illuminated manuscripts.

Museo delle Sinopie★

This museum contains the sketches or *sinopie* (sketches in a reddish-brown pigment, which came from Sinope on the Black Sea) that were under the frescoes and were brought to light by a fire following the bombing in 1944. They give a good idea of the free draughtsmanship of these 13C-15C painters.

Piazza dei Cavalieri★

This, the historic centre of Pisa, gets its name from the Cavalieri di Santo Stefano (Knights of St Stephen), a military order that specialised in the struggle against the infidel. Around the square are: the **Palazzo dei Cavalieri** with

a **façade**★ decorated by Vasari; the **church of Santo Stefano** built in 1569 with its white, green and pink marble façade and dedicated to St Stephen; and the **Palazzo Gherardesca** designed in 1607 by Vasari to stand on the site of a prison, Torre della Fame, where Count Ugolino della Gherardesca and his children were condemned to die by starvation, having been accused of treason after the naval defeat at Meloria.

Museo Nazionale di San Matteo★★

🕐*Open Tue-Sat, 8.30am-7pm, (Sun and public holidays 1pm).* 🕐*Closed Mon, 1 Jan, 1 May, 15 Aug and 25 Dec.* ⊙*5€.* ☎*050 54 18 65.*
The National Museum houses 13C-15C works, created in Pisa. Of note are the **Virgin Mary Nursing** by Nino Pisano and Masaccio's **St Paul**.

Chiesa di Santa Maria della Spina★★

This 14C church, dedicated to St Mary of the Thorn, resembles a reliquary shrine with its pinnacles and statues by the Pisano and their assistant. Some originals have been replaced by replicas.

♿ S. Caterina (façade★), S. Michele in Borgo (façade★), Lungarni (Palazzo Agostini★), S. Sepolcro (chancel★), S. Paolo a Ripa d'Arno (façade★).

Excursions

Basilica di San Piero a Grado★

6km/4mi southwest.
This Romanesque church stands on the spot on which St Peter is said to have landed when he came from Antioch.

Livorno

24km/14mi southwest of Pisa.www. comune.livorno.it.
Cosimo I de' Medici started rebuilding Livorno's harbour to replace the silted-up Porto Pisano, and it was finished in 1620 under Cosimo II. In the Piazza Micheli stands the **monument**★ to the last prominent Medici, the Grand Duke Ferdinand. The four bronze Moors (1624) were the work of Pietro Tacca.

PISTOIA★★

POPULATION 85 273
MICHELIN MAP 563 K 14
SEE THE GREEN GUIDE TUSCANY.

Pistoia's historic centre is evidence of its importance in the 12C-14C. Both Lucca and Florence coveted Pistoia, but it was Florence who annexed it in 1530.

- **Information:** Piazza S.Leone 1. ☎ 0573 37 43 11. www.provincia.pistoia.it.
- **Orient Yourself:** Between Florence and the coast (36km/22mi from Florence).
- **Don't Miss:** The birthplace of Leonardo Da Vinci.
- **Organizing Your Time:** Half a day for Pistoia, plus a day excursion to Vinci.
- **Also See:** *FIRENZE, MONTECATINI TERME, PRATO.*

Visit

Piazza del Duomo★★

This is a most attractive and well-proportioned square lined with elegant secular and religious buildings.

Duomo★

🕐 *Cappella di S. Jacopo: Open 8.30am-12.30pm and 3.30-7pm. ⊛2€. ☎0573 25 095 (Curia Vescovile di Pistoia); www.diocesi.pistoia.it.*

Rebuilt in the 12C and 13C, the cathedral has a **façade**★ that is a harmonious blend of the Pisan-Romanesque style (tiers of colonnaded galleries) and the Florentine-Renaissance style (porch with slender columns added in the 14C). The interior was remodelled in the 17C. Inside is the **altar of St James**★★★, a 13C masterpiece of silversmith work. The saints surround the Apostle seated in a niche, with Christ in Glory above. Scenes from the Old and New Testaments complete the composition. In the chapel is a **Madonna in Majesty**★ (c 1480) by Lorenzo di Credi.

Battistero★

🕐*Open Tue-Sat 10am-1pm and 3-6.15pm. 🕐Closed Mon. ☎0573 21 622.*

This Gothic baptistery dates from the 14C. The tympanum of the central doorway bears a statue of the Virgin and Child attributed to Nino and Tommaso Pisano.

Palazzo Pretorio

This palace was built in the 14C as the residence of the governing magistrate

(*podestà*) and remodelled in the 19C.

Palazzo del Comune – The Town Hall was built from 1294 to 1385 and has a graceful arcaded **façade**★ with elegant paired windows or triple bays. The palace houses the **Museo Civico** with its collection of paintings and sculptures from the 13C-20C Tuscan school.🕐*Open 10am-5pm. 🕐Closed Sun afternoon, Mon, 1 Jan, 1 May, 25 Dec. ⊛3.50€. ☎0573 37 12 96.*

Chiesa di Sant'Andrea★

This church dedicated to St Andrew is in the pure Pisan-Romanesque style and has a **pulpit**★★ executed (1298-1308) by Giovanni Pisano in his dramatic manner: the panels represent scenes from the Life of Christ. The **crucifix**★ in gilded wood is by Giovanni Pisano *(beyond the first altar on the right).* Palazzo del Tau, Ospedale del Ceppo (frieze★★ by Giovanne della Robbia), S. Giovanni Forcivitas (north façade★, pulpit★, *Visitazione*★★ by Luca della Robbia).

Excursions

Vinci★

24km/15mi south.

Leonardo da Vinci was born not far from this town. The **Museo Leonardiano**★ is in the castle. 🕐*Open Mar-Oct daily 9.30am-7pm (Nov-Feb 6pm). 🕐Closed 25 Dec. ⊛5€. ☎0571 56 055. The birthplace of the artist lies 2km/1.2mi to the north. 🕐Open daily 9.30am-6pm. 🕐Closed Mon. ☎0571 56 055.*

GOLFO DI **POLICASTRO**★★
GULF OF POLICASTRO

MICHELIN MAP 564 G 28 – CAMPANIA – BASILICATA – CALABRIA.

This gulf extending from Infreschi to Praia a Mare is backed by austere mountains. The lower slopes are planted with olive groves and chestnut trees.

- **Information:** Comune di Praia a Mare Infoline. ☎039 09 85. www.comune.praia-a-mare.cs.it.
- ▶ **Orient Yourself:** The access roads to the Gulf of Policastro are A 3 and S 18.
- **Don't Miss:** The panorama of the Gulf of Policastro from Maratea.
- **Also See:** *CALABRIA*.

Visit

Between **Sapri** and **Praia a Mare** the corniche road overlooks the green waters. A series of small villages lie along this enchanting coast.

Maratea⌂⌂
www.costadimaratea.com.
This seaside resort has many beaches and hotels hidden behind lush vegetation. The village is spread over Monte Biagio, with the basilica of San Biagio on the summit, and the figure of the Statue of the Redeemer (22m/72ft tall), the work of Innocenti (1965). Nearby there is a superb **panorama**★★ of the Gulf of Policastro.

Calabrian curing

Calabria differs from most other Italian regions in its traditional emphasis on preserving food. As a result, you will find a host of local sausages and cold cuts (Sopressata, 'Nduja), vegetables and meats packed in olive oil, and cured fish such as swordfish, sardines (sardelle rosamarina) and cod (Baccalà). Such preservation techniques helped the Calabrians cope with the climate and potential crop failures.

Address Book

For coin ranges see the Legend on the cover flap.

WHERE TO STAY
Hotel Germania – *Via Roma 44 – 87028 Praia a Mare – 12km/7mi southeast of Maratea on S 18 – ☎0985 72 016 – Fax 0985 72 755 – Closed Oct-Mar – ▣ ⌂ – 60 rm – ⌂. An unpretentious establishment. Shame about the furnishings and decor which are a little dated. Lovely location right on the beach and a huge sun terrace.*
Hotel Martino – *Via Citrosello 16, Località Marina di Maratea – 85046 Maratea – 7km/4mi southeast of Maratea – ☎0973 87 91 26 – www.hotelmartino. net – ▣⌂ – 33 rm – ⌂. This hotel has a lovely setting. Good-sized rooms that*

have been tastefully furnished. Try and get one with a private terrace. Indoor swimming pool and private beach.

WHERE TO EAT
Taverna Antica – *Piazza Dei Martiri 3 – 87028 Praia a Mare – 12km/7mi southeast of Maratea on S 18 – ☎0985 72 182 – Closed Tue (except Jun-Oct) – ▤ – Reservations recommended. Here you can enjoy excellent fish cuisine, the type of fish dependent on availability.*
La Tana – *Località Castrocucco – 85040 Maratea Porto – South of Maratea – ☎0973 87 17 70 – latana@ tiscalinet.it – Closed Thu (except 15 Jun-15 Sep). Imaginative cooking and dishes are attractively presented. Accommodation also available.*

POMPEI★★★
POMPEII

MICHELIN MAP 564 E 25 – CAMPANIA.

Pompeii, the opulent town that was buried in AD 79 in one of the most disastrous volcanic eruptions in history, provides important evidence of the ancient way of life. The extensive and varied ruins of the dead city, in its attractive setting, movingly evoke on a grand scale a Roman city at the time of the Empire. Pompeii was included in UNESCO's World Heritage List in 1997.

- **Information:** Via Sacra 1, 80045 Pompei (NA). ☎081 85 75 331; www.pompeiisites.org, www.arethusa.net.
- ▶ **Orient Yourself:** Pompeii is situated at the foot of Vesuvius, the volcano to which it owes its fame. The main access road is A3.
- **Don't Miss:** The Foro (the Forum), Terme Stablane (baths) and the splendid fresco at the Villa del Misteri.
- **Organizing Your Time:** The site is extensive so allow a day to see it all.
- **Also See:** *COSTIERA AMALFITANA, CAPRI, ERCOLANO, ISCHIA, NAPOLI, Golfo di NAPOLI.*

A Bit of History

Pompeii was founded in the 8C BC by the Oscans, but by the 6C BC a Greek influence was already prevalent in the city from its neighbour Cumae, then a powerful Greek colony. From the end of the 5C BC, when it came under Samnite rule, to the beginning of the 1C AD, the city knew great prosperity; town planning and art flourished. In the year 80 BC, the town fell under Roman domination and soon became a favourite resort of rich Romans. Roman families settled there. Pompeii adopted Roman organisation, language, lifestyle, building methods and decoration. When the eruption of Vesuvius struck, Pompeii was a booming town with a population of about 25 000. The town was situated in a fertile region, trade flourished and there was even some industrial activity; it also had a port. The numerous shops and workshops that have been uncovered, its wide streets and the deep ruts made in the cobblestones by chariot wheels are evidence of the intense activity that went on in the town.

The people had a lively interest in spectacles, games and active politics, as can be seen in a fresco housed at the Archaeological Museum in Naples. In AD 59, after a fight between rival supporters, the amphitheatre was closed for 10 years and re-opened after Nero's wife Poppea interceded. In the year AD 62, an earthquake extensively damaged the town but before it could be put to rights, Vesuvius erupted (August AD 79) and also destroyed Herculaneum and Stabiae. In two days Pompeii was buried under a layer of cinders 6m to 7m/20ft to 23ft deep. Bulwer-Lytton describes

A girl – who may represent Dionysus herself – reading the rites under the watchful gaze of two women priests, Villa dei Misteri.

R. Mattes/MICHELIN

TAKING A BREAK

Snack wine's Todisco –
Piazza Schettini 19 – Pompeii –
☎*081 85 05 051 – Closed Mon –* ✉.
Having satisfied your thirst
for knowledge, now is the time to
replenish your weary body with
something to eat and drink. This
simple café, near the Sanctuary,
is the perfect spot. Shaded by a
perfumed citrus grove, it is popular
with the people who work on the
site. Serves good food at extremely
reasonable prices. A cut above the
other bars and cafés here.

these events in his novel **The Last Days of Pompeii.**

It was only in the 18C, under the reign of Charles of Bourbon, that systematic excavations began.

Architecture and Decoration

Building methods – Pompeii was destroyed before a degree of uniformity in building methods had been achieved and it presents examples of the diverse methods and materials used: *opus quadratum* (large blocks of freestone piled on top of one another, without mortar of any kind); *opus incertum* (irregularly shaped blocks of *tufa* or lava bonded with mortar); *opus reticulatum* (small square blocks of limestone or tufa arranged diagonally to form a decorative pattern); *opus testaceum* (walls are faced with triangular bricks laid flat with the pointed end turned inwards). Sometimes the walls were faced with plaster or marble. There are several types of dwelling in Pompeii: the sober and austere house of the Samnites,

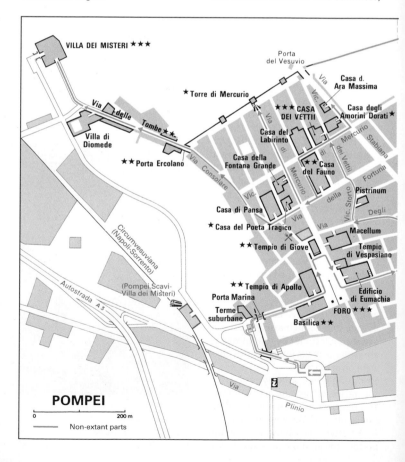

POMPEI

0 — 200 m

Non-extant parts

which became larger and more richly decorated through Greek influence. With the arrival of the Romans and the problems arising from a growing population, a new kind of house evolved in which limited space is compensated for by rich decoration.

Pompeiian Painting – A large number of paintings, which adorned the walls of the dwellings, have been transferred to the Archaeological Museum in Naples. However, a visit to the dead city gives a good idea of the pictorial decoration of the period. There are **four different styles**. The 1st style by means of relief and light touches of colour imitates marble. The 2nd style is by far the most attractive: walls are divided into large panels by false pillars surmounted by pediments or crowned by a small shrine, with false doors all designed to create an illusion of perspective.

The artists show a partiality for Pompeiian red, cinnabar obtained from mercury sulphide, and a dazzling black. The 3rd style abandoned trompe-l'œil in favour of scenes and landscapes painted in pastel colours. Most of the frescoes uncovered at Pompeii belong to the 4th style. It combines elements from the 2nd style with the 3rd style to produce ornate compositions.

Visit

Allow 1 day. Open daily, Apr-Oct 8.30am-7.30pm (last admission 6pm), Nov-Mar 8.30am-5pm (last admission 3.30pm). Access from Porta Marina (Via Villa dei Misteri or Piazza Esedra) or from Piazza Anfiteatro. Closed 1 Jan, 1 May, 25 Dec. 11€, 20€ combined ticket (valid 3 days) for Pompeii, Oplonti, Stabia and

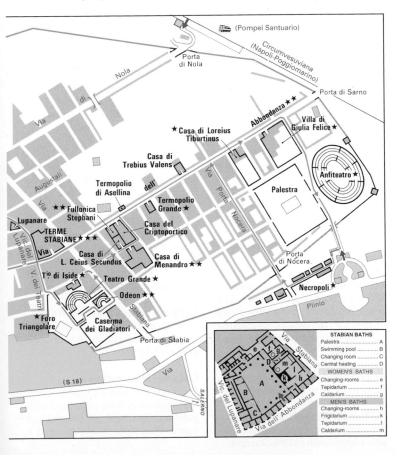

Boscoreale. Information desk at Porta Marina (9am-5pm). ☎ 081 85 75 347; www.pompeiisites.org. ⚠Some of the houses listed may occasionally be closed for cleaning and maintenance.

Porta Marina

The road passed through this gateway down to the sea, with separate gates for animals and pedestrians.

Streets

The streets are straight and intersect at right angles. They are sunk between raised pavements and are interrupted at intervals by blocks of stone to enable pedestrians to cross without getting down from the pavement when the roadway was awash with rain.

Foro★★★

The forum was the centre of the town and the setting for most of the large buildings. In this area, religious ceremonies were held, trade was carried out and justice was dispensed. The immense square, closed to traffic, was paved with large marble flagstones and adorned with statues of past emperors. A portico enclosed it on three sides.

The **Basilica**★★ is the largest building (67m by 25m/220ft by 82ft) in Pompeii and is where judicial affairs were conducted.

The **Tempio di Apollo**★★ is a temple dedicated to Apollo, built before the Roman occupation, which stood against the background of Vesuvius. The altar was placed in front of the steps leading to the shrine (*cella*). Facing each other are copies of the statues of Apollo and Diana found on the spot (the originals are in the Naples Museum).

The **Tempio di Giove**★★, in keeping with tradition, has pride of place. The temple dedicated to the Capitoline Triad (Jupiter, Juno and Minerva) is flanked by two triumphal arches, formerly faced with marble.

The **Macellum** was a large covered market lined with shops. In the centre, a kiosk crowned by a dome contained a basin used for cleaning fish.

The **Tempio di Vespasiano**, dedicated to the Emperor Vespasian, contained an altar adorned with a sacrificial scene.

A fine **doorway**★ with a marble frame decorated with carvings gives access to the **Edificio di Eumachia** (Building of Eumachia), built by the priestess Eumachia for the powerful guild of the *fullones*, of which she was the patron.

Foro Triangolare★

There are several Ionic columns of a majestic propylaeum that preceded the Triangular Forum. A few vestiges of its **Doric temple** provide evidence of the town's existence in the 6C BC.

Teatro Grande★

The Great Theatre was built in the 5C BC, remodelled in the Hellenistic period (200-150 BC) and again by the Romans in the 1C AD. It was an open-air theatre that could hold 5 000 spectators.

Caserma dei Gladiatori

The gladiators' barracks has an esplanade bounded by a gateway, originally used as a foyer for the theatres.

Odeion★★

Odeums, or covered theatres, were used for concerts, oratorical displays and ballets. This held only 800 spectators. It had a wooden roof and it dates from the early days of the Roman colonisation.

Tempio d'Iside★

The cult of the Egyptian goddess Isis spread in the Hellenistic period thanks to contact with the Orient and Egypt. The small building stands in the middle of an arcaded courtyard. To its left is the *purgatorium*, a site set aside for purification ceremonies that contained water from the Nile. The pictorial decorations of the temple are housed in the Archaeological Museum in Naples.

Casa di Lucius Ceius Secundus

This interesting house has a façade faced with stucco in imitation of stone as in the 1st style.

Casa del Menandro★★

This large patrician villa named after Menander, was richly decorated with paintings (4th style) and mosaics and had its own baths. In the atrium is a *lararium* (shrine to the household gods) arranged as a miniature temple.

The house opens onto **Via dell'Abbondanza**★★, a commercial street, evocative with its shops and houses.

Casa del Criptoportico

After passing through the peristyle (note the painting in the *lararium*: *Mercury with a Peacock, Snakes and Foliage*), go down to the Cryptoporticus, a wide underground passage surmounted by a fine barrel vault and lit by small windows. This type of corridor, popular in Roman villas during the Empire, was used as a passage and for exercise as it was sheltered from the sun and rain.

Fullonica Stephani★★

No 7. This is an example of a dwelling-house converted into workshops. The clothing industry flourished in Roman times as the full, draped costume required a lot of material. In the *fullonicae*, new fabrics were finished and clothes were laundered. Several of these workshops have been uncovered in Pompeii. The *fullones* (fullers) cleaned the cloths by trampling them with their feet in vats that were filled with water and soda or urine.

Termopolio di Asellina

This was a bar which also sold precooked dishes (*thermopolium*). A stone counter giving directly onto the street formed the shop front; jars embedded in the counter contained food for sale.

Termopolio Grande★

This bar, which is similar to the previous one, has a painted *lararium*.

Casa di Trebius Valens

The inscriptions on the wall are electoral slogans.

Casa di Loreius Tiburtinus★

This was a rich dwelling, judging from the fine marble *impluvium*, the triclinium adorned with frescoes and the **decoration**★ against a white background of one of the rooms, which is among the best examples of the 4th Pompeian style. But its most luxurious feature was the splendid **garden**★, which was laid out for water displays.

Villa di Giulia Felice★

Built just within the town boundary, it has three main parts: the dwelling, the baths, which the owner opened to the public, and a section for letting, including an inn and shops. The large garden is bounded by a fine **portico**★ and embellished by basins.

Anfiteatro★

This is the oldest Roman amphitheatre known (80 BC). It was built away from the city centre to enable easy access. On hot days spectators were protected from the heat by a linen drape held up by wooden poles. Alongside is the **palestra**, a training ground for athletes.

Necropoli Fuori Porta Nocera★

Tombs line one of the roads leading out of town, via the Nocera Gate.

▷ *Take the Via di Porta Nocera to return to the Via dell' Abbondanza, then turn left.*

Terme Stabiane★★★

These are the oldest baths in Pompeii (2C BC), and divided into sections for men and women. The entrance is through the gymnasium (*palestra*); to the left are changing-rooms (*spogliatoio*), and a swimming pool (*piscina*).

The **women's baths** begin at the far end on the right, with changing-rooms and lockers, a *tepidarium* (lukewarm bath) and a *caldarium* (hot bath). The men's baths have changing-rooms, a *frigidarium* (cold bath), a *tepidarium* and a *caldarium*. There is stucco decoration on the coffered ceiling.

Lupanare

The official brothel of Pompeii is decorated with licentious subject matter, illustrating the "specialities" of the prostitutes. Wall graffiti provides customers' opinions on services received.

Pistrinum

The baker's oven and flourmills.

Casa dei Vettii★★★

The Vettii brothers were rich merchants. Their dwelling, the most lavishly decorated in the town, is the finest example of a faithfully restored house and garden. The reroofed *atrium* opens onto the peristyle surrounding a garden with statues, basins and fountains.

The **frescoes** in the *triclinium*, on the right of the peristyle, depict mythological scenes and friezes of cupids, and are among the finest from Antiquity.

Casa degli Amorini Dorati★

This house shows the refinement of the owner, who probably lived during the reign of Nero, and his taste for the theatre. The glass and gilt medallions depicting cupids *(amorini)* have deteriorated. But the building as a whole, with its peristyle with one wing raised like a stage, is well preserved. There is an obsidian mirror set in the wall between the peristyle and *atrium*.

Casa dell'Ara Massima

There are well-preserved **paintings**★ (one in trompe l'oeil).

Casa del Labirinto

One of the rooms opening onto the peristyle has a mosaic of the Labyrinth with Theseus killing the Minotaur.

Casa del Fauno★★

This vast, luxurious house had two atriums, two peristyles and dining rooms for all seasons. The bronze original of the famous statuette of the faun that adorned one of the impluviums is in the Naples Museum. The rooms contained admirable mosaics including the famous *Battle of Alexander and Darius* (Naples Museum) which covered the area between the two peristyles.

Casa della Fontana Grande

Its main feature is the large **fountain**★ *(fontana)* shaped as a niche decorated with mosaics and fragments of coloured glass in the Egyptian style.

Torre di Mercurio★

A tower on the town wall, dedicated to the god Mercury, now affords an interesting **view**★★ of the excavations.

Casa del Poeta Tragico★

This house takes its name from a mosaic now in the Naples Museum. A mosaic of a watchdpg at the threshold bears the inscription *Cave Canem* (Beware of the dog).

Casa di Pansa

A spacious house partly converted for letting.

Porta Ercolano★★

The Herculaneum Gate was the main gateway of Pompeii, with two gates for pedestrians and one for vehicles.

Via delle Tombe★★

A great melancholy feeling pervades this street lined with monumental tombs and cypresses. There are examples of all forms of Greco-Roman funerary architecture: tombs with niches, round or square temples, altars resting on a plinth, drum-shaped mausoleums, simple semicircular seats or *exedrae*.

Villa di Diomede

This important dwelling dedicated to Diomedes has a loggia overlooking the garden and the swimming pool.

Villa dei Misteri★★★

Located outside the city centre this ancient patrician villa is comprised of a luxurious residential part (west) and the eastern half reserved for agricultural work and servants' quarters. In the area inhabited by the owners, the dining room *(from the apsed room in the west of the villa, enter the tablinium, turn right into the cubiculum and right again into a room leading to the triclimium)* contains the splendid **fresco** from which the villa derives its renown and name. This composition, which fills the whole room, depicts the initiation of a young bride to the mysteries (misteri) of the cult of Dionysus (from left: Child reading rites; offerings, sacrifices and Dionysian rites; flagellation of a girl; dancing Bacchante; dressing of the bride). The mistress of this house was probably a priestess of the Cult of Dionysus, which was then very popular in southern Italy. There is a fine peristyle and underground passage *(criptoportico)*.

PROMONTORIO DI **PORTOFINO**★★★
PORTOFINO PROMONTORY
MICHELIN MAP 561 J 9 – LIGURIA.

This rocky, rugged promontory offers one of the most attractive landscapes on the Italian Riviera. The coastline is dotted with small villages in sheltered bays. Part of the peninsula has been designated as a nature reserve (Parco Naturale) to protect the fauna and flora. By taking the corniche roads and the numerous footpaths the visitor can discover the secret charms of this region.

- **Information:** Via Roma 35, 16034 Portofino (GE). ☎0185 26 90 24; www.comune. portofino.genova.it. Ente Parco di Portofino, viale A. Rainusso 1, 16038 Santa Margherita Ligure (GE). ☎0185 28 94 79. www.parcoportofino.org.
- ▶ **Orient Yourself:** The promontory is 40km/24mi from Genoa, just off S 1.
- **Don't Miss:** Glamorous, hideaway, Portofino or the pretty village of Fruttuoso.
- **Organizing Your Time:** Allow a day for Portofino and excursions to the surrounding area.
- **Also See:** *GENOVA, RIVIERA LIGURE.*

Portofino★★★

Access by sea: From Rapallo, Santa Margherita and S. Fruttuoso from ⚓4€ (one-way) and 13.50€ (round trip). For information, contact Servizio Marittimo del Tigullio, ☎0185 28 46 70; www.traghettiportofino. it. From Camogli to S. Fruttuoso: ⚓6.50€ (one-way) and 9€ (round trip). For information, contact Trasporti Marittimi Turistici Golfo Paradiso, ☎0185 77 20 91; www. golfoparadiso.it.
To reach the port which gave the peninsula its name, take the road that passes

via **Santa Margherita Ligure**⚓⚓ *(5km/ 3mi)*, a fashionable seaside resort, and the **corniche road**★★ (Strada Panoramica), which affords lovely views of the rocky coast. This small, colourful fishing village lies at the head of a sheltered creek. The **walk to the lighthouse**★★★ *(1hr on foot there and back)* is beautiful, especially in the evening, when the setting sun shines on the Gulf of Rapallo. Wonderful views unfold between the olive trees, yews and sea pines. From the **castle** – formerly Castello San Giorgio *(take the stairway which starts near the harbour*

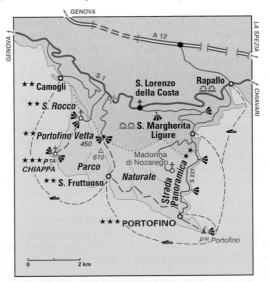

Address Book

For coin ranges see the Legend on the cover flap.

WHERE TO STAY

Albergo La Camogliese – *Via Garibaldi 55 – 16032 Camogli – ☎0185 77 14 02 – www.lacamogliese.it – Closed 15-30 Nov and 10-25 Jan – 21 rm*. The entrance to the hotel is shared with the building's other tenants but it has its own elegant hallway with a breakfast area and some of the rooms leading off it. The other rooms have a sea view and in the background you can hear the waves. Good value for the money.

Bed & Breakfast Villa Gnocchi – *Via Romana 53 – 16030 S. Lorenzo della Costa – 3km/1mi west of Santa Margherita Ligure – ☎0185 28 34 31 –Closed 18 Oct-Easter – – 9 rm*. Wonderful setting overlooking Santa Margherita and the Gulf of Tigullio, with magnificent views from the lovely terrace-garden. The well-kept rooms are light and tastefully decorated, and furnished with solid wooden furniture. Half-board rates available.

WHERE TO EAT

Oca Bianca – *Via XXV Aprile 21 – 16038 Santa Margherita Ligure – ☎0185 28 84 11 – Closed Mon and lunchtimes (except Sat and Sun), Jul and Aug, open evenings only; 7 Jan-13 Feb – – Reservations recommended*. Very pleasant establishment with a menu that focuses on meat, vegetables and cheese. Dishes have been imaginatively put together. Very reasonable prices.

---

and the church of San Giorgio) – there are splendid **views**★★★ of Portofino and the Gulf of Rapallo. Continue along the pathway to the lighthouse, from where the view extends right round the coast as far as La Spezia. *Open Mar-Oct 10am-7pm; Nov-Feb 10am-5pm. 3.50€. ☎0185 26 90 46.*

Excursion

San Fruttuoso★★

On foot: take the signposted footpath starting in Portofino (5hr there and back) or another from Portofino Vetta, but the final stages are difficult (3hr there and back). By boat: services operate from Rapallo, Santa Margherita Ligure, Portofino and Camogli. This small village stands at the head of a narrow cove in the shadow of Monte Portofino. There is a beautiful abbey, **Abbazia di San Fruttuoso**, built from the 13C to 14C.

From Portofino to Camogli★★

20km/12.5mi. *Allow half a day at least.*

Chiesa di San Lorenzo della Costa

10km/6mi north.
At Santa Margherita Ligure take the scenic **road**★★ for lovely views over the Gulf of Rapallo. The church of San Lorenzo contains a **triptych**★ (1499) by an artist from Bruges.

Portofino Vetta★★

14km/9mi.
From this elevated site (450m/1 476ft) there is a lovely view of the peninsula and the Ligurian coast.

Belvedere di San Rocco★★

13km/8mi northwest.
From the terrace beside the church there is a view of Camogli and the western coast, Punta della Chiappa, right round to Genoa. A path leads to **Punta della Chiappa**★★★ (2hr30min there and back by a stepped footpath to the right of the church). There are unforgettable views of the peninsula and the Genoa Coast.

Camogli★★

15km/9mi northwest.
Tall houses crowd round a small harbour.

PRATO★★

POPULATION 180 674
MICHELIN MAP 563 K 15
SEE ALSO THE GREEN GUIDE TUSCANY.

For a long time Prato was in conflict with Florence, but in 1351 the town fell under the sway of its illustrious neighbour until the 18C. In the 14C a fortified wall in the form of a hexagon was erected around the old town.

- **Information:** Via Luigi Muzzi 38, 59100 Prato. ☎ 0574 35 141; www.prato.turismo.toscana.it.
- ▶ **Orient Yourself:** Prato is only 17km/10mi from Florence. The main access roads are A 1 (Bologna-Florence), and the road that links Florence with the coast.
- **Don't Miss:** Frescoes by Fra Filippo Lippi in the Duomo.
- ○ **Organizing Your Time:** Allow half a day.
- **Also See:** *FIRENZE, PISTOIA.*

Worth a Visit

Duomo★

The cathedral, built in the 12C and 13C and extended in later centuries, blends of Romanesque and Gothic styles. The façade owes its elegance to its lofty central part and the graceful pulpit (15C) by Michelozzo and Donatello.

The sober interior of the church has columns of green marble and works of art: the **Capella del Sacro Cingolo** (Chapel of the Holy Girdle) is enclosed by delicately worked bronze **screens★** decorated with frescoes (1392-95) by Agnolo Gaddi. The **Virgin and Child★** (1317) is by sculptor Giovanni Pisano.

In the axial chapel are **frescoes★★** by **Filippo Lippi**. Note the **Banquet of Herod★★★** and *Salome's Dance*. Note also the marble **pulpit★** with the shape of a chalice, and in a niche the moving **Virgin of the olive tree★**, a terracotta statue (1480) by Benedetto da Maiano.

Palazzo Pretorio★

This austere and massive building, a curious mixture of the Romanesque and Gothic styles, overlooks a charming square, **Piazza del Comune**, with a bronze fountain (1659) by Tacca. Three floors of the building are occupied by the **Galleria Comunale**, which presents works by the 14C and 15C Tuscan school, notably an important collection of **polyptychs★**.

Castello dell'Imperatore, S. Maria delle Carceri, S. Francesco (frescoes★), Museo dell'Opera del Duomo (panels★ carved by Donatello).

PUGLIA

MICHELIN MAP 988 D-H 29-37.

With the exception of the Gargano Promontory and the limestone Murge Hills which rise behind Bari, Puglia is a flat plain planted with cereals, olive trees and vines. Away from the main tourist haunts, Puglia offers the visitor beautiful yet austere scenery, quiet beaches and religious and military architectural gems.

- **Information:** Via XXIV Maggio 26, 73100, ☎0832 23 00 33; pugliaturismo.com.
- ▶ **Orient Yourself:** This region takes its name from the ancient Roman province of Apulia. It extends from the spur of the Italian "boot" right down to the heel, along the Adriatic coast in the south of the country. The main access roads are A 14 from the north and A 16 from Naples.

- ▣ **Parking:** There is a car park at Castel del Monte.
- ◉ **Don't Miss:** The Castel del Monte, Ostuni and unusual Trulli residences in Alberobello.
- ◷ **Organizing Your Time:** Allow at least 1-2 days to see the region.
- ▦ **Especially for Kids:** The stalactites and stalagmites at the Grotte di Castellana.
- ◔ **Also See:** *BRINDISI, Promontorio del GARGANO, LECCE, TARANTO, Isole TREMITI.*

A Bit of History

In the late 8C BC, Greeks from Laconia and Sparta founded the towns of Gallipoli, Otranto and Taranto on the Apulian coast. In the 5C and 4C BC Taranto was the most prosperous town in Magna Graecia. The local tribe, the Lapyges, resisted Greek colonisation, but in 3C BC the Greek cities and Italiots came under Roman rule.

Taranto declined as Brindisi, a trading post facing the eastern part of the Mediterranean, flourished. The latter was linked to Rome when Trajan prolonged the Appian Way. Christianity was first introduced to the area in the 3C and strengthened in the 5C with the appearances of the Archangel Michael at Monte Sant'Angelo.

The area was occupied successively by the Byzantines, Lombards and Arabs before Puglia sought help in the 11C from the Normans who then dominated the entire area. Puglia greatly increased its trade and its architectural heritage thanks to the early Crusades, most of which embarked from the Apulian ports, and to the reign of Roger II of Sicily (1095-1154).

It was under the Emperor Frederick II of Hohenstaufen, a cultured and highly intelligent ruler, that the region had a golden period in the first-half of the 13C. His son Manfred continued his work but had to submit to Charles of Anjou in 1266. The French lost interest in the region and it began to lose its prestige. Puglia then passed to the Aragon dynasty who, by isolating the region, contributed to its decline.

After a period of Austrian domination, the Bourbons of Naples improved to some small extent the stagnation. The brief Napoleonic period followed a similar policy. In 1860 Puglia was united with the rest of unified Italy. During the 20C Puglia has achieved a certain vigour and now claims two thriving industrial towns, Taranto and Lecce, a Trade Fair in Bari and several universities.

Driving tours
Sights given in alphabetical order.

Altamura

This large market town in the Murge Hills has an old hilltop quarter. The 13C **Duomo** forms the focal point of the main street. The façade is pierced by a delicate 13C **rose window**★ and a sculptured 14C-15C **doorway**★.

Off the coast of Puglia

G. Bludzin/MICHELIN

Address Book

For coin ranges see the Legend on the cover flap.

WHERE TO STAY

Agriturismo Curatori – *Via Conchia 227, Contrada Cristo delle Zolle – 70043 Monopoli – 15km/9mi northeast of Castellana Grotte on S 377 – ☎080 77 74 72 – www.agriturismocuratori.it – 2 rm – .* An 18C farm, surrounded by old olive trees. Accommodation extends to studios with kitchens and simple rooms lovely wrought-iron beds). Cosy, family atmosphere. Meals are on request, prepared with produce made on the farm.

Hotel Rosa Antico – *Strada statale 16 – 73028 Otranto – ☎0836 80 15 63 – www.hotelrosaantico.it – P – 12 rm - .* More like staying at a friend's house than going to a hotel, such is the warmth of the welcome you are likely to receive. The rooms are simple but attractive, with great attention paid to detail. Delicious breakfasts, served in generous portions.

Hotel Lo Scoglio – *On a small islet which you can get to by car – 73010 Porto Cesareo – 30km/18mi north of Gallipoli – ☎0833 56 90 79 – www.isolaloscoglio.it – P – 47 rm - 7 €.* Situated on two islets linked to the coast by a wharf. The hotel is tucked away among luscious vegetation in a garden almost entirely surrounded by the sea.

Hotel Novecento – *Contrada Ramunno – 72017 Ostuni – 1.5km/1mi south of Ostuni – ☎0831 30 56 66 – www.hotelnovecento.com – P – 16 rm.* A real oasis of peace and quiet. Although it has been modernised, this splendid villa has retained its former charms and ambience. Half- and full-board rates available.

Hotel Orsa Maggiore – *Coastal road towards Santa Cesarea Terme 303 – 73030 Castro Marina – 18km/11mi south of Otranto on S 173 – ☎0836 94 70 28 – www.orsamaggiore.it – P – 30 rm.* This hotel is situated near the famous Grotta di Zinzulusa, overlooking the sea from its clifftop position. Wonderful views which lift the spirit. Very reasonably priced meals: the cooking is at its best in the fish dishes. Simple rooms, with panoramic views.

Grand Hotel D'Aragona – *Strada provinciale, towards Cozze – 70014 Conversano – 10km/6mi northwest of Castellana Grotte on S 634 – ☎080 49 52 344 – www.grandhotel daragona.it – P – 68 rm.* A little off the beaten track but you are unlikely to be disappointed. There are bathing facilities to suit everybody: experienced swimmers, beginners and children are all catered for. Rooms are spacious with modern furnishings. Large, well-tended garden, ideal for relaxing.

WHERE TO EAT

Trattoria Iolanda – *Via Montanara 2 – 73014 Lucugnano – 12km/7mi north of Santa Maria di Leuca on S 275, then turn left – ☎0833 78 41 64 – Closed Wed (except 16 Jun-Sep) – – Reservations recommended.* You have been warned: there's no sign-board, the striped awning is made out of plastic, the bread is served in baskets made of the same material and you have no say in what you choose to eat. It's a sort of initiation ritual but worth the effort required. There are very few establishments like this left.

Trattoria delle Ruote – *Via Monticello 1 – 74015 Martina Franca – 4.5km/3mi east of Martina Franca – ☎080 48 37 473 – Closed Mon – – Reservations recommended.* This trattoria is housed in a 19C *trullo* which has been modernised. The proprietor and his family are most welcoming and offer good, home-cooked food which is steeped in tradition. Agricultural implements and wheels hang on the walls.

U.P.E.P.I.D.D.E. – *Corso Cavour, ang. Trapp. Carmine – 70037 Ruvo di Puglia – ☎080 36 13 879 – www.pepidde.it – Closed Mon, 10 Jul-10 Aug.* The cuisine is traditional but has a very distinctive personal touch. Flame-grilled dishes are the house speciality. With their uneven ceilings and stone walls, the dining rooms have a cosy feel to them and are very atmospheric. Good selection of regional and other Italian wines.

⊜**Osteria del Tempo Perso** – *Via Tanzarella Vitale 47 – 72017 Ostuni – ☎0776 638 039 – www.osteriadeltempoperso.com – Closed Mon, lunchtime (except Sun and public holidays), 10-31 Jan – Reservations recommended*. Have you ever eaten in a cave? Well, this is as good a time as any. The authentic, traditional food complements the rustic setting beautifully. There is also a second dining room which, while less "cavelike," has a certain rusticity. Farm workers' tools (and religious items!) decorate the walls.

⊜**Baccosteria** – *Via San Giorgio 5 – 70051 Barletta – ☎0883 53 40 00 – Closed Mon, Sun evenings, 1-20 Aug – ▦ – Reservations recommended*. Fortunately for us, nostalgia got the better of this dynamic American couple and they returned to their homeland to set up a rather smart bistro. Specialities include spaghetti with sea urchins (ricci di mare) and squid (calamari) stuffed with ricotta cheese. The glass floor that allows diners to see into the wine cellar below is a nice touch.

⊜⊜**Da Mimì** – *Via del Mare – 73053 Patù – 5km/3mi north of Santa Maria di Leuca – ☎0833 76 78 61 – Closed Nov - Reservations recommended*. Panoramic clifftop setting, with lovely shady terrace overlooking the sea. Fish dishes are served here, prepared with fresh, good quality ingredients. Very reasonable prices.

SHOPPING

The little terracotta whistles *(figuli)* with their colourful designs make lovely gifts. They are produced in Rutigliano, near Bari.

Bari Ⓖ*see BARI.*

Barletta ⌂

In the 12C and 13C Barletta was an embarkation port for the Crusades and many military or hospitaller Orders chose this as the site for an institution. Now a commercial and agricultural centre, the town has a fine historic nucleus comprising medieval religious and secular buildings. The symbol of the town is the **Colosso**★★ or Statua di Eraclio, a gigantic statue over 4.5m/15ft tall of a Byzantine emperor whose identity is uncertain. Probably 4C, this work marks the transition from decadent Roman to early Christian art. The figure's stiffness is offset by its intense expression.

The statue stands in front of the basilica of **San Sepolcro**, which dates from the 12C-14C and possesses a fine **reliquary**★, with Limoges enamels on the base.

The **Castello**★, an imposing fortress built by the Emperor Frederick II of Hohenstaufen, houses a **pinacoteca** exhibiting a **collection**★ of paintings by the local artist, Giuseppe de Nittis (1846-84).

In Via Cialdini, the ground floor of the 14C Palazzo di Don Diego de Mendoza is where the Barletta challenge, **la Disfida di Barletta**, was issued.

The Barletta Challenge

In 1503 the town, which was held by the Spanish, was besieged by French troops. The Italians, accused of cowardice by a French prisoner, issued a challenge, following which 13 Italian knights led by **Ettore Fieramosca** met and defeated 13 French knights in single combat.

In the 19C this deed was deemed a fine example of patriotism and Ettore Fieramosca became a heroic figure. In 1833 the author Massimo d'Azeglio based a novel on this event, Ettore Fieramosca or the Tournament of Barletta (Ettore Fieramosca o la disfida di Barletta).

Further along is the 17C Palazzo della Marra; its façade is richly decorated in the Baroque style.

Bitonto

17km/11mi southwest of Bari. www.comune.bitonto.ba.it.

Set amid olive groves, this small town has a fine **Duomo**★ that strongly resembles those in Trani and Bari. The fine pulpit dates from 1229.

Frederick's Castles

A cultivated and eclectic man, **Frederick II of Hohenstaufen** (1194-1250) had numerous castles and fortresses built in Puglia, and was closely involved in their construction. Their basic plan is the square, deriving from the Roman castrum as well as symbolising the number four, which was considered a magical number in the Middle Ages. The square and the circle were considered symbols of the earth and the sky, Man and God. This magical and practical synthesis reached a peak in the octagonal plan of Castel del Monte. The octagon was considered a perfect balance between the circle and the square, the form that blended and united the human and the divine. Eight is the number which comes up almost obsessively in this building: the castle is eight-sided, there are eight towers and each floor has eight rooms.

Among Frederick's memorable castles in Puglia are those in Bari, Barleta, Brindisi, Castel del Monte, Gioia del Colle, Lagopesole, Manfredonia (erected by Frederick's son Manfred) and Trani.

Brindisi 👁 see BRINDISI

Canosa di Puglia

23km/14mi southwest of Barletta. www. canosadipuglia.org.

The inhabitants of this Greek, then Roman, city were known for their ceramic vases (*askoi*). The 11C Romanesque **Duomo,** which shows Byzantine influence, was remodelled in the 17C following an earthquake. The façade is 19C. Inside note the 11C episcopal throne and the **tomb**★ of Bohemond, Prince of Antioch (d 1111), the son of Robert Guiscard (1015-85), a Norman adventurer who campaigned in southern Italy. In the Via Cadorna there are three 4C BC hypogea, the **Ipogei Lagrasta**, and to the right of the Andria road, the remains of the palaeo-Christian basilica of **San Leucio**, built on the site of a Roman temple. 🕐Ipogei: *Hypogea open daily Mar-Oct 9am-1pm and 4-6pm (5-7pm in summer); Nov-Feb and Sun, 8am-2pm.*🕐*Closed Mon.*☎*0883 61 11 76; www.canusium.it.*

Canne della Battaglia

▶*12km/8mi southwest of Barletta.*

The strategic importance of the site in late Antiquity is evidenced by a battle in AD 216 when the Carthaginians led by Hannibal won a victory over the Roman army under Scipio. There are ruins of a medieval necropolis and of an Apulian village; and on the opposite slope, a stronghold where the main Roman axis, the *decumanus*, intersected by

streets (*cardi*) is still visible, as well as the remains of a medieval basilica and of a Norman castle.

Castel del Monte★★

▶*29km/18mi south of Barletta.* 🚹🕐*Open daily Mar-Sept 10.15am-7.45pm, rest of the year 9am-6.30pm.*🕐*Closed 1 Jan, 1 May, 15 Aug, 25 Dec.*🎫*3€.*☎*080 56 99 97.* The last section of the road is closed to vehicles. 🅿Car park 3€.

The Emperor Frederick II of Hohenstaufen built this castle c 1240 on the summit of one of the Murge Hills. With its octagonal plan the Castel del Monte is the exception in 200 quadrilateral fortresses built by this sovereign on his return from the Crusades.

Grotte di Castellana★★★

40km/25mi southeast of Bari, at Castellana-Grotte. 🚶*Guided tours only.* 🕐*Open daily 8.30am-7pm. 13€.*☎*0532 54 40 724;www.grottedicastellana.it.*

These vast chambers have magnificent concretions: curtain and richly coloured stalactites and stalagmites. They climax at the White Cave, **Grotta Bianca**★★★, which glistens with calcite crystals. 🚑*Tour not recommended for visitors with heart conditions.* 🧒*The caves are enchanting for older children.*

Foggi

Town plan in the Michelin Atlas Italy. www.comune.foggia.it.

Foggia is set in the heart of a vast cereal-growing plain, the Tavoliere.

Its present **Duomo** incorporates parts of an earlier building (13C), notably the lower walls with some blind arcading. This earlier structure, destroyed by the 1731 earthquake, has been rebuilt.

Galatina

www.comune.galatina.le.it.

This craft and wine-making centre stands on the Salento Peninsula. The 14C church of **Santa Caterina di Alessandria**★, commissioned by Raimondello del Balzo Orsini, is decorated with a marvellous cycle of **frescoes**★ by 15C artists. Many of the women depicted in the frescoes bear the features of Maria d'Enghien, Raimondello's wife.

Galatone

24km/15mi southwest of Lecce.

The **Church of the Crocifisso della Pietà** has a **façade**★ in the Baroque style typical of the Lecce area.

Gallipoli ⌂

The old town with its small port is set on an island and linked to the modern town by a bridge. Note the imposing 16C **castle** and the **cathedral** with a Baroque façade (the interior contains many paintings of the 17C and 18C). Along the Riviera, which follows the outline of the old city wall, stands the **Church della Purità**; the **interior**★ has a remarkable ceramic floor.

Promontorio del Gargano★★★

see PROMONTORIO DEL GARGANO

Gioia del Colle

In the centre of the town stands the massive **Norman castle** built on the site of a Byzantine fortress. The ground floor rooms house the Archaeological Museum (note the fine 4C BC Apulian red-figure bowl depicting a burial temple at the centre), as well as the old bakery and prison. On the upper storey is the **throne room**. ⌂ ⊙*Open daily 8.30am-7.15pm.* ⊙*Closed 1 Jan, 1 May, 25 Dec.* ⊚*2.50€.* ☏*080 34 81 305.*

Lecce★★ *see LECCE.*

Lucera

Already important in Roman times, Lucera was ceded by the Emperor Frederick II of Hohenstaufen to the Saracens of Sicily, who in turn were expelled by Charles II of Anjou. Lucera has an imposing 13C **fortress**★ built by the Angevins, which affords a fine **panorama**★ of the Tavoliere Plain. The historic centre is dominated by the 14C **Duomo** which overlooks a fine square, the focal point of the town. Nearby a fine palace, unfortunately in poor condition, houses the **Museo Civico G. Fiorelli** which displays a marble **Venus**★, a Roman replica of a model by the school of Praxiteles. ⚷*Closed for restoration at the time of going to press.* ☏*0881 54 70 41.*

A short distance from the centre stands a well-preserved Roman **amphitheatre**★ built during Augustus' reign.

Manfredonia ⌂

Manfred, the son of the Emperor Frederick II of Hohenstaufen, founded the port in the 13C. It is guarded by a fine 13C **castle**. The **Church of Santa Maria di Siponto**★ *(3km/2mi south by S 89)* is an 11C building in the Romanesque style which shows Oriental (square plan and terraced roof hiding the dome), and Pisan (blind arcades with columns enclosing lozenges) influences.

The late-11C church of **San Leonardo** *(beyond the church of Santa Maria, take the Foggia road to the right)* has a fine delicately sculptured 13C **doorway**★.

Ostuni★

35km/22mi west of Brindisi. This large market town spreads over several hillsides. At the centre of the old town with its white alleyways and Aragonese ramparts stands the late-15C **Cattedrale**. The **façade**★ is crowned by an unusual pattern of concave (central section) and convex (side sections) lines. In the centre there is a beautiful **rose window**★ with complex symbolism relating to the passage of time: 24 external arcades, standing for the hours in a day, 12 internal ones standing for the months of the year, while Christ, in the centre, is surrounded by seven angels' heads which stand for the days of the week. Nearby the church of San Vito houses

Santa Maria di Leuca

an **archaeological museum**, which displays the plaster cast of **Delia**, a young pregnant woman who lived about 25 000 years ago (her skeleton shows the foetus' tiny bones). ♿⏰*Open 10am-1pm and 5-8pm.* ⏰*Closed Mon (winter).* ✆*1.50€.* ☎*0831 33 63 83.*

Otranto

Otranto lies on the Adriatic coast of the "heel" of the peninsula. This fishing port was once capital of "Terra d'Otranto," the last remaining Byzantine stronghold, and resisted the Lombards and then the Normans for some considerable time. In the 15C when the town was besieged by the troops of the Turkish ruler Mohammed II the townspeople took refuge in the cathedral where they were massacred. Survivors were taken prisoner and killed on the summit of a hill, Colle della Minerva, where a sanctuary was built to the memory of the martyrs. Greek influence has been so strong in the "Terra d'Otranto" that even today inhabitants speak a dialect, similar to Greek.

Città Vecchia

There is a good view of the old town from the northeast pier; to the left is the 15C **Castello Aragonese**. To reach this stronghold pass through the Porta di Terra and the 15C Porta Alfonsina.

Cattedrale★

This 12C cathedral was altered in the late 15C. The interior is remarkable for its astonishing mosaic **floor**, executed between 1163 and 1165 by Pantaleone, a priest. The central nave portrays the Tree of Life, held up by two Indian ele-

phants. The tree's outstretched branches embrace biblical scenes, creatures from a medieval bestiary, heroes of courtly poems, mythological images and the cycle of months and astrological signs. At the end of the aisles there are two other trees and representations of Paradise and Hell. The vast **crypt** is sustained by ancient capitals.

Chiesetta di San Pietro

This 9C church has frescoes of the same period; sadly in poor condition.

The Coast to the South★

Between Otranto and **Santa Maria di Leuca** *(51km/32mi)* the road offers fine views of this wild coastline. At the head of an inlet is a cave, **Grotta Zinzulusa**, with salt water and freshwater lakes, inhabited by rare marine species. ⏰*Guided tours only (20min), no tours when sea is rough. www.grottazinzulusa.it.*

Ruvo di Puglia

34km/21mi west of Bari.

On the edge of the Murge Hills, Ruvo has an Apulian-style Romanesque **cathedral★**. The **Museo Archeologico Jatta** has a fine collection of Attic, Italic and Apulian **vases★**. Of these the **Crater of Talos★★**, a red-figured vase with a black background, is particularly notable. (♿⏰*Open Mon-Thu, 8.30am-1.30pm, Fri-Sun 8.30-7.30pm.* ⏰*Closed 1 Jan, 1 May, 25 Dec.* ☎*080 36 12 848; www.palazzojatta.org.*)

▶ Take Via De Gaspari, with its 16C clock tower, the Torre dell'Orologio

– to reach Piazza Matteotti, flanked by palaces and medieval ruins.

San Giovanni Rotondo
43km/27mi northeast of Foggia on S 89 and S 272.
This is a site of pilgrimage dear to devotees of **Padre Pio** (1887-1968). The Capuchin monk from **Pietrelcina**, near Benevento, was ordained and lived here. In 1918 Stigmata appeared on his body, disappearing on his death. He was canonised in 2002.

Trani
This wine-growing town has an ancient port and a 11C-13C Romanesque **cathedral**★★dedicated to St Nicholas the Pilgrim, a Greek shepherd who arrived in Trani on the back of a dolphin. It has a fine 12C **bronze door**★ and a nave and aisles built over two immense crypts.
From the **public gardens**★, east of the port, there is a view of the old town.

Troia
17km/11mi southwest of Foggia.
This market town overlooks the Tavoliere plain. The Romanesque **cathedral**is embellished with a lovely **rose window**★ and 12C **bronze door**★.

Taranto★ *see TARANTO.*

Isole Tremiti★
see IsoleTREMITI.

Terra dei Trulli★★★
This region between Fassano, Ostuni, Martina Franca and Alberobello takes

The conical roofs of the trulli: Alberobello

its name from the curious buildings, the *trulli*, found almost everywhere. These square structures have conical roofs covered with *chiancarelle*, local grey limestone roof slabs. Originally built without using mortar, the walls and the edges of the roof are whitewashed. They are crowned by differently-shaped pinnacles, each with a magical significance. Each dome corresponds to a room and each abode usually comprises three or four *trulli*.

Alberobello★★★
Visit the 12-coned Trullo Sovrano.
This town has an entire district of *trulli* (about 1 400), spread over the hillside to the south of the town (Zona Monumentale, Rioni Monti and Aia Piccola). The hilltop church of **Sant'Antonio**, is also a *trullo (Via Monte Sant'Angelo).*
It is possible to visit some of these strange dwellings. A good example is at the **Museo del Territorio** (in the new quarter, Piazza XXVII Maggio), a large 18C *trullo*, now used for exhibitions. The **Trullo Sovrano**★, the largest in Alberobello, stands near the principal church on Piazza Sacramento. Built in the mid-18C it has 12 cones. *Open daily May-Sept 10am-6pm, 1.50€. Closed: 25 Dec. 080 43 26 030; www.alberobellonline.it.*

Locorotondo
www.comune.locorotondo.ba.it.
This town takes its name from its alleyways, which wind in concentric circles (*loco rotondo*: round place) around the hill. In the **historic centre**★ is the neo-Classical church of San Giorgio.
The road from Locorotondo to Martina Franca follows the **Valle d'Itria**★★, a vast and fertile plain dotted with *trulli*.

Martina Franca★
www.comune.martina-franca.ta.it.
This white city in the Murge Hills has an old town, girdled by ramparts. **Piazza Roma** is bordered by the 17C Palazzo Ducale. Head toward Corso Vittorio Emanuele and Piazza del Plebiscito. The adjacent Piazza Maria Immacolata, leads into **Via Cavour**★, lined by Baroque palaces.

RAVENNA★★★

POPULATION 147 000

MICHELIN MAP 562, 563 I 18.

In the peaceful provincial-looking town of Ravenna, the sober exteriors of its buildings belie the wealth of riches accumulated initially when Ravenna was the capital of the Western Empire and later when it was an Exarchate of Byzantium. The mosaics that adorn the city's ecclesiastical buildings are breathtakingly beautiful in the brightness of their colours and powerful symbolism.

- **Information:** Via Salara 8, ☎0544 35 404; www.turismo.ravenna.it.
- **Orient Yourself:** Ravenna lies south of the Po Delta which is crossed by S 309. Other access roads include A 14: exit just after the junction for Imola.
- **Don't Miss:** The mosaics in St Andrew's Chapel, the Mausoleo di Galla Placida, Basilica di Sant'Apollinare in Classe and Basilica di Sant'Apollinare Nuovo.
- **Organizing Your Time:** Allow at least one day to see all of Ravenna's riches.
- **Also See:** *DELTA DEL PO, FAENZA, RIMINI.*

A Bit of History

After the division of the Empire in AD 395 by Theodosius, Rome, already in decline, was abandoned in AD 404 by the Emperor Honorius who made Ravenna the capital of the Roman Empire. Honorius' sister, **Galla Placidia**, governed the Western Empire before the barbarian invasions brought the Ostrogoth kings Odoacer (476-93) and **Theodoric** (493-526) to Ravenna; they embellished Ravenna in their turn. The strategic location of Ravenna's port, Classis, on the Adriatic sea, inevitably led to trading with Byzantium, which had become the Imperial capital in 476. Ravenna came under Byzantine rule in 540 in the reign of the **Emperor Justinian** (482-565). From then on it exercised considerable influence over much of the Italian peninsula.

The Mosaics

The oldest mosaics are in the Neonian Baptistery and the Tomb of Galla Pla-

---

Address Book

<table>
<tr><td colspan="2">

For coin ranges see the Legend on the cover flap.

WHERE TO STAY

☞**Residenza Galletti Abbiosi** – *Via di Roma 140 – ☎0544 31 313 – www.galletti.ra.it – – 70 beds .* This 19C palazzo has been restored to its former glory. One of the best features is the wonderful staircase up to the rooms which tend to be rather plain and functional (although some have a frescoed ceiling!).

☞**Hotel Ravenna** – *Via Maroncelli 12 – Ravenna – ☎0544 21 22 04 – Fax 0544 21 20 77 – – 26 rm.* This well-

</td><td>

maintained, home-from-home hotel would appeal to those not wanting to spend a fortune but looking for value for money. Simple, uncluttered rooms.

WHERE TO EAT

☞**Ca' de' Vén** – *Via C. Ricci 24 – ☎0544 30 163 – Closed Mon – – Book.* Once the smartest grocer's shop in Ravenna – with origins dating back to 1876 – now a trattoria-wine bar where diners are seated at long wooden tables. Renowned for its wonderful *piadine* (flatbread toasted sandwiches), a regional speciality.

</td></tr>
</table>

C. Guégan/MICHELIN

The mosaics in St Andrew's Chapel: the Museo Arcivescovile

Combined ticket for entrance to all dioc-esan monuments in Ravenna. ☎ 0544 54 16 88.
Battistero degli Ariani: ♿ ⓒOpen daily, 8.30am-7.30pm. ☎0544 34 424.
Museo Nazionale: ♿ⓒOpen daily except Mon, 8.30am-7pm. ⓒClosed 1 Jan, 1 May, 25 Dec. 4€; 5€ Combined ticket including entrance to Mausoleo di Teodorico. ☎0544 68 28 75.
S. Apollinare in Classe: ⓒOpen daily, 8.30am-7pm ⌾2€; 6.50€ Combined ticket including entrance to Museo Nazi onale and Mausoleo di Teodorico. ☎0544 47 35 69.

cidia (5C). Next in chronological order are those adorning the Baptistery of the Arians, St Apollinaris the New, St Vitalis, and finally St Apollinaris in Classe (6C). The mosaic heritage of the city combines the two great schools of the Ancient world: The Hellenic-Roman School, characterised by a realistic ren-dition of figure and landscape, and the Byzantine School whose rarefied and stylised figures seem to be fixed on their gold background. In 1996 UNESCO reco-gnized these early Christian monuments on the World Heritage List.

Visit

Below are the opening times for the build-ings with mosaics. Basilica di S. Vitale, Mausoleo di Galla Placidia; ⓒOpen daily Apr-Sep 9am-7pm, rest of the year 10am-5pm. Battistero Neoniano, Museo Arcivescovile and Basilica di S. Apollinare Nuovo; ⓒOpen daily Apr-Sep 9am-7pm, (Mar & Oct 5.30pm), rest of the year 9am-5.30pm. ⓒAll closed 1 Jan, 25 Dec. ⌾7.50€

What is Arianism?

The spread of Arianism began in the 4C following the preaching of the Alexandrian priest Arius (280-336). The Arian heresy maintained that Christ was not fully divine. Condem-ned by the Council of Nicaea in 325, Arianism flourished in the East in the 4C and among Goths, Vandals and Lombards until the 6C.

Sights

Basilica di San Vitale★★★

Access to the basilica affords a view of the fine recomposed **fresco** by Pietro da Rimini (c 1320), originally in the Church of Santa Chiara. Consecrated in 547 by Archbishop Maximian, the basilica is an architectural masterpiece; the splendour, originality and light effects are typical features of the later period of Ancient art. The church, dedicated to St Vitalis, has an octagonal plan, two sto-reys of concave exedrae encircled by an ambulatory and a deep apse. The richly decorated interior is dazzling: precious marbles, splendidly carved Byzantine capitals, frescoes and especially the **mosaics** of the apse with their brilliant colours. The chancel is adorned with sacrificial scenes from the Old Testa-ment; on the side walls of the apse are wonderful groups representing the **Empress Theodora** with her retinue and the **Emperor Justinian** attended by his court. These works display the splendour, hieratic power and strong outlines, which are typical of Byzantine art. On the ceiling **Christ in Majesty** is between St Vitalis and Bishop Ecclesio (on the right), the church's founder.

Mausoleo di Galla Placidia★★★

This mid-5C mausoleum is embellished by mosaics. On the tympanum and pen-dentives the symbolic scenes are full of serenity. Note the Good Shepherd, on the west wall. The sarcophagi in the mausoleum were made to house Galla Placidia and her family.

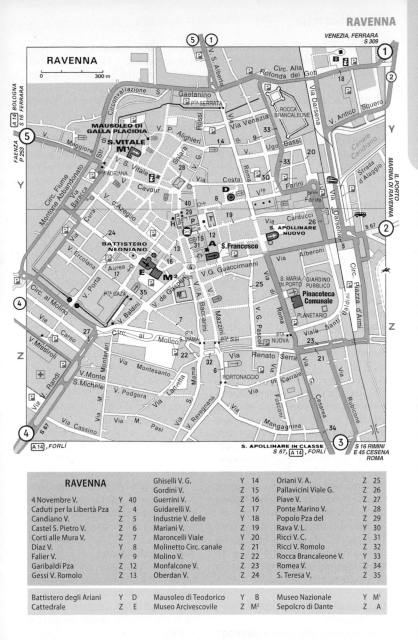

The Benedictine monastery adjacent to the basilica houses the **Museo Nazionale**, which has some fine displays, particularly those of late-Roman and palaeo-Christian artefacts, textiles, ivories and Cretan-Venetian icons.

Battistero Neoniano (or degli Ortodossi)★

The baptistery, erected in the 5C by Bishop Neoni, is also known as the Orthodox Baptistery in contrast to the Arian baptistery erected by the Goth Theodoric. It has a vault that is covered in splendid mosaics: in the dome there is a portrayal of the **Baptism of Christ** accompanied by the Apostles; the lower section portrays eight small temples with altars and thrones surmounted by the cross, an Eastern iconography which refers to the preparation of the Almighty's throne for the Last Judgement. Around the side windows there are Byzantine low relief sculptures depicting the prophets.

Museo Arcivescovile

The Episcopal Palace museum displays a small lapidary collection and Archbishop Maximian's **throne**★★ (6C), a masterpiece in carved ivory. The **Capella di Sant'Andrea**★ contains remarkable mosaics.

Battistero degli Ariani

The **Arians' Baptistery** was built by the Goth Theodoric in the 6C. The dome is decorated with **mosaics** that make use of the same iconography, if less elegantly, as the Neoniano Baptistery.

Basilica di Sant'Apollinare Nuovo★★

Erected between 493 and 526 by Theodoric, probably as a Palatine church, St Apollinaris is divided into a nave and two aisles articulated by beautifully crafted columns in Greek marble with Corinthian capitals. The north and south walls are decorated with a series of **mosaics** on a gold background distributed over three sections: the upper sections date from Theodoric's reign while the lower section was remodelled under Justinian who eliminated any reference to Arianism. The lower registry on the south side shows a **Procession of martyrs** leaving Theodoric's palace led by St Martin making their way towards Christ the King. The opposite side shows a **Procession of virgins** led by the Magi leaving the city of Ravenna and the port of Classis with its three anchored ships.

Basilica di Sant'Apollinare in Classe★★

▶ 5km/3mi south. Leave Ravenna by S 67.
The basilica stands in open country not far from the sea. The basilica was begun in 534 and consecrated in 549; a cylindrical campanile was added in the 11C. The majestic interior is composed of a nave and two aisles separated by arches on marble columns with Corinthian capitals. In the aisles lie Christian sarcophagi (5C-8C). The triumphal arch and apse

feature 6C-7C **mosaics** with a lovely harmony of colour. The triumphal arch shows Christ the Saviour surrounded by symbols representing the Evangelists; underneath there are two groups of six lambs (the Apostles) leaving two towered cities (Bethlehem and Jerusalem). The vaulting of the apse shows the Transfiguration: dominated by the hand of God. At the ends of the arms the Greek letters alpha and omega indicate that Christ is the beginning and the end. There are depictions of the prophets Moses and Elijah; the three sheep represent St Peter, St James and St John, witnesses of the Transfiguration. Below Apollinaris is surrounded by his sheep (the flock of the faithful).

Additional Sights

Mausoleo di Teodorico★

◔Open daily, Mar-Sep 8.30am-6.30pm, rest of the year 8.30am-4.30pm. ◔Closed 1 Jan, 1 May, 25 Dec. ◔2€; 5€; including Museo Nazionale; 6.50 € including Museo Nazionale and S. Apollinare in Classe. ☎0544 68 40 20.
This curious mausoleum, erected by Theodoric around 520, is built of huge blocks of freestone assembled without mortar. The two-storey building is covered by a remarkable monolithic dome. Inside, the decoration includes a Romanesque porphyry basin that has been transformed into a sarcophagus.

Sepolcro di Dante

The writer Dante was exiled from the city of Florence and took refuge first at Verona and then at Ravenna, where he died in 1321. The Classical building in which the tomb now stands was erected in 1780.

Chiesa di San Francesco

This 10C Romanesque church, dedicated to St Francis, is flanked by a campanile of the same period. Remodelled after the Second World War, it still retains some fine Greek marble columns, a 5C high altar and a 10C crypt.
ᚼMuseo d'Arte della Città (recumbent effigy★ of Guidarello Guidarelli).

REGGIO DI CALABRIA

POPULATION 183 041

MICHELIN MAP 564 M 28

TOWN PLAN IN THE MICHELIN ATLAS ITALY – CALABRIA.

Reggio, which backs against the Aspromonte Massif, is a pleasant town, rebuilt after the earthquake of 1908. Reggio is surrounded by groves of olives, vines, orange and lemon trees, and fields of flowers used for making perfume. Half the world production of bergamot (a citrus fruit) comes from Reggio.

- **Information:** Via S. Nicola, Galleria Mancuso, 88100 Catanzaro. ☎0961 74 78 98. www.turismo.regione.calabria.it.
- **Orient Yourself:** Reggio sits right at the bottom of A 3.
- **Organizing Your Time:** Spend a couple of hours at least in the Museo Nazionale Archeologico.
- **Also See:** *CALABRIA, MESSINA.*

Visit

Lungomare★

This elegant seafront promenade lined with palm trees affords views of the Sicilian coastline and Etna. Join locals at dusk for a promenade along this favoured spot.

Museo Nazionale Archeologico★★

&⊙ Open daily except Mon, 9am-7.30pm. ⊙ Closed 1 Jan, 1 May, 25 Dec. ◉4€. ☎0965 81 22 55.

Although most visitors come to this museum wanting to look at the mysterious bronze warriors it would be a pity not to have a look at other exhibits, including the **pinakes**★, terracotta low reliefs used in Locri as ex-votos in the 5C BC. They were dedicated to Persephone,

A City Rebuilt

Founded as a Rhegion by Greek settlers in the 8th century BC, Reggio has been destroyed by nature and rebuilt by man several times over the centuries. The worst earthquakes came in 1783 and on December 28, 1908. The latter quake was the most devastating and remains the worst on record in modern western European history. Some 80 percent of all buildings in Reggio collapsed and thousands were killed. It took Reggio a generation to fully recover.

bride of Hades who carried her off to the Underworld while she was picking flowers. The lower floor is "home" to the two **Riace Warriors**★★★, found in the sea of Riace in 1972.

A Few Minutes in Front of the Riace Warriors

Made in Greece in the 5C BC, the bronze statues are 1.98m/6.5ft and 2m/6.6ft tall respectively. Cleaned of marine sediment and hollow inside, they each weigh 250kg – 550lb. Their "names" – A and B – are clinical in the extreme but their expressions are anything but anonymous. Their eyes (B is missing one) have ivory and limestone irises and pupils made from a vitreous paste; the eyelashes are silver, as are the teeth, which are revealed only through the lips of A. Both hold, on their folded left arms, the holding straps of shields and in their right hands a lance. But each warrior seems troubled by different thoughts and feelings: A seems aggressive and indomitable and has been captured while thrusting his left leg forward. He has just turned his head and seems about to speak. B has a frightened and tentative expression, the position of his shoulders suggests he is reluctant to progress.

RIETI

POPULATION 46 500

MICHELIN MAP 563 O 20 – LAZIO.

Rieti is the geographical centre of Italy, and a good centre from which to follow in the footsteps of St Francis of Assisi, who preached locally.

- **Information:** Via Cintia 87. ☎0746 20 11 46. www.apt.rieti.it.
- **Orient Yourself:** Rieti lies at the foot of Mount Terminillo. The main access roads are S 4, the Via Salaria, which links the town to L'Aquila the A 1, and S 79, which goes to Terni.
- **Don't Miss:** The Convento di Fonte Colombo and the caves of St Francis at Convento di Poggio Bustone.
- **Organizing Your Time:** Allow a day to see the town and surrounding monasteries.
- **Also See:** *ABRUZZO.*

Sights

Piazza Cesare Battisti

This is the centre of the town, where the most important buildings are to be found. Take the gateway by the 16C-17C Palazzo del Governo to reach the **public garden**★, from where there is a lovely view of the town.

Duomo

This cathedral has a 15C porch and a lovely Romanesque campanile dating from 1252. Inside, the fresco of the Madonna dates from 1494 while the **crypt** is 12C.

Palazzo Vescovile

Behind the cathedral. This 13C episcopal building has heavily ribbed **vaulting**★ over the two vast naves.

Excursions

Convento di Fonte Colombo

5km/3mi southwest. Take the Contigliano road and after 3km/2mi turn left.
It was in the old monastery that **St Francis** underwent an eye operation. He dictated the Franciscan Rule in the grotto after having fasted for 40 days. Note the 12C Chapel of St Mary Magdalene adorned with frescoes depicting the "T," the emblem of the Cross designed by St Francis, the grotto where the saint fasted and the tree-trunk in which Jesus appeared to him.

Convento di Greccio★

15km/9mi northwest. Take the road via Contigliano to Greccio and continue for 2km/1.2mi. Leave the car on the esplanade at the foot of the monastery. This 13C monastery clings to a rocky overhang. It was here that St Francis celebrated Christmas in 1223 and said Mass at a manger (presepio) between an ox and an ass, thus starting the custom of Christmas Nativity scenes. Visitors have access to the Chapel of the Crib (Cappella del Presepio – which has some fine frescoes by the school of Giotto) and the areas where St Francis and his companions lived.

Convento di Poggio Bustone

10km/6mi north by the Terni road. Open daily, 8.30am-1pm and 3-7.30pm (5.30pm winter). ☎0746 68 89 16.
Perched at 818m/2 684ft, the monastery consists of a 14C church, with its 15C to 17C frescoes, 15C-16C cloisters, a 14C refectory and two caves in which St Francis is said to have lived.

Convento La Foresta

5km/3mi north. Open daily, summer 8.30am-noon and 2.30-7.30pm, winter 8.30am-noon and 2.30-6.30pm. Guided tours only. ☎0746 20 00 85.
It was in this retreat that St Francis wrote his Canticle of the Creatures and performed the miracle of the vine. In the wine cellar is the vat which was filled by the miraculous grape. The cave where St Francis stayed is also open.

RIMINI☼☼☼

POPULATION134 500
MICHELIN MAPS 562, 563 J 19
TOWN PLAN IN THE MICHELIN ATLAS ITALY.

Once the destination for the rich and famous, today Rimini is a seaside resort with modern hotels and a great beach. Its illustrious past is documented in its pretty historic centre.

- **Information:** Piazzale Federico Fellini 3. ☎0541 43 82 11/ Piazzale Cesare Battisti 1. ☎0541 51 331; www.riminiturismo.it.
- **Orient Yourself:** The main access roads are A 14, S 9 (the Via Emilia), and S 16.
- **Don't Miss:** Tempio Malatestiano.
- **Organizing Your Time:** Allow half a day.
- **Also See:** *RAVENNA, SAN MARINO, URBINO.*

A Bit of History

This Umbrian and Gallic colony, with its strategic situation, flourished during the Roman Empire. In the 13C the town grew to fame with the notoriety of its ruling house, the **Malatesta**. In *The Divine Comedy* Dante immortalised the fate of the tragic lovers, Paolo Malatesta and Francesca da Rimini, who were murdered by Gianni Malatesta (brother of Paolo and husband of Francesca). In the 16C Rimini became a papal town.

Giotto's work in the church of St Francis (now the Tempio Malatestiano) engendered the development of a **Riminese school** in the 14C.

More recently, the city has achieved international fame as the birthplace of the film director **Federico Fellini** (1920-93).

Sights

Tempio Malatestiano★★

Built in the 13C by the Franciscans the church became the Malatesta mausoleum in the 14C. It was remodelled from 1447 by **Leon Battista Alberti** on Sigismondo I's orders. Based on the principal that the church was to glorify Sigismondo and his beloved wife Isotta by housing their tombs, Alberti decided to adopt the Classical model of a triumphal arch and Classical elements.

The **interior** includes an allegorical decoration crafted by Agostino di Duccio who used medieval elements updated with pagan and Classical influences (note the enchanting **Childhood games** in the second chapel on the right). The south aisle houses Sigismondo's tomb and the reliquary chapel with the portrait **Sigismondo Malatesta and St Sigismondo**★★ by Piero della Francesca. In the adjacent chapel, Isotta's tomb rests on elephants holding Sigismondo's crest (SI). In the third chapel on the right, the signs of the zodiac celebrate the divine creation, contrasting with human activity, represented by the liberal arts in the opposite chapel in the north aisle. Behind the altar is Giotto's **painted 14C crucifix**★★.

Arco d'Augusto

Piazzale Giulio Cesare.

The majestic arch of Augustus was built in 27 BC.

The historic centre

Piazza Cavour is bordered by the Town Hall (Palazzo Comunale), Palazzo dell'-Arengo and the Palazzo del Podestà, all 13C-14C. Turn into Via Cairoli for the **church of Sant'Agostino,** with examples of 14C Riminese painting.

Ponte di Tiberio

The bridge was begun under Augustus, completed under the emperor Tiberius in AD 21, and built from massive blocks of Istrian limestone.

Museo della Città (Pietà★ by Giovanni Bellini).

Address Book

🪙 *For coin ranges, see the Legend on the cover flap.*

WHERE TO STAY

Hotel Diana – *Via Porto Palos 15 – 47811 Viserbella – 8km/5mi north of Rimini* – ☎0541 73 81 58 – www. hoteldiana-rimini.com – Closed Nov-Feb – 🅿🗻🎠(payment) – 38 rm– 🍴. The well-kept rooms overlook the swimming pools that back onto the beach. Courteous, friendly staff.

Hotel Giglio – *Viale Principe di Piemonte 18 – 47831 Miramare di Rimini – 7km/4mi south of Rimini* – ☎0541 37 20 73 – www.hotelgiglio.it – Closed Oct-Easter – 🅿🗻🎠(payment) – 42 rm– 🍴 – Restaurant. Directly on the beach, it has a lovely sunbathing terrace and you can get from the rooms (modern) to the sea in a nanosecond. Friendly, family atmosphere and good food.

Hotel Avila In – *Via San Salvador 192 – 47812 Torre Pedrera – 9km/5mi north of Rimini* – ☎0541 72 01 73 – www.hotelavila.it – Closed Nov – 🅿🗻🎠 – 65 rm 🍴 – Restaurant. A very comfortable hotel right on the seafront. There are swimming pools, a tennis court, facilities for children and a health club.

Grand Hotel – *Parco Fellini 1 – 47900 Rimini* – ☎0541 56 000 – Fax 0541 56 866 – 🅿🗻🎠♿ – 164 rm – 🍴 – Restaurant. Inextricably linked to the great film-maker Federico Fellini, this establishment has an elegant interior with 15C furnishings.

WHERE TO EAT

La Baracca – *Via Marecchiese 373 – 47037 Vergiano – 4.5km/3mi southwest of Rimini* – ☎0541 72 74 83 – www. labaracca.com – Closed Wed. A simple, little restaurant with a friendly, family atmosphere. Offers a traditional meat-based menu.

Dei Cantoni – *Via Santa Maria 19 – 47020 Longiano – 22km/13mi northwest of Rimini off the Via Emilia* – ☎0547 66 58 99 – Closed Wed, 15 Feb-15 Mar – 🍴. This lovely restaurant is situated in the historic centre. Delicious, seasonal regional cuisine. Al fresco dining.

Osteria la Sangiovesa – *Piazza S. Balacchi 14 - 47822 Santarcangelo di Romagna – 13km/8mi west of Rimini on the Via Emilia* – ☎0541 62 07 10 – www. sangiovesa.it – Closed lunchtime, 1 Jan, 25 Dec – 🍴. A gastronomic experience, as recommended by many hotels on the Riviera. The excellent cuisine draws on tradition. Good selection of wines.

TAKING A BREAK

Bounty – *Via Weber 6* – ☎0541 39 19 00 – www.bountyrimini.it – Open Jun-Sep 7.30am-3am; Oct-May, Tue and Wed, Fri-Sun. The largest pub in Rimini and the town's main nightspot, this vast bar has been decked out like a sailing vessel.

GOING OUT

Antica Drogheria Spazi – *Piazza Cavour 5* – ☎0541 23 439 – Open 11am-3pm and 6pm-midnight. An elegant winery/wine bar in the upper part of the town. Away from the crowds and the beach, there is plenty of space and it has a lovely outdoor area.

Club Paradiso – *Via Covignano 260* – ☎0541 75 11 32 – Open daily 5-20 Aug 9pm-5am; rest of the year Fri and Sat. With its luxuriant gardens and Baroque furnishings, the Paradise club is the most attractive discotheque in Rimini.

SHOPPING

Stamperia Ruggine – *Via Bertani 36* – ☎0541 50 811 – Open Tue-Sat 9am-1pm and 3.30-7.30pm. This is the place to watch the local craftsmen at work.

SPORT AND LEISURE

Blue Beach Center – *Zona Pascoli* – ☎0541 38 24 56 – www.spiaggia63a.it –Open 8am-7.30pm – Closed 20 Sep-May. Of all the private swimming pools, this is the best. As well as activities for children, a treatment (massage) room, fitness centre, television room and various other sports facilities you can also learn to water ski and jet ski here!

Delfinario – *Lungomare Tintori 2* – ☎0541 50 298 – www.delfinariorimini.it – Closed Nov-Mar. This little dolphinarium has a live show (40min) with five dolphins performing. These dolphins are also used in therapy for autistic children.

RIVIERA LIGURE★★

MICHELIN MAP 561 I-K 4-12 – LIGURIA.

The enchanting Italian or Ligurian Riviera is like the French Riviera, a tourist paradise. The mild climate makes it particularly popular in winter. The coast is dotted with popular resorts with good amenities and a wide range of hotels. The hinterland provides walks for those who prefer solitude.

- ⓘ **Information:** Regione Liguria, via Fieschi 15, 16121 Genova, ☎010 54 851; www.turismoinliguria.it.
- ▸ **Orient Yourself:** rom Ventimiglia to the Gulf of La Spezia, the coast describes a curve backed by the slopes of the Alps and the Ligurian Apennines, with Genoa in the middle.cela vient des premières lignes The coastal roads include A 10 (Riviera di Ponente), A 12 (Riviera di Levante) and S 1 (Via Aurelia).
- 🅿 **Parking:** Parking is difficult along the Cinque Terra. it is best to visit the villages on foot via the coastal path or by public transport.
- 🚫 **Don't Miss:** The Cinque Terra, Portofino and San Remo.
- 🕐 **Organizing Your Time:** Allow four days to the Riviera (excluding Genova).
- 🧒 **Especially for Kids:** The caves of Grotte di Toirano.
- 👁 **Also See:** GENOVA, Promontorio di PORTOFINO.

1 Riviera di Ponente★

Ventimiglia to Genoa - *175km/109mi. Allow a day.*

The main road of the Riviera, the Via Aurelia, is of Roman origin. It is difficult, as it is winding, narrow, and car- ries heavy traffic. Nevertheless, there are remarkable viewpoints from the corniche road or when the road runs close to the Ligurian Sea. Inland the A 10 motorway runs parallel. The road passes through resorts with villas screened by luxuriant vegetation, or crosses coastal plains traversed by mountain torrents.

Address Book

For coin ranges see the Legend on the cover flap.

WHERE TO STAY

Albergo Rosita – *Via Mànie 67 – 17024 Finale Ligure – 3km/2mi northeast – ☎019 60 24 37 –www.hotelrosita.it – Closed 5-20 Jan, Nov –* 🅿 *– 9 rm – Restaurant.* Splendid clifftop location in a verdant setting. Light, airy public areas furnished in wood. Rooms are com-fortable and have a balcony with sea view. Breakfast served on the veranda.

Hotel Delle Rose – *Via de Medici 17 – 18014 Ospedaletti – 6km/4mi northeast of Bordighera on the Via Aurelia – ☎0184 68 90 16 – Fax 0184 68 97 78 – 14 rm – Restaurant.* The main attractions here are the lovely garden full of exotic plants and the warmth and hospitality of the family owners. Classic, if slightly old-fashioned rooms and public lounges. Off the beaten track.

Hotel Ca' d'Andrean – *Via Discovolo 101 – 19010 Manarola – ☎0187 92 00 40 – www.cadandrean.it – Closed 10-25 Nov – 10 rm –.* This small, charming hotel is situated in the pedestrianised area in the upper part of the village. Modern-style rooms. Pleasant lounge area with lovely fireplace. Beautiful garden with lemon trees.

Hotel Due Gemelli – *Via Litoranea 9, Località Campi – 19017 Riomaggiore – 4.5km/3mi east of Riomaggiore – ☎0187 92 01 11 – www.duegemelli.it – 🅿 – 13 rm – Restaurant.* You may not have direct access down to the sea, but there are splendid panoramic views from the balconies in the rooms and the terrace restaurant. A simple, family establishment that would make an ideal base for exploring the Cinque Terre.

WHERE TO EAT

Luchin – *Via Bighetti 51 – 16043 Chiavari – ☎0185 30 10 63 – Closed Sun –.* With origins dating back to 1907, this establishment has a reputation for authentic Ligurian cooking: specialities include *farinata di ceci* (chickpea polenta). Welcoming ambience with large refectory-style tables.

La Favorita – *Località Richelmo – 18030 Apricale – 16km/10mi north of Ventimiglia – ☎0184 20 81 86 – Closed 24 Jun-8 Jul, 12 Nov-6 Dec – Book.* What was once an old farmhouse is now a great restaurant run with tremendous enthusiasm by the family owners.

U Giancu – *Via San Massimo 78 – 16035 Rapallo – ☎0185 26 05 05 – www.ugiancu.it – Closed Wed (except Aug), Mon (Jan-Easter), lunchtimes for 10 days in Dec – Book.* With its splendid collection of old cartoons on the walls and a country-style ambience outside, it is easy to forget that the sea is only minutes away. There is a children's area and the train where they can take their meals is a nice touch.

Quintilio – *Via Gramsci 23 – 17041 Altare – 12km/7mi northwest of Savona on S 29 – ☎019 58 000 – Closed Sun evening, Mon, lunchtime (except Sun), Jul.* A mixture of elegant and rustic, simply decorated and furnished. Home cooking focuses on regional (Ligurian and Piedmontese) specialities prepared with flair and imagination. Accommodation also available.

TAKING A BREAK

Caffè Gino – *Piazza Milite Ignoto 1 – 17026 Noli – ☎019 74 84 57 – 8am-1am. Closed mid-Jan to mid-Feb.* From the tables set out in the piazza (pedestrians only) you have a great view of the red clock tower and the flower-filled balconies of the old houses. An oasis of peace in this charming little village.

Enoteca Marone – *Via San Francesco 61 – 18038 San Remo – ☎0184 50 69 16 – Mon 4-7.30pm, Tue-Sat 8.45am-12.30pm and 4-7.30pm.* For 18 years the dynamic, knowledgable owners of this wine bar have been choosing the wines direct from the producers. The cellar extends to around 1 200 different wines.

Enoteca Olioteca San Giorgio – *Via Volta 19 – 18010 Cervo – ☎0183 40 01 75 – Tue-Mon 9am-3pm and 5.30pm-3am.* This wine bar also specialises in olive oil products (including the regional delicacy, pesto). Good choice of traditional wines from Liguria including Vermentino, Pigato, Vignamare, Ormeasco and Rosolio.

Gelatomania – *Via Cavour 56/D – 18039 Ventimiglia* – ☎*0184 35 26 16*. This is the oldest gelateria in town, as well as one of the best. Give yourself plenty of time to choose from the 44 flavours which include seasonal fruits and meringue.

Mondino – *Via Roma 38/B – 18039 Ventimiglia* – ☎*0184 35 13 61 – Mon-Sat 7am-1pm and 3.30-7.30pm; closed mid-Sep to mid-Oct*. Excellent pasticceria (confectioner's and pastry shop) which sells delicious panettoni (cakes) and other regional specialities.

Pasticceria-Focacceria Scalvini – *Via Colombo 3 – 17026 Noli – ☎019 74 82 01 – Summer, 7.15am-1pm and 3.30-8pm; rest of the year, Wed-Mon 8am-1pm and 3.30-7.30pm*. Founded in 1820, specialities here include *torta di mandorla* (almond tart), different Genoese-style breads, amaretti, and pastries made with fruit.

U Gumbu – *Via Matteotti 31 – 18010 Cervo – Tue-Mon 10am-noon and 3-6pm*. This house includes the Museo dell'Oliva. On sale are artisanal products including extra virgin olive oil, pesto and jams.

Vino e Farinata – *Via Pia 15/r – 17100 Savona – Tue-Sat noon-2pm and 6-9.30pm; Closed 10 days in Aug-Sep*. As you walk through the tiled doorway to the oldest bakery in town nothing has changed here for 130 years. Pastries, such as those made with farina di ceci (chickpea flour) are prepared according to age-old recipes.

GOING OUT

Bagni Miramare – *Corso Bigliati 10 – 17012 Albissola Marina – Opposite Piazza del Popolo*. – ☎*019 48 02 85 – Closed Oct-Feb*. While the children throw themselves off the diving-board, their parents can sip cocktails at the Bali-style bar. In the evening the Miramare transforms itself into a discotheque.

Casinò Municipale di San Remo – *Corso Inglesi 18 – 18038 San Remo – ☎0184 53 40 01 – 10am-2.30am*. This is the town's main nightspot. The casino is housed in a rather grand building with original early-19C furnishings.

LEISURE

La Superba – *Pontile Marinetta – 17100 Savona – Beneath the Torre Pancaldo – ☎010 26 57 12 – Bookings only*. Day trips to Genoa (visiting the Acquario and the Lanterna), Portofino (and San Fruttu-oso), or the Cinque Terre (including a tour of Isola Palmaria). Of particular interest are the whale watching trips accompanied by experts from the WWF.

With its exceptional exposure to the sun the Riviera specialises in flower growing.
The hinterland provides tranquillity with wild, forested landscapes.

Ventimiglia

Not far from the French border, Ventimiglia has an old quarter (Città Vecchia) criss-crossed by narrow alleyways, the 11C-12C Duomo, an 11C octagonal baptistery, the 11C-12C church of San Michele and the 17C Neri Oratory. The **Giardini Hanbury**★★ (Hanbury Gardens) in Mortola Inferiore *(6km/4mi west, towards the French border)*, with their varied and exotic vegetation, are laid out in terraces, overlooking the sea. ♿🕒*Open daily 9.30am-dusk.* ☎*7.50€*. ☎*0184 22 95 07; www.amici hanbury.com*

Bordighera☖☖
The villas and hotels of this resort are scattered among flower gardens. The old town still has fortified gateways.

San Remo☖☖
www.sanremoguide.com/inglese.
The capital of the Riviera di Ponente enjoys the highest number of sunshine hours on the Ligurian coast, and boasts thermal establishments, pleasure boat harbour and cultural events.
San Remo is the main Italian flower market and millions of roses, carnations and mimosa flowers are exported worldwide. 🖐*Enjoy the fragrance and spectacle of the Oct-June flower market.*

Corso Imperatrice
Liguria's most elegant seafront promenade is known for its Canary palms.

La Pigna★

La Pigna has a medieval aspect, its winding alleys lined with narrow houses. From Piazza Castello climb up to the church of the Madonna della Costa, for an attractive bay **view**★.

Stop and take in the fine panorama from Monte Bignone★★.

Bussana Vecchia

The medieval village was destroyed by an earthquake in 1887 and lay deserted until the 1960s, when artists set about restoring the houses and opening up shops selling their work and crafts.

Taggia

Taggia, set amid vineyards and olive groves, commands the Argentina Valley. In the 15C and 16C Taggia was an important art centre frequented by Louis (Ludovico) Bréa from Nice and the Piedmontese artist Canavese.

The church of **San Domenico** has a fine collection of **works**★ by Louis Bréa (*Virgin of Pity and the Baptism of Christ*).

Diano Marina

From here, visit the fortified village of Diano Castello and 12C Chapel of the Knights of Malta (Cappella dei Cavalieri di Malta) with its multicoloured roof.

Albenga

Albenga lies a short distance inland, in an alluvial plain with rich market gardens. The medieval **old town**★ is clustered round the **Cattedrale** whose octagonal 5C baptistery has a palaeo-Christian mosaic.

Grotte di Toirano★

Guided tours only in Jul and Aug 9.30am-12.30pm and 2-5.30pm (rest of the year 2-5pm). Closed mid-Dec-mid-Jan. 9€. 0182 98 062; www.toirano grotte.it.

The caves were inhabited in the late-Neolithic period. There are traces of human footprints, torch marks, the remains and prints of bears, and mud balls used as missiles Kids. The caves open into a series of chambers bristling with stalagmites and stalactites.

Finale Ligure

Finale Marina has a basilica with a fanciful Baroque façade. In **Finale Pia** the abbey church is graced with an elegant late-13C campanile. The old town of **Finale Borgo**★, 2km/1.2mi inland, still has its town walls and its collegiate church of San Biagio has an elegant 13C polygonal campanile. Inside are a polyptych of St Catherine (1533) and a 16C painting of St Blaise.

From **Castel San Giovanni** (1hr on foot there and back; start from Via del Municipio) there is a **view**★ of Finale Ligure, the sea and the hinterland. **Castel Gavone** retains a 15C round tower with diamond-shaped rustication.

Noli★

This fishing village still has ancient houses, 13C towers and a Romanesque

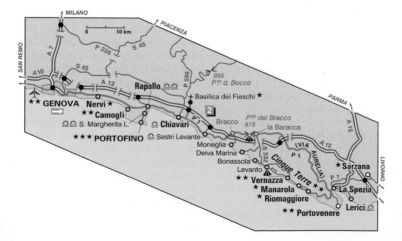

Riomaggiore

church with a huge wooden statue of Christ, also of the Romanesque period.

Savona

Savona's old town has Renaissance palaces, its 16C Duomo and a 16C fortress, **Fortezza Priamar**, where Italian patriot Mazzini was imprisoned in 1830.

Albissola Marina⌂

This town is known for its production of ceramics, which carries on a 13C tradition. At the end of the 16C a Duke of Nevers, a member of the Italian Gonzaga family, summoned the Conrade brothers from Albisola to Nevers to found a faïence factory. The 18C Villa Faraggiana with its exotic **park**★, now houses the Ligurian Ceramics Centre. The exhibits include: the rich Empire furnishings, ceramic pavements and flooring, and the superb **ballroom**★ with its stucco and fresco decoration. ♿☉⌚⤴*Guided tours only 3-7pm.* ⊘*Closed Mon, Easter, Oct-Feb.* ⛵*4.20€; garden only €2.* ☎*019 48 06 22; www.villafaraggiana.it.*

Genoa★★ ♿see GENOVA

②Riviera di Levante★★★

Genoa to La Spezia - *173km/108mi. Allow one day.*

This stretch of coast has more character and is wilder than the Riviera di Ponente. Sharp promontories, little sheltered coves, tiny fishing villages, wide sandy bays, cliffs, the pinewoods and olive groves of the hinterland, all lend it charm. The road is often winding and hilly but there are fewer stretches of corniche road and the road often runs much further from the coast. ♿*Don't miss the beautiful villages of the Cinque Terra.*

Nervi⌂

This little seaside resort with its multi-coloured houses was very fashionable in the early 20C. The lovely *passeggiata* **Anita Garibaldi**★ is a pleasant walk along the coast and affords fine views from the Alpi Marittimieto Portofino. Nervi's **public parks** comprise the gardens that belonged to three villas.

Portofino★★★ ♿*see Promontorio di PORTOFINO.*

Rapallo⌂⌂

This sophisticated seaside resort is admirably situated at the head of a bay to the east of the Portofino peninsula. The Lungomare Vittorio Veneto is a lovely palm-shaded **promenade**★ along the seafront.

Chiavari⌂

This seaside resort has a vast beach and a pleasure-boat harbour. In San Salvatore 2km/1.2mi to the northeast is the small 13C **Basilica dei Fieschi**★ with its courses of black and white marble.

Cinque Terre★★

www.cinqueterre.it.

Lying northwest of the Gulf of La Spezia, the Cinque Terre (Five Lands) is, even today, an isolated region best reached by train or boat. This coast is wild but hospitable, with its vineyards and fishing villages where the people remain strongly attached to old customs and traditions. In 1997 Cinque Terre, Portovenere and the Palmaria, Tino and Tinetto islands, were included in UNESCO's World Heritage List.

A coastal path linking Riomaggiore, Manarola, **Corniglia**, Vernazza and **Monterosso** affords fine views.

Vernazza★★ – This is the most attractive village with its tall colourful houses and its church clustered together at the head of a well-sheltered cove.

Manarola★ – This fishing village with its small 14C church is set in a landscape of terraced vineyards. Starting from the station there is a splendid **walk**★★ (15min on foot) offering lovely views of the coast and other villages.

Riomaggiore★ – Take the branch road off the La Spezia-Manarola road. The houses of this medieval village lie in a narrow valley.

Take a walk along the coastal path. Parking is difficult. Proceed on foot or public transport.

La Spezia

▶*Town plan in the Michelin Atlas Italy. viale Mazzini 47. www.laspezia.net.*

This is Italy's largest naval dockyard and specialises in the manufacture of arms.

Museo Lia★★ – *Open Tue-Sun, 10am-6pm. Closed 1 Jan, 1 May, 15 Aug, 25 Dec. For information and reservations ☎0187 73 11 00; www.laspezia. net/museolia.*

Housed in a restored 17C monastery, this collection was accumulated by Amedeo Lia who amassed 1 110 works of art, dating from Roman times to the 18C. The museum has important sections on ivory, enamels, crosses, devotional objects, illuminated manuscripts, paintings, glass and rock crystal. Do not miss some of the most significant pieces such as an Umbrian *Virgin and Child* in polychrome wood (13C), an **amethyst head**, probably a portrait of one of Caligula's sisters, as well as a 13C Limoges cross (516). Illuminated manuscripts and numerous illuminated pages, mostly Italian (14C-16C) as well as paintings (13C-18C) mark the beginning of the visit. Painters from the 16C include Giampietrino *(Madonna and Child with St John)*, Bellini and **Pontormo** (self-portrait). The 17C and 18C are represented respectively by followers of Caravaggio and Venetian landscapes and portraits (Longhi, Guardi). Rooms XI and XII show bronze figures, rock crystal and Roman glass – note the 1C bottle with gilded bands. Maritime artefacts at the Museo Navale.

Sarzana★

▶*16km/10mi north.*

The busy town of Sarzana was once an advance base of the Republic of Genoa, a rival of Pisa, and its numerous historic buildings bear witness to its past importance. The **Cattedrale** has a marble **altarpiece**★ (1432) delicately carved by Riccomani. In a chapel to the right of the chancel is a phial that is said to have contained the Blood of Christ. In the chapel to the left is a **Crucifixion**★ (1138) by the artist, Guglielmo.

The **Fortezza di Sarzanello**★ (1322) is a fortress built to the northeast of the town, by the *condottiere* (leader of a mercenary army) from Lucca, Castruccio Castracani. It is a curious example of military architecture with moats and curtain walls guarded by round towers. *For information on admission times, charges and events, contact ☎339 41 30 037 (mobile) or 0187 62 20 80; www.for tedisarzanello.com.*

From the top of the keep there is a magnificent **panorama**★★ of the town and the Apennine foothills.

Enjoy views from Fortezza di Sarzanello.

Portovenere★★

From the terrace of the church of San Lorenzo there is a fine view of the Cinque Terre region.

ROMA★★★
ROME
POPULATION 3 700 000
MICHELIN MAP 563 Q 19
MICHELIN MAP 38 ROME – SEE ALSO THE GREEN GUIDE ROME.

The "Eternal City" is rich in monuments of its ancient history, which justify its renown. Today it's no longer the marble city left behind by Augustus and the Emperors, nor is it the opulent court of the Papal era: since 1870, the year when it was proclaimed capital of Italy. Rome has seen a widespread and, especially after the Second World War, uncontrolled urban expansion. Her monuments – famous the world over – continue to delight tourists: the Pantheon and Forum, the majestic Colosseum, St. Peter's, Castel Sant'Angelo, Piazza Navona, Spanish Steps, Trevi Fountain and Villa Borghese.

- **Information:** Via Parigi 5, 00185 Roma, ☎06 48 89 91 and Aeroporto di Fiumicino, International Arrival Hall, ☎06 65 95 60 74, www.romaturismo.it.
- **Orient Yourself:** "All roads lead to Rome", so they say. In fact, Rome lies at the hub of a complicated motorway network with the traffic from A 1, A 12, A 24 all converging on the very busy Raccordo Anulare (ringroad).
- **Parking:** There are few private car parks in Rome and they are extremely expensive and access to the city centre by car is restricted (a permit is required). There are two underground car parks in the centre: under the Villa Borghese gardens, near the Porta Pinciana, and Parking Ludovisi, Via Ludovisi 60.
- **Don't Miss:** The Forum and the Colossseum, Trevi fountain, the views from the Janiculum (Gianicolo) and Aventine (Aventino) belvederes, and the Pincio hills.
- **Organizing Your Time:** Allow at least three days.
- **Especially for Kids:** Bikes and pedal cars in the Pincio, the hot air balloon at the Villa Borghese, Ostia and the Ostia Lido.

Colosseum detail

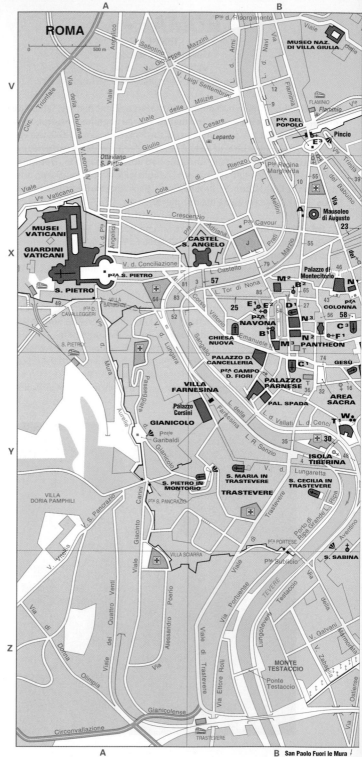

ROMA

0   500 m

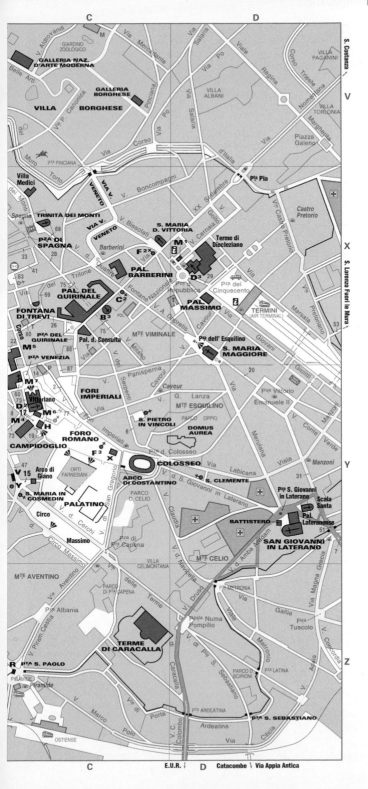

ROMA

Name	Grid	No.
20 Settembre V.	CDX	
24 Maggio V.	CX	88
4 Novembre V.	CXY	87
Acaia V.	DZ	
Adriana Pza	BX	
Aldrovandi V. U.	CV	
Alessandra V.	CY	2
Altoviti Lungotevere degli	BX	3
Amba Aradam V. d.	DY	
Angelico Viale	AV	
Anguillara Lungotevere degli	BY	4
Annibaldi V. degli	CY	6
Appia Nuova V.	DY	7
Aracoeli Pza e V.	CY	8
Armi Lungotev. d.	BV	
Arnaldo da Brescia L.	BV	9
Augusta Lungotevere. in	BX	10
Aventino Lungotev.	BYZ	
Aventino Viale	CZ	
Azuni V. D. A.	BV	12
Babuino V. del	BX	
Battisti V. C.	CXY	14
Belle Arti Viale d.	BCV	
Bissolati V. L.	CX	
Bocca della Verità Pza della	CY	15
Boncompagni V.	CX	
Botteghe Oscure V. d.	BY	16
Campidoglio Pza d.	CY	17
Campidoglio V. del	CY	19
Campo dei Fiori Pza	BY	
Canonica Viale P.	CV	
Carini Viale G.	AYZ	
Carlo Alberto V.	DY	20
Castello Lungotev.	BX	
Castro Pretorio Viale	DX	
Cavour Pza	BX	
Cavour V.	CDXY	
Cenci Lungotev. d.	BY	
Cerchi V. d.	CY	
Cernaia V.	DX	
Cilicia V.	DZ	
Cinquecento Pza d.	DX	
Circo Massimo V. d.	CY	
Claudia V.	CDY	
Cola di Rienzo V.	ABX	
Collegio Romano Pza del	CX	22
Colombo V. Crist.	DZ	
Colonna Pza	BX	
Colosseo Pza d.	CDY	
Conciliazione V. d.	AX	
Concordia V.	DZ	
Condotti V. dei	BCX	23
Conte Verde V.	DY	
Coronari V. dei	BX	25
Corso V. del	BCX	
Crescenzio V.	ABX	
Dataria V. della	CX	26
Depretis V. A.	CDX	
Dogana Vecchia V. della	BX	27
Donna Olimpia V. di	AZ	
Druso V.	DZ	
Due Macelli V.	CX	28
Einaudi Viale L.	DX	29
Esquilino Pza d.	DX	
Fabricio Ponte	BY	30
Farnesina L. della	BY	
Filiberto V. E.	DY	31
Flaminia V.	BV	
Florida V.	BY	32
Fori Imperiali V. d.	CY	
Frattina V.	BCX	33
Gallia V.	DZ	
Galvani V.	BZ	
Garibaldi Piazzale	AY	
Garibaldi Ponte	BY	35
Gianicolense Circ.	AZ	
Gianicolo Passeggiata di	AY	
Giolitti V. G.	DXV	
Giubbonari V. dei	BY	36
Giuliana V. della	AV	
Giulio Cesare Viale	ABV	
Goito V.	DX	
Italia Cso d'	CDV	
Labicana V.	DY	
Lanza V. G.	CDY	
Leone IV V.	AX	
Lungara V. d.	AXY	
Lungaretta V. d.	BY	
Magna Grecia V.	DYZ	
Manzoni Viale	DY	
Marco Polo V.	CZ	
Margutta V.	BX	39
Marmorata V. della	BZ	
Marsala V.	DX	
Marzio Lungotev.	BX	
Mazzini Viale G.	ABV	
Mellini Lungotev.	BX	
Mercadante V.	CV	
Mercede V. della	CX	41
Merulana V.	DY	
Metronia Porta	DZ	
Metronio Viale	DZ	
Milano V.	CX	
Milizie Viale d.	ABV	
Montecitorio Pza di	BX	43
Mura Aurelie Viale d.	AXY	
Muro Torto Viale d.	BCVX	
Navi Lungotev. d.	BV	
Navicella V. d.	DYZ	
Navona Pza	BX	
Nazionale V.	CX	
Nomentana V.	DV	
Numa Pompilio Piazzale	DZ	
Ostiense V.	BZ	
Panisperna V.	CY	
Parlamento Pza del	BX	46
Petroselli V. L.	CY	47
Pierleoni L. dei	BY	48
Pinciana V.	CV	
Piramide Cestia V.	CZ	
Po V.	CDV	
Poerio V. A.	AZ	
Popolo Pza d.	BV	
Porta Angelica V. del	AX	
Porta Ardeatina Viale d.	CDZ	
Porta Capena Pza di	CY	
Porta Cavalleggeri V. di	AX	49
Porta S. Giovanni Pza di	DY	51
Portal S. Sebastiano V.	DZ	
Portuense V.	BZ	
Prati Lungotevere	BX	
Pretoriano Viale	DX	
Principe A. Savoia Aosta Ponte	AX	52
Quattro Fontane V. d.	CX	
Quattro Venti Viale dei	AYZ	
Quirinale Pza d.	CX	
Ramni V. dei	DX	53
Regina Margherita Ponte	BX	
Regina Margherita Viale	DV	
Repubblica Pza	DX	
Rinascimento Cso d.	BX	54
Ripa Lungotev.	BY	
Ripa Grande Porto di	BY	
Ripetta V. di	BX	55
Risorgimento Ponte d.	BV	
Rolli V. E.	BZ	
Rotonda Pza d.	BX	56
S. Angelo Ponte	BX	57
S. Giovanni in Laterano Pza	DY	
S. Giovanni in Laterano V. d.	DY	
S. Gregorio V. d.	CY	
S. Ignazio Pza	BX	58
S. Marco Pza di	CY	60
S. Pancrazio V.	AY	
S. Pietro Pza	AX	
S. Silvestro Pza	CX	63
Sabotino V.	AV	
Salaria V.	DV	
Sangallo Lungotevere. d.	ABX	
Sanzio L. R.	BY	
Sassia Lungotevere in	AX	64
Scrofa V. della	BX	65
Serpenti V. dei	CXY	
Settembrini V. L.	ABV	
Sistina V.	CX	68
Spagna Pza di	CX	
Stamperia V. della	CX	69
Sublicio Ponte	BZ	
Teatro di Marcello V. del	CY	73
Terme di Caracalla Viale delle	CDZ	
Testaccio L.	BZ	
Testaccio Ponte	BZ	
Tor di Nona Lungotevere	BX	
Torre Argentina Largo di	BY	74
Traforo V. del	CX	75
Trastevere Vle di	BYZ	
Trieste Cso	DV	
Trinità dei Monti Viale	BVX	
Trionfale Cir.	AV	
Tritone V. del	CX	
Tulliano V. del	CY	77
Turati V. F.	DY	
Tuscolo Pza	DZ	
Umberto I Pza	BX	79
Umiltà V.	CX	80
Vallati L. d.	BY	
Vaticano Lungotevere	ABX	81
Vaticano Viale	AX	
Veneto V. Vittorio	CX	
Venezia Pza	CXY	
Vitellia V.	AZ	
Vittorio Emanuele II Cso	BX	
Vittorio Emanuele II Ponte	AX	83
Vittorio Emanuele II Pza	DY	
Zabaglia V.	BZ	
Zanardelli V.	BX	85

Ara Pacis Augustae	BX	A	Palazzo Corsini	ABY		S. Lorenzo fuori le Mura	DX	
Arco di Costantino	CY		Palazzo Doria Pamphili	CX	M[5]	S. Luigi dei Francesi	BX	D[1]
Arco di Giano	CY		Palazzo Farnese	BY		S. Maria Maggiore	DX	
Area Sacra	BY		Palazzo Lateranense	DY		S. Maria Sopra Minerva	BX	F[1]
Aula Ottagona	DX	M[1]	Palazzo Madama	BX	N[3]	S. Maria d'Aracœli	CY	D[2]
Battistero	DY		Palazzo Massimo	DX		S. Maria d. Vittoria	CDX	
Campidoglio	CY		Palazzo Nuovo	CY	M[6]	S. Maria degli Angeli	DX	D[3]
Castel S. Angelo	BX		Palazzo Senatorio	CY	H	S. Maria del Popolo	BV	E[3]
Catacombe	DZ		Palazzo Spada	BY		S. Maria dell'Anima	BX	E[2]
Chiesa Nuova	BX		Palazzo Venezia	CY	M[7]	S. Maria della Pace	BX	E[1]
Colosseo	CDY		Palazzo d. Cancelleria	BY		S. Maria in Cosmedin	CY	
Domus Aurea	DY		Palazzo d. Consulta	CX		S. Maria in Trastevere	BY	
E.U.R.	DZ		Palazzo dei Conservatori	CY	M[4]	S. Paolo fuori le Mura	AZ	
Fontana di Trevi	CX		Palazzo del Quirinale	CX		S. Pietro	AX	
Fori Imperiali	CY		Palazzo della Sapienza	BX	N[2]	S. Pietro in Montorio	ABY	
Foro Romano	CY		Palazzo di Montecitorio	BX		S. Pietro in Vincoli	CY	
Galleria Borghese	CV		Pantheon	BX		S. Sabina	BZ	
Galleria Nazionale d'Arte			Pincio	BV		S. Susanna	CX	F[2]
Moderna	CV		Piramide di Caio Cestio	CZ	R	S.S. Cosma e Damiano	CY	F[3]
Gesù	BY		Porta Pia	DX		Scala Santa	DY	
Gianicolo	AY		Porta S. Paolo	CZ		Teatro di Marcello	BY	T[1]
Giardini Vaticani	AX		Porta S. Sebastiano	DZ		Tempio della Fortuna Virile	CY	V
Isola Tiberina	BY		S. Agnese in Agone	BX	B[1]	Tempio di Apollo Sosiano	BY	W
Mausoleo di Augusto	BX		S. Agostino	BX	B[2]	Tempio di Venere e Roma	CY	X
Musei Vaticani	AX		S. Andrea al Quirinale	CY	B[3]	Tempio di Vesta	CY	Y
Museo Nazionale di			S. Andrea della Valle	BY	C[1]	Terme di Caracalla	CZ	
Villa Giulia	BY		S. Carlo alle Quattro Fontane	CXC[2]		Terme di Diocleziano	DX	
Palatino	CY		S. Cecilia in Trastevere	BY		Trastevere	BY	
Palazzo Altemps	BX	M[2]	S. Clemente	DY		Trinità dei Morti	CX	
Palazzo Barberini	CX		S. Costanza	DV		Via Appia Antica	DZ	
Palazzo Braschi	BX	M[3]	S. Giovanni in Laterano	DY		Villa Borghese	CV	
Palazzo Chigi	BX	N[1]	S. Ignazio	BX	C[3]	Villa Farnesina	BY	
						Villa Medici	CX	
						Vittoriano	CY	

A Bit of History

No other city in the world has managed to combine so successfully such a diverse heritage of Classical antiquities, medieval buildings, Renaissance palaces and Baroque churches. Far from being discordant, they constitute a logical continuity where revivals, influences and contrasts are evidence of the ingenuity of Roman architects and builders. Of course, the ruins no longer present the splendour of the Empire, when they were faced with marble. Only a few of the palaces have retained the painted decoration of their façades. And even the city more recently acclaimed by Goethe and Stendhal has changed, due to the damage caused by heavy traffic and the modernisation of a busy capital city.

However, Rome still impresses, both as the great centre of ancient civilisation and a lively urban core. The best overall views of this complex – sprawling over the seven hills – are from the belvederes with the numerous domes and bell towers in the distance. Rome is the city of churches with over 300 edifices –some even side by side. It is often impossible to stand back and admire their façades, but the richness of the decoration and the ingenious use of *trompe l'oeil* tend to compensate for this drawback. Often the interiors are astonishing for their silence and light and the inventiveness and audacity of the ultimate design. In the older districts of Rome (centro storico) around the Pantheon, the Piazza Navona and the Campo dei Fiori, there is a wealth of fine palaces. Wander the back alleys for a glimpse, between ochre-coloured façades, of a small market square, or stairways descending to a fountain. In the evening, these areas are bathed in a soft glow by tall street lights – a sharp contrast to the bustling main arteries.

Luxury shops are to be found around the Piazza del Popolo, Via del Corso, Piazza di Spagna and the streets which open off them. Via Veneto – lined with cafés and luxurious hotels –was the epicentre of *la Dolce Vita* and remains a tourist centre. Piazza Navona is another fashionable meeting-place. Antique and second-hand shops line Via dei Coronari. Romans tend to dine in **Trastevere**, once home to artisans and foreigners, across the river from the main Campo dei Fiori market. And, of course, a visit to the Fountain of Trevi is required. Legend claims that a coin thrown backward over the left shoulder ensures a return to the Eternal City.

Legend and Location

The legendary origins of Rome were perpetuated by historians and poets, such as Livy and Virgil. Both claimed that Aeneas, son of the goddess Aphrodite, fled from Troy when it was captured, and landed at the mouth of the Tiber. Having defeated the local tribes, he founded Lavinium. His son Ascanius (or Iulus) founded Alba Longa. There Rhea Silvia the Vestal, following her union with the god Mars, gave birth to the twins Romulus and Remus, who were abandoned on the Tiber.

The twins, transported by the current of the river, came to rest at the foot of the Palatine, and were nursed by a wolf. Later Romulus marked a furrow round the sacred area where the new city would stand. Jesting, Remus stepped over the line; Romulus killed him for violating the sacred precinct. He populated his village with outlaws who married women seized from the Sabines. An alliance grew between the two peoples, ruled by a succession of kings, alternately Sabine and Latin, until the Etruscans arrived.

But beyond legend, modern historians emphasise the strategic location of Rome's seven hills especially the Palatine, which was a staging-post on the salt road (Via Salaria) and was first settled in the 8C BC.

Two centuries later the Etruscans had transformed these shacks into a well-organised town, with a citadel on the Capitoline. The last Etruscan king, Tarquin the Superb, was thrown out in 509 BC and the Consulate was instituted.

The Republican era was an ambitious one of territorial expansion. During the 2C and 1C BC, civil war tore the regime to pieces. **Julius Caesar** (101-44 BC) emerged as leader because of his audacious strategies (he conquered the whole of Gaul in 51 BC), his grasp of political affairs, his talents as an orator and his unbounded ambition. Appointed consul and dictator for life, he was assassinated on the Ides of March, 15 March 44 BC.

He was succeeded by his great-nephew, **Octavian**, a young man who was of delicate health and had won no military glory. Octavian was to demonstrate tenacity of purpose and political genius, ably vanquishing possible rivals. In 27 BC the Senate granted him the title **Augustus**, which conferred an aura of holiness. He soon became the first Roman emperor. His achievements were considerable: he extended Roman government and restored peace to the whole of the Mediterranean basin.

Among Augustus' successors were those driven by madness and cruelty (Caligula, Nero and Domitian). Others continued the work of Roman civilisation: the good administrator, Vespasian; Titus who was known as the love and delight of the human race; Trajan, the "best of Emperors" and great builder; and Hadrian, an indefatigable traveller and passionate Hellenist.

Christianity

The old order passed away, undermined within by economic misery and the concentration of authority in the hands of one man, and from without by barbarian attacks. A new force – Christianity – began to emerge. The religion of Jesus of Nazareth originated in Palestine and Syria, and first reached Rome in the reign of Augustus. During the last years of the 1C and the early years of the 2C, the Christian Church became organised, but transgressed the law from the beginning because the Emperor embodied religious power. It was not until the **Edict of Milan** (313), which allowed Christians to practise their religion openly, and the conversion of **Constantine** (314), that the Church could come out into the open.

From the first days of Christianity, the bishop was Christ's representative on earth. Gradually the name "Pope", once used for all pontiffs, was reserved for the Bishop of the Empire's capital alone. For 19 centuries, these leaders have influenced the history of Christianity and given the Eternal City its character.

Address Book

GETTING THERE

By car – Driving in Rome is not advisable as parking in the city can be a major problem (visitors should note that most of the hotels in the city centre do not have private garages or parking). The few private car parks that do exist are extremely expensive and access to the city centre by car is severely restricted (a special permit is required). There are two large underground car parks in central Rome: under the Villa Borghese gardens, near the Porta Pinciana, and Parking Ludovisi, Via Ludovisi 60. Most city traffic makes use of two ring roads: the outer ring road (Grande Raccordo Anulare), lies on the outskirts of the city at a junction of main national roads as well as A 1, A 2, A 24, A 18 motorways; the second ring-road is the Tangenziale Est which forms part of the traffic network within the city. It connects the Olympic stadium to Piazza San Giovanni in Laterano, passing through the eastern quarters of the city (Nomentano, Tiburtino, Prenestino).

By train – The mainline national and international trains arrive at Stazione Termini or Tiburtina, which are linked to the city centre on both Metro lines A and B. *For information contact: ☏89 20 21, or consult the website www.trenitalia.com.*

By air – The main airport is Leonardo da Vinci, at Fiumicino (26km/16mi southwest of Rome; www.adr.it). It is linked to the centre by train, with services from Stazione Termini (9.50 €), and from the stations at Tiburtina, Tuscolana, Ostiense (line FM 5€). There is also a night bus service to the airport from Stazione Tiburtina (45min).

GETTING ABOUT

By taxi – Radiotaxi telephone numbers are: ☏*06 66 45, 06 49 94, 06 55 51. 06 35 70, 06 41 57. Use only the official metered taxis, usually painted white.*

By bus, tram or underground – City route plans are on sale in bookshops and kiosks; the plan Rete dei Trasporti Urbani di Roma, published by ATAC *(Azienda Tramvie e Autobus del Comune di Roma, ☏06 46 951),* is sold at the information kiosk in Piazza dei Cinque-cento. Tickets should be purchased before the beginning of the journey and punched in the machine in the bus and on the underground to be validated. Different tickets are available, including the BIT *(valid for 75min; 1€)*, BIG *(valid until noon on the day stamped; 4€)* Tickets are also available for three-day and weekly periods.

SIGHTSEEING

The city of Rome has information booths located at strategic points of the city centre (Largo Goldoni, Piazza Sonnino, Piazza Cinque Lune, corner of Via Minghetti (zona Fontana di Trevi). These offer information on all cultural and tourist events in the capital. Open Tuesday to Saturday from 10am to 6pm and on Sundays from 10am to 1pm, up-to-the-minute information is provided.
Internet users can visit the website: www.comune.roma.it
Combined tickets – The Roma Archeologia Card *(20€, valid 7 days)* includes entrance to the following museums and monuments: Museo Nazionale Romano *(Palazzo Massimo alle Terme, Terme di Diocleziano, Palazzo Altemps and Crypta Balbi),* the Colosseum, Palatino, Terme di Caracalla, Tomba di Cecilia Metella and Villa dei Quintili. The card can be purchased at the relevant sites *(with the exception of Tomba di Cecilia Metella and Villa dei Quintili)* and from the information centre on Via Parigi 5. There is also a combined ticket for the museums of the Museo Nazionale Romano *(Museum Card 6€, valid for 7 days).*
For coin ranges see the Legend on the cover flap.

B. Pérousse/MICHELIN

WHERE TO STAY

Visitors can book hotel rooms through the **Hotel Reservation Service**, ☎06 69 91 000, www.hotelreservation.it. This service offers a choice of 500 hotels in the capital. Visitors booking any of these hotels may also take advantage of a shuttle service from Fiumicino airport, at a cost of €12.50 per person.

For accommodation in convents and monasteries contact the Peregrinatio ad Petri Sedem, **Piazza Pio XII 4** (Vaticano – San Pietro district), ☎06 69 88 48 96; Fax 06 69 88 56 17 or **CITS** (Centro Italiano Turismo Sociale), Viale Monte Oppio 28, ☎06 48 73 145, 06 47 44 090; Fax 06 47 44 432.

SELECTING A DISTRICT

A good selection of pensioni and hotels can be found in the **historic centre**, where the atmosphere and high concentration of tourist sights and shops make it particularly popular with visitors; however, many of these establishments have limited capacity and as a result are often full. The attractive village-like quarter of **Trastevere**, with its lively nightlife, would also be a pleasant area in which to stay, although accommodation options here are somewhat limited.

The **Vatican and Prati** districts are close to the centre and are quieter and more reasonably priced than the historic centre and Trastevere (especially the Prati district, which has a good choice of hotels). The choice of accommodation around **Via Cavour** (near the Rione Monti district), between **Termini Station** and the Fori Imperiali, is also good for mid-range hotels. Many of the cheaper pensioni and smaller hotels are concentrated in the area around Termini Station. The majority of the city's luxury hotels can be found on the Via Veneto and in the area around Villa Borghese.

⊖**Pensione Ottaviano** – Via Ottaviano 6, Vatican district – ☎06 39 73 81 38 – www.pensioneottaviano.com – ⊟ – 25 rooms. Particularly popular with young foreign visitors, this cheerful pensione is decorated with paintings and posters left by previous guests. After 8.30pm guests can check their e-mail free of charge. Breakfast not available.

⊖**Hotel Pensione Tizi** – Via Collina 48, Porta Pia district – ☎06 48 20 128 – Fax 06 47 43 266 – ⊟ – 25 rooms. – ⊠ The lobby of this small pensione is similar to the entrance hall in houses belonging to a typical Roman family. The hotel is named after the owner's daughter, Tiziana, who is usually at reception to welcome guests. Quiet, attractive rooms, both with and without bathrooms. Good value for money.

⊖**Accommodation Planet 29** – Via Gaeta 29, Termini district – ☎06 48 65 20 – http://planet29.hotelinroma.com – ⊠. This simple hotel, run by a family with a passion for art, is popular with tourists and business travellers alike.

⊖**A Roma San Pietro Bed & Breakfast** – Via Crescenzio 85, Vatican district – ☎06 68 78 205 – Fax 06 68 13 19 32 – ftraldi@tiscali.it – 6 rooms – ⊠. This simple hotel with just half a dozen rooms enjoys an excellent location near the Vatican.

⊖⊖**Bed & Breakfast Maximum** – Via Fabio Massimo 72, Vatican district – ☎06 32 42 037 – Fax 06 32 42 156 – bbmaximum@tiscalinet.it – ⊟ – 4 rooms. ⊠. This B&B situated close to St Peter's offers colourful rooms fitted with ceiling fans. The rooms and bathrooms, one of which has a hydromassage tub, are arranged allong an arched corridor. Breakfast is served in the rooms.

⊖⊖**Pensione Panda** – Via della Croce 35, Piazza di Spagna district – ☎06 67 80 179 – Fax 06 69 94 21 51 – www.pensionepanda.com – 20 rooms.. This well-kept pensione in a 17C palazzo not far from the Spanish Steps has quiet, simply furnished rooms, some with shared bathroom. Although lacking in overall charm, the hotel is recommended for its excellent location and reasonable rates.

⊖⊖**Hotel Perugia** – Via del Colosseo 7, Colosseo district – ☎06 67 97 200 – Fax 06 67 84 635 – htlperugia@iol.it – 13 rooms. ⊠. Given its excellent location close to the Colosseum, this small hotel is reasonably priced. One of the rooms on the fourth floor has a small balcony with views of the amphitheatre.

Hotel Trastevere Manara – *Via Luciano Manara 24/A-25, Trastevere district – ☎06 58 14 713 – Fax 06 58 81 016 – hoteltrastevere@tiscalinet.it – 9 rooms.* An excellent location, just a stone's throw from the attractive Piazza Santa Maria in Trastevere. The hotel rooms, all furnished in modern style, include individual safety deposit boxes.

Hotel Navona – *Via dei Sediari 8, Piazza Navona district – ☎06 68 64 203 – www.hotelnavona.com – 30 rooms.* This delightful hotel has cool, attractive rooms decorated in English style. The hotel is located in a 16C palazzo which was built on top of much older foundations. Breakfast is served at a long table.

Hotel Due Torri – *Vicolo del Leonetto 23, Piazza Navona district – ☎06 68 76 983 – www.hotelduetorre.com – 26 rooms.* Once the residence of high prelates, this delightful centrally located hotel is situated in a quiet, attractive street. Each room has its own unique decor and is furnished with a parquet floor and high quality furniture, including some genuine antiques. One of our favourite addresses in Rome.

Hotel Lord Byron – *Via De Notaris 5, Parioli district – ☎06 32 20 404 – www.lordbyronhotel.com – 27 rooms.* This small, elegant hotel overlooks the Villa Borghese gardens and has an attractive 1920s atmosphere. The hotel restaurant, the Relais Le Jardin, serves fine cuisine.

WHERE TO EAT

PIZZERIAS

Al Forno della Soffitta – *Via dei Villini 1e, Porta Pia district – ☎06 44 04 642 – Closed Sun morning.* Genuine Neapolitan pizza is the speciality of this restaurant, where all the ingredients used come from the Campania region. Neapolitan-style pizzas have a rim and are thicker than the Roman variety. They are served on a round, wooden board, then cut into segments, each covered with the different ingredients chosen.

Da Baffetto – *Via del Governo Vecchio 114, Piazza Navona district – ☎06 68 61 617.* Excellent crispy pizza served in a traditional pizzeria that has been popular with students since the 1960s. Expect to queue, but once you're seated the service is remarkably swift.

Est Est Est – *Via Genova 32, Quirinale district – ☎06 48 81 107 – Closed Mon and Aug.* One of the oldest pizzerias in Rome, it is known for its interior decor dating from the beginning of the 20C, and for the small cherub shown pouring the so-called "mayor's water". The white wine which gives its name to the restaurant is highly recommended.

RESTAURANTS AND TRATTORIAS

Filetti di Baccalà – *Largo dei Librari 88, Piazza Navona district – ☎06 68 64 018 – Closed Sun and Aug.* A typical local trattoria, with simple decor and a warm atmosphere. As the name suggests, the house speciality is dried cod (baccalà), which is served breaded and fried, accompanied by a traditional side dish of salad flavoured with garlic and anchovies (puntarelle).

Enoteca La Bottega del Vino da Anacleto Bleve – *Via S. Maria del Pianto 9/a, Torre Argentina district – ☎06 68 65 970 – Closed evenings and public holidays – Booking recommended.* This wine bar is situated in the heart of the Jewish quarter. Before sitting down, choose from the delicate soufflés, roulades, salads and cheeses displayed at the bar. Delicious lemon or coffee ice cream. Family run with attentive service.

Augusto – *Piazza de' Renzi 15, Trastevere district – ☎06 58 03 798 – Closed Sat evening and Sun, one week in Feb, mid-Aug to mid-Sep.* During the summer this family-run restaurant has large wooden tables outside, overlooking one of the most typical squares in this district. The food here is simple and the atmosphere warm and informal. Expect to wait for a table.

Da Lucia – *Vicolo del Mattonato 2, Trastevere district – ☎06 58 03 601 – Closed Mon, two weeks in Aug and one week at Christmas – Booking recommended.* This simple restaurant, founded in 1938, serves traditional Roman cuisine. Dishes include the local spaghetti *cacio e pepe*, spaghetti *alla gricia*, gnocchi and baccalà.

Eau Vive – *Via Monterone 85, Pantheon district* – ☎06 68 80 10 95 – *eauvive@pcn.ne* – *Closed Sun and Aug* – *Booking recommended* . This restaurant is run by missionary nuns of different nationalities and is located inside the 16C Palazzo Lante, near the Pantheon. French specialities can be sampled in the large, frescoed dining room on the first floor.

Trattoria dal Cavalier Gino – *Vicolo Rosini 4, Montecitorio district* – ☎06 68 73 434 – *Closed Sun and Aug* – 🚭. A friendly atmosphere and good food at affordable prices make this trattoria a popular choice with office workers of the surrounding neighbourhood. For this reason, and because of the restaurant's limited capacity, it can be difficult to get a table here at lunchtime.

Ditirambo – *Piazza della Cancelleria 74, Campo dei Fiori district* – ☎06 68 71 626 – *Closed Mon lunchtime and Aug* – 🚭 – *Booking recommended*. Situated directly behind Campo dei Fiori, this friendly restaurant has two small, well-furnished rooms where a range of sophisticated dishes are served. The different types of bread, the pasta and the desserts are home-made. A popular choice.

La Penna d' Oca – *Via della Penna 53, Piazza del Popolo district* – ☎06 32 02 898 – *Closed lunchtime, Sun, for 10 days in Jan and 20 days in Aug* – *Booking recommended*. Not far from Piazza del Popolo, this charming restaurant serves traditional cuisine, innovative fish and seafood dishes, savoury pies and home-made bread and soup. Meals are served on a pleasant veranda in summer.

Checchino dal 1887 – *Via Monte Testaccio 30, Testaccio district* – ☎06 57 46 318 – *checchino-roma@tin.it* – *Closed 24 Dec-2 Jan, Aug, Sun and Mon* – 🚭 – *Booking recommended*. A good address for quality Roman cuisine, accompanied by the best Italian wines. Specialities include *rigatoni all pajata*, sweetbreads in a white wine sauce and oxtail. Cheaper meals based on cheese and vegetables available at lunchtime.

Sora Lella – *Via di Ponte Quattro Capi 16, Torre Argentina district* – ☎06 68 61 601 – *www.soralella.com* – *Closed Sun, 1 Jan, Easter, Aug and 24-26 Dec.* – 🍽. This famous restaurant was once run by Lella Fabrizi, the sister of the actor Aldo. It is now managed by her son, who has extended the traditional range of family recipes to include new specialities. Don't miss the *formaggi alle marmellate* (cheese with sweet fruit jelly) and the home-made desserts.

La Pergola – *Via Cadlolo 101, Vatican district* – ☎06 35 09 21 52 – *district* – ☎06 35 09 21 52 – *www. cavalieri-hilton.it* – *Closed Sun, Mon, lunchtimes, Jan and two weeks in Aug* – 🍽 – *Booking recommended*. Located in the roof garden of the Cavalieri Hilton Hotel, this elegant restaurant offers modern, innovative cuisine with attention to detail and impeccable service. The magnificent panorama of Rome is one of the most evocative views in Italy.

TAKING A BREAK

Antico Caffè della Pace – *Via della Pace 5, Piazza Navona district* – ☎06 68 61 216 – *Closed Mon morning and for a week in mid-Aug*. Situated in a lovely little square near the main piazza, the two rooms inside this café have a Central European feel, with padded sofas, soft lights and tinted mirrors.

Caffè Greco – *Via dei Condotti 86, Piazza di Spagna district* – ☎06 67 91 700. The café was founded by a Greek in 1760 and was frequented by writers and artists such as Goethe, Berlioz, Leopardi, D'Annunzio, Andersen and Stendhal, whose last Roman residence was at no 48. On 24 March 1824, Pope Leo XII forbade his citizens to enter the café, subject to a term of three months' imprisonment. This decision proved so unpopular that the café owner continued to serve customers through an opening in the window. The long, narrow, inner room known as the "omnibus" contains portraits of famous people.

Il Gelato di S. Crispino – *Via della Panetteria 42, Fontana di Trevi district* – ☎06 67 93 924 – *www.ilgelatodisancrispino.com – Closed Tue*. The owners of this gelateria, considered to be one of the best in Rome, only make flavours that they like themselves. Try the ice cream with honey, ginger and cinnamon, cream with Armagnac, liquorice, meringue with hazelnut or chocolate and cream with Pantelleria raisin wine.

Rosati – *Piazza del Popolo 5 – ☎06 32 25 859 – 7.30am-midnight.* This traditional, elegant café/restaurant and terrace is situated right on the piazza and is a pleasant meeting-place.

Sant'Eustachio Il Caffé – *Piazza S. Eustachio 82, Pantheon district – ☎06 68 61 309 – www.santeustachioilcaffe.it – 8.30am-1am.* This café is famous for its creamy coffee known as a gran caffè speciale, the secret recipe of which is jealously guarded by its creator. Let the waiter know if you prefer coffee unsweetened *(senza zucchero)*, as it's served with the sugar already added.

GOING OUT

Nightlife in Rome is mainly concentrated in three areas. The district between **Piazza Campo dei Fiori** and **Piazza Navona** has a wide choice of pubs and bars, drawing a mix of young students, foreign tourists and the theatre crowd. On the streets of **Trastevere**, the bars and restaurants are generally typically Roman in character and host shows with live music. The majority of the city's most popular nightclubs are concentrated in the Testaccio district, particularly in Via di Monte Testaccio, and more recently, in the nearby Via di Libetta.

Big Mama – *Vicolo S. Francesco a Ripa 18, Trastevere district – ☎06 58 12 551 – www.bigmama.it – Closed Mon and mid-Jun to mid-Sep.* For more than 10 years, this nightclub has been a venue for some of the world's best blues and jazz musicians.

Goa – *Via di Libetta 13, Piramide Cestia-Testaccio district – ☎06 57 48 277 – Closed Mon.* This large loft, in a street lined with bars and clubs, is now one of the most popular nightclubs in the area, largely the result of the well-known DJs who perform here.

Jonathan's Angels – *Via della Fossa 16, Piazza Navona district – ☎06 68 93 426.* It's often difficult to find a seat in this popular piano bar, which is deliberately kitsch in style and decorated with paintings by the owner, an enigmatic figure who dominates from behind the till.

It's worth a visit to the toilets to admire the decor.

Vineria Reggio – *Piazza Campo dei Fiori 15 – ☎06 68 80 32 68 – Closed Sun morning.* Situated opposite the statue of Giordano Bruno, this typical wine bar, has wooden benches in front of the long bar and its outdoor terrace.

SHOPPING

FASHION

Many luxury stores are located in **Via Veneto**, while some of the best-known names in the Italian fashion world can be found in the area between **Via del Corso** and **Piazza di Spagna**, especially in Via Frattina, Via Borgognona (Laura Biagiotti, Versace, Fendi etc) and Via Bocca di Leone (Versace). Particularly worthy of mention in this district is **Bulgari**, one of the original goldsmiths in Rome, which is situated on **Via dei Condotti**. Other famous names in this district include Armani, Gucci, Prada and Valentino.

MARKETS

Mercato di Via Sannio – *Via Sannio, San Giovanni in Laterano district – Mon-Sat, 10am-1pm.* A choice of new and second-hand clothes.

Porta Portese – *Trastevere district – Sun, from dawn to 2pm.* This market sells a bit of everything and is often referred to as the flea market. It opened officially during the Second World War, formed by stalls from other local markets, and is held along Via Portuense.

In the 11C **Gregory VII** restored order to the Christian Church, which had by then an appalling reputation. He dealt with two scourges: the buying and selling of church property, and the marriage of the clergy. In so doing he started the **Investiture Controversy**, which set in opposition the Sovereign Pontiff and the Holy Roman Emperor.

During the Renaissance, numerous popes patronised the arts, bringing to their court such artists as Raphael and Michelangelo, whose genius contributed to the embellishment of the capital. They included Pius II, Sixtus IV (who built the Sistine Chapel, Santa Maria della Pace and Santa Maria del Popolo), Julius II (who commissioned Michelangelo to decorate the ceiling of the Sistine Chapel), Leo X (who had a great personal fortune and nominated Raphael as intendant of the arts), Clement VII, Sixtus V (a great builder) and Paul III who built the Farnese Palace.

The French, Spanish and Austrians ruled, prior to the Unification of Italy in 1871. Giuseppe Garibaldi led the revolt that led to the new state. Rome was – and still is – its capital. The World Wars and the rise of Facist Dictator Benito Mussolini brought hardship and horrors to Rome. The climate of fear continued during the 1970s and 80s, as communists and conservatives vied for power, often employing terrorist tactics. Recent decades have seen calm and safety once again restored to this magnificent city.

Main Sights

No other city in the world has such a wealth of Classical antiquities, medieval buildings, Renaissance palaces and Baroque churches. With this in mind, a minimum stay of two or three days is recommended. The following paragraphs give general information on some 20 of the best-known sights. The section entitled "Additional Sights" lists by type other highlights.

Campidoglio★★★

On the hill that symbolised the power of ancient Rome, there now stand the city's administrative offices, the church of Santa Maria d'Aracoeli, Piazza del Campidoglio and its palaces, and pleasant gardens. The Capitoline was known as the *caput mundi* in ancient times. The **view**★★★ over the Roman Forum is superb, especially at night.

Chiesa di Santa Maria d'Aracoeli★★

The church has a lovely staircase built as a votive offering after the plague

of 1346, and a beautiful, austere façade. It was built in 1250 on the spot where the Sibyl of Tibur (Tivoli) announced the coming of Christ to Augustus. In the first chapel on the right are **frescoes**★ painted by Pinturicchio in about 1485.

Piazza del Campidoglio★★★

Michalangelo masterminded the exquisite square – framed by three palaces and a balustrade with statues of the Heavenly Twins or Dioscuri – from 1536 onwards. Its crowning glory is an equestrian statue of the Emperor Marcus Aurelius, celebrated on Italy's version of the €0.50 coin. The Capitoline Museums now house the original sculpture.

Musei Capitolini★★★

Open daily 9am-8pm (ticket office closes 7pm). Closed Mon, 1 Jan, 1 May, 24-25 Dec. 6.20€, 10€ combined ticket with Centrale Montemartini (valid for 7 days). 06 39 96 78 00; www.musei capitolini.org.

The museums are housed in the **Palazzo Nuovo** (New Palace), built in 1655 by Girolamo Rainaldi, the 12C **Palazzo Senatorio**, remodelled between 1582 and 1602 by Giacomo della Porta and Girolamo Rainaldi, and the **Palazzo dei Conservatori**. Some sections of the collection, particularly the Roman remains, are housed in the **Centrale Montemartini**★★, at Viale Ostiense 106. *Open daily 9.30am-6.30pm. Closed Mon, 1 Jan, 1 May, 24-25 and 31 Dec. 6.50€, 10€ combined ticket with Musei Capitolini (valid for 7 days). 06 39 96 78 00.*

Of note in the Palazzo Nuovo are the **equestrian statue of Marcus Aurelius**★★ (late 2C); the **Dying Gaul**★★★, a Roman sculpture based on a bronze of the Pergamum school (3C-2C BC); the **Sala degli Imperatori**★★ (Emperors' Room) with portraits of all the emperors; the **Capitoline Venus**★★, a Roman work inspired by the Venus of Cnidus by Praxiteles; and the **Mosaic of the Doves**★★ from Hadrian's Villa at Tivoli. The Palazzo dei Conservatori, built in the 15C and remodelled in 1568 by Giacomo della Porta, houses the **She-Wolf**★★★

The Dioscuri and the Palazzo Senatorio

(6C-5C BC), the **Boy Extracting a Thorn**★★, a Greek original or a very good copy dating to the 1C BC, and a **Bust of Junius Brutus**★★, a remarkable head dating from the 3C BC placed on a bust in the Renaissance period. The picture gallery or **pinacoteca**★ *(2nd floor)* contains mainly 14C to 17C paintings (Titian, Caravaggio, Rubens, Guercino, Reni).

From Via del Campidoglio there is a beautiful **view**★★★ of the ruins. The excellent cafe in Palazzo Caffarelli (behind the Palazzo dei Conservatori) unfurls a vista in the opposite direction and is accessible without a ticket.

Terme di Caracalla★★★ (Baths of Caracalla)

&. ⏰*Open daily 9am-1hr before dusk.* ⏰*Closed Mon pm, 1 Jan, 25 Dec. Tours with archaeologist available Sat-Sun at 10.30am and noon; book in advance.* ✆*5€. ☎06 39 96 77 00; www.pierreci.it* These baths built by Caracalla in AD 212 extend over more than 11ha/27 acres and could take 1 600 bathers at a time. The main rooms (*caldarium, tepidarium* and *frigidarium*) occupy the middle part of the central section; the secondary rooms (vestibule, palaestra and *laconicum*) are symetrically positioned at the sides. The ruined caldarium for the very hot bath, a circular room (34m/112ft in diameter), is the setting for operatic performances in summer.

Catacombe★★★

There are numerous underground Christian cemeteries alongside the Via **Appia Antica**★★. In use from the 2C they were rediscovered in the 16C and 19C. They consist of long galleries radiating from an underground burial chamber (hypogeum) which belonged to a noble Roman family of the Christian faith. They permitted fellow Christians to use the galleries. The decorations of the catacombs (carvings or paintings of symbolic motifs) are precious examples of early Christian art.

▶ *The 110 bus passes many of catacombs, as does the Archaeobus, which departs from Piazza Venezia and circles 14 major sites each hour.* **Kids** *Cycle along the traffic-free Via Appia on Sundays. Rental shops around the* Sede il Parco *(Park Seat).* ⏏*The visitor with little time to spare should visit the following catacombs:*

Catacombe di San Callisto★★★ (*Via Appia Antica 110,* ☎06 51 30 15 80), **Catacombe di San Sebastiano**★★★, (*Via Appia Antica 136,* ☎06 78 50 350), **Catacombe di Domitilla**★★★ (*Via delle Sette Chiese 282,* ☎06 51 10 342). *Guided tours only (45min), available in several languages,* ⏰*8.30am-noon and 2.30-5.30pm (5pm in winter). 5 €.* ⏰*Closed: San Callisto, Wed and Feb; San Sebastiano, Sun and 10 Nov-10 Dec; Domitilla, Tue and Jan.*

Castel Sant'Angelo★★★

🕐 *Open daily except Mon 9am-7pm.*
🕐 *Closed 1 Jan, 25 Dec.* 👓 *5€.* ☎ *06 39 96 76 00; www.pierreci.it*

The imposing fortress was built in AD 135 as a mausoleum for the Emperor Hadrian and his family. In the 6C, Gregory the Great erected a chapel on top of the mausoleum to commemorate the apparition of an angel who, by putting his sword back into its sheath, announced the end of a plague. In the 15C Nicholas V added a brick storey to the ancient building and corner towers to the surrounding wall. Alexander VI (1492-1503) added octagonal bastions. In 1527, during the sack of Rome, Clement VII took refuge in the castle and installed an apartment which was later embellished by Paul III; the **Popes' Apartment**★ stands isolated at the summit of the fortress and testifies to the graciousness of the popes' life style.

A long passageway (Il Passetto) links the fortress to the Vatican palaces. A fine spiral ramp dating from antiquity leads to the castle. From a terrace at the summit there is a splendid **panorama**★★★ of the whole town. The Castel Sant'Angelo is linked to the left bank of the Tiber by

The angel standing watch over Castel Sant'Angelo

L. Pessina/MICHELINO

the graceful **Ponte Sant'Angelo**★, which is adorned with Baroque angels by Bernini and with statues of St Peter and St Paul (16C).

Domus Aurea★★

Entrance on Viale Domus Aurea, below the gardens of Colle Oppio. ♿🕐 *Open daily except Tue, 9am-7.45pm (ticket office closes 6.45pm).* 🕐 *Closed 1 Jan, 25 Dec.* 👓 *5€ + 1.50€ for reservation (required).* ☎ *06 39 96 77 00; www.pierreci.it.*

This was the luxurious residence erected by Nero after the fire of AD 64. The grotto-like underground rooms are decorated with geometric designs, grapes, faces and animals. These "grotesques" were a great source of inspiration to Renaissance artists.

Colosseo★★★ (Colosseum)

♿🕐 *Open daily 9am-1hr before dusk.* 🕐 *Closed 1 Jan, 25 Dec.* 👓 *€11 including Palatino. Visit the ruins on the hill first, then – combination ticket in hand – bypass the summer crowds outside the Colosseum kiosks.* ☎ *06 39 96 77 00; www.pierreci.it.*

This amphitheatre, inaugurated in AD 80, is also known as the Flavian Amphitheatre after its initiator, Vespasian, first of the Flavian emperors. It took the name of the Colosseum either because it stood near the huge bronze statue of Nero, the Colosseum, which was 36m/120ft high (its position is marked by a few slabs of stone on the ground near the beginning of Via dei Fori Imperiali), or because of its own colossal dimensions (527m/576yds in circumference and 57m/187ft high). With its three superimposed Classical orders (Doric, Ionic and Corinthian), it is a masterpiece of classical architecture. The projections supported wooden poles inserted through holes in the upper cornice: the poles carried a linen awning which could be extended over the amphitheatre to protect the spectators from sun or rain. In all there was probably space for about 50 000 spectators. Fights between men and beasts, gladiatorial contests, races and mock naval battles took place in the arena. The excavations revealed an underground warren where the wild animals waited before being brought to the surface by a system of ramps and lifts.

Now an integral part of the Coliseum, the **arco di Costantino**★★★ is an arch erected to commemorate Constantine's victory over Maxentius in AD 315. Some of the low reliefs were removed from other 2C monuments erected in honour of Trajan, Hadrian and Marcus Aurelius.

Fori Imperiali★★★

To visit the Imperial Fora, contact the Visitor Center dei Fori Imperiali (in front of the Chiesa dei S.S. Cosma e Damiano), which organises guided tours and audio-guides of the sites. The centre also displays useful information panels relating to the site. ◷*Open daily except Mon, 9.30am-6.30pm.* ◷*Closed 1 Jan, 2 Jun, 25 Dec.* ☎*06 67 97 702; www.capi tolium.org*

Caesar, Augustus, Trajan, Nerva and Vespasian built these forums, though hardly any remains of the latter two's efforts. The Via dei Fori Imperiali, laid out in 1932 by Mussolini, divides the imperial forums.

The **Mercati Traianei**★★, which have kept their semicircular façade, were a distribution and supply centre as well as a retail market. They comprised about 150 shops. ♿◷*Open daily except Mon, 9am-6.30pm (4.30pm in winter).* ◷*Closed 1 Jan, 1 May, 25 Dec, afternoons of public holidays.* ☞*6.20€. Torre delle Milizie: open by prior arrangement only.* ☎ *06 67 90 048; www.comune.roma. it/cultura.*

The **Torre delle Milizie**★ (Tower of the Militia) is part of a 13C fortress. All that remains of the finest of the imperial forums, **Foro di Traiano**★★★ (Trajan's Forum), is the **Colonna Traiana**★★★ (Trajan's column) which depicts, in over 100 scenes, episodes of the war waged by Trajan against the Dacians. It is an unrivalled masterpiece.

Of the Augustan Forum, **Foro di Augusto**★★ *(view from Via Alessandrina)*, there remain a few columns of the Temple of Mars the Avenger, and vestiges of the stairway and of the wall enclosing the forum (behind the temple). The forum is dominated by the House of the Knights of Rhodes (Casa dei Cavalieri di Rodi), built in the Middle Ages and rebuilt in the 15C amid the ancient ruins. Of Caesar's Forum, the **Foro di Cesare**★★ (view from Via del Tulliano), there remain three lovely columns from the Temple of Venus Genitrix.

Foro Romano★★★

The public toilets (poorly signposted) are near the Temple of Castor and Pollux. ♿◷*Open daily 9am-1hr before dusk.* ◷*Closed 1 Jan, 25 Dec.*☎*06 39 96 77 00; www.pierreci.it; www.capitolium.org.*

The remains of the Roman Forum, the religious, political and commercial centre of ancient Rome, reflect the 12 centuries of history that created Roman civilisation. The forum was excavated in the 19C and 20C.

The **Basilica Emilia** was the second basilica to be built in Rome (170 BC).

Take the Sacred Way, **Via Sacra**★, along which victorious generals marched in triumph to the **Curia**★★, rebuilt in the 3C by Diocletian. Senate meetings were held here; nowadays it houses the **Plutei di Traiano**★★), low reliefs sculpted low-relief panels depicting scenes from the life of the Emperor Trajan, and sacrificial animals.

After the Romans attacked Antium (modern Anzio) in 338 BC and captured the prows (*rostra*) of the enemy ships which they fixed to the **orators' platform**★; this then became known as the Rostra.

Nearby rises an imposing Triumphal Arch, **Arco di Settimio Severo**★★, built in AD 203 to commemorate the Emperor's victories over the Parthians. At the foot of the Capitol stood some remarkable monuments: the late 1C **Tempio di Vespasiano**★★ (Temple of Vespasian) of which only three elegant Corinthian columns remain; the **Tempio du Saturno**★★★ (Temple of Saturn) which retains eight 4C columns; and the **Portico degli Dei Consentis**★, a colonnade of pillars with Corinthian columns dating back to restoration work of AD 367 – the portico was dedicated to the 12 principal Roman deities.

The **Colonna di Foca**★ (Column of Phocas) was erected in AD 608 in honour of the Byzantine Emperor Phocas who presented the Pantheon to Pope Boniface IV. The **Basilica Giulia**★★, which has five aisles, was built by Julius Caesar and completed by Augustus. It served as a law court and exchange.

Almost nothing is left of the **Tempio di Cesare** which started the cult of Emperor worship. It was consecrated by Octavian in 29 BC to the "god" Julius Caesar.

Three beautiful columns with Corinthian capitals remain of the **Tempio di Castore e Polluce**★★★ (Temple of Castor and Pollux). The circular **Tempio di Vesta**★★★ stands (Temple of Vesta) near the Casa delle Vestaliaaa (House of the Vestal Virgins).

The **Regia** was held to have been the residence of King Numa Pompilius, who succeeded Romulus and organised the State religion.

The **Tempio di Antonino e Faustina**★★ (Temple of Antoninus and Faustina) was dedicated to the Emperor Antoninus Pius and his wife (note the fresco of grotesques and candelabra). The temple now houses the church of San Lorenzo in Miranda rebuilt in the 17C.

The remains of the **Tempio di Romolo** (the Romulus to whom the temple is thought to be dedicated was not the founder of Rome but the son of the Emperor Maxentius who died in 307) include the concave façade and the bronze doors between two porphyry columns.

The grandiose **Basilica di Massenzio**★★ (Basilica of Maxentius) was completed by the Emperor Constantine. The **Arco di Tito**★★ (Triumphal Arch of Titus), erected in 81, commemorates the capture of Jerusalem by this emperor, who reigned for only two years.

Palatino★★★
Access from the Roman Forum or from Via S. Gregorio 30. ⚐⚐Open daily, 9am-1hr before dusk. ⚐Closed 1 Jan, 25 Dec. ⚐11€ combined ticket with Colosseum (lines for tickets are much shorter here). ☎06 39 96 77 00, www.pierreci.it. Book at least one day in advance for the Casa dei Grifi.

The **Palatine Hill**, where Romulus and Remus were discovered by the wolf, was chosen by Domitian as the site for the Imperial Palace. The **Domus Flavia**★ (or official state apartments) was made up of three main areas: the basilica, where the Emperor dispensed justice, the throne room and the *lararium*, the Emperor's private chapel. Also of note were the peristyle courtyard and the dining room or triclinium which opened onto two small leisure rooms, *nymphaea*. The rooms in the **Domus Augustana**★★ (private imperial apartments) are arranged around two peristyles on two floors. Then there was the **Stadium**★ designed to stage private games and spectacles for the Emperor.

The **Casa di Livia**★★ (House of Livia) (⚐ *closed for restoration at the time of writing*) probably belonged to Augustus (fine vestiges of paintings). The **Orti Farnesiani** (Farnese Gardens), laid out in the 16C on the site of Tiberius' palace,

It is hard to imagine the feverish activity that surrounded the forum and Capitol

Piazza di Spagna, one of the most atmospheric "stage sets" in Italy

J. Malburet/MICHELIN

afford **views**★★ of the Forum and town. *The Farnese Gardens offer a shady and beautiful place to walk.*

▶ *Leave the Palatine and head along Clivus Palatinus then turn into Via Sacra near the Arco di Tito.*

Tempio di Venere e di Roma★

The Temple of Venus and Rome, built between 121 and 136 by Hadrian, was the largest in the city (110m/361ft by 53m/174ft). It was unique in that it comprised two *cellae* with apses back to back. One was dedicated to the goddess of Rome and faced the Forum; the other was dedicated to Venus and faced the Colosseum.

Chiesa del Gesù★★★

The mother-church of the Jesuits in Rome, built by Vignola in 1568, is a typical building of the Counter-Reformation. On the outside, the engaged pillars replace the flat pilasters of the Renaissance, with light and shade effects and recesses. The interior, spacious and ideal for preaching, was lavishly decorated in the Baroque style: on the dome, the **Baciccia frescoes**★★ illustrate the *Triumph of the Name of Jesus* (1679); the **Cappella di Sant'Ignazio**★★★ *(north transept)*, a chapel where the remains of St Ignatius Loyola rest, is the work (1696-1700) of the Jesuit Brother Andrea Pozzo and is sumptuously decorated.

Pantheon★★★

The Pantheon, an ancient building perfectly preserved, founded by Agrippa in 27 BC and rebuilt by Hadrian (117-125), was a temple which was converted into a church in the 7C.
Access is through a porch supported by 16 single granite columns, all ancient except for three on the left. The doors are the original ones. The **interior**★★★, a masterpiece of harmony and majesty, is dominated by the **ancient dome**★★★, the diameter of which is equal to its height. The side chapels, adorned with alternately curved and triangular pediments, contain the tombs of the kings of Italy and that of Raphael *(on the left)*. *The Roma musicians that play in the Piazza della Rotunda.* Bernini's elephant obelisk outside Santa Maria Sopra Minerva, just southeast of the Pantheon.

Piazza del Popolo★★

The **Piazza del Popolo** was designed by Giuseppe Valadier (1762-1839). The **Porta del Popolo**★ was pierced in the Aurelian wall in the 3C, and adorned with an external façade in the 16C and with an inner façade designed by Bernini in the 17C.
The Renaissance church of **Santa Maria del Popolo**★★ was remodelled in the Baroque period. It contains 15C **frescoes**★ by Pinturicchio *(first chapel on the right)*; two **tombs**★ by Andrea Sansovino *(in the chancel)*; two **paintings**★★★ by **Caravaggio**: *the Crucifixion*

of St Peter and the Conversion of St Paul (first chapel to the left of the chancel); and the **Cappella Chigi**★ (2nd on the left), a chapel designed by Raphael. Leading off the Piazza del Popolo is the main street of central Rome, **Via del Corso**, lined with handsome Renaissance palaces and fashionable shops.

Pincio
This fine public park was laid out in the 19C by Giuseppe Valadier. It is bordered by the gardens of the Villa Borghese and affords a magnificent **view**★★★ particularly at dusk when the golden glow so typical of Rome is at its mellow best. Bike and pedal-car rentals, as well as the ethered hot air balloon in the Villa Borghese.

Piazza di Spagna★★★
This square, a popular tourist attraction, was so named in the 17C after the Spanish Embassy occupied the Palazzo di Spagna. It is dominated by the majestic **Spanish Steps**, the **Scalinata della Trinità dei Monti**★★★, built in the 18C by the architects De Sanctis and Specchi, who adopted the baroque style of perspective and trompe l'oeil. At the foot of the stairway are the **Fontana della Barcaccia**★ (Boat Fountain) by Bernini's father, Pietro (17C), and Keats' House where the poet died in 1821.
At the top of the stairs, the church of the **Trinità dei Monti**★ is the French church, built in the 16C and restored in the 19C. It contains a **Deposition from the Cross**★ (2nd chapel on the left) dating from 1541 by Daniele da Volterra, a great admirer of Michelangelo.
Leading off from this square is **Via dei Condotti** lined with elegant shops. It is also renowned for the Caffè Greco (see p 407), a famous establishment which was opened in 1760 and frequented by celebrities (Goethe, Berlioz, Wagner, Stendhal etc).

Piazza Navona★★★
The square built on the site of Domitian's stadium retains its shape. A pleasant and lively pedestrian precinct, it is adorned at the centre with Bernini's Baroque masterpiece, the **Fontana dei Fiumi**★★★ (Fountain of the Four Rivers), completed

in 1651. The statues represent the four rivers – Danube, Ganges, Rio de la Plata and Nile – symbolising the four corners of the earth.
Among the churches and palaces lining the square are **Sant'Agnese in Agone**★★ with a Baroque façade by Borromini and attractive **interior**★ on the plan of a Greek cross, and the adjoining 17C **Palazzo Pamphili**. A two-month winter fair celebrates Befana, the Christmas witch.

Piazza Venezia★
This Piazza in the centre of Rome is lined with palaces: Palazzo Venezia, Palazzo Bonaparte, where Napoleon's mother died in 1836, and the early-20C Palazzo delle Assicurazioni Generali di Venezia.

Palazzo Venezia★
Open daily except Mon, 8.30am-7.30pm. Closed 1 Jan, 1 May, 25 Dec. 4€. 06 32 81 01. The **basilica di San Marco**, which was incorporated within the palace in the 15C, has a fine Renaissance **façade**★ overlooking Piazza di San Marco. This palace, built by Pope Paul II (1464-71), is one of the first Renaissance buildings. A **museum**, on the first floor, presents collections of medieval art (ivories, Byzantine and Limousin enamels, Italian Primitive paintings on wood, gold and silver work, ceramics and small bronzes of the 15C-17C.

Monumento a Vittorio Emanuele II (Vittoriano)
Open daily 9.30am-5.30pm (4.30pm in winter). 06 69 91 718.
This much-criticised memorial by Giuseppe Sacconi, begun in 1885 in honour of the first king of a united Italy, Victor Emanuel II, overshadows the other monuments of Rome by its sheer size and dazzling white colour. It affords a **view**★★ of the Eternal City. Don't msis the great view from atop the monument.

Basilica di San Giovanni in Laterano★★★
St John Lateran, the cathedral of Rome, is among the four major basilicas in

Rome. The first basilica was founded by Constantine prior to St Peter's in the Vatican. It was rebuilt in the Baroque era by Borromini and again in the 18C.

The main façade by Alessandro Galilei dates from the 18C and the central door has bronze panels that originally belonged to the Curia of the Roman Forum. The grandiose interior has a 16C **ceiling**★★, restored in the 18C. In the nave the **Statues of the Apostles**★ by pupils of Bernini stand in niches. The **Cappella Corsinia** (first in the north aisle) was designed by Alessandro Galilei. The transept **ceiling**★★ dates from the end of the 16C.

The **Cappella del Santissimo Sacramento** (Chapel of the Blessed Sacrament – north transept) has fine ancient **columns**★ in gilded bronze. The pretty **cloisters**★ are by the Vassalletto (13C), marble-masons who were associates of the Cosmati. The **baptistery**★ is decorated with 5C and 7C mosaics.

In **Piazza di San Giovanni in Laterano** rises a 15C BC Egyptian obelisk, the tallest in Rome.

The **Palazzo Lateranense** (Lateran Palace), rebuilt in 1586, was the papal palace until the papal court returned from Avignon. The staircase, **Scala Sancta**, is a precious vestige from the medieval papal palace and is traditionally identified as the one Christ used in the palace of Pontius Pilate. Worshippers climb the stairs on their knees. At the top is the papal chapel, called the Sancta Sanctorum, with its many precious relics.

Basilica di Santa Maria Maggiore★★★

This is one of the four major basilicas in Rome. It was built by Pope Sixtus III (AD 432-440) and is dedicated to St Mary Major. It has since undergone extensive restoration. The campanile, erected in 1377, is the highest in Rome. The façade is the work of Ferdinando Fuga (1743-1750). The adjoining **loggia** is decorated with **mosaics**★ by Filippo Rusuti (end 13C), much restored in the 19C.

The **interior**★★★ contains remarkable **mosaics**★★★: in the nave, those above the entablature are among Rome's most ancient Christian mosaics (5C).

The coffered **ceiling**★ is said to have been gilded with the first gold brought from Peru. The floor, the work of the **Maestri Cosmati** (12C) was subject to much restoration in the 18C. The **Cappella di Sisto V** (south aisle) and the **Cappella Paolina** (north aisle) were both built in the form of a Greek cross and surmounted by a cupola. Another chapel was added at the end of the 16C and one in the 17C: they were richly decorated in the Baroque style. Popes Sixtus V, Pius V, Clement VIII and Paul V are buried here.

▷ *Leave the church by the door at the far end of the south aisle.*

From **Piazza dell'Esquilino**, with its Egyptian obelisk, there is a **view**★★ of the church's imposing 17C chevet.

Basilicia di San Paolo Fuori Le Mura★★

One of the four major basilicas, St Paul's "Outside the Walls", was built by Constantine in the 4C on the site of St Paul's tomb. It was rebuilt in the 19C, after it had been wholly destroyed by fire in 1823, on the original basilical plan of early Christian churches.

The impressive **interior**★★★ contains: an 11C bronze door cast in Constantinople *(at the entrance of the first south aisle)*; and a Gothic **ciborium**★★★ (1285) by Arnolfo di Cambio, placed on the high altar which stands above a marble plaque inscribed with the name Paul and dated 4C. In the **Cappella del Santissimo Sacramento**★ (Chapel of the Blessed Sacrament) *(left of the chancel)* are: a 14C wooden figure of Christ attributed to Pietro Cavallini; a statue of St Brigitta kneeling, by Stefano Maderno (17C); a 14C or 15C statue of St Paul; and the **paschal candelabrum**★★, a 12C Romanesque work by the Vassalletto. The **cloisters**★ are also attributed to this family of artists.

Fontana di Trevi★★★

A late-Baroque creation, the Trevi Fountain was commissioned from Nicola Salvi in 1762 by Pope Clement XIII. The central figure, the Ocean, rides in a chariot drawn by seahorses and tritons. Tourists continue the tradition of throwing two coins over their shoulders into the fountain – one coin to ensure their return to Rome and the other for the fulfilment of a wish. The money is donated to charities. *Watch your wallet in the thick crowds here.*

The Vatican

The Vatican City is bounded by a wall, overlooking Viale Vaticano, and to the east by the colonnade of St Peter's Square. This makes up the greater part of the Vatican state as laid down in 1929 in the Lateran Treaty. The Vatican City, now reduced to only 44ha/109 acres and with less than a thousand inhabitants, stems from the Papal States, a donation made in the 8C by Pepin the Short to Pope Stephen II, and lost in 1870 when Italy was united into one kingdom with Rome as its capital. The Vatican State, with the Pope as ruler, has its own flag and anthem and prints its own stamps. In 1970, Pope Paul VI dissolved the armed forces, retaining only the Swiss Guard who wear a colourful uniform said to have been designed by Michelangelo.

The Pope, who is the Head of State, is also the Supreme Head of the Universal Church, and from this very small State, the spiritual influence of the Church radiates throughout the world through the person of the Sovereign Pontiff. When the Pope is in residence, he grants **public audiences** on Wednesdays.

Giardini Vaticani★★★

€9. Reservations required at Vatican Museums. 06 69 88 44 66; www. vatican.va
The vast, magnificent gardens are adorned with fountains and statues, gifts from various countries.

Piazza San Pietro★★★

This architectural masterpiece was begun in 1656 by Bernini. The two semicircles of the colonnade which adorn the square and frame the façade of the basilica form an ensemble of remarkable sobriety and majesty. At the centre of the square stands a 1C BC obelisk brought from Heliopolis in Egypt to Rome in AD 37 by order of Caligula. It was erected here in 1585 on the initiative of Sixtus V by Domenico Fontana. At the top is a relic of the Holy Cross. *The speedy Vatican Post has an office on the piazza's south side.*

Basilica di San Pietro★★★

Michelangelo's Pietà.
Constantine, the first Christian Emperor, decided in AD 324 to build a basilica on the site where St Peter was buried after he had been martyred in Nero's circus. In the 15C it proved necessary to rebuild.

For two centuries, the plan of the new basilica was constantly revised. The plan, of a Greek cross surmounted by a dome designed by Bramante and adopted by Michelangelo, was altered to a Latin cross at the behest of Paul V in 1606, when he instructed Carlo Maderna to add two bays and a façade to Michelangelo's square plan. From 1629 onwards, the basilica was decorated in a sumptuous Baroque style by Bernini.

The **façade** (115m/377ft long and 45m/151ft high) was completed in 1614 by Carlo Maderna; it is surmounted by colossal figures. In the centre is the balcony from which the Sovereign Pontiff gives his benediction Urbi et Orbi (to the City and the World).

Under the **porch**, the first door on the left has bronze panels carved by Giacomo Manzù (1964); the bronze central door dates from the Renaissance (1455); the door on the right, or Holy Door, is opened and closed by the Pope to mark the beginning and end of a Jubilee Year.

Inside, it is customary to first approach the stoups in the nave which at first glance appear of normal size but are in fact huge. Such size emphasises the gigantic dimensions of the basilica, otherwise not apparent because of the harmony of its proportions. The length of St Peter's can be compared to that of other great basilicas throughout the world by means of markers inlaid in the pavement of the nave.

The first chapel on the right contains the **Pietà**★★★, the moving and powerful masterpiece carved by Michelangelo in 1499-1500, which shows his genius.

In the right aisle, adjoining the Cappella del SS Sacramento, **Gregory XIII's Monument**★ is adorned with low reliefs illustrating the institution of the Gregorian calendar devised by that pope. Immediately beyond the right transept, **Clement XIII's Monument** ★★★ is a fine neo-Classical design by Canova dating from 1792. The apse is dominated by the **Cattedra di San Pietro**★★★ (St Peter's Throne) by Bernini (1666), a great carved throne in bronze encasing a 4C episcopal chair but symbolically attributed to St Peter.

In the chancel on the right is **Urban VIII's Monument**★★★, again by Bernini (1647), a masterpiece of funerary art. On the left stands **Paul III's Monument**★★★ by Guglielmo della Porta (16C), a disciple of Michelangelo.

St Leo the Great's Altar (chapel to the left of the chancel) has a fine Baroque **altarpiece**★ carved in high relief by Algardi. Nearby, Alexander VII's Monumenta, characterised by extreme exuberance, is a late work by Bernini (1678) assisted by his pupils. The **baldaquin**★★★ which crowns the pontifical altar and is 29m/95ft tall (the height of the Farnese Palace) was strongly criticised: partly because the bronze had been taken from the Pantheon and partly because it was thought to be too theatrical and in bad taste.

The **dome**★★★ designed by Michelangelo, which he himself built as far as the lantern, was completed in 1593 by Giacomo della Porta and Domenico Fontana. From the **summit** (leave the basilica by the right aisle for access) there is a **view**★★★ of St Peter's Square, the Vatican City and Rome from the Janiculum to Monte Mario. ☉Open daily, Apr-Sep 8am-5.45pm, Oct-Mar 8am-4.45pm. ☞€5 in lift, 4€ on foot (over 300 steps up a narrow, one-way staircase). For information ☎06 69 88 16 62 (Centro Servizi-Informazioni).

The 13C bronze **Statue of St Peter**★★ overlooking the nave is attributed to Arnolfo di Cambio and is greatly venerated by pilgrims, who come to kiss its feet. **Innocent VIII's Monument**★★★ (between the second and third bays in the left aisle) is a Renaissance work (1498) by Antonio del Pollaiuolo. The **Stuart Monument** (between the first and second bays in the left aisle) carved by Canova is adorned with beautiful **angels**★ in low relief. The **Museo Storico**★ (Historical Museum) (entrance in the left aisle, opposite the Stuart Monument) has many treasured items from St Peter's. ☉Open daily, Apr-Sep 8.30am-6pm; Oct-Mar 8.30am-5pm. ☞5€. ☎06 69 88 16 62.

Musei Vaticani★★★

Entrance in Viale Vaticano. Queue early (or queue forever). ♿Two itineraries available for disabled visitors. Itinerary A: Classical and Etruscan antiquities. Itinerary B: Palazzi Vaticani – Pinacoteca. ☉Open Mar-Oct Mon-Fri, 8.45am-4.45pm (ticket office closes at 3.20pm), Sat, last Sun of the month and Nov-Feb, 8.45am-1.45pm (ticket office closes 12.20pm). ☉Closed Sun (except last Sun of month), 1 and 6 Jan, 11 Feb, 19 Mar, Easter and Easter Mon, 1 and 20 May, 10 and 29 Jun, 14-15 Aug, 1 Nov, 8, 25 and 26 Dec. Audioguide tours in various languages. ☞12€, no charge last Sun of the month. Loggia di Raffaello: open for specialists only. Museo delle Carrozze: open by prior arrangement. Bar, coffee shop and self-service facilities. ☎ 06 69 88 49 47; www.vatican.va

The museums of the Vatican occupy part of the palaces built by the popes from the 13C onwards, which have been extended and embellished to the present day.

These include on the first floor the **Museo Pio-Clementino**★★★ (Greek and Roman antiquities) with its masterpieces: the **Belvedere Torso**★★★ (1C BC), greatly admired by Michelangelo; the **Venus of Cnidus**★★, a Roman copy of Praxiteles' Venus; the **Laocoon Group**★★★, a 1C BC Hellenistic work; the **Apollo Belvedere**★★★, a 2C Roman copy; **Perseus**★★, a neo-Classical work by Canova, which was purchased by Pius VII; **Hermes**★★★, a 2C Roman work inspired by the work of Praxiteles; and the **Apoxyomenos**★★★, the athlete scraping his skin with a strigil after taking exercise, a 1C Roman copy of the Greek original by Lysippus.

B. Morandi/MICHELIN

Who will dare place a hand in the notorious Bocca della Verità?

The **Museo Etrusco**★, on the second floor, has a remarkable 7C BC gold **fibula**★★ adorned with lions and ducklings (Room II) and the **Mars**★★ found at Todi, a rare example of a large bronze statue from the 5C BC (Room III).

The **Sala della Biga** derives its name from the **two-horse chariot**★★ (*biga*), a 1C Roman work.

The four **Stanze di Rafaello**★★★ (Raphael Rooms), the private apartments of Julius II, were decorated by Raphael and his pupils from 1508 to 1517. The frescoes are remarkable: *the Borgo Fire, the School of Athens, Parnassus, the Expulsion of Heliodorus from the Temple, the Miracle of the Bolsena Mass and St Peter delivered from prison.* The **Collezione d'Arte Moderna Religiosa**★★ is displayed in the apartment of Pope Alexander VI.

On the first floor the **Cappella Sistina**★★★ (Sistine Chapel) is open to the public; its splendid vault, painted by **Michelangelo** from 1508 to 1512, illustrates episodes from the Bible, with the Creation, the Flood and, above the altar, the Last Judgement, which was added by the artist in 1534. The lowest sections of the side walls were decorated by Perugino, Pinturicchio and Botticelli. The **Pinacoteca**★★★ (Picture Gallery) also contains: three **compositions**★★★ by **Raphael** (*The Coronation of the Virgin, The Madonna of Foligno* and *The Transfiguration* – Room VIII); **St Jerome**★★ by Leonardo da Vinci (Room IX) and a

Descent from the Cross★★ by Caravaggio (Room XII).

Additional Sights

Churches: Chiesa Nuova★, S. Andrea al Quirinale★★, S. Andrea della Valle★ (façade★★, dome by Maderno★★), S. Agnese Fuori le Mura★, S. Agostino★ (*Madonna of the Pilgrims*★★★ by Caravaggio), S. Carlo alle Quattro Fontane★★, S. Cecilia in Trastevere★ (*Last Judgement*★★★ by Cavallini), S. Clemente★★ (mosaics★★★ in the apse), S. Ignazio★★, S. Lorenzo Fuori le Mura★★, S. Luigi dei Francesi★★ (works★★★ by Caravaggio), S. Maria degli Angeli★★, S. Maria in Cosmedin★★ ("Bocca della Verità"), S. Maria sopra Minerva★, S. Maria della Pace★, S. Maria in Trastevere★★ (Mosaics★★★ in the chancel), S. Maria della Vittoria★★ (Ecstasy of St Teresa★★★ by Bernini), S. Pietro in Montorio★ (Bramante's tempietto★★), S. Pietro in Vincoli★ (Moses★★★ by Michelangelo), S. Sabina★, S. Susanna★★.

Museums and palaces: Galleria Borghese★★★ (www.galleriaborghese.it), Museo Nazionale Romano★★★ (Palazzo Massimo alle Terme★★★, Palazzo Altemps★★★, Aula Ottagona★★★), Museo Nazionale di Villa Giulia★★★, Palazzo Barberini★★ (Galleria Nazionale di Arte Antica★★), Palazzo della Cancelleria★★, Palazzo Farnese★★ (www.farnese.net), Palazzo del Quirinale★★, Villa Farnesinaaa, Palazzo Braschi★ (Museo di Roma★), Palazzo Doria Pamphili★ (art gallery★★), Palazzo della Sapienza (S. Ivo★★), Palazzo Spada★, Galleria Nazionale d'Arte Moderna★.

Monuments from Antiquity: Ara Pacis Augustae★★, Area Sacra del Largo Argentina★★, Tempio di Apollo Sosiano★★, Piramide di Caio Cestio★, Tempio della Fortuna Virile★, Tempio di Vesta★, Tomba di Cecilia Metella★.

Squares, streets, parks and gardens: Piazza del Quirinale★★, Villa Borghese★★, Piazza Bocca della Verità★, Piazza Campo dei Fiori★, Piazza Colonna★(Colonna di Marco Aurelio★), Piazza S. Ignazio★, Porta S. Paolo★, Porta di S. Sebastiano★, Via dei Coronari★, E.U.R.★ (Museo della Civiltà Romana★★), Isola Tiberina★ (Ponte Fabricio★), Gianicolo★ (views★★★).

 See the *Green Guide Rome* for details.

Excursions

Castelli Romani★★

Castelli Romani, or Roman Castles, is the name given to the Alban Hills (Colli Albani), to the southeast of Rome. In the Middle Ages, while anarchy reigned in Rome, noble families sought refuge in the outlying villages. Each of these villages was set on the outer rim of an immense crater, itself pitted with secondary craters, some of which now contain lakes (Albano and Nemi).

Nowadays the Romans leave the capital in summer for the "Castelli" where they find walking trails and country inns.

Tour of the Castles

122km/76mi, allow half a day.

Leave Rome by the Via Appia in the direction of **Castel Gandolfo★★**, now the Pope's summer residence. It is thought that Castel Gandolfo was built on the site of ancient Alba Longa, the traditional and powerful rival of Rome. Their rivalry led to the famous combat of the Horatios for Rome and the Curiaces for Alba, as recounted by the Roman historian Livy. **Albano Laziale** was built on the site of Domitian's villa. Today the town boasts an attractive church, **Santa Maria della Rotonda★**, which has a Romanesque campanile, the **Villa Comunale★**, once a villa belonging to Pompey (106-48 BC). Close to Borgo Garibaldi is the **tomb of the Horatios and the Curiaces★**.

Velletri is a prosperous town lying south of the Alban Hills in the heart of a wine-producing region.

▶ *Take Via dei Laghi out of Velletri.*

This scenic road winds through groves of chestnut and oak trees to reach **Nemi**, a small village in a charming **setting★★** on the slopes of the lake of the same name. The road then climbs to **Monte Cavo** (alt 949m/3 124ft) which

was crowned by the Temple of Jupiter. First a monastery and now a hotel have occupied the buildings. From the esplanade there is a fine **view★** of the Castelli region with Rome on the horizon. Beyond the attractively set **Rocca di Papa**, facing the Alban lakes, the road passes through **Grottaferrata** with its **abbey★** which was founded in the 11C by Greek monks. **Tusculo** was the fief of the powerful Counts of Tusculum who governed the Castelli region. Next comes **Frascati★** pleasantly situated on the slopes facing Rome. It is known for its wines and its 16C and 17C villas, particularly the **Villa Aldobrandini★** set above its terraced gardens. *Gardens only: open Mon-Fri, 9am-1pm and 3-6pm (5pm winter).* *Closed Sat, Sun and public holidays. Permit required for visit, to be picked up at IAT, Piazza Marconi 1.* ☎*06 94 20 331.*

The road back to Rome passes **Cinecittà**, the Italian Hollywood.

Ostia Antica★★

The train from Stazione Ostiense (metro Pyramide) is the easiest option. Ostia's roads, near the main airport, can grow crowded and intense.

Ostia, at the mouth of the Tiber, takes its name from the Latin word ostium meaning mouth. According to Virgil, Aeneas landed here but its foundation dates in reality back to the 4C BC when Rome embarked on her conquest of the Mediterranean. From that time on, Ostia's development has reflected that of Rome: a military port during the period of expansion, a commercial port once Rome had established an organised system of trade. At first there was simply a castle to protect the port from pirates but by the IC BC Ostia had become a real town around which Sulla built ramparts in 79BC. Like Rome, Ostia began to decline in the 4C.

Slowly the harbour silted up and malaria decimated the population. Ostia was soon covered by alluvium deposited by the Tiber. It was 1909 before Ostia was discovered and regular excavations began.

Discover a variety of interesting remains: warehouses (*horrea*); baths; sanctuaries; examples of the substantial dwell-

Priceless Mushrooms

White truffles are an underground mushroom tuber which grow in symbiosis with the roots of oaks, willows or poplars in damp, clay soil which has little exposure to the sun. They are mainly composed of water and mineral salts which are absorbed through the roots of the trees. They are hunted out by "trifolai" (from "trifola", a dialect word for truffle), accompanied by highly trained dogs who must find the truffles without damaging them.

ing-house, the domus built around its atrium or courtyard; and the more usual blocks of flats, several storeys high (*insula*). They were nearly all built of brick and unrendered. Some had elegant entrances framed by a triangular pediment resting on two pillars. Here and there a porch or a balcony added interest to the street front.

In addition there is the forum, the political and social hub. Kids Children enjoy exploring this ghost town, and the beach – Ostia Lido –nearby.

Excavations

Allow at least half a day. ⊙*Open daily Apr-Oct 8.30am-7.30pm (ticket office closes 6pm); Nov-Mar 8.30am-dusk.* ⊙*Closed Mon, 1 Jan, 1 May, 25 Dec.* ⊛*4€.* ☎*06 56 35 80 99; www.ostia-antica.org.* Once past the **Via delle Tombe**, just outside the **Porta Romana** (the main town entrance coming from Rome) is the **Decumanus Maximus**, the east-west axis of all Roman towns; in Ostia it was paved with slabs and lined with porticoed houses and shops.

On the right are the **Terme di Nettuno**. This 2C baths building has a terrace with a view of the fine **mosaics**★★, which depict the marriage of Neptune and Amphitrite. A little further on, on the opposite side is the **Horrea di Hortensius**★, grand 1C warehouses built round a pillared courtyard which is lined with shops. The theatre has been much restored but is nevertheless very evocative of life in a Roman city.

The **Piazzale delle Corporazioni**★★★ was surrounded by a portico housing the offices of the 70 trading corporations which represented the trading links with the Roman world. The mosaic pavement portrays their emblems, which in turn indicate the commodity they traded in and the country of origin. The temple in the centre of the square is sometimes attributed to Ceres, goddess of the harvest.

On the right is the Casa di Apuleio and then the **Mitreo**, a temple to Mithras. The **Thermopolium**★★ was a bar with a marble counter where hot drinks were served (hence its name).

The **Casa di Diana**★ is an example of an *insula* (block of flats) with rooms arranged around an inner courtyard.

The **Museo**★ displays objects found in Ostia: crafts, oriental religious cults, sculptures and **portraits**★.

Dedicated to the Capitoline triad (Jupiter, Juno and Minerva) the **Capitolium**★★ was the largest temple in Ostia, built in the 2C. Some of the pillars of the surrounding portico in the **forum** (extended in the 2C) are still standing. At the far end stands the 1C Temple of Rome and Augustus (Tempio di Roma e Augusto), faced with marble.

Beyond the **Casa del Larario**★, so-called because of the ochre brick decoration, is the **Horrea Epagathiana**★, a warehouse with a fine doorway.

Built in the 4C facing the seashore, the **Casa di Amore e Psiche**★★ has interesting remains of mosaic and marble floors and a lovely nymphaeum.

There is a series of baths (*terme*) starting with the **Terme di Mitra** with traces of the steps and *frigidarium*. Further along are the **Insula del Serapide**★ and the Terme dei **Sette Sapienti**★ – there is a handsome mosaic floor in the large circular room. Beyond the walls are the **Terme della Marciana** with a beautiful **mosaic**★ in the *frigidarium*.

The **Schola del Traiano**★★ is a 2C to 3C building which was the headquarters of a guild of merchants. An inscription on a colonnade marks the entrance to the 4C **Basilica cristiana**.

Further on are the **Terme del Foro**★, the largest baths in Ostia. In the rectangular enclosure of the **Campo della Magna Mater** are the remains of a temple dedicated to Cybele (or the Magna Mater, the Great Mother).

Cerveteri

The ancient Caere was a powerful Etruscan centre. Within the fortress, Palazzo Ruspoli houses the Museo Archeologico Nazionale. &.◔*Open daily 9am-6.30pm.* ◔*Closed Mon, 1 Jan, 1 May, 25 Dec.* ◌*4€.* ☎*06 99 41 354; www.pierreci.it*
In the 4C BC Caere began to decline. It was only at the beginning of the 20C that excavation work began on this site. Most of the finds are now displayed in the Villa Giulia in Rome. (&*see The Green Guide Rome.*) &*Another outstanding Etruscan site is TARQUINIA*

Necropoli della Banditacci★★★

▶*2km/1mi to the north of Cerveteri and signposted from the main piazza.* ◔*Open daily 8.30am-1hr before dusk.* ◔*Closed Mon, 1 Jan, 1 May, 25 Dec.* ◌*4€.* ☎*06 99 40 001.*
The splendid necropolis is an important testimonial to Etruscan burial cults. It is laid out like a city with numerous tumuli lining a main street.The tombs generally date from the 7C BC. These conical earth mounds rest on a stone base, with the burial chambers underneath. Other tombs consist of underground burial

chambers reached through simply decorated doors. A vestibule leads into the burial chambers, which often contain two funeral beds placed side by side: one is adorned with a small column if the deceased was a man (the breadwinner) and the other with a small canopy in the case of a woman (guardian of the home). One of the tombs without a tumulus is the **Tomba delle Rilievi**★★ with its low-relief stuccoes giving a picture of everyday Etruscan life. &*Tombs are opened in rotations. Highlights include the Tomba Bella, Tomb dei Letti Funebri, Tomba delle Rilievi and Tomba dei Capitelli.*

Tour around Lake Bracciano★★

From Cerveteri go 18km/11mi north to Bracciano (&see Green Guide Rome).
Bracciano★*is dominated by* **Castello Orsini Odescalchi**★★★ (14C-15C). **The interior** has lovely frescoed rooms. The jewel of this place is the enchanting **Central Courtyard**★. ◔*Guided tours only (1hr).* ◔*Closed Mon, 1 Jan, 25 Dec.* ◌*7 €. For information on opening times, call* ☎*06 99 80 43 48; www.odescalchi.it.*
Clinging to the promontory, the medieval village of **Anguillara Sabazia**★ offers magnificent lake views.
Trevignano Romano is a medieval village with fishermen's houses arranged in a herringbone pattern.

SALUZZO★

POPULATION 16 000
MICHELIN MAP 561 I 4 – PIEDMONT.

This pretty town, situated on the slopes of a hill, has an imposing castle at the heart of its medieval buildings. From the 12C-16C Saluzzo was the seat of a powerful marquisate making it a prosperous centre of art and culture, and also the birthplace of the patriot and writer Silvio Pellico (1789-1854), author of *My Prisons.*

- **Information:** Piazzetta dei Mondagli 5 (Casa di Silvio Pellico), 12037 Saluzzo (CN), ☎175 46 710; www.comune.saluzzo.cn.it.
- ▶ **Orient Yourself:** Saluzzo is situated between Cuneo and Turin, the main link roads to these towns being S 20 and S 662.
- **Don't Miss:** Casa Cavassa.
- **Organizing Your Time:** Allow two days for the whole region.
- **Also See:** *CUNEO, LANGHE E MONFERRATO, TORINO.*

Priceless Mushrooms

White truffles are an underground mushroom tuber which grow in symbiosis with the roots of oaks, willows or poplars in damp, clay soil which has little exposure to the sun. They are mainly composed of water and mineral salts which are absorbed through the roots of the trees. They are hunted out by "trifolai" (from "trifola", a dialect word for truffle), accompanied by highly trained dogs who must find the truffles without damaging them.

Visit

Casa Cavassa★

⏱Open Apr-Sep daily 10am-1pm and 2-6pm (rest of the year 2-5pm). ⏱Closed Mon, 1 Jan, 1 May, 25 Dec. 👛4€; 5€ including Torre Civica. ☎0175 41 455; www.comune.saluzzo.cn.it.

The Renaissance portal of this elegant 15C house is surmounted by the motto "droit quoy qu'il soit" (forward at all costs) and by the emblem of the Cavassa family, a fish swimming upstream. The gallery of the panoramic loggia has a grisaille decoration depicting the Labours of Hercules by the Flemish-Burgundian artist Hans Clemer. Note his altarpiece, **Madonna della Misericordia**★ in one of the rooms opening onto the loggia.

Chiesa di San Giovanni

The austere façade of this 14C church conceals a rich interior. In the north aisle there is a fine cycle of 15C **frescoes**★. The masterpiece of the church is the extraordinary **apse**★★, a jewel of Burgundian Gothic art, "embroidered" in green Sampeyre stone. Near the church, on the other side of the square, stands the 15C **Torre Civica**. The effort required to reach the top of the tower is rewarded by the **view**★. ⏱Open Thu, Sat and Sun 9.30am-12.30pm and 2.30-6.30pm; Tue, Wed and Fri by reservation only. ⏱Closed Mon, 1 Jan, 1 May, 25 Dec. 4€; 5€ including Casa Cavassa. ☎0175 41 455; www.comune.saluzzo.cn.it.

Excursions

Abbazia di Staffarda★

10km/6mi north on S 589. ⏱Open daily 9am-12.30pm and 3-5.30pm. 👛5.20€. ☎0175 27 32 15; www.mauriziano.it.

This imposing monastery was erected by Cistercian monks in the 12C-13C and constituted an important economic centre that hosted fairs and markets.

Castello della Manta

4km/2.5mi south of Saluzzo on S 589. Open Feb-Sept daily 10am-6pm (rest of the year 5pm). ⏱Closed Mon, Jan, last 2 weeks Dec. 👛5€. ☎0175 87 822; www.fondoambiente.it.

This 12C stronghold was turned into an aristocratic residence in the 15C. The **frescoes**★★★ in the Baronial Room depict the Procession of Heroes and Heroines from the courtly poem The Wandering Knight, by Tommaso III.

On the return journey, a short detour to **Savigliano** (13km/8mi east of Saluzzo on S 662) is recommended. Note the atmospheric **Piazza Santarosa**★.

Le Langhe

From Bra to Alba, a 90km/56-mile itinerary. www.langhe.it.

The River Tanaro and River Bormida di Spigno mark the borders of this region of limestone hills. The vineyards here produce prized wines such as Barolo and Nebbiolo. Other typical products include white truffles from Alba and hazelnuts. This route starts from Bra and, passing through La Morra, Monforte, Dogliani, Belvedere Langhe, Bossolasco, Serralunga d'Alba and Grinzane Cavour, finally reaches **Alba**. The landscape is dominated by castles and vineyards and affords panoramic **views**★. The castle at Grinzane Cavour has hosted the literary prize of the same name since 1982.

Alba was the ancient Roman city of Alba Pompeia, the birthplace of the Roman Emperor Pertinax (AD 126-193). It is a gourmet centre famous for its delicious **tartufi bianchi** or white truffles (annual truffle fair in autumn) and its wines.

SAN GIMIGNANO★★★

POPULATION 7 383
MICHELIN MAP 563 L 15
SEE ALSO THE GREEN GUIDE TUSCANY.

Rising up from the Val d'Elsa, San Gimignano is surrounded by rolling country-side dotted with vines and olive trees. Its 14 grey stone towers set on a hilltop are enclosed within an outer wall. Built mainly of brick, it has all the charm of a small medieval town, and has been amazingly well preserved.

- **Information:** Piazza Duomo 1, 53037 San Gimignano (SI). ☎0577 94 00 08; www.comune.sangimignano.si.it, www.sangimignano.com.
- **Orient Yourself:** Frtom Florence take the Florence-Siena dual carriageway as far as Poggibonsi; follow the signs *(13km/8mi from Poggibonsi)*.
- **Don't Miss:** Collegiata frescoes and the view from the Palazzo del Popolo tower.

Visit

Piazza della Cisterna★★

The square is paved with bricks laid in a herring-bone pattern and derives its name from a 13C cistern or well (cisterna). It is one of the most evocative squares in Italy with its tall towers and austere 13C-14C mansions all around.

Piazza del Duomo★★

The collegiate church, palaces and seven towers line this majestic square.

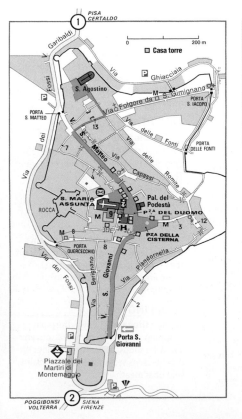

SAN GIMIGNANO	
20 Settembre V.	13
Bonda V. di	2
Castello V. del	3
Diacceto V.	4
Mainardi	7
Pecori Pza Luigi	9
Quercecchio V. di	8
Santo Stefano V.	12
Palazzo del Popolo (Municipio)	H

Collegiata★
(Santa Maria Assunta)

🕐 *Open Apr-Oct 9.30am-7.10pm (5.10pm Sat); Nov-Mar 9.30am-4.40pm.* 🚫*Closed Sun morning and 21 Jan-Feb .* 🎫*3.50€.* ☎*0577 94 00 08; www.sangimignano. com.*

This 12C Romanesque church was extended in the 15C by Giuliano da Maiano. The façade was restored in the 19C. Inside are a **Martyrdom of St Sebastian** (1465) by Benozzo Gozzoli and an **Annunciation** by Jacopo della Quercia *(west wall)*.

The walls of the left aisle are adorned with **frescoes**★ evoking scenes from the Old Testament by Bartolo di Fredi (14C), while the **frescoes**★★ (c 1350) of the right aisle are by Barna da Siena and depict scenes from the Life of Christ *(start at the top)*. In the **Cappella di Santa Fina** (railings) designed by Giuliano da Maiano, the harmonious **altar**★ is by his nephew Benedetto da Maiano and the **frescoes**★ (1475) by Domenico Ghirlandaio.

Palazzo del Popolo★

The 13C-14C Town Hall is dominated by a tall **tower** with a **view**★★over roofs and towers. The Council Chamber has a remarkable **Maestà**★ (Madonna and Child enthroned in Majesty, 1317) by Lippo Memmi, restored c 1467 by Benozzo Gozzoli. **The Museo Civico**★ is on the second floor.

♿ Palazzo del Podestà, S. Agostino (frescoes★★, tomb★ of St Bartolo, the work of Benedetto da Maiano).

Excursions

San Vivaldo★
17km/10mi northwest.
In 1500 Franciscan monks settled here to honour the body of St Vivaldo who died

---

Address Book

WHERE TO STAY

🍽**A La Casa de' Potenti** – *Piazza delle Erbe 10* – ☎*0577 94 31 90* – *www. casadeipotenti.com* – ▭ – *9 rm* – ▱. This 14C palazzo is as central as it gets in San Gimignano. Some of the rooms overlook the piazza and have a view of the Duomo. You cannot fail to be impressed by the position, the decor (very atmospheric) and the prices!

🍽🍽**Agriturismo Il Casale del Cotone** – *Via Cellone 59* – *2.5km/1mi north of San Gimignano in the direction of Certaldo* – ☎*0577 94 32 36* – *www.casaledelco-tone.com* – *Closed 2 Nov-23 Dec* – ⛷ – *11 rm* ▱. An elegant farmhouse which dates back to the 18C. Tasteful mixture of antiques and country furnishings. Nearby is also an annexe with apartments to rent. An ideal base for a relaxing holiday in a rural setting.

WHERE TO EAT

🍽**Osteria del Carcere** – *Via del Castello 3* – ☎*0577 94 19 05* – *Closed Wed, Thu (winter only), Jan and Feb* – ▱ . This simple rustic-style eatery is situated in the vicinity of the Piazza della Cisterna.

Check the blackboard for the day's specials. Excellent meat dishes prepared with stuffed joints of meat from the famous butcher in Panzano in Chianti. Good selection of wines and cheeses.

TAKING A BREAK

Caffè delle Erbe – *Via Diacceto 1* – ☎*0577 90 70 83* – *Jun-Oct, Wed-Mon 8am-midnight, rest of the year 8am-8pm.* The smartest café in town: its warm and friendly ambience make it a very popular place. Musicians come and play in the small bar area with wrought-iron furniture and paintings on the walls. Lovely intimate but airy dining room upstairs (you get a glimpse of it through the skylight in the bar downstairs). There are also tables outside in the piazza.

SHOPPING

Via San Giovanni – This is the main shopping street with plenty of souvenir and wine shops, as well as a number of delicatessens selling the local speciality, wild boar meat.

R. Mattes/MICHELIN

here in 1320. They built a monastery and a series of chapels, **sacro monte,** (17 are still extant) recreating the holy places of Jerusalem in miniature. *By appointment* ☏*0571 68 01 14.*

Certaldo

13km/8mi north.
It was in this village, in the wooded Elsa Valley, that **Giovanni Boccaccio** (1312-75) spent the last years of his life. Along with Dante and Petrarch, he was one of the three great Italian writers. In the upper town are the **Casa del Boccaccio**, now converted into a museum, the church of San Jacopo where the writer is buried and the **Palazzo Pretorio**, which was rebuilt in the 16C. *House-museum:* 🕐*Open daily Apr-Sep 10am-7pm; Oct-Mar, 10.30am-4.30pm.* 🚫*Closed Mon (winter), Tue, 25-26 Dec.* ✎*3.10€.* ☏*0571 66 12 19; www.comune.certaldo.ft.it.*

REPUBBLICA DI SAN MARINO★
SAN MARINO REPUBLIC
POPULATION 29 000
MICHELIN MAPS 562, 563 K 19
TOWN PLAN IN THE MICHELIN ATLAS ITALY.

One of the smallest states in the world (61km2/23sqmi), San Marino stands in an admirable site★★★ on the slopes of Monte Titano. This ancient republic had its own coinage, postage stamps and army and police force.
San Marino is believed to have been founded in the 4C by a pious mason, Marinus, who was fleeing from the persecutions of the Emperor Diocletian. The system of government has changed little in nine centuries, and the leading figures are still the two Captains Regent, who are chosen from among the 60 members of the Grand Council and installed every six months during a colourful ceremony (see Events and Festivals in the Practical Points section). San Marino produces a pleasant wine, Moscato.

- 🛈 **Information:** Piazza della Liberta, Repubblica di San Marino, ☏0549 88 29 14; www.visitsanmarino.com.
- ▶ **Orient Yourself:** San Marino is 22km/13mi from Rimini, on S 72.
- 👁 **Don't Miss:** The views from the Rocche and the panorama from San Leo.
- 🕐 **Organizing Your Time:** Allow a day.
- 👣 **Also See:** *RIMINI.*

A Bit of History

Officially, the Republic was founded in 301AD. Marino's inaccessible location and relative poverty helped it to maintain its independence, which was recognised in 1631 by the papacy. Even during World War II this small state was able to remain neutral. Axis forces retreated through the country with British and American forces in hot pursuit, leaving the area a few weeks later. San Marino was the world's smallest republic from 301 until 1968, until Nauru gained independence. The state became a member of the Council of Europe in 1988 and of the United Nations in 1992.

Worth a Visit

Palazzo Pubblico

Piazza della Libertà. 🕐*Open daily 8am-8pm (summer), rest of the year 9am-5pm.* 🕐*Closed 1 Jan, 25 Dec, 2 Nov.* 🎫*4.50€ (includes Museo di S. Francesco).* ☎0549 88 53 70; www.museidistato.sm. Government House was rebuilt in the Gothic style in the late 19C. The Great Council Chamber is open to visitors.

Basilica di San Marino

The basilica contains the relics of St Marinus. In the nearby church of San Pietro there are two niches hewn in the rock, in which St Marinus and his companion St Leo are said to have slept.

"Rocche" (Guaita, Cesta and della Fratta, Montale)

These three peaks are crowned with three towers (torri), which are linked by a watchpath. From the towers there are splendid **views**★★★ of the Apennines, the plain, Rimini and the sea as far as the Dalmatian coast. In the Torre Cesta there is a museum, **Museo delle Armi Antiche**, with a collection of firearms. 🕐*Open daily, mid-Jun to Sep 8am-8pm, rest of year 9am-6pm.* 🕐*Closed 1 Jan, 25 Dec.* 🎫3€. ☎0549 99 12 95; www.museidistato.sm.

Museo-Pinacoteca di San Francesco

🕐*Open daily 8am-8pm (summer), rest of the year 9am-5pm.* 🎫*4.50€ (includes Museo di S. Francesco).* ☎0549 99 51 32; www.museidistato.sm.
Paintings from the 12C to 17C and 20C, Etruscan pottery and funerary objects.

Excursions

San Leo★★

16km/10mi southwest. Leave to the north then take the road to the left leading down to the Marecchia Valley. Just before Pietracuta and S 258 bear left.
A steep winding road climbs to the summit of the huge limestone rock (alt 639m/2 096ft) in an impressive **setting**★★, made famous by Dante in his Divine Comedy, with the historic village of San Leo and its 15C **fortress**★, designed by Francesco di Giorgio Martini, where the charlatan Count Cagliostro (18C) was imprisoned and died. From the fortress, which houses a **museum**, there is an immense **panorama**★★★ of the Marecchia Valley, Montefeltro and San Marino.
The cathedral, which is in the Lombard-Romanesque style (1173), and the pre-Romanesque parish church (restored) are noteworthy. The 16C Palazzo Mediceo *(Piazza Dante Alighieri 14)* houses the **Museo d'Arte Sacra**, with works from the 14C-18C. Museums: 🕐*Open 9am-6.30pm (11pm Jul and Aug). Last admission 30min before closing time.* 🕐*Closed 1 Jan, 25 Dec am. Museo della città: 3€; Museo d'Arte Sacra: 3€; Forte di San Leo: 8€.* ☎800 55 38 00 (Free phone); www.comune.san-leo.ps.it.

SANSEPOLCRO ★

POPULATION 15 923

MICHELIN MAP 563 L 18 –

SEE ALSO THE GREEN GUIDE TUSCANY.

This small industrial town (famous for its pasta) retains its old town walls and numerous old houses★dating from the Middle Ages to the 18C. The finest streets are the Via XX Settembre and the Via Matteotti. However, Sansepolcro's main claim to fame is as the birthplace of the most important artist of the Italian Quattrocento (15C), **Piero della Francesca**.

- **Information:** Piazza Garibaldi 2, 52037 Sansepolcro (AR), ☎0575 74 05 36; www.sansepolcro.net.
- ▶ **Orient Yourself:** Sansepolcro is off the dual carriageway that links Cesena with Perugia. The town is on the border with Umbria.
- **Don't Miss:** Piero della Francesa paintings in the Museo Civico.
- **Organizing Your Time:** Allow a couple of hours.
- **Also See:** AREZZO.

Worth a Visit

Museo civico★★

Via Aggiunti 65. ⏰*Open July-Sept daily 9am-1.30pm and 2.30-7pm (rest of the year 6pm).* ✎*6.20€.* ☎*0575 73 22 18; www.sansepolcro.net.*
The most interesting exhibits are the **paintings★★★** by **Piero della Francesca**: his *Resurrection* (an impressive example of a mature style of art), the beautiful polyptych of the *Virgin of Mercy* and two fragments of frescoes, one of *St Julian* and the other of *St Ludovic*. The museum also has works by Bassano, Signorelli, and the Della Robbia School. From the upper floor, there is a beautiful view of Via Matteotti and 14C sinopies (red chalk drawings).

S. Lorenzo (*Descent from the Cross★* by Rosso Fiorentino).

Excursions

Camaldoli★★

76km/47mi northwest. www.camaldoli. it. Camaldoli, situated in a great forest in the heart of the mountains, was the cradle of the Camaldulian Order, founded in the 11C by St Romuald. The monastery, standing at the head of an austere valley, was rebuilt in the

13C. Higher up in a grim, isolated site is the **Hermitage★** *(Eremo)* a cluster of buildings encircled by ramparts. These include St Romuald's cell and a fine 18C church.

Convento della Verna★

36km/22mi northwest. The monastery, pleasantly situated, was founded in 1213 and it was here that St Francis of Assisi received the Stigmata. The basilica and the small church of Santa Maria degli Angeli are adorned with terracottas by Andrea della Robbia.

Poppi★

61km/38mi northwest.
This town overlooks the Arno Valley. It's crowned by its 13C **castello★**, former seat of the Counts of Guidi, with a **courtyard★**. ⏰*Open daily, mid-Mar to Oct 10am-6pm; rest of year, call for opening times.* ✎*4€.* ☎*0575 52 05 16; www.castellodipoppi.it.*

Monterchi

17km/11mi south. The cemetery cha... has a strange but compelling wor... Piero della Francesca, the **Mad... del Parto★**, which has been de... and placed above the altar. ... rare depiction of the pregna... in Italian art.

SIENA★★★

POPULATION 54 498

MICHELIN MAP 563 M 15/16

SEE ALSO THE GREEN GUIDE TUSCANY.

More than anywhere else Siena embodies the aspect of a medieval city. With its yellowish-brown buildings (from which the colour "sienna" is named) the city, encircled by ramparts, extends over three converging clay hills. As a centre for the arts, Siena is an enticing maze of narrow streets, lined with tall palaces and patrician mansions, that come together on the famous Piazza del Campo.

- **Information:** Piazza del Campo 56, ☎0577 28 05 51; www.comune.siena.it.
- ▶ **Orient Yourself:** Siena is 68km/41mi from Florence. There is a dual carriageway linking Siena with the region's capital.
- **Don't Miss:** Piazza del Campo, the Palazzo Publico and Signorelli frescoes in the Abbazia di Monte Oliveto Maggiore.
- **Organizing Your Time:** Allow a day.
- **Also See:** *VOLTERRA*.

A Bit of History

Siena's greatest period of prosperity was the 13C-14C, when it was an independent republic with a well-organised administration of its own. During the Guelphs versus **Ghibellines** conflict, Siena was opposed to its powerful neighbour Florence. One of the most memorable episodes of this long struggle was the Battle of Montaperti (1260), when the Sienese Ghibellines defeated the Florentine Guelphs. During this time Siena acquired her most prestigious buildings, and a local school of painting evolved that played a notable part in the development of Italian art.

In 1348 the plague decimated Siena's population and the city began to decline as dissension continued to reign among the rival factions. By the early 15C Siena's golden era was over.

The mystical city of Siena was the birthplace in 1347 of **St Catherine**. By the age of seven, it seems, she had decided on her spiritual marriage with Christ. She entered the Dominican Order aged and had many visions and trances throughout her life. She is said to have received the Stigmata at Pisa. In 1377 worked to bring the popes back from to Rome, which they had left **Bernardine** (1380-1444) is venerated in Siena. He gave to help the victims of the plague in the city. At the age of 22, he entered the Franciscan order and was a leader of the Observants, who favoured a stricter observance of the rule of St Francis. A great preacher, he spent much of his time travelling throughout Italy.

Sienese Art

It was not only in political matters that Siena opposed Florence. In Dante's city, Cimabue and Giotto were innovators, but were greatly influenced by the Roman traditions of balance and realism which led to the development of Renaissance art in all its glory. Siena, on the other hand, remained attached to the Greek or Byzantine traditions, in which the graceful line and the refinement of colour gave a certain dazzling elegance to the composition, which was one of the chief attractions of Gothic painting. **Duccio di Buoninsegna** (c 1255-1318/19) was the first to experiment with this new combination of inner spirituality and increased attention to space and composition.

Simone Martini (c 1284-d 1344 in Avignon) followed in Duccio's footsteps and had a considerable reputation in Europe, working at the Papal Court in Avignon. His contemporaries **Pietro** and **Ambrogio Lorenzetti** introduced an even greater realism with minute delicate

Address Book

⚙ *For coin ranges see the Legend on the cover flap.*

WHERE TO STAY

⊖**Bed & Breakfast Casa per Ferie Convento San Francesco** – *Piazza San Francesco 5/6 – ☎0577 22 69 68 – Fax 0577 22 69 68 – Closed 20 days in Jan – ♿ – 16 rm – ⊑.* Located within the Basilica complex, this small but welcoming establishment is in keeping with the simple tenets of the Franciscan order. Modern, functional rooms: one bathroom for every two rooms. No specific restrictions.

⊖**Santuario Casa di S. Caterina Alma Domus** – *Via Camporegio 37 – ☎0577 44 177 – Fax 0577 47 601 – ⊠ – 30 rm – ⊑.* If luck is on your side you may get one of the rooms with a little balcony overlooking the Duomo. Whatever happens you can always repair to the lovely reading room or the little chapel (access on the second floor). Ask for a "room with a view"!

⊖⊖**Albergo Cannon d'Oro** – *Via Montanini 28 – ☎0577 44 321 – www.cannondoro.com – 30 rm 60/95 € – ⊑.* This was once the home of Sapia, who appears in Dante's Divine Comedy (Purgatory, Canto XIII). Guests must still negotiate the three flights of old stairs, although rooms are available on the ground floor.

WHERE TO EAT

⊖**Osteria la Chiacchiera** – *Costa di Sant'Antonio 4 – ☎0577 28 06 31.* Be patient – there's not much room inside and you may have to wait a long time for a table but it's worth it. During the summer when there are tables out in the little street that runs between Santa Caterina and the Piazza del Campo, service is much quicker. Traditional Tuscan cooking.

⊖**Hosteria Il Carroccio** – *Via Casato di sotto 32 – ☎0577 41 165 – Closed Wed, 3 weeks in Jan, Feb.* This establishment is renowned for its authentic Sienese cooking and delicious salads. A small but welcoming rustic-style trattoria which is popular with the locals. Located a few minutes' walk from the Piazza del Campo.

⊖**Trattoria Papei** – *Piazza del Mercato 6 – ☎0577 28 08 94 – Closed Mon, except public holidays, and 10 days in Jul.* Classic Sienese trattoria, with a lively and friendly atmosphere. Simple, unpretentious decor. In the summer meals are served outside in the busy Piazza del Mercato, with the Torre del Mangia in the background. Represents good value for money.

⊖⊖⊖**Antica Trattoria Botteganova** – *Strada statale 408, per Montevarchi – ☎0577 28 42 30 – www.anticatrattoriabotteganova.it – Closed Mon – ▤ – Book. 10% service charge.* This is deemed to be one of the best restaurants in town and worth the detour even if it is a little out of the way. Stylistically it is somewhere between rustic and elegant.

TAKING A BREAK

Piazza del Campo – It is difficult to choose from the large number of cafés that surround this wonderful square. Look for the most comfortable chairs and get a table in the sun!

Nannini – *Via Banchi di Sopra 22/24 – ☎0577 23 60 09 – open 7.30am-midnight.* Probably the most famous café in town and its association with various Sienese specialities extends throughout Italy as well as internationally. Push the boat out and treat yourself to a pastry or an ice cream. It's an experience you won't forget.

Pasticceria Bini – *Via Stalloreggi 91/93 - ☎0577 28 02 07 – Tue-Sun 7am-1.30pm and 3.30-8pm.* Founded in 1943, this pasticceria remains one of the best in Siena. Specialities include panforte margherita (cake with honey, almonds and candied citrus fruit), panforte oro (with candied melon), copate (small white wafer biscuits) and cannoli (pastries filled with ricotta and candied fruit).

WINE BARS

Enoteca Italiana – *Fortezza Medicea – ☎0577 22 8 8 11 – www.enoteca-italiana.it. Mon noon-8pm, Tue-Sat noon-1am, Closed 10 days in Jan.* Set up with the aid of State funding in the castle ramparts, this wine cellar/bar promotes Italian and especially Tuscan wines. Organises tastings of more than 1 000 wines. Also hosts lectures for the larger wine-growers.

Antica Drogheria Manganelli – *Via di Città 71/73* – ☎*0577 28 00 02 – 9am-8pm, closed Jan.* With origins dating back to 1879, this splendid delicatessen sells a marvellous selection of quality products supplied by some of the best producers in the area. As well as wine you can buy cantucci (little biscuits made with almonds), pasta and even a wonderful 80 year-old balsamic vinegar made with hazelnuts!

EVENTS AND FESTIVALS

Twice a year, on 2 July and 16 August, Siena becomes a hotbed of feverish anticipation, excitement and vociferous rivalry when the famous bareback horse race, the **Palio delle Contrade** takes place; www.ilpalio.org, www.sienaol.it

details. A favourite theme of the Sienese school was the Virgin and Child.

The Sienese artists of the Quattrocento (15C) continued in the spirit of the Gothic masters. While Florence concentrated on rediscovering antiquity's myths, minor masters such as **Lorenzo Monaco, Giovanni di Paolo** and **Sassetta** continued to emphasise precision, flexibility and subtlety of colour.

In secular architecture, the Gothic style gave Siena its own special character. Windows became numerous, especially in the Sienese style with a depressed triple arch supporting a pointed one.

Building activity was concentrated on the cathedral, over two centuries. Sculpture, also influenced by the building of the cathedral, was enriched by the output of two Pisan artists, Nicola and Giovanni Pisano. The most important figure in Sienese sculpture is **Jacopo della Quercia** (1371-1438), who combined Gothic traditions with the Florentine Renaissance style.

Piazza del Campo★★★

Visit: 1hr15min.

This piazza forms a monumental ensemble. It is shaped like a scallop and slopes down to the façade of the Palazzo Pubblico. Eight white lines radiate outwards dividing the area into nine segments, each symbolising one of the forms of government that ruled Siena from the late-13C to the mid-14C.

At the upper end is the **Fonte Gaia** (Fountain of Joy) so-called because of the festivities which followed its inauguration in 1348. Fountains were at that time a symbol of the city's power.

Twice annually the Piazza del Campo hosts the popular festival **Palio delle Contrade**, which recalls the medieval administrative organisation of Siena with its three main quarters, subdivided into parishes (contrade). The festivities begin with a procession of the costumed contrade, who then compete in a dangerous horse race round the square. The palio, a standard bearing the effigy of the Virgin, the city's protectress, is awarded to the winner.

Palazzo Pubblico★★★

🕐*Open daily 10am-6pm (5pm Nov to mid-Mar). ☜7€. ☎0577 22 62 30; www.comune.siena.it.*
The Town Hall, built between the late-13C and mid-14C in the Gothic style, has numerous triple bays under supporting arches. From one end of the façade rises the **Torre del Mangia**, a tower (88m/289ft high) designed by Lippo Memmi. At the foot of the tower, **Cappella di Piazza** is a chapel in the form of a 14C loggia, built to mark the end of the plague. 🕐*Tower: Open daily 9.30am-7.30pm (10am-4pm Nov to mid-Mar). ☜6€. ☎0577 22 62 30; www.comune.siena.it.*
This palace was the seat of Siena's governments, and most great Siennese artists contributed to its decoration.
Sala dei Priori: Frescoes (1407) by Spinello Aretino recount the struggles between Pope Alexander III and the Emperor Frederick Barbarossa.
Cappella★: Frescoes by di Bartolo, a **railing★** and early-15C **stalls★★**.

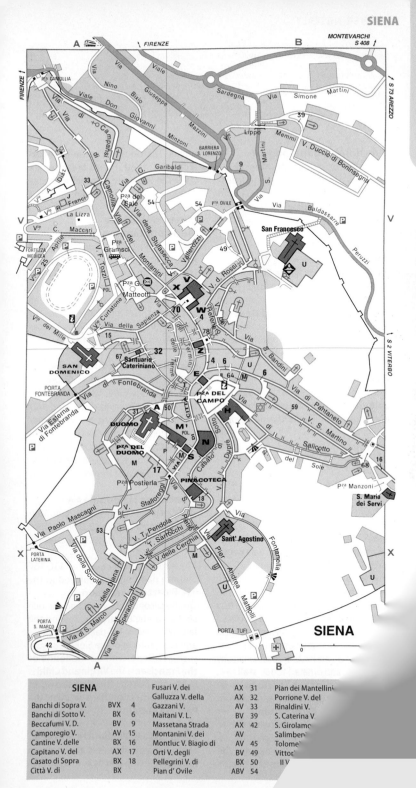

SIENA

Battistero S. Giovanni	AX	A	Palazzo Piccolomini	BX	S	Pinacoteca		BX
Duomo		AX	Palazzo Pubblico	BX	H	San Domenico		AX
Loggia dei Mercanti	BX	E	Palazzo Salimbeni	BV	V	San Francesco		BV
Museo dell'Opera			Palazzo Spannocchi	BV	W	Sant' Agostino		BX
Metropolitana	BX	M¹	Palazzo Tantucci	BV	X	Santa Maria dei Servi		BX
Palazzo Chigi-Saracini	BX	N	Palazzo Tolomei	BV	Z	Santuario Cateriniano		AX

Sala del Mappamondo★★

in the Globe Room the **Maestà**★★ (1315) is Simone Martini's earliest known work, and opposite is the famous **equestrian portrait**★★ of the Sienese general, Guidoriccio da Fogliano, by the same artist.

Sala della Pace★★

in the Peace Room are the famous frescoes, although badly damaged (1335-40), of Ambrogio Lorenzetti, entitled **Effects of Good and Bad Government**★★, where the artist has combined a scholarly allegorical approach with meticulous narrative detail.

Torre★★

From the top there is a superb **panorama**★★ of Siena's chaotic rooftops and the gently-rolling countryside beyond.

Visit

Duomo★★★

Libreria Piccolomini: ⏱*Open 10.30am-7.30pm (July -Aug 8pm).* ⏱*Closed Sun morning, 1 Jan, 25 Dec.* ☞*3€.* ☎*0577 28 30 48; www.operaduomo.siena.it.*

The façade of the cathedral was begun in the 13C by Giovanni Pisano.
The walls of the **interior** are faced with black and white marble. The 15C-16C **paving**★★★ is unique. About 40 artists ~~i~~ncluding **Beccafumi** worked on the 56 ~~mar~~ble panels portraying mythological ~~figure~~s such as Sibyls and Virtues.
~~The ch~~ancel is a 15C bronze tabernacle by ~~Vecchietta~~ and ornate 14C-16C **stalls**★★.
~~The entr~~ance to the north transept ~~holds a p~~**ulpit**★★★ carved from ~~marble by~~ **Nicola Pisano**.
~~From the left ai~~sle a doorway leads to ~~the Libreria Picc~~**omini**, built in 1495 ~~by Cardinal Todeschini~~ Piccolomini, the ~~future Pius III, to~~ house his uncle's

books. The Umbrian painter **Pinturicchio** adorned it with **frescoes**★★ (1502-09) depicting episodes in the life of Aeneas Silvius Piccolomini (Pius II).

Museo dell'Opera Metropolitana★★

⏱*Open daily 9.30am-8pm.* ⏱*Closed 1 Jan, 25 Dec.* ☞*6€.* ☎*0577 28 30 48.*
The museum is in the extant part of the vast building started in 1339. The present cathedral was to have been its transept. The museum contains the **Maestà** (Virgin in Majesty) by Duccio, originally painted on both sides.

Battistero di San Giovanni★

⏱*Open daily 9.30am-8pm.* ⏱*Closed 1 Jan, 25 Dec.* ☞*2.50€.* ☎*0577 28 30 48.*
This 14C baptistery is decorated with 15C frescoes. The **font** ★★ is adorned with panels by Jacopo della Quercia. The bronze panels are by Tuscan masters like Lorenzo Ghiberti and Donatello. Note the latter's Feast of Herod.

Pinacoteca Nazionale★★

♿⏱*Open Tue-Sat 8.15am-7.15pm, Mon, Sun and public holidays 8.15am-1.15pm.* ⏱*Closed 1 Jan, 1 May, 25 Dec.* ☞*4€.* ☎*0577 28 11 61.*
The extensive collection of 13C-16C Sienese paintings is displayed in the 15C **Palazzo Buonsignori**★.
On the second floor you'll find the rich section of the **Primitives**. Beyond the late-12C to early-13C painted Crucifixes are masterpieces of the Sienese school such as Duccio, with the **Madonna of the Francisans**. The **Virgin and Child** is by Simone Martini. There are also works by the Lorenzetti brothers including the **Pala del Carmine**.

Via di Città★, Via Banchi di Sopra

These flagstoned streets are bordered by remarkable **palaces**★. in the Via di

B. Morandi/MICHELIN

Piazza del Campo as seen from the top of the tower.

Città is the 15C **Palazzo Piccolomini**, its lower façade rusticated in the Florentine manner. Opposite stands the **Palazzo Chigi-Saracini**, now the Academy of Music. The **Loggia dei Mercanti** is the Commercial Courts.

The **Piazza Salimbenia** is enclosed by the 14C Gothic **Palazzo Salimbeni**, 15C Renaissance **Palazzo Spannocchi** and 16C Baroque **Palazzo Tantucci**.

Basilica di San Domenico★

St Catherine experienced her trances in this 13C-15C Gothic conventual church. Inside, there is an authentic portrait by her contemporary, Andrea Vanni.

In the Cappella di Santa Caterina (halfway down the south aisle) is a Renaissance **tabernacle**★ containing the head of the saint. The wall **frescoes**★ depict scenes from the life of the saint.

Casa di Santa Caterina

In the basement of St Catherine's house is the cell where she lived. Above is the 13C crucifix in front of which the saint is said to have received the Stigmata.

Chiesa di Sant'Agostino

This 13C church has a remarkable **Adoration of the Crucifix**★ by Perugino, and **works**★ by Ambrogio Lorenzetti, Matteo di Giovanni and Sodoma.

Excursions

Abbazia di Monte Oliveto Maggiore★★

36km/22mi southeast of Siena. ⏱*Open daily, 9.15am-noon and 3.15-6pm (5pm winter).* ☎*0577 70 76 11; www.abbazie. com/mom.*

Cypresses hide this rose-coloured **abbey**, the Mother House of the Olivetans, part of the Benedictine Order. ⏍*The Signorelli frescoes.*

Chiostro Grande

The cloisters are decorated with a cycle of 36 **frescoes**★★ depicting the life of St Benedict by **Luca Signorelli** from 1498 and by **Il Sodoma** from 1505 to 1508. The frescoes begin by the west door, with two of Sodoma's masterpieces: *Christ of the Column* and *Christ bearing His Cross*. The majority are by Il Sodoma, who was influenced by Leonardo da Vinci an Perugino *(see Index).* Note in partic no 12 the saint greeting two young no 19 where courtesans have be to seduce the monks and no 2 St Benedict resuscitates a r cloisters lead to the refe library and pharmacy.

Chiesa abbaziale

This abbey church (1505) by Fra Giov

SPOLETO★

POPULATION 38 563

MICHELIN MAP 563 N 20 – UMBRIA.

This former Roman municipium became the capital of an important Lombard duchy from the 6C to the 8C. The town covers a hill crowned by the Rocca dei Papi. The city was dear to St Francis, who loved its austere character, tempered by graceful narrow alleys, palaces and numerous medieval buildings.

- **Information:** Piazza Libertà 7, ☎0743 23 89 20; www.spoleto.umbria2000.it and for Norcia and the Parco dei Monti Sibillini: Casa del Parco, Via Solferino 22, 06046 Norcia (PG), ☎0743 81 70 90; www.sibillini.net.
- **Orient Yourself:** Spoleto lies off S 3, the Via Flaminia, which links Foligno with Terni.
- **Don't Miss:** The Duomo's Fra Filippa Lippi frescoes, Cascata delle Mamore.
- **Organizing Your Time:** Allow a couple of hours.
- **Also See:** *ASSISI.*

Visit

Duomo★★

Flanked by a baptistery, the cathedral provides the focal point of **Piazza del Duomo**★. The façade is fronted by a fine Renaissance porch and adorned above by a rose window and 13C mosaic. Inside note the altar cross painted on parchment applied to wood by Alberto Sozio (1187), frescoes *(first chapel on the south side)* by Pinturicchio, Fra Filippo Lippi's burial monument *(south transept)* and in the apse **frescoes** depicting the life of the Virgin by Fra Filippo Lippi and his assistants. In the episode depicting the Dormition of the Virgin, note the self-portrait of Lippi dressed in Dominican vestments.

Ponte delle Torri★★

A pleasant walk leads to the 13C Bridge of Towers (80m/262ft high, 230m/755ft long), built over a Roman aqueduct which was used as a foundation. The bridge with its ten Gothic arches is guarded by a fortified gatehouse.

Basilica di San Salvatore★

St Saviour's Basilica, one of the first Christian churches in Italy, was built by Oriental monks in the 4C and modified in the 9C. Roman materials were re-used in later building.

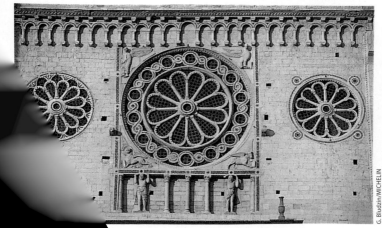

...omo

G. Bludzin/MICHELIN

Address Book

WHERE TO STAY

It is worth noting that during the trade fairs and exhibitions, the hotels tend to put their prices up. Enquire when you make your booking.

Hotel Aurora – Via Apollinare 3 – ☎0743 22 03 15 – www.hotelauroraspoleto.it – – 23 rm . Tucked away in a quiet corner of town is this lovely little family-run hotel which represents very good value for money. Modern rooms. Full- or half-board rates with meals at the adjacent Apollinare restaurant (see above).

WHERE TO EAT

Apollinare – Via Sant'Agata 14 – Spoleto – ☎0743 22 32 56 – www.ristoranteapollinare.it – .
An elegant, very reputable restaurant which is popular with the locals. The subtle yellow and blue decor provides a harmonious contrast to the old stone walls and beamed ceilings. Evening meals served by candlelight. The excellent cuisine draws on tradition but is also innovative.

EVENTS AND FESTIVALS

Each summer the town hosts an international arts festival, the Spoleto Festival, originally set up by the Italian-American impresario and composer Giancarlo Menotti. ☎800 56 56 00 or 0743 22 03 20, www.spoletofestival.it.

Chiesa di San Gregorio Maggiore★

This 12C Romanesque church, dedicated to St Gregory Major, was modified in the 14C. The 14C baptistery to the left of the entrance porch has walls covered with frescoes (Massacre of the Innocents). The campanile is built of stone from ancient buildings.

Arco di Druso

This arch was built in AD 23 in honour of Tiberius' son, Drusus.

Chiesa di San Domenico

This lovely 13C church, dedicated to St Dominic, is built of alternating courses of white and pink stone. The nave is decorated with 14C and 15C frescoes and the south transept contains a canvas by Lanfranco.

Excursions

Fonti del Clitunno★

13km/8mi north. For information on opening times, call ☎0743 52 11 41; www.fontidelclitunno.com. 2€. Tempietto: Open daily 8.45am-7.45pm (rest of the year 5.45pm). Closed Mon. ☎0743 27 50 85.

These crystal-clear waters were sacred to the Romans, who plunged animals into the water for purification prior to sacrifice. About 1km/0.6mi below stands the **tempietto**★ of Clitumnus, a minuscule early Christian building dating from the 5C.

Monteluco road★

8km/5mi east.
A winding road leads up to **Monteluco**. On the way up, the church of **San Pietro** has a 13C Romanesque **façade**★ with relief sculptures. On the summit, Montelucoa, once the seat of an ancient cult, is now a health resort. The monastery founded by St Francis still exists.

Driving tours

Southern Umbria

This long (155km/93mi) sc
in southern Umbria ends
Sibillini. From Spoleto he
along S 418 and con
Gemini and San Ge

Roman ruins

▸ 16km/1
S. Gem
These ar
destro

T. Zane/MICHELIN

Castelluccio: little hilltop village which is renowned for its lentil production

▶ *Head in the direction of Terni along S 3 bis.*

Terni

Terni, an important industrial centre, has an old town with several fine palaces. The town centre comprises Piazza della Repubblica and Via Roma.

▶ *Follow S 79 as far as Cascate delle Marmore.*

Cascata delle Marmore★★

▶*The waterfall can be reached either via the S 209 to Macerata (7km/4mi east of Terni) or via the S 79 to Rieti (9km/5.5mi east, then 30min on foot there and back).* ⏲*For information on admission times and charges, contact Infopoint* ☎*0744 62 982; www.cascatamarmore.it*

This artificial waterfall created by the Romans falls in three successive drops down sheer walls of marble (marmore). Take the Macerata road, S 209 (7km/4mi ⁀st of Terni), or the Rieti road, S 79 ⁀/6mi to the east plus 30min there ⁀ck on foot).

⁀209 as far as Ferentillo.

⁀heast. www.comune.

⁀ is dominated by here (5km/3mi ⁀er by a poor ⁀he solitary ⁀e★. The ⁀scoes

and there are Roman sarcophagi. ⏲*Open daily summer 10am-5pm; rest of the year by reservation only.* 💶 *Donation recommended.* ☎*0744 78 03 16.*

▶ *Proceed along S 209 as far as the junction with S 320. Head in the direction of Norcia.*

Norcia★

www.norcia.net.

The walled town of Norcia is located within the **Parco dei Monti Sibillini**, whose highest peak is Monte Vettore (2 476m/8 170ft). St Benedict, patriarch of Western monasticism and patron saint of Europe, was born here in 480.

The walk along the Corso Sertorio towards Piazza S. Benedetto is a delight, with shop windows piled high with truffles, cheeses, salamis and pasta.

Overlooking Piazza S. Benedetto is the 16C **Castellina** fortress, which now houses the **Museo Civico-Diocesano**, and the 13C church of **San Benedetto**, with its Gothic façade. The frescoes inside date back to the 14C.

La montagna a ridosso di Norcia – Around 20km/12mi from Norcia, in the direction of Ascoli Piceno, the hilltop village of **Castelluccio** looms up (1 453m/4 790ft) against a backdrop of tundra-like scenery, heralding the beginnings of the immense upland plain of the **Piano grande★★**, which is carpeted with flowers in spring. Look out for the inscriptions on the limewashed walls of the stables and their ironic comments on village life.

SULMONA★

POPULATION 25 276

MICHELIN MAP 563 P 23 – ABRUZZI.

Sulmona was the birthplace of the Roman poet Ovid, who immortalised his origins in the verse "Sulmo mihi patria est" (hence the acronym SMPE of the town's emblem). Sulmona is a lively crafts centre, renowned for its goldsmiths' workshops.

- **Information:** Corso Ovidio 208, 67039 Sulmona (AQ), ☎ 0864 53 276; www.comune.sulmona.aq.it.
- ▶ **Orient Yourself:** Sulmona lies at the head of a fertile basin framed by majestic mountains. The main access roads are A 25 from Pescara, or S 5, the *Via Tiburtina Valeria.*
- **Don't Miss:** Local goldwork, lively markets in Piazza Garibaldi and the Palazzo dell'Annunziata.
- ☉ **Organizing Your Time:** Allow a couple of hours.
- **Also See:** *ABRUZZO, L'AQUILA*

Worth a Visit

Porta Napoli★

Southern town gateway. This Gothic gate has historiated capitals (14C). The exterior has decoration of gilded bosses, Angevin coats of arms and Roman low reliefs. **Corso Ovidio**, which cuts through the medieval heart of the city, commences here.

Piazza Garibaldi

This square is the scene of a large, colourful market on Wednesdays and Saturdays. The square is bordered by the

> **SHOPPING**
> **Confetti Pelino** – *Via Stazione Introdacqua 55 – 67039 Sulmona* – ☎ 0864 21 00 47 – *www.pelino.it.* Well-stocked with presents for a wedding, baptism or anniversary.

pointed arches of the 13C **aqueduct**★, the Baroque corner of Santa Chiara and the Gothic doorway of San Filippo. At the corner of the aqueduct by Corso Ovidio is the Renaissance fountain, **Fon-**

Colorful Little Delicacies

From the windows of Corso Ovidio colourful and unusual bunches of flowers peep out: these are the famous Sulmona sweets which were created at the end of the 15C. A taste of these little sweets will hold some pleasant surprises in store: a glacé of pure sugar hides Sicilian almonds, hazelnuts, chocolate, candied fruit and rosolio.

To find out more, go to the small museum, Museo dell'Arte e della Tecnologia confettiera, at the Pelino factory in Via Introdacqua 55. *Via Stazione Introdacqua 55. Tours only, Mon-S and 3.30-6.30pm. Closed Sun and public holidays.* ☎ 0864 21 00 47; ww

Sugared almonds from Confetti P

tana del Vecchio. On Easter Sunday, the feast of the "Madonna che scappa in piazza" is celebrated in Piazza Garibaldi: the statue of the Virgin is borne to a meeting with the Risen Christ.

Chiesa di San Francesco della Scarpa

This church was erected in the 13C by Franciscan monks who had shoes (hence its name, *scarpa* being the Italian for "shoe"). It has a Romanesque doorway★ on Corso Ovidio.

Palazzo dell'Annunziata★★

This monumental construction documents four centuries of Sulmonese art. Built by a Brotherhood of Penitents from 1415, the palace constitutes a synthesis of Gothic (the doorway with statues of the Virgin and St Michael, the ornate trefoil openings★ and statues of four Doctors of the Church), Renaissance (the middle doorway, the right portal and the twin openings) and Baroque art (the theatrical façade of the adjacent church). There is a carved frieze★ halfway up the façade

depicting hunts and love scenes. Inside, the palace houses the Museo Civico. ◷Open daily 9am-1pm. ⊚1€. ☎0864 21 02 16; www.comune.sulmona.aq.it.

Excursions

Basilica di San Pelino★

▶13km/8mi northwest, near the village of Corfinio. ◷Open daily summer 8.30am-noon and 3-6.30pm, rest of year by appointment only. ⊚Donation recommended. ☎0864 72 81 20.
This bishop's seat was erected in the 11C and 12C. The rear of the basilica offers a good view of the apse complex★. The interior houses a 12C ambo.

Popoli

▶17km/10mi northwest. www.comune.popoli.pe.it.
This pretty town is clustered around Piazza Matteotti. Next to the square stands the Taverna Ducale★, an elegant 14C Gothic building, which was once used a storeroom for tithes.

TARANTO★

POPULATION 199 012
MICHELIN MAP 564 F 33
TOWN PLAN IN THE MICHELIN ATLAS ITALY –PUGLIA.

Taranto is a naval base, closed at the seaward end by two fortified islands. Taranto was founded in the 7C BC and was one of an important colony of Magna Graecia. During Holy Week many impressive ceremonies take place in the town, including several processions between Thursday and Saturday, one lasting 12 hours and another 14 hours, which go from church to church at a very slow pace.

- **Information:** Corso Umberto 113, ☎099 45 32 392; www.comune.taranto.it.
- ▶ **Orient Yourself:** Tucked away behind the "heel", Taranto lies off S 106 (if you are travelling from Calabria), S 7, Via Appia and S 172.
- **Don't Miss:** During Holy Week many processions take place.
- **Organizing Your Time:** Allow half a day.
- **Also See:** *BRINDISI.*

h a Visit

zionale★★
restoration at time of pub-
ion temporarily located
eo, Lungomare Vittorio
715

A good collection of local archeological finds including a Poseidon★★ discovered at Ugento, a collection of ceramics★★ and Hellenic gold jewellery★★★(4C and 3C BC).

TARQUINIA

Giardini comunali Villa Peripato★
Municipal Gardens; **Lungomare Vittorio Emanuele★**:This is a long promenade planted with palm trees and oleanders.

La città vecchia
The old city is an island connected to the mainland by two bridges, one of which is a revolving bridge. At the eastern extremity of the island stands the **Aragonese Castle,** which is the seat of the Navy today.

Duomo
The 11C-12C cathedral with a Baroque façade has been greatly remodelled. The nave and two aisles are separated by ancient columns with Romanesque or Byzantine capitals and the ceiling is 17C. The chapel of **San Cataldo★** was faced with polychrome marble and embellished with statues in the 18C.
Chiesa di San Domenico Maggiore – This 14C church was remodelled in the Baroque era. There is a fine, if damaged, façade with an ogival portal surmounted by a rose-window.

TARQUINIA★
POPULATION 16 000
MICHELIN MAP 563 P 17 – LAZIO.

The town of Tarquinia crowns a rocky platform, facing the sea, in a barley- and corn-growing region interspersed with olive groves. As D. H. Lawrence noted in 1932 travelogue *Etruscan Places*: "Tarquinia, its towers pricking up like antennae on the side of a low bluff of a hill, is some few miles inland from the sea. And this was once the metropolis of Etruria, chief city of the great Etruscan League." Today, all that remains of this ancient civilisation – that flourished from the 10C BC – are the necropolis and its famous frescoes, column stubs on the acropolis and superb art work in museums (both here and in Rome's Villa Giulia).

Information: Piazza Cavour 23, ☎0766 84 92 82; www.tarquinia.net.
▶ **Orient Yourself:** Tarquinia is located off S 1 (the Via Aurelia) in northern Lazio.
Don't Miss: The Necropoli dio Monterozzi and the Museo Nazionale Tarquiniese.
Organizing Your Time: Allow a day.
Especially for Kids: Etruscopolis.
Also See: *Promontorio dell'ARGENTARIO, VITERBO.*

A Bit of History

According to legend, the town was founded in the 12C or 13C BC. Archaeologists have found 9C BC vestiges of the Villanovian civilisation which derived its name from the village of Villanova near Bologna, and developed around the year 1000 BC in the Po Plain, in Tuscany and in the northern part of Latium, where the Etruscans later settled. Standing on the banks of the River Marta, Tarquinia was a busy port and in the 6C BC ruled the coast of Etruria. Under Roman rule, Tarquinia was decimated by malaria in the 4C BC and was sacked by the Lombards in the 7C AD. The inhabitants

then moved to the present site about two kilometres to the northeast of the original position. Special Features

Etruscan Tarquinia

Necropoli di Monterozzi★
4km/2.5mi southeast. Oper
Sept 8.30am-7.30pm (Oct 6.3
the year 8.30am-2pm.
Jan, 1 May, 25 Dec. 4€
Museo Nazionale. 07
The burial ground e
5km/3mi long an
It contains 6 00°

6C-1C BC. There are remarkable **paintings**★★★ in the burial chambers.

The most important tombs include: the **Tomba del Barone** (tomb of the Baron), dating from the 6C BC; the 5C BC **Tomba del Leopardi** (tomb of the Leopards), in which are depicted leopards and scenes of a banquet and dancing; the 6C BC **Tomba dei Tori** (tomb of the Bulls) with its erotic paintings; the **Tomba delle Leonesse** (tomb of the Lionesses) dating from around 530-520 BC; the 4C BC **Tomba Gigliogi** (Giglioli tomb) decorated with *trompe l'oeil* paintings; and the late-6C BC **Tomba delle Caccia e della Pesca** (tomb with Hunting and Fishing Scenes).

 Children may prefer Etruscopolis. The exhibits are more hands-on, but otherwise are pale imitations. Via delle Pietrare. ○*Open Mon, Tues & Thurs–Sun 9am–1pm and 4.30–8.30pm, Sun 9.30–8.30pm.* ✆*7€.* ☎*0766 85 51 75; www.etruscopoli.it*

Museo Nazionale Tarquiniese★

Piazza Cavour 1. ♿○*Open daily 8.30am-7.30pm.* ○*Closed Mon, 1 Jan, 1 May, 25 Dec.* ✆*4€; 6.50€ including Necropoli di Monterozzi.* ☎*0766 85 60 36.*

The National Museum is housed in the **Palazzo Vitelleschi**★, built in 1439. It contains a most remarkable collection of Etruscan antiquities originating from the excavations in the necropolis. Note especially the two admirable **winged horses**★★★ in terracotta.

Walking About

Chiesa di Santa Maria n Castello★

visit, contact the houses to the left of hurch. ✆ *Donation recommended.*

omanesque church (1121-1208) of the fortified citadel. Its doorecorated by Cosmati.

as

avecchia.com.
nan *Centumcel-*
f Rome since

the reign of Trajan and now handles maritime traffic with Sardinia. The port is guarded by the Fort of Michelangelo, a massive Renaissance construction begun by Bramante, continued by Sangallo the Younger and Bernini, and completed by Michelangelo in 1557.

Museo Nazionale Archeologico

Largo Plebiscito no 2 A. ♿○*Open daily 8.30am-7.30pm.* ○*Closed Mon.* ☎*0766 23 604.*

A fine display of local Etruscan and Roman collections.

Terme di Traiano (or Terme Taurine)

3km/2mi northeast. ○*Open daily 9am-1pm and 3pm-dusk.* ○*Closed Mon.* ✆*5€.* ☎*0766 20 299; www.prolococivitavecchia.it.*

The two groups of baths (terme) date first *(to the west)* from the Republican period and the second was built by the Emperor Hadrian.

Tuscania★

25km/16mi north.

Tuscania was a powerful Etruscan town, a Roman municipium and an important medieval centre.

Chiesa di Santa Maria Maggiore★ and Chiesa di San Pietro★

South-east of the old town, on the road to Viterbo. ○*Open daily 9am-1pm and 3-7pm (2-5pm Oct-Apr).* ○*Closed Mon.* ☎*0761 43 63 71.*

The façade of St Peter's stands on the site of the Etruscan acropolis. To the right is the former bishop's palace, whose interior was built by Lombard masons in the 11C. The **crypt**★★ is a forest of columns of various periods.

Chiesa di Santa Maria Maggiore★

This 12C church, dedicated to St Mary Major, is modelled on St Peter's. The **13C Romanesque doorways**★★ are decorated with masterly sculptures.

TIVOLI★★★
POPULATION 49 254
MICHELIN MAP 563 Q 20 – LAZIO.

The villas testify to Tivoli's importance as a holiday resort from the Roman period through to the Renaissance. Tivoli or Tibur in antiquity came under Roman control in the 4C BC. The poet Virgil described it as "proud Tivoli... making every kind of weapon with 1,000 anvils." Legend claims a Sibyl prophesied the coming of Jesus Christ to the Emperor Augustus there. Famous for its sunsets, Tivoli also has two famous and contrasting gardens: the groomed Villa d'Este and wild Villa Gregoriana. Its true glory, however, is the Imperial Villa Adriana (Hadrian's villa), a 2C pastoral palace complex.

- **Information:** Piazza Garibaldi, 00019 Tivoli (RM). ☎0774 31 12 49; www.tibursuperbum.it
- **Orient Yourself:** Tivoli, a small town on the lower slopes of the Apennines where the River Aniene plunges in cascades into the Roman plain prise des premières lignes, lies off S 5, the Via Tiburtina, 36km/22mi from Rome.
- **Don't Miss:** Villa Adriana and Villa d'Este.
- **Organizing Your Time:** Allow a day for Tivoli and excursions.
- **Also See:** ANAGNI, ROMA.

Villa Adriana★★★

6km/4mi southwest of Tivoli.

Before visiting the villa, visitors are advised to buy a detailed map of the site (on sale at the ticket office). A large model of the villa is on display in the room next to the cafe. *Information panels placed around the site mark out itineraries of different length (1hr-2hr 30min). Visitors with less time at their disposal can finish their tour at the Canopo.* ⊙*Open daily 9am-1hr before dusk (last admission 1hr 30min before closing time).* ⊙*Closed 1 Jan, 25 Dec.* ⊕*8.50€.* ☎*06 39 96 79 00; www.villa-adriana.net.*
This was probably the richest building project in antiquity and was designed entirely by the Emperor **Hadrian** (AD 76-138), who had visited every part of the Roman Empire. He had a passion for both art and architecture and he wished to recreate the monuments and sites he had visited during his travels. In AD 134 the villa was almost finished, but the 58 year-old Hadrian, ill and grief-stricken by the death of his young favourite Antinoüs, was to die four years later. Although later emperors probably continued to visit Tivoli, the villa was soon forgotten and fell into ruin. The site was explored from the 15C to the 19C and the recovered works were dispersed to various museums and private collections. It was only in 1870 that the Italian government organised the excavation of Tivoli, thus revealing this complex. Before exploring the site, study a model of the villa displayed in a room next to the bar.

The Canopo: Villa Adriana

Pecile★★

The water-filled Pecile takes its name from a portico in Athens. It was built in the shape of a large rectangle with slightly curved ends and is lined with a portico; it was oriented so that one side was always in the shade. The apsidal chamber called the **Sala dei Filosofi** (philosophers' room) was perhaps a reading room.

Teatro Marittimo★★★

The circular construction consists of a portico and a central building surrounded by a canal. It provided an ideal retreat for the misanthropic Hadrian. Bear south to pass the remains of a **nymphaeum** (ninfeo) and the great columns which belonged to a building comprising three semicircular rooms round a courtyard (cortile).

Terme★★

The layout of the baths shows the high architectural standards attained in the villa. First come the Small Baths and then the Great Baths with an apse.
The tall building, the **Pretorio** (Praetorium), was probably a storehouse.

Canopo★★★

Beyond the **museum** is a complex which evokes the Egyptian town of Canope with its famous Temple of Serapis. The route to Canope from Alexandria consisted of a canal lined with temples and gardens. At the southern end of this site is a copy of the Temple of Serapis.
Having reached the ruins overlooking the nymphaeum, turn right before skirting the **fishpond** and portico.

Palazzo imperiale

The palace complex extended from ʹiazza d'Oro to the Libraries. The rectangular **Piazza d'Oro**★★ was surrounded by a double portico and was ʹthetic indulgence serving no useʹ ʹose. On the far side are traces ʹgonal chamber and a domed ʹpposite.

ʹstri Dorici★★

ʹts name from the surʹcomposed of pilasters ʹd capitals.

Also visible are the **Caserma dei Vigili** (firemen's barracks), remains of a summer dining room and a nymphaeum. These buildings overlook a courtyard which is separated from the **library court** by a cryptoporticus, part of a network of underground passages which ran from one villa to another without emerging above ground.

The suite of ten rooms along one side of the library court was an infirmary. Note the fine mosaic **paving**★. According to custom the **library** was divided in two for a Greek section and a Latin section. The route to the **Terrazza di Tempe** goes past rooms paved with mosaic that belonged to a dining room. The path runs through the trees on the slope above the valley past a **round temple** attributed to the goddess Venus, and skirts the site of a **theatre**, on the left, before ending at the entrance.

Villa d'Este★★★

Head to the centre of Tivoli and park in the car park in Largo Garibaldi. Entrance on Piazza Trento. ♿ 🕐 *Allow 1hr 30min. Open daily except Mon, 8.30am-1hr before dusk.* 🕐 *Closed 1 Jan, 25 Dec.* ✆ *9€.* ☎ *0774 31 20 70; www.villadeste tivoli.info.*

In 1550 Cardinal Ippolito II d'Este –raised to great honours by François I of France but disgraced when the king's son Henri II succeeded to the throne – decided to retire to Tivoli. He immediately began to convert the former Benedictine convent into a pleasant country seat. The Neapolitan architect Pirro Ligorio was invited to prepare plans. The simple architecture of the villa contrasts with the elaborate terraced gardens. The statues, pools and fountains enhance the natural beauty with all the grace of the Mannerist style. Small wonder UNESCO added this watery spectacle to its World Heritage List.

To the left of the main entrance stands the old abbey church of **Santa Maria Maggiore** with its attractive Gothic façade and a 17C bell tower. Inside, in the chancel, are two 15C triptychs: above the one on the left is a painting of the Virgin by Jacopo Torriti, who also worked in mosaic in the 13C.

Palace and gardens★★★

From the former convent cloisters go down through the elaborately-decorated Old Apartments. From the ground-floor level there is a pleasant **view**★ of the gardens and Tivoli itself. A double flight of stairs leads to the upper garden walk. A fountain with a shell-shaped basin, Fontana del Bicchierone, is attributed to Bernini. To the left the Fontana Rometta, or "Mini Rome", reproduces some of the well-known monuments of Classical Rome. From here a splendid avenue lined with fountains, **Viale delle Cento Fontane**★★★, leads to the Oval Fountain, **Fontana dell'Ovato**★★★, dominated by a statue of the Sibyl. At a lower level the Fishpond Esplanade, **le Peschiere**, is overlooked at one end by the Organ Fountain, **Fontana dell' Organo**★★★, in which a concealed water-powered organ once played music.

Right at the very bottom of the garden is the Nature Fountain, **Fontana della Natura**, with a statue of Diana of Ephesus. Return by the central avenue to admire the Dragon Fountain, **Fontana dei Draghi**, built in 1572 in honour of Pope Gregory XIII, then turn right to pass the Bird Fountain, **Fontana della Civetta**, which used to produce birdsong, and finally the Fountain of Proserpina, **Fontana di Proserpina**.

Villa Gregoriana★

Enter from Piazza Tempio di Vesta, exit from Largo Massimo. ◷*Open March 10am-2.30pm, Apr-mid-Oct 10am-6.30pm. Open 16 Oct-30 Nov 10am-2.30pm.* ◷*Closed Mon.* ⊚*€4. www. villagregoriana.it*
This wooded park has a tangle of paths that wind down the steeply wooded slopes to the River Aniene where it cascades through the ravine. The waters of the Aniene plunge down at the Great Cascade, the **Grande Cascata**★★, disappear out of sight at the Siren's Cave or **Grotta della Sirena** and burst from the rock-face in Neptune's Cave, **Grotta**

di Nettuno. Climb the slope overlooking the ravine to leave the Villa Gregoriana and visit the **Tempio della Sibilla** (Sibyl's Temple), also known as the Temple of Vesta. This elegant Corinthian-style structure dates from the end of the Republic. An Ionic temple stands alongside.

Excursion

Palestrina★

▶*23km/14mi southeast.*
With its panoramic position overlooking the Prenestini mountains, an old historic centre and the remains of the celebrated Temple of Fortuna Primigenia, Palestrina makes for an extremely pleasant excursion. This splendid town flourished from the 8C to 7C BC; after various vicissitudes it submitted to Roman domination. The Romans turned it into a holiday resort for emperors and nobles. The cult of the goddess Fortuna prospered until the 4C AD when the sanctuary was abandoned and the medieval city born on its remains.

Palazzo Barberini★ and Museo Archeologico Prenestino★

♿ ◷*Open daily, 9am-7.30pm.* ⊚*3€.* ☎*06 95 38 100; www.comune.palestrina.rm.it.*
The museum has artefacts from several necropoleis as well as objects from the Barberini collection. The museum's masterpiece is the magnificent Nile **mosaic**★★, which portrays Egypt with the Nile flooding.

Tempio della Fortuna Primigenia★

This magnificent sanctuary, one of the finest examples of Hellenic architecture in Italy, dates from the 2C-1C BC and ori inally comprised a series of descend esplanades. In the Lower Sanctua Basilical Room remains as well side buildings, a grotto and Room from where the celeb fresco was taken. The Upp was built on the temple's nade (now Piazza della 11C Palazzo Colonn now the archaeolo built here. From fine **view of th**

TODI★★

POPULATION 17 075

MICHELIN MAP 563 N 19 – UMBRIA.

Todi, a charming old town perched on an attractive site, has retained walls from the Etruscan (Marzia Gateway), Roman and medieval periods.

- **Information:** Piazza Umberto I 6, 06059 Todi (PG) ☎075 89 43 395; www.comune.todi.pg.it.
- ▶ **Orient Yourself:** Todi is roughly the same distance from Perugia, Terni, Orvieto and Spoleto. The main road to Perugia is S 3 bis.
- **Don't Miss:** Piazza del Popolo and the Chiesa di San Fortunato.
- **Organizing Your Time:** Allow a couple of hours to sightsee.
- **Also See:** *PERUGIA, ORVIETO, SPOLETO.*

Worth a Visit

Piazza del Popolo★★

This square is surrounded by buildings that mark the town's flourishing commercial life in the Middle Ages. The 13C Gothic **Palazzo dei Priori**★, formerly the seat of the governor (podestà), is dominated by a 14C tower on a trapezoidal plan.

The 13C **Palazzo del Capitano**★ has attractive windows in groups of three flanked by small columns. The adjoining **Palazzo del Popolo**★, one of the oldest communal palaces in Italy (1213), houses a lapidary museum, a picture gallery and a museum of Etruscan and Roman antiquities. &⊙*Open daily 10.30am-1pm and 2.30-6.30pm (2.30-5pm Nov-Mar).* ⊙*Closed Mon, 1 Jan, 25 Dec.* ⊕*3.50€.* ☎075 89 44 148; www.sistemamuseo.it.

Chiesa di San Fortunato★★

Piazza della Repubblica.

Building on the church lasted from 1292 to 1460; the structure combines Gothic and Renaissance features. The **central doorway**★★ is delicately decorated. The lofty interior has **frescoes** (1432) by Masolino (fourth chapel to the south) and the tomb of **Jacopone da Todi** (1230-1307), a Franciscan monk, a poet and author of the *Stabat Mater.*

Duomo★

This early-12C Romanesque building is preceded by a staircase leading up to the pink and white marble façade, whose great rose window is pierced and fretted in the Umbrian manner.

Piazza Garibaldi

This square adjoining the Piazza del Popolo is graced with a monument to

Address Book

& *For coin ranges see the Legend on the* over flap.

ERE TO STAY

Bed & Breakfast San Lorenzo
a San Lorenzo 3 (2nd floor) – Todi 075 89 44 555 – sanlorenzotre@ losed Jan, Feb – ⌀ *– 6 rm.* ooking for a quiet, elegant with historic overtones J, this is the place for hich are all very indi- tefully furnished

with period pieces.
Ask for a room with a view out over the countryside.

WHERE TO EAT

☞**Antica Osteria De La Valle** – *Via Ciuffelli 19 – Todi –* ☎075 89 44 848 *– Closed Mon.* A one-room rustic-style establishment complete with bar and bottles on display. The owner, who is also in charge of the cooking, offers a variety of dishes drawing inspiration from seasonal, local produce.

Garibaldi. From the terrace, there is a pretty **view**★★ of the valley.

Rocca
Pass to the right of St Fortunatus and walk up to the ruins of the 14C castle. There is a shady public garden.

Chiesa di Santa Maria della Consolazione★
1km/0.6mi west on the Orvieto road

This Renaissance church was built between 1508 and 1609 by several architects who drew inspiration from Bramante's designs. The dome, whose drum is designed in accordance with Bramante's rhythmic principle, was decorated in the 16C and the 12 statues of the Apostles are by Scalza (16C).
 Cisterna romana; Campanile S. Fortunato.

TORINO★★
TURIN

POPULATION 868 000
MICHELIN MAP 561 G 4-5

Turin is unwilling to reveal its true character to the rushed visitor who will almost certainly fail to capture the profound contrasts that comprise the soul and charm of this city. On two occasions Turin has had to reinvent itself as a capital: first of the newly created Kingdom of Italy and more recently of the automobile industry. Now the city is attempting to shake off the role of "factory-city" and become an important cultural centre for the new millennium.

The military tradition of the ruling Savoy dynasty has given Turin a rather severe imprint, reflected in its restrained Baroque architecture. For centuries the city has jealously guarded the Turin Shroud at the same time cherishing a vocation for the esoteric that has attracted personalities such as Paracelsus, Nostradamus and Cagliostro. Nietzsche lived his last years in Turin where he wrote his major works. He claimed that "Turin is the first place where I am possible."

- **Information:** Atrium Torino, piazza Solferino 10100 Torino, ☏011 53 51 81; Stazione Porta Nuova, ☏011 53 13 27; www.turismotorino.org.
- **Orient Yourself:** Situated at the foot of the Alps, against a backdrop of wonderful alpine scenery, Turin lies at the hub of a motorway network which takes in A 4, as well as A 5 (to the Valle d'Aosta), A 32 (to the Val di Susa) and A 32 (to Moncenisio), A 21 (to Piacenza) and A 6 (to Cuneo).
- **Parking:** If arriving by car, park and explore the city on foot or on the extensive public transport system.
- **Don't Miss:** The Holy Shroud, the Galleria di Sabauda, Museo del Cinema and the Galleria Civica di Arte Moderna e Contemporane.
- **Organizing Your Time:** Turin is a good weekend destination and two days is the minimum to see the city - allow 3-4 days for a more thorough exploration.
- **Especially for Kids:** The Mole Antonelliana chair lift.
- **Also See:** *LANGHE E MONFERRATO, SALUZZO, VALLE D'AOSTA, VERCELLI.*

A Bit of History

During the 1C the capital of the Celtic tribe, the Taurini, was transformed by the Romans into a military colony and given the name of Augusta Taurinorum. Converted to Christianity, it became the seat of a bishopric in the early 5C and a

century later a Lombard duchy passing under Frankish rule. F 11C onwards and for nearly turies the destiny of Turin to that of the **House of S** Italy's reigning royal fam to 1946). They were skil siding with the pope

G. Bressi/Archivio Turismo Torino

The elegance and clean lines of Juvarra's Stupinigi Hunting Lodge

emperor, and playing France off against the Dukes of Milan. In the early 18C that Charles Emmanuel II and Victor Amadeus II embellished their adopted city with buildings by Guarini and Juvarra. Charles Emmanuel III increased the importance of Turin during his long reign (1732-73) by reorganising the kingdom's administration and by establishing in his capital a court with very formal etiquette, similar to the one at Versailles. In 1798 Charles Emmanuel IV was expelled from Turin by French troops who wanted to impose a regime based on the revolutionary principles of 1789. On the fall of Napoleon Bonaparte, Victor Emmanuel I was restored to his kingdom and promoted a policy against foreign interference in Piedmontese affairs. Turin then became the centre of the struggle against the Austrians, and for the unification of Italy.

Following the reorganisation of Piedmont by Camillo Cavour, the Franco-Piedmontese alliance against Austria and the victories at Solferino and Magenta (1859) Victor Emmanuel II was proclaimed the first King of Italy and Turin became the seat of the Italian government, to be replaced by Florence in 1865. The House of Savoy reigned over Italy until the proclamation of an Italian Republic in 1946.

Economy

The intense activity of its suburban industries has made Turin the capital of Italian engineering. It was in the Piedmontese capital that the **Italian motor industry** was born with FIAT, founded in 1899 by Giovanni Agnelli, and Lancia, created in 1906 by Vincenzo Lancia and

Not Just Fiat

For many Turin is synonymous with FIAT but numerous companies known all over the world were born here or have their central offices in or around the city. Among these are: Lavazza, Cinzano, Martini & Rossi, Gancia, Caffarel and Peyrano in the food and drink sector; the textile group GFT, producers of the Armani, Valentini-Cerruti and Ungaro brands; the Istituto Bancario San Paolo and the Cassa di Risparmio di Torino (the second largest bank in Italy) in the banking sector; SAI, and Reale Mutua Assicurazioni in the insurance sector; STET-Telecom Italia in the communications sector; Robe di Kappa, Superga and Invicta in the sports sector and De Fonseca in the shoe manufacturing industry. Without forgetting Michelin naturally, who opened their first factory outside France in 1906 a building on Via Livorno.

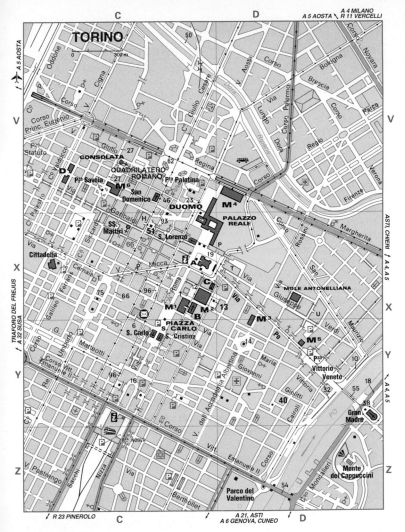

Address Book

GETTING ABOUT

By car – In spite of its decentralised position (the city is only about 100km/62mi from the French border) there is a good network of motorways linking Turin to various cities. Furthermore, thanks to its famous octagonal plan and wide 19C avenues, traffic, although heavy at times, is manageable and it is easier to travel in and around Turin by car than it is in many other Italian cities.

Bus – The terminus is in Corso Inghilterra at the corner of Corso Castel Fidardo, ☎011 53 52 47.

By train – The main railway stations in the city are:

Porta Nuova, Corso Vittorio Emanuele II 53, i ☎8488 88088 (toll-free number);

Porta Susa, piazza XVIII Dicembre 8, ☎8488 88088 (toll-free number).

By air – Turin's international airport is situated 11km/7mi north of the city in Caselle (www.aeroportoditorino.it). It is served by national and international airline companies.

Buses operated by Sadem ensure connections to the city every 45min, from 5.15am to 10.30pm (departs from Porta Nuova – Corso Vittorio Emanuele II at the corner of Via Sacchi – and Porta Susa – Corso San Martino at the corner of Piazza XVIII Dicembre) and from 6.30am to 11.30pm (departs from the airport, arrivals floor, opposite the national flights exit). Tickets can be purchased from ticket counters adjacent to the terminals or on the vehicle when leaving from Turin and from the newspaper stand in the departure lounge, the automated ticket machine or the ticket office in the National Arrivals lounge when departing from the airport.

TORINO CARD (and museums)

The card includes free transport for 48hrs and 72hrs (from the date on the back of the card) on all public transport in the city as well as free entrance to all the museums, discounts for concerts and various other events. The card costs €15/17 (one adult and child under 12). For information contact Turismo Torino, ☎011 53 13 27; www.turismotorino.org

ENJOYING TURIN BY DAY...

The best way of discovering the city is on foot. The historic centre is compact and can be covered on foot; pedestrians are protected from inclement weather by the arcades lining the main streets.

Public transport – ATM (City transport company) has its head office in Corso Turati 19/6, ☎800 019 152 (toll-free number), www.comune.torino.it/atm Tickets can be purchased at tobacconists, newspaper stands and authorised bars. There are various types of tickets: the biglietto ordinario urbano (€0.90) is valid for 70min, a biglietto giornaliero (one-day ticket – 3€) allows unlimited travel all day, the Shopping ticket (1.80€) is valid for four hours from when it is stamped, from 9am to 8pm, the Shopping insieme ticket (4€) is valid only on Saturdays and allows unlimited travel for three people from 2.30pm to 8pm.

Taxi – Central Taxi Radio ☎011 57 30, Centrale Radio ☎011 57 37, Radio Taxi ☎011 57 30 or 33 99.

DISCOVERING THE CITY

Boat trips on the Po – Boat trips are operated along the Po (departure from the river bank at Lungopo Diaz). For information ☎011 4 48 92.

Touristbus – This service operates tours of the city, the hills and the Savoy residences. ☎011 58 11 900; www.turismotorino.org

Get on your bike – Cycle through the magnificent Mandria a Venaria Reale Park (1340 ha/3311 acres of parkland 15km/9mi northwest of the city centre); bicycles can be rented. The park also offers excursions on horseback and nature walks. For information call ☎800 48 66 64 (toll-free number).

WHERE TO STAY

For coin ranges see the Legend on the cover flap.

It is worth noting that during the trade fairs and commercial exhibitions, the hotels tend to put their prices up.

Hotel Centrale – Via Mazzini 13 – Torino – ☎011 81 24 182 – Fax 011 88 33 59 – 12 rm. The rooms are modern and functional but comfortable. Very reasonably priced.

◎🛏**Hotel Magenta** – *Corso Vittorio Emanuele II 67 – Torino – ☎011 54 26 49 – Fax 011 54 26 49 – 18 rm.* A stone's throw from the Porta Nuova station and very convenient for anyone arriving by train. Fine period palazzo with basic rooms. Some have shared bathrooms.

◎🛏**Hotel Dogana Vecchia** – *Via Corte d'Appello 4 – Torino – ☎011 43 66 752 – www.hoteldoganavecchia.com – ℙ – 50 rm. ☕.* The inn of the old customs-house, built at the end of the 18C, was a stopping place for travellers, including Mozart, Napoleon and Verdi. The prettiest rooms are those decorated with antique furnishings, but there are a few modern, functional rooms.

◎◎🛏**Hotel Roma e Rocca Cavour** – *Piazza Carlo Felice 60 – Torino – ☎011 56 12 772 – www.romarocca.it – 90 rm – ☕.* Elegant hotel: antique furniture, magnificent wood or marble floors, precious rugs, Murano glass chandeliers. The hotel offers excellent discounts on weekends, in the month of August and during the Easter and Christmas holidays. In August 1950 Cesare Pavese put an end to his tormented life in room 346.

◎◎🛏**Relais Villa Sassi** – *Strada al Traforo del Pino 47 – Torino – ☎011 89 80 556 – www.villasassi.com – Closed Aug – ℙ☷ – 16 rm – ☕ – Restaurant €49/67.* An exclusive retreat of faded grandeur. Situated just 4km/2.5mi from the historic centre this 17C villa is surrounded by parkland (over 2ha/5 acres). Spacious rooms with period furnishings.

WHERE TO EAT

◎**Pizzeria La Stua** – *Via Mazzini 46 – Torino – ☎011 81 78 339 – Closed Mon, Sun lunchtime – ☷ – Book.* During the winter the regular customers in the know head for the little dining room on the ground floor where there is a lovely fire crackling in the fireplace.

◎**Porto di Savona** – *Piazza Vittorio Veneto 2 – Torino – ☎011 81 73 500 – Closed Mon, Tue lunchtime – ☷ ☷.* A typical old-fashioned trattoria. A good selection of traditional, regional dishes on the menu.

◎◎**Del Cambio** – *Piazza Carignano 2 – Torino – ☎011 54 37 60 – Closed Sun, 12-18 Aug, 1-7 Jan – ☷ – Book. 15% service charge.* Valuable works of art, Baroque mirrors and gilded stuccowork all make for a very refined ambience where time seems to have stood still.

TAKING A BREAK

Baratti & Milano – *Piazza Castello 29 – Torino – ☎011 44 07 138 – Open Mon and Tue, Thu-Sat 8.30am-7.30pm, Sun 8.30am-1pm and 3.30-7.30pm.* Founded in 1875, this was originally a confectionery shop. With its elegant Art Nouveau rooms the café was a favourite with the ladies of Turin's high society.

Caffè San Carlo – *Piazza San Carlo 156 – ☎011 56 17 748 – Open Tue-Sun 7am-midnight.* This opulent café, founded in 1822, was a patriotic stronghold during the Risorgimento and later became a salon frequented by artists, literary personalities and statesmen.

Caffè Torino – *Piazza San Carlo 204 – ☎011 54 51 18 – www.caffe-torino. it – Open 8am-1am.* Founded in 1903, this Art Nouveau café was frequented by actors such as James Stewart, Ava Gardner and Brigitte Bardot.

Fiorio – *Via Po 8 – ☎011 81 73 225 – Open Tue-Sun 8am-1am.* Founded in 1780, this was the traditional meeting-place for aristocrats and conservative intellectuals. Its ice cream is one of the glories of Turin.

Mulassano – *Piazza Castello 15 – ☎011 54 79 90 – Open 7.30am-9pm.* Founded in 1907, this charming café was frequented by members of the Savoia family and performers from the nearby Teatro Regio. It counted the comedian Macario and the poet Guido Gozzano among its habitués.

GOING OUT

Tre Galli – *Via Sant'Agostino 25 – ☎011 52 16 027 – www.3galli.com – Open 7pm-2am.* A wine bar-restaurant with a rustic-minimalist atmosphere.

ENTERTAINMENT

Music lovers... – There are several prestigious concert halls in Turin including the **Auditorium Giovanni Agnelli del Lingotto**, Via Nizza 262/43, ☎011 66 77 415 (classical music) and the

Conservatorio Giuseppe Verdi, Via Mazzini 11, ☎011 81 78 958. Without forgetting the Teatro Regio, in Piazza Castello 215, ☎011 88 15 241.

SHOPPING

There are 18km/11mi of arcades in the historic centre. On Via Roma, which the architect Piacentini modernised in the 1930s, there are luxurious shops and the elegant San Federico gallery.

Art and antique lovers should head for the nearby Via Cavour, Via Maria Vittoria and Via San Tommaso. Most antiquarian bookshops are concentrated around Via Po, Via Accademia Albertina and Piazza San Carlo, while Via Lagrange is a gourmet's paradise. Turin specialities include agnolotti pasta, bagna cauda, grissini breadsticks and chocolate (chocolates with fillings, hazelnut-chocolate *gianduiotti*, bonet). All of which can be accompanied by local wines or vermouth, created in Turin at the end of the 18C.

Two streets lead off Piazza Castello: the Via Po and the Via Garibaldi, one of the longest pedestrian streets in Europe. On the second Sunday of the month is the Balôn in Porta Palazzo, Turin's traditional flea market, in existence since 1856.

Caffè Torino

L. Pessina/MICHELIN

eventually taken over by the FIAT group in 1969. The Lingotto, the famous FIAT factory which was built in 1920 with such avant-garde technical features as the spectacular test ramp on the roof, was defined by Le Corbusier as "one of the most striking spectacles provided by industry." When production ceased, the building was transformed by Renzo Piano into a highly modern conference and exhibition centre with an auditorium and a commercial area. Important tyre manufacturers and well-known coachbuilders (one of the most famous was the great Pinin Farina) have contributed to the prosperity of the motor industry in Turin itself.

But Turin boasts other very solid traditions. There are numerous publishing companies such as Bollati Boringhieri, Einaudi, Lattes, Loescher, Paravia, SEI and UTET as well as one of the major national newspapers, *La Stampa*, founded in 1895. Music also thrives in Turin thanks to the presence of the RAI National Symphony Orchestra and the prestigious *Teatro Regio*.

These diverse traditions are all displayed in the numerous fairs and exhibitions hosted by the city: the *Salone [dell'] Automobile* (every two years), the *Salone del Libro* (Book Fair), the *Salone della Musica* and the *Settembre Musica festival* which also encompasses the prestigious *Cinema Giovani* (Young cinema) festival, a homage to the "tenth art" in a city which until the First World War was the Italian capital of cinema.

Historic Centre

Piazza San Carlo★★

This is a graceful example of town planning. The churches of San Carlo and Santa Cristina, symmetrically placed on the south side, frame the Via Roma. The curious façade of Santa Cristina (on the left), surmounted by candelabra, was designed by the famous Sicilian-Turinese architect Juvarra, who was responsible for many of Turin's lovely buildings. On the east side is the 17C palace which was the French Ambassador's residence from 1771 to 1789. In the centre of the square stands the famous "bronze horse" by C Marocchetti (1838), an equestrian monument to Emanuele Filiberto of Savoy who, after defeating the French at the battle of San Quintino in 1557, salvaged his states after 25 years of French occupation (Treaty of Cateau-Cambrésis).

Palazzo dell'Accademia delle Scienze

This 17C palace by Guarini now houses two major Italian museums.

Palazzo Carignano★★

Victor Emmanuel II (1820-78), responsible for the Unification of Italy and the country's first king (1861), was born in this beautiful Baroque palace by **Guarini**. The palace is now home to the **Museo del Risorgimento Italiano** (🛈 see Worth a Visit for a description of the museum).

Piazza Castello

The political and religious heart of the city, this square was designed by the architect Ascanio Vitozzi (1539-1615). The main city streets lead off this square and it is bordered by the Royal Palace and the arcades of the **Teatro Regio**, inaugurated in 1740. Severely damaged by bombardments in the Second World War, it was rebuilt and opened to the public in 1973. In the theatre's atrium there is a gateway designed by the artist Umberto Matroianni entitled **Musical Odyssey**. In the centre of the square stands the imposing castle from which it derives its name. The castle was later named Palazzo Madama.

Palazzo Madama★

The palace derives its name from the two "Madame Reali" who stayed here in the 17C-18C: Maria Cristina of France, widow of Victor Amadeus I and Giovanna of Savoia-Nemours, widow of Charles Emmanuel II. The castle was erected in the 14C and 15C on the remains of the Roman gateway, Porta Pretoria, which formed part of the Augustan ramparts, while the west façade was designed in the 18C by Juvarra. Across from its hall is the Sala del Voltone, once the courtyard of the medieval castle, where the ruins of the Roman doorway can still be seen. The palace is now home to the **Museo di Arte Antica** (🛈 see below).

Palazzo Reale★

The princes of the House of Savoy lived in this plain building until 1865. The façade was designed by Amedeo di Castellamonte in the 17C. The sumptuous **apart-ments (appartamenti)** are accessed by the fine staircase, **Scala delle Forbici**, designed by Filippo Juvarra and are decorated in the Baroque, Rococo and neo-Classical styles. &🛈Telephone for opening times. 🕐Closed Mon, 1 Jan, 25 Apr, 2 and 24 Jun, 25 Dec. ≈6.50€ (first floor); 4€ (second floor, ground floor). ☎011 43 61 455; www.ambienteto.arti.beniculturali.it.

The Royal Armoury, **Armeria Reale**★, contains a splendid collection of arms and armour and military memorabilia dating from the 13C to 20C. 🕐Closed Mon, 1 Jan, 25 Dec. ≈ 4€. For information on opening times, call ☎011 51 84 358; www.artito.arti.beniculturali.it

To the left of the palace stands the **church of San Lorenzo** to which the architect Guarini added a dome and rather daring crenellations.

Duomo★

🛈The Shroud of Turin.

This Renaissance cathedral, dedicated to St John, Turin's patron saint, was built at the end of the 15C for Cardinal Della Rovere. The façade has three carved doorways; the crown of the campanile was designed by Juvarra.

Inside, behind the high altar surmounted by a dome, a Baroque masterpiece by Guarini, is the **Cappella della Santa Sindone** (Chapel of the Holy Shroud), which enshrined the precious but much-contested **Holy Shroud**★★★ in which Christ is said to have been wrapped after the Descent from the Cross. In 1997 a raging fire caused grave damage to Guarini's dome (temporarily replaced by a trompe-l'œil) but fortunately the urn containing the precious relic was saved.

Archaeological area

There are some interesting Roman remains near the cathedral: remains of a 2C AD theatre and the **Porta Palatina** (1C AD), a fine Roman city gateway. Via IV Marzo crosses the oldest part the city and leads to the harmoni elegant Piazza del Palazzo di Città, inated by the 17C Town Hall whi erected by Francesco Lanfranch Nearby (turn right onto Via stands **San Domenico** (14C) only Gothic church. inside, the church has works by Ferrari and Spanzotti and a beautiful cycle of 14C frescoes.

From Piazza Castello to the Po

Via Po★

Created between the 17C and 18C to connect the historic centre to the River Po and bordered by harmoniously arranged palaces and arcades, this is one of Turin's most beautiful streets. Nearby stands the **Pinacoteca Albertina**, a picture gallery with collections of Piedmontese, Lombard and Venetian painting, a section on Flemish and Dutch painting as well as a fine group of **cartoons★** by Gaudenzio Ferrari and his school. ○*Open daily 10am-6pm.* ○*Closed Mon, 25 Dec.* ✆*4€.* ☎*011 81 77 862; www.accademialbertina.torino.it*

Mole Antonelliana★

This unusual structure, towering 167m/548ft up into the air, is the symbol of Turin. Its daring design was the work of the architect Alessandro Antonelli (1798-1888). Originally destined to be a temple for the Jewish community (1863), it was ceded to the city in 1877. The summit affords a vast **panorama★★** of Turin. ○*Lift operates 10am-8pm (11pm in summer).* ○*Closed Mon.* ✆*€3.62.* ☎*011 57 64 733.*

Piazza Vittorio Veneto

This large 19C square affords a wonderful **view★★** of the hills and dips down towards the river, which can be reached by going down to the Murazzi (Lungopo Diaz), ramparts erected in the 19C. Beyond the Victor Emmanuel I bridge, erected by Napoleon, stands the church of the Gran Madre. To the right of the church, Monte dei Cappuccini (alt. 284m/932ft) affords an exceptional **anorama★★★** of the city.

co del Valentino★★

wooded park extends along the about 1.5km/1mi and affords a t walk along the river. To the ands the **Castello del Valen-**

tino, erected in the first half of the 17C for Duchess Marie Christine of France. There is also the Palazzo delle Esposizioni (Exhibition Hall), the Teatro Nuovo and the **Borgo Medievale★**, an interesting reconstruction of a medieval town and Fénis Castle. ○*Open 9am-6pm.* ○*Closed Mon, 25 Dec.* ✆*No charge for Borgo; 5€ for fortress.* ☎*011 44 31 701; www.comune.torino.it/musei/civici/bm.*

Sights

Museo Egizio★★★

Via Accademia delle Scienze 6. ♿○*Open daily 8.30am-7.30pm (ticket office closes 6.30pm).* ○*Closed Mon, 1 Jan, 1 May, 25 Dec.* ✆*6.50€; 8€ including Galleria Sabauda.* ☎*011 56 17 776; www. museoegizio.org.*

The Egyptian Museum is one of the richest collections of Egyptian antiquities in the world. The basement houses the finds from the excavations carried out in 1911 by two Italian archaeologists, Schiaparelli and Farina. On the ground floor is the section on statuary art with 20 seated or standing figures of the lion-headed goddess Sekhmet from Karnak, and an important series of statues of Pharaohs of the New Kingdom (1580-1100 BC), Egypt's Golden Age. The Rock Temple of Thutmose III (c 1450 BC), a gift from the United Arab Republic, originated from Ellessya 200km/124mi to the south of Aswan.

The collections on the first floor represent all aspects of Egyptian civilisation, in particular: the sarcophagi – simple examples dating from the Middle Kingdom (2100-1580 BC) and sculpted ones during the New Kingdom; and an important number of mummies and copies of funerary papyri rolls known as the Book of the Dead. In addition to the recreated funeral chambers (mastabas, Giza 2500 BC), there is an exceptional collection of funerary steles dating from the Middle and New Kingdoms. Jewellery and pottery from the pre-dynastic civilisations, known as Nagadian, date from 4000-3000 BC. The influence of the Greek world made itself felt from the 4C BC following the conquest by

Alexander the Great (masks and statu-ettes), followed by the Romans from 30 BC (bronze vases).

Galleria Sabauda★★★

Via Accademia delle Scienze 6. ⏱*Open Tue, Fri-Sun, 8.30am-2pm, Wed 2-7.30pm, Thu 10am-7.30pm (In winter telephone for opening hours).* ⏱*Closed Mon, 1 Jan, 1 May, 25 Dec.* ∞*4€; 8€ including Museo Egizio.* ☎*011 54 74 40; www.museitorino. it/galleriasabauda.*

The gallery houses the collections of the House of Savoy and is divided into the-matic and chronological sections.

On the second floor, the section on 14C to 16C **Piedmontese painting**★ has works by Martino Spanzotti (1455-1528), the principal exponent of the Late Gothic Piedmontese school, his pupil Defendente Ferrari (1510-31), Macrino d'Alba (1495-1528) and Gaudenzio Fer-rari (1475-1546), an artist closely linked to the Milanese school. One of his masterpieces is the **Crucifixion**★. The section on 14C to 16C **Italian painting** includes works by Fra Angelico, Antonio and Piero Pollaiolo (Tuscan school), Ber-gognone (Lombard school), Bartolomeo Vivarini and Giovanni Bellini (Venetian school). The **Prince Eugene Collection** has both Italian and European painting including a collection of **Dutch and Flemish painting**★★. One of the rich-est in Italy, it includes the *Stigmata of St Francis* by Van Eyck (1390-1441), *Scenes from the Passion of Christ* by Hans Mem-ling (c 1435-94), the *Old Man Sleeping* by Rembrandt (1606-69) and enchant-ing **landscapes** by Jan Brueghel (1568-1625).

On the third floor the **Dynastic Collec-tions,** divided into three sections pre-sented in chronological order, include fine examples of Italian and European painting from the 15C to 18C. Some of the most notable works include the **Visitation**★ by the Flemish artist Van der Weyden (1400-64), **The Meal at the House of Simon**★, an early work of Veronese (1528-1588), the *Trinity* by Tintoretto (1519-94), the great canvases by the **Bassano** family (16C) whose dynamic use of light heralds the work of Caravaggio, the **Assumption**★★ by

Orazio Gentileschi (1563-1639), one of the artist's masterpieces characterised by a violent realism, the **Sons of Charles I of England**★, a fine portrait by Van Dyck (1599-1641), *The Four Elements* by the Bolognese painter F. Albani (1578-1660) whose classicism derives from the work of the Carracci and Guido Reni, the portrait of *Philip IV of Spain* by Velasquez (1599-1660), *The Triumph of Aurelius* by Tiepolo (1696-1770) and the beautiful **views**★ by the Venetian painter Bel-lotto (1720-80), a nephew of Canaletto. The fine **Gualino Collection** includes works from the fine and decorative arts of various nationalities, among which is some fine Chinese sculpture.

Museo del Cinema★★★

♿⏱*Open daily except Mon, 9am-8pm (11pm Sat).* ∞*5.20€; 6.80€ museum and panoramic lift.* ☎*011 81 38 560; www. museonazionaledelcinema.org.*

This museum is home to a vast col-lection of films, documents and other items relating to the history of cinema. A spiral staircase leads up to the heart of the Mole Antonelliana and the museum, where an exhibition explores various cinematic themes.

Museo di Arte Antica★★

Palazzo Madama, Piazza Castello. ⏱*Tele-phone for opening times and prices.* ⏱*Closed Mon.* ☎*011 44 29 912; www. comune.torino.it/palazzomadama.*

There is a museum of ancient art, the **Museo d'Arte Antica**★, on the ground floor. Exhibits include Gothic carvings, work by the 15C-16C Piedmontese school (Gian Martino Spanzotti, Macrino d'Alba, Defendente and Gaudenzio Ferrari), a Portrait of a Man (1475) by Antonello da Messina and a 14C Madonna by Barnaba da Modena.

Museo Nazionale del Risorgimento Italiano★★

Via Accademia delle Scienze 5. ⏱ *for restoration at the time o...* *press.* ☎*011 56 21 147; ww...* *piemonte.it/cultura/risorgi...*

This museum houses a... of documentation pe... history of Italy from...

to the Second World War. The museum includes the **Sala del Parlamento Subalpino**★, where speakers included Cavour, Garibaldi, Verdi and Manzoni.

GAM – Galleria Civica di Arte Moderna e Contemporanea★★

Via Magenta 31. ♿️🕐*Open daily 10am-7pm.* 🕐*Closed Mon.* ➿*7.50€(Tue no charge).* ☎*011 44 29 546; www.gam torino.it.*

This ample collection of fine art gives a good overview of Italian art and its main exponents, focusing on the 19C and 20C Piedmontese schools. The second floor, devoted to 19C art, has the largest body of work by the Reggio artist Antonio Fontanesi (1818-82), whose landscapes are notable for their solemn compositions, veiled light and dense, rich colours. The first floor, devoted to the 20C, shows the development of Italian and European art through the work of the more significant artists and movements: Balla, Casorati, Martini, the Milanese Novecento group, the Ferrara metaphysical paintings (Carlo Carrà, Giorgio de Chirico), the Roman school (Scipione, Mafai), Turin's "Gruppo dei Sei" (Jessie Boswell, Gigi Chessa, Nicola Galante, Carlo Levi, Francesco Menzio and Enrico Paolucci), examples of Informal Art and "Arte Povera" from the 1960s. The ground floor has collections of international art of the last 30 years.

Museo dell'Automobile Carlo Biscaretti di Ruffi★★★

South of the town. Take Corso Massimo d'Azeglio and then follow the plan of the built-up area in the Michelin Atlas Italy. The address is Corso Unità d'Italia 40. ♿️🕐*Open daily 10am-6.30pm.* 🕐*Closed Mon, 1 Jan, 25 Dec.* ➿*5.50€.* ☎*011 67 76 66; www.museoauto.it.*

A vast modern building houses an extensive collection of cars, chassis and engines, as well as graphic documents outlining the history of the auto from its beginnings to the last 20 years.

Another room devoted to the history of tyre manufacture traces the tremendous development of materials, structure, technology and research, famous car races and types of vehicle. The museum also includes a library and archives (open by appointment only).

Hills around Turin★

50km/31mi. Take Corso Regina Margherita and turn left into Corso Casale after crossing the River Po. Take the next right onto the Circuito della Maddalena.

Basilica di Superga★

🕐*Basilica: open Mon-Fri 9am-noon and 3-5pm (Apr-Oct 6pm), Sat-Sun 9am-12.45pm and 3-5,45pm (Apri-Oct 6.45pm).* 🕐*Closed 1 Jan (morning).* 👣*Tours of*

...omage to Turin's motor industry: the Museo dell'Automobile ...fia

Museo dell'Automobile Carlo Biscaretti di Ruffia

royal tombs 👓*3€.* ☎*011 89 97 456; www. basilicadisuperga.com.*

This masterpiece was built by Juvarra from 1717 to 1731 on a hill (670m/2 198ft high). The basilica is circular in plan and roofed with a dome and its most remarkable feature is its monumental façade. The chapel dedicated to the Virgin, in the chancel, is a pilgrimage centre. The basilica is the Pantheon of the Kings of Sardinia.

Tombe dei Reali

The royal tombs in the crypt include that of Victor Amadeus II, who built the basilica to fulfil a vow made when his capital was being besieged by a French and Spanish army in 1706. Alongside are the tombs of Charles-Albert and other princes of the House of Savoy. From the esplanade there is a fine **view**★★★ of Turin, the Po Plain and the Alps.

Chieri

This town is known for its cuisine. It has some fine Piedmontese Gothic monuments such as the 15C cathedral flanked by the Romanesque-Gothic baptistery and the 13C-15C church of San Domenico with its fine campanile.
Follow directions for Castelnuovo Don Bosco (4km/2.5mi south at **Colle Don Bosco** is the house where St John Bosco was born) and Albugnano.

Colle della Maddalena★

From Superga take the scenic route via Pino Torinese which affords good **views**★★ of Turin. From Pino Torinese continue to the hilltop, Colle della Maddalena, and the Parco della Rimembranza, commemorating those who died in the First World War. On the way down there are more lovely views★. The Parco Europa at Cavoretto overlooks the southern part of the town.

Val di Susa★★

150km/93mi, allow one day. From Turin take the west exit in the direction of Corso Francia

▶ *Take S 25. From S 25 follow the turn-off 6km/4mi after Rivoli.*

4 May 1949

Heavy rain and fog over Turin. An aeroplane flies over Superga with its illustrious passengers: 18 players from Grande Torino, the legendary football team who won five championships in a row and provided Italy's national team with ten players. They were on their way back from Lisbon where they had played a friendly and were accompanied by technicians, executives and journalists. With zero visibility, at 5.05pm the plane loses radio contact and plunges down, its left wing hitting the basilica, finally crashing to the ground. The city of Turin is paralysed with grief, the Grande Torino team dies and its memory is imbued with a sense of nostalgia and the desire to make the sport live forever.

Abbazia di Sant'Antonio di Ranverso★

🕐*Open Apr-Oct 9am-noon and 2.30-5.30pm, Nov-Mar 9am-noon and 2-4.30pm.* 👓*€2.60.* ☎*011 93 67 450; www. mauriziano.it.*

This abbey was a pilgrims' resting place and a centre for curing "St Anthony's Fire" (egotism). The church, founded in the 12C, has three 15C doorways adorned with gothic pediments and pinnacles. The interior has **frescoes**★ by **Giacomo Jaquerio** (1401-53). The frescoes in the sacristy are better preserved; the scene of two peasants offering two pigs refers to the tradition of curing St Anthony's fire with pork fat.

Avigliana

Until the 15C this town was one of the Savoia family's favourite residences. The heart of the historic centre is the pretty square, **Piazza Conte Rosso**, dominated by the ruins of a **Castle** (15C). Nearby stands the Romanesque-Gothic parish church of San Giovanni. Southeast of the ruins stands the church of **San Pietro**★ (10C-11C) which has a fine cy of frescoes (mainly 14C-15C). *To visi church, contact the parish priest launderette on Via San Pietro.* ☎ 28 300.

Sacra di San Michele: a magnificent but haunting sight.

A scenic road skirts the two lakes of Avigliana, originally glaciers, eventually leading up to the abbey of San Michele. (13.5km/8mi).

Sacra di San Michele★★★

🕐*Open daily 9.30am-12.30pm and 3-6pm (closes at 5pm in winter).* 🕐*Closed Mon.* ⊕*4€.* ☎*011 93 91 30; www.sacra disanmichele.com.*

This Benedictine abbey, perched on a rocky site (alt 962m/3 156ft), was a powerful establishment in the 13C with over 100 monks and 140 sister houses. It was built at the end of the 10C by Hughes de Montboissier from Auvergne and its layout bears a strong resemblance to the abbey at Mont Saint Michel in France. Climb the great staircase leading to the Zodiac Door; its pilasters and capitals were decorated by the famous Master Nicolò (1135). The Romanesque-Gothic church built on top of the rocky eminence has 16C **frescoes**. The early-16C triptych on the high altar is by Defendente Ferrari.

From the esplanade there is a lovely **view**★★★ of the Alps.

▶ *Head back along S 25 or A 32 through the Fréjus tunnel.*

sa★

ated at the foot of an impressive ntain range dominated by the melone (3 538m/11 608ft) stands Susa, at a junction of two roads which lead to France. This has resulted in its being referred to as "Italy's gateway". Because of its strategic position Susa, was destroyed by Constantine in 312 and by Barbarossa in 1174.

The symbol of the city is the **Savoy Door**★, which takes its name from the French region and dates from the late 3C to early 4C AD when the ramparts were built. Next to the door stands the **Cathedral**, founded in the years 1027-29 with Gothic additions made in the 14C. To the south side of the church Piazza San Giusto is dominated by the **Romanesque campanile**★★.

In a delightful corner stands the elegant **Arco di Augusto**★, the oldest monument in the city (8 BC). In front of the arch there are remains of the **Roman Aqueduct** (4C AD); beyond stand the Celtic **rocks** (6C-5C BC), used by Druid priests for sacrificial rites.

To the south, in a typically decentralised position stands the **amphitheatre**, erected in the 1C-2C AD.

Abbazia della Novalesa

8km/5mi northeast. 🕐*Open daily Jul and Aug for ↰⌐guided tours at 10.30am and 4.30pm), Sep-Jun Sat-Sun only 9-11.30am.* 🕐*Due to the fragility of the frescoes, the Cappella di S. Eldrado is not open to visitors during snow or rain.* ⊕*Donation recommended.* ☎*0122 65 32 10; www. abbazianovalesa.org.*

This powerful Benedictine abbey was founded in the 8C and destroyed by Saracens in the 10C. The real jewel of this abbey are the **frescoes**★★in the **Cappella Sant'Eldrado** (12C).

Monteferrato★

150km/93mi, allow one day. From Turin head east on S 10.
The proposed itinerary takes the visitor through this attractive region of limestone hills, bordered to the north by the Po, to the east by the plains of Alessandria and to the southwest by the Langhe hills. The valley of Villafranca d'Asti and the lower part of the River Tanaro divide the area into Lower and Upper Monferrato. Defended by numerous strongholds, Monferrato has given Piedmont some of its finest wines: Barbera, Dolcetto and Grignolino among red wines, Cortese and Gavi among white wines and the dessert wines Asti Spumante, Moscato and Brachetto.

Abbazia di Vezzolano★

17km/10mi northeast of Chieri. ⏱*Open daily summer 9.30am-12.30pm (winter 9.30am-noon) and 2-6pm.* ⏱*Closed Mon, 1 Jan, 1 May, 26 Dec.* ☎*011 99 20 607.*
This abbey is one of the finest examples of Piedmontese Romanesque-Gothic architecture. Beyond its façade stands the real jewel of Vezzolano, the splendid 12C **jubé**★★(rood screen), whose polychrome low reliefs depict the life of the Virgin. These structures separated the faithful from the monks. At the end of the south aisle are the **cloisters**★ with 13C-14C fresco remains.

▶ *Rejoin S 458.*

Asti

38km/24mi southeast on S 458.
The home town of the tragic poet, Vittorio Alfieri (1749-1803), is the scene of an annual horse race *(palio),* which is preceded by a procession with over 1 000 participants in 14C and 15C costume. The 12C **baptistery of San Pietro**★, the 15C church of San Pietro and the Gothic cloisters form an attractive group.

▶ *Take E 74 dual-carriageway and then S 456 for Acqui Terme.*

Strada dei castelli dell'Alto Monferrato★

From Acqui Terme to Gavi *(24km/15mi to Ovada on S 456 and another 24km/15mi to Gavi on minor roads)* this scenic route, also known as the wine route, follows the crest of the hillsides covered with vineyards. **Acqui Terme**♨♨, famous in Roman times for its healing mud and spa water, is a pleasant town with Roman remains and medieval architecture. Along the road the hilltop villages include Visone, Morsasco, Cremolino, Molare, Tagliolo, Lerma, Casaleggio, Mornese and, to the northeast, Montaldeo, Castelletto d'Orba and Silvano d'Orba.

Excursions

Castello di Rivoli and Museo d'Arte Contemporanea★★

Victor Amadeus II commissioned Juvarra to build a grandiose residence (18C) in the Baroque style. Only the left wing and the lower part of the central range were built. The château now houses a museum of contemporary art, **Museo d'Arte Contemporanea**★★ (1960 to the present day). ♿⏱*Open Tue-Thu 10am-5pm, Fri-Sun 10am-9pm.* ⏱*Closed Mon, 1 Jan, 1 May, 25 Dec. 6.50€.* ☎*011 95 65 222, Fax 011 95 65 230; www.castel lodirivoli.org.*

Palazzina di Caccia di Stupinigi★

Return to the ring-road and follow signs to Savona/Alessandria. Exit at Stupinigi. ⏱*Telephone for current opening times.* ⏱*Closed Mon and public holidays. 3.10€.* ☎*011 35 81 220; www.mauriziano.it.*
This huge building was a hunting lod built by Juvarra for Victor Amadeus Savoy. Napoleon stayed here before ming the crown of Italy. The pala houses a **Museo d'Arte e del** (Fine Arts and Furniture Mus apartments are decorated in style of the 18C. A magnifi rounds the *palazzina.*

ISOLE **TREMITI**★
TREMITI ISLANDS
POPULATION 370
MICHELIN MAP 564 A 28 – PUGLIA.

This tiny archipelago, the only one on the Adriatic coast, comprises two main islands, San Nicola and San Domino as well as two uninhabited isles, Capraia and Pianosa. The boat trip out from Manfredonia offers unforgettable **views**★★★of the Gargano coastline. As the boat rounds the promontory there are also good views★★★of the coastal towns of Vieste, Peschici and Rodi Garganico.

- **Information:** Isola di San Nicola. ☎0882 463 002; www.comune.isoletremiti.fg.it.
- **Orient Yourself:** The Tremiti islands lie offshore from the Gargano Promontory and belong to the same geological formation.
- **Don't Miss:** A boat trip around the island.
- **Organizing Your Time:** Allow half a day.
- **Also See:** *Promontorio del GARGANO, PUGLIA.*

Islands

San Nicola★
On the clifftop stands the **Abbazia di Santa Maria al Mare**, a 9C Benedictine abbey. Of particular interest are the remains of an 11C mosaic pavement, a 15C Gothic polyptych and a 13C Byzantine crucifix. From the cloisters there are views of the second island, San Domino *Open Jun-Sep daily, 9.30am-7.30pm, Oct-May 8.30am-2pm. ☎0882 46 30 63.*

San Domino★
A boat trip round this island reveals its rugged coasts (*for archipelago tours contact Società Cooperativa AMAR BLU, ☎0360 37 35 27 or 348 01 66 961*).

TRENTO★
TRENT
POPULATION 110 142
MICHELIN MAP 562 D 15
TOWN PLAN IN THE MICHELIN ATLAS ITALY – TRENTINO-ALTO ADIGE.

Austrian and Italian influences meet here. This agricultural and industrial centre stands at an important crossroads with the converging of routes from the Brenner Pass, Brescia and Venice.

- **Information:** Via Manci 2 38100 Trento. ☎0461 21 60 00. www.apt.trento.it.
- **Orient Yourself:** Trent, capital of Trentino, stands on the Adige not far from the Brenta Massif and is encircled by rocky peaks and valleys. The town lies off A 22, the Brenner transalpine pass.
- **Don't Miss:** Il Castello del Buonconsiglio.
- **Organizing Your Time:** Allow half a day.
- **Also See:** *BOLZANO, DOLOMITI, Regione dei LAGHI.*

f History

...colony under the Empire ...scopal see in the 4C, was ...ively by the Ostrogoths under Theodoric, and by the Lombards in the 6C before being united to the Holy Roman Empire in the late 10C. From 1004 to 1801 the town was governed by a succession of prince-bishops. The

Address Book

♿ *For coin ranges see the Legend on the cover flap.*

WHERE TO STAY

🛏️ **Hotel Aquila d'Oro** – *Via Belenzani 76 – Trento – ☎0461 98 62 82 – www. aquiladoro.it – Closed 23 Dec-7 Jan – ⌷ – 19 rm* ⌷. This little hotel is situated in the heart of the historic centre, a stone's throw from the Duomo. If the public areas are rather cramped the rooms are spacious with modern furnishings. Pleasant bar (with the same name) next door open to the public.

🛏️ **Hotel America** – *Via Torre Verde 50 – Trento – ☎0461 98 30 10 – www. hotelamerica.it – P⌷ – 67 rm.* ⌷ *– Restaurant.* Wood and pale colours throughout – from the public lounges to the rooms – creating a very relaxing atmosphere. Lovely views over the town and the Castello del Buonconsiglio and out over the surrounding mountains. A very pleasant spot.

WHERE TO EAT

🍴 **Antica Trattoria Due Mori** – *Via San Marco 11 – Trento – ☎0461 98 42 51 – Closed Mon, 15-30 June –* ▭. Rustic setting – with 15C wooden barrel-vaulted ceilings – for a classical restaurant. The menu focuses largely, but not exclusively, on traditional dishes and draws inspiration from produce that is in season.

🍴 **Osteria a Le Due Spade** – *Via Don Rizzi – angolo Via Verdi 11 – ☎0461 23 43 43 – www.leduespade.com – Closed Sun and Mon lunchtime – Book.* A culinary experience not to be missed, if you can get a table that is. With origins dating back to the 16C, this small, charming establishment -housed in what was an old cellar – offers regional dishes with an innovative flair. Attentive service.

Council of Trent (1545-63), called by Pope Paul III to study methods of combating Protestantism, met in the town. These important deliberations marked the beginning of the Counter-Reformation and the findings were to change the character of the Church. The main decisions which aimed at the re-establishment of ecclesiastical credibility and authority, concerned compulsory residence for bishops and the abolition of the sale of indulgences. After a period of Napoleonic rule in the 19C, Trent was ceded to the Austrians in 1814. In 1918, the town was liberated, after a long hard struggle, by Italian troops.

Visit

Piazza del Duomo★

This cobbled square is the town centre. Around it stand the cathedral, the Palazzo Pretorio (13C, restored), the belfry and the Rella houses painted with 16C frescoes.

Duomo★

The 12C-13C cathedral is in the Lombard-Romanesque style. The façade of the north transept is pierced with a window representing the Wheel of Fortune. To the right, in the 17C Chapel of the Crucifix (Cappella del Crocifisso), is a wooden Christ in front of which decrees of the Council of Trent were proclaimed. In the south transept is the tomb of the Venetian mercenary leader Sanseverino, killed in 1486.

The remains of a 5C early-Christian basilica, **basilica paleocristiana**★, lie beneath the chancel. 🕐*Open 10amnoon and 2.30-6pm (winter 5.30pm).* 🎫*1.50€; 4€ combined ticket with Museo Diocesano.* ☎*0461 23 44 19; www.museo diocesanotridentino.it*

Museo Diocesano★

♿🕐*Open daily 9.30am-12.30p* 2.30-5.30pm. 🕐*Closed Tues* ☎*0461 23 44 19; www.museod tridentino.it.*

The Diocesan Museum in the torio displays the most im from the cathedral's tre

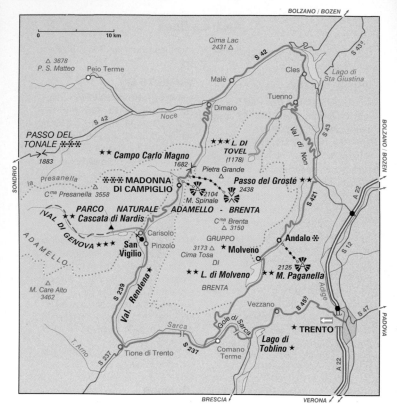

wooden panels★, **altarpiece**★ and eight early-16C **tapestries**★, woven in Brussels by Pieter Van Aelst.

Via Belenzani

This street is lined with palaces in the Venetian style. Opposite the 16C town hall (Palazzo Comunale) stand houses with walls painted with frescoes.

Via Manci

The Venetian (loggias and frescoes) and mountain (overhanging roofs) styles intermingle along the street.

astello del Buon Consiglio★★

⊙ Open daily 9am-6pm, rest of the 9.30am-5pm. ⊙ Closed Mon. ☎0461 23 37 70; www.buoncon-

13C to the dawn of the 14C this
he residence of Trent's prince-
telvecchio (Old Castle), as its
, is the oldest part of the
porates the **Torre Aquila**

(☏there are excellent guided tours of the tower: contact the guard at the Loggia del Romanino), which an artist of Bohemian origin decorated with frescoes depicting the **months**★★ in a fine expression of the International Gothic Style. Everyone will have a favourite: the month of January portrays the inhabitants of the castle throwing snowballs; the month of May depicts the season of love; and the month of December shows the gathering of fire-burning wood for the winter months.
The prince-bishop who most influenced life in Trent in the 16C was Bernardo Cles who enlarged the castle adding the Magno Palazzo. Cles was a true Renaissance prince, calling renowned artists to decorate his residence. The Ferrarese painters Dosso and Battista Dossi adorned the most important rooms, such as the Sala Grande. The frescoes on the vaulting and lunettes of the **loggia** depict biblical and mythological scenes and are by the Brescian artist Gerolamo Romanino.

The castle also houses collections of paintings, coins and archaeological artefacts as well as a Risorgimento Museum.

Palazzo Tabarelli★

This remarkable building is in the Venetian-Renaissance style, with pilasters, pink marble columns and medallions.

Chiesa di Santa Maria Maggiore

Numerous meetings of the Council of Trent were held in this Renaissance church, dedicated to St Mary Major, with its Romanesque campanile. The elegant marble organ loft (1534) in the chancel is by Vincenzo and Girolamo Grandi. At the second altar on the right, in the nave, is a 16C altarpiece of the *Madonna and saints* by Moroni.

Chiesa di Sant'Apollinare

This Romanesque church on the west bank of the Adige has a pointed roof covering two Gothic domed vaults.

Gruppo del Brenta Driving Tour★★★

▶ *Round trip starting from Trent: 233km/145mi. Allow 2 days.*

The wild limestone Brenta Massif prolongs the Dolomites beyond the Adige Valley. Its characteristic features are deep valleys, lakes and eroded rocks. *The map above locates the towns and sites described in the guide and also indicates other beauty spots in small black type. Take S 45b in the direction of Vezzano.*

Lago di Toblino★

www.parks.it/biotopo.lago.toblino.
This charming lake fringed with tall rushes, stands against a background of rocky walls. An attractive castle, once the summer residence of the bishops of Trent, stands on a small peninsula.

Val Rendena★

www.valrendena.com.
This valley clad with firs has charming villages with fresco-covered churches, protected by overhanging roofs.

The church of **San Vigilio** near Pinzolo has a remarkable *Dance of Death* (1539) by Simone Baschenis.

Val di Genova★★★

www.campiglio.it/info/valgenova.
The valley crosses the granite Adamello Massif and is known for its wild grandeur. The road follows a fast-flowing river as it tumbles and foams along the rock-strewn bed to reach a waterfall, **Cascata di Nardis★★**, where the waters drop over 100m/330ft.

Madonna di Campiglio★★★

This pleasant resort and winter sports centre has many hotels and numerous possibilities for excursions.

Campo Carlo Magno★★

A supposed visit by Charlemagne gave this place its name. It has become a winter sports centre. From the **Passo del Grosté** – *cable car and then on foot* – there is a fine **panorama★★** of the Brenta Massif. *Cable car: For information on cableway schedule* ☏*0465 44 77 44.*

▶ *Continue to Dimaro and Malè and at Cles turn right towards Tuenno.*

Lago di Tovel★★★

www.parcoadamellobrenta.tn.it.
Pass through wild gorges to reach this lake fringed by wooded slopes. In hot weather the lake waters take on a reddish tinge due to microscopic algae.

Andalo✳

This small holiday resort is set in majestic scenery amid a great pine forest and overlooked by the crests of the Brenta Massif. From the summit of **Monte Paganella** *(cable car)* at 2 125m/6 972ft there is a splendid **panorama★★** of the whole region, and in clear weather as far as Lake Garda. *Access for cableway c chairlift from Jul to mid-Sep and from [to Apr. Access also possible from Fai c Paganella by chairlift. For inform* ☏*0461 58 55 88; www.paganella*

Molveno★

This resort is situated amic at the north end of a **lake** on the floor of a cirque.

TREVISO★

POPULATION 82 112

MICHELIN MAP 562 E-F 18

TOWN PLAN IN THE MICHELIN ATLAS ITALY –VENETO.

Treviso is an important agricultural and industrial centre, but has retained its old walled town. Since the 14C its fortunes have been linked with those of Venice.

- 🔲 **Information:** Piazza Monte di Pietà 8. ☎*0422 54 76 32*; http://turismo.provincia.treviso.it.
- ▶ **Orient Yourself:** Treviso is close to Venice, linked by the S 13.
- 😊 **Don't Miss:** Chiesa di San Nicolo and the villa at Maser.
- 🕐 **Organizing Your Time:** Allow a day to visit the city.
- 👁 **Also See:** *LAGUNA VENETA, PADOVA, VENEZIA.*

A Bit of History

Treviso flourished under Carolingian rule in the early Middle Ages. In 1164 the Emperor Frederick I recognized the city as a free commune; Treviso extended its domain, built new churches and buildings, and held feasts hosting poets and troubadours, which earned it the name of "Joyous and harmonious March." However, in 1237 the city fell under the tyranny of Ezzelino da Romano and subsequently endured over a century of torment and civil war as authority passed from hand to hand. Treviso made a pact with Venice in 1389, which heralded a long period of prosperity and saw another period of construction, this time in the Venetian Gothic style. In 1509 the city began to play a key role in Venice's defence of the south and was given new fortifications. The current walls and gates date back to this period.

In 1797 Treviso - and Venice itself - fell to Napoleon, and was subsequently subsumed into the Austrian domain until 15 July 1866, when it was liberated by Italian bersaglieri. American bombings in 1944 saw Treviso suffer heavy losses; ʰousands of were killed and many his- ⁻ic landmarks were destroyed.

...t

...ei Signori★

...the historic centre of Treviso,
...impressive monuments: the
...odestà with its belltower,

the **Palazzo dei Trecento**★ (1207) and the Renaissance Palazzo Pretorio. In Piazza del Monte di Pietà is the former municipal pawn shop, the Monte di Pietà and Chapel of the Rectors (Cappella dei Reggitori). In Piazza San Vito there are two adjoining churches **San Vito** and **Santa Lucia,** the latter adorned with **frescoes**★ by Tommaso da Modena, one of the finest 14C artists.

Chiesa di San Nicolò★

This large Romanesque-Gothic church contains interesting frescoes, especially those on the columns by Tommaso da Modena. In the Onigo Chapel there are portraits of people from Treviso by Lorenzo Lotto (16C). The *Virgin in Majesty* at the far end of the chancel is by Savoldo (16C). The adjoining **monastery** has portraits of famous Dominicans by Tommaso da Modena.

Museo Civico Bailo★

Borgo Cavour 22. ⚿*Closed for restoration at the time of going to press. Most important works on display in Santa Caterina in Via S. Caterina.* ☎*0422 54 48 64.* In the municipal museum are works by Tommaso da Modena, Girolamo da Treviso (15C) and others of the Venetian school such as Cima da Conegliano, Giovanni Bellini, Titian, Paris Bordone, Jacopo Bassano and Lorenzo Lotto.

Duomo

The 15C and 16C cathedral has seven domes, a neo-Classical façade and a Romanesque crypt. Left of the cathedral stands an 11C-12C baptistery. In the Chapel of the Annunciation (Cappella dell'Annunziata) there are Mannerist frescoes by Pordenone and on the altarpiece an *Annunciation* by Titian.

Chiesa di San Francesco

Viale Sant'Antonio da Padova.

This church in the transitional Romanesque-Gothic style has a fine wooden ceiling, the tombstone of Petrarch's daughter and the tomb of one of Dante's sons, as well as frescoes by Tommaso da Modena in the first chapel to the left of the chancel.

Excursions

Maser

29km/18mi northwest by S 348.

This small agricultural town is known for its famous **villa**★★★ built in 1560 by Palladio for the Barbaro brothers: Daniele, Patriarch of Aquileia, and Marcantonio, ambassador of the Venetian Republic. The interior was decorated from 1566 to 1568 with a splendid cycle of **frescoes**★★★ by Veronese. ◷*Open Mar-Oct, Tue, Sat, Sun and public holidays, 3-6pm; Nov-Feb Sat-Sun and public holidays only 2.30-5pm.* ◷*Closed Easter, 24 Dec to 6 Jan.* ⊜*5€. Visitors are advised to call to check opening times.* ☎*0423 92 30 04; www.villadimaser.it.*

Not far from the villa is a **Tempietto**, a graceful circular chapel with a dome, also the work of Palladio.

Conegliano

28km/17mi north.

Conegliano is surrounded by hills clad with vineyards that produce an excellent white wine. This was the birthplace of **Cima da Conegliano** (1459-1518), a superb colourist who introduced idealised landscapes bathed in a crystal-clear light. The **Duomo** has a fine **Sacra Conversazione**★ by this artist. ◷*Open Mon-Fri, by appointment only.* ☎*0438 22 606.* The **castello** houses two small **museums** and affords a lovely **panorama**★of the town. ◷*Museo Civico del Castello: Open Apr-Sept daily 10am-12.30pm and 3.30-7pm (Oct-Mar 6.30pm).* ◷*Closed Mon, Nov.* ☎*0438 22 871.*

Next to the cathedral the **Scuola dei Battuti** has 15C and 16C **frescoes**★ in Venetian and Lombard styles.

Vittorio Veneto

41km/26mi north.

The name of this town recalls the great victory of the Italians over the Austrians in 1918. In Ceneda to the south of the town, the **Museo della Battaglia**, which presents documents on this victory, is installed in a 16C loggia (Loggia Cenedese) with a frescoed portico by Sansovino. ◷ *Open daily Apr-Oct 9.30am-12.30pm and 4-7pm (Nov-Mar 2-5pm).* ◷*Closed Mon, 1 Jan, Easter, 1 Nov, 25 Dec.* ⊜*3€.* ☎*0438 57 695.*

The suburb of Serravalle in the north has retained a certain charm. The church of **San Giovanni** *(take Via Roma and then Via Mazzini)* has interesting **frescoes**★ attributed to Jacobello del Fiore and Gentile da Fabriano (15C).

Portogruaro★

56km/35mi east. www.comune.portogruaro.ve.it

The town grew up from the 11C onwards along the banks of the River Lemene, a trade route that brought the town its wealth. Two fine main streets lined with attractive porticoes flank the river banks and there are numerous palaces built in a style that is typically Venetian, dating from the late Middle Ages and the Renaissance (14C-16C). On the **Corso Martiri della Libertà**★★ (the busiest of the shopping streets) not far from the 19C cathedral and its leaning Romanesque campanile is the strange **Palazzo Municipale**★, built in a late-Gothic style (14C), on which the façade is crowned with Ghibelline merlons. Behind the palace is the river: note, to the right, the two 15C watermills (now restored) and a small 17C fishermen's chapel (Oratorio del Pesce) with its own landing-stage. In the Via ⌐ Seminario the main street on the op⌐ site bank) stands the **Museo Nazi⌐ Concordiese** (at no 22). This has ⌐ exhibits (small bronze of Diane ⌐ tress) and palaeo-Christian arte⌐ Concordia Sagittaria *(3km/2⌐ Roman colony founded in 4⌐ daily 9am-8pm.* ◷*Closed ⌐ Dec.* ⊜*2€.* ☎*0421 72 6⌐

TRIESTE ★

POPULATION 207 069

MICHELIN MAP 562 F 23 – FRIULI-VENEZIA GIULIA.

With its lively cultural life, there is something of the Central European city about Trieste. It is also the largest seaport on the Adriatic, whose 12km/7.5mi of quays stretch as far as the Slovenian border. An oil pipeline links Trieste to refineries in Austria and Bavaria. The vast shipyards are vital to the local economy.

- **Information:** Piazza dell'Unità d'Italia. ☎040 34 78 312; www.triestetourism.it.
- ▶ **Orient Yourself:** Trieste is a modern town which stands at the head of a bay of the same name and at the foot of the Carso Plateau. The edge of the latter forms a steep coast with magnificent white cliffs as far as Duino in the north. The A 4, which begins in Turin and then crosses the Po Valley, ends here.
- **Don't Miss:** The Colle di San Giusto and the Grotta Gigante.
- **Organizing Your Time:** Allow one day.
- **Also See:** *LAGUNA VENETA.*

A Bit of History

Trieste is of ancient origin; the Celts and Illyrians fought over the town before the Romans made it their great trading centre of Tergeste, which had the important role of defending the eastern frontiers of the Empire. In the Middle Ages it came under the sway of the Patriarch of Aquileia and then, in 1202, under Venice. In 1382 Trieste rebelled and placed itself under the protection of Austria and it played

the role of mediator between the two powers until the 15C. In 1719 Charles VI declared it a free port and established the headquarters of the French trading company Compagnie d'Orient et du Levant in the city. Trieste then enjoyed a second period of prosperity and was embellished by numerous fine buildings. Many political exiles sought refuge in the city. It was only in 1919 after fierce fighting that Trieste was united with the Kingdom of Italy. At the beginning of the 20C Trieste boasted an active literary group under the leading influence of the novelist Italo Svevo and the poet Umberto Saba. James Joyce lived in the town for some years until 1914.

Visit

Colle di San Giusto★★

This hilltop was the site of the ancient city and today the **Piazza della Cattedrale**★ is lined with the ruins of a Roman basilica, a 15C-16C castle, a 1560 Venetian column, the altar of the Third Army (1929) and the basilica of San Giusto.

Basilica di San Giusto★

It was founded in the 5C on the site of a Roman building, but the present buildings date in large part from the 14C. The massive campanile has fragments of Roman columns built into its lowest storey. From the top there is an attractive **view**★ of Trieste.
The **interior**★ has a magnificent 12C **mosaic**★★ in the north apse showing the Virgin in Majesty, Archangels Michael and Gabriel, and the Apostles.

Castello di San Giusto

🕐*Castle: open daily except Mon, Apr-Sep 9am-7pm; Oct-Mar 9am-5pm. Museum: open daily except Mon, 9am-1pm.* ⊗*2€.* ☎*040 30 93 62; www.triestecultura.it.*
The castle houses a **museum** of furniture and a fine collection of **arms**★.

Museo di Storia e d'Arte

The Museum of History and Art contains a remarkable collection of red-figured **Greek vases**★ and charming **small bronzes**★ dating from the Roman Archaic period. 🕐*Open daily except Mon, 9am-1pm (7pm Wed).* 🕐*Closed public holidays.* ⊗ *2€.* ☎*040 31 05 00; www.triestecultura.it.*

Teatro romano

The remains of a 2C Roman theatre lie at the foot of the Colle di San Giusto.

Piazza dell'Unità d'Italia★

Three early-20C palaces line this square: the Palazzo del Governo (Government Palace), Palazzo del Comune (Town Hall) and the offices of Lloyd Trieste.

Museo del Mare★

Via Campo Marzio. Access in Riva Nazario Sauro. 🕐*Open daily 8.30am-1.30pm.* 🕐*Closed Mon, public holidays.* ⊗*3€.* ☎*040 30 49 87.* The history of seafaring is traced from its beginnings to the 18C. The fishing **section**★★ is of special interest.

Excursions

Santuario del Monte Grisa

▶*10km/6mi north. Leave by Piazza della Libertà in the direction of Prosecco and then Villa Opicina and follow the signposts to "Monte Grisa."*
This modern sanctuary is dedicated to the Virgin. From the terrace there is a splendid **panorama**★★ of Trieste.

Villa Opicina

9km/6mi north. www.tramdeopcina.it. Leave by Via Fabio Severo. After 4.5km/3mi turn left off S 14 to take S 58. It is also possible to take the funicular which leaves from Piazza Oberdan in Trieste. 🕐*Open daily, 7am-8pm.* ☎*800 01 66 75.*
Villa Opicina stands on the edge of the Carso Plateau (alt 348m/1 142ft). From the belvedere there is a magnificent **view**★★ over Trieste and its bay.

Grotta Gigante★

13km/8mi north. Follow the above directions to Villa Opicina and then turn left to Borgo Grotta Gigante. ⤳*Guided tours only (50min).* 🕐*Closed Mon (except in summer), 1 Jan, 25 Dec. 8.50€. For opening times call* ☎*040 32 73 12; www.grottagigante.it.*
An impressive stairway leads down to this immense chamber. There is a **speleological museum** (Museo di Speleologia) at the entrance to the cave.

Castello di Miramare★★

8km/5mi northwest by the coas▪ ♿🕐*Open daily 9am-6.30pm* ☎*040 22 41 43; www.castello-mi*
Standing on a headland, this with its terraced **gardens** Archduke Maximilian of was shot in Mexico in 18 Princess Charlotte, wh

UDINE

POPULATION 96 402

MICHELIN MAP 562 D 21

TOWN PLAN IN THE MICHELIN ATLAS ITALY – FRIULI-VENEZIA GIULIA.

This charming town was the seat of the Patriarchs of Aquilea from 1238 to 1420 when it passed under Venetian rule. Udine nestles round a hill encircled by a picturesque lane, Vicolo Sottomonte, and with a castle on its summit. The charm of Udine lies in its secluded squares and narrow streets, often lined with arcades. The town was badly damaged, like most of Friuli, by the 1976 earthquake.

- **Information:** Piazza I Maggio 7, 33100. ☎0432 29 59 72. www.comune.udine.it.
- **Orient Yourself:** Udine is connected to A 4 by A 23, the road that links up with the Tarvisio pass.
- **Also See:** *LAGUNA VENETA*.

Visit

Piazza della Libertà★★

This harmonious square has kept its Renaissance character and is bordered by several public buildings. The former town hall is also known as the **Loggia del Lionello** (1457), from the name of its architect. Its Venetian-Gothic style is characterised by the elegant arcades and its white and rose-coloured stonework. Opposite on a slightly higher level is the 16C **Loggia di San Giovanni**, a Renaissance portico surmounted by a 16C clock tower, with Moorish jacks *(Mori)* to strike the hour, similar to the ones in Venice. A 16C fountain plays in the centre of the square, not far from statues of Hercules and Cacus and the columns of Justice and St Mark.

Castello

○*Open Tue-Sat 9.30am-12.30pm and 3-6pm.* ○*Closed Sun pm, Mon, 1 Jan, Easter, 1 May, 25 Dec.*⊕*2.55€.* ☎*0432 27 15 91.*

This imposing early-16C castle is preceded by an esplanade from which there is a good view of Udine and the surrounding Friuli countryside. This was the seat of the representatives of the Serene Republic (Venice).

Here is the 13C church of **Santa** ... **Castello** with a 16C façade ... which bears a statue ... Angel Gabriel at its summit ... is a 13C fresco of the ... *Cross.*

Duomo

This 14C Gothic cathedral has a Flamboyant-Gothic doorway. Inside, there is attractive **Baroque decoration**★: organ loft, pulpit, tombs, altarpieces and historiated stalls. Tiepolo painted the *trompe l'oeil* frescoes in the Chapel of the Holy Sacrament (Cappella del Santo Sacramento).

The oratory **della Purità**, to the right of the cathedral, has a ceiling decorated with a remarkable Assumption (1757) by Tiepolo. ○*Open Mon-Sat 9am-noon and 4-6pm, Sun and public holidays 4-6pm.* ⊕*Donation recommended.* ☎*0432 50 68 30.*

Palazzo Arcivescovile

○ *Open Wed-Sun, 10am-noon and 3.30-6.30pm.* ○*Closed Mon, Tue.* ⊕*€5.* ☎*0432 25 003.*

The 16C-18C Archbishop's Palace boasts **frescoes**★ by Tiepolo. The ceiling of its grand staircase depicts the *Fall of the Rebel Angels*, while the apartments are decorated with scenes from the Old Testament.

Piazza Matteotti

This lovely square bordered by arcaded houses is the site of a lively open-air market. Also of interest are: the elegant 16C Baroque church of San Giacomo, a 16C fountain and a 15C column of the Virgin. It is pleasant to stroll in Via Mercato Vecchio and Via Vittorio Veneto with their shops beneath the arcades.

Address Book

For coin ranges see the Legend on the cover flap.

WHERE TO STAY

Hotel Clocchiatti – *Via Cividale 29* – ☎0432 50 50 47 – www.hotelclocchiatti.it – Closed 20 Dec-15 Jan – P ▤ – 13 rm – ☕ 8 €.
A cosy and welcoming little hotel. Simply furnished rooms with all the basics (the rooms in the attic on the second floor are particularly attractive). The small bar area where breakfast is served leads out to an outdoor terrace.

WHERE TO EAT

Al Vecchio Stallo – *Via Viola 7* – ☎0432 21 296 – Closed Sun, 25 Dec-4 Jan, 1-15 Aug, Easter – ⌷. A real find indeed: a good old-fashioned eatery which has been in the same family for generations. Rustic-style ambience in this 17C palazzo (note the horses' harnesses on the walls). Authentic regional cooking at reasonable prices.

Alla Vedova – *Via Tavagnacco 9* – ☎0432 47 02 91 – zamarian@libero.it – Closed Sun evening, Mon, 10-25 Aug.
The profusion of objects on the walls (copper utensils, hunting trophies, old

Prosciutto di San Daniele: the famous dry-cured ham

L. Pessina/MICHELIN

firearms and an odd collection of little spoons) bear witness to the passing of time at this century-old establishment. Divided up into several small dining rooms (some with fireplace). Specialises in grilled meats and game.

SHOPPING

When it comes to dry-cured ham two names spring to mind: *prosciutto di Parma* and the famous *San Daniele*, which originated in San Daniele del Friuli, near Udine.

Villa Manin★★

30km/18mi southwest, in Passariano.
⌷ ⌚For opening times call ☎0432 90 66 57.
Having lived in the Friuli area (territory under Venetian control) since the 13C, the Manin family occupied very high-ranking positions in the service of the Republic. The villa was a summer residence, the counterpart of their palace on the Grand Canal. The 16C villa was rebuilt in the 17C and rapidly completed with two wings set at right angles to the main part of the building, recalling the grandeur of Versailles. Finally, it was extended by semi-circular outbuildings based, in design, on St Peter's Square in Rome. It was here that Napoleon stayed prior to the Treaty of Campoformio (8km/5mi southwest of Udine) marking the end of the Venetian Republic: an

irony given that this was the residence of the last Doge, Ludovico Manin.
In the right wing of the villa, visitors can see the magnificent chapel and its sacristy, the stables with their 18C and 19C coaches and carriages, and the weapons room (15C-18C arms). The superb grounds are decorated with statues.

Cividale del Friuli★

16km/10mi west. www.cividale.net.
This is the *Forum Julii*, which gave the town, situated high above the River N... sone its modern name. The Lomba... who came from Scandinavia, se... here in the 6C and founded th... of their many duchies. The to... became the residence of the ... of Aquileia. From the 15C... belonged to Venice.

Duomo

The Duomo contains the **Museo Christiano**, a museum of Lombard art containing the octagonal baptismal font of the Patriarch Callisto and the 8C "altar" of Duke Ratchis. ◷Museum: *Open Mon-Sat, 9.30am-12.30pm and 3-6pm.* ◷*Closed Sun, public holidays am.* ☎*0432 73 11 44.*

Museo Archeologico Nazionale★★

To the left of the cathedral. ♿◷*Open Tue-Sun, 8.30am-7.30pm.* ◷*Closed Mon afternoon, 1 Jan, 25 Dec.* ⊜*2€.* ☎*0432 70 07 00.*

Housed in a 16C palace the museum displays items discovered in Lombard graveyards in Cividale including jewellery and weaponry. Note the Roman sarcophagus, later re-used, and objects from the grave of Duke Gisulfo (7C).

Tempietto★★

Near Piazza San Biagio. ◷ *Open 9.30am-12.30pm and 3-5pm.* ⊜ *2€.* ☎*0432 70 08 67; www.cividale.net.*
This 8C building has a Lombard **decoration** of friezes, a unique example of the architecture of this period.

URBINO★★

POPULATION 15 500
MICHELIN MAP 562, 563 K 19 – MARCHES.

The walled town of Urbino, with its rose-coloured brick houses, is built on two hills overlooking the undulating countryside bathed in a glorious golden light. Urbino was ruled by the Montefeltro family from the 12C onwards and reached its peak in the reign (1444-82) of Duke Federico da Montefeltro, a wise leader, man of letters, collector and patron of the arts. Urbino was the birthplace of Raphael (Raffaello Sanzio) (1483-1520). In 1998 Urbino's evocative historic centre was added to UNESCO's World Heritage List.

- **Information:** Piazza Rinascimento 1, 61029 Urbino (PU), ☎0722 26 13; www.comune.urbino.ps.it ; www.regione.marche.it.
- ▶ **Orient Yourself:** Urbino is 36km/22mi from Pesaro, to which it is linked by S 423.
- **Don't Miss:** Palazzo Ducale and Galleria Nazionale delle Marche.
- **Organizing Your Time:** Allow two days.
- **Also See:** *RIMINI, SAN MARINO.*

Visit

Palazzo Ducale★★★

Visit: 1h30min. The palace (1444-72), started by order of Duke Federico by the Dalmatian architect **Luciano Laurana** and completed by the Sienese **Francesco di Giorgio Martini**, is a masterpiece of harmony and elegance. The design hinges on the panorama to the ... of the old town, and the original ... overlooking the valley is pierced ... rimposed loggias and flanked by ... round towers.

... courtyard, inspired by earlier ... models, is a classic example ... ce harmony with its pure, delicate lines, serene architectural rhythm and subtle combination of rose-coloured brick and white marble.
On the ground floor are a museum, the **Museo Archeologico** (lapidary fragments: inscriptions, steles, architectural remains etc), a library, the **Biblioteca del Duca**, and cellars or **cantine.**

Galleria Nazionale delle Marche★★

♿◷*Open Tue-Sun 8.30am-7.15pm (ticket office closes 6.15pm).* ◷*Closed Mon, 1 Jan, 1 May, 25 Dec.* ⊜*€4.* ☎*0722 27 60.*
The palace's first-floor rooms with their original decoration are the setting for the National Gallery of the Marches which

G. Bludzin/MICHELIN

The grandeur and magnificence of the Palazzo Ducale

contains several great **masterpieces**★★★: a predella of the *Profanation of the Host* (1465-69) by Paolo Uccello, *Madonna di Senigallia* and a curious *Flagellation of Christ* by Piero della Francesca (see Index), the *Ideal City* (see PIENZA) by Laurana and the portrait of a woman, known as **The Mute**, by Raphael. Duke Federico's **studiolo**★★★ is decorated with magnificent intarsia panelling.

A collection of 16C-17C Italian paintings and 17C-18C maiolica is on the second floor.

To the north of the palace stands the early-19C cathedral built by Valadier.

Casa di Raffaello★

57 Via Raffaello. ○*Open Mar-Oct daily 9am-1pm and 3-7pm, Sun and public holidays 10am-1pm, rest of the year 9am-2pm and 10am-1pm.* ○*Closed 1 Jan, 25 Dec.* €3€. ☎0722 32 01 05; www.accademiaraffaello.it.*

Raphael lived here up to the age of 14. This typical 15C house belonged to the boy's father, Giovanni Sanzio or Santi, and contains mementoes and period furniture.

Chiesa di San Giovanni Battista e San Giuseppe

Via Barocci. ○*Open Mar-Oct Mon-Sat 10am-12.30pm and 3-5.30pm, Sun and public holidays 10am-12.30pm (afternoons by appointment only); Nov-Feb, 10am-12.30pm (afternoons by appointment only).* €2€. *For further information, contact Sig. Angelo ☎347 67 11 181 (mobile).*

Of these two adjacent churches, the first is 14C and contains curious **frescoes**★★ by the Salimbene brothers depicting the life of St John the Baptist. The second, dating from the 16C, has a colossal statue of St Joseph (18C) painted in grisaille, and a life-size stucco **crib**★ by Federico Brandani (1522-75).

Strada panoramica★★
Starting from Piazza Roma, this scenic road skirts a hillside and affords admirable **views**★★ of the lower town.

In the footsteps of the Malatesta Tour

▶ *60km/37mi. Allow at least one day.*

▶ *Follow the SS 423 to Montecchio, then turn left to Gradara.*

Gradara
15km/9mi northwest.
Gradara is a medieval town, almost intact. **The Rocca**★ is a well-preserved example of military architecture in the 13C and 14C. It is here that Gianni Malatesta is said to have come upon and then murdered his wife, Francesca da Rimini, and her lover, his brother Paolo Malatesta, who were in the throes of passion while reading a courtly romance. Dante portrayed the inseparable couple in his Divine Comedy. ◐*Open Mon 8.30am-1.30pm, Tue-Sun 8.30am-7pm.* ◐*Closed 1 Jan, 1 May, 25 Dec.* ▨ *4€.* ☎ *0541 96 41 15; www.gradara.org.*

▶ *Head to the SS 16 and follow signs south to Pesaro.*

Pesaro⌂⌂
Situated on the Adriatic coast and at the mouth of the smiling Foglia Valley, Pesaro was the birthplace of the composer Gioacchino Rossini. The compos-'s house (at no 34 Via Rossini) is now useum. ◐*Same admission times and es as the Musei Civici.*

chino Rossini Tour

792-Passy 1868)

er was characterised by which catapulted him

from Pesaro into a realm of the most prestigious recognition, first from the important Italian cities and later from the principal European courts. He is often hastily labelled as a "light" composer but in reality his work contains a kind of aloof sense of irony about the worries of the world, in the context of a typically theatrical humour, and ultimately attains a pessimistic view similar to that of Leopardi, who was also from the Marches. Aged 37 Rossini stopped composing and retired from public life. Among his most celebrated works are The Italian Girl in Algiers, The Barber of Seville, Cinderella and William Tell.
An attractive stretch of **coastline**★ extends between Pesaro and Gabicce *(15km/9mi north).*

Palazzo Ducale
The great mass of the Ducal Palace, built for a member of the Sforza family in the 15C, overlooks the Piazza del Popolo with its fountain adorned with tritons and sea horses. The crenellated façade has an arcaded portico, with windows adorned with festoons and cherubs.

Museums★
The picture gallery in the Municipal Museum contains several works by the Venetian, Giovanni Bellini. The famous Pala di Pesaro (1475) is an immense altarpiece representing the Virgin being crowned on the central panel, and other scenes on the predella.
In the **ceramics section**★★, the Umbrian potteries are well represented but there are also examples of work from the Marches region. ◐*Open Jul and Aug daily 9.30am-12.30pm and 4-7pm (10.30pm Tue and Thu).* ◐*Closed Mon, 1 Jan, 25 Dec. 4 €, 7 €, including Casa Rossini.* ☎ *0721 38 74 74; www. museicivicipesaro.it*
⛪ Museo Oliveriano (archaeological items), remains of the old church of S. Domenico.

▶ *Continue south on the SS 16.*

Fano⌂
▶ *1 1km/7mi southeast. This town, now a seaside resort, was ruled by the Malatesta family from Rimini in the 13C-15C.*

Corte Malatestiana★

This 15C Renaissance ensemble includes a courtyard-garden and palace, and would make an ideal theatrical set. Inside is a museum, the Museo Civico. *Open mid-June-mid Sept Tue-Sat 9.30am-12.30pm and 4-7pm, Sun 10am-1pm, rest of the year telephone for opening times. Closed Mon and public holidays.* 3.50€. 0721 82 83 62; www.turismofano.com.

Chiesa di Santa Maria Nuova

16C-18C. This contains works a by Perugino, which are admired for their fine draughtsmanship and their delicate colours.

Fontana della Fortuna

Piazza XX Settembre.
This 16C fountain presents the protecting goddess Fortune, perched on a pivoting globe, with her billowing cloak acting as a weather-vane.

Arco d'Augusto

At the far end of the street of the same name. This 1C arch has a main opening and two side ones for pedestrians. A low relief on the façade of the church of San Michele nearby portrays the arch in its original form. To the left of the arch are the remains of the Roman wall.

VALLE D'AOSTA
AOSTA VALLEY
MICHELIN MAP 561 E 3-4.

With its castles and villages of balconied houses roofed with flat stone slabs (lauzes), the Valle d'Aosta is one of Italy's most attractive tourist areas offering numerous possibilities for excursions and scenic routes leading up to glaciers. This region comprising the Dora Baltea and adjacent valleys is surrounded by French and Swiss Alpine peaks: Mont Blanc, the Matterhorn (Cervino), Monte Rosa, Grand Combin, Dent d'Hérens, Gran Paradiso and Grande Sassière.
Since 1948 the Valle d'Aosta has been, for administrative purposes, an autonomous region: inhabitants speak a Franco-Provençal dialect and public documents are published in Italian and French.

- **Information:** Piazza Chanoux 2, 11100 Aosta, 0165 23 66 27; www.regione.vda.it/turismo.
- ▶ **Orient Yourself:** Flanked by France and Switzerland, the Valle d'Aosta covers the northwest corner of the Italy. It is crossed by A 5.
- **Don't Miss:** Skiing in Courmayer and the beautiful Parco Nazionale del Gran Paradiso.
- **Organizing Your Time:** Dedicate three days to exploring the region.
- **Especially for Kids:** This area is famous for its wooden toys.

Parco Nazionale del Gran Paradiso★★

The Gran Paradiso National Park Department organises outings in each valley with park guides who will help visitors discover the unique features of the protected area. Contact the appropriate Park Office. 011 86 06 233; www.pngp.it. Valle d'Aosta: Rhêmes-Notre Dame (fr. Chanavey), open all year; Valsavaranche, fr. Degioz, open Jul-Sep, 25 Dec and Easter; Giardino Botanico Alpino Paradisia, fr. Valnontey (Valle di

The unmistak...

Address Book

For coin ranges see the Legend on the cover flap.

WHERE TO STAY

Hotel Miravalle – *Località Porossan – 11100 Aosta – ☎0165 23 61 30 – Fax 0165 35 705 – 🅿 – 24 rm €53/73.* Of note are the fireplace (a fire is lit in the evenings) and the light and spacious breakfast room with lovely picture windows (fine views) as well as the sun terrace. The harmonious, if unusual, decor (complete with porcelain ornaments and some beautiful dolls) and the courteous service enhance the old-fashioned ambience.

A l' Hostellerie du Paradis – *Eau Rousse – 11010 Eau Rousse – 3km/1.8mi south of Valsavarenche – ☎0165 90 59 72 – www.hostellerieduparadis.it – 30 rm – Restaurant.* Entirely in keeping with its surroundings this hotel is situated in a charming and quiet mountain hamlet. Facilities include a reading room and snooker room. Rooms are very welcoming and all individually decorated: some have a fireplace. Traditional fare.

Albergo La Barme – *Località Valnontey – 11012 Cogne – 4km/2.5mi southeast of Cogne – ☎0165 74 91 77 – www.hotellabarme.com – Closed Oct and Nov – 15 rm – Restaurant.* A small, family-run hotel ideally situated for excursions into the Parco del Gran Paradiso in summer and for cross-country skiing in winter. Complementing the stone and wooden structure are the pale furnishings. Complete with restaurant, garden and a sauna.

Albergo Dei Camosci – *Località La Saxe – 11013 Courmayeur – ☎0165 84 23 38 – www.courmayeur-hotel-camo*... *it – Closed May, mid-Jun, 23 Sep-3*... *– 🅿 – 23 rm – Restaurant.* ... mountain-style hotel: stone and ... ructure with functional but ... rooms. Comfortable public ... views of Mont Blanc. The ... e also in charge of the ... ocuses on regional ... ities.

... **ta Parey** – *Località* ... *mes-Notre-Dame* ... *mes-Notre-*

Dame – ☎0165 93 61 04 – www.rhemes-grantaparey.com – Closed Nov – 🅿 – 27 rm – Restaurant. Children are particularly welcome in this family-run hotel which is situated very near the ski-lifts. Comfortable rooms with parquet floor and pine furniture. Separate dining room for guests.

Hotel Tourist – *Via Roma 32 – 11028 Valtournenche – 8km/5mi south of Cervinia – ☎0166 92 070 – Fax 0166 93 129 – Closed Oct and Nov – 🅿 – 34 rm – Restaurant.* A welcoming, airy establishment (pale walls and lots of wood and stone) – spacious rooms with furniture in cherrywood. Cuisine typical of the region is served in the restaurant and a free shuttle-bus to the nearby ski-pistes is available.

WHERE TO EAT

Hotel Casale – *Frazione Condemine 1 – 11020 Saint Christophe – 4km/2.5mi northeast of Aosta – ☎0165 54 12 03 – www.hotelristorantecasale.it – Closed Sun evening, Mon (winter), 5-20 Jan, 5-20 Jun – 25 rm.* Good food that is a mixture of the traditional and original. Welcoming, family atmosphere. Helpful proprietor. Comfortable rooms on the first floor. Lovely terrace with views over the valley.

Hostellerie de la Pomme Couronnée – *Frazione Resselin 3 – 11020 Gressan – 3km/1.8mi southwest of Aosta – ☎0165 25 10 10 – www.lapommevda.com – Closed Tue, Wed lunchtime – Book.* Situated in a small, rural farmhouse which has been restored with as many original features as possible including the entrance and the stone walls in the dining room. Apples reign supreme and are a key feature of the cuisine here.

TAKING A BREAK

La Bottega degli Antichi Sapori – *Via Porta Praetoria 63 – ☎0165 23 96 66 – Mon-Sat 8am-1pm and 3-7.30pm.* Cheeses, hams, wines... there's no shortage of specialities in the Aosta region. This lovely grocer's (air-conditioned) has a fine selection of them, along with various types of pasta and delicious sauces.

Old Distillery Pub – *Via Près Fosses 7* – ☎*0165 23 95 11* – *Summer, Tue-Sun 6pm-2am; daily, rest of the year.* The coloured glass, flowery curtains and old tables combine to create an authentic-seeming Scottish pub: a little piece of Scotland transported to Italy.

GOING OUT

Caffè della Posta – *Via Roma 51 – 11013 Courmayeur* – ☎*0165 84 22 72* – *Thu-Tue 8.30am-2.30am, closed 2 weeks in winter and summer.* Housed in a stone building, this lovely café is just the place to gather your strength for the long winter ahead. Cosy up to the wonderful fireplace that has been warming its visitors since 1911.

Cogne), open in summer. Piedmont: Noasca (Valle Orco), Ronco Canavese (Valle Soana), Piazza del Municipio; Ceresole Reale, fr. Pian della Balma (Valle Orco); Locana, the old church of San Francesco (Valle Orco). ⏱The centres are open daily in Jul and Aug and Sat-Sun Jun-Sep, 25 Dec and Easter. For further information, contact the Segreteria Turistica del Parco in Noasca: ☎/Fax 0124 90 10 70; www. pngp.it.

This national park (70 000ha/270sqmi) includes an area previously preserved as a royal hunting ground. It can be reached by the Rhêmes, Savarenche, Cogne and Locana valleys or the Nivolet Pass road. The park is rich in wildlife and important as a reserve for endangered species, such as the ibex, and rare specimens of alpine flora.

Facilities

Owing to its marvellous situation the Valle d'Aosta offers some splendid **viewpoints**★★★. It is also a ski-lover's paradise (resorts at **Breuil-Cervinia**★★★, **Courmayeur**★★★, **La Thuile**★★, **Gressoney, Champoluc**★). The slopes wind down through breathtaking landscapes comprised of woods, forests and glaciers, such as the stunning one at Monte Rosa. Ski-lovers can immerse themselves in the heart of the Parco Nazionale del Gran Paradiso (**Cogne**★★).

Economic activities in the region include woodcarving. Furniture, typical grolle (wooden goblets), sculptures and toys (particularly animals such as cows and donkeys) can all be found.

Tour from Courmayeur to Ivrea

▶*160km/100mi. Allow one day*

Courmayeur★★★

Plans of the town and surrounding areas in the Michelin Atlas Italy. This well-known mountaineering and winter sports resort is a good excursion centre. Take a cable car to the Cresta d'Arp and to cross the Mont Blanc Massif and make a short detour into France *(for the area beyond La Palud see The Green Guide French Alps).* By car you can explore the following valleys: Veny, Ferret or Testa d'Arpi and the road to the Little St Bernard Pass, one of the busiest transalpine routes which was used by the Romans in ancient times.

Once through St-Pierre and past the road south up the Cogne valley, on the left stands **Castello di Sarre**, the former summer residence of the Counts of Savoy. Further on, to the right, is the 14C **Fortezza d'Aymavilles**, impressively quartered with great round crenellated towers.

Aosta★

Aosta stands in the valley of the sa name and is the capital of the re It has retained the geometric a military camp (castrum) a interesting monuments from period. Aosta, an active reli in the Middle Ages, was th the theologian St Anse Archbishop of Canter in 1109. Today it is town and, since th Blanc Tunnel in

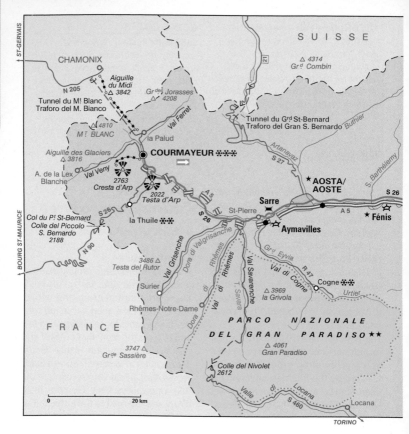

rist centre, at the junction of the trans-alpine routes to France and Switzerland Via the St Bernard Tunnel.

Roman Monuments★

These are grouped in the centre of Aosta and include the **Porta Pretoria**, a majestic 1C BC arch, **Arco di Augusto**, a **Roman bridge**, a **theatre** and the ruins of an **amphitheatre**.

mplesso Ursino – The church has
e lovely carved 15C **stalls** and a
ue rood screen. Beside the 11C
a doorway opens onto Roman-
sters with historiated **capi-**
e Priorato di Sant'Orso is a
tyle priory with elegant
Open Mon-Sat Oct-
l and Aug 9am-8pm.
iew frescoes of the
e custodian. ☎01
e.vda.it.

Cattedrale

The 12C cathedral now has a neo-Classical façade (1848) and contains the 14C tomb of Thomas II of Savoy.

Castello di Fénis★

⏱*Open daily Mar-Jun & Sep 9am-7pm, Jul and Aug 9am-8pm; rest of year, daily except Tue, 10am-12.30pm and 1.30-5pm, Sun 10am-12.30pm and 1.30-6pm.* ⏱*Closed 1 Jan, 1 May and 25 Dec.* ⊚5€. ☎0165 23 66 27 or 0165 76 42 63; www.regione.vda.it.

This fortress contains carved furniture in the local style. The courtyard's frescoes portray the Golden Legend.

Breuil-Cervinia★★★

This winter sports resort is situated at 2 050m/6 822ft. Cable cars climb up to the Rosa Plateau (Plan Rosa) and the Furggen Pass at 3 491m/11 453ft.

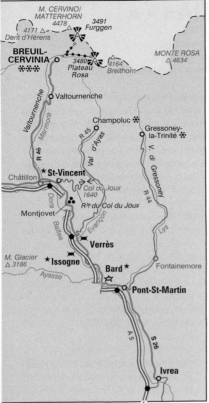

Saint-Vincent★
The Casino de la Vallée in its fine park is very popular. The road passes Castello di Montjovet and **Castello di Verrès**.

Castello d'Issogne★
🕑*Open Mon-Sat Mar-Jun & Sep 9am-6.30pm, July and Aug 9am-7.30pm; rest of year 10am-12.30pm and 1.30-4.30pm, Sun and public holidays 10am-12.30pm and 1.30-5.30pm (closed Wed in this season).* 🕑*Closed public holidays.* 🎟*5€.* ☎*0165 23 66 27 or 0125 92 93 73; www.regione.vda.it.*
The 15C castle has a fine courtyard with a fountain surmounted by a wrought-iron pomegranate tree.

Fortezza di Bard★
The fortress, dismantled on the orders of Napoleon in 1800 and rebuilt during the 19C, commands the upper Dora Baltea Valley.

Pont-Saint-Martin
The village is named after the Roman bridge that was guarded by a chapel dedicated to St John Nepomuk.

Ivrea
This busy industrial town stands ⁀ mouth of the Valle d'Aosta. To t' of Ivrea is the largest moraine i' the Serra d'Ivrea.

VENEZIA ★★★
VENICE

POPULATION 271 251
MICHELIN MAP 562 F 18-19 –
SEE ALSO THE GREEN GUIDE VENICE.

Venice is a legendary city, presiding regally over the lagoon for more than a thousand years. The same water that saved her from the clutches of time now threatens her very being. The stone palaces lining the canals are slowly sinking, as the sea floods ever higher. *La Serenissima* – "the most serene" – has a multitude of moods: labyrinthine streets, lively wine bars *(bacari)*, lavish ballrooms, and broody landscapes a la *Death in Venice.* Painting has flourished here, alongside the exquisite glass art of Murano island. Yet the true attraction is always Venice itself, which Lord Byron dubbed "a fairy city of the heart."

- ▣ **Information:** Castello 4421. ☎041 52 98 711, www.turismovenezia.it
- ▶ **Orient Yourself:** The main road to Venice is A 4. It is linked to Mestre by the Ponte della Libertà. The Grand Canal – 4km/2.5mi – divides central Venice.
- ⊜ **Don't Miss:** Piazza San Marco, Ponte dei Sospiri and Collezione Peggy Guggenheim.
- ⊙ **Organizing Your Time:** A week offers a real feel for the place, time to stroll the narrow streets and explore the lagoon islands.
- 🄺🄸🄳🅂 **Especially for Kids:** A gondola ride and glassworks at Murano Island
- ⚲ **Also See:***Riviera del BRENTA, LAGUNA VENETA, PADOVA, TREVISO.*

A Bit of History

Venice is built on 117 islands; it has 150 canals and 400 bridges. A canal is called a rio, a square a campo, a street a *calle* or *salizzada*, a quay a *riva* or *fondamenta*, a filled-in canal *rio Terrà*, a passageway, a *sottoportego*, a courtyard a *corte* and a small square a *campiello*.

Gondolas – For centuries gondolas have been the traditional means of transport in Venice. The gondola is an austere and sober craft except for its typical iron hook, which acts as a counterweight to the gondolier. The curved fin is said ⌐o echo the doge's *corno* (horn-shaped ⌐t) and the prongs to represent the *ses-* ⌐ or districts of the city. The prong ⌐e back of the stern symbolises the ⌐a.

⌐etians** – The Venetians are ⌐d and fiercely traditional, ⌐eir commercial and prac- ⌐ "**bautta**" (black velvet ⌐nino (a wide hooded ⌐ popular with the ⌐ in Venice at Carni- ⌐lusiveness. Skilled ⌐and spies have

given Venice a reputation for intrigue. Venetian is a very lively dialect which is used in place of Italian.

Venice was founded in AD 811 by the inhabitants of Malamocco, near the Lido, fleeing from the Franks. They settled on the Rivo Alto, known today as the Rialto. In that year the first doge – a name derived from the Latin dux (leader) – Agnello Partecipazio, was elected and thus started the adventures of the Venetian Republic, known as La Serenissima, which lasted 1 000 years. In 828 the relics of St Mark the Evangelist were brought from Alexandria; he became the town protector.

The Venetian Empire – From the 9C to the 13C Venice grew steadily richer as it exploited its position between East and West. With its maritime and commercial power it conquered important markets in Istria and Dalmatia. The guile of Doge Dandolo and the assistance of the Crusaders helped the Venetians capture Constantinople in 1204. The spoils from the sack of Constantinople flowed to Venice, while trade in spices, fabrics and precious stones from markets established in the East grew apace.

Address Book

The hub of public life is Piazza San Marco (☞ see below) where tourists and citizens sit on the terraces of the famous Florian and Quadri cafés. The Florian is the most celebrated of all the cafés in Venice; founded in 1720 it has received Byron, Goethe, George Sand, Musset and Wagner within its mirrored and allegory-painted walls.

The shops in St Mark's have sumptuous window displays of lace, jewellery, mirrors and the famous glassware from Murano. The Mercerie – shopping streets – lead to the Rialto Bridge. On the far side of this are the displays of greengrocers' (erberie) and fishmongers' shops (pescherie).

GETTING ABOUT

It goes without saying that in Venice all public transport is water-borne. It is important to bear in mind that heavy traffic on the Grand Canal and the fact that stops do not always take one "door to door" mean that walking can sometimes be quicker. However, on arrival in the city, the very sight of the first bridge (Ponte degli Scalzi, opposite the station, is particularly steep) can be tiring for visitors carrying heavy luggage. Likewise, walking up and down bridges all day can put even the most energetic walker to the test.

Visitors will find that they will happily make use of the famous Venetian waterboats, the **vaporetti**.

Listed below are the two most convenient routes:

– **Line 1** stops at all stops along the Grand Canal. Terminates at the Lido after stopping at Piazzale Roma, the station and San Marco.

– **Line 82** is faster than Line 1 as it makes fewer stops. Stops at Tronchetto, Piazzale Roma, the Giudecca, San Giorgio, San Marco and the Lido.

A single ticket on the fast line costs 5€. 24hr (12€) and 72hr (25€) tickets can also be purchased, these need be stamped only on the initial journey. Visitors who opt to walk will be relieved to learn that as well as a choice of three bridges crossing the Grand Canal (Scalzi, Rialto, Accademia) they can be "ferried" across the canal in a gondola.

This service is available at eight points along the Grand Canal (Station, S. Marcuola, S. Sofia, al Carbon, S. Tomà, S. Samuele, S. Maria del Giglio and Dogana): it is a very rapid journey and costs only 0.40€ (except when exhibitions are on at Palazzo Grassi, in which case the S. Samuele crossing costs 0.52 €). Be careful to keep your balance!

GONDOLAS

Visitors who want to enjoy the full experience of a gondola ride must be prepared to spend considerably more: a 40 minute journey through canals costs 80€ (official starting price which does not include musical accompaniment). This price can be divided among six people who can be accommodated in a gondola. Each 20min after the initial 50min costs 40€. A tour in a gondola by night is an unforgettable experience but incurs considerable costs: from 8pm to 8am a 40min journey costs 100€, each 20min thereafter costs 50€.

For more information contact the Istituzione per la Conservazione della Gondola e la Tutela del Gondoliere, ☎041 52 85 075.

VENICE-CARD

The Comune di Venezia has recently introduced a pre-paid ticket for visitors to Venice which includes public transport and/or entry to some of the city's museums. The Venice-card is available in different formats, with a Senior ticket for visitors over 30 and a Junior ticket for those under 30. For information on prices and to book a ticket, call ☎041 24 24 or log onto www.venicecard.it (up to 48 hours before your arrival in Venice). The tickets are also available at Ve.La. ticket offices and APT and AVA information points. As the number of tickets issued is limited, visitors are advised to book in advance.

FOR YOUNG VISITORS

For those who are lucky enough to be aged between 14 and 29 Rolling Venice card (cost €4) range of discounts on you hotels, campsites, univer restaurants, museums shops taking part in t

entitles holders to a reduction on the three-day vaporetto ticket. Cards can be purchased with proof of identity at the following places:
Ve.La. ticket offices and agents (various locations around the city); APT tourist offices (various locations around the city); Associazione Italiana Alberghi per la Gioventù (the Italian Youth Hostel Association), Calle dei Amai 197/i, Santa Croce; Agenzia Arte e Storia, Corte Canal 659, Santa Croce.
👌 *For coin ranges, see the Legend at the back of the guide.*

WHERE TO STAY

The accommodation listed below also includes information on religious orders (addresses with no description) which offer reasonably priced rooms to visitors. The only drawback is that guests are usually expected to be back in the evening by a specified hour.

Casa Capitanio – *S. Croce 561 – ☎041 52 03 099 – Fax 041 52 23 975 – 🛏 – 12 rooms.*

Casa Cardinal Piazza – *Cannaregio 3539/A – ☎041 72 13 88 – Fax 041 70 02 33 – 🛏 – 24 rooms.*

Casa Murialdo – *Circolo ANSPI – Cannaregio 3512 – ☎041 71 99 33 – Fax 041 72 00 02 – 🛏 – 12 rooms.*

Istituto San Giuseppe – *Ponte della Guerra 5402, Castello – ☎041 52 25 352 – 🛏 – 11 rooms.*

Patronato Salesiano Leone XIII – *Castello 1281 – ☎041 24 03 611 – Fax 041 24 03 610 – 🛏 – 15 rooms.*

Ostello della Giudecca – *Fondamenta Zitelle 86, Isola della Giudecca – ☎041 52 38 211 – Fax 041 52 35 689 – Closed for 20 days in Dec – 260 beds 🍴.* An excellent base for exploring (by vaporetto!) one of the most fascinating cities in the world and without burning a hole in your pocket. ... arvellous situation – on the Giudecca, ...rlooking the lagoon and the city.

...nta Fosca – *Cannaregio 2372 ...1 71 57 33 – www.santafosca.it ...' for 10 days in Dec – 30 beds.*

...ria Valdese – *Castello 5170 ...6 797 – Fax 041 24 16 238 ...iavaldese.org/venezia. ...*

...a – *S. Polo 3082 – ...ax 041 52 27 139*

– *Closed mid-Sep to May – 🛏 – 100 beds 25/27 €.*

⊖**Hotel Bernardi** – *Semenzato – Calle dell'Oca 4366 – Vaporetto Cà d'Oro – ☎041 52 27 257 – www.hotelbernardi. com – Closed for 10 days in Jan – 25 rooms.* 🍴. A no-frills hotel (stylewise the rooms leave a bit to be desired) but it is well situated (in a small street behind Campo S.S. Apostoli, near the Rialto bridge) in a less touristy part, although right at the heart, of the city.

⊖**Pensione Seguso** – *Zattere 779 – ☎041 52 86 858 – www.pensioneseguso.it – Closed Dec-Feb – 34 rooms.* 🍴. Whether it is the wooden panelling or the round windows, there is something pleasantly old-fashioned and Anglo-Saxon about this hotel. Previous visitors include Italo Calvino and Ezra Pound.

⊖**Hotel La Residenza** – *Campo Bandiera e Moro 3608, Castello – ☎041 52 85 315 – www.venicelaresidenza.com – 🖥 – 15 rooms.* 🍴. A stone's throw from Piazza San Marco, this splendid 16C palazzo has been lovingly restored to its former glory – the perfect setting for a dream holiday. Features include 18C stuccowork, along with period furnishings. The other main attraction is the wonderful view of the campo. Reasonably priced.

⊖⊖**Casa Caburlotto** *"Casa per Ferie"* – *Fondamenta Rizzi 316/318, S. Croce – ☎041 71 08 77 – Fax 041 71 08 75 – 🛏 – 30 rooms.* 🍴.

⊖⊖**Locanda Cà Foscari** – *Calle della Frescade 3887/B – Vaporetto San Tomà – ☎041 71 04 01 – www.locandacafoscari. com – Closed 20 Nov-20 Jan and 25 Jul-8 Aug – 11 rooms.* 🍴. A very simple but pleasant establishment with light, airy rooms and a family atmosphere. Offers extremely good value for money – a very rare thing in Venice.

⊖⊖**Hotel Serenissima** – *Calle Goldoni 4486, San Marco – ☎041 52 00 011 – www.hotelserenissima. it – Closed mid-Nov to mid-Feb – 🖥 – 37 rooms* 🍴. This unpretentious hotel is ideally located between the Rialto Bridge and St Mark's Square. The rooms are simply furnished but tastefully decorated (some in Venetian style) and well kept. One of the main attractions here is the staff who are very pleasant, creating a friendly, family atmosphere.

Hotel Abbazia – *Calle Priuli dei Cavalletti 68, Cannaregio – ☎041 71 73 33 – www.abbaziahotel. com – Closed 7 Jan-7 Feb –* 📺 ✕ *– 50 rooms.* 🍴. An ideal location for visitors wishing to stay near the station. This hotel once housed a Carmelite monastery and retains many of its original features including the pulpit in the hall, from where the monks would preach during meals. Attentive, professional staff. The rooms are plain but spacious and there is a lovely garden.

La Calcina – *Fondamenta Zattere ai Gesuati 780, Dorsoduro – Vaporetto Zattere – ☎041 52 06 466 – www. lacalcina.com –* 📺 *– 28 rooms.* 🍴 *– Restaurant 40/46€.* Only a photograph remains in the hallway of the "La Calcina" inn where Ruskin stayed in 1876, but this hotel, completely remodelled, stands on that very site. The fine location on the Canale della Guidecca adds to its charm as does the light which floods in, a rarity in Venice's narrow streets.

Hotel Paganelli – *Riva degli Schiavoni 4687, Castello – ☎041 52 24 324 – www.hotelpaganelli. com –* 📺 ✕ *– 22 rooms.* 🍴. This family-run hotel overlooks the Bacino di San Marco. Some rooms (all decorated in the Venetian style) enjoy this view, others (in an adjoining building) look out onto Campo San Zaccaria.

Hotel Locanda Fiorita – *Campiello Novo 3457/A, San Marco – ☎041 52 34 754 –www.locandafiorita. com –* 📺 *– 10 rooms* 🍴. A good little hotel housed in a lovely old building. It is situated in one of the city's most attractive little squares, just a stone's throw from the very famous Piazza S. Marco. The rooms are rather functional and the public areas could be better but who wants to stay in their room when there is the whole of Venice to explore?

Hotel Danieli – *Riva degli Schiavoni 4196, Castello – ☎041 52 26 480 – www.starwoodhotel. com –* 📺 ✕ *– 233 rooms –* 🍴 *– Restaurant.* Possibly the most famous hotel in the world! The legendary 14C Palazzo Dandolo, a symbol of the powerful Venetian Republic, has housed the Hotel Danieli since 1822. Over the years,

guests have included monarchs and ambassadors, as well as famous writers and musicians such as Dickens, Wagner, Balzac, Proust, George Sand and Alfred Musset.

WHERE TO EAT

Lunch or dinner in one of the trattorias is one of the pleasures of Venetian life. High up the list of things to try are the fish and seafood (in particular the squid, cuttlefish, eels and mussels), as well as fegato alla veneziana (calf's liver fried with onions). There are some excellent local wines to accompany these dishes including Valpolicella, Bardolino and Amarone (red) along with Soave and Prosecco (white).

Gam-Gam – *Fondamenta Pescaria 1122 – ☎041 71 52 84 – www.jewishven-ice.org – Closed Fri, Sat lunch (Sat evening in summer) –* ✕ *– Reservation recommended.* For anyone looking for something a little different or even a complete change of scene, you could try this rather pleasant Jewish restaurant. Modern, if austere decor. Strictly kosher food.

Alla Patatina – *San Polo 2741/A, Calle Saoneri – ☎041 52 37 238 – www.lapatatina.it – Closed Sun – Reservation recommended* . Pleasant 1950s-style establishment with a lively atmosphere. On offer at the bar are plenty of vegetable antipasti (including, of course, the delicious roast potatoes they do so well here) along with polpette al sugo (meatballs with sauce). Standard table service also available.

S. Trovaso – *1016, Dorsoduro – ☎041 52 03 703 – giorgiocassan@tin. it – Closed Mon, 31 Dec – Reservation recommended – .* This establishment is conveniently situated near the Acca-demia. It is always very crowded so remember to book! Good selection of dishes as well as pizzas.

La Zucca – *Sestiere S. Croce 1762 – ☎041 52 41 570 – www.lazucca.it – Closed Sun, 1 week in Aug and Dec – Reservation recommended* . If you in the mood for more varied and dishes, prepared with a lightnes touch, this is the place to go. A trattoria, it offers a particula selection of vegetables dis decor itself is a celebration of the pumpkin (zucca)!

Ai Frati – *Fondamenta Venier 4 – 30141 Murano – ☎041 73 66 94 – Closed Thu, for two weeks in Feb and Jul. 12% service charge.* Originally founded as a wine shop in the mid-19C, this restaurant has been serving good, authentic home cooking for more than half a century. The dining room is very pleasant but for a real treat try and get a table on the terrace overlooking the canal.

Alle Testiere – *Calle del Mondo Novo 5801, Castello – ☎041 52 27 220 – Closed Sun and Mon, 24 Dec-12 Jan, 25 Jul-25 Aug –* 🔲 ✖– *Reservation recommended.* A small, informal establishment. The napkins might be made of paper but the cooking is a rather gastronomic affair. The menu, which focuses mostly on fish dishes, depends on what was on sale at the market that morning. A real treat for you (and your wallet!).

Harry's Dolci – *Fondamenta San Biagio 773, Giudecca – ☎041 52 24 844 – www.cirpiani.com –Closed Tue, 8 Nov-26 Mar. 12% service charge.* Both restaurant and pasticceria, this is a little less expensive than its more famous sister establishment near Piazza San Marco. Stylistically it owes much to the Harry's tradition with diners seated close together in comfy chairs at low tables. Spectacular view from the large terrace overlooking the Canale della Giudecca.

TAKING A BREAK

Al Volto – *San Marco 4081 – La Fenice – ☎041 52 28 945.* With its collection of vintage wines, this wine bar is popular with serious wine buffs. Warm, welcoming atmosphere – can get very busy.

Caffè Florian – *Piazza San Marco 55. – ☎041 52 05 641 – www.caffeflorian. com* With its elegant 18C salons, smart waiters and magnificent exterior, this famous café is a throw-back to its past even with all the hustle and bustle. Also hosts renowned classical music concerts.

Caffè Quadri – *Piazza San Marco 120 – ☎041 52 89 299– www.quadrivenice. com.* You will need a break from all that sightseeing so why not treat yourself to a top-quality cup of coffee? In the 1830s, this was one of the first cafés in Venice to serve Turkish coffee.

Harry's Bar – *San Marco (Calle Vallaresso) 1322 – Piazza San Marco. – ☎041 52 85 777 – www.cipriani.com – 10.30am-11pm.* Not far from the Piazza San Marco is the legendary Harry's Bar. Opened in 1931 by Giuseppe Cipriani, it boasted the writer Ernest Hemingway as one of its regulars. These days, it is popular with the locals and tourists alike who come and enjoy the elegant surroundings while sipping the house cocktail, a "Bellini", which is made with champagne and peach juice. The hot chocolate served with cream is sheer decadence, although rather expensive.

Paolin – *Sestiere San Marco 3464 – La Fenice. – ☎041 52 20 710 – Sun-Fri.* Offers an imaginative selection of delicious ice creams. Flavours include Tiramisù, Torrone (nougat) and Yogurt. For an even more luxurious experience there are a number of extras on offer including candied fruit, whipped cream, custard and there is even a liquorice/aniseed topping for the more adventurous.

Piero e Mauro – *Calle dei Fabbri 881 – Piazza San Marco. – ☎041 52 37 756 – Open 6.30am-2am.* Good selection of sandwiches, crostini (toasted bread snacks) and beers. The decor is fun too: the rather cramped room is decorated like the interior of a boat.

Rosa Salva – *Calle delle Locande – ☎041 52 25 385.* You might have to stand up but it's worth it. They say this place serves the best cappuccino in Venice. Why not have a delicious pastry with it?

R. Mattes/MICHELIN

GOING OUT

Devil's Forrest – *San Marco (Calle degli Stagneri) 5185 – S. Giorgio degli Schiavoni.* – ☎041 52 00 623. Beer, beer and more beer. You can even play darts here!

Il Paradiso perduto – *Cannaregio (Fondamenta della Misericordia) 2540 – Ca' D'Oro* – ☎041 72 05 81 – *Mon-Fri 7pm-1am, Sat 7pm-2am – Closed Wed.* An unusual establishment with live music, poetry readings and good food.

Linea d'Ombra – *Dorsoduro (Punta della Dogana) 19 – La Salute.* – ☎041 52 04 720 – *Open 8pm-2am – Closed Wed and Sun evening.* This rather elegant piano bar is situated round the corner from the Dogana del Mar, on the Zattere. Wonderful views of the Giudecca. Serves good cocktails.

The Fiddler's Elbow – *Cannaregio (Corte dei Pali) 3847 – Ca' D'Oro* – ☎041 52 39 930 – *5pm-1am.* If you fancy an Irish coffee or a pint, how about a trip to this Irish pub?

ENTERTAINMENT

Gran Teatro La Fenice – *Campo S. Fantin* – ☎041 78 65 11 or 041 24 24 – *www.teatrolafenice.it.*

Teatro a l'Avogaria – *Calle Avogaria 1617, Dorsoduro* – ☎041 52 09 270 – *www.teatroavogaria.it.*

Teatro Fondamenta Nuove – *Cannaregio – Fondamenta Nuove 5013* – ☎41 52 24 498 – *www.teatrofondamentanuove.it.* Situated on the Fondamenta Nuove, near the Sacca della Misericordia. Plays, concerts and dance.

Teatro Goldoni – *Calle Goldoni 4650B* – ☎041 24 02 011. Situated on the Calle del Teatro. Offers a rich season of plays and concerts.

SHOPPING

Marchini – *San Marco 2769 – La Fenice* – ☎041 52 29 109 – *www.golosessi.com.* Elegant pasticceria with a very inviting window display!

SIGHTSEEING

Combined tickets – The Museum Pass includes entrance to the museums on Piazza San Marco (Palazzo Ducale, Palazzo Correr and Biblioteca Nazionale Marciana), as well as to Ca' Rezzonico, Ca'Pesaro, the Museo del Vetro on Murano and the Museo del Merletto on Burano (18€, valid for three months). A Museum Card for the museums on Piazza San Marco only costs 12€ and is valid for three months.

Marco Polo (1254-1324) returned from China with fabulous riches. The 14C war with Venice's rival Genoa ended in victory for the Venetians in 1381.

The first half of the 15C saw Venetian power at its peak: the Turks were defeated at Gallipoli in 1416 and the Venetians held the kingdoms of Morea, Cyprus and Candia (Crete) in the Levant. In mainland Italy, from 1414 to 1428, they captured Verona, Vicenza, Padua, Udine, and then Brescia and Bergamo. The Adriatic became the Venetian Sea from Corfu to the Po.

The capture of Constantinople by the Turks in 1453 started the decay. The discovery of America caused a shift in the patterns of trade and Venice had to keep up an exhausting struggle with the Turks who were defeated in 1571 in the naval battle of **Lepanto**, in which the Venetians played an important part.

Their decline, however, was confirmed in the 17C when the Turks captured Candia (Crete) after a 25-year siege.

The "Most Serene Republic" came to an end in 1797. Napoleon Bonaparte entered Venice and abolished a thousand year-old constitution. Then, by the **Treaty of Campoformio**, he ceded the city to Austria. Venice and the Veneto were united with Italy in 1866.

The government of the Republic, was from the earliest, organised to avoid the rise to power of any one man. The role of doge was supervised by several councils: the Grand Council drew up laws; the Senate was responsible for foreign affairs, military and economic matters; the Council of Ten, responsible for security, kept a network of spies and informers that ensured all aspects of city life.

Venetian Painting

The Venetian school of painting with its marked sensuality is characterised by the predominance of colour over draughtsmanship, and by an innate sense of light in hazy landscapes with blurred outlines. Art historians have often noted the contrast between the scholarly and idealistic art of the Florentines and the freer, more spontaneous work of the Venetians, which later influenced the Impressionists.

The real beginnings of Venetian painting are exemplified by the **Bellini** family: Jacopo, the father, and Gentile (1429-1507) and **Giovanni** (or **Giambellino**, 1432-1516), his sons. The latter, the younger son, was one of the first Renaissance artists to integrate landscape and figure compositions harmoniously. In parallel, their pupil **Carpaccio** (1455-1525) recorded Venetian life with his usual care for detail while **Giorgione** remained an influence. His pupil, **Lorenzo Lotto**, was also influenced by the realism of Northern artists.

The Renaissance came to a glorious conclusion with three artists: Titian (c 1490-1576) who painted dramatic scenes where dynamic movement is offset by light effects; Paolo **Veronese** (1528-88), whose rich colours reflected the splendour of La Serenissima; and **Tintoretto** (1518-94), whose dramatic technique reflects an inner anxiety.

The artists of the 18C captured Venice and its peculiar light, grey-blue, iridescent and slightly misty: **Canaletto** (1697-1768) whose works won favour with English Grand Tourists, and his pupil Bellotto (1720-80), were both inspired by townscapes; Francesco **Guardi** (1712-93) who painted in luminous touches; Pietro Longhi (1702-58), e artist of intimate scenes; **Giovanni tista (Giambattista) Tiepolo** (1696-), a decorator who painted frescoes t and movement.

neity and colour are also found
's musicians; the best known is
'ivaldi (1678-1741), who was
olin and viola at a hospice,
a Pietà. (Hospices were also
usic and drama).

San Marco, the Drawing Room of Venice

Piazza San Marco★★★
St Mark's Square is the heart of Venice, where the covered galleries of the **Procuratie** (procuratorships) shelter famous cafés (F lorian, Quadri), and luxury shops.
The square opens on the Grand Canal through the **Piazzetta San Marco**. The two granite columns crowned by "Marco" and "Todaro" (St Mark and St Theodore) were brought from the East in 1172.

Basilica★★★
St Mark's combines the Byzantine and Western styles. Building was carried out throughout the 11C and when the basilica was consecrated in 1094, the body of St Mark, stolen from Alexandria in 828, had been miraculously recovered.
Built on the plan of a Greek cross, the basilica is crowned by a bulbous dome flanked by four smaller domes of unequal height placed on the cross.

Façade
This is pierced by five large doorways adorned with sculptures. Above the central doorway are copies of the four **bronze horses** (the originals are in the gallery of the basilica).
On the first arch on the left is depicted the Translation of the Body of St Mark. On the south side near the Doges' Palace stands the porphyry group, known as the **Tetrarchs**★ (4C). At the corner is the proclamation stone (pietra del bando), where laws were proclaimed.

Atrium
As an introduction to the narrative told in mosaic inside the basilica, the mosaics in the atrium depict Old Testament scenes. The atrium gives access to the **Galleria e Museo marcian,** which displays the **gilded bronze horses**★★. &○Open daily Apr-Oct 9.45am-5pm (Nov-Mar 4pm), Sun and public holidays 2-4pm 3€. 041 52 25 205; www. museosanmarco.it.

Interior

The dazzling decoration of St Mark's combines the mosaics (1071) by artists from Constantinople and a 12C pavement decorated with animal and geometric motifs. An iconostasis separates the raised presbytery (sanctuary) from the nave. Beyond, a ciborium raised on **alabaster columns**★★ precedes the **Pala d'Oro**★★★ (Golden Altarpiece), a masterpiece of Gothic art dating from the early 10C. The relics of St Mark rest under the high altar. **Pala d'Oro:** ◐*Open Mon-Sat Apr-Sep 9.45am-5pm (Oct-Mar 4pm), Sun and public holidays 2-5pm. ☞1.50€. ☎041 52 25 205; www.basilicasanmarco.it.*

The mosaic decoration depicts the New Testament, starting with the dome of the apse with Christ as Pantocrator (ruler of all) and ending with the Last Judgement in the area above the atrium. Near the entrance, the Arch of the Apocalypse illustrates the visions described in the gospel of St John. The dome nearest the doorway is dedicated to Pentecost. As one approaches the central dome, the west arch presents a synthesis of the Passion and Death of Christ. The south arch opening onto the south transept depicts the Temptation of Christ and His Entry into Jerusalem, the Last Supper and the Washing of the Feet. In the centre is the Dome of the Ascension depicting the Apostles, the Virgin, the Virtues and the Beatitudes. Christ in Benediction dominates the scene. The Presbytery Dome is dedicated to the Season of Advent. The mosaics on the north arch giving onto the north transept, are after cartoons by Tintoretto (St Michael, Last Supper and Marriage at Cana) and Veronese (Healing of the Leper). The Dome of St John the Evangelist in the left transept illustrates the Sermon on the Mount and the Life of St John the Evangelist.

The south transept gives access to the **treasury**★. ♿◐*Open daily Apr-Sep 9.45am-5pm, Oct-Mar 9.45am-4pm. ◐Closed Sun morning. ☞2€. ☎041 52 22 205; www.basilicasanmarco.it.*

Campanile★★

◐*Open daily Jul-Sep 9.45am-8pm; Apr-Jun, 9.30am-5pm; Oct-Mar 9.45am-4pm. ☞6€. ☎041 52 25 205; www.basilicasanmarco.it.*

The bell tower (99m/325ft high) is the symbol of Venice and a reconstruction of the 15C campanile, which collapsed in 1902. The **panorama**★★ from the top extends from to the Grand Canal.

At the base is the **Loggetta Sansoviniana**; statues of Minerva, Apollo, Mercury and Peace adorn the niches.

Palazzo Ducale★★★

♿◐*Open daily, Apr-Oct 9am-6pm, Nov-Mar 9am-4pm. ◐Closed 1 Jan, 25 Dec. ☞11€ (Museum Card for all museums in*

The delicate tracery work of the windows of a palace on the Gr

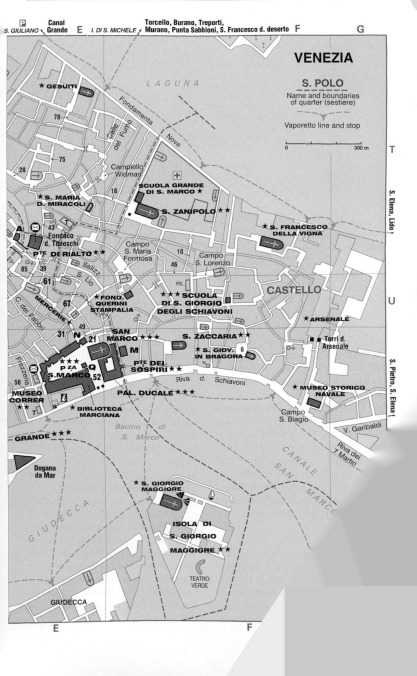

Angelo Raffaele	AV		Murano	FT		S. Francesco della Vigna	FT	
Arsenale	FGU		Museo Correr	EV		S. Giacomo dall'Orio	BT	
Biblioteca Marciana	EV		Museo Diocesano di			S. Giorgio Maggiore	FV	
Burano	FT		Arte Sacra	FV	M	S. Giovanni in Bragora	FV	
Ca' Corner della Regina	DT		Museo Ebraico	BT		S. Lazaro d. Armeni	GV	
Ca' Dario	DV		Museo Storico Navale	FV		S. Marco	EFV	
Ca' Foscari	BV		Palazzo Balbi (Pal. della			S. Maria d. Miracoli	ET	
Ca' Pesaro	CDT		Ragione)	BV	B	S. Maria della Salute	DV	
Ca' Rezzonico	BV		Palazzo Bernardo	CU		S. Pantalon	BU	
Ca' d'Oro	DT		Palazzo Corner delta Ca'			S. Pietro	GV	
Campanile	EV	Q	Granda (Prefettura)	DV	P	S. Sebastiano	ABV	
Canal Grande	BDTV		Palazzo Ducale	FV		S. Servolo	GV	
Collezione Peggy			Palazzo Fortuny	DUV		S. Stefano	CDV	
Guggenheim	CDV		Palazzo Grassi	BCV		S. Trovaso	BV	
Dogana da Mar	EV		Palazzo Labia	BT		S. Zaccaria	FV	
Fondaco d. Tedeschi	ET		Palazzo Lando			S. Zanipolo	FT	
Fondaco dei Turchi (Museo di			Corner Spinelli	CDU	E	Scala del Bovolo	DV	
Storia Naturale)	BT	M⁵	Palazzo Loredan			Scuola Grande dei		
Fondazione Querini			(Municipio)	DU	H	Carmini	ABV	
Stampalia	FU		Palazzo Loredan			Scuola Grande di S. Marco	FT	
Gallerie dell'Accademia	BV		dell'Ambasciatore	BV		Scuola Grande di S. Rocco	BU	
Gesuiti	ET		Palazzo Mocenigo	BCV		Scuola di S. Giorgio degli		
Ghetto	BT		Palazzo Vendramin			Schiavoni	FU	
I Frari	BTU		Calergi	CT		Sinagoga Spagnola	BT	
Isola di S. Giorgio			Palazzo dei Camerlenghi	ET	A	Teatro Goldoni	DU	T¹
Maggiore	FV		Ponte dei Sospiri	FV		Torcello	FT	
La Fenice	DV		S. Alvise	BT		Torre dell'Orologio	EV	N
Lido	GV		S. Clemente	FV		Torri d. Arsenale	FV	
Madonna dell'Orto	DT		S. Elena	GV		Treporti	FT	
Mercerie	EU		S. Francesco d. Deserto	FT		Zattere	BDV	

Piazza S. Marco). ☎*041 27 15 911; www. museicivicivenziani.it*

The palace was a symbol of Venetian power and glory, residence of the doges and seat of government and the law courts as well as being a prison. It was built in the 12C but was transformed between the 13C and the 16C.

A pretty, geometric pattern in white and pink marble lends great charm to the two **façades**. The groups at the corners of the palace represent, from left to right, the **Judgement of Solomon** (probably by Bartolomeo Bon), *Adam and Eve*, and **Noah's Drunkenness** (14C-15C Gothic sculptures).The main entrance is the **Porta della Carta★★**. ~~as~~ on its tympanum a Lion of St Mark ~~re~~ which kneels Doge Foscari (19C The gateway leads into the Por- ~~scari~~; opposite is the **Scala dei** ~~Giants'~~ Staircase) dominated ~~of~~ Mars and Neptune.

~~of~~ Sansovino's **Scala** ~~ircase)~~ and pass ~~oms~~ as follows: ~~Porte~~ (Room ~~the ambas-~~ ~~ience with~~

the doge; an antechamber, the **Sala dell'Antecollegio**, for diplomatic missions and delegations; the **Sala del Collegio** where the doge presided over meetings; the Senate Chamber, **Sala del Senato** or **"dei Pregadi"**, where the members of the Senate submitted their written request to participate in the meetings. The **Sala del Consiglio dei Dieci** (Chamber of the Council of Ten) is where the council met the powerful magistrates who used the secret police and spies to safeguard the institutions. Beyond the **Sala della Bussola**, the waiting-room for those awaiting interrogation and the armoury (Armeria) is the **Sala del Maggior Consiglio** (Grand Council Chamber). In this vast room (1 300m2 – 14 000sq ft) sat the legislative body which appointed all public officials; here also the constitutional election of the new doge was conducted. In the chamber hang portraits of 76 doges as well as Tintoretto's **Paradise**. Proceed to the **Sala dello Scrutinio** (Ballot Chamber); the **Prigione Nuove** (new prisons) and the Bridge of Sighs (Ponte dei Sospiri). Further along are the Censors' Chamber **(Sala dei Censori)**, the seat of the judiciary, and the **Sala dell'Avogaria**.

The view from Piazza San Marco: San Giorgio Maggiore

Ponte dei Sospiri★★

The 16C Bridge of Sighs connects the Doges' Palace with the prisons. It owes its name to romantic literary notions that held that the prisoners would suffer their final torment at the enchanting view of Venice from the window.

Torre dell'Orologio

🔒 *Closed for restoration at time of publication. For information ☎041 27 15 911.*

At the top of the late 15C Clock Tower are the Moors (Mori), a pair of bronze jacks that strike the hours.

Museo Correr★★

&⏱ *Open daily, Apr-Oct 9am-6pm; Nov-Mar 9am-4pm.* ⊘*Closed 1 Jan, 25 Dec.* ⊜*11€ (Museum Card for all museums in Piazza S. Marco).* ☎*041 24 05 211; www.museicivicivenezian.it.*

Interesing paintings and artefacts.

Libreria Sansoviniana★

This noble building was designed by Sansovino in 1553. At No 7 is a library, **Biblioteca Nazionale Marciana**.

Canal Grande★★★

(Grand Canal)

The Grand Canal (3.8km/2.3miles long, between 30m and 70m/100-230ft wide and 5.5m/18ft deep) is an inverted S and affords the best view of the palazzi. On the left bank you will see:

Palazzo Vendramin Calergia

An early-16C mansion, residence of the Codussi, where Wagner lived and died.

Ca' d'Oro★★★

Although it has lost the gilded decoration which gave it its name, the mansion retains an elegant façade in the ornate Gothic style. It houses the **Galleria Franchetti** which displays a fine **St Sebastian**★ by Mantegna. *Gallery:* &⏱*Open 8.15am-6.15pm.* ⊘*Closed Mon afternoon, 1 Jan, 1 May, 25 Dec.* ⊜*3€.* ☎*041 52 00 345; www.cadoro.org.*

Ponte di Rialto★★

The Rialto Bridge, built by Antonio da Ponte, was opened in 1591. The present structure is the sixth version and the first to be built from stone.

Palazzo Grassi★

It was built in the 18C by Giorgio Massar' and was the last great Venetian pala to be constructed before the fall of Republic. It is the venue for major ex tions. On the right bank are:

Ca' Pesaro★

The palace built by Longhe home of the **Museo d'Arte** (Museum of Oriental Art) **leria Internazionale di A**

The Venetian Scuole

Instituted during the Middle Ages, the *scuole* (literally meaning schools) were lay guilds drawn from the middle classes which were active in all aspects of life, be it devotional, charitable or professional, until the fall of the Republic. Each school had its own patron saint and mariegola, a rule book and constitution of the guild. In the 15C the scuole were housed in magnificent palaces with their interiors decorated by famous artists.

To appreciate the rich artistic heritage of the guilds, visit the **Scuola di San Rocco★★★**, decorated with scenes from the Old and New Testaments by Tintoretto, and the **Scuola di San Giorgio degli Schiavoni★★★**, a perfect setting for the exquisite paintings in warm colours by Carpaccio relating the lives of St George, St Tryphon and St Jerome. S. *Rocco:* ⚅🕐*Open daily, Apr–Oct 9am–5.30pm; Nov–Mar 10am–4pm.* 🕐*Closed 1 Jan, Easter, 25 Dec. 5.50€.* ☎*041 52 34 864; www.scuola grandesanrocco.it*

S. *Giorgio degli Schiavoni:* ⚅🕐*Open Tue–Sun, Apr–Oct 9.30am–12.30pm and 3.30–6.30pm; Nov–Mar 10am–12.30pm and 3–6pm.* 🕐*Closed Sun pm, Mon, public holidays. 3€. The Scuola is occasionally closed for Confraternita meetings.*

(International Gallery of Modern Art). *Museo di Arte Orientale:* ⚅🕐*Open daily except Mon, 10am–5pm (4pm Nov–Mar).* 🕐*Closed 1 Jan, 1 May, 25 Dec.* 🎫*5.50€.* ☎*041 52 41 173 and 041 52 04 69 95; www.museicivicivenezian.it.*

Ca' Rezzonico★★

This was the last palace designed by Longhena which was completed by Massari. It houses the **Museo del Settecento Veneziano** (Museum of 18C Venice). ⚅🕐*Open daily except Tue, Apr–Oct 10am–5pm; Nov–Mar 10am–4pm.* 🕐*Closed 1 Jan,1 May, 25 Dec.* 🎫*6.50€.* ☎*041 24 10 100; www.museiciviciven eziani.it*

Ca' Dario★

The late-15C palazzo has gained a sinister reputation owing to the suspicious deaths of several of its owners.

Venice on Canvas

Gallerie dell'Accademia★★★

Open 8.15am–6.15pm. 🕐*Closed Mon*
...oon, 1 Jan, 1 May, 25 Dec. 🎫*6.50€*
...2 00 345; www.gallerieaccademia.

...my presents the most impor-
...ion of Venetian art from the
...3C. Masterpieces include a
...throned and the **Virgin**

and Child between St Catherine and Mary Magdalene by Giovanni Bellini; the **Calling of the Sons of Zebedee** by Marco Basaiti; **St George** by Andrea Mantegna; **The Tempest** by Giorgione; a **Portrait of a Young Gentleman in His Study** by Lorenzo Lotto; a sinister **Pietà** by Titian; **Christ in the House of Levi** by Veronese; the cycle of of the **Miracles of the Relics of the True Cross** by Gentile Bellini and Carpaccio. The latter also painted the magical canvases relating the **Story of St Ursula**.

Churches

Santa Maria della Salute★★

The church, dedicated to St Mary of Salvation, was built to mark the end of a plague epidemic (1630). Designed by Longhena, it is a landmark with its modillions and concentric volutes (known as *orrechioni* – big ears). In the sacristy hangs a **Wedding at Cana** by Tintoretto in which the artist included himself as the first Apostle on the left.

San Giorgio Maggiore★

The church on the island of San Giorgio, was designed by Palladio. The top of the tall **campanile** affords the finest **view★★★** of Venice. In the presbytery (sanctuary) hang two large paintings by Tintoretto, the Last Supper and the

Harvest of Manna. ⏱*Campanile: Ascent daily, 9.30am-12.30pm and 2.30pm to 30min before dusk.* 🚶*3€ (with lift).* ☎*041 52 27 827.*

San Zanipòlo★★
The square boasts an **equestrian statue**★★of the mercenary leader Bartolomeo **Colleoni** by Verrocchio and is flanked by the **Scuola Grande di San Marco**★to one side, and dominated by the Gothic church of Santi Giovanni e Paolo, dedicated to St John and St Paul (in the Venetian dialect Zanipòlo is a contraction of the two names) and the burial place for the doges.

I Frari★★
⏱*Open daily 9am (1pm Sun and public holidays)-6pm.* 🚶*2.50€.* ☎*041 27 28 611; www.chorusvenezia.org*
This great Franciscan church – its name is derived from the abbreviation of Fra*(ti Mino)*ri – can be compared to San Zanipòlo on account of its imposing appearance and its funerary monuments. The focal point of the perspective is an **Assumption of the Virgin** by Titian in the Cappella Maggiore.

San Zaccaria★★
The interior of the Renaissance-Gothic Church of St Zachary is covered with paintings; the most important is Giovanni Bellini's **Sacra Conversazione**.

Other Areas and Museums of Venice

Arsenale★
There was a dockyard in Venice as early as 1104 when the crusades stimulated shipbuilding. The Arsenal has two entrances: the land gateway marked by lions from Ancient Greece, and the watergate marked by two towers through which the *vaporetto* passes.

Ghetto★★
The Jewish quarter (ghetto), in the Cannaregio district, was the first to be differentiated as such in Western Europe. In the Venetian dialect the term *geto* referred to a mortar foundry. The g,

pronounced soft (as in George) was hardened by the first Jews who came from Germany. A museum, the Museo Ebraico and synagogues, **sinagoghe** are open to visitors.

Giudecca
Giudecca Island offers a glorious view of Venice and the Palladian church of **Il Redentore**★*(Fondamenta S. Giacomo).*

Collezione Peggy Guggenheim★
⏱*Open daily except Tue, 10am-6pm.* ⏱*Closed 25 Dec.* 🚶*10 €.* ☎*041 24 05 411; www.guggenheim-venice.it.*
An 18C palazzo where the American Peggy Guggenheim lived until her death, is the setting for an interesting collection of art by 20C artists

Excursions

Lido♨♨
Venice's seaside resort has a casino, and hosts a prestigious annual film festival.

Murano★★
By the end of the 13C, the threat of fire was constant in Venice with its wooden buildings, and so the Grand Council moved the glassworks to Murano. This glassmaking island has a museum, **Museo di Arte Vetraria**★, with displays of exquisite glassware. The apse of the basilica, **Santi Maria e Donato**★★, is a masterpiece of 12C Veneto-Byzantine art and the **mosaic floor**★★ recalls that of St Mark's. *Museo di Arte Vetraria:* ⏱*Open daily Apr-Oct 10am-5pm (Nov-Mar 4pm).* ⏱*Closed Wed 1 Jan, 1 May* 🚶*4€; 6€ combined ticket with Mus del merletto.* ☎*041 73 95 86; www.m civiciveneziani.it.*

Burano★★
This is the most colourful o in the lagoon. At the do women are engaged i

Torcello★★
A ghost island, To decimated by Venetian rul

VERONA★★★

POPULATION 259 068
MICHELIN MAPS 561, 562 F 14-15 –
TOWN PLAN IN THE MICHELIN ATLAS ITALY.

Verona stands on the banks of the Adige against a hilly backdrop. It is the second most important art centre in the Veneto region after Venice. The fashionable Piazza Bra is linked by Via Mazzini to the heart of the old town.

- **Information:** Via degli Alpini 9. ☎045 80 68 580; Stazione Porta Nuova, 37138 *Verona*, ☎045 80 00 861; www.tourism.verona.it.
- ▶ **Orient Yourself:** Verona is very well situated with easy access to Venice (take A 4) and the Brenner transalpine pass (take A 22). Also nearby are Lake Garda and the Euganean Hills (Colli Euganei).
- ☺ **Don't Miss:** Castelcecchio and Ponte Scaligero, theatrical performances at Teatro Romano and Chiesa di San Zeno Maggiore.
- **Kids** **Especially for Kids:** Roman amphitheatre and the Tomb of Juliet

A Bit of History

This Roman colony under the Empire was coveted by the Ostrogoths, Lombards and Franks. The town reached the peak of its glory under the Scaligers who governed for Holy Roman Emperor from 1260 to 1387. Then it passed to the Visconti of Milan before submitting to Venetian rule from 1405. Verona was occupied by Austria in 1814 and became part of the Veneto with Italy in 1866.

Pisanello – Artists of the Veronese school were influenced by Northern art from the Rhine Valley and they developed a Gothic art which combined flowing lines with a meticulous attention to detail. Antonio Pisanello (c 1395-c 1450), a great traveller, active painter, prodigious medal-maker and enthusiastic draughtsman, was the greatest ~ponent of this school. His painting, with soft colours, meticulous details and flowing lines, was reminiscent of the rapidly disappearing medieval world and heralded the realism typical of the Renaissance.

Walking About

Our route starts in Piazza Bra in the heart of the city. This large square is dominated by Verona's Roman amphitheatre.

Arena★★

♿ ⊙ *Open daily 8.30am-6.30pm.* ⊙*Closed Mon morning, 1 Jan, 25 Dec.* ⊜*3.10€.* ☎*045 59 29 85; www.arena.it.* This amphitheatre, among the largest in the Roman world, could accommodate 25 000 spectators with its 44 tiers of seats. It is built of blocks of pink marble, flint and brick; this indicates that it prob-

R. Mattes/MICHELIN

...na

Address Book

🪙 *For coin ranges see the Legend on the cover flap.*

WHERE TO STAY

It is worth noting that during trade fairs and exhibitions the hotels tend to put their prices up. Do enquire about this when you make your booking.

🛏️🛏️**Cavour** – *Vicolo Chiodo 4 – Verona – ☎045 59 01 66 – Fax 045 59 05 08 – Closed 9 Jan-9 Feb – 🍴 🖳 – 22 rm – 🖳 12 €.* The main benefit of this hotel is its quiet, central location. Simple rooms with modern furnishings (some have exposed beamed ceilings). In fact, you could quite happily stay in your room and listen to opera were it not such a magical experience going to the Arena.

🛏️🛏️**Hotel Torcolo** – *Vicolo Listone 3 – ☎045 80 07 512 – www.hoteltorcolo.it – Closed 7 Jan-8 Feb – 🖳 – 19 rm – 🖳 €12.* Having trouble finding a decent hotel in the centre without facing financial ruin? Look no further... and the staff are keen to please. Pleasant rooms (some with a slightly retro feel). Breakfast served in your room or, when possible, outside.

WHERE TO EAT

🍽️**La Stueta** – *Via Redentore 4/B – ☎045 80 32 462 – Closed Mon, Tue lunchtime, 7-14 Jan, 4-25 Jul.* A reasonably priced trattoria not far from the Roman amphitheatre. Traditional decor and cooking. Polenta lovers will not be disappointed.

🍽️**San Basilio alla Pergola** – *Via Pisano 9 – Verona – ☎045 52 04 75 – Closed 15 days in Jan and 15 days in Sep.* With its rustic-style dining rooms and splendid wooden floors, there is a pleasant, country feel to this restaurant. Complementing the ambience is the chef's traditional but imaginative cooking. Good value.

🍽️🍽️**Ciccarelli** – *Via Mantovana 171, Località Madonna di Dossobuono – 8km/5mi southwest of Verona on S 62 in the direction of Mantua – ☎045 95 39 86 – www.ristorantecicca relli.it – Closed Sat, mid-Jul-mid- Aug – 🖳.* It almost goes without saying that the dishes done best by this very traditional trattoria are roast and boiled meats (accompanied by a wide selection of cooked or raw vegetables). The puddings are all home-made. Solo diners may have to share a table.

EVENTS AND FESTIVALS

The opera and theatre summer seasons both draw large crowds.

ably dates from the late 1C. In summer it is the venue for a prestigious opera season. From the topmost row there is a good **panorama**★★ of the town in its hilly setting, which on a clear day reaches as far as the Alps.

Castelvecchio and Ponte Scaligero★★

This splendid fortified complex was built in 1354 by Cangrande II Scaliger. The castle itself is divided into two parts separated by a passageway guarded by a keep.

The castle contains the **Museo d'Arte**★★created by the architect Carlo Scarpa (🪙*see Worth a Visit*).

▸ Follow Corso Cavour, home to the church of San Lorenzo (🪙*see Worth*

Romeo and Juliet

The setting for this apocryphal drama was Verona in 1302 when political conflict raged. The tragic young coupl[e] immortalised by Shakespeare belon[g] to rival families: Romeo to the M[onte]chi (Montagues), who were [...] and supported the Pope, a[nd...] the Capuleti (Capulets), w[ho...] bellines and supported [...]

a Visit), then
dei Borsari [...]
along Co[...]

Piazza
The S[...]
Ro[...]

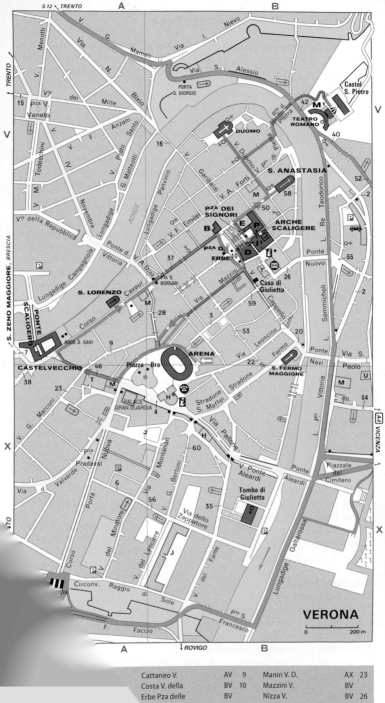

VERONA

0   200 m

Redentore V.	BV	40	S. Cosimo V.	BV	53	SS. Trinità V.	BX	56
Regaste Redentore	BV	42	S. Francesco V.	BX	54	Stella V.	BV	59
Roma V.	AVX	46	S. Tomaso Pza	BV	55	Tezone V.	BX	60
S. Anastasia Cso	BV	50	Signori Pza dei	BV				
S. Chiara V.	BV	52	Sottoriva V.	BV	58			

Loggia del Consiglio	BV	E	Palazzo Maffei	BV	B	Palazzo del Comune	BV	D
Museo Archeologico	BV	M¹	Palazzo dei Tribunali	BV	J¹	Palazzo del Governo	BV	P

and lively, especially on market day. In line, down the middle of the square, stand the market column; the *capitello* (a rostrum from which decrees and sentences were proclaimed) of the 16C governors *(podestà)*; the fountain known as the Verona Madonna, with a Roman statue symbolising the town; and a Venetian column surmounted by the winged Lion of St Mark (1523).

Palaces and old houses, some with pink marble columns and frescoes, frame the square: on the north side is the Baroque **Palazzo Maffei**.

In Via Cappello (No 23) is the **Casa di Giulietta** (Juliet's House); in fact it is a Gothic palace which is said to have belonged to the Capulet family; the famous balcony is in the inner courtyard. *Open daily 8.30am-6.30pm.* ◐*Closed Mon morning, 1 Jan, 25 Dec.* ▰4€. ☎045 80 34 303; www.comune.verona.it.

Piazza dei Signori★★

Take Via della Costa to reach this elegant square which resembles an open-air drawing-room. On the right is the 12C **Palazzo del Comune** (Town Hall), also known as the Palazzo della Ragione dominated by the **Torre dei Lamberti**, a tower built of brick and stone and with an octagonal upper storey. This building is connected by an arch with the **Palazzo dei Tribunali** (Law Courts), formerly the Palazzo del Capitano (Governor's Residence) which is also flanked by a massive brick tower, Torrione Scaligero. The **Loggia del Consiglio** on the opposite side is an elegant edifice in the Venetian-Renaissance style. *Tower:* ◐*Open daily 8.30am-6.30pm.* ◐*Closed Mon morning, 1 Jan, 25 Dec.* ▰3€. ☎045 80 32 726; www.comune.verona.it.

At the far end of the square, the late-13C **Palazzo del Governo** with its machicolations and fine Classical doorway (1533) by Sammicheli was initially a Scaliger

residence before it became that of the Venetian Governors.

Arche Scaligere★★

The Scaliger built their tombs between their palace and their church. The sarcophagi bear the arms of the family, with the symbolic ladder *(scala)*.

The elegant Gothic mausolea are surrounded by marble balustrades and wrought-iron rails, and are decorated with carvings of religious scenes and statues of saints in niches.

Over the door of the Romanesque church of **Santa Maria Antica** is the tomb of the popular Cangrande I (d 1329) with his equestrian statue above *(the original is in the Castelvecchio Museum).*

Teatro Romano★

◐*Open daily 8.30am-6.30pm.* ◐*Closed Mon morning, 1 Jan, 25 Dec.* ▰3€. ☎045 80 00 360; www.comune.verona.it.

The Roman theatre dates from the time of Augustus but has been heavily restored. Theatrical performances are still given here. A former monastery, **Convento di San Girolamo** *(access by lift)* has the small **Museo Archeologico** and there is a lovely view over the town. ◐Museum: *Open daily 8.30am-6.30pm.* ◐*Closed Mon morning, 1 Jan, 25 Dec.* ▰3.10€. ☎045 80 00 360.

Castel San Pietro

Take the stairway which leads off Redentore. St Peter's Castle dat the Visconti and the period rule. The terraces afford sp ★★of Verona.

Art and Re

Admission to nastasia, San and San Ze

churches: €5). Associazione Chiese Vive; ☏045 59 28 13; www.chieseverona.it.

Museo d'Arte★★

🕑Open daily 8.30am-6.30pm. 🕑Closed Mon morning, 1 Jan, 25 Dec. 🌐 4€. ☏045 80 62 611; www.comune.verona.it/ castelvecchio/cvsito.

The art museum's collection shows the development of Veronese art from the 12C to 16C and its links with Venice and the International Gothic. There are frescoes by local artists and canvases by Stefano da Verona, Pisanello, Giambono, Carlo Crivelli (splendid Madonna of the Passion), Mantegna and Carpaccio as well as the Bellinis.

The rooms on the upper floor contain works from the Renaissance period by Veronese artists: Morone, Liberale da Verona (Virgin with a Goldfinch), Girolamo dai Libri and Veronese. There are also Venetian works by Tintoretto, Guardi, Tiepolo and Longhi. Also on display are jewellery and sculpture.

Chiesa di Sant'Anastasia★

www.chieseverona.it.
This church was begun at the end of the 13C and completed in the 15C. The campanile is remarkable and the façade is pierced with a 14C double doorway adorned with frescoes and sculpture. The lofty interior contains several masterpieces: four figures of the Apostles by Michele da Verona; Pisanello's famous fresco (above the Pellegrini Chapel, to the right of the high altar) of St George delivering the Princess of Trebizondaa (1436), which has an almost surreal combination of realistic precision and Gothic fantasy; ⁷ terracottasa by Michele da Firenze in Cappella Pellegrini; and the fresco ing Knights of the Cavalli family resented to the Virgina (1380) ronese artist, Altichero (first e south transept). 🕑Pisanel-

Fermo Maggiore★
it.
d to St Firmanus e 11C-12C and te. The façade othic styles. ered by a

stepped, keel-shaped roof. By the west door the Brenzoni mausoleum (1430) is framed by a fresco of the Annunciation★by Pisanello.

Duomo★

The cathedral has a 12C Romanesque chancel, a Gothic nave and a Classical-style tower. The remarkable main doorway in the Lombard-Romanesque style is adorned with sculptures and low reliefs by Maestro Nicolò. The interior has pink marble pillars. The altarpiece (first altar on the left) is decorated with an Assumption by Titian. The marble chancel screen is by Sammicheli (16C). The canons' quarters are pleasant.

Chiesa di San Zeno Maggiore★★

Access via Largo D. Bosco. 🕑Plan of the built-up area in the Michelin Atlas Italy-www.chieseverona.it.

St Zeno is one of the finest Romanesque churches in northern Italy. It was built on the basilical plan in the Lombard style in the 12C. The façade is decorated with Lombard bands and arcading; the side walls and campanile have alternate brick and stone courses. In the entrance porch resting on two lions, there are admirable bronze doors★★★ (11C-12C) with scenes from the Old and New Testaments. On either side are low reliefs by the master sculptors Nicolò and Guglielmo (12C). On the tympanum of the doorway is a statue of St Zeno, patron saint of Verona.

The imposing interior has a lofty, bare nave with a cradle roof flanked by aisles with shallow roofing. On the high altar is a splendid triptych★★ (1459), a good example of Mantegna's style characterised by precise draughtsmanship and rich ornamentation. There are 14C statues on the chancel screen and a curious polychrome statue of St Zeno laughing in the north apse.

Tomba di Giulietta

Via del Portiere. 🕑Open daily 8.30am-6.30pm. 🕑Closed Mon morning, 1 Jan, 25 Dec. 🌐3€. ☏045 80 00 361.
Juliet's tomb is in the cloisters of the church of San Francesco al Corso, where, it is said, Romeo and Juliet were married.

VERSILIA ★

MICHELIN MAP 563 J 12 – K12/13
SEE ALSO THE GREEN GUIDE TUSCANY.

Versilia is a district with a mild climate and contrasting landscapes lying between the sea coast and the mountains, which form a natural barrier against the north wind. The gently rolling hills give way to the lush coastal plain, which was formed in the Quaternary Era by the alluvium deposited by the streams tumbling down from the mountain peaks.

Along the coast is a string of superb resorts boasting fine sandy beaches (up to 100m/110yd wide), which slope gently into the sea and are ideal for families with young children. In the distance one can see the Apuan Alps which give Upper Versilia its natural resources of white and red marble and slate. In the hinterland and on the mountains Nature has the upper hand and the traditional villages, surrounded by olive and chestnut trees, provide a contrast to the crowded coast.

The Apuan Alps are a Parco Naturale, which includes Camaiore, Pietrasante, Seravezza and Stazzema. The park is an ideal place for outdoor activities – hiking, climbing, gliding, pony trekking, mountain biking and caving.

- **Information:** Consorzio di Promozione Turistica della Versilia Arte Mare, Piazza America 2, 55044 Marina di Pietrasanta (LU), ☎0584 20 331, www.artemare.net and Viale Carducci 10, 55049 Viareggio (LU), ☎0584 96 22 33.
- ▶ **Orient Yourself:** Versilia is easily accessible from the motorways that link Genoa to Livorno and Florence to the coast.
- **Don't Miss:** Cave dei Fantiscritti and the Migliarino-San Rossore-Massaciuccoli Country Park.
- **Especially for Kids:** Sandy beaches at Marina di Pietrasanta.

Tour from Quarry to Quayside

▶ *50km/30mi. Allow half a day.*

Cave di Carraracela

The wild countryside and gigantic nature of the quarrying operations afford a spectacular sight. The impressive quarries, **Cave dei Fantiscritti**★★*(5km/3mi northeast)* and the **Cave di Colonnata**★ *(8.5km/5mi east)* are both actively worked and regularly despatch quantities of marble *(marmo)* to the port of **Marina di Carrara** *(7km/4mi southwest)*.

Marina di Massa and Marina di Carrara

A deserted stretch of coast precedes these two resorts, which have a number of fine turn-of-the-century buildings. Between them is the harbour from which marble is exported.

Forte dei Marmi ⌂⌂⌂

www.versilia.org/turismo.

This elegant resort is popular with artists and the Italian jet set. The beach has regular rows of colourful little cabins. To the north the mountains of Liguria turn west towards the coast and plunge into the sea, marking the end of the gentle Versilian coastline.

Marina di Pietrasanta ⌂⌂

www.toscanamare.com.

The seaside resort has a long beach (o▮ 5km/3mi), delightful paths thro▮ the pine woods for walking or c▮ a wide range of sports amenit▮ excellent nightlife.

On the outskirts of Marina di P▮ on the other bank of the F▮ back from the beach, is **V▮** (80ha/200 acres of woo▮ Gabriele D'Annunzio ▮ tor to the early-20C ▮ the park hosts cult▮

The stylish Viale Regina Margherita in Viareggio

Kids *Beaches at Marina di Pietrasanta.*

Lido di Camaiore
Lido di Camaiore is more modern and more of a family resort than Viareggio, its prestigious neighbour, but they are so close that they tend to run into one another. It has the same fine sandy beach, the same pine woods and a delightful esplanade.

Viareggio
This fashionable seaside resort, on the Tyrrhenian Coast, has lovely beaches and plenty of amenities for holidaymakers. Viale Regina Margherita and its prolon-

gation, Viale Guglielmo Marconi provide fine examples of the architectural style of the late 1920s, somewhere between art nouveau and Art Deco, such as the splendid Gran Caffè Margherita. At **Torre del Lago Puccini** (5km/3mi to the southeast) the composer Puccini wrote the majority of his operas. The **Villa Puccini** contains the tomb and other mementoes of Puccini. *Villa:* Open June-Oct daily 10am-12.30pm and 3-6.30pm(Apr and May 6pm, rest of the year 5.30pm). Closed Mon, Nov, 25 Dec. 7€. 0584 34 14 45; www.giacomopuccini.it.

Massaciuccoli★
Head for the Via Aurelia (SS 1) going north towards Viareggio; left to Torre del Lago. This road crosses part of the **Migliarino-San Rossore-Massaciuccoli** Country Park including the lake (average depth 1.60m/5ft), the Massaciuccoli Marshes and all that remains of the ancient Pisan Forest which used to stretch from La Spezia *(north)* to Castiglioncello *(south of Livorno)*. The lake is stocked with fish and turtles. Over 250 species of birds, some rare, live and nest or visit here during migration.

Address Book

For coin ranges see the Legend on the cover flap.

WHERE TO STAY
Hotel Grande Italia – *Via Torino 5 – 55044 Marina di Pietrasanta* – 0584 20 046 – Fax 0584 24 350 – Closed 20 Sep-May – 28 rm – Restaurant. Dating back to the early 20C this hotel remains largely unchanged and would appeal to retro enthusiasts. Simple surroundings and a family atmosphere. The lovely pinewood which surrounds hotel enhances the sense of peace quiet.
Hotel Arcangelo – *Via Carrara 49 Viareggio* – 0584 47 123 elarcangelo.com – Closed rm – Restaurant. This d in what was once a private benefits from a peaceful the location in a street ovely garden at the

back. 1950s-style rooms (simple) and public areas (well kept). Friendly staff.
Hotel Pardini – *Viale Carducci 14 – 55049 Viareggio* – 0584 96 13 79 – Fax 0584 96 16 79 – hotelpardini@virgilio.it – Closed Nov – 14 rm – . A family-run hotel on the main drag, within easy reach of restaurants, shops and bathing areas. Pleasant ambience and peaceful atmosphere. Spacious rooms, with simple, modern furnishings. Attentive, courteous service.

WHERE TO EAT
Rino – *Via della Chiesa 8 – 55040 Bargecchia – 4km/2.5mi south of Camaiore* – 0584 95 40 00 – Closed Tue (Sept-May). Right in the heart of the village is a very traditional establishment (both in terms of decor and cuisine). Specialities include fresh pasta and grilled meats. There is a lovely garden where meals are served in summer.

Accommodation also available.

Mokambo – *Viale della Repubblica 4 – 55042 Forte dei Marmi – ☎0584 89 446 – Closed Wed –* 🖩 ⌧ *– 10% service charge.* After a day in the sun by the sea, this is the ideal spot for a quick pizza, a sandwich or even a proper meal (fish of course!). With its cheerful ambience and spacious surroundings, this place is popular with families and groups of youngsters.

Osteria alla Giudea – *Via Barsanti 4 – 55045 Pietrasanta – ☎0584 71 514 –Closed Mon –* 🖩 *– Book – 10% service charge.* The proprietors are also the chefs here – you will see them hard at work in the kitchen which is on show. With its marble and wrought-iron tables there is a French bistro feel to the place, but the cooking is firmly rooted in the traditions of the region. The dishes of the day are written up on the blackboard near the entrance.

Il Puntodivino – *Via Mazzini 229 – 55049 Viareggio – ☎0584 31 046 – Closed lunchtime Jul to Aug, 7-28 Jan –* 🖩. A great place for a quick lunch – the dishes of the day are written up on a blackboard near the entrance. In the evening, there is more choice and you can sample several dishes if you choose the menu degustazione. Good selection of wines which you can also buy. Young, trendy ambience.

Trattoria al Porto – *Via Coppino 319 – 55049 Viareggio – ☎0584 38 38 78 – Closed Sun and Mon lunchtime, 20 Dec-15 Jan, mid-Sept-mid-Oct –* 🖩 *– Book.* You will have to book several days in advance if you want to dine here – this establishment is always busy! Jovial, lively atmosphere (the menu will be read out to you in a rather flamboyant manner…). Specialises in seafood, the dishes prepared with the freshest of ingredients.

TAKING A BREAK

Pasticceria Bar Fappani – *Viale Marconi, Lungomare – 55049 Viareggio – ☎0584 96 25 82 – Tue-Sun 8am-midnight.* With its large terrace area overlooking the sea, this is a good spot to indulge any yearnings for something sweet. A family-run establishment since 1921, it has a relaxing, cosy atmosphere.

GOING OUT

Discotheques in Versilia – *Seafront between Lido di Camaiore and Forte dei Marmi – 55042 Forte dei Marmi.* Every night the seafront is transformed into one long dance hall. From Viareggio to Forte dei Marmi, there is one disco–theque after another – and they are all very different. It was actually La Bussola, which opened back in 1970, that established Versilia's reputation for its lively nightlife. Generally speaking the younger generation (aged between 25 and 30) head for the Seven Apples (which has a swimming pool) or the Capannina which organises theme nights. The local youth tend to hang out at the Faruck, the Agorà and the Midho' (where the Kupido annex is given over to tecno music). Last of all, as you head out of Forte dei Marmi, there is the Canniccia, which is popular with the over-30s: it has four dance floors and a large garden.

Agorà – *Viale Cristoforo Colombo 666 – 55043 Lido di Camaiore – ☎0584 61 04 88 – Open Wed-Thu and Sat 9pm-4am.*

Faruk – *Viale Roma 53/55, Tonfano – 55044 Marina di Pietrasanta – ☎0584 21 57 8/ 05 84 21 744 – Open Thu-Sat midnight-4am.*

La Bussola – *Viale Roma 44 – 55044 Marina di Pietrasanta – ☎0584 22 737 – Open Thu-Sun 10pm-4am.*

Midho' and Kupido – *Viale Achille Franceschi 12 – 55042 Forte dei Marmi – ☎0584 89 114 – www.midho.com – Open Fri-Sat and Tue 11.30pm-4am.*

Seven Apples – *Viale Roma 109, Focette – 55044 Marina di Pietrasanta – ☎0584 20 458/ 0584 22 433 – www.sevenapples. it – Open Fri-Sun 8.30pm-4am.*

SHOPPING

Laboratorio di Cartapesta – *Via Morandi – 55049 Viareggio – Guid tours of the papier- mâché work Information in Piazza Mazzini carnival in Viareggio is inte famous for the processio papier-mâché floats (s large). Visitors are we see how they are m*

VICENZA★★

POPULATION 113 483
MICHELIN MAP 562 F 16
TOWN PLAN IN THE MICHELIN ATLAS ITALY –VENETO.

Strategically located at the crossroads of the routes that link the Veneto with the Trentino, the proud and noble city of Vicenza is now a busy commercial and industrial centre. In addition to its traditional textile industry, and newer mechanical and chemical industries, Vicenza has a reputation as a gold-working centre. The gastronomic speciality of Vicenza is baccalà alla Vicentina, salt cod with a sauce served with slices of polenta (maize semolina), which is best with wine from the Berici Mountains (Barbarano, Gambellara and Breganze).

- **Information:** Piazza Matteotti 12. ☎0444 32 08 54. www.vincenzae.org.
- **Orient Yourself:** Vicenza lies in a pretty setting at the foot of the Berici Mountains. phrase prise des premières lignes The main access road is A 4.
- **Don't Miss:** Piazza dei Signori, the Teatro Olimpico and splendid frescoes by Giovanni Battista at the Villa Valmarana ai Nani.
- **Organizing Your Time:** Allow a day for a visit.
- **Also See:** LAGUNA VENETA, PADOVA, VERONA.

A Bit of History

The ancient Roman town of Vicetia became an independent city state in the 12C. After several conflicts with the neighbouring cities of Padua and Verona, Vicenza sought Venetian protection at the beginning of the 15C. This was a period of great prosperity, when Vicenza counted many rich and generous art patrons among its citizens and it was embellished with an amazing number of palaces.

Andrea Palladio

Vicenza was given the nickname of "Venice on *terra firma*" due to an exceptionally gifted man, Andrea di Pietro, known as Palladio, who spent many years in Vicenza. The last great architect of the Renaissance, Palladio was born in Padua in 1508 and died at Vicenza in ... succeeded in combining, in ... harmonious idiom, the present art with the contemporary ...tions. Encouraged by the ..., he made several visits ...her monuments and ... a Roman architect ...us. He perfected ... 1570 published ...**ture**, in four

volumes, which made his work famous throughout Europe.

The **Palladian style** is characterised by rigorous plans where simple and symmetrical forms predominate and by harmonious façades which combine pediments and porticoes, as at San Giorgio Maggiore in Venice (*see VENEZIA*). Palladio was often commissioned by wealthy Venetians to build residences in the countryside around Venice. He combined architectural rhythm, noble design and, in the case of the country mansions, a great sense of situation, decoration and height, so that the villas seemed to rise like a series of new temples on the banks of the Brenta (*see Riviera del BRENTA*) or the slopes of the Berici Mountains. His pupil, Vicenzo Scamozzi (1552-1616), completed several of his master's works and carried on his style.

Visit

Piazza dei Signori★★

Like St Mark's Square in Venice, it is an open-air meeting-place recalling the forum of Antiquity. As in the Piazzetta in Venice, there are two columns, here bearing effigies of the Lion of St Mark and the Redeemer.

Address Book

For coin ranges see the Legend on the cover flap.

WHERE TO STAY

Hotel Victoria – *Strada Padana (in the direction of Padua) 52 – 7km/4mi east of Vicenza on SS 11* – ☎0444 91 22 99 – www.hotelvictoria vicenza.com – ⓟ▤& – *123 rm* ⌁. Combines reasonable prices with comfortable surroundings – a rare thing in Vicenza. Offers good-sized rooms and apartments: stylewise they are somewhere between classical and functional. Given its situation – not far from the motorway and yet a few minutes' from the centre – this hotel would be a good solution for anyone arriving by car.

Giardini – *Via Giuriolo 10* – ☎0444 32 64 58 – www.hotelgiardini. com– *Closed 23 Dec-3 Jan* – ⓟ▤& – *17 rm* ⌁. Situated just a stone's throw from the Teatro Olimpico, is this little hotel that from the outside – Venetian villa in style – pays homage to the great Palladio. Inside it is comfortable with attractive, modern rooms.

WHERE TO EAT

Al Pestello – *Contrà Santo Stefano 3* – ☎0444 32 37 21 – *Closed Sun, 15 May and 15 Oct*. Serves tasty food in lovely surroundings – note the huge fresco in the dining room. There is also a lovely outdoor area. The menu (in dialect!) includes a number of traditional, local specialities.

Antica Osteria da Penacio – *Via Soghe 22, località Soghe – 36077 Arcugnano – 10km/6mi south of Vicenza on S 247* – ☎0444 27 30 81 – *Closed Wed, Thu lunchtime, 20-30 Jan, 20-30 Jul, 20-30 Oct* – ▤. From the outside it looks like a rather old taverna but the interior is surprisingly elegant. Both dining rooms are modern in style and there is a small but well-stocked wine cellar which adds to the atmosphere. The cuisine is of a high standard.

With the lofty **Torre Bissara**★, a 12C belfry, the **Basilica**★★ (1549-1617) occupies one whole side of the square. The elevation is one of Palladio's masterpieces, with two superimposed galleries in the Doric and Ionic orders, admirable for their power, proportion and purity of line. The great keel-shaped roof, destroyed by bombing, has been rebuilt. The building was not a church but a meeting-place for the Vicenzan notables. *Telephone for openings times and prices.* ☎0444 32 36 81; www. vicenzae.org.

The 15C **Monte di Pietà** (municipal pawn shop) opposite, its buildings framing the Baroque façade of the church of San Vincenzo, is adorned with frescoes. The **Loggia del Capitano**★, formerly the residence of the Venetian Governor, which stands to the left, at the corner of the Contrà del Monte, was begun to the plans of Palladio in 1571 and left unfinished. It is characterised by its colossal orders with composite capitals and its statues and stuccoes commemorating the naval victory of Lepanto (*see Index*).

Teatro Olimpico★★

Open Tue-Sun Jul and Aug 9am-7pm, rest of year 9am-5pm. Closed Mon, 1 Jan, 25 Dec. 8€. ☎0444 22 28 00; www. vicenzae.org.

This splendid building in wood and stucco was designed by Palladio in 1580 on the model of the theatres of Antiquity. The tiers of seats are laid out in a hemicycle and surmounted by a lovely **colonnade** with a balustrade crowned with statues. The **stage**★★★ is one of the finest in existence with its superimposed niches, columns and statues and its amazing perspectives painted in trompe l'oeil by Scamozzi who completed the work.

Corso Andrea Palladio★

This, the main street of Vic several neighbouring stree lished by many palace Palladio and his pupil ning is the **Palazzo** *below*), an imposin at No 147 the 15C the Venetian-G known as the because it was covered with frescoes with gilded backgrounds. The west front of **Palazzo Thiene** overlooking Contrà S. Gaetano Thiene was by Palladio, while the entrance front at No 12 Contrà Porti is Renaissance, dating from the late 15C.

The **Palazzo Porto-Barbaran** opposite is also by Palladio. At No 98 the **Palazzo Trissino** (1592) is one of Scamozzi's most successful works. Next is the Corso Fogazzaro, where the **Palazzo Valamarana** (1566) at No 16 is another work by Palladio.

Museo Civico★

On the first floor of Palazzo Chiericati. ♿ 🕐*Open daily 9am-7pm 9am-5pm.* 🕐*Closed Mon, 1 Jan, 25 Dec.* ✎*8€ including other Vicenza museums. For information* ☎*0444 32 13 48.*

The collection of paintings includes Venetian Primitives (*The Dormition of the Virgin* by Paolo Veneziano); a **Crucifixion**★★by Hans Memling; canvases by Bartolomeo Montagna (pupil of Giovanni Bellini), Mantegna and Carpaccio, one of the most active artists in Vicenza. There are Venetian works by Lorenzo Lotto, Veronese, Bassano, Piazzetta, Tiepolo and Tintoretto as well as Flemish works by Brueghel the Elder and Van Dyck.

Chiesa della Santa Corona

Opposite Santa Corona.

The church was built in the 13C in honour of a Holy Thorn presented by St Louis, King Louis IX of France, to the Bishop of Vicenza. The nave and two aisles have pointed vaulting while the chancel is Renaissance. Works of art include: a **Baptism of Christ**★★ by Giovanni Bellini *(fifth altar on the left)* and **Adoration of the Magi**★★ (1573) by ese *(third chapel on the right).* The chapel on the right has a coffered adorned with gilded stucco, Magdalene and Saints by Montagna.

lt between the 14C actively colourful Renaissance east lyptch★ (1356)

Giardino Salvi

This garden is attractively adorned with statues and fountains. Canals run along two sides of the garden and two lovely Palladian 16C and 17C loggias are reflected in the waters.

Excursions

Villa Valmarana ai Nani★★

2km/1mi south by the Este road and then the first road to the right. 🕐*Open mid-Mar-Oct 10am-noon and 3-6pm (rest of the year 4pm).* 🕐*Closed Mon.* ✎*6€.* ☎*0444 32 18 03; www.villavalmarana. com.*

The villa dates from the 17C. Both the Palazzina and the Forestiera buildings were adorned with splendid **frescoes**★★★ by Giovanni Battista (Giambattista) Tiepolo and his son Giovanni Domenico.

La Rotonda★

2km/1mi southeast by the Este road and then the second road to the right. 🕐*Open mid-Mar-Oct daily 10am-noon and 3-6pm (rest of the year 2.30-5.30pm).* 🕐*Closed Mon.* ✎*10€ for interior and garden, 5€ for garden* ☎*0444 32 17 93; www. vicenzae.org.*

The Rotonda is one of Palladio's most famous creations and the plan of Chiswick House in London was inspired by it. The gracefully proportioned square building is roofed with a dome and fronted on each side by a pedimented portico, making it look like an ancient temple.

Basilica di Monte Berico and Monti Berici★

2km/1mi south by Viale Venezia and then Viale X Giugno.

As the Viale X Giugno climbs uphill, it is lined with an 18C portico and chapels. On the summit is the Baroque basilica roofed with a dome. From the esplanade there is a wide **panorama**★★ of Vicenza, the Venetian plain and the Alps. Inside, there is a Pietà (1500) by Bartolomeo Montagna.

From here the road runs southwards to Arcugnano and Barbarano, where one can catch occasional glimpses of former patrician villas now used as farmhouses in this countryside of volcanic hills.

Montecchio Maggiore

13km/8mi southwest by S 11. www.comune.montecchio-maggiore.vi.it. The ruins of these two castles brings to mind Romeo and Juliet. There are good **views**★ of the Po Plain and Vicenza.

On the outskirts of Montecchio on the Tavernelle road the **Villa Cordellina-Lombardi** has one room entirely covered with frescoes★ by Tiepolo. ♿ ⏱️*Open Apr-Oct daily except Mon, 9am-1pm and 3-6pm; Nov-Mar by appointment only.* 🎫*2.10€.* ☎*0444 69 60 85; www.provincia.vicenza.it.*

VIPITENO
STERZING

POPULATION 5 931

MICHELIN MAP 562 B 16 – TRENTINO-ALTO ADIGE.

Only 15km/9mi from the Austrian border, Vipiteno is a pretty town grouped around one street lined with typical Tyrolean houses (Erker) and arcading. Vipiteno's long history began in the Bronze Age. In Roman times there was a road station named Vipitenum and in 1180 the town was documented as Stercengum (from which Sterzing derives). Vipiteno flourished between the 15C and 16C when silver and lead were mined in nearby valleys (a visit to the mines in the nearby Val Ridanna and Valle Aurina, in Predoi, will provide an insight into mining activity in the Alto Adige).

- ℹ️ **Information:** Piazza Città 3, ☎0472 76 53 25; www.sterzing.net.
- ▶ **Orient Yourself:** Vipiteno is the last exit off A 22, the Brennero transalpine pass.
- 🎯 **Don't Miss:** Cascate di Stanghe
- ⏱️ **Organizing Your Time:** Allow a couple of hours for the town, and a day for excursions.
- 👓 **Also See:** *DOLOMITI, MERANO.*

Walking About

The 15C tower, Torre dei Dodici, cuts the street in half, the more picturesque **Città Nuova**★ (New City) street lying to the south and the **Città Vecchia** (Old City) street to the north. On Via Città Nuova stands the 16C town hall.

In the square where the two streets converge stands the church of the Holy Spirit (Chiesa dello Spirito Santo), richly decorated with 15C frescoes.

Excursions

Cascate di Stanghe

Road to Racines; follow Stanghe signs. ⏱️*Open daily Mar-Oct 9am-5.30pm (Aug 6pm).* 🚫*Closed Nov-Apr.* 🎫*2.60€.* ☎*0472 76 06 08; www.racines.info.*

This waterfall descends a narrow gorge that, having been eroded by the water, is coloured white and green. Walking through the winding gorge is facilitated

Vipiteno: the Val...

by the presence of long passageways and small wooden bridges attached to the rocks. A walk through the ravine and the wood near the town is pleasant and can be done uphill (obviously more tiring) or downhill. To vary the excursion it is possible to descend via the waterfall (leaving the car at the top where there is a cafeteria and a small chapel) and return up via footpath no 13 which passes through meadows and affords fine views of the pastures. Whether one chooses the waterfall or footpath route, the journey time is roughly the same: about an hour to ascend and three quarters of an hour to descend.

Montecavallo

Along the Brennero road, just after Via Città Vecchia, there is a cable car to Montecavallo (alt 2 000m/6 500ft). On arrival there is a wide choice of footpaths and walks.

VITERBO

POPULATION 60 000
MICHELIN MAP 563 O 18 – LAZIO.

Viterbo, still encircled by its walls, has kept its medieval aspect, notably in the San Pellegrino quarter★★, a working-class area that houses many craftsmen. Here there are typical vaulted passageways, towers and external staircases.

- **Information:** Piazza San Carluccio, 5, 01100 Viterbo, ☎0761 30 47 95; www.apt.viterbo.it; www.comune.viterbo.it.
- ▶ **Orient Yourself:** 20km/12mi southeast of Lago di Bolsena. Access to A 1 is by dual carriageway.
- **Don't Miss:** Piazza San Lorenzo, Villa Lante di Bagnaia and the Palazzo Farnese di Caprarola.
- **Especially for Kids:** The 16C theme park of Bomarzo.
- **Also See:** *ORVIETO, Lago di Bracciano e Cerveteri (around ROMA), TARQUINIA.*

Visit

Piazza San Lorenzo★★

This medieval square, which occupies the site of the former Etruscan acropolis, has a 13C house on Etruscan foundations (now a chemist's), a cathedral ...ing from 1192 and adorned with a ...othic campanile, and a 13C papal **Palazzo dei Papi**★★, one of the ...resting examples of medieval ...hitecture in Lazio. From the ...ri d'Ungheria there is a ...he piazza.

...d for restoration at ...61 34 08 10.

...onastery of ... collection ...s discov-... grave

artefacts from the tombs. The picture gallery, on the first floor, has a terracotta by the Della Robbia as well as works by Salvator Rosa, Sebastiano del Piombo and a local painter, Pastura (15C-16C).

Excursions

Teatro Romano di Ferento★

9km/6mi north. ⊶Closed for restoration at time of publication. For information ☎0761 32 59 29; www.ferento.it.
The 1C Roman theatre is well preserved and is the most important vestige of the Ancient Ferentium, the ruins of which lie scattered over a melancholy plateau. The theatre ruins stand between the road and the Decumanus (main road) and consist of a brick back wall as well as a portico of blocks without mortar, and 13 tiers of seats. The site hosts summer concerts.

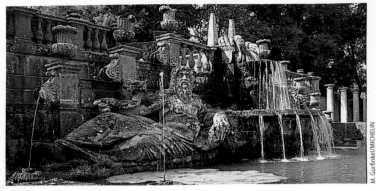

One of the fountains at Villa Lante di Bagnaia

M. Gurfinkel/MICHELIN

Santuario della Madonna della Quercia

3km/2mi northeast. The church, dedicated to the Madonna of the Oak (quercia), is in the Renaissance style with a rusticated façade and tympana by Andrea della Robbia.

Villa Lante di Bagnaia★★

5km/3mi northeast. ⚓🕐*Open daily midApr to mid-Sep 8.30am-7.30pm; mid-Sep to mid-Apr 8.30am-1hr before dusk.* 🕐*Closed Mon, 1 Jan, 1 May, 25 Dec.* ✍2€. ☎*0761 28 80 08; www.bagnaia.vt.it.*
This elegant 16C villa was built to the designs of Vignola and became the residence of several popes. A lovely Italian terraced garden with geometric motifs and numerous fountains makes an ideal setting for the villa. Mannerist highlights include a grotto, the Cardinal's table and a crayfish-shaped waterfall. Sacheverell Sitwell – the eccentric English art historian – was moved to hail this small estate as "the most lovely place of the physical beauty of nature in all Italy or in all the world."

Bomarzo Parco dei Mostri★★

21km/13mi northeast by S 204. 🕐*Park Open daily, 8am-dusk.* ✍8€. ☎*0761 92 40 29; http://www.bomarzo.net.*
Extending below the town is the Parco dei Mostri or **Sacro Bosco** (Monster Park/Sacred Wood), a Mannerist creation that Vicino Orsini adorned with fantastically shaped **sculptures**★. This 16C theme parks includes whales, dragons, harpies, nymphs, and a cavernous or head so large that tourists cluster in

mouth for group photos. A crooked little house, two stories of slanting stone, is especially popular. Kids *Stand inside the orc's mouth or race in the slanted house.*

Lago di Vico★

18km/11mi southeast by the Via Santa Maria di Gradi. This solitary but charming lake occupies a forested crater.

Palazzo Farnese di Caprarola★

18km/11mi southwest. ⚓🕐*Open daily, 8.30am-6.45pm (🚶guided tours every 30min).* 🕐*Closed 1 Jan, 1 May, 25 Dec.* ✍2€. ☎*0761 64 60 52.*
The five-storey building is arranged around a delightful circular inner courtyard. To the left of the entrance hall is Vignola's **spiral staircase**★★, which rises majestically through tiers of 30 paired Doric columns, and is decorated with grotesques and landscapes by Antonio Tempesta. The paintings which adorn several rooms are by the Zuccaro brothers, Taddeo (1529-66) and Fede... 1540-1609) as well as Bertoja (... These are typical of the r... sophisticated Mannerist s... Italian Renaissance pe...

Civita Castell...

36km/22mi so...
Civita Cast...
the Etru...
was d...
bu...
...

VOLTERRA★★

POPULATION 11 309
MICHELIN MAP 563 L 14
SEE ALSO THE GREEN GUIDE TUSCANY.

A commanding position★★ overlooking beautiful countryside makes a harmonious setting for the Etruscan and medieval town of Volterra with its well-preserved walls. To the northwest of the town there is a view of the Balzea, impressive precipices, which are part of a highly-eroded landscape furrowed by gully erosion. Large salt pans to the west are used in the manufacture of fine salt and soda.

- **Information:** Piazza dei Priori 20, 56048 Volterra (PI). ☎0588 86 150; www.comune.volterra.pi.it.
- ▶ **Orient Yourself:** Volterra rises up the summit of a hill that separates the Cecina and Era valleys. The main access road is S 68 which links Poggibonsi with Cecina.
- ⊛ **Don't Miss:** The Duomo and battistero and the Etruscan displays at the Museo Etrusco Guarnacci.
- ⊙ **Organizing Your Time:** Allow half a day.
- ⦿ **Also See:** *SAN GIMIGNANO, SIENA*.

Visit

Piazza dei Priori★★

The piazza is surrounded by austere palaces. The 13C Palazzo Pretorio has paired windows and is linked with the Torre del Podestà, also known as Torre del Porcellino because of the wild boar sculpted high up on a bracket. The early-13C Palazzo dei Priori, opposite, is decorated with terracotta, marble and stone shields pertaining to the Florentine governors.

Duomo and battistero★

The cathedral in the Pisan-Romanesque ~~de~~, although it has been remodelled several times, stands in the picturesque Piazza San Giovanni. The interior comprises a nave and two aisles with monolithic columns and 16C capitals. On the second altar in the nave, on the left is a lovely late-15C *Annunciation*. The transept contains a 13C painted wooden sculpture **Descent from the Cross**★★ in the south arm. The nave has a superb 17C pulpit with 12C low reliefs. The octagonal bapistery dates from 1283.

Via dei Sarti

This street is lined with palaces: No 1, Palazzo Minucci-Solaini attributed to Antonio da Sangallo now houses the

B. Morandi/MICHELIN

art gallery (*see below*), and No 37, the **Palazzo Viti** with its superb Renaissance façade designed by Ammanati. In 1964 Luchino Visconti shot some scenes from his film *Vaghe stelle dall'orsa* here. Some beautiful Indian robes that belonged to Giuseppe Viti, a trader in alabaster who was also the Emir of Nepal, are conserved here. *Open Apr-Oct daily 10am-1pm and 2.30-6pm. rest of the year by appointment only. Closed 5 Nov-29 Mar. 4€. 0588 84 047; www.palazzoviti.it.*

Pinacoteca

Via dei Sarti 1. Open daily mid-Mar to Oct 9am-7pm, rest of year 9am-2pm Closed 1 Jan, 25 Dec. 7€ including Museo Etrusco and Museo di Arte Sacra. 0588 87 580; www.comune.volterra. pi.it. The Art Gallery displays works of art by 14C to 17C Tuscan artists, notably an Annunciation by Luca Signorelli and a Descent from the Cross, a masterpiece of Mannerism by Rosso Fiorentino.

Museo Etrusco Guarnacci★

Open daily mid-Mar to Oct, 9am-7pm, rest of year 9am-2pm. Closed 1 Jan, 25 Dec. 7€ including Pinacoteca and Museo di Arte Sacra. 0588 86 347; www.comune. volterra.pi.it. More than 600 Etruscan funerary urns, made of tufa, alabaster and terracotta, make up the exhibition.

Porta all'Arco★(Etruscan gateway), Teatro romano, Porta Docciola, Viale dei Ponti (views★★).

Excursion

Larderello

33km/21mi south.

Larderello is situated Set in the heart of the **Colline Metalliferi**★, the "metal-bearing hills", mined for iron ore, copper and pyrites. Larderello is one of Tuscany's more unusual places; desolate landscapes, the hissing of its volcanic steam jets and belching smoke from the blast furnaces.

G. Simeone/MICHELIN

SARDEGNA
SARDINIA

Sardinia offers an almost primeval landscape of rocks sculpted by the wind and sea, forests of holm and cork oaks, oleander, aromatic plants and shrubs, the clear blue waters of the Mediterranean and the silence of an earlier age broken only by the sounds of nature.

- **Information:** Viale Trieste 105, 09123 Caligari. ☎070 606 7005; www.sardegnaturismo.it.
- ▶ **Orient Yourself:** Sardinia is the largest island in the Mediterranean after Sicily. It is surrounded by the Tyrrhenian sea to the east and south, the Mediterranean Sea to the west and the Straits of Bonifacio, which divide it from Corsica, to the north.
- ☺ **Don't Miss:** Alghero, Barumini and the Costa Smeralda.
- ⏱ **Organizing Your Time:** Allow a minimum of four days, preferably a week.

A Bit of History

Earliest inhabitants

Sardinia has traces of human settlement dating back to prehistoric times – *domus de janas* (fairies' houses) with their disturbing human-like features, dolmens standing alone in the middle of fields and ancient *nuraghi*.

The Nuraghic civilisation lasted from 1800 to 500 BC; its golden age is considered have lasted from 1200 to 900 BC. The island has over 7 000 **nuraghi** or fortified tower houses, structures in

Address Book

TRAVELLING IN SARDINIA

Sardinia offers endless opportunities for visitors with its rugged scenery, views of the sea and megalithic remains. Allow at least a week in order to explore the island fully. When exploring the east side of the island it is advisable to leave with a full tank of petrol, as petrol stations are few and far between.

GETTING THERE

Ferries leave from Civitavecchia, Genoa, La Spezia, Livorno, Palermo and Trapani for the ports of Cagliari, Golfo Aranci, Olbia, Porto Torres and Arbatax *(see Planning Your Trip section at the beginning of the guide)*. Visitors are advised to book in advance if travelling in the summer season. Sardinia can also be reached by **air**, with airports in Alghero, Cagliari, Olbia and Sassari.
♿ Consult *The Michelin Guide Italia and Michelin map 566* for further information on companies and specific routes.

WHAT TO EAT

The traditional recipes of Sardinia are simple but tasty, flavoured with the many aromatic plants and herbs that grow in profusion on the island.
Bread is often the soft-doughed *carasau,* known as *carta da musica* in the rest of Italy. *Gnocchetti sardi,* a type of pasta shell which has nothing to do with the traditional Italian gnocchi, are also known as *mallureddus,* and are often served with a sausage and tomato sauce. Meat-lovers should try the suckling pig *(porchetto da latte)* roasted on a spit. The island has many different varieties of cheese, including goats' cheese, Sardinian *fiore* and Sardinian *pecorino*.

B. Morandi/MICHELIN

Colourful Sardinian costume

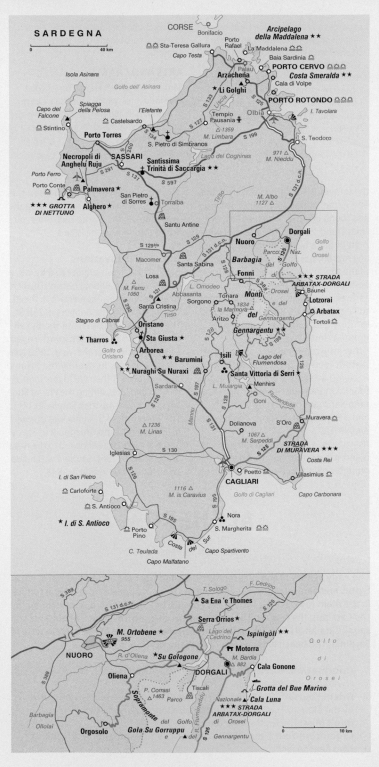

SARDEGNA

CORSE

Bonifacio

0   40 km

Arcipelago della Maddalena ★★

CORSE
Sta-Teresa Gallura
Porto Rafael
La Maddalena
Capo Testa
Palau
PORTO CERVO ⌂⌂⌂
Baia Sardinia
Costa Smeralda ★★
Cala di Volpe
PORTO ROTONDO ⌂⌂⌂
Arzachena
★ *Li Golghi*
S 133
Olbia
I. Tavolara
Tempio Pausania †
△ 1359
M. Limbara
S. Teodoro
971 △
M. Nieddu

Isola Asinara
Golfo dell'Asinara

Capo del Falcone
Spiaggia della Pelosa
l'Elefante
Castelsardo
S 127
Stintino
Porto Torres
S 134
S. Pietro di Simbranos
S 199
S 131 d.c.n.
S 200
SASSARI
Lago del Coghinas
Santissima Trinità di Saccargia ★★
Necropoli di Anghelu Ruju
S 291
S 131
M. Albo
1127 △
Porto Ferro
Porto Conte
★ **Palmavera**
S 597
San Pietro di Sorres †
Torralba
★★★ *GROTTA DI NETTUNO*
★ **Alghero** ★
Santu Antine

S 129bis
S 129
Nuoro
Dorgali
Golfo di Orosei
S 125
Parco Naz.
Macomer
Santa Sabina
Barbagia
del
S 128
Fonni
STRADA ARBATAX-DORGALI ★★★
Losa
△ 1050
M. Ferru
S 131
L. Omodeo
Abbasanta
Tonara
1834 △
P. la Marmora
Golfo di Orosei
e del
Baunei
Monti
Lotzorai
Santa Cristina
Tirso
Sorgono
del
Arbatax
Stagno di Cabras
Oristano
Aritzo
Tortolì
★ **Tharros**
Gennargentu ★★
S 126
★ **Sta Giusta** ★
Golfo di Oristano
Arborea
S 128
Isili
Lago del Flumendosa
★ **Barumini** ▲
★★ **Nuraghi Su Nuraxi** ⌂
Santa Vittoria di Serri ★
Sardara
S 197
L. Mulargia
Menhirs
S 128
S 125
Goni
△ 1236
M. Linas
S 131
Dolianova
1067 △
M. Serpeddi
S'Oro
Muravera ⌂
STRADA DI MURAVERA ★★★
Iglesias
S 130
Costa Rei
Villasimius ⌂
I. di San Pietro
S 126
Poetto ⌂
CAGLIARI
⌂ Carloforte
1116 △
M. is Caravius
S 195
Golfo di Cagliari
Capo Carbonara
⌂ S. Antioco
S 195
Nora
★ *I. di S. Antioco*
Porto Pino
S. Margherita ⌂
Costa del Sur
Capo Spartivento
C. Teulada
Capo Malfatano

S 389
T. Sologo
F. Cedrino
▲ **Sa Ena 'e Thomes**
S 131 d.c.n.
S 129
Serra Orrios ★
Lago del Cedrino
Ispinigòli ★★
M. Ortobene ★
955
Golfo
di
NUORO
R. d'Oliena
★ *Su Gologone*
▲ **Motorra**
M. Bardia
882
Cala Gonone
Orosei
S 389
Oliena
DORGALI
P. Corrasi
1463
Tiscali
Grotta del Bue Marino
Parco
Nazionale ▲ ★ **Cala Luna**
Barbagia
Ollolai
Soprammonte
del Golfo
★★★ STRADA ARBATAX-DORGALI di Orosei
Orgosolo
Gola Su Gorruppu
R. Flumineddu
S 125
Gennargentu
0   10 km

Local desserts include the rhomboid-shaped *papassinos,* which are often covered with icing and sprinkled with small coloured sugar balls, and sebadas, round doughnuts which are fried and covered with honey. The best-known local wines are the Anghelu Ruju and Cannonau; Mirto is an excellent local liqueur.

Our recommendations for restaurants in Sardinia are listed in the relevant sections.

ARTS AND CRAFTS

Sardinia is also well known for its cottage industries, which produce a range of products including goldwork, ceramics, leather, wood and cork, tapestries and basketware.

the form of a truncated covered cone. The name comes from the root nur, also found in nurra, which means both "mass" and "cavity." The nuraghi were built of huge blocks of stone without any mortar, possibly using an inclined plane along which they would have been pushed or rolled. They were used as dwellings, as watchtowers from which to keep an eye on both livestock and territory and, when built together as a group, as fortresses.

Other structures remain from this prehistoric period, including dolmens, "covered avenues" or *allées couvertes*, funeral monuments comprising a rectangular room covered by stone slabs and a tumulus, and Giants' Tombs *(see ARZACHENA).*

As water was a rare commodity on the island, it played an important part in the nuraghic religion. The god who lived in the wells and rivers and who had the power to overcome periods of drought was represented by the bull, often pictured throughout the island.

Successive invasions

Sardinia has been subject to a number of invasions throughout history. The first to arrive were the Phoenicians in the 8C BC, followed by the Romans in 238 BC, the Vandals in AD 455 and the Byzantines in AD 534. The Saracens arrived in the 7C and after the year 1000 the island was fought over by the Pisans and Genoese. It then fell to the Spanish in 1295 and later, during the War of Succession, to the Austrian Empire in 1713. The Kingdom of Sardinia was created in 1718 by Vittorio Amedeo II of Savoy and the island was annexed to the new united Italy in 1861. Sardinia was made an autonomous region in 1948.

ALGHERO ★

POPULATION 40 257

MICHELIN MAP 566 F 6.

The early history of this pleasant little walled port set amid olive trees, eucalyptus and parasol pines is unknown. Coral divers operate from the port which is the main town on the Riviera del Corallo. In 1354 Alghero was occupied by the Catalans; the town still has a Catalan-Gothic centre and its inhabitants still speak Catalan. Its Spanish air has earned it the nickname of the Barcelonetta of Sardinia. The beach extends 5km/3mi to the north of the village.

- **Information:** Piazza Portaterra 9, 07041 Alghero (SS), ☎ 079 97 90 54; www.comune.alghero.ss.it.
- ▶ **Orient Yourself:** Alghero is located 35km/21mi southwest of Sassari and served by the Alghero-Fertilia airport *(www.aeroportodialghero.com)*
- ☺ **Don't Miss:** The Grotta di Nettuno.
- ⏰ **Organizing Your Time:** Allow a day, with a visit to the Grotta di Nettuno.
- ✦ **Also See:** *SASSARI.*

Alghero: the splendid tiled dome of San Michele

Walking About

Città vecchia★

The fortifications encircle a network of narrow streets in the old town. The **Duomo** (*Via Roma*) has a beautiful doorway and a campanile in the Catalan-Gothic style. The 14C-15C church of **San Francesco** has **cloisters** in golden-coloured tufa.

The fishing harbour is the embarkation point for the boat trips to the **Grotta di Nettuno**★★★ (Neptune's Cave). *For information on opening times and prices call ☎079 94 65 40; www.infoalghero.it.*

Excursions

Grotta di Nettuno★★★

▶*27km/17mi west; access also possible by boat.* The road out to the headland, Capo Caccia, offers splendid **views**★★ of the rocky coast. Neptune's Cave is on the point. A stairway (654 steps) leads down the cliff face. There are small inner lakes, a forest of columns, and concretions in the form of organ pipes.

Nuraghe Palmavera★

▶*10km/6mi on the Porto Conte road. Open daily Apr-Oct 9am-7pm, Nov-Mar 9.30am-4pm. 3€. ☎079 98 00 40 or 348 43 85 947 (mobile); www.coopsilt.it.*

This nuraghe is surrounded by the remains of a prehistoric village, formed by approximately 50 individual dwellings crowded closely together.

Necropoli di Anghelu Ruju

▶*10km/6mi from Alghero on the Porto Torres road. Open daily Apr-Oct 9am-7pm, Nov-Mar 9.30am-4pm. 3€. ☎079 98 00 40 or 348 52 43 735 (mobile); www.coopsilt.it.*

This necropolis comprises 38 hypogea (underground chambers) dating from the Neolithic era (c 3000 BC).

ARZACHENA

POPULATION 11 701
MICHELIN MAP 566 D 10.

Arzachena, once an agricultural market town, owes its fame to its position in the heart of the Costa Smeralda hinterland at the foot of a mushroom-shaped rock (Fungo) and its proximity to important archaeological remains.

- 🛈 **Information:** Via Lungomare Andrea Doria, 07020 Cannigione (SS). ☎0789 89 20 19; www.arzachena.net.
- ▶ **Orient Yourself:** Arzachena is on S 125.
- 🕐 **Organizing Your Time:** Allow half a day.
- 🕑 **Also See:** *COSTA SMERALDA*.

Megalithic Stones

The remains of a **Giants' Tomb** (Tomba dei Giganti di Li Muri) and a necropolis can be seen not far from Arzachena.

Address Book

🕑 *For coin ranges see the Legend on the cover flap.*

WHERE TO STAY

▭**Centro Vacanze Isuledda** – *07020 Cannigione* – *6.5km/4mi northeast of Arzachena* – ☎*0789 86 003* –*www.isuledda.it.* Great position overlooking the Maddalena archipelago with accommodation to suit the most and least adventurous travellers: there are tents, bungalows, rooms, mobile homes and "tukul". Other facilities include supermarkets, shops and various essential services. Lively atmosphere.

▭**Hotel Citti** – *Viale Costa Smeralda 197* – *07021 Arzachena* – ☎*0789 82 662* – *Closed 25 Dec-6 Jan* – 🄿🄴 – *50 rm* ▭. One of the main attractions of this establishment is that if offers excellent value for money, making it a good base for exploring the entire Costa Smeralda. The street on which it is situated may be slightly busy but the rooms are spacious and comfortable and there is a lovely lounge with a pool at the back.

▭**Hotel Selis** – *Località Santa ... a – 07021 Arzachena – Strada ...ale (in the direction of Porto ... 0789 98 630 – www.selishotel. ... 18 rm: half-board.* ▭ The splendid stone building which houses this hotel is off the beaten track. The good-sized rooms are light and airy, with tiled floors and wrought-iron beds: some have a small garden-terrace which makes a lovely children's play area or a sunbathing place (and would also suit anyone travelling with their dog).

▭▭**Residence Hotel Riva Azzurra** – *Località Banchina – 07020 Cannigione – 6.5km/4mi northeast of Arzachena* –☎*0789 89 20 05/6 – www.riva-azzurra. it – Closed 15 Apr-15 Oct –* 🄿🄴🄴🄴 *– 29 apartments for 4 people.* Attractive pastel-coloured, Mediterranean-style hotel which blends in well with the setting. The comfortable, two-roomed apartments laid out in an arc around a lovely garden, a stone's throw from the beach. Friendly, welcoming atmosphere.

WHERE TO EAT

▭**Pinocchio** – *Località Cascioni – 07021 Arzachena – Strada provinciale (in the direction of Porto Cervo)* – ☎*0789 98 886*. A traditional establishment which specialises in fish, the dishes inspired by traditional recipes of the area. Also serves excellent pizzas cooked in a wood-fired oven. Reasonably priced accommodation available: simple, comfortable rooms with private access from the garden. Not far from the Costa Smeralda.

Giants' Tombs

Popular tradition gave the name Giants' tomb to these tombs dating from the nuraghic period. The funeral chambers lined and roofed with megalithic slabs (like a dolmen) were preceded by an arc of standing stones forming the exedra or area of ritual. The front of the structure is formed by a central stele with fascia in relief, which leads to the corridor of stones. This "false door" may have symbolised the connection with the afterlife.

BARBAGIA

MICHELIN MAP 566 G-H 9-10.

Wild and evocative, this area is full of steep ravines, known only to local shepherds, and has a wide variety of flora (holm oak, chestnut, hazelnut, thyme and yew) and fauna (golden and bonelli eagle, peregrine falcon, golden kite, wild boar, fox and moufflon). The Monti del Gennargentua★ and Supramonte, a limestone plateau in the Orgosolo, Oliena and Dorgali areas, are also situated in this region.

▶ **Orient Yourself:** This region of Sardinia lies behind the immense Gennargentu massif.
◉ **Don't Miss:** Grotta di Ispinigòli.
Kids Especially for Kids: The stalagmites at Grotta di Ispinigòli.
◷ **Organizing Your Time:** The itinerary covers 160km, allow a couple of days.
◔ **Also See:** *NUORO.*

Wild Landscapes, History and the Sea

Tortolì

Tortolì is the main town of **Ogliastra**, a wild region characterised by cone-like rocks known as "Tacchi". The sea is calm along this coastline, especially at Gairo, where the pebbles are called "*coccorocci*" (coconut rocks). Juniper plants grow at **Orrì**.

Arbatax

This isolated port is situated in a beautiful mountain setting overlooking the Tortolì sea. A secluded bay can be found at Cala Moresca *(follow signs)*. The magnificent stretch of **road**★★★ between Arbatax and Dorgali *(70km/43 miles)* skirts impressive gorges.

Between Lotzorai and Baunei

The SS 125 road **from Arbatax to Dorgali**★★★ passes through an increasingly atmospheric landscape as it runs further into the Barbagia region. Stop at the road's highest point (1 000m/3 300ft) to admire the view.

Dorgali

www.dorgali.it.

This town, the main resort in the Barbagia, lies in the bay of Cala Gonone and is the cultural, culinary and craftwork centre of the region. Its main street, via Lamarmora, offers traditional shops selling local rugs made with a distinctive knot. The local *cannonau* grape has been producing excellent wine for two thousand years.

The nuraghic village of **Serra Orrios**★ lies not far from Dorgalio on the road leading to S 129, while the Giants' Tomb **Sa Ena 'e Thomes** is situated on the

Domus de Janas

These attractively named hypogea (*domus de janas* means "house of fairies") were built from the beginning of the fourth to the middle of the third millennium.

They are constructed from sandstone, granite, limestone and basaltatic rock and some are decorated with drawings of oxen and goats.

Address Book

🪙 *For coin ranges see the Legend on the cover flap.*

WHERE TO STAY

😐😐**Hotel L'Oasi** – *Via Garcia Lorca 13 – 08020 Cala Gonone –* ☎*0784 93 111 – www.loasihotel.it – Closed 10 Oct-Easter –* 🅿️ ▦ *(payment) – 30 rm* *–* 🍴 *– Restaurant.* A small hotel which offers good-sized rooms and apartments, attractively furnished. The main attraction is the building that houses the restaurant: perched on the cliff, overlooking the sea with a splendid view of the bay.

WHERE TO EAT

😐😐**Ristorante presso Hotel Monteviore** – *On S 125 (at the 196km/118mi point), Località Monteviore – 08022 Dorgali – 9km/5mi south of Dorgali –* ☎*0784 96 293.* Off the beaten tourist track is this old farmhouse which has been tastefully restored. Authentic, traditional cooking. There is accommodation: rooms are spacious and attractive. Also has a naturists campsite in the area.

Lula road. This tomb has the traditional layout of a Giants' Tomb. The funerary chamber, a passage roofed with large slabs, is preceded by stones forming the arc of a circle.

Cala Gonone

A winding **road**★★ leads to this resort built in an attractive bay. Boat trips leave from the harbour.

Cala Luna

This sandy beach is lapped by calm water and backed by oleanders. There are a number of caves around the bay.

Grotta del Bue Marino

🕐*For information on opening times and prices* ☎*0784 96 243 or 0784 93 305.* The *bue marino* or sea ox refers to the monk seal that occupied this cave until the end of the 1970s.

Dolmen Mottorra

▶*Head north. After a bend in the road, at the km 207 point on S 125, a sign marks the path to the dolmen.* The dolmen is situated in the middle of a field which is reached after a five-minute walk. It consists of an almost circular slab of schist supported by seven upright stones and dates from the third millennium BC.

spirit: a mural in Orgosolo

B. Morandi/MICHELIN

Grotta di Ispinigòli★★

▶The road to the cave is approximately 7km/4mi from Dorgali on S 125. ◷Open Apr to mid-Nov 9am-noon and 3pm-dusk (entrance every hr); mid-Nov to Mar, by appointment only. For information, call ☎0784 96 243.

On entering the cave, the visitor realises that the cave is formed by an immense cavity and not by a tunnel. The eye is caught by a **stalagmite column**, (38m/125ft) the second tallest in the world. The cave is now a fossil, as there is no more water to form concretions, which are lamellar (in the shape of knives or drapes) or cauliflower (formed under water, like coral) in form.

The abundant flow of water in the past quickly built up deposits on the floor of the cave; as a result the stalagmites are much larger than the stalactites.

Phoenician jewellery and human bones have been found in the cave, suggesting that it was perhaps used for sacrificial purposes or as a burial chamber.

Kids Gaze in wonder at the world's second-tallest stalagmite

Su Gologone★

▶20km/12.5mi to the southeast of Nuoro, on the Oliena-Dorgali road. The large town of **Oliena** stands at the foot of a steep slope of the Sopramonte.
Just beyond Oliena take a local road to the right for about 6km/4mi. The lovely spring at Su Gologone gushes from a rocky face (300 litres per second).
Not far from Supramonte di Dorgali a cave open to the sky hides the **nuraghic village of Tiscali.**

Orgosolo

▶20km/12mi south.

This market town is notorious for being the stronghold of bandits and outlaws (popularised by the Italian film producer Vittorio de Seta in his film Banditi a Orgosolo made in 1961). Today it is a pleasant town with bright murals.

BARUMINI★★

POPULATION 1 395
MICHELIN MAP 566 H 9.

The town of Barumini is surrounded by numerous traces of the earliest period of Sardinian history.

- 🛈 **Information:** www.sardegna.com.
- ▶ **Orient Yourself:** Barumini is in the heartland of Sardinia, 10km/6mi north of Villanovaforru, off S 197.
- ◷ **Organizing Your Time:** Allow an hour.
- ⚲ **Also See:** ORISTANO.

Nuraghe Su Nuraxi★★

▶2km/1.2mi west, on the left-hand side of the Tuili road. ◷Open daily, 9am-1hr before dusk. ⏷4.20€. ☎070 93 68 128 or 337 81 30 87 (mobile).

The oldest part of Su Nuraxi dates from the 15C BC. The fortress was consolidated due to the threat posed by the Phoenician invaders between the 8C and 7C BC and was taken by the Carthaginians between the 5C and 4C BC and abandoned in the 3C with the arrival of the Romans.

Santa Vittoria di Serri★

38km/24mi east by the Nuoro road and a road to the right in Nurallao.

There are remains of a prehistoric religious centre. On the way out, the road passes through the crafts village of **Isili** (furniture-making and weaving).

Nuraghic settlement: Su Nuraxi

CAGLIARI

POPULATION 161 465
MICHELIN MAP 566 J 9.

Cagliari is the capital of the island. It is a modern town with a busy harbour and an old nucleus surrounded by fortifications, built by the Pisans in the 13C. Before becoming Roman it was a flourishing Carthaginian city called Karalis. The Terrazza Umberto 10 affords a fine **view**★★ of the town, harbour and bay.

- **Information:** Piazza Matteotti 9, ☎ 070 66 92 55.
- ▶ **Orient Yourself:** Cagliari is located in the south of the island, overlooking the Golfo di Cagliari. The road network that converges on the town includes S 195, S 130, S 131, S 125 and the coastal road to Villasimius.
- **Don't Miss:** Strada di Muravera.
- ◯ **Organizing Your Time:** Allow a day.
- **Also See:** *Isola di SANT'ANTIOCO.*

Worth a Visit

Cattedrale
Built in the 13C Pisan style, the cathedral was remodelled in the 17C. Inside are magnificent **pulpits**★★ (1162) by Guglielmo of Pisa. A little door on the right of the choir leads down to the Sanctuary or **Santuario**, a crypt that contains the remains of 292 Christian martyrs in urns placed along the walls. A door opens on the right into a chapel containing the tomb of Marie-Louise of Savoy, the wife of the future King Louis XVIII of France and sister of the King of Sardinia.

Museo Archeologico Nazionale★
&. ◯ *Open daily 9am-7pm.* ◯ *Closed Mon, 1 Jan, 1 May, 25 Dec.* ᏅᏅ*4 €.* ☎*070 65 59 11 or 070 68 40 00.*
The National Archaeological Museum has a large collection of arms, pottery and small **bronzes**★★★, grave artefacts from the earliest period of Sardinian history. Phoenician, Punic and Roman art are represented in the other rooms.

WHERE TO EAT
◯◯**Lillicu** – *Via Sardegna 78 – 09124 Cagliari* – ☎*070 65 29 70 – Closed Sun, 10 Aug-1 Sep –* ▦.
You could easily get round Cagliari in a day and this is the place to head for lunch or supper. Authentic, local cooking: dishes are well prepared and not too heavy. Diners are seated together at large marble tables – all very cosy.

Torre dell'Elefante and Torre San Pancrazioa

The 14C Elephant and St Pancras towers were part of the Pisan fortifications.

Anfiteatro Romano

This amphitheatre is the most important Roman monument in Sardinia.
& Orto Botanico

Excursion

Strada di Muravera★★

▶ Some 30km/19mi from Cagliari, the SS 125 road enters wild gorges with reddish walls of porphyritic granite, dotted with oleander and prickly pear cacti.

COSTA SMERALDA★★
EMERALD COAST
MICHELIN MAP 566 D 10.

This wild and undulating region is a succession of pink granite headlands, covered with maquis scrub overlooking the sea, which is a clear emerald green. Once a region of farmers and shepherds, it was discovered in 1962 by the international jet set. The development of the Emerald Coast was promoted by a consortium originally presided over by the Aga Khan. This peninsula of the Gallura region now offers tourist facilities, including windsurfing, sailing, golf and tennis. The main resorts are Porto Cervo⌂⌂⌂, Cala di Volpe and Baia Sardiniae.

- **Information:** www.mondosardegna.net.
- ▶ **Orient Yourself:** The Costa Smeralda lies towards the northeast of the island.
- **Don't Miss:** The Maddalena Archipelago.
- **Organizing Your Time:** Allow a couple of days.
- **Also See:** *ARZACHENA.*

Arcipelago della Maddalena★★

The Maddalena Archipelago consists of the islands of Maddalena, Caprera, Santo Stefano, Spargi, Budelli, Razzoli, Santa Maria and other islets in the **Straits of Bonifacio.**
These isolated islands, occasionally frequented by Corsican shepherds, were annexed to the Kingdom of Sardinia in 1767. Maddalena then became a military base. The archipelago was made a **national park** in 1996.

Maddalena★★

A lovely scenic route *(20km/12mi)* follows the coastline of this small island.

Caprera★

This island was once the home of Garibaldi and is connected to Maddalena by the Passo della Moneta causeway. It now houses a sailing centre.

Casa di Garibaldi★

& For opening times call ahead. Closed Mon, 1 Jan, 1 May, 25 Dec. ⌂2€.
☎0789 72 71 62.
The tree planted by Garibaldi (1807-82) on the birth of his daughter Clelia (1867) can be seen in the garden of his one-time home, where he is also buried.

Crystal-clear water

DISCOVERING ITALY

Address Book

⚱️*For coin ranges, see the Legend on the cover flap.*

WHERE TO STAY

Hotel Da Cecco – *Via Po 3 – 07028 Santa Teresa di Gallura – 17km/10mi west of Palau on S 133b – ☎0789 75 42 20 – www.hoteldacecco.com – Closed Nov-24 Mar – ☐ – 32 rm – 🍽️. From the rooms and the sun lounge there is a magnificent view over the Straits of Bonifacio beyond the Saracen tower. This is a small, modern hotel which would suit visitors looking for a relaxing holiday and the best of Sardinian hospitality.

Hotel Villa Gemella – *Baia Sardinia – 07020 Baia Sardinia – ☎0789 99 303 – www.hotelvillagemella.com – ☐🍽️ – 26 rm 🍽️ – Restaurant*. One of the main attractions of this hotel is the lovely flower-filled garden which is a great spot for relaxation. There is also a swimming pool… not to mention the sea (the Bay of Sardinia) nearby. The rooms, which are light and airy, have been tastefully furnished; some have a terrace and a view (ask when booking).

WHERE TO EAT

Panino Giusto – *Piazetta Clipper – 07020 Porto Cervo – ☎0789 91 259 – Closed Nov-May – 🍽️* Situated at the entrance to Porto Cervo Marina, overlooking the yachting harbour, this establishment would suit anyone looking for a snack or a light meal but who does not want to stray far from the beach. Open all day, it serves simple meals, salads and sandwiches. You can eat outside looking out over the boats moored in the harbour, or inside where there is a pub-style dining area.

La Vecchia Costa – *07021 Arzachena – 5km/3mi southwest of Porto Cervo (in the direction of Arzachena) – ☎0789 98 ..88 –* 🍽️. If you are in the mood for a ...d pizza, this is the place to head for. ...e with the soft-doughed bread, ..."carasau", that is peculiar to ..., the pizzas are deliciously ...crispy, as well as vast! Very ... prices, unusual in this area.

Tattoo – *Liscia di Vacca Alta – 07020 Porto Cervo – 2km/1.2mi from Porto Cervo – ☎0789 91 944 – Closed Oct-Mar – 🍽️ 🍽️*. Surrounded by smart pastel-coloured, Mediterranean-style villas, this establishment is not far from the beach (very exclusive!) at Liscia di Vacca. The Tattoo is also fashionable enough to hold its own and is popular with the jet set.

La Terrazza – *Via Villa Glori 6 – 07024 La Maddalena – ☎0789 73 53 05 – Closed Sun (except May-Sep) – 🍽️*. Having fallen in love with Sardinia, the dynamic owners (originally from Bologna) have adopted the island's delicious gastronomy as their own. The varied menu focuses on fish – always super-fresh and of the best quality – and includes a number of regional specialities. Meals are served out on the terrace which boasts a wonderful panoramic view.

OFF THE BEATEN TRACK

Terza Spiaggia – *Località Terza Spiaggia – 07020 Golfo Aranci – 44km/27mi southeast of Arzachena – ☎0789 46 485 – www.terzaspiaggia.com – Closed Oct-Mar*. What could be better than relaxing on the beach next to the crystal-clear sea and with a wonderful view of the Golfo degli Aranci, while tucking into a delicious sandwich? Or maybe you would prefer a simple fish dish (prepared with fish caught by the owners themselves earlier that day). Meals are served inside (simple beach-style café interior).

Il Portico – *Via Nazionale 107 – 08020 Budoni – 34km/20mi southeast of Olbia on S 125 – ☎0784 84 44 50 – Closed Mon (winter), 10 Oct-10 Dec – 🍽️*. Creative home cooking with lots of seafood and Sardinian specialities prepared with the freshest of ingredients. The dining facilities extend to a large veranda, small outdoor terrace and dining room inside. In summer, they also serve pizzas cooked in a wood-burning oven.

NUORO

POPULATION 36 678

MICHELIN MAP 566 G 9-10.

Nuro lies at the foot of Monte Ortobene, on the borders of the Barbagia region. In this large central Sardinian town the customs and folklore have remained unchanged since ancient time – including the splendid Sagra del Redentore (Feast of the Redeemer), an annual costumed procession through the town. The author Grazia Deledda, a native of Nuoro, won the Nobel Prize for Literature in 1926 for her descriptions of Sardinian life.

- **Information:** Piazza Italia 19. ☎0784 30 083. www.comune.nuoro.it. www.festeinsardegna.it.
- **Orient Yourself:** Nuoro is situated off S 131
- **Don't Miss:** Views from Monte Ortobene.
- **Organizing Your Time:** Allow a couple of hours.
- **Also See:** *BARBAGIA.*

Visit

Museo della Vita e delle Tradizioni Popolari Sarde

Via A Mereu 55. &. ◔*Open daily mid-Jun to Sep 9am-8pm, rest of year 9am-1pm and 3-7pm.* ☞3€. ☎*0784 25 70 35 or 0784 292 900; www.itresardegna.org.*

The museum has a fine collection of Sardinian costumes.

Excursion

Monte Ortobene★

9km/6mi east.
The summit affords good viewpoints.

ORISTANO

POPULATION 32 781

MICHELIN MAP 566 H 7.

Oristano is the main town on the west coast and was founded in 1070 by the inhabitants of nearby Tharros.

- **Information:** Via Ciuttadella de Menorca 14, ☎0783 70 621.
- **Orient Yourself:** The main access road is S 131.
- **Don't Miss:** Tharros.
- **Organizing Your Time:** Allow one day, with excursions.
- **Also See:** *BARUMINI.*

Walking About

Piazza Roma

The crenellated tower, Torre di San Cristoforo was originally part of the 13C town wall. Off Piazza Roma is **Corso Umberto**, the main shopping street.

Chiesa di San Francesco

The church has some interesting **works of art**★including a wooden statue of Christ by the 14C Rhenish school and a statue of *St Basil* by Nino Pisano (14C).

Excursions

Basilica di Santa Giusta★

▶*3km/2mi south.*
This church, built between 1¹ and 1145, stands in the town of same name.

WHERE TO STAY

Hotel La Caletta – *Località Torre dei Corsari – 09031 Marina di Arbus – 20km/12mi south of Arborea through Stagno di Marceddi – ☎070 97 70 33 – www.lacaletta.it – Closed Oct-Easter –* 📄📺 *– 32 rm* 🛏 *– Restaurant.* The hotel may not be in keeping with the landscape, but it boasts a magnificent clifftop location with views over the sea.

The sober elegance of Santa Giusta is characteristic of all Sardinian churches with Pisan and Lombard influences.

Tharros★

On Capo San Marco, on the northern side of the gulf. The Phoenicians founded Tharros in the 8-7C BC. It was a depot on the Marseilles-Carthage trading route, before it was conquered by Rome c 3C BC.

Zona archeologica

🕐*Open daily 9am to 1hr before dusk.* ☎0783 37 00 19; www.ilportalesardo.it/archeo.

The excavation site lies near a hill crowned by a Spanish tower (Torre di San Giovanni). Here are remains of Punic fortifications, tanks, baths, a Punic temple with Doric half-columns and, on the hilltop, a tophet (🕐*see SANT'ANTIOCO).*

Arborea

18km/11mi south.

This town was laid out in 1928 by the Fascist government, following the draining of the marshes and the extermination of the malaria mosquito.

ISOLA DI **ANT'ANTIOCO**★

POPULATION 11 756

MICHELIN MAP 566 J-K 7.

This volcanic island is the largest of the Sulcis Archipelago. It has a hilly terrain with high cliffs on the west coast. The chief town, also called Sant'Antioco, is linked to the mainland by a road. Catacombs, some of which have been transformed from Punic hypogea, can be seen under Sant'Antioco church. They date from the 6C and 7C AD.

- **Information:** Piazza Repubblica 31/A, ☎078 18 20 31. www.comune.santantioco.ca.it
- ▶ **Orient Yourself:** Sant'Antioco lies off Sardinia 's southwest coast. The main access road is S 126.
- 🕐 **Organizing Your Time:** Allow a day.
- 🕐 **Also See:** *CAGLIARI.*

Vestigia di Sulcis★

&🕐*Open daily 9am-7pm.* 🕐*Closed 1 Jan, Easter, 8, 25/26 Dec.* 📷*8€.* ☎0781 80 05 96; www.archeotur.it.

The ancient town of Sulci, founded by the Phoenicians in the 8C BC, gave its name to this group of islands.

The archaeological site is divided into different areas. The tombs in the necropolis, carved out of volcanic tufa, were used by the Carthaginians. The archaeological museum includes a fine collection of steles★. The archaeological area comprises the Phoenician-Punic topheta, once believed to be where the first-born male child was sacrificed, but now understood to be a cemetery for children who died in infancy.

Excursions

Monte Sirai

19km/12mi from Sant'Antioco.

Traces of a Phoenician-Punic settlement remain on this hill. The Phoenicians arrived here in 750 BC. Their city was destroyed by the Cathaginians in 520 BC, who built a new fortress, in turn destroyed by the Romans in 238 BC.

SASSARI

POPULATION 124 929
MICHELIN MAP 566 E 7
TOWN PLAN IN THE MICHELIN ATLAS OF ITALY.

Sassari is the second largest town in Sardinia. Its airy modern quarters contrast with its medieval nucleus, around the cathedral. The busiest thoroughfares are the Piazza d'Italia and the Corso Vittorio Emanuele II.

▪ **Information:** Via Roma, 62, ☎079 23 17 77.
▶ **Orient Yourself:** Sassari is situated about 20km/12mi from the Golfo dell'Asinara. The main access roads are S 131, S 291 and S 597.

Worth a Visit

Museo Nazionale Sanna★

🕐*Open daily 9am-8pm.* 🕐*Closed Mon, 1 Jan, 25 Dec.* ✎*2 €.* ☎*079 27 22 003.*
The museum contains rich archaeological collections, including an interesting section devoted to Sardinian ethnography and a small picture gallery.

Duomo

The cathedral is built in many styles and has a 13C campanile with a 17C upper storey, a late-17C Spanish Baroque **façade**★ and a Gothic interior.

Excursions

Santissima Trinità di Saccargia★★

17km/11mi southeast by the Cagliari road, S 131, and then the road to Olbia, S 597.
This former 12C Camaldulian abbey church was built in courses of black and white stone, typical of the Pisan style. The elegant façade includes a porch added in the 13C and is flanked by a campanile. Inside, the apse is adorned with fine 13C frescoes depicting scenes of the Passion.

Chiesa di San Gavino★

The church was built at the end of the 11C by the Pisans and is a fine example of medieval Sardinian art. Inside, a large **crypt** enshrines the relics of St Gavin and a Roman **sarcophagus**★, decorated with the Muses.

The Symbol of Sassari

This is the Fontana di Rosello, the huge fountain near the church of the Holy Trinity. It is a rather grand and elaborate Renaissance structure which was erected by the Genoese in 1605, although records show that there has been a fountain on this spot since the end of the 13C.

A Romanesque jewel: Santissima Trinità di Saccargi

SICILIA
SICILY

From sun-scorched earth in the summer, the land turns a brilliant green as soon as the spring rain arrives. With its mountainous terrain at the heart of the island, and glorious coastline, Sicily has much to offer. Visitors who come to relax by the sea or marvel at the island's rich artistic heritage and traditional way of life, are rewarded with a marvellous collage of colourful images and sensations.

- **Information:** Via Nicolo Garzilli 34, 90141 Palermo. ☎091 70 77 364. www.regione.sicilia.it.
- **Orient Yourself:** Sicily, the largest of the Mediterranean islands, has an area of 25 709km2/9 927sq miles. It is triangular and was named Trinacria ("three points") under Greek rule. The island generally mountainous and reaches at its highest point, Mount Etna (an active volcano), an altitude of 3 340m/10 958ft.
- **Don't Miss:** The Valley of the Temples at Agrigento, the splendour of Mt Etna, the beautiful Eolie and Egadi Islands, and visits to cosmoplitan Palermo, Siracusa and Taormina.
- **Organizing Your Time:** Allow 3-4 days to explore the island.

A Bit of History

Sicily has been a constant pawn for marauding forces in the Mediterranean because of its strategic location, lying, as it does, near the Italian peninsula and controlling the Mediterranean. First came the Greeks in the 8C BC who discovered an island divided between two ethnic groups: the Sicani, the oldest inhabitants, and the Siculi (Sicels) who came from the mainland.

The Carthaginians were for several centuries the main rivals of the Greeks. They were finally pushed back to the western part of the island, where they remained until the siege of Motya by Dionysius I of Syracuse in 397 BC.

The 5C BC, excluding the rules of the tyrants of Gela and Syracuse (see SIRA-CUSA), was the apogee of Greek rule in Sicily (Magna Graecia). After erecting some magnificent buildings, they neutralised their enemies and Syracuse ˙rew to become the rival of Athens.

˙is fragile peace was broken by the ˙val of the Romans who coveted the ˙d for the richness of its soil.

˙ BC, at the end of the First Punic ˙ whole of Sicily had been con-˙nd it became a Roman prov-˙ned by a praetor. The Romans ˙e island's resources to the ˙elp of dishonest officials.

The island was also a victim of barbarian invasions.

In 535 the island passed to the Byzantines and in the 9C the Muslims of the Aghlabid dynasty (Tunisia) – who were then expelled by the Normans (11C).

The son of the Great Count Roger I of Sicily, Roger II (1095-1154), created the Norman Kingdom of Sicily. He established his court at Palermo and during his reign the island was to enjoy a prosperous period of considerable political power and cultural influence.

The name of the Hohenstaufen Emperor Frederick II dominated the reign of this Swabian dynasty. The house of Anjou followed in 1266; however, Charles of Anjou was expelled following the Palermo revolt of 1282 known as the Sicilian Vespers. Power passed to the Aragon dynasty and it was Alfonso V the Magnanimous who reunited Naples and Sicily and took the title of King of the Two Sicilies (1442).

The island passed to the Bourbons of Naples by marriage until they were overthrown by the Expedition of Garibaldi and the Thousand (1860).

The Second World War left its mark on Sicily; the Anglo-American landings between Licata and Syracuse in 1943 ended in the abandonment of the island by the Germans after more than a month of heavy fighting.

Address Book

GETTING ABOUT

The main connections to Sicily by boat leave from Cagliari, Genoa, Livorno, Naples, Reggio di Calabria, Villa San Giovanni.

If you are travelling by air you will arrive at either Palermo or Catania, the island's two main airports. There are also airports at Trapani, Pantelleria and Lampedusa and there are connecting flights to these airports at busy times of the year (Easter and in summer). Another possibility is the airport at Reggio di Calabria, which, although not in Sicily itself, is very near the Straits of Messina. See the Practical Points section at the beginning of the guide for further details.

SIGHTSEEING

You could just about get round the island in a week. In addition to the places and areas that are described in this guide, the map highlights other areas of interest and beauty (indicated in small, black type).

SHOPPING

Ceramics are perhaps the island's most celebrated artisanal trade: the most important centres are Caltagirone, Santo Stefano di Camastra and Sciacca. If, on the other hand, you are in the Trapani area, you might be interested in the necklaces and other objects made out of coral, and in Erice there is a rug-making tradition. Natural sponges are the thing to buy on Pantelleria, and in Syracuse the papyrus may be of interest. The antique and junk shops are a good place to look for Sicilian puppets and carts.

Each period has left its mark on the island's heritage. The Greeks built admirable Doric temples and also splendid theatres. During the brief period when the Normans dominated the island, Sicily knew an era of economic prosperity. This style was unique for its blending of a variety of different influences. The architectural style was still essentially Norman but the decoration (horseshoe-shaped arches, bulbous bell towers and intricately decorated ceilings) showed a strong Moorish influence, while the decoration of the walls with dazzling mosaics on golden backgrounds was Byzantine.

Known variously as Sicilian-Norman or Arab-Norman, this style can be seen at Palermo, Monreale, Cefalù and Messina. If the Renaissance has left few traces in the island – with some outstanding exceptions by **Antonello da Messina** who usually worked on the mainland – the Sicilians adopted the Spanish-influenced Baroque style with great fervour in the late 18C. The main exponents were the architects Rosario Gagliardi in Noto and Ragusa, Vaccarini in Catania, and Giacomo Serpotta who embellished oratories in Palermo with his sculpted fantasies.

Sicilian literature is particularly rich, especially in the 19C, with Giovanni Verga who created a new form of Italian novel, and Luigi Pirandello. Noteworthy among the 20C writers to describe contemporary life are Elio Vittorini (1908-66) and Leonardo Sciascia (1921-89). Other writers include Gesualdo Bufalino (1920-96) and the poet Salvatore Quasimodo (1901-68).

Sicily Today

The long period of foreign domination in Sicily has left its imprint not only on the art, culture and literature of the island but also on its economy. Following the Arab invasions, the island's economy was neglected by its foreign rulers, with the exception of the Normans and Swabians. Forests were cleared, the locals exploited, and the island prevented from developing.

Today Sicily survives on an assisted economy. New development projects hope to stem the emigration of Sicily's young people and restore former glory.

Geographically and economically Sicily can be divided into three regions. The first region comprises the provinces of

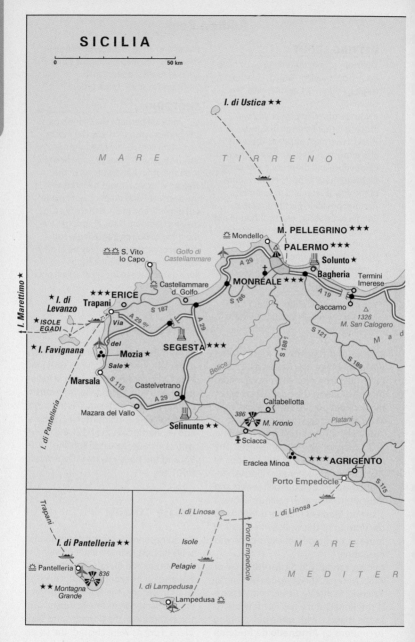

Catania, Syracuse and the southern part of Messina. The agriculture of the region tends to be intensive and of high quality. Palermo, Trapani and the north of Messina have a highly developed services sector and building industry. Finally, the poorest part of Sicily consists of the provinces of Agrigento, Caltanissetta and Enna. The fishing industry is still of prime importance to local economy.

Traditions
Folk traditions and customs have almost completely disappeared. It is only on

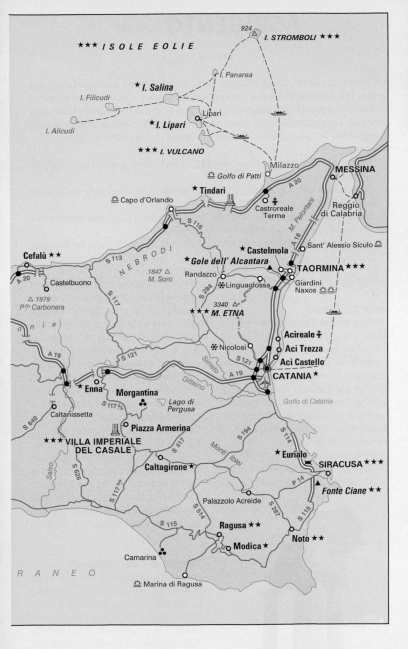

★★★ *I S O L E   E O L I E*

924

I. STROMBOLI ★★★

I. Panarea

★ **I. Salina**

I. Filicudi

Lipari

I. Alicudi

★ **I. Lipari**

★★★ **I. VULCANO**

Golfo di Patti

Milazzo   A 20   **MESSINA**

Capo d'Orlando

★ **Tindari**

Castroreale Terme

Reggio di Calabria

M. Peloritani

Cefalù ★★

N E B R O D I

S 116

S 113

Castelbuono

1847 △ M. Soro

Randazzo

★ **Castelmola**

Sant' Alessio Siculo

★ **Gole dell' Alcantara**

TAORMINA ★★★

△ 1979 Pᶻᵒ Carbonara

S 117

S 284

❀ Linguaglossa

Giardini Naxos

A 20

3340 △ ★★★ **M. ETNA**

S 121

S 121

❀ Nicolosi

Acireale ♓

Aci Trezza

Aci Castello

Simeto

A 19

A 19

CATANIA ★

★ **Enna**

Morgantina

Lago di Pergusa

Dittaino

Golfo di Catania

S 640

S 117

Caltanissetta

★★★ **VILLA IMPERIALE DEL CASALE**

Piazza Armerina

S 626

S 417

Caltagirone ★

Monti Iblei

★ **Eurialo**

S 194

S 114

SIRACUSA ★★★

Salso

S 117

P 14

Fonte Ciane ★★

Palazzolo Acreide

S 574

S 267

S 115

Ragusa ★★

Noto ★★

S 115

Modica ★

Camarina

R A N E O

Marina di Ragusa

feast days and in the museums that the visitor can now see the famous Sicilian carts, which were gaily decorated with intricate wrought-iron work, that were the main method of transport for over a century, until the end of the 1950s. In Palermo the popular puppet (pupi) theatres can still be seen showing their dramatised versions of the 12C Song of Roland and Ariosto's Orlando Furioso (Roland the Mad) can still be seen.

AGRIGENTO★★★

POPULATION 55 000

MICHELIN MAP 565 P 22.

Agrigento, the Greek city of Akragas, is attractively set on a hillside facing out to sea. The Greek poet Pindar referred to Agrigento as "man's finest town". It includes a medieval quarter on the upper slopes above the modern town, and impressive ancient ruins strung out along a ridge below, erroneously called the Valley of the Temples (declared a UNESCO World Heritage Site in 1997).

- **Information:** Piazza A. Moro. ☎0922 20 454. www.comune.agrigento.it, www.agrigentonatura.it.
- ▶ **Orient Yourself:** Agrigento is linked to Palermo by S 189 and the north coast of the island by S 640 and A 19.
- **Don't Miss:** Giardino della Kolymbetra, Tempio della Concordia and the fine exhibits at the Museo Archeologico Regionale.
- **Organizing Your Time:** Allow at least half a day for the Valley of the Temples.

Special Features

Valle dei Templi
(Valley of the Temples)★★★

Allow half a day. Archaeological site: open daily 9am-dusk. Museo Archeologico: open 9am-7pm; ⊘*Closed Mon afternoon, Sun and afternoons of public holidays.* ⊘*Antiquaria: open 9am-dusk.* ⊗*6€ archaeological site, 10€ combined ticket with Museo Archeologico and Antiquaria.* ☎*0922 26 191 or 0922 62 16 11; www.lavalledeitempli.it.*

The monuments in the Valley of the Temples are grouped in two areas: the first includes the actual temples, the Gia-

rdino della Kolymbetra, the antiquaria and the palaeo-Christian necropolises. The second comprises the archaeological museum, the Chiesa di San Nicola, the Oratorio di Falaride and the Greco-Roman quarter. To walk from one area to the other, visitors may either follow the very busy main road or the quiet road within the park. Car parks are located near to the Temple of Zeus and the archaeological museum.

Of the many temples from the late 6C to the late 5C BC, parts of nine are still visible. The destruction of the temples was for long thought to have been caused by earthquakes but is now also attributed to the anti-pagan activities of the early Christians. Only the Temple of Concord was spared when it became a church in the late 6C AD.

Tempio di Zeus Olimpio★

Had this now-ruined temple been completed, its size (113m/371ft long by 56m/184ft wide) would have made it one of the largest in the ancient world. The entablature of the Temple of Olympian Zeus (Roman Jupiter) was supported by 20m/66ft tall columns, between which stood **telamones** (columns in the form of male figures). One of these colossal statues, standing 7.5m/25ft high, has been reconstructed and is now on view in the Archaeological Museum *(see below)*.

B. Kaufmann/MICHELIN

Temple of Castor and Pollux

Tempio dei Dioscuri★★

Of the hexastyle temple of Castor and Pollux, only four columns supporting part of the entablature remain.

Alongside is a **sacred area** dedicated to Demeter and Persephone: there are two sacrificial altars, one with a holy well.

Giardino della Kolymbetra★

🕐*Open Apr-Dec 10am-7pm, rest of the year 10am-1hr before dusk.* 🕐*Closed Mon, 7-31 Jan.* 🪙*2€.* ☎*335 12 29 042 (mobile).*

This 5-ha/12-acre "basin" has developed over the centuries into a fertile grove of fruit and citrus trees. After years of neglect, the Kolymbetra, now restored and managed by the FAI, is planted out with olive trees, prickly pear, poplar, willow, mulberry, orange, lemon and mandarin trees. Paths laid out in the garden make this a pleasant area for a stroll.

▶ *Return to the square and take Via dei Templi.*

Tempio di Eracle★★

Dating from the late 6C, the Temple of Hercules is probably the oldest of the Agrigento temples and is built in the ancient Doric style. Eight of its columns have been raised.

Farther on to the left can be seen the deeply grooved ruts thought to have been made by ancient wheeled vehicles. The deep marking is possibly due to the ruts having been used at a later date as water channels.

Tempio della Concordia★★★

The Temple of Concord is the most massive, majestic and best preserved of the Doric temples in Sicily. It has a peristyle of 34 tufa limestone columns, the original stucco facing having disappeared. The internal arrangement dates from the Christian period (mid-5C).

Tempio di Hera Lacinia★★

Set on the edge of the ridge, this temple, dedicated to Hera (Roman Juno), conserves part of its colonnade. On the east side there is a sacrificial altar and behind the temple an ancient cistern.

From the Antiquarium di Casa Pace a small road leads up the Collina di San Nicola, crossing fields of prickly pears, pistachio and olive trees.

▶ *As you approach the top of the hill, continue straight on. This path leads to the Greco-Roman Quarter.*

The **Greco-Roman quarter**★ is an extensive urban complex of ruined houses, some adorned with mosaics.

Chiesa di San Nicola

For information on opening times, call ☎0922 20 014.

This church contains a magnificent Roman **sarcophagus**★ on which the death of Phaedra is portrayed. From the terrace there is a fine temple **view**★.

Oratorio di Falaride

Legend has it that the palace of Phalaris, the first tyrant of Agrigento, was in the

---

Address Book

🪙*For coin ranges see the Legend on the cover flap.*

WHERE TO STAY

🛏️🍽️**Hotel Villa Eos** – *Contrada Cumbo, villaggio Pirandello* – *On S 115* – ☎*0922 59 71 70* – *www.hotelvillaeos. it* – 🅿️🛏️🖥️ *– 23 rm* 🍽️ *– Restaurant.* After a tiring day's sightseeing what could be more restorative than a dip in the swimming pool, or a game of tennis if you still have the strength. Well

situated just a stone's throw from the sea and not far from Pirandello's house. Attractive, well-kept rooms.

WHERE TO EAT

🍽️**Kokalo's** – *Via Cavaleri Magazzeni 3, Valle dei Templi* – ☎*0922 60 64 27* – *www.ristorante-kokalos.com* – *Book.* Having satisfied your thirst for learning in the Valley of the Temples, this rustic-style establishment, could be just the place to quench your less spiritual thirst with a refreshing drink.

Tyrants, Philosophers and Writers

The town was founded in 580 BC by people from Gela who originated from Rhodes. Of the governing "tyrants", the cruellest in the 6C was Phalaris, while Theron (5C) was renowned as a great builder. The 5C philosopher Empedocles was a native of Agrigento, as was Luigi Pirandello (1867-1936), winner of the Nobel Prize for Literature in 1934 and innovator in modern Italian drama (Six Characters in Search of an Author), whose plays were woven around the themes of incomprehension and absurdity.

vicinity. The building is in fact a Roman-Hellenistic temple transformed during the Norman period.

Museo Archeologico Regionale★★

The museum contains a fine collection of **Greek vases**★ including the Dionysius Cup and the Perseus and Andromeda Cup on a white background. One room is devoted to the **telamones**★ from the Temple of Zeus. There are also the 5C BC marble statue of a youth, the *Ephebe of Agrigento*★★ (Room 10) and the *Gela Cup*★★ (Room 15), which illustrates a centaur and the battle between the Greeks and the Amazons.

Walking About

Town centre

The centre of the town is concentrated around the **Piazzale Aldo Moro**, which leads into the **Via Atenea**, a busy shopping street. On the way back down to Piazzale Aldo Moro visit a small abbey church, **Abbaziale di Santo Spirito**★, which has four **high reliefs**★ in stucco attributed to Giacomo Serpotta.

Excursions

Tomba di Terone

Visible from the Caltagirone road.
The tomb (3m/10ft high), said to be that of Theron, Tyrant of Agrigento, in fact dates from the Roman era and is thought to have been erected in honour of soldiers from the Second Punic War.

Casa di Pirandello

6km/4mi west by the Porto Empedocle road, S 115. Turn left shortly after the Morandi viaduct. Open daily 9am-1pm and 2-dusk. 2€. 0922 51 18 26; www.regione.sicilia.it.
This small house was the birthplace of the dramatist Luigi Pirandello (1867-1936), buried under a nearby pine tree.

CALTAGIRONE★

POPULATION 37 475
MICHELIN MAP 565 P 25.

Caltagirone is famous for its pottery, which is displayed in profusion in the local shops and on bridges, balustrades, balconies (notably 18C Casa Ventimiglia), and the façades of palaces lining Via Roma in the town centre.

- **Information:** Palazzo Libertini, 0933 53 809; www.comune.caltagirone.ct.it.
- **Orient Yourself:** Caltagirone lies just off S 417 which links Catania with Gela.
- **Don't Miss:** A history of local ceramics at the Museo della Ceramica.
- **Organizing Your Time:** Allow a couple of hours.
- **Also See:** *CATANIA, RAGUSA, Villa Imperiale del CASALE.*

Visit

Santa Scala di S. Maria del Monte★

The stairway built in the 17C to join the old and new town, has 142 steps in volcanic stone; the risers are decorated with polychrome ceramic tiles with geometric, floral and other decorative motifs. On 24 and 25 July the stairway is covered in lights which form different patterns: the most frequent is the symbol of the town, an eagle with a shield on its breast.

Villa Comunale★

This beautiful garden was designed in the mid-19C by Basile as an English garden. The side flanking Via Roma is bounded by a balustrade adorned with maiolica vases. On an esplanade stands the delightful Arab-style **palchetto della musica** (bandstand) decorated with ceramics.

Museo della Ceramica

Via Roma (Giardini Pubblici). ♿ ⏰*Open daily 9am-6.30pm.* ☎*0933 58 418; www.regione.sicilia.it/beniculturali.*
The **Teatrino**, a curious little 18C theatre decorated with ceramics, houses an interesting museum that traces the history of local ceramics from prehistory to the early 20C. There is a fine 5C **cup**★ depicting a potter.

VILLA IMPERIALE DEL CASALE★★★

MICHELIN MAP 565 0 25.

This immense 3C or 4C Roman villa (3 500m2/37 670sq ft) probably belonged to some dignitary and is important for its mosaic pavements which cover almost the entire floor space. These picturesque mosaics, in a wide range of colours, were probably the work of African craftsmen and portray scenes from mythology, daily life, and events such as hunts or circus games.
UNESCO declared the Villa Romana del Casale a World Heritage Site in 1997.

- 🛈 **Information:** Via Generale Muscara, Piazza Amerina (EN). ☎ 0935 68 02 01. www.piazza-armerina.it.
- ▶ **Orient Yourself:** The villa is situated near Piazza Armerina, off S 117b.
- 😊 **Don't Miss:** The mosaics in the Sala della Piccola Caccia, Ambulacro della Grande Caccia and the triclinium.

Visit

Mosaics★★★

⏰*Open daily, summer 8.30am-6pm; winter 8am-1hr before dusk. 4.53€.* ☎*0935 68 00 36.*
The most noteworthy mosaics portray **cupids**★★ fishing or playing with dolphins, a hunting scene in the **Sala della Piccola Caccia**★★★, the capturing and selling of wild animals for circus use in the **Ambulacro della Grande Caccia**★★★ and sports practised by young girls who appear to be wearing modern swimwear in the **Sala delle Dieci Ragazze in Bikini**★★. Finally, the mosaics of the **triclinium**★★★ portray the **Labours of Hercules**.

Excursion

Piazza Armerina

5km/3mi southwest.
The **medieval centre**★ of Piazza Armerina huddles round its Baroque **cathedral** the pleasantly green slopes of a va...

CATANIA★

POPULATION 308 000

MICHELIN MAP 565 O 27 (INCLUDING A PLAN OF THE BUILT-UP AREA).

Catania is a busy seaport and industrial town that has developed considerably in recent years, despite being destroyed several times by the eruptions of Mount Etna. This fine city has wide, regular streets overlooked by numerous Baroque buildings by the architect Vaccarini, who rebuilt Catania after the 1693 earthquake. Natives of the town include the musician Vicenzo Bellini (1801-35), composer of the opera Norma, and the novelist, Giovanni Verga.

- 🛈 **Information:** Via Cimarosa 10, 95124. ☎095 73 06 222. www.apt.catania.it.
- ▶ **Orient Yourself:** Catania is situated on the east coast, overlooking the Ionian Sea. The main access roads are A 18 (from Messina), A 19 (from Enna), and S 114, which links the town with Syracuse.
- 🏛 **Don't Miss:** The elegant Piazza del Duomo and Palazzo Biscaria, Castello Ursino.
- 🕐 **Organizing Your Time:** Catania gets very hot in summer, with searing temperatures. Sightsee in the early morning if possible.
- 🧒 **Especially for Kids:** The Elephant Fountain in Piazza del Duomo.
- ♿ **Also See:** *CALTAGIRONE, ETNA, SIRACUSA, TAORMINA.*

Visit

Piazza del Duomo★

This square is the centre of town and is surrounded by a Baroque ensemble designed by Vaccarini which includes the **Fontana dell'Elefante** (Elephant Fountain) dating from 1735, the **Palazzo Senatorio or degli Elefanti** (town hall) with its well-balanced façade, and the **Duomo**★ dedicated to St Agatha, the town's patron saint. The cathedral, built at the end of the 11C by the Norman, Roger I, was remodelled after the 1693 earthquake and has an elegant **façade**★ by Vaccarini. To the left of the cathedral, the beautiful abbey church **Badia di Sant'Agata**★ contributes to the harmony

of the square. Not far from here, in via Museo Biscari, stands **Palazzo Biscaria**, one of the most beautiful examples of civil architecture in the city. The south side of the mansion has a decorated **façade**★★ with figures, cherubs and scrolls.

Via Etnea★

The town's main shopping artery is over 3km/2mi long. All the way along it affords a view of Etna. It is bordered by numerous palaces and churches and the **Villa Bellinia** gardens.

Quartiere Occidentale

This district to the west of the town runs through Via Vittorio Emanuele II, along which the old theatre, **Teatro Antico**,

Address Book

WHERE TO STAY

☎☎**Hotel La Vecchia Palma** – *Via Etnea 668 – 95100 Catania – ☎095 43 20 25 – www.lavecchiapalma.it –* ▭ *– 11 rm* ▭. An Art Nouveau-style building with many of the original features, this hotel offers good-sized, comfortable rooms with modern amenities. It is a family-run establishment and guests are made to ... at home. Definitely one for the book.

WHERE TO EAT

☎☎**Cantine del Cugno Mezzano** – *Via Museo Biscari 8 – 95100 Catania – ☎095 71 58 710 – Closed Sun lunchtime, 10-28 Aug.* This is a very trendy, fashionable establishment housed in an old 18C palazzo in the centre of town. Rustic-style ambience, with large wooden tables, but a modern approach to the cuisine. Also has a good wine list.

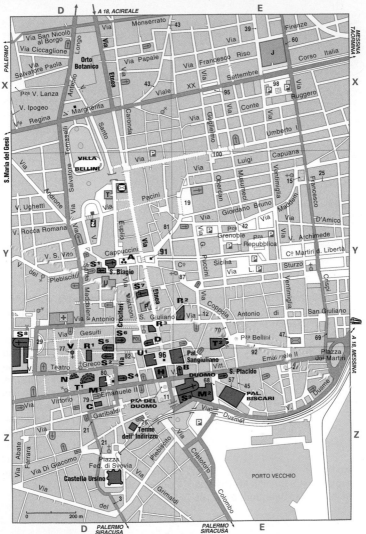

Rapisardi V. Michele	EY	70	S. Giuseppe al Duomo V.	DZ	82	Tomaselli V. S.	DXY		
Regina Margherita Viale	DX		S. Maddalena V.	DY		Trento Pza	EX	95	
Repubblica Pza	EY		S. Nicolò al Borgo V.	DX		Ughetti V.	DY		
Riso V. F.	EX		S. Vito V.	DY		Umberto I V.	DEX		
Rocca Romana V.	DY		Sicilia Cso	DEY		Università Pza dell'	DZ	96	
Rotonda V. d.	DYZ	77	Spirito Santo Pza	EY	87	Ventimiglia V.	EXY		
S. Anna V.	DZ	79	Stesicoro Pza	DY	91	Verga Pza	EX	98	
S. Eupilio V.	DXY		Sturzo V.	EY		Vittorio Emanuele II V.	DEZ		
S. Francesco d'Assisi Pza	DZ	80	Svevia Pza F. d.	DZ		Vittorio Emanuele III Pza	EY	100	
S. Gaetano alle Grotte V.	DEY	81	Teatro Greco V.	DZ		XX Settembre Viale	DEX		
S. Giuliano V. A. d.	DEY		Teatro Massimo V.	EYZ	92				

Anfiteatro	DY	A	Palazzo Biscari	EZ		S. Michele Arcangelo	DY	S[7]
Badia di S. Agata	EZ	B	Palazzo Manganelli	EY	R[2]	S. Nicolò l'Arena	DY	S[8]
Casa di Verga	DZ	C	Palazzo S. Demetrio	DY	R[3]	S. Placido	EZ	
Castello Ursino	DZ		Palazzo Sangiuliano	DEZ		Seminario Arcivescovile	EZ	S[3]
Collegiata	DY	D	Palazzo Senatorio o degli Elefanti	DZ	H	Teatro Antico	DZ	T[1]
Duomo	EZ		S. Agata al Carcere	DY	S[1]	Teatro Bellini	EY	T[2]
Museo Belliniano	DZ	M[1]	S. Benedetto	DZ	S[2]	Terme dell'Indirizzo	DZ	
Museo Diocesano	EZ	M[2]	S. Biagio	DY		Terme della Rotonda	DZ	V
Museo Emilio Greco	DZ	M[1]	S. Francesco	DZ	S[4]	Università	DZ	U[1]
Odeon	DZ	N	S. Francesco Borgia	DYZ	S[5]	Villa Bellini	DXY	
Orto Botanico	DX		S. Giuliano	DY	S[6]			
Palazzo Asmundo	DZ	R[1]						

can be seen. It is is crossed by **Via Crociferi**★, one of the best examples of Baroque architecture in Catania.

Castello Ursino

☎095 34 58 30.
This bare, grim castle, fortified by four towers, was built in the 13C by the Emperor Frederick II of Hohenstaufen.

Acireale

17km/11mi north.
The route passes through **Aci Castello**, with its **castle**★ built from black volcanic rock, and **Aci Trezza**, a small fishing village. Offshore, the **Faraglioni dei Ciclopia** (Cyclops' Reefs) emerge from the sea. These are supposed to be the rocks hurled by the Cyclops Polyphemus after Ulysses had blinded him by thrusting a blazing stake into his single eye. The road leads to **Acireale**, a modern town with numerous Baroque buildings which include those of the **Piazzo del Duomo**★ with the Basilica of St Peter and St Paul and the Town Hall, as well as the church of **San Sebastiano** with its harmonious **façade**★embellished with columns, niches and friezes.

CEFALÙ ★★

POPULATION 13 480
MICHELIN MAP 565 M 24.

Cefalù is a small fishing town in a fine setting★★, hemmed in between the sea and a rocky promontory. It boasts a splendid Romanesque cathedral.

Information: Corso Ruggero 77, 900 15 Cefalù (PA), ☎0921 42 10 50. www.cefalu-tour.pa.it.
Orient Yourself: Cefalù is situated on the north coast, overlooking the Tyrrhenian Sea. The main access roads are A 20 (from Palermo), and S 113 ʹrom Messina)
ɔn't Miss: The Duomo.
ᵃnizing Your Time: Allow a couple of hours.
See: *PALERMO.*

Duomo★★

🕐 *Open daily, summer 8am-noon and 3.30-7pm, rest of year 8am-noon and 3.30-5pm.* ☎*0921 92 20 21.*

Built of a golden-tinted stone which blends in with the cliff behind, this cathedral was erected to fulfil a vow made by the Norman King, Roger II (12C), when in danger of shipwreck. The church (1131-1240) has well-marked Norman features in its tall main apse flanked by two slightly projecting smaller ones and especially in its façade, abutted by the two square towers. The portico was rebuilt in the 15C by a Lombard master. The timber ceiling of the two aisles and the transept galleries are also Norman. The

columns are crowned with splendid **capitals**★★ in the Sicilian-Norman style.

The presbytery is covered with beautiful **mosaics**★★ on a gilded background, displaying a surprising variety of colour and forming an admirable expression of Byzantine art. Above is Christ Pantocrator (Ruler of All) with underneath, on three different levels, the Virgin with four archangels and the 12 Apostles. In the choir, the angels on the vaulting and the prophets on the side walls date from the 13C. Note the episcopal throne (south side) and the royal throne (north side), both in marble and mosaic.

👛 Museo Mandralisca (*Portrait of an Unknown Man*★ by Antonello da Messina).

ISOLE EGADI★
EGADI ISLANDS
POPULATION 4000
MICHELIN MAP 565 M-N 18-19.

The islands are popular for their wild aspect, clear blue sea and beautiful coastlines. It was here in 241 BC that the treaty ending the First Punic War was concluded, in which Carthage surrendered Sicily to Rome.

- 🅸 **Information:** Largo Marina 14, 91023 Favignana (TP), ☎0923 92 21 21. Piazza Madrice 8, ☎0923 92 16 47, www.egadiweb.it.
- ▶ **Orient Yourself:** The three islands – Favignana, Levanzo and Marettimo – which make up this small archipelago lie offshore from Trapan
- ⊝ **Don't Miss:** The Grotta Azzurra at Favignana, the Grotta del Genovese on Levanzo and the caves around Marettimo.
- 🕐 **Organizing Your Time:** Allow a day to explore the caves on the islands.
- 🄺🄸🄳🅂 **Especially for Kids:** A boat trip to the Grotta Azzurra.
- 👛 **Also See:** *ERICE, TRAPANI, SEGESTA.*

Visit

Favignana★

▶*The island covers an area of 20km2/8 sq miles and is butterfly-shaped. www. isoladifavignana.com.*

The **Montagna Grossa** culminating at 302m/991ft runs right across the island and ends as an indented coastline. The islanders were masters in the art of tuna fishing which took place for about 50 days between May and June. Having captured the tuna in a series of nets, they would perform a dangerous manoeuvre

and pull in the fish towards the shore where they were harpooned.

The main town of the group of islands, **Favignana**, is guarded by the fort of Santa Caterina, a former Saracen lookout tower, which was rebuilt by the Norman King, Roger II, and served as a priso under the Bourbons. To the east of t harbour are the former **tufa quarri** now drowned by the sea. Boat trip visitors to the various caves (cont fishermen at the harbour), inclu **Grotta Azzurra**★, which is sit the west coast.

Address Book

GETTING ABOUT

There are daily departares from Trapani: ferries (1-2hr 45min) and hydrofoils (20min-1hr).

Shipping company: **Siremar** (Gruppo Tirrenia, www.tirrenia.it), ☎892 1232 or 081 01 71 998; www.siremar.it

WHERE TO STAY

⊖**Hotel Egadi** – *Via Cristoforo Colombo 17 – 91023 Favignana – ☎0923 92 12 32 – www.albergoegadi.it – Closed Oct-mid May – 12 rm ⊑.* This hotel has become something of an institution on the island, such is the level of hospitality and courtesy.

The rooms are simple but spotlessly clean and the cooking is good. In the evening there is a wide selection of imaginative dishes, carefully put together and prepared with good quality ingredients.

⊖⊖**Hotel Aegusa** – *Via Garibaldi 11/17 – 91023 Favignana – ☎0923 92 24 30 – www.aegusahotel.it – ▤ – 28 rm ⊑ – Restaurant.* This hotel has a real holiday feel about it. Inviting (and reasonably priced) menu with a good selection of fish and other traditional dishes. Meals served in the lovely courtyard-garden. Rooms are light and airy with wicker furniture.

Kids *Take a boat trip to Grotta Azzurra.*

Levanzo★

This tiny island is only 6km²/2sq miles in size. In 1950 traces of life in prehistoric times were found in the **Grotta del Genovese**★, which is reached on foot or by boat from Cala Dogana. *To visit, contact Sig. Castiglione, Via Calvario, Levanzo. ☎0923 92 40 32 or mobile 339 74 18 800.*

Marettimo★

Off the beaten tourist track, Marettimo with its attractive **harbour** *(no landing stage, rowing boats take visitors to the quay)* has several restaurants but no hotels. Take a **trip**★★ around the island in a boat (contact the fishermen at the harbour) to discover the numerous caves that riddle the cliff faces.

re of Levanzo

M. Reitano/Lara Pessina/MICHELIN

ENNA★

POPULATION 28 424

MICHELIN MAP 565 O 24.

Surrounded by a sun-scorched landscape, Enna's isolated but panoramic site★★ has earned it the nickname of the Belvedere of Sicily. According to legend it was on the shores of a lake, Lago di Pergusa, (10km/6mi to the south), that Pluto carried off the youthful Proserpine (or Persephone), future Queen of the Underworld.

- **Information:** Via Roma 411. ☏0935 52 82 88. www.apt-enna.com.
- **Orient Yourself:** At the centre of the island, Enna rises to an altitude of 942m/ 3 091ft. The main access road is A 19.
- **Don't Miss:** Panorama from the tallest tower of the Castello di Lombardia.
- **Organizing Your Time:** Allow half a day.
- **Also See:** *Villa Imperiale del CASALE*

Worth a Visit

Castello di Lombardia★

Open daily, mid-Apr to mid-Oct 8am-8pm, rest of year 8am-1hr before dusk. ☏0935 50 09 62.
This medieval castle has six of its original 20 towers. From the top of the tallest there is an exceptional **panorama**★★★ of the hilltop village of Calascibetta, Mount Etna and most of the Sicilian mountain peaks. Beyond the castle, the **belvedere**, once the site of a temple to Demeter, offers a fine **view**★ of Calascibetta and of Enna itself.

Duomo

Open daily, 8am-1pm and 4-7pm. 0935 50 31 65.
The cathedral was rebuilt in the Baroque style in the 16C and 17C and has a carved coffered **ceiling**★ with winged creatures at the end of each beam.

Torre di Federico★

At the far end of Via Roma facing the castle. In the past Enna could have been described as the town of towers. The town's strategic, defensive function accounts for the large number of these.

ISOLE **EOLIE**★★★

AEOLIAN OR LIPARI ISLANDS

POPULATION 12 000

MICHELIN MAP 565 L 25-27 AND K 27.

The Aeolian Islands, also known as the Lipari Islands, are so called because the ancients thought Aeolus, the God of the Winds, lived there. The archipelago comprises seven main islands, Lipari, Vulcano, Stromboli, Salina, Filicudi, Alicudi and Panarea, all of exceptional interest for their volcanic nature, their beauty, their light and their climate. A deep blue, warm, clear sea, ideal for underwater fishing, interesting marine creatures including flying fish, swordfish, turtles, sea horses and hammerhead sharks, make the islands a refuge for those who like to live close to nature. Boat trips provide good views of the beautiful indented coastlines and hidden coves and bays. The inhabitants of the islands fish, grow vines and quarry pumice stone.

- **Information:** Corso Vittorio Emanuele 202, Lipari. ☏090 98 52 028 and Via Levante 4 (July-Sept), Vulcano. www.aasteolie.info.
- **Orient Yourself:** The Aeolian Islands lie off the coast near Milazzo, in the Tyhrrenian sea.

- 😊 **Don't Miss:** A glass of local Malvasia wine, Stromboli and the Great Crater on Vulcano.
- 🕐 **Organizing Your Time:** Allow 3-4 days to explore the islands.
- 👶 **Especially for Kids:** Older children will find the volcanic activity of Stromboli exciting.

Worth a Visit

Lipari★
www.comunelipari.it.

This, the largest island in the archipelago, is formed of volcanic rock dipping vertically into the sea. In ancient times Lipari was a source of obsidian, a glassy black volcanic rock, from which pumice stone was quarried on the east coast (the industry is now in decline). Today the islanders fish and grow cereals and capers.

Two bays (Marina Lunga with its beach and Marina Corta) frame the town of Liparia, dominated by its old quarter encircled by 13C-14C walls. Inside is the castle rebuilt by the Spaniards in the 16C on the site of a Norman building. The castle houses the **Museo Archeologico Eoliano**★★, which exhibits a re-creation of Bronze Age necropoli, a lovely collection of red-figure **kraters**★, **amphorae**★ and terracotta theatrical **masks**★★. ♿🕐*Open daily 9am-1.30pm and 3-7pm.* 🎫*6€.* ☎*090 98 80 174; www.regione.sicilia.it.*

There are **boat trips**★★ leaving from Marina Corta which take the visitor round the very rugged southwest coast of the island. When making a tour of the island by car, stop at Canneto and Campo Bianco to visit the pumice stone quarriesa. The splendid **view**★★ from the Puntazze headland includes five of the islands: Alicudi, Filicudi, Salina, Panarea and Stromboli. However, it is the belvedere at Quattrocchi which affords one of the finest **panoramas**★★★ of the whole archipelago.

Vulcano★★★
www.isoladivulcano.com.

This 21km2/8sq mile island is in reality four volcanoes. According to mythology it is here that Vulcan, the god of fire, had his forges – whence the term volcanism. Although there has been no eruption on the island since 1890 there are still important signs of activity: fumaroles (smokeholes), spouting steam-jets often underwater, hot sulphurous mud flows greatly appreciated for their therapeutic properties. The island has a wild but forbidding beauty, with its rugged rocky shores, desolate areas and strangely coloured soils due to the presence of sulphur, iron oxides and alum. The island's main centre, Porto di Levantee, stands below the great crater. The beach is known for its particularly warm water due to the underwater spouting steam-jets. Excursions to the **Great Crater**★★★ *(about 2hr on foot there and back)* are interesting for the impressive views they afford of the crater and of the archipelago. The headland Capo Grillo affords a view of several islands.

A tour of the island by boat *(starting from Porto Ponente)* offers the visitor many curious views, especially along the northwestern coast, which is fringed with impressive basalt reefs.

The sulphurous vapours of Vulcano

Address Book

GETTING ABOUT

Ferries run regularly from Milazzo, Messina, Reggio di Calabria, Palermo and Naples. i Siremar (Gruppo Tirrenia; www.tirrenia.it), ☎091 74 93 111; www.siremar.it SNAV, Stazione Marittima, Napoli, ☎081 42 85 555; www. snav.it

For coin ranges, see the Legend on the cover flap.

WHERE TO EAT

E Pulera – *Via Diana – 98055 Lipari – ☎090 98 11 158 – Closed lunchtime; Nov-May – Book. 12% service charge.* One of the main attractions is the beautiful flower-filled garden where guests have dinner (authentic local fare). In July and August diners are entertained with live music and folk dancing displays.

Filippino – *Piazza Municipio – 98055 Lipari – ☎090 98 13 600 – www. pulera.it – Closed Mon (except Jun-Sep), 16 Nov-15 Dec – . 12% service charge.* With its large open-air area in Piazza della Rocca, this place has become something of an institution throughout the archipelago and, indeed, the whole of Sicily. The menu (mostly fish) is dicated by the morning's catch, the dishes cooked according to tradition. Informal ambience and excellent (quick and efficient) service.

Punta Lena – *Via Marina, località Ficogrande – 98050 Stromboli – ☎090 98 62 04 – puntalena@libero. it – Closed Nov-Mar.* The fish is always ultra-fresh and of very good quality, and the dishes are tasty, but if the seafood specialities lack a little imagination, you will be consoled by the setting. Meals are served under a lovely pergola with a splendid view of the sea.

WHERE TO STAY

Hotel Ericusa – *98050 Alicudi – ☎090 98 89 902 – www.alicudihotel. it –Closed Oct-May – – 20 rm – Restaurant.* This simple, small hotel is the only accommodation on the island. It is right on the beach and the rooms have their own private entrance. On the menu are lots of vegetables and fish (caught that morning). Would appeal to those looking for a sunny, seaside vacation and, most of all, peace and solitude!

Hotel La Canna – *Contrada Rosa – 98050 Filicudi – ☎090 98 89 956 – www.lacannahotel.it – Closed Nov – – 8 rm .* Housed in an Aeolian-style building which is in keeping with the landscape, this hotel enjoys a panoramic setting overlooking the port and the sea. There are two very romantic rooms with a little terrace reserved for "honeymoon couples," but the wonderful swimming pool and sun lounge are open to everybody.

Hotel Poseidon – *Via Ausonia 7 – 98055 Lipari – ☎090 98 12 876 – www. hotelposeidonlipari.com – Closed Nov-Feb – – 18 rm – .* Very centrally located. A small, Mediterranean-style establishment – lots of white and blue. Light and airy rooms with modern, functional furnishings. Sun lounge. Helpful staff.

Locanda del Barbablù – *Via Vittorio Emanuele 17/19 – 98050 Stromboli – ☎090 98 61 18 – www.barbablu.it – Closed lunchtime, Nov and Feb – – 6 dbl rm – Restaurant.* You will receive a warm welcome here. Attractive, stylish rooms which successfully combine antique pieces with artisanal works. Imaginative and varied menu with something for everyone.

Don't miss the impressive views from Great Crater.

Stromboli★★★

The volcano of Stromboli, with its plume of smoke, has a sombre beauty and is a wild island with steep slopes. There are very few roads and such soil as can be cultivated is covered with vines yielding a delicious golden-coloured Malvasia wine. Visit the little square, with its white houses that are markedly Moorish in style.

The **crater**★★★, in the form of a 924m/3 032ft cone, has frequent minor eruptions with noisy explosions and accompanying flows of lava. To see the **spectacle**★★★ climb up to the crater *(about 5hr on foot there and back, difficult climb, visitors are advised to make the ascent in the company of a guide)* or watch from a boat the famous flow of lava along the crevasse named Sciara del Fuoco towards the sea. Excursions: *Authorised CAI-AGAI guides, Porto di Scari and Piazza San Vincenzo, Stromboli.* ☎/Fax 090 98 62 11, 090 98 62 63, 368 66 49 18 or mobile 330 96 53 67. *Visitors are recommended to book authorised guides only.*

Salina★

The island is formed by six extinct volcanoes of which two have retained their characteristic outline. The highest crater, Monte Fossa delle Felci (962m/ 3 156ft) dominates the archipelago. There is a pleasant panoramic road round the island. Caper bushes and vines grow on the lower terraced slopes. The latter yield the delicious golden Malvasia wine.

ERICE★★★

POPULATION 29 000
MICHELIN MAP 565 M 19.

Occupying a unique and beautiful setting★★★ this ancient Phoenician and Greek city presents two faces. During the hot summers, it is bright and sunny and the sun-drenched streets of the village, strategically located, offer splendid views★★ over the valley. In winter Erice is wreathed in mist and seems a place lost in time. In Antiquity this area was a religious centre famous for its temple consecrated to Astarte, then to Aphrodite and finally Venus, who was venerated by mariners of old.

- **Information:** Via Tommaso Guarrasi 1, 91016 Erice (TP). ☎0923 86 93 88; www.regione.sicilia.it/turismo.
- **Orient Yourself:** Erice, rising almost vertically (750m/2 461ft) above the sea, lies about 14km/8mi from Trapani, on the western side of the island.
- **Don't Miss:** Views from Castello di Venere.
- **Organizing Your Time:** Allow a couple of hours.
- **Also See:** *SEGESTA, TRAPANI.*

Address Book

WHERE TO STAY

Azienda Agricola Pizzolungo – *Contrada S. Cusumano – 96016 Erice Casa Santa – ☎0923 56 37 10 – www. pizzolungo.it – – 6 apartments (per head charge).* A stone's throw from the sea is this 19C farmhouse surrounded by a lovely garden. A romantic and rustic establishment – how about a refreshing dip in an old stone trough? Apartments for 2, 4 and 6 people, complete with kitchen and private access.

Hotel Baglio Santacroce – *91019 Valderice – 2km/1.2mi east of Valderice – ☎0923 89 11 11 – www.bagliosanta croce.it – – 25 rm – Restaurant.* What was once a 17C farmhouse is now

a charming, small hotel. Glorious, verdant setting with wonderful views of the Golfo di Cornino. The rooms may not be spacious but have plenty of character with exposed beams and tiled floors.

WHERE TO EAT

Monte San Giuliano – *Vicolo San Rocco 7 – ☎0923 86 95 95 – www. mon-tesangiuliano.it – Closed Mon, 7-25 Jan and 5-23 Nov – Book .* Located at the heart of the village is this lovely little establishment which serves authentic, local fare. Fine, rustic-style dining room but perhaps even more appealing is the pergola in the internal courtyard – very light and airy.

Walking About

Castello di Venere

This castle, built by the Normans in the 12C, crowns an isolated rock on Monte Erice, on the site of the Temple of Venus (Venere). From here and the nearby gardens (Giardino del Balio) there are admirable **views**★★: in clear weather the Tunisian coast can be seen in the distance.

Chiesa Matrice★

This church was built in the 14C using stones quarried from the Temple of Venus. The porch was added in the 15C and flanked by the square battlemented bell tower (13C).

ETNA★★★

MICHELIN MAP 565 N-O 26-27.

Etna is the highest point in the island (3 340m/10 950ft), and is snow-capped for most of the year. It is still active and it is the largest and one of the most famous volcanoes in Europe. Etna was born of undersea eruptions that also formed the Plain of Catania, formerly covered by the sea.

- 🛈 **Information:** Parco dell'Etna, Via del Convento 45, Monastero di San Nicolo La Rena, 90035 Nicolosi (CT). ☎095 82 11 11; www.parcoetna.it.
- ▶ **Orient Yourself:** Etna dominates the Ionic coastline between Catania and Taormina.
- 😊 **Don't Miss:** An ascent of Mt Etna.
- 🕐 **Organizing Your Time:** Allow a day.
- 🧒 **Especially for Kids:** Older children will enjoy scaling a volcano.
- ⏱ **Also See:** *CATANIA, TAORMINA.*

A Bit of History

In 1987 the Parco dell'Etna was created, covering an area of 59 000ha/145 790 acres; in the centre of the park, the mountain has the appearance of a huge, black, distorted cone which can be seen from a distance of 250km/155 miles. On its lower slopes, which are extremely fertile, orange, mandarin, lemon and olive trees

Etna

The Giant Awakes

Etna's eruptions were frequent in ancient times: 135 are recorded. But the greatest disaster occurred in 1669, when the flow of lava reached the sea, largely devastating Catania as it passed.

The worst eruptions in recent times occurred in 1910, when 23 new craters appeared, 1917, when a jet of lava squirted up to 800m/2 500ft above its base, and 1923, when the lava ejected remained hot 18 months after the eruption. Since then, stirrings of Etna have been numerous... the last, in 2001, which involved the crater on the southeast side, swept away the lifts and the funicular platform and threatened to destroy the Sapienza Refuge and the town of Nicolisi.

flourish as well as vines which produce the delicious Etna wine. Chestnut trees grow above the 500m/1 500ft level and give way higher up to oak, beech, birch and pine. Above 2 100m/6 500ft is the barren zone, where only a few clumps of Astralagus siculus (a kind of vetch) will be seen scattered on the slopes of secondary craters, among the clinker and volcanic rock.

Via Cimarosa 10, 95124 Catania, ☎095 73 06 211, apt@apt-catania.it, www.turismo.catania.it.

Via Garibaldi 63, 95030 Nicolosi (CT), ☎095 91 15 05.

Piazza Annunziata 7, 95015 Linguaglossa (CT), ☎095 64 30 94.

Piazza Luigi Sturzo 3, 95019 Zafferana Etnea (CT), ☎095 70 82 825.

Special Features

Ascent of the volcano★★★

🕒 *By the south face from Catania via Nicolosi, or by the northeast face from Taormina via Linguaglossa. As the volcano may ~upt at any time, tourist facilities (roads, ~ths, cable cars and refuge huts) may ~losed, moved or withdrawn. Excursions may be cancelled in the case of bad weather (fog) or volcanic activity. The best time for the ascent is early morning. Wear warm clothing even in summer (anorak, thick pullover) and strong shoes (no heels – the stony terrain of the paths through the lava can cause injuries, particularly to ankles). Wear sunglasses to avoid the glare. Gruppo Guide Alpine Etna Sud, via Etnea 49, Nicolosi, ☎095 79 14 755*

South face

🕒 *Depending on snow conditions, excursions take place from the week before Easter to 31 Oct, 9am-4pm. Duration: approx 2hr round trip.* 🚠 *around €40-45 including insurance and guide. Gruppo Guide Alpine Etna Sud, Via Etnea 49, Nicolosi, ☎095 79 14 755 or Funivia dell'Etna, Piazza V. Emanuele 45, Nicolosi, ☎095 91 41 41/42; www.funiviaetna.com. Another option is to book a private trip with one of the alpine guides who organise trekking, alpine skiing and expeditions into the caves created by the lava flow.*

The ascent depends on the conditions on the volcano and stops close to the grandiose valley, Valle del Bove, which is hemmed in by walls of lava (1 200m/3 900ft high) pierced with pot holes and crevasses belching smoke.

Northeast face

🕒*May-Oct, 9am-4pm. Excursions leave from Piano Provenzana. Duration: approx 2hr round trip.* 🚠*35€, including alpine guide. STAR, Via Santangelo Fulci 40, ☎095 37 13 33.*

The road goes through Linguaglossa, a lovely pinewood and the winter sports resort of Villaggio Mareneve.

The surfaced road ends at Piano Provenzana (1 800m/5 900ft). There is a magnificent **view**★★from the area around the new observatory. The climb ends amid an extraordinary landscape of lava, which still smokes at times.

Circumetnea

This road runs around Etna, offering varied views of the volcano and passing through a number of interesting villages.

MESSINA

POPULATION 249 351
MICHELIN MAP 565 M 28 (INCLUDING TOWN PLAN).

Despite having been destroyed numerous times throughout the centuries, including weathering a devastating earthquake in 1908, Messina – the ancient Zancle of the Greeks – is today a thriving market town.

- **Information:** Via Calabria, isol 301 bis, 98122 Messina. ☎090 67 42 36; www.azienturismomessina.it.
- **Orient Yourself:** Messina overlooks that stretch of sea that separates Sicily from the main land.
- **Don't Miss:** The Museo Regionale and The Duomo.
- **Organizing Your Time:** Allow half a day.
- **Also See:** *TAORMINA*.

Visit

Museo Regionale★

North of the town at the end of the Viale della Libertà. ⚙ ⏱*Open Tue-Sat, 9am-1.30pm, also 4-6.30pm Tue, Thu and Sat (3-5.30pm in winter); Sun and hols 9am-12.30pm.* ⏱*Closed Mon.* ☎*090 36 12 92.*
The museum comprises an art gallery and a sculpture and decorative arts section. The painting section displays a **polyptych of St Gregory** (1473) by Antonello da Messina, a remarkable composition that combines the Tuscan idiom with the earliest Flemish influences, a remarkable **Descent from the Cross** by the Flemish artist Colin van Coter (15C); and two Caravaggios, **Adoration of the Shepherds** and **Resurrection of Lazarus**, both painted towards the end of his life from 1608 to 1610. The **Berlina del Senato**★ painted in 1742 is worthy of note.

Duomo

⏱*Open Mon-Sat 9.30am-7pm, Sun 10.30-11am and 4-7pm.* ☎*090 77 48 95.*
To the left of the campanile (60m/196ft tall) has an astronomical clock★ made in Strasbourg in 1933 and believed to be the world's largest.

Santissima Annunziata dei Catalani

Take the Via Cesare Battisti from the south side of the cathedral.
The church which was built in 1100 during the Norman reign and altered in the 13C, takes its name from the Catalan merchants who owned it. The **apse**★ is characteristic of the composite Norman style which blends Romanesque (small columns supporting blind arcades), Moorish (geometric motifs and polychrome stonework) and Byzantine (dome on a drum) influences.

Excursion

Tindari★

▶*62km/37mi west.*
The ancient Greek Tyndaris, founded in 396 BC, is perched on the cape of the same name.The **ruins** *(rovine)* are essentially those of the city **ramparts**, the **theatre** and the so-called **Basilica**, an arcaded Roman building. ⏱*Open daily, 9am to 2hr before dusk.* ☎*0941 36 90 23; www.regione.sicilia.it*

Antonello da Messina

Born in Messina in 1430, he studied in Naples where he was influenced by the then popular Flemish art. Later, he was attracted by the innovations of Tuscan painting which emphasised volume and architectural details. His works show a complete mastery of his art: forms and colours, skilfully balanced, enhance an inner vision which greatly influenced the Venetian painters of the Renaissance, notably Carpaccio and Giovanni Bellini. Antonello died on his native island around 1479.

NOTO★★

POPULATION 22 971
MICHELIN MAP 565 Q 27.

Noto, dating from the time of the Siculi, was destroyed by the earthquake of 1693. It was rebuilt on a new site 10km/6mi from the original town. Lining the streets, laid out on a grid plan, are palaces and churches in local white limestone. Several Sicilian architects worked on this project, including Rosario Gagliardi.

- **Information:** Piazza XVI Maggio, 96017 Noto (SR). ☎0931 83 67 44; www.regione.sicilia.it/turismo.
- **Orient Yourself:** Noto is situated in the south of the island. The main access road is S 115.
- **Don't Miss:** The Baroque centre.
- **Organizing Your Time:** Allow a couple of hours.
- **Also See:** *RAGUSA, SIRACUSA.*

Walking About

The Baroque centre★★

The hub of the town is **Corso Vittorio Emanuele**, which widens into three squares overlooked by the monumental façades of churches designed in an imposing but flexible Baroque style: **San Francesco all'Immacolata** and the **cathedral**★★ (the cupola and much of the central nave collapsed in 1996) in the attractive **Piazza Municipio**★, and **San Domenico**★.

To the right of San Domenico is **Via Corrado Nicolaci**★, a gently sloping street which offers an enchanting vista with the church of Montevergine as focal point. It is lined with palaces sporting splendid balconies; the most notable is **Palazzo Nicolaci di Villadorata** with exuberantly fanciful **balconies**★★★.

PALERMO★★★

POPULATION 682 000
MICHELIN MAP 432 M 21-22 (INCLUDING PLAN OF BUILT-UP AREA).

Palermo, the capital and the chief seaport of Sicily, is built at the head of a wide bay enclosed to the north by Monte Pellegrino and to the south by Capo Zafferano. It lies on the edge of a fertile plain bounded by hills and nicknamed the Conca d'Oro (Golden Basin), where lemon and orange groves flourish.

- **Information:** Piazza Castelnuovo 34, ☎091 60 58 111, www.aapit.pa.it.
- **Orient Yourself:** Palermo is situated on the northern coast. The main access roads is A 19.
- **Parking:** Traffic in Palermo is congested and parking is difficult. Walk or use public transport. Large car parks can be found on the city outskirts.
- **Don't Miss:** Capella Palatina, Galleria Regionale della Sicilia, Chiesa di San Giovanni degli Eremiti, Catacombe dei Cappuccini, Monreale.
- **Organizing Your Time:** Allow two days to see Palermo and one more for the surrounding area.
- **Especially for Kids:** Puppets at the Museo Internazionale delle Marionette.
  Also See: *CEFALÙ, USTICA.*

A Bit of History

Palermo was founded by the Phoenicians, conquered by the Romans and later came under Byzantine rule. From 831 to 1072 it was under the sway of the Saracens, who gave the city its special atmosphere suggested today by the luxuriance of its gardens and the shape of the domes on some buildings. Conquered by the Normans in 1072, Palermo became the capital under Roger II, who took the title of King of Sicily. This great builder succeeded in blending Norman architectural styles with the decorative traditions of the Saracens and Byzantines: his reign was the golden age of art in Palermo. Later the Hohenstaufen and Angevin kings introduced the Gothic style (13C). After three centuries of Spanish rule, the Bourbons gave Palermo its Baroque finery.

The Sicilian Vespers

Since 1266 the brother of Louis IX of France, Charles I of Anjou, supported by the pope, had held the town. But his rule was unpopular. The Sicilians had nicknamed the French, who spoke Italian badly, the *tartaglioni* or stammerers. On the Monday or Tuesday after Easter 1282, as the bells were ringing for vespers, some Frenchmen insulted a young woman of Palermo in the church of Santo Spirito. Insurrection broke out, and all Frenchmen who could not pronounce the world *cicero* (chick-pea) correctly were massacred.

Palazzo dei Normanni★★

Only the central part and the Pisan Tower are of the Norman period, built on the site of an earlier Moorish fortress,

Cappella Palatina★★★

1st floor of Palazzo dei Normanni. Built in the reign of Roger II from 1130 to 1140, it is a wonderful example of Arab-Norman decoration. The upper walls, dome and apses are covered with dazzling **mosaics★★★**, which, along with those of Constantinople and Ravenna, are the finest in Europe. This decoration is complemented by the carved stalactite ceiling, marble paving, ornate pulpit and paschal candelabrum.
🕐 *Open Mon-Sat 8.30am-noon and 2-5pm, Sun 8.30am-noon.* 🚫*Closed public holidays.* 🎫*4€.* ☎*091 70 54 879.*
On the second floor the old royal apartments, **Antichi appartamenti reali★★**, house the 12C King Roger's chamber, **Sala di re Ruggero**, which is adorned with mosaics of the chase. (👣*Guided tours only.*)
The attractive gardens, **Villa Bonanno★**, boast superb palm trees.

Flavour of the East: San Giovanni degli Eremiti

Address Book

GETTING THERE

The easiest and quickest way to get to Palermo is by **air**. The city airport, Falcone-Borsellino (www.gesap.it), named after two judges who were murdered in 1992 (and formerly known as Punta-Raisi), is situated 30km/18mi north of Palermo, off the A 29 dual carriageway It is served by various airlines including Alitalia, Alpi Eages, Air Sicilia, Med Air-lines, Meridiana and Air Europe. A bus links the airport with the city centre every 30min, stopping in Via le Lazio, Piazza Ruggero Settimo in front of Hotel Politeama, and at the main railway station. The 45min journey costs 4.50€ (single). The island can also be reached by **ferry** from **Genoca, Livorno and Napoli**:

Grandi Navi Veloci, Via Fieschi 17, Genova, ☎010 55 091, www1.gnv.it.

Tirrenia, Molo Angioino, Napoli, ☎892 123 or 081 01 71 998; www.tirrenia.it.

SNAV, Stazione Marittima, Napoli, ☎081 42 85 555, www.snav.it.

Getting around – It is best to avoid driving in Palermo because of traffic congestion and the difficulty of finding somewhere to park. Large car parks can be found on the outskirts of the city (marked by a 🅿 on the map). There is also a free car park in Piazza Maggiore, 300m from the Botanical Gardens. Other parking facilities (for which there is a charge) include Piazza Giulio Cesare 43, Porto, Via Guardione 81, Porto and Via Stabile 10. However, by far the best way to see the city is by public transport and taxi for longer distances and on foot once in the old town.

Bus – There are two types of ticket: tickets valid for 120min cost 1€ and the daily tickets (which expire at mid-night) ost 3.50€ and are a good option if you nd to use public transport more than times during the course of

utoradio Taxi ☎091 51 27 27
Taxi Trinacria ☎091 22 54 55.

STAY

s, see the Legend on the

Lampedusa – Via
ith lift) – 16 rm �.

Puppets

Housed in a palazzo right in the historic centre, this establishment would appeal to visitors looking for the real Palermo and a bit of local colour. No-frills rooms with basic facilities. Offers good value for money.

⊜**Hotel Moderno** – *Via Roma 276* – ☎*091 58 86 83* – ▤ – *38 rm* – ☐ *2.58 V*. The main attraction here is the warm, friendly welcome from the staff who will do their utmost to make guests feel at home. Simple, good-sized rooms although the modern furnishings are possibly just a little too spartan.

⊜⊜**Hotel Gardenia** – *Via Mariano Stabile 136 – 90100 Palermo –* ☎*091 32 27 61 – www.gardeniahotel.com –* ▤ *– 16 rm* ☐. A small, family-run hotel housed on the upper floors of an old palazzo in the city centre. Simple rooms (some have a balcony overlooking the city). Reasonably priced.

⊜⊜⊜**Massimo Plaza Hotel** – *Via Maqueda 437 –* ☎*091 32 56 57 – www. massimoplazahotel.com –* ▤ *– 15 rm* ☐. Small but elegant and stylish, this hotel is situated opposite the neo-Classical Teatro Massimo. Very attentive service. The rooms (spacious) and the public areas are all tastefully decorated with warm colours, attractive furnishings and wooden floors.

⊜⊜⊜**Centrale Palace Hotel** – *Corso Vittorio Emanuele 327 – 90134 Palermo –* ☎*091 33 66 66 – www.centrale palacehotel.it –* 🅿▤⅊ *– 63 rm –* ☐ *10.33 € – Restaurant*. The elegant, tasteful Centrale Palace is located in a 17C mansion and offers excellent hospitality. This hotel has attractive public areas, including a panoramic restaurant on the top floor.

WHERE TO EAT

Pizzeria Tonnara Florio – *Discesa Tonnara 4, zona Arenella* – ☎*091 63 75 611* – *www.tonnaraflorio.com* – *Closed Mon*. This attractive Liberty-style building, unfortunately in need of restoration, has a beautiful garden and a number of rooms once used for processing tuna and repairing fishing boats. The old tuna room in the building now houses a pizzeria. There is also a nightclub.

Antica Focacceria San Francesco – *Viale Sandro Paternostro 58 – 90100 Palermo* – ☎*091 32 02 64* – *www.afsf.it* – *Closed Tues (except Mar-Oct)*. This establishment is situated in the heart of the medieval quarter, in front of the church of San Francesco. With its marble tables and an unusual counter carved out of an old cast-iron stove, it has a pleasantly old-fashioned feel about it. Specialities include focaccie farcite (flat-pizza dough baked with various fillings, arancini (deep-fried rice balls) and torte salate (savoury pastries).

Di Martino – *Via Mazzini 54 – 90100 Palermo* – ☎*091 58 59 90* – *andreadimartino@libero.it*. After a morning's sightseeing – taking in 19C Palermo and maybe the Museo d'Arte Moderna – you will probably have worked up an appetite. If you are not in the mood for a full-blown lunch, this is the place to head for a sandwich: they are both exquisitely presented and delicious. Tables outside.

Capricci di Sicilia – *Via Istituto Pignatelli 6, angolo piazza Sturzo* – ☎*091 32 77 77*. A rather unusual establishment – you will probably see the odd mime artist and even the street vendors poking their head round the door. Simple surroundings and informal service, but its main attraction is the excellent quality of the cooking which draws its inspiration from the cuisine and produce of the area.

Bye Bye Blues – *Via del Garofalo 23, zona Mondello* – ☎*091 68 41 415* – *www.byebyeblues.it* – *Closed at lunchtime (except Sun and public holidays), Tue* – *Book*. This is a must – as much for the ambience as the food. The menu is imaginative, the dishes (both fish and meat, in equal measure) are well put together and there is an excellent wine list.

TAKING A BREAK

Bar Costa – *Via G. d'Annunzio 15* – Wed-Mon 8am-9pm. Specialises in all kinds of cakes and pastries (especially lemon and orange mousses).

Mazzara – *Via Generale Magliocco 15* – ☎*091 32 14 43* – Sun-Fri 8am-9pm, Sat 8am-11.30pm. The long-established pasticceria (pastry shop), where Giuseppe Tomasi di Lampedusa, the author of Il Gattopardo (The Leopard) used to stop for breakfast.

Oscar – *Via Mariano Migliaccio 39* – ☎*091 68 22 381* – Wed-Mon 8am-9pm. The best-known speciality here is a Devil's food cake.

SHOPPING

The food markets in Palermo are full of life and regional character, with a range of colourful lamp-lit stalls selling fresh fruit, vegetables and local fish. The most famous is without a doubt **Vucciria** market, a vibrant, colourful food market which is held every morning (except Sunday) until 2pm not far from the quayside in Via Cassari-Argenteria and the surrounding area (almost up to Piazza San Domenico). Other lively markets include the **Ballarò** food market in the area around Piazza del Carmine, and **Capo** market, the most interesting part of which sells food (Piazza Beati Paoli) and the second section of which sells a variety of clothing (Via San Agostino and Via Bandiera).

From Palazzo dei Normanni to the Cala

Visit: 3hr. The route begins at Palazzo dei Normanni, the focus of Sicilian politics, both past and present, pas two pretty squares which centre of Palermo and e the old harbour of the

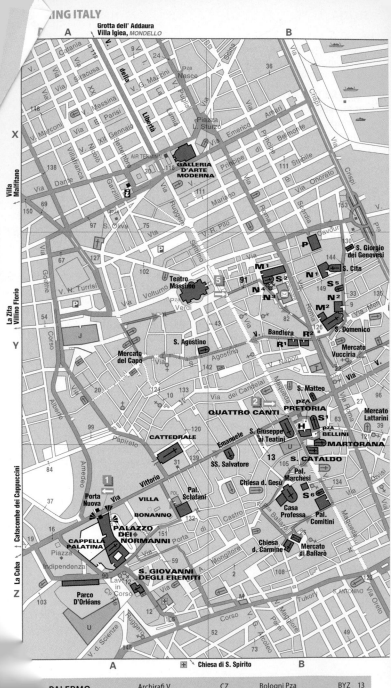

ING ITALY

Grotta dell' Addaura
Villa Igiea, MONDELLO

Chiesa di S. Spirito

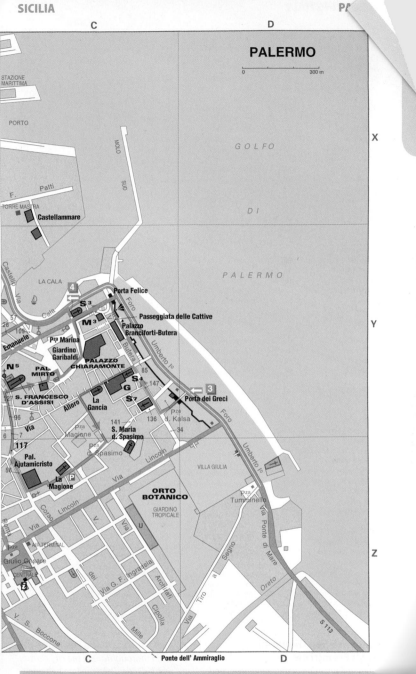

SICILIA

PALERMO

PALERMO

0   300 m

X

GOLFO

DI

PALERMO

Y

Z

STAZIONE MARITTIMA

PORTO

MOLO SUD

F. Patti

TORRE MASTRA

Castellammare

LA CALA

4

Porta Felice

S 3

Passeggiata delle Cattive

M 3

Palazzo Branciforti-Butera

Pza Marina

Giardino Garibaldi

PALAZZO CHIARAMONTE

Foro

Butera

Umberto I°

N 5

PAL. MIRTO

S. FRANCESCO D'ASSISI

Alloro

La Gancia

S 4

G

S 7

85

147

3

Porta dei Greci

Pza d. Kalsa

Foro

Umberto I°

Via

Pza Magione

S. Maria d. Spasimo

141

136

34

Pal. Ajutamicristo

Pza di Spasimo

Lincoln

VILLA GIULIA

La Magione

P

Via

ORTO BOTANICO

GIARDINO TROPICALE

Pza Tumminello

Via Ponte di Mare

Corso Lincoln

Via

Via

U

Pza Giulio Cesare

AUTOTERMINAL

CENTRALE

Via G. F. Ingrassia

Archirafi

Cipolla

Mille

Via al Tiro a Segno

Oreto

S 113

V. S. Boccone

Ponte dell' Ammiraglio

C   D

Carmine Pza d.	BZ	25	Cervello V.	CY	34	Donizetti V. G.	ABY	43
Cassa di Risparmio Pza	BY	27	Cipolla V.	CZ		Errante V. V.	BZ	
Cassari V.	BCY	28	Collegio di Maria V.	BX	36	Filiciuzza V.	ABZ	
Castello Pza	BCY		Colonna Rotta V.	AZ	37	Finocchiaro Aprile Cso C.	AY	
Castelnuovo Pza	AX	30	Crispi V.	BX		Fonderia Pza	C	
Catania V.	AX		Croce dei Vespri Pza d.	BY	39	Garibaldi V.		
Cattedrale Pza d.	AZ	31	Dante V.	AX		Garzilli V. N.		
Cavalieri di Malta Largo	BY	33	Divisi V.	BZ		Gasometro Pza		
Cavour V.	BXY		Don Sturzo Pza	ABX		Generale Cadorna V.		

Street	Code	No.	Street	Code	No.	Street	Code	No.
Giudici Discesa d.	BY	63	Paternostro V. A.	BCY	96	S. Isidoro alla Guilla Pza	AY	133
Giullio Cesare Pza	CZ		Paternostro V. P.	AX	97	S. Oliva Pza	AX	
Goethe V.	AY		Patti V. F.	BCX		S. Orsola Vicolo	BZ	134
Indipendenza Pza	AZ		Peranni Pza D.	AY	99	S. Sebastiano V.	BY	135
Ingrassia V. G. F.	CZ		Pignatelli d'Aragona V.	AY	102	S. Teresa V.	CY	136
Juvara Cluviero V.	AY	67	Pilo V. R.	BXY		Sammartino V.	AX	138
Kalsa Pza d.	CY		Pisani Cso P.	AZ	103	Scienze V. d.	AZ	
La Lumia V. I.	AX		Ponte di Mare V.	DZ		Scina V.	BX	
Latini V. B.	AX	69	Ponticello V.	BZ	105	Scuole V. d.	AZ	139
Libertà V. d.	AX		Porta di Castro V.	ABZ		Siracusa V.	AX	
Lincoln V.	CZDY		Porta Montalto Pza	AZ	106	Spasimo Pza d.	CYZ	
Maggiore Perni V.	BZ		Porta S. Agata V.	BZ	108	Spasimo V. d.	CY	141
Magione Pza d.	CYZ		Porto Salvo V.	CY	109	Spirito Santo V. d.	ABY	142
Maqueda V.	BYZ		Pretoria Pza	BY		Squarcialupo V.	BY	144
Marconi V.	AX		Principe di Belmonte V.	BX		Stabile V. M.	AYBX	
Marina Pza	CY		Principe di Scordia V.	BX		Stazzone Pza	AZ	145
Marino V. S.	BZ	73	Principe Granatelli V.	ABX	111	Tiro a Segno V.	DZ	
Mazzini V. G.	AX		Puglisi V.	AX		Torremuzza V.	CY	147
Meccio V. S.	AX	75	Quattro Canti Pza Vigliena	BY		Tukory Cso	ABZ	
Meli V.	BY		Rao V. C.	CZ		Tumminello Pza	DZ	
Messina V.	AX		Rivoluzione Pza	CZ	117	Turrisi V. N.	AY	
Mille Cso d.	CZ		Roma V.	BXCZ		Turrisi Colonna V.	AX	148
Mongitore V. A.	ABZ		Ruggero Settimo Pza	AX	118	Umberto I Foro	CYDZ	
Monteleone V.	BY	82	Ruggero Settimo V.	AXY		Valverde V.	BY	149
Mosca V. G.	AZ	84	S. Agata V.	AY	120	Verdi Pza	ABY	
Mura del Cattive Salita	CY	85	S. Agostino V.	AYZ		Villafranca V.	AX	
Napoli V.	BY		S. Anna Pza	BY	121	Virgilio Pza	AX	150
Nasce Pza	AX		S. Antonino Pza	BZ	123	Vittoria Pza d.	AZ	151
Onorato V.	BX		S. Domenico Pza	BY	126	Vittorio Emanuele V.	AZCY	
Oreto V.	BZ		S. Francesco da Paola Pza	AY	127	Volturno V.	AY	
Orleans Pza	AZ	90	S. Francesco d'Assisi Pza	CY	129	XII Gennaio V.	AX	
Orlogio V.	BY	91	S. Giorgio dei Genovesi Pza	BY	130	XIII Vittime Pza	BX	153
Papireto V.	AYZ		S. Giovanni			XX Settembre V.	AX	
Parisi V. E.	AX		Decollato Piazzetta	AZ	132			

Monument	Code	Ref	Monument	Code	Ref	Monument	Code	Ref
Cappella Palatina	AZ		Oratorio del Rosario di S. Cita	BY	N[1]	Porta dei Greci	CY	
Casa Professa	BZ		Oratorio del Rosario di			Prefettura	BY	P
Castellammare	CXY		S. Domenico	BY	N[2]	Quattro Canti	BYZ	
Cattedrale	AZ		Oratorio di S. Caterina			S. Agostino	AY	
Chiesa del Carmine	BZ		d'Alessandria	BY	N[3]	S. Cataldo	BZ	
Chiesa del Gesù	BZ		Oratorio di S. Filippo Neri	BY	N[5]	S. Caterina	BY	S[1]
Galleria Regionale di Sicilia			Oratorio di S. Lorenzo	CY	N[4]	S. Cita	BY	
(Palazzo Abatellis)	CY	G	Orto Botanico	CDZ		S. Domenico	BY	
Galleria d'Arte Moderna			Palazzo Ajutamicristo	CZ		S. Francesco d'Assisi	CY	
(Teatro Politeama)	AX		Palazzo Branciforti-Butera	CY		S. Giorgio dei Genovesi	BY	
Giardino Garibaldi	CY		Palazzo Chiaramonte	CY		S. Giovanni degli Eremiti	AZ	
La Gancia	CY		Palazzo Comitini	BZ		S. Giuseppe ai Teatini	BY	
La Magione	CZ		Palazzo Marchesi	BZ		S. Ignazio all'Olivella	BY	S[2]
La Martorana	BY		Palazzo Mirto	CY		S. Maria della Catena	CY	S[3]
Mercato Vucciria	BY		Palazzo Oneto di Sperlinga	BY	R[1]	S. Maria della Pietà	CY	S[4]
Mercato Lattarini	BY		Palazzo Pretorio (Municipio)	BY	H	S. Maria dello Spasimo	CYZ	
Mercato di Ballarò	BZ		Palazzo Sclafani	AZ		S. Maria di Valverde	BY	S[5]
Mercato di Capo	AY		Palazzo Termine	BY	R[2]	S. Matteo	BY	
Museo Archeologico			Palazzo dei Normanni	AZ		S. Orsola	BZ	S[6]
Regionale	BY	M[1]	Parco d'Orléans	AZ		S. Teresa alla Kalsa	CY	S[7]
Museo Internazionale			Passeggiata delle Cattive	CY		SS. Salvatore	BZ	
delle Marionette	CY	M[3]	Porta Felice	CY		Teatro Massimo	AY	
Museo del Risorgimento	BY	M[2]	Porta Nuova	AZ		Villa Bonanno	AZ	
						Vucciria	BY	

Chiesa di San Giovanni degli Eremiti★★

ⓘ For information on opening times and prices call ☎091 65 15 019.

Close to the Palazzo dei Normanni, this church, with its surrounding gardens, is an oasis. The church was built with the aid of Arab architects in 1132 and is topped with pink domes. Beside it is a lovely garden with 13C **cloisters★**.

▶ Turn into Via Vittorio Emanuele, the main thoroughfare in the city centre, which divides Palermo into two parts. The cathedral is on the left.

Cattedrale★

Founded at the end of the 12C, the cathedral is built in the Sicilian-Norman style but has often been modified. The

apses★ of the east end have retained their Sicilian-Norman decoration.

In the interior, which was modified in the 18C in the neo-Classical style, note the tombs of the Emperor Frederick II and other members of the Hohenstaufen dynasty as well as of Angevin and Aragonese rulers. The **Treasury** (Tesoro) displays the ornate **imperial crown**★ that belonged to Constance of Aragon. *Treasury:* ⏰*Open Mon-Sat, 8am-6pm.* ☎*091 33 43 763.*

Quattro Canti★

Two main streets, Via Vittorio Emanuele and Via Maqueda, intersect to form this busy crossroads decorated with statues and fountains. The church of **San Giuseppe ai Teatini** has an astonishingly decorative **interior**★.

La Martorana★★

⏰*Open Mon-Sat 9am-1pm and 3.30-6.30pm, Sun and public holidays 8.30am-1pm.* ✍*Donation recommended.* ☎*091 61 61 692.*

The real name of this church is Santa Maria dell'Ammiraglio (St Mary of the Admiral). It was founded in 1143 by the Admiral of the Fleet to King Roger II and altered in the 16C and 17C by the addition of a Baroque façade on the north side. Pass under the 12C belfry-porch to enter the original church, decorated with Byzantine **mosaics**★★ depicting scenes from the New Testament and in the cupola, the imposing figure of Christ Pantocrator (Christ as Ruler of All). At the very end of the two side aisles note the two panels depicting *Roger II crowned by Christ (right),* and *Admiral George of Antioch kneeling before the Virgin (left).*

Chiesa di San Cataldo★★

⏰*Open Mon-Sat 9.30am-12.30pm and 3.30-6.30pm.* ✍*1€.* ☎*091 63 75 622.*

This splendid church, founded in the 12C, recalls Moorish architecture with its severe square shape, its domes and the traceried openings of the façade. The two churches face each other on the small **Piazza Bellini**★. The Moorish and Norman features of the square are particularly evident in the three rose-coloured cupolas of San Cataldo.

Piazza Pretoria★★

The square has a spectacular **fountain**★★ surmounted by numerous marble statues, the work of a 16C Florentine artist. The **Palazzo Pretorio**, now the town hall, occupies one side of this square. Immediately to the north of the last stretch of Corso Vittorio Emanuele, is a lively food market, the **Vucciria**, which is open every morning except Sunday.

Chiesa di San Francesco d'Assisi★

The church was built in the 13C. After its destruction during the Second World War it was rebuilt in the original style. Particu-

Piazza Pretoria at night

larly noteworthy are the **portal** (original) and the rose window on the façade.

Palazzo Chiaramonte★

This fine Gothic palace (1307) served as a model for many buildings in Sicily. In the gardens, **Giardino Garibaldi**, opposite there are two spectacular **magnolia-fig trees**★★ (Ficus magnolioides).

The Cala

The old harbour is known as the cala, once enclosed by chains, now in the church of **Santa Maria alla Catena**★.

A Riot of Baroque Stucco

Oratorio del Rosario di San Domenico★★★

Tours: ☎329 61 90 318. The stucco decor of this church was the work of **Giacomo Serpotta**, an important artist of the Baroque period.

Oratorio del Rosario di Santa Cita★★★

Tours: ☎091 33 27 798. This church is considered to be the masterpiece of **Giacomo Serpotta**, who worked on it between 1686 and 1718. Panels depicting the Mysteries are framed by rejoicing angels.

Oratorio di San Lorenzo★★★

Chiesa di S. Francesco d'Assisi: ☎091 61 58 351. A late work and masterpiece of **Giacomo Serpotta** decorated with stuccowork is an imaginative riot of rejoicing putti.

Palazzi and Museums

Galleria Regionale della Sicilia★★

Via Alloro. ⏰Open 9am-1.30pm, Tue-Fri also 2.30-7.30pm (ticket office closes 30min early). 6€. ☎091 62 30 011.; www.regione.sicilia.it/beniculturali. This museum and gallery is housed in the attractive 15C **Palazzo Abatellis**★. includes a medieval art section and picture gallery featuring works from 11C to the 18C. Outstanding works

include the dramatic fresco of **Death Triumphant**★★★from Palazzo Sclafani and a very fine **bust of Eleonora of Aragon**★★by Francesco Laurana. Paintings of note include the **Annunciation**★★by Antonello da Messina and a triptych, the **Malvagna Altarolo**★★, by the Flemish artist Mabuse.

Museo Internazionale delle Marionette★★

Piazzetta Niscemi 5 (entrance Via Butera 1). ⏰Open Mon-Fri 9am-1pm and 4-7pm. ⏰Closed Sat-Sun and public holidays. 5€. ☎091 32 80 60; www.museomarionettepalermo.it. This museum is a testament to the tradition of puppet (marionette) shows in Sicily. Shows concentrated on chivalric themes, in particular the adventures of two heros, Rinaldo and Orlando. The museum houses a splendid collection of Sicilian puppets. The delicate features of Gaspare Canino's puppets are admirable: these puppets are among the oldest in the collection (19C). The second part of the museum is dedicated to European and non-European craftsmanship with puppets from Asia and Africa. Kids See the puppet collection in action in a chivalric show.

Museo Archeologico Regionale★

Piazza Olivella 24. ⏰Open daily 8.30am-6.45pm. 6€. ☎091 61 16 805; www.regione.sicilia.it/beniculturali. The archaeological museum, which is housed in a 16C convent, contains the finds from excavations in Sicily. On the ground floor are displayed two Phoenician sarcophagi, an Egyptian inscription known as the Palermo Stone and pieces from Selinus. These last include a fine series of twin stelae and the reconstruction of a temple pediment (Sala Gabrici) and especially the **metopes**★★from the temples (6C and 5C BC). On the first floor are displayed bronzes including **Heracles with stag**★and the famous **Ram**★★, a Hellenistic work from Syracuse, and marble statues, notably **Satyr**★, a copy of an original by Praxiteles. On the second floor are two fine mosaics (3C BC), **Orpheus with animals** and the Mosaic of the seasons.

Palazzo Mirto★

Via Merlo 2. ⏰*Open Mon-Sat 9am-7pm, Sun and public holidays 9am-1.30pm. 3€.* ☎*091 61 67 541.*

The main residence of the Lanza-Filangieri princes contains its original 18C and 19C furnishings. Outside, the 19C **stables**★are of interest. The piano nobile *(1st floor)* is open to visitors. The splendid **Salottino cinese** (Chinese Room) has leather flooring and silk wall coverings depicting scenes from everyday life, while the walls in the **Smoking Room**★are decorated with engraved leather. Exhibits of note include a 19C Neapolitan dinner service. *(in the passageway facing the Chinese Room).*

Teatro Massimo★

⏰ *Guided tours, 10am-3.30pm.* ⏰*Closed Mon.* ☎*091 58 89 58; www.teatromassimo.it*

This opera house is a neo-Classical structure modelled on the pronaos of an ancient temple. The initial design was completed by Giovanni Battista Basile in 1875; building work was concluded by his son Ernesto.

Additional Sights

Villa Malfitano★★

Off the map. Follow Via Dante. ⏰*Open Mon-Sat 9am-1.30pm.* ⏰*Closed Sun and public holidays.*☎*091 68 20 522.*

Surrounded by beautiful **gardens**★★, this Liberty-style villa has retained many Oriental furnishings. Paricularly worthy of note is the **decoration** of the **Sala d'estate** (Summer Room) by Ettore de Maria Bergler; the *trompe- l'œil* effect transforms the room into a cool veranda surrounded by greenery.

Catacombe dei Cappuccini★★

Access by Via dei Cappuccini, at the bottom of Corso Vittorio Emanuele. ⏰*Open daily 9am-noon and 3-5pm.* ☎*091 21 21 17.*

These Capuchin catacombs are an impressive sight. About 8 000 mummies were placed here from the 17C to 19C, preserved by the very dry air.

La Zisa★

♿ ⏰*Open Mon-Sat 9am-7pm, Sun and public holidays 9am-1pm.* ☞*4.50€.* ☎*091 65 20 269; www.regione.sicilia.it/beniculturali*

This magnificent palace now houses a collection of Egyptian works from the Mameluke and Ottoman periods.

Orto Botanico★

⏰*For information on opening times call.* ☎*091 62 38 241; www.ortobotanico.palermo.it/principale.php.*

A garden with a fine collection of exotic flora, including magnificent magnolia-fig treesaa (Ficus magnolioides).

Parco della Favorita

3km/2mi north along Via Diana.

This 18C park was laid out for the Bourbons. Beside the Chinese pavilion (Palazzina Cinese) is a museum, the **Museo Etnografico Pitrè**, which displays traditional Sicilian objects. ♿⏰*Open daily 7.30am-7.30pm.* ⏰*Closed Fri.* ☞ *5€.* ☎*091 61 77 004.*

Excursions

Monreale★★★

8km/5mi southwest. www.monreale.net.

The town, dominating the Conca d'Oro (Golden Basin) of Palermo, grew up around the 12C Benedictine abbey founded by Norman King, William II.

Duomo★★★

⏰*Open daily 8am-6pm.* ☞*2.60€. Lift to terraces: 9.30am-5.45pm. 2€.* ☎*091 64 04 413.*

The central doorway of the cathedral has beautiful **bronze doors**★★ (1185), which were carved by Bonanno Pisano. The Byzantine north **doorway**★ is the work of Barisano da Trani (12C). The decoration of the **chevet**★★ blends Moorish and Norman styles.

The cathedral has a basilical plan. The interior is dazzling with multicoloured marbles, paintings, and especially the 12C and 13C **mosaics**★★★.

A gigantic **Christ Pantocrator** (Ruler of All) is enthroned in the central apse. Above the episcopal throne, in the

choir, a mosaic represents King William II offering the cathedral to the Virgin. A mosaic opposite, shows King William receiving his crown from Christ.
From the **terraces**★★★ there are magnificent **views**★★ over the fertile plain of the Conca d'Oro.

Chiostro★★★
&♿ ⏱*Open Mon-Sat 9am-6.30pm, Sun and public holidays 9am-1pm . ⊜6€. ☎091 64 04 403.*
The cloisters to the right of the church are as famous as the mosaics. On the south side there is a fountain that was used as a lavabo by the monks.

Monte Pellegrino
14km/9mi north.
The road out of the city affords splendid **glimpses**★★★ of the Conca d'Oro.

Bagheria
16km/10mi east.
Bagheria is known for its Baroque villas and especially for the **Villa Palagonia**★, which is decorated with **sculptures**★ of grotesques and monsters.

Villa Cattolica houses the **Civica Galleria d'Arte Moderna e Contemporanea Renato Guttuso** as well as the tomb of the painter himself by Giacomo Manzù (1912-1987). ⏱*Villa Palagonìa: Open daily Apr-Oct 9am-1pm and 4-7pm, Nov-Mar 9am-1pm and 3.30-5.30pm. ⊜ 4€. ☎091 93 20 88; www.villapalagonia.it, &♿ Galleria d'Arte Moderna e Contemporanea: Open daily 9.30am-6pm (summer), rest of the year 9am-1.30pm and 2.30-7pm. ⏱Closed Mon, public holidays. ⊜2€. ☎091 94 39 02.*

Rovine di Solunto★
19km/12mi east. ⏱Open Mar-Oct, Mon-Sat, 9am-6pm, Nov-Feb 9am-4.30pm, Sun and public holidays 9am-1pm. ⊜€2. ☎091 90 45 57.
Soluntum has a splendid site overlooking a headland, Capo Zafferano
The site **(zona archeologica)** includes ruins of the baths, forum and theatre. Take Via Ippodamo da Mileto to the summit for a lovely **view**★★.

ISOLA DI **PANTELLERIA**★★
PANTELLERIA ISLAND
POPULATION 7 000
MICHELIN MAP 565 Q 17-18.

Known as the "Black Pearl of the Mediterranean", the island is full of character with its indented coastline, steep slopes covered with terraces under cultivation, and its Moorish-looking cubic houses (dammusi).

The highest point of this volcanic island is Montagna Grande (836m/2 743ft). The vineyards produce wines such as Solimano and the muscat Tanit. Capers are also grown here.

Pantelleria has remains of prehistoric settlements and, like Sicily, later suffered invasions by the Phoenicians, Carthaginians, Greeks, Romans, Vandals, Byzantines, Moors and Normans who in 1123 united the island with Sicily.

- 🛈 **Information:** Piazza Cavour 1, 91017 Pantelleria (TP), ☎0923 91 18 38; www.pantelleria.it/proloco.
- ▸ **Orient Yourself:** Situated in the Sicilian Channel, the Island of Pantelleria is only 84km/52miles away from Cape Bon in Tunisia. It is the westernmost island of the Sicilian group and lies on the same latitude as Tunis.
- ⏱ **Organizing Your Time:** Allow half a day.

Excursions

Tour of the island by car★★

▶About 40km/24mi: 3hr. The picturesque coastal road gives the visitor a chance to discover the beauty of the indented coastline, thermal springs and lakes. Driving south from Pantelleria, road signs indicate a Neolithic village, where the **sese grande**★, an elliptic funerary monument can be seen. Further along the road, the village of **Scauri**★ boasts a lovely site. On the south coast towards **Dietro Isola** the corniche road affords plunging **views**★★ of this coastal area. The cape, **Punta dell'Arco**★, is terminated by a natural rock arch known as the **Arco dell'Elefante**★ (Elephant Arch). On the northeast coast the inlet **Cala dei Cinque Denti**★, and the rest of the coastline further north make a lovely volcanic landscape. From here, you can

GETTING THERE

The quickest way to reach the island is by air with connecting flights from Trapani and Palermo. There are also direct flights from Rome and Milan during the summer. **Airone** ☎199 20 70 80; www.flyairone.it. Ferries (5-6hr) and hydrofoils (2hr 30min) leave from Trapani. **Ustica Lines,** ☎0923 87 38 13; www.usticalines.it.

go on to visit the **Specchio di Venere**★ (Venus' Mirror), a beautiful green lake.

Montagna Grande★★

▶13km/8mi southeast of Pantelleria. From the summit of this peak there is a splendid **panorama**★★ of the island, as far as Sicily and Tunisia.

RAGUSA★

POPULATION 69 000
MICHELIN MAP 565 Q 26.

Ragusa, partly rebuilt following the 1693 earthquake, boasts a splendid setting on a plateau between deep ravines. The modern town lies to the west while the old town, Ragusa Ibla, clusters on an outlie of the hills, Monti Iblei, to the east. The Syracuse road offers magnificent **views**★★ of the old town.

-  **Information:** Palazzo La Rocca, via Capitano Bocchieri 33, 97100 Ragusa Ibla. ☎0932 22 15 11. www.ragusaturismo.it.
- ▶ **Orient Yourself:** Ragusa is situated at the southernmost point of the island. The main access road is *S 115*.
- ☺ **Don't Miss:** A walk in Ragusa Ibla and a visit to pretty Modica.
- 🕐 **Organizing Your Time:** Allow a day, and two days including the surrounding region.
- 🍃 **Also See:** *NOTO*.

Worth a Visit

Ragusa Ibla★★

The medieval area is a maze of streets, but much of the old town was rebuilt in the Baroque style. The hub of the town is Piazza del Duomo, where the elegant Baroque church of **San Giorgio**★★ stands. The church was designed by Rosario Gagliardi who also worked in Noto.

The nearby church of **San Giuseppe**★ shares certain similarities with San Giorgio and may be by the same architect.

Città nuova

The new town is laid out in a grid pattern around the 18C cathedral of **San Giovanni**, which is fronted by a wide terrace. Not far away, the **Museo Archeologico Ibleo** (*Palazzo Mediterraneo, Via Natalelli*) contains the finds from excavations undertaken locally, notably from the ancient Greek city of Camarina. ⏱*Open daily 9am-1.30pm and 4-7.30pm.* ⊚€2. ☎0932 62 29 63.

Excursion

Modica★

▶*15km/9mi south.*
This village, situated in a narrow valley, has retained many of its magnificent Baroque buildings, the most impressive of which is the majestic church of **San Giorgio**, preceded by a long flight of stairs.

The **Museo delle Arti e Tradizioni Popolari**★ offers interesting reconstructions of old workplaces, including workshops and a farm. ♿ ⏱ *Open daily except Mon, 10am-1pm and 4.30-7.30pm (winter 3.30-6.30pm).* ⏱*Closed 1 Jan, 15 Aug.* ⊚€2.50. ☎0932 75 27 47.

SEGESTA★★★

MICHELIN MAP 565 N 20.

Splendidly situated against the hillside, its ochre colours in pleasant contrast to the vast expanse of green, the archaeological park is dominated by a fine Doric temple standing in an isolated site. Probably founded, like Erice, by the Elimi, Segesta soon became one of the main cities in the Mediterranean under Greek influence, rivalling Selinus in importance.

- **Information:** www.regione.sicilia.it/turismo.
- ▶ **Orient Yourself:** Segesta is 35km/21mi southeast of Trapani.
- **Don't Miss:** The temple of Segesta.
- **Also See:** *ERICE, SELINUNTE, TRAPANI.*

Visit

Tempio★★★

⏱*Open daily summer 9am-7pm (ticket office closes 6pm), rest of year 9am-5pm (ticket office closes 4pm).* ⊚€ *4.50. There is a shuttle bus to the theatre.* ☎*0924 95 23 56.*

The temple of Segesta stands alone, encircled by a deep ravine, in a land-

The elegant Doric temple at Segesta

scape of receding horizons. The Doric building (430 BC), pure and graceful, is girt by a peristyle of 36 columns in golden-coloured limestone. The road leading up to the theatre *(2km/1mi; shuttle bus available, see above)* affords a magnificent **view**★★ of the temple.

Teatro★
This Hellenistic theatre (63m/207ft in diameter) is built into the rocky hillside. The tiers of seats are orientated towards the hills, behind which, to the right, is the Gulf of Castellammare.

ANTICA CITTÀ DI **SELINUNTE**★★
SELINUS (ANCIENT CITY)
MICHELIN MAP 565 O 20.

Selinus was founded in the mid-7C BC by people from the east coast city of Megara Hyblaea and destroyed twice, in 409 and 250 BC, by the Carthaginians. The huge ruins of its temples with their enormous platforms are impressive.

- **Information:** www.regione.sicilia.it.
- **Orient Yourself:** Selinus is situated on the south coast. The main access roads are S 115 and S 115d.
- **Also See:** *SEGESTA.*

Special Features

Zona archeologica
Open daily, 9am to 3hr before dusk. € 4.50. ☎0924 46 277.
Visitors to the site first reach an esplanade around which are grouped the remains of three **temples**. The first to come into view is **Temple E** (5C BC) which was reconstructed in 1958. To the right stands **Temple F**, completely in ruins. The last of the three, **Temple G** was one of the largest in the ancient world. It was over 100m/330ft long; its columns were built of blocks each weighing several tonnes.

Cross the depression, Gorgo Cottone, to reach the **acropolis**. The site is dominated by the partially reconstructed (1925) columns of **Temple C** (6C BC), the oldest. There are four more ruined temples nearby. To the west, across the River Modione are the remains of a sanctuary to Demeter Malophoros (the dispenser of pomegranates).

SIRACUSA★★★
SYRACUSE
POPULATION 122 000
MICHELIN MAP 565 P 27.

Syracuse is superbly situated at the head of a beautiful bay. It was one of Sicily's, if not Magna Graecia's, most prestigious cities and at the height of its splendour rivalled Athens.

- **Information:** Via S. Sebastiano 43, 96100 Siracusa, ☎0931 48 12 00; www.apt-siracusa.it.
- **Orient Yourself:** Syracuse is situated on the east coast, overlooking the Io Sea. The main access roads are S 114 (from Catania) and S 115 (from the s
- Don't Miss: L'Ortigia and the Museo Archaeologico Regionale Paolo Orsi
- **Especially for Kids:** Orecchio di Dionisio grotto.
- **Also See:** *CATANIA, NOTO.*

A Bit of History

Greek colony

Syracuse was colonised in the mid-8C BC by Greeks from Corinth who settled on the island of Ortigia. It soon fell under the yoke of the tyrants, and it developed and prospered. In the 5C-4C BC the town had 300 000 inhabitants. Captured by the Romans during the Second Punic War (212 BC), it was occupied by the barbarians, Byzantines (6C), Arabs (9C) and Normans.

Tyrants and intellectuals

In the Greek world, dictators called tyrants (from the Greek word *turannos*) exercised unlimited power over certain cities, in particular Syracuse. Already in 485 BC **Gelon**, the tyrant of Gela, had become master of Syracuse. His brother **Hiero** an altogether more unpleasant person, nonetheless patronised poets and welcomed to his court **Pindar** and **Æschylus**, who died in Gela in 456.

Dionysius the Elder (405-367 BC) was the most famous but even he lived in constant fear. He had a sword suspended by a horsehair above the head of Damocles, a jealous courtier, to demonstrate to the many dangers which threatened a ruler. He rarely left the safety of his castle on Ortigia, wore a shirt of mail under his clothing and changed his room every night. He had Plato expelled from the city when he came to study the political habits of the people under his dictatorship.

Archimedes, the famous geometrician born at Syracuse in 287 BC, was so absent-minded that he would forget to eat and drink. It was in his bath that he discovered his famous principle: any body immersed in water loses weight equivalent to that of the water it displaces. Delighted, he jumped out of the bath and ran naked through the streets shouting "Eureka" (I have found it!). When defending Syracuse against ▪e Romans, Archimedes set fire to the ▪my fleet by focusing the sun's rays ▪a system of mirrors and lenses. But ▪the Romans succeeded in entering ▪n by surprise, Archimedes, deep ▪lculations, did not hear them, ▪an soldier ran him through.

L'Ortigia★★★

Visit: 45min. Ortigia boasts numerous medieval and Baroque palaces, the latter mainly in **Via della Maestranza**★. The **Piazza Duomo**★ is particularly attractive, lined by palaces adorned with wrought-iron balconies and the monumental façade of the **Duomo**★. It was built in the 7C on the foundations of a temple dedicated to Athena, some columns of which were re-used in the Christian building *(north and interior)*.

Fonte Arethusa★

This is the legendary cradle of the city. The nymph Arethusa, pursued by the river-god Alpheus, took refuge on the island of Ortigia where she was changed into a spring *(fonte)* by Artemis. The **Passaggio Adorno**, a favourite walk for the Syracusans, starts below.

Galleria Regionale di Palazzo Bellomo★

⚷ *Closed for restoration.* ☎ *0931 69 511.* The museum is housed in a beautiful 13C palace. The art gallery has an admirable **Annunciation**★(damaged) by Antonello da Messina and The **Burial of St Lucy**★ by Caravaggio. There is also a collection of goldsmiths' work, Sicilian cribs, liturgical objects and furniture.

Parco Archeologico della Neapolis★★★

Access by Via Rizzo or Via Paradiso. 2hr on foot. ♿ ⏱*Open daily 9am-1 hour before dusk.* ▪*6€ .* ☎*0931 65 068; www.regione. sicilia.it/turismo.*

Teatro greco★★★

The Greek theatre dates from the 5C BC and is one of the largest of the Ancient world. The tiers of seats are hewn out of the rock. The first performance of The Persians by Æschylus was held here. Behind the theatre stretches the road of the tombs, **Via dei Sepolcri**.

Latomia del Paradiso★★

This former quarry, now an orange grove, dates from ancient times. Part of its roof fell in during the 1693 earthquake.

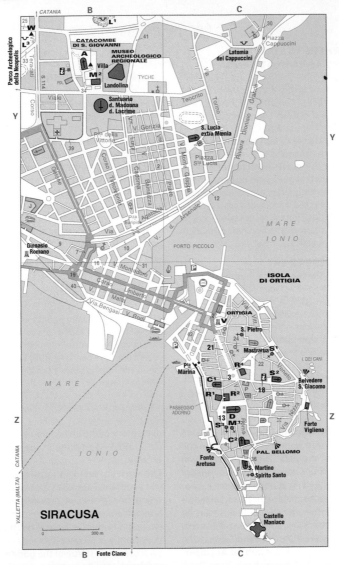

SIRACUSA

SIRACUSA

Agrigento V.	BCY	2	Foro Siracusano	BYZ	16	Regina Margherita Viale	BYZ	31
Archimede Pza	CZ	3	Gelone Cso	BY		Romagnoli V.	BY	33
Capodieci V.	CZ	4	Maestranza V. d.	CZ	18	S. Giovanni Viale	BY	34
Castello Maniace V.	CZ	6	Marconi Piazzale	BZ	19	S. Martino V.	CZ	36
Catania V.	BY	7	Matteotti Cso G.	CZ	21	Svevia Pza F. d.	CZ	38
Crispi V. F.	BY	9	Mergulensi V.	CZ	22	Testaferrata V. G.	BY	39
Diaz Viale A.	BY	10	Mirabella V.	CZ	24	Tripoli V.	BZ	40
Dionisio il Grande Riviera	CY	12	Necropoli Groticelle V. d.	BY	25	Umberto I Cso	BZ	
Duomo Pza	CZ	13	Pancali Pza	CZ	27	Von Platen V. A.	BY	41
			Puglia V.	CY	30	XX Settembre V.	CZ	42

Basilica di S. Giovanni Evangelista	BY	A	Latomia di S. Venera	BY	L³	S. Benedetto	CZ	C
Chiesa dei Gesuiti	CZ	C¹	Museo del Papiro	BY	M²	S. Filippo Neri	CZ	
Duomo	CZ	D	Palazzo Beneventano del Bosco	CZ	R¹	S. Francesco all'Immacolata	CZ	
Galleria Civica d'Arte Moderna	CZ	M¹	Palazzo Mergulese-Montalto	CZ	R⁴	S. Lucia	C	
Latomia del Casale	BY	L¹	Palazzo del Senato	CZ	R²	Tempio di Apollo	C	
						Tomba di Archimede		

Address Book

WHERE TO STAY

Agriturismo La Perciata – *Via Spinagallo 77 – 10km/6mi southwest of Syracuse on the Maremonti road (in the direction of Canicattini, Floridia junction) – b0931 71 73 66 – www.perciata.it – ⚞ 📖 – 11 rm ⚌ Restaurant.* There is a very Mediterranean feel to this villa which enhances the very relaxing ambience. The hotel's rural location also means that guests can go horse riding if they wish. Other attractions include a tennis court and hydromassage facilities. Elegant, rustic-style rooms and apartments which have all modern conveniences.

WHERE TO EAT

Darsena-Da Jannuzzo – *Riva Garibaldi 6 – As soon as you reach the island of Ortigia, turn right – ☎0931 61 522 – Closed Wed – 📖.* You only need to cast your eye over the display of fresh fish at the entrance to know that you are in for a treat. The cooking is simple and tasty, the dishes prepared with fish caught that morning. Meals are served either inside (simple surroundings) or

out on the veranda with views over the waterfront.

Bed & Breakfast Dolce Casa – *Via Lido Sacramento 4, Località Isola – S 115 (in the direction of Noto, heading off left for Isola – ☎0931 72 11 35 – www.bbdolcecasa.it – ⚞📖 – 10 rm.* What was once a private dwelling has been transformed into a very pleasant and welcoming B&B halfway between Syracuse, with all its various attractions, and the sea. The good-sized rooms are light and airy, with rustic-style furnishings, and have a rather romantic feel to them. There is also a lovely garden with lots of palm trees and a pinewood.

Albergo Domus Mariae – *Via Vittorio Veneto 76 – ☎0931 24 858 – www.sistemia.it/domusmariae – 📖 – 12 rm ⚌ – Restaurant.* This is a hotel with a difference run by nuns. In every other respect it is a very traditional establishment. The rooms (spacious) and public areas (a little cramped) are elegant and have been tastefully furnished and there is a lovely sun lounge with sea views.

The **Orecchio di Dionisio**★★★ (Ear of Dionysius) is an artificial grotto in the form of an earlobe. The grotto was named in 1608 by Caravaggio as a reminder of the legend recounting how the exceptional echo enabled the tyrant Dionysius to overhear the talk of the prisoners he confined below. 🄺🄸🄳🅂 *Children will love testing the echo in the Orecchio di Dionisio.* The park tour concludes with the **Ara di Ierone II,** a rock-hewn altar (c 200m/656ft long) used for public sacrifices.

Museo Archeologico Regionale Paolo Orsi★★

🕐*Open daily 9am-6pm, Sun and public days 9am-1pm.* 🕐*Closed Mon.* ⚌6€. *☎931 46 40 22; www.regione.sicilia.it/ ...lturali*

...charming grounds of the **Villa ...na** stands the museum built

in memory of the archaeologist Paolo Orsi (1859-1935); it presents the history of Sicily.

The museum features local geology and early fauna as well as Greek colonisation (from mid-8C BC onwards); many artefacts were salvaged in the Lentinoi excavations (marble kouros) but more importantly at Megara Hyblaea and at Syracuse: chalk statue of the **goddess-mother**★, architectural fragments and small-scale replicas of the great sanctuaries of Ortigia. The **Venus Anadiomede**★, a Roman copy of a Greek statue by Praxiteles, is on temporary display. The third part of the museum is devoted to the various Syracusan colonies.

Catacombe di San Giovanni★★

🕐*Open daily 9am-12.30pm and 2.30-dusk.* 🕐*Closed Mon.* ⚌€ 4. *☎0931 64 694; www.kalosnet.it.*

After the catacombs in Rome, these are the finest examples in Italy. Big enough to hold up to seven tombs, they consist of a main gallery off which branch secondary galleries ending in circular chapels or rotundas.

Excursions

Fonte Ciane★★

▶8km/5mi southwest. It is best to visit by boat. Reservation required out of season. Sig. Vella. ☎0931 39 889 or 368 72 96 040 (mobile).

The River **Ciane**★★, rising here, is lined with papyrus beds, which are unique in Italy. It was here that the nymph Ciane was changed into a spring when she opposed the abduction of Proserpine by Pluto.

Castello Eurialo★

9km/6mi northwest of the plan. ◷Open daily 9am-1hr before dusk. ☎0931 71 17 73.

This was one of the greatest fortresses of the Greek period; it was built by Dionysius the Elder. Fine **panorama**★.

TAORMINA★★★

POPULATION 10 000
MICHELIN MAP 565 N 27
TOWN PLAN IN THE CURRENT MICHELIN ITALY ATLAS.

Taormina stands in a wonderful site★★★ at an altitude of 250m/820ft and forms a balcony overlooking the sea and facing Etna. It is renowned for its peaceful atmosphere and its beautiful monuments and gardens. The nearby seaside resort of Giardini Naxos also hosts a number of cultural and musical events.

- **Information:** Piazza S. Caterina (Palazzo Corvaja), 98039 Taormina (ME), ☎0942 23 243; www.gate2taormiina.it.
- **Orient Yourself:** Taormina is situated on the east coast, overlooking the Ionion Sea. The main access road is A 18.
- **Don't Miss:** Teatro Greco and the waterfalls at Gole dell'Alcantara.
- **Organizing Your Time:** Allow a day.
- **Also See:** CATANIA, ETNA, MESSINA.

Visit

Teatro greco★★★

◷Open daily 9am-2hr before dusk. €6. ☎0942 23 220; www.regione.sicilia.it/turismo.

The Greek theatre dates from the 3C BC but was remodelled by the Romans who used it as an arena for their contests. Performances of Classical plays are given in summer. From the upper tiers there is an admirable **view**★★★ between the stage columns of the coastline and Etna.

Corso Umberto★

The main street of Taormina has three gateways along its course: Porta Catania; the middle one, Porta di Mezzo, with the Torre dell' Orologio (Clock Tower); and Porta Messina. The Piazza del Duomo is overlooked by the Gothic façade of the **cathedral**.

Almost halfway along, the **Piazza 9 Aprile**★ forms a terrace, which affords a splendid **panorama**★★ of the gulf. The Piazza Vittorio Emanuele was laid out on the site of the forum and is overlooked by the 15C **Palazzo Corvaja**.

Giardino di Villa Comunale★★

From these terraced public gardens there are views of the coast and sea.

Excursions

Castello

4km/2.5mi northwest by the Castelmola road, and then a road to the right. It is also

B. Morandi/MICHELIN

The theatre and Mount Etna, Taormina

possible to walk up (1hr there and back). The castle was built in the medieval period on the summit of Monte Tauro (390m/1 280ft), on the remains of the former acropolis. There are splendid **views**★★ of Taormina.

Castelmola★
5km/3mi northwest.
This tiny village is strategically located near Taormina and enjoys a splendid **site**★and views. The focus of the village

is the Piazzetta del Duomo. From points there are fine **views**★ of Etna.

Gole dell'Alcantara★
17km/11mi west. ○*Open daily 9am-1h before dusk.* ○€*2.50, plus rental of boots and overalls.* ☎*0942 98 50 10; www.golealcantara.it*
The volcanic walls of these gorges are formed by irregular geometrical shapes, turning the waterfalls that cascade down the rock into prisms of light.

Address Book

WHERE TO STAY
○**Bed & Breakfast Villa Regina**
– Punta San Giorgio – 98030 Castelmola – 5km/3mi northwest of Taormina – ☎0942 28 228 – Fax 0942 28 083 – 10 rm – � €7. A very simple but charming establishment, with a lovely little shady garden, that boasts wonderful views of Taormina and the coast. Definitely one for the address book especially for couples looking for a bit of privacy and romance.
○○**Andromaco Palace Hotel** –
Via Fontana Vecchia – ☎0942 23 834 – www.andomaco.it – 🍴 ▣ *– 24 rm.* ☒. Notwithstanding the rather grandiloquent name, this is a small, rather gracious, family-run hotel. Panoramic position not far from the centre. Comfortable rooms. Warm welcome assured.

WHERE TO EAT
○○**Vicolo Stretto** – *Via Vicolo Stretto 6 – ☎0942 23 849 – Closed Mon (except 15 Jun-15 Sep), 9-20 Dec, 8 Jan-12 Feb –* ▣ *– Book.* Wherever you are seated, whether it is in the lovely little dining room (warm and welcoming) inside or the terrace (open and airy) overlooking the rooftops of Taormina, just sit back and relax. The cooking – mostly fish – draws inspiration from the cuisine in the Trapani area (where the chef comes from) and includes dishes such as tuna fish with couscous.

TAKING A BREAK
Caffè San Giorgio – *Piazza S. Antonio 1 – 98030 Castelmola –* 🍴. revious habitués of this cafe include a number of famous personalities (among them Rolls and Royce as well as Rockefeller). One of the main attractions is the breathtaking view of Taormina from the splendid terrace area.

TRAPANI

POPULATION 68 000

MICHELIN MAP 565 M 19.

Situated within sight of the Egadi Islands, Trapani has a sheltered port which is important to the salt trade.

- **Information:** Piazza Saturno. ☎0923 29 000; www.apt.trapani.it.
- ▶ **Orient Yourself:** Trapani is situated at the westernmost point of the island. The main access roads are A 29 and S 113.
- **Don't Miss:** Museo del Sale, Isola di Mozia.
- **Especially for Kids:** The restored windmill near Mozia.
- **Organizing Your Time:** Allow half a day.
- **Also See:** *Isole EGADI, ERICE, SEGESTA*

Worth a Visit

Santuario dell'Annunziata★

 Open daily 7am-noon and 4-7pm.
☎0923 53 91 84.
Built in the 14C, the church was remodelled and enlarged in the 17C. On the north side the **Cappella dei Marinai** (Renaissance Sailors' Chapel) is crowned with a dome. Inside, access to the **Cappella della Madonna**★ is through a 16C Renaissance arch; the chapel contains the statue of the Virgin (14C) known as the **Madonna di Trapani** and attributed to Nino Pisano.

Museo Pepoli★

 Open Mon-Sat, 9am-1.30pm, Sun and public holidays 9am-12.30pm. €2.50 ☎0923 55 32 69.
The Pepoli Museum is located in the former Carmelite convent which adjoins the Annunziata. The works include sculpture (by the Gagini) and paintings, such as the 15C Trapani polyptych, a **Pietà**★ by Roberto di Oderisio.

Centro storico★

The old town is built on the promontory, with the Villa Margherita to the east.

Excursions

Salt pans

30km/18mi from Trapani to Marsala. Allow one day, including a trip to Mozia. The coastal road which leads from Trapani to Marsala is lined with salt pans (*saline*) and fine open **views**★★; the water is divided into a multicoloured grid by strips of land. In places there are windmills, a reminder of times gone by when they were the main way to pump water and grind the salt. The view is even more evocative in the summer, at harvest time, when the rose-coloured tint of the water in the basins is more intense (the colour changes as the saline content increases) and the shimmering pools of water inland are drying out in the sun. At Nubia there is the small, but interesting **Museo del Sale**. *Open Mon-Sat, 9.30am-1pm and 3.30-6.30pm (5pm winter), Sun am only. Guided tours available (30min).* € 2. ☎0923 86 74 42.

 Wind permitting, the windmill operates in summer, Wed and Sat 4-6pm, rest of year Sat-Sun and public holidays only on request. €3.50€ .Saline Ettore and Infersa, ☎0923 96 69 36.

M. Magni/MICHELIN

The salt pans which date back to the Phoenicians

Kids A restored **mill** can be visited not far from Mozia *(see below)*.

Isola di Mozia★

▶*14km/9mi south of Trapani.* Leave the car at the jetty. Fishermen provide a ferry service to the island. This ancient Phoenician colony was founded in the 8C BC on one of the four islands of the **Laguna dello Stagnone**. Visitors can explore the ruins of the Phoenician city by following the path around the island *(about 1hr30min; anti-clockwise direction recommended)*. A small **museum** houses exhibits found on the island, including the magnificent **Ephebe of Mozia★★**, a noble figure of rather haughty bearing clothed in a long, pleated cloak which shows an obvious Greek influence. ♿🕐*Access to island and visit to museum daily 9am-1pm and 3pm to 1hr before dusk.*☎*0923 71 25 98.*

Marsala

Marsala, the ancient Lilybaeum on Capo Lilibeo, the westernmost point of the island, owes its present name to the Saracens, who first destroyed and then rebuilt the city, calling it Marsah el Ali (Port of Allah). It is known for its sweet Marsala wine which an English merchant, John Woodhouse, rediscovered in the 18C.

Piazza della Repubblica is the hub of city life, lined by the cathedral and Palazzo Senatorio.

A former wine cellar, near the sea, now houses a museum, the **Museo Archeologico di Baglio Anselmi** *(Via Boeo)*: the exhibits include the wreck of a **warship★**that fought in the Punic War and was found off the coast near Mozia. ♿🕐*Open daily 9am-6pm.* 🎫€6. ☎*0923 95 25 35; www.regione.sicilia.it/beniculturali.*

USTICA★★

POPULATION 1 348

MICHELIN MAP 565 K 21.

This small volcanic island boasts an indented coastline which hides magnificent caves, inlets and bays. It has been a marine reserve since 1987.

🛈 **Information:** Piazza Umberto I, 90010 Ustica (PA), ☎091 84 49 456; www.comune.ustica.pa.it.

▶ **Orient Yourself:** Ustica is situated off the coast around Palermo. There are regular ferry departures from Palermo. During the summer months there is also a hydrofoil service (route: Trapani-Favignana-Ustica-Napoli). 🛈*Via Amm. Staiti 23, Trapani,* ☎*0923 22 200; Ustica Lines www.usticalines.it.*

😊 **Don't Miss:** Snorkelling in the Riserva marina.

🕭 **Also See:** *PALERMO.*

Special Features

Island

The village of **Ustica★** is built overlooking the bay. A **prehistoric village★**dating from the Bronze Age has been discovered in the Colombaia district. The coastline is dotted with rocky inlets, such as the **piscina naturale★**, known as the natural swimming pool.

Riserva marina

☎*091 84 49 456 or 091 84 49 045.*

This marine reserve was established in 1987 to protect the natural marine environment around Ustica, where the sea is particularly free of pollution (Ustica is located in the middle of the Atlantic current). The reserve organises guided tours to caves around the island and snorkelling trips. Experienced divers can enjoy a spectacular **underwater show★★** near **Scoglio del Medico**.

For the best little places, follow the leader.

Looking for the latest news on today's best hotels and restaurants? Pick up the Michelin Guide and look for the Bib Gourmand and Bib Hotel symbols. With 45,000 addresses in Europe, in every category and price range, the perfect place to dine or stay is never far away.

INDEX

INDEX

INDEX

WHERE TO EAT

INDEX

WHERE TO STAY

MAPS AND PLANS

LIST OF MAPS

COMPANION PUBLICATIONS

Companion publications Internet users can access personalised route plans, Michelin maps and town plans, and addresses of hotels and restaurants featured in The Michelin Guide Italia through the website at: **www.ViaMichelin.com**

All Michelin publications are cross-referenced. For each sight covered in the Selected Sights section of the guide, a map reference is given under the heading "Location". From our range of products we recommend the following:

◆ Michelin map 735 Italy, a practical map on a scale of 1:1 000 000 which shows the whole Italian road network

◆ Michelin Atlas Italy, a practical, spiral-bound road atlas, on a scale of 1:300 000, with an alphabetical index of places and maps of 70 cities and conurbations.

◆ Michelin map 561, Italy North-West (Lombardy, Piedmont, Valle d'Aosta, Liguria), on a scale of 1:400 000 which gives detailed information on the area you wish to tour.

◆ Michelin map 562, Italy North-East (Veneto, Trentino-Alto Adige, Friuli-Venezia Giulia, Emilia-Romagna), on a scale of 1:400 000 which gives detailed information on the area you wish to tour.

◆ Michelin map 563, Italy Centre (Tuscany, Umbria, Lazio, Marches, Abruzzi, Repubblica di San Marino), on a scale of 1:400 000 which gives detailed information on the area you wish to tour.

◆ Michelin map 564, Italy South (Puglia, Molise, Campania, Calabria, Basilicata), on a scale of 1:400 000 which gives detailed information on the area you wish to tour.

◆ Michelin map 565, Sicily, on a scale of 1:400 000 which gives detailed information on the area you wish to tour.

◆ Michelin map 566, Sardinia, on a scale of 1:400 000 which gives detailed information on the area you wish to tour.

LEGEND

	Sight	Seaside resort	Winter sports resort	Spa
Highly recommended	★★★	⚠⚠⚠	✻✻✻	‡‡‡
Recommended	★★	⚠⚠	✻✻	‡‡
Interesting	★	⚠	✻	‡

Selected monuments and sights

◉ ▭	Tour - Departure point
⛪ ✝	Catholic church
⛪ ✝	Protestant church, other temple
✡ ▣ ▤	Synagogue - Mosque
▬	Building
■	Statue, small building
✝	Calvary, wayside cross
◎	Fountain
●▬►	Rampart - Tower - Gate
✕	Château, castle, historic house
∴	Ruins
◡	Dam
✿	Factory, power plant
☆	Fort
∩	Cave
▣	Troglodyte dwelling
⋔	Prehistoric site
▼	Viewing table
⋙	Viewpoint
▲	Other place of interest

Special symbols

⬦	Police station (Carabinieri)
⌂	Nuraghe
⌂	Palace, villa
⚏	Temple, Greek and Roman ruins

Additional symbols

🛈	Tourist information
═══ ═	Motorway or other primary route
❶ ❶	Junction: complete, limited
⬌ ═	Pedestrian street
⌶═════⌶	Unsuitable for traffic, street subject to restrictions
⌷⌷⌷ ----	Steps – Footpath
🚆 🚉	Train station – Auto-train station
🚌 🚌	Coach (bus) station
⊶⊷	Tram
Ⓜ	Metro, underground
P R	Park-and-Ride
♿	Access for the disabled

Sports and recreation

🏇	Racecourse
⛸	Skating rink
≋ ⛱	Outdoor, indoor swimming pool
🎬	Multiplex Cinema
⟁	Marina, sailing centre
⛺	Trail refuge hut
▫▪▪▫	Cable cars, gondolas
▫┼┼┼▫	Funicular, rack railway
🚂	Tourist train
◈	Recreation area, park
🎡	Theme, amusement park
¥	Wildlife park, zoo
❀	Gardens, park, arboretum
❁	Bird sanctuary, aviary
🧍	Walking tour, footpath
😊	Of special interest to children

Abbreviations

H	Town hall (Municipio)
J	Law courts (Palazzo di Giustizia)
M	Museum (Museo)
P	Local authority offices (Prefettura)
POL.	Police station (Polizia) (in large towns: Questura)
T	Theatre (Teatro)
U	University (Università)

✉	Post office
☎	Telephone
▭	Covered market
⋅✕⋅	Barracks
△	Drawbridge
∪	Quarry
✕	Mine
B F	Car ferry (river or lake)
⛴	Ferry service: cars and passengers
⛵	Foot passengers only
③	Access route number common to Michelin maps and town plans
Bert (R.)...	Main shopping street
AZ B	Map co-ordinates

Michelin Apa Publications Ltd

A joint venture between Michelin and Langenscheidt

Suite 6, Tulip House, 70 Borough High Street, London SE1 1XF, United Kingdom

No part of this publication may be reproduced in any form
without the prior permission of the publisher.

© 2007 Michelin Apa Publications Ltd
ISBN 978-1-906261-13-9
Printed: September 2007
Printed and bound in Germany

575